# The Recognition Sūtras

Also by Christopher D. Wallis:

*Tantra Illuminated: The Philosophy, History, and Practice of a Timeless Tradition*
Mattamayūra Press

# The Recognition Sūtras

A complete translation and explanation of

the 1,000-year-old spiritual masterpiece

the *Pratyabhijñā-hṛdaya*

by Rājānaka Kṣemarāja

Christopher D. Wallis

Mattamayūra
PRESS

The Recognition Sūtras



Mattamayūra Press
3950 Colorado Ave, Unit B
Boulder, CO 80303
press@mattamayura.org

Cover illustration by Greg R. Perkins
Cover design, interior design, and typesetting by Jeff Werner
Copy-editing by Amy Haagsma
Proofreading by Roma Ilnyckyj
Indexing by Catherine Plear

Publisher's Cataloging-In-Publication Data
(Prepared by The Donohue Group, Inc.)

Names: Kṣemarāja, active 11th century. | Wallis, Christopher D., author, translator.
Title: The recognition sūtras : a complete translation and explanation of the 1,000-year-old spiritual masterpiece the Pratyabhijñā-hṛdaya by Rājānaka Kṣemarāja / Christopher D. Wallis.
Other Titles: Pratyabhijñāhṛdaya. English & Sanskrit
Description: Boulder, CO : Mattamayūra Press, [2017] | In English and Sanskrit. | Includes bibliographical references and index.
Identifiers: ISBN 978-0-9897613-7-6 (hardcover) | ISBN 978-0-9897613-8-3 (paperback) | ISBN 978-0-9897613-9-0 (ePub) | ISBN 978-0-9986887-0-1 (mobipocket) | ISBN 978-0-9986887-1-8 (PDF)
Subjects: LCSH: Kashmir Śaivism--Doctrines--Early works to 1800.
Classification: LCC BL1281.1545 .K7413 2017 (print) | LCC BL1281.1545 (ebook) | DDC 294.5/95--dc23

10 9 8 7 6 5 4 3

Printed in the United States of America on acid-free paper

# TABLE OF CONTENTS

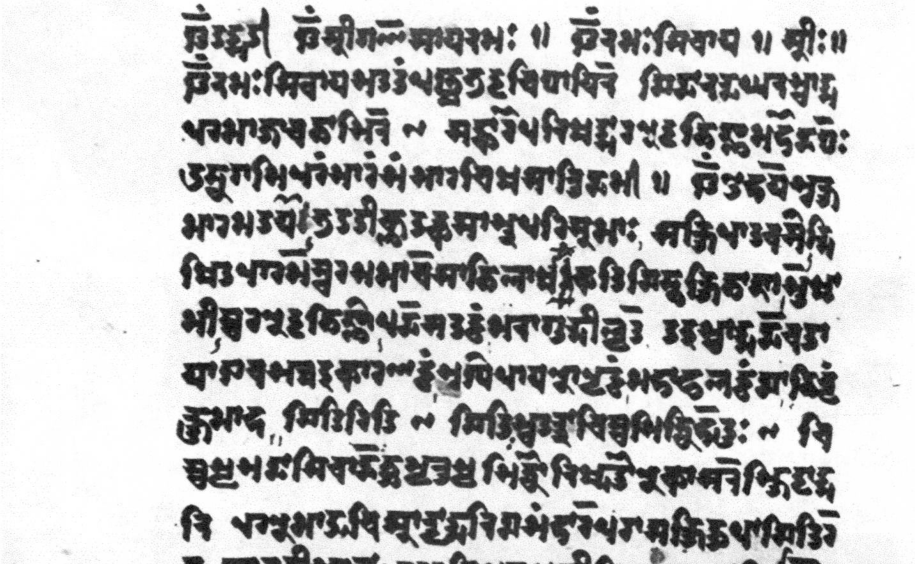

First page of a Śāradā manuscript of the Pratyabhijñā-hṛdaya

# Preface

## *(especially for scholars and academics)*

This is something new. At least, I haven't seen anything quite like it. It's new insofar as it joins together two kinds of writing that have, until now, remained mostly distinct: (1) an academically rigorous, philologically informed, complete, and thorough English translation of a Sanskrit text, and (2) an explicit and unashamed work of constructive theology that encounters that same text as a living document capable of instigating spiritual awakening, spiritual epiphanies, and even radical transformation of one's experience of reality. As a scholar-practitioner, I hold that the potential of #2 is in part predicated upon the rigor and fidelity of #1: a surprisingly uncommon claim.

By 'constructive theology' I do not at all mean 'imaginative theology', for I attempt to stay as true to the original author's vision as I can. I mean rather that this book attempts to make a meaningful *contribution* to the spiritual dimension of human life. It does not merely report what was taught by a professional *tāntrika* in the Valley of Kashmīr 1,000 years ago (though it does do that); it also attempts to show how what Kṣemarāja wrote constitutes a cutting-edge contribution to spiritual discourse in the first quarter of the twenty-first century—but only when we unpack his meaning in terms of concepts, metaphors, and analogies that are current in our present culture. So this book walks a precarious tightrope: to what extent is it possible to be faithful to Kṣemarāja's intended meaning, insofar as it can be discerned, while engaging in discourse that is compelling for twenty-first-century readers of English? Since I feel a kind of devotion and loyalty (*bhakti*) to the original author and his lineage, I have done my best to convey accurately the insights that crystallized in his awakened awareness and that he transcribed in the Sanskrit language; however, whenever the intent of his language was not completely clear, I have interpreted it in the manner that seemed to me most likely to be spiritually relevant and impactful today. Fortunately for us, his command of Sanskrit was such that his meaning usually is clear, allowing for that degree of ambiguity that invites deeper contemplation in a way that pedantry cannot.

The book is therefore divided into two distinct registers: the literal translation of Kṣemarāja's words and my explanation of what he means.

Having studied with the best in the field, I feel fairly confident in the former, and history shall judge the validity and usefulness of the latter. The translation appears in two forms: on its own and interleaved with explanation.

Those who seek an intellectual justification for both writing and reading this kind of book need look no further than Jeffrey Kripal's cogent definition of 'hermeneutical mysticism':

> *Hermeneutical mysticism* ... [is] a disciplined practice of reading, writing, and interpreting through which intellectuals actually come to experience the religious dimensions of the texts they study, dimensions that somehow crystallize or linguistically embody the forms of consciousness of their original authors. In effect, a kind of initiatory transmission sometimes occurs between the subject and object of study...[1]

It is my hope that both scholars and practitioners who read this book feel at least an inkling of that initiatory transmission from the great sage Rājānaka Kṣemarāja and his lineage.

# How to Read This Book

Unlike *Tantra Illuminated,* this book is not a reference work; it is a journey, with a beginning, middle, and end. I would say that it is best read cover to cover if you already have some background in Tantrik philosophy. However, I want to alert you to the fact that some chapters are much more relevant to the culture of India 1,000 years ago, while other chapters have content that is more universal. Inconveniently, some of the former come closer to the beginning, such as Chapters Three and Eight, while some of the most powerful and universal content occurs in chapters toward the end. It would be such a pity if you got bogged down in the first ten chapters and missed the gems in the second half. So, as with *Tantra Illuminated,* I encourage you to simply skip ahead when you feel stuck. You will want to read this book a second time anyway, I assure you.

The designer, Jeff Werner, and I have striven to present the text in such a way that it is always clear when you are reading a translation of Kṣemarāja and when you are reading my explanation. In each of the twenty chapters, as well as the prologue and epilogue, you first encounter Kṣemarāja's text without explanation or embellishment. It will necessarily be somewhat opaque on the first reading, yet suggestive and intriguing. Then you move on to my detailed explanation, within which the original text repeats in full. This style of writing—carefully explaining each sentence of a primary source in order—is called *exegesis,* and it was once commonplace in both Europe and India but is now a virtually lost art in both. To do it well one must be trained in *philology* (the art and science of the interpretation of texts written in classical languages), which 100 years ago in Europe was considered the most important of the academic disciplines. Today the word, let alone the disciplined and careful way of thinking it denotes, is largely unknown to the general public. (Under the name *vyākaraṇa,* it was also considered the foundation of all clear thinking in classical India.) Suffice to say that the very act of reading this book will teach you about the art of exegesis, so long as you read critically. Reading critically simply means actively engaging with the ideas presented, rather than passively taking them in in the way one does with most television: wrestling with them, subjecting them to inquiry, and investigating their truth-value experimentally and experientially.

Though the finer points of this book will be more easily understood by those who have read my first book, *Tantra Illuminated*, such prior reading is not required. In terms of the writing style, just as in *Tantra Illuminated*, parenthetical material can be ignored by the reader new to this philosophy, as it generally provides information more relevant to the specialist or experienced reader (such as the specific Sanskrit word being translated). Endnotes also provide more references and nuances of thought that would interrupt the flow of the main text. Unlike in *Tantra Illuminated,* we also provide a brief glossary to help you recall the meaning of the various Sanskrit technical terms which necessarily appear from time to time. Finally, I use a couple of special punctuation conventions. Single quotes ('example') are used for emphasis, definitions of Sanskrit words, or scare quotes, whereas double quotes ("example") are reserved for actual quotations from the primary source or from other sources, when those quotations are not formally set off from the main text. Lastly, an ampersand (&) is sometimes used to link two words or phrases that both translate a single Sanskrit word, when that word cannot be captured by a single English word (example: vibrate & shine for the verb *sphurati*).

***Quick 'n' Easy Guide to Sanskrit Pronunciation***

» c is always pronounced as 'ch,' as in the Italian cioccolato;
so candra = chandra and vāc = vaach
» ph is always as in upheaval, never as in phrase
» ś and ṣ are both pronounced 'sh' as in sugar
» jñ is pronounced gnya, so yajña is 'yag-nya' and jñāna is 'gnyaana'

Also please note the convention of bolding that we use in the main body of the book: in the 'original text' sections, the main sūtra of each chapter is bolded, and when the words of that sūtra repeat in Kṣemarāja's commentary, they are again bolded; by contrast, in the 'explanation' sections, all of Kṣemarāja's words are bolded, to distinguish them clearly from my words. When he quotes a primary source, it is bolded and offset; when I quote a primary source other than our main source, it is offset and in a slightly different font, but not bolded. All translations are my own unless otherwise noted.

# Acknowledgments

I first encountered the *Pratyabhijñā-hṛdaya* two and a half decades ago, at age seventeen. I remember exactly where I was when I first saw the cover of the Jaideva Singh edition: standing beside the front desk of the Seattle Siddha Yoga Meditation Center. I was immediately intrigued by this book with a ridiculously long Sanskrit title, though Jaideva Singh's mid-twentieth-century Indian English translation of it—the only translation that existed up till now—was of course more or less incomprehensible to me (and to many others, I later learned).

I received my first coherent explanation of select sūtras of the text from Swāminī Chidvilāsānandā (also known as Gurumayī), who gave me a sense of the work's profundity and importance: I thank her deeply for that. I subsequently heard some talks on the text from Sally Kempton (then Swāminī Durgānandā) as well as Paul Muller-Ortega, my first mentor and best model for being a scholar-practitioner, under whose tutelage I earned my undergraduate degree in religion and classics.

For my scholarly understanding of the text and its language, I am deeply indebted to the most accomplished living scholar of Shaivism, Alexis Sanderson, professor emeritus of All Souls College, Oxford, with whom I was fortunate to read much of the text during his residency at the University of Leipzig some years ago. Sanderson's careful reading and exposition of the text not only clarified many points of confusion, but also shed much light on the modes of thinking and writing prevalent in the wider Śaiva philosophical milieu. Several of his emendations to the received text restored sense to corrupted passages; these are duly noted in the edition found in the appendix of the book. It is not an exaggeration to say that much of whatever merit exists in my translation of Kṣemarāja's words is due to Sanderson's patient tutelage, while its faults are mine alone.

Finally, this book would not have been possible without the incredible support of so many people. Foremost among them is one of my most loyal friends, global yoga teacher Janet Stone, who provided me with accommodation at a number of different retreat sites over the past six years, sites where significant progress was made on this book, due in no small part to the inspiration of the spiritual community she creates through her dedicated practice and teaching. Also foremost among them is my longtime business partner, Cristina Star Ryan, who ably organized and lovingly hosted all of the classes I held on this text (off and on from 2011 through the present), classes which were instrumental in refining the translation and discovering through conversation with students which ways of explaining the text made sense and which didn't. I offer an especially deep bow to that amazing community of students and practitioners who gathered over the course of the first three years of Heart of Recognition classes at the San Francisco home of those radiant beings, Matthew and Alejandra Sosa Siroka, which we called the Shānta Shālā. Their questions made me refine my understanding of Kṣemarāja's teachings, and their love for this text inspired this book in the first place.

Though I cannot possibly thank all the friends who gave me moral support during the six years it took to write this book, special mentions go to Mark Haviland for his unparalleled bodywork skills, my mother, Katherine Dobson (Surabhi), for her undying support, and to Lisa Chloé Marie Larn, who put up with far too much work and too little fun during the time I was finishing this book.

Third, a very successful Indiegogo campaign raised the funds for the production and publication of this book, and I would like to acknowledge the six 'benefactors' who gave extra generously: Adria Badagnani, Darcy Gray, Duncan Kennedy and Katherine Bash, Andreas Schindler, and Mark Davis, as well as more than ninety contributors whose generosity literally made possible the book you are holding: Stephen Thomas, Andrew Smith, Virgine Lamotte, Natalie Horscroft, Sally Kempton, Adam Bauer, Iain Bryson, Henry Wetz, Vickie Ropp, Dena Evans, Briala da Silva, Kurt Keutzer, William Watson, ClayBear Campbell, Hrönn Sigurðardóttir, Jackie Hutchings, Malu Renzo (Āgamā), Stefanie Suschenko, Ewan Rayment, Luis Gonzalez Deleze, Zoe Lamaera, Jenni Smallshaw, Luke Reichelt, Christian de Vietri, Ulrik Notlev, Rich Swan (Nityabodha), Kevin Taplin, Daniel Copper Crow, Harmit Kaur Bajaj, Maria da Silva, Joachim Meire, Peter Cornish, Mark Wells, Peter Hengstler, Brian McKenney, Andra Tellervo Väänänen, Lee Brock, Aneesh Mulye, Anna Punsal, Archimedes Bibiano, Benjamin Peterson, Carisa Bishop, Chris Westin, Christine Krejca, Colby Graham, D'Arcy Swanson, David Cates, Heather Gallagher, Henry Folse, Jill Manske, Karen Greenwood, Kate Zulaski, Katherine Cain, Kathy Kunitake, Kelly Blaser, Laura Huckeba, Laura Jarrait, Ruth Vilders, Lucia Walker, Lynn

Otterson, Maeghan Moore, Mark Garner, Mary Richter, Michael Aquino, Michael Bowden, Noelani Fielder, Patricia Salzillo, Patrick O'Connor, Peter Monteparo, Roberto Lim, Romy Toussaint, Rudy Ramsey, Saran Saund, Scott Gordon, Sheldon Thieszen, Shivā Reinhardt, Sila Sayan, Susan Gantt, Sweat Yoga Studio, Trudy Rolla, and Yvonne Palka.

And of course, humble acknowledgements to the great Kaula master who revealed the Recognition Sūtras, Mahāmahopādhyāya Rājānaka Kṣemarāja, the King of Contentment, holder of the Trika and Krama lineages, and to his guru, Mahāmahopādhyāya Rājānaka Abhinava Gupta, and to all the other masters of those lineages, who were both fully awake and fully embodied. May we follow in their light-filled footsteps.

*Jaya jaya Karuṇābdhe Śrī Mahādeva Shambho!*

~ Hareesh Saurabh (Christopher Wallis)
Spring Equinox, 2017, Hafnarfjörður, Iceland

THE

# PRATYABHIJÑĀ HṚIDAYA

BEING

**a Summary of the Doctrines of the Advaita Shaiva Philosophy of Kashmir**

BY

KṢHEMARĀJA

अथ

# प्रत्यभिज्ञाहृदयम् ।

श्रीनगर

( कश्मीर )

**SRINAGAR,**

KASHMIR.

**1911.**

Title page of the 1911 edition of the Sanskrit text

# Introduction: History and Context

You hold in your hands a translation and explanation of a short book written in Sanskrit 1,000 years ago in the Valley of Kashmīr. The author, Rājānaka Kṣemarāja, called it *Pratyabhijñā-hṛdaya*, which means 'the Essence of the Recognition philosophy' or 'the Heart of the teachings on Recognition'—recognition, that is, of oneself and all beings as expression of the singular, universal, divine Consciousness.

The Recognition philosophy is the most fully developed body of teachings in nondual Śaiva Tantra. It arose in Kashmīr in the early 900s and eventually spread through the whole Indian subcontinent, being especially well studied in the far south as well as the far north. Even back then, it was considered an intellectually challenging philosophy—I think it's among the most sophisticated and intellectually challenging in any language—and so to make its teachings more approachable, Rājānaka Kṣemarāja composed this short work, about fifty pages in the original Sanskrit (see the appendix). It is a concise primer, written, he tells us, to introduce spiritual seekers to the Recognition philosophy in more accessible language, language that doesn't require a degree in philosophy to understand (see "Prologue"). What he created turned out to be one of the great spiritual masterpieces, breathtaking in its brevity but stunning in its power. It came to be considered equivalent to scripture itself by later generations, because of its undeniable inspiration. I think it's one of the greatest spiritual works of all time, at least equal in value to the *Bhagavad-gītā* or the *Yoga-sūtra*, but less well-known due solely to the vicissitudes of history.

The present work, then, is classed not as a *śāstra* (work of philosophy or science), but as an *upadeśa* (wisdom-teaching) that serves as a direct means to liberation when put into practice. Therefore, I encourage you to read and reread it, ponder and wrestle with it, until its teachings come alive for you on a nonconceptual level. I've been doing precisely that for the past seven years, and it has been the most wonderful and revelatory seven years of my life.

So the text itself is extraordinary, but the fact that we're able to read *The Recognition Sūtras* today—that it exists at all, in *any* language, let alone in English—is nothing short of a miracle.

### *The Story of a Miracle*

The lush and verdant Valley of Kashmīr, at the cultural crossroads far to the north of the Indian subcontinent, was one of the key heartlands of nondual Śaiva Tantra, and the original setting for the development of its Recognition school of philosophy. The writings of Tantrik authors from Kashmīr are often collectively referred to as 'Kashmir Shaivism', but this is a modern term (originating in the early twentieth century), and in fact there was nothing specifically Kashmiri about the Śaiva Tantrik tradition. However, certain schools of thought within nondual Śaiva Tantra, like the Recognition and Spanda schools, did originate in the Valley of Kashmīr, where the rulers were faithful patrons of the tradition up until the Muslim conquest in the early 1300s.

The valley was and is incredibly beautiful, with its towering mountains, verdant hardwood forests, waterfalls, and rivers, and modest homes built from native woods. Think Switzerland for its natural beauty and craftsmanship, but with a much more diverse culture that derived from being a meeting point for travelers and merchants from India, Persia, China, Mongolia, Tibet, and Chinese Turkestan.

In the time of Kṣemarāja, Kashmīr was a Tantrik kingdom, which means the rulers were (usually) Tantrik initiates who generously patronized the tradition—and therefore indirectly made possible this book! At that time there were many Tantrik kingdoms in the Asian world, such as those of Bali, Champa (coastal Vietnam), Angkor Wat (in Cambodia), and Tibet, and many more in India, Nepāl, and what is now Pakistān. Until just a few years ago Nepāl was a Tantrik kingdom, and nearby Bhūtān is the last of the Tantrik kingdoms existing today.

Less than 100 years ago, nearly all those who had heard of Tantra, both in India and in the West, thought it was a weird, marginal, superstitious sect concerned with magical powers and strange sexual rites. Today, after decades of groundbreaking research, we know that it was an influential and highly developed pan-Asian spiritual movement with many branches that flourished for more than six centuries (c. 600–1200 CE), as I've documented in *Tantra Illuminated.* Not only Shaivism, but *all* the Indian religions of that era developed a Tantrik component, which was seen by its adherents as the fastest track to spiritual liberation. Though comparatively little of this massively complex religious culture survives today, its influence was enormous: the whole character of Tibetan Buddhism, and a sizable chunk of modern Hinduism, was shaped by Tantra. Tantrik practices, imagery, and aesthetics survive today in lands as distant as Japan and Bali.

How have we only recently come to this knowledge of the huge historical significance of what was previously thought to be esoteric, bizarre, and idiosyncratic? And how did this spiritual philosophy survive the ravages of conquest and colonialism? Let's briefly trace the plot of this fascinating story.

In the days of our author, 1,000 years ago, the Kashmiri kings funded festivals and temples, but also supported philosophical study and spiritual practice, even paying stipends to those philosophers and contemplatives who explored the inner landscape and wrote about their insights (some of these, like our author, were given the title *rājānaka* to indicate the king's favor and patronage). Given today's impoverished academic climate, we may find the idea of government funding for spiritual research and writing astonishing (though exactly that is now happening through the European Research Council), but what is even more impressive, I think, is the manner in which this spiritual literature survived to the present day—though only just.

As with many beautiful places, Kashmīr has been under many rulers. In the three centuries after our author, the Muslims invaded again and again, regularly looting and destroying temples, holy places, and monasteries, believing as they did that all non-Muslim religion was an offense to God. In this period, untold numbers of Śaiva Tantrik manuscripts written in Sanskrit were destroyed, but many were saved, held by devoted Kashmiri *paṇḍit* families and passed down reverently, whether or not anyone in the family could read them. Kashmīr was finally permanently conquered in 1339, after which time ten different Muslim rulers persecuted Shaivism and other non-Muslim religions over a period of 400 years (late fourteenth to late eighteenth century). Finally, Kashmīr fell into Sikh hands in 1819, and after a Sikh rebellion in British-ruled India of the mid-nineteenth century, the region came into the hands of the British. For political reasons the Brits wanted a Hindu head of state—and so for a period that would last 100 years, Kashmīr once again, after five centuries, had Hindu rulers who would support the study of Śaiva Tantra.

But there had been much destruction, and much sacred knowledge had been lost. The new Hindu kings ruled a population that was 95% Muslim. When Sir Pratāp Singh Sāhib Bahādur assumed his throne in 1885, there were only about forty Śaiva *paṇḍit* families left in the region (it was these families whose duty it was to preserve the ancient knowledge). Fortunately, these families held a substantial number of manuscripts of original Tantrik texts (scriptures, commentaries, and original works, including the text you're about to read), but most of them did not understand the content of these texts, not being able to read Sanskrit. As a Hindu, King Pratāp Singh was aware of the treasure trove of scriptures that had been preserved under Muslim rule through painstaking recopying for nearly six centuries.

Sir Pratāp Singh Sāhib Bahādur

Singh's government engaged representatives from the remaining *paṇḍit* families to gather these original manuscripts: written on birch bark, partially eaten by ants, or rotting in moldy attics. Almost no one had been actually *reading* these scriptures, but there were a few *paṇḍit*s left who fulfilled the original meaning of their name and were scholars of the Sanskrit language written in the Śāradā script. These scholars compared multiple manuscripts of each work in an effort to correct errors that had crept in over the centuries of copying, and thereby created rough editions for publication (though many copyist errors remained). Between 1911 and 1947, the government of Kashmīr published about fifty works of Śaiva Tantra, all in the original Sanskrit, as the Kashmir Series of Texts and Studies (KSTS). This is, amazingly, only about 3% of the Tantrik literature that once existed. Another approximately 20% exists in handwritten manuscript form only, still held in government archives in Kashmīr and Nepāl. About 75% of the original body of literature has been lost, probably forever. Fortunately, many (but not all) of the really important and valuable sources survived, since they were copied more frequently, and many of these sources were published in the KSTS series.

In the early twentieth century, the Kashmīr government had stacks of these printed Sanskrit books, commissioned by the king, that virtually no one in Kashmīr actually read. Fifty texts comprising eighty volumes of Sanskrit from a tradition that influenced all of Asian spirituality, now obscure and forgotten by the world. Did these texts contain valuable material? In 1947, when India attained independence and the series finished publication (having lost its funding in the upheaval of independence and Partition), no one really knew of their value aside from the handful of scholars who edited them. However, someone in the Kashmiri government of the time had the thought that Western universities might appreciate having them, and so eighty-volume KSTS sets were mailed to various universities around the world. Onto the shelves they went, where they immediately began collecting dust.

The stage was set for the 1960s. When interest in Eastern philosophy suddenly boomed in America throughout that decade and the following, these encyclopedic scriptures of the spiritual life were just sitting there in university library stacks, awaiting discovery. Some of the students at these universities, influenced by the Beat Generation's appreciation of Indian spirituality, were meditating, experiencing awakenings, and hearing Hindu teachings laced with Tantrik philosophy (though that wasn't known at the time) from the likes of Swāmī Satchitānanda and Maharishi Mahesh Yogī. A few of these students were so captivated that they signed up to study Sanskrit so they could better understand the roots of the spirituality they had been exposed to. One of these young Sanskrit scholars was my former teacher Paul Muller, who as a freshman heard Maharishi speak at Yale. It so happened that Paul's graduate school mentor, Sanskrit professor Gerry Larson, had had a look at the KSTS volumes in the university library stacks, and felt that they might be important. He was too far along in his career to change gears, but he pointed them out to a handful of students like Paul, who became utterly fascinated with them and is still working with them forty years later.

Others, like my former teacher Alexis Sanderson of Oxford, were drawn by intellectual curiosity more than spiritual yearning. Sanderson, like some other young European Sanskritists interested in Śaiva philosophy, journeyed to Kashmīr in the early 1970s so that he could learn directly from the last living guru of the Trika branch of the tradition, Swāmī Lakṣman-jū. Sanderson read all eighty volumes of the KSTS with Lakṣman-jū, then realized that to have the deep understanding he craved, he needed to turn to the original manuscript sources, which were far more numerous. Fast-forward forty-four years (exactly my age, as it happens) to the present: Sanderson has now read thousands of crumbling, handwritten Sanskrit manuscripts and published over 2,000 pages of path-breaking academic work showing that Shaivism was the dominant religious tradition of the Indian subcontinent for 1,000 years (about 400 to 1400 CE), and that its esoteric Tantrik component had an incalculable impact on all the other Indian religions, especially Buddhism. The primary elements of Śaiva Tantrik yoga—including teachings on the 'subtle body', *cakra*s, *kuṇḍalinī*, Tantrik mantras, *mudrā*s, and Deity Yoga—not only have survived, but today pervade the entire world of modern yoga, albeit usually in highly simplified or distorted forms, accompanied by a near-total ignorance of the tradition from which they are derived.

So this treasure trove of spiritual literature just managed to survive into the digital age, and now it will never be lost (at least as long as our technological civilization persists). It's possible that without the publication of the KSTS series—which only happened through the historical accident of the British needing a Hindu king to rule Muslim Kashmīr to preserve their balance of power—no one in the modern age would have taken any interest in the spiritual philosophy of Śaiva Tantra, which 100 years ago was considered obscure, difficult, and not particularly worthy of study by the few scholars who were aware of it. We are fortunate indeed that this formerly secret knowledge was transmitted to the world before the Śaiva tradition evaporated in Kashmīr. In 1991 the last Kashmiri guru of this tradition, Swāmī Lakṣman-jū, died. The following year, virtually all the remaining *paṇḍit* families in Kashmīr left in an veritable exodus driven, at least in part, by fear. Now Kashmīr is wholly in Muslim hands—1,000 years after the first Muslim incursion by Maḥmūd of Ghazni in 1014. Of course most of the Muslims who live there nowadays are gentle and kind people, unaware of the devastation wrought by some of their ancestors. Having visited there, I can attest that some of the generous spirit and open-mindedness of the Kashmiris of old can be found among Muslim Kashmiris today.

Now that I've outlined the history (in a grossly simplified way, of course) of the transmission of the text you're about to read, what about its teachings? Why should we study them? What relevance could they have for our modern lives? Great relevance, as it turns out: many of the teachings that most captivate modern yoga practitioners come straight out of nondual Tantra, but are encountered as mere fragments, having lost the context within which their full power can be felt. Tantrik teachings that are presented without the benefit of understanding the coherent and comprehensive spiritual tradition from which they spring become reduced to what I think of as 'bumper stickers' or fortune-cookie platitudes—vague, appealing yet ambiguous statements like *We're all connected* and *It's all one Consciousness* and *You create your own reality*. Hearing such a teaching, you might well wonder, "What does that really mean? Is there anything more to it than just a New Age, feel-good affirmation? And how does one actually experience the reality that these phrases glibly allude to?"

Understood in the proper context, these teachings of classical nondual Tantra are not at all vague or nebulous. They precisely map the subtle and intricate processes of awareness, and they pay impeccable attention to detail in answering fundamental questions like *What is the fundamental nature of a human being? Is consciousness a static witness or a dynamic process? How do we acquire valid insight, undistorted by our past conditioning?* and *How do we become free of suffering?* Careful answers to these questions informed by direct spiritual realization is the gift we have received from the Tantrik sages who composed and transmitted texts such as the one you're about to read. The specific scripture we're going to explore, the *Pratyabhijñā-hṛdaya*, or 'Heart of the Teachings on Recognition', is not hard to understand for those already comfortable with the fundamental Tantrik teachings (such as those presented in

*Tantra Illuminated*), but for those who are new to this philosophy, it can feel like rather a deep dive into the ocean of classical Tantra. Therefore, the following section, "Spiritual Introduction", lays the groundwork and presents the spiritual teachings that help orient you to the work that follows. In fact, for anyone reading this book with the intention of furthering their awakening and learning to abide fully in their essence-nature, I recommend reading it. In it, I take off my 'scholar' hat and put on my 'practitioner' hat; subsequently, I will (attempt to) wear both simultaneously.

What follows in the next few pages is an edited transcript of a live teaching session. Note how the style of language is different; it is (or can be) what the tradition calls 'direct transmission'. It occurs when lineage teachings that have been fully internalized flow forth spontaneously in response to the presence of those who are open to receiving them. Though the tone of the language might sound authoritative and universal, it still needs to be investigated, explored, and tested in your direct experience, rather than received as a dogma. But this exploration can and should be nonconceptual as well as conceptual. In other words, don't just think about the teachings that follow; try to *sense* where they're coming from. In yourself, feel into the place from which these teachings arose. Because the truth to which they point exists within you if it exists anywhere at all.

*Dedicated to all my teachers and my students*

Parā Devī, ‘the Supreme Goddess’ of the Trika lineage

# Spiritual Introduction: The Heart of the Tantrik Way

You are reading this book for exactly the same reason I wrote it: because of the innate desire within Consciousness to wake up to itself. To know itself as it truly is.

In the Tantrik View, each of us is a complete expression of the energy of Consciousness. Each of us is a perfect movement in its endless dance of self-exploration, self-realization, and self-love. Let us then celebrate the fact that the opportunity has been given us to become *aware* of what we are. Our awakening to our true nature is integral to the energy of life and instrumental to its unfolding. Whether you can sense it right now or not, you long to awaken to your total being, and by so doing, to fall in love with the whole of reality, which is nothing but an expression of your own Self.

You are the one Divine Consciousness made flesh. Your task is simply to become aware of this miracle, this fundamental fact of your being. *Life has created a form by which it may know itself, and that form is you.* Take this statement in; absorb it in its fullness. Become aware that the disparate currents of energy in your being—what you call *thoughts, feelings, sensations, memories, perceptions*—are all simply vibrations of energy, flowing within a field of awareness. You are awareness, and you are the vibrating patterns of energy that manifest within it. Awareness and energy entwined in perfect union: that's all that is ever happening, and that's all that 'you' are.

Once you become aware of the true nature of reality, everything you do becomes an act of reverence. Simply living your ordinary daily life with full awareness becomes a complete practice of meditation, a perfect form of worship, an offering to all beings and to Being itself. Tantra teaches that because there is only One in the universe, all actions are in truth the Divine exploring itself, reverencing itself, worshiping itself.

Needless to say, not all actions seem like an expression of the Divine to the conditioned mind. This is because we do not comprehend the Five Acts that constitute a central teaching of the text that follows. Consciousness not only creates, sustains, and dissolves the worlds of its experience, but also conceals itself from itself as well as reveals itself to itself once again.

### *But if I'm Perfect Right Now...*

The central tension of spiritual life is this: the urge, desire, even need we feel to *transform* ourselves and the equally pressing urge, desire, or need *to accept and love ourselves exactly as we are*. These two vectors of the spiritual life seem to be at odds, don't they? It appears that you could do one but not both. You could either change, or you could honor yourself exactly as you are at this moment. The paradox is that we are apparently being asked to do both. Simultaneously. The Tantrik tradition makes a careful exploration of this dilemma and comes to an insightful conclusion.

The tradition tells us that when you open to the possibility of honoring yourself exactly as you are at every moment, that attitudinal stance necessarily includes honoring your transformation, because you are not a static entity! Truly accepting yourself as you are clearly encompasses accepting change. But what kind of change? With self-acceptance, you no longer seek to force change upon yourself out of a sense of not being good enough; rather, the change and growth of which we speak is simply what naturally wants to happen. In other words, accepting yourself includes accepting whatever Life most naturally wants to do through you, moment to moment.

The tradition also suggests that the process by which Consciousness awakens to itself through you is inevitable and that *everyone is involved in this process of self-discovery*. If you think about it, this claim is quite startling. Not only is there in truth only one spiritual path, dressed up in different cultural costumes, but everyone is on that path. There's only one game in town, and everybody's a part of it, even if they don't know it yet. This game is the process by which life comes to fully know and love and celebrate the whole of itself.

Some people, of course, don't know they're on the path. Either they are still accumulating enough pleasure to realize that accumulated pleasure doesn't lead to fulfillment, or they are still in the process of accumulating enough suffering to motivate themselves to seek a different paradigm. Once you have accumulated a certain amount of suffering (or pleasure, for that matter), something inside you says, *This is just not working.* At this point an opening occurs deep inside (which the tradition calls *śaktipāta*), and what emerges is a willingness to approach life in a way you never before sensed clearly, except perhaps inchoately and fleetingly, as a child. And no matter what you think you know about life, once this opening takes place, whatever you thought you knew has run its course. Something else begins, and continues to unfold.

Some arrive at this point by living the dream of whomever they feel they are supposed to be—right up to the moment when everything they do seems forced, hollow, or somehow pointless. Some arrive at this point by rebelling against society until that doesn't work either. Others may go back and forth between trying to live up to something and trying to tear everything apart.

The great Tantrik master Abhinava Gupta, the guru of the author of our text, taught that deep inside your being, at some point there is a turn, an opening, an expansion. It's subtle at first; it may take the conscious mind months, or even years, to comprehend that this turn has taken place—though if the turn is a sharp one, usually you will become aware of it within a year.

*A turn toward what?* you might ask. With this turn, you may find yourself thinking things like, *There must be more than this. I don't know what this life is about. I don't know what I am supposed to be doing. But I know that no one else really knows either, however much they pretend otherwise. It's like everyone's playing a game without being sure of the rules and without knowing how to win.*

Realizing the truth of *not knowing* gives rise to a longing that you experience more deeply, perhaps even more painfully, than you ever experienced the desire to live up to the programmed standards that were set for your life. The programming ceases to matter much anymore. Now, you experience an openness, a willingness, a humility, and a coming to the path.

Before you embark on the spiritual path *per se*, you may see the world as a big scary place where everyone is trying to persecute you, or you may see it as a game in which you're striving to win a huge prize. Or both. Either way, once you come to the path, you see through your fruitless attempts to be 'safe' or to 'succeed', and a deeper awareness arises—*there's something else going on. Something utterly beyond my programming, and yet much more real. I want to know what that is.*

This initial spiritual opening is often accompanied with immaturity—such as harsh judgments of your previous way of life, of the way others are living, of family and friends who are still 'sleepwalking', and of yourself whenever you fall back into your old ways, as you must at times do. The harshness comes up because in the beginning you haven't yet softened into compassion, in true self-acceptance, which is the maturation of your awakening.

In our immature stage we say, *I have to* ***do*** *this spiritual work; I have to* ***make*** *myself one with God*, and, further, *The people I know should to do it, too. My partner should be doing it. I can't even talk with someone who's not doing this.* At this point in our spiritual work, nothing very deep can happen for us yet. We have made ourselves the agents of our own transformation, taken on responsibility for something that we don't really know how to do, something that doesn't need to be 'done' but rather needs to be allowed, served, facilitated. In the language of yoga, when you make yourself the doer that must act on and forcibly manipulate reality (whether that 'reality' is your mind, your body, or your life situation), no real transformation can take place.

Eventually, our immaturity gives way to a stage in which we're willing to embrace the whole of our being and allow a natural process to unfold. Now, real transformation can happen. Now we get out of our own way and surrender our mental images of the spiritual life to the inner intuitive power known as *kuṇḍalinī.*

Probably the most precise definition of Kuṇḍalinī Shakti is *the innate intelligence of embodied Consciousness.* In spiritual work, the true task of the mind is to get out of the way so that the innate intelligence, *kuṇḍalinī*, can work through the body-mind unimpeded. This is particularly challenging for those who think they *are* the body-mind, which is nearly everyone. We look at the shape of our body and the contents of our mind—the thoughts, the beliefs, the feelings—and we have the notion that this defines who and what we are. This conviction is so deep that it's not even in our conscious awareness. It is challenging, to say the least, for a mind conditioned to believe in its own centrality to accept the invitation to get out of the way.

Wake up to the truth that what you think and believe is not that important, and it doesn't define you. It doesn't point toward reality, because reality is nonverbal and nonconceptual. So you cannot look at the contents of the mind to discover who you are. If you explore your mind, your only discovery will be what you have been conditioned to believe. The mind is, prior to awakening, just an organ that regurgitates conditioning. Subsequent to the onset of awakening, little by little the mind can become a servant of the awakening process. Not so much through embracing new beliefs (which is just trading old concepts for new ones), but more through the power of its attention. What you choose to pay attention to can, over time, radically alter your experience of reality more than anything else.

***A Gentle Lean into Loving Awareness***

The Tantrik tradition offers us an option that makes the whole spiritual path gel into coherence: the gentle effort of leaning into a loving awareness of what is. This means using the power of the will, gently but persistently, to open into nonjudgmental intimacy with whatever is happening in this moment. For example, let's say you're meditating on the breath. Ask yourself: *What is the minimum effort I can expend to be fully present with the movement of my breath?* I phrase it this way because being in real presence requires *softening* into what is, opening to it, becoming intimate with it, until there's no 'it' separate from 'you'. Working with the breath in this way is good practice for more challenging forms of presence. Let's say you're experiencing emotion. Ask yourself: *Can I relax into intimacy with what is right now, and let it all the way in, even if it's painful at first?* For this to work, you must soften into intimacy with the raw feeling rather than your story about the feeling. (Notice how this Tantrik approach is markedly different from what we learn in other forms of yoga.)

Almost any spiritual practice can be performed with this sort of loving awareness, this curious exploration. Anything from yoga postures to meditation to exploring your feelings to walking down the street can become motivated by a sense of wonder, and therefore become part of this process of deeper inquiry into what is. This process, when it's working, is not motivated by the desire to become different from how you are or a 'better person'. You're just following the natural flow of awareness becoming more intimate with itself. And that, as it happens, tends to make you more present, more compassionate, more curious, and more caring, and most people happen to call that being a 'better person'.

Once begun, you cannot stop this process of self-discovery. It's a natural part of your being. But you can definitely slow it way down, if you feed habitual thought patterns and unconscious behavior patterns. This process can take a very long time or happen fairly quickly, depending in part on your ability to be gentle with yourself yet absolutely relentless and persistent with your inquiry.

### *Self-Acceptance and Unconditional Love for What Is*

Loving your own being; fully accepting yourself; accepting what Life wants to do through you; releasing your ambition to transform yourself into someone or something else, some imagined ideal; and, at the same time, fully allowing and making space for your *natural* process of transformation to unfold—this is the heart of the spiritual life.

Be aware that this gentle yet persistent lean into your natural unfolding process is not going to take you somewhere, other than deeper into yourself, or *get* you something, other than self-awareness. All striving to obtain or acquire—whether we're talking about spiritual experiences, dramatic realizations, money, or power, it's all the same—only moves you around on the horizontal plane. There is no paradigm shift. With this gentler Way I've been talking about, you are moving in the vertical plane: deepening your sense of the real.

This is the goal of Tantra: we seek to pierce through and break out of our mental conditioning—like a new butterfly breaks free of the cocoon of its long slumber—and live day by day, even moment to moment, from the deepest place in our being: from Being itself. No words can begin to describe the subtle glory, the beauty, and the quiet joy of living that way. It's a state in which nothing need be added or subtracted. It's like you're gently riding the crest of a wave and can surrender into its flow, and it brings you to anything you need, and bears away what you don't.

The ocean offers a perfect metaphor for this paradigm shift. The ocean is a hugely complex system of fluid dynamics, constantly moving. Sometimes the tide is in; sometimes it's out; sometimes the waves are high; sometimes they're low. Whatever the configuration, there is a pattern: the waves come minute by minute, cresting, breaking, and then folding back to return to the sea. This unceasing movement is like a single complex Pattern, and it's all a part of the same whole. You don't pick and choose a favorite section of a wave and try to hang on to it, do you? It's like that in the awakened life. Once you sense the pattern of life's energy, its flux, how it endlessly ebbs and flows, how could you continue with your picking-and-choosing strategy, or your managing-and-controlling strategy? You can't, and you wouldn't want to. The whole of life is revealed as beauty and rhythm and a thrilling energy—and opening to it, surrendering to and aligning with its ceaseless movement, brings both joy and peace. Joy and peace in boredom, in grief, and in desolation, as well as in happiness. Joy in the dance of the Pattern, and peace in forever releasing resistance to it. *That* is the peace that passeth understanding.

But we cannot come to abide in that paradigm without support. For this process to work, we need powerful teachings that are precisely articulated, that we can contemplate, that are durable, that don't fall apart when we use them in intensely and challenging personal inquiry. Such teachings have the power to destabilize the deep-seated programming that doesn't allow us to experience things the way they really are. Once they have done that work, the teachings can dissolve. We don't need to hang on to them.

### *Set an Intention for This Course of Study*

Let the teachings you are about to encounter be the 'acid bath' to dissolve the calcified structures of your identity and your conditioned ideas about reality. Let them create porosity, movement, and flow. Let them open you to wonder. Take the sūtras deep inside and let them marinate; let them work within you. Come at them from every angle. Hold them up to your own experience. Explore the feelings, the textures, the colors, and the flavors of the teachings. Ask yourself again and again, *What would it be like if I directly realized the truth of this teaching? What might it feel like to abide in the wordless place this teaching arose from?*

Here is one possible sacred intention (*sankalpa*) for reading this book and absorbing its teachings and practices. You can of course compose your own as well.

**_Sankalpa_**

*In the days ahead I'll allow myself to feel into the deepest, purest yearnings of my heart. I will allow those yearnings to bring me into spaces of stillness; spaces of gentle, wordless inquiry; and spaces of opening to whatever lies within. And I further resolve to explore, with loving awareness, whatever I discover within myself until it integrates and shines as one with the light of my innate being. I will not fear. I will not shy away from that light, whether gloriously or painfully bright. Inspired by the teachings of the scripture, I'll look inside and welcome what I see, opening ever deeper day after day, with gentle effort, with sweet effort, allowing the spiritual unfolding that wants to happen and is ready to occur.*

### *Blessings of Gratitude*

Blessings of gratitude and love to all the saints, sages, siddhas, yoginīs, gurus, and wisdom masters—may all those great ones continue to benefit all beings in all times and places. May we fully receive the incredible blessings of their teachings, their practices, their insights, and their shared intention for each of us to realize our true nature. May we walk the path in their footsteps together, never accepting any excuse not to treat ourselves with love and respect. May we honor and serve the unfolding of the awakening process and may we offer the fruit of that process for the benefit of all beings in all times and spaces.

Here and now, extend your awareness out into the world, to all who are suffering, to all who are struggling to awaken. Let us together flow loving compassion toward them and toward all beings, understanding that we are not and never have been separate.

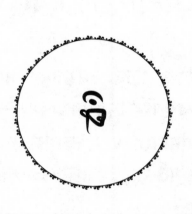

ओं नमो मङ्गलमूर्तये ।

अथ

# प्रत्यभिज्ञाहृदयम् ।

नमः शिवाय सततं पञ्चकृत्यविधायिने ।
चिदानन्दघनस्वात्मपरमार्थावभासिने ॥ १ ॥
शांकरोपनिषत्सारप्रत्यभिज्ञामहोदधेः ।
क्षेमेणोद्ध्रियते सारः संसारविषशान्तये ॥ २ ॥

इह ये सुकुमारमतयोऽकृततीक्ष्णतर्कशास्त्रपरिश्रमाः शक्तिपातोन्मिषित-पारमेश्वरसमावेशाभिलाषिणः कतिचित् भक्तिभाजः, तेषाम् ईश्वरप्रत्यभिज्ञोपदेशतत्त्वं मनाक् उन्मील्यते ।

# PROLOGUE

*Kṣemarāja's original text*

*Oṃ. Reverence to the One who is the embodiment of auspiciousness.*

*Now begins*

## The Heart of the Teachings on Recognition

Reverence to the Divine, which constantly performs the Five Acts [of creation, preservation, reabsorption, concealment, and revelation]—and which, by so doing, reveals the ultimate reality of one's own Self, which is nothing but the Joy of Awareness. || 1 ||

I will here extract for you the ultimate essence from the great ocean of the Recognition philosophy, which is itself the essence of the esoteric teachings of the Auspicious One; for it neutralizes the poison of the cycle of suffering. || 2 ||

Here, the essential substance of the teachings on the Recognition of oneself as God will be gently and concisely opened up for the benefit of those rare devotees whose minds are childlike, who have not labored in the science of rigorous philosophical reasoning, and whose longing for total immersion into the Highest Divinity continues to grow through the influence of their initial awakening experience (*śaktipāta*). |

# PROLOGUE

*with explanation*

*First Introductory Verse*

*[Oṃ] namaḥ śivāya satataṃ pañca-kṛtya-vidhāyine* |
*cid-ānanda-ghana-svātma-paramārthāvabhāsine* || 1 ||

> **Reverence to the Divine, which constantly performs the Five Acts** [of creation, preservation, reabsorption, concealment, and revelation]—**and which, by so doing, reveals the ultimate reality of one's own Self, which is nothing but the Joy of Awareness.**

Kṣemarāja begins his work with the auspicious word *namaḥ*,* 'reverence', 'obeisance', or 'homage', from the root *nam*, 'bow'. To bow is the beginning and the ending of the spiritual path. It is to humble oneself, to acknowledge the infinite majesty of the Divine. It is awe in the face of the great mystery. It is the recognition that one's mind, with all its power, is merely the most ephemeral and fleeting expression of the one Consciousness that pervades all of reality (this is why we lower the head when we bow). That divine Consciousness is the object of Kṣemarāja's devotion, for he initiates his auspicious opening verse with the words *namaḥ śivāya*, 'reverence to Śiva', and in his tradition of nondual Śaiva Tantra, the name Śiva denotes the single all-pervasive divine Awareness that is both the ground and substance of the whole of reality.

As a nondualist, Kṣemarāja holds that Śiva constitutes the essential nature of every conscious being. In this view, there is no 'other' to bow to, so Kṣema understands the real meaning of *namaḥ śivāya* to be 'I merge my awareness in my Divine nature'. We know from other

* *Namaḥ* is a form of the word *namas* (as in *namaste*).

works of his that he explicitly takes *namaḥ* to be equivalent to the word *samāveśa*,[2] which in Śaiva Tantra denotes the experience of oneness with the Absolute, or more accurately the experience of being totally immersed in Divinity, that is, of sharing a single Self with God.* Arguing for the equivalence of these two terms is not such a stretch, for what greater act of reverence is there than to merge oneself with the object of one's devotion? What greater act of humility than to dissolve one's sense of separateness? What greater obeisance than acknowledging that only the Divine truly exists? Such obeisance is in truth nothing but the release of all that holds you back from falling into the very Heart of your essence-nature.

*Contemplation Exercise*

Whisper softly to yourself, "*Oṃ namaḥ śivāya.* I allow my awareness to merge into my real divine nature." Take a deep breath, and let yourself open to the sacred core of your being. Quietly treasure the barest glimpse of it, yet without grasping at it. The moment the experience is no longer fresh, let it go and return to the book.

Now go back and read the opening verse again, and see if you have a deeper feel for it.

As is traditional, this verse is an invocation to the Divine that (a) serves to invoke grace and bless the work it prefaces with auspiciousness and (b) contains allusions to the primary teachings of the work. So let's investigate what the verse is teaching us, with the understanding that these concepts will be unpacked more thoroughly throughout the book. In the verse, Kṣema describes what Śiva, the divine Self, *is* (i.e., *cid-ānanda*, 'the Joy of Awareness') and also what it *does* (constantly performs the Five Acts). He implies that the true nature of the Self is revealed through the constant performance of the Five Acts—because

* As we will learn later, this experience is, in this tradition, said to be due to the temporary falling away of one's false identification with the limited body-mind, which obscures the ever-present true reality of oneness.

when you realize that the Five Acts of God are precisely what you yourself are doing all the time, there is the possibility of a flash of recognition: that you are nothing other than a contracted or condensed form of the one universal Awareness. (This is the Recognition that gives this school of thought its name.) God, or Divine Consciousness, is constantly performing the Five Acts, not on some grandiose cosmic stage, but through *you*.*

*The Five Acts*

| | |
|---|---|
| *sṛṣṭi* | creation, emission, manifestation, flowing forth |
| *sthiti* | stasis, maintenance, preservation |
| *saṃhāra* | dissolution, retraction, reabsorption |
| *nigraha* | concealment, occlusion, forgetting |
| *anugraha* | grace, revelation, remembering |

The performance of these Five Acts through you (and all sentient beings) takes place on all scales and in all spheres. For example, in the social sphere, you contribute to creating some social constructs (from modes of behavior to institutions) and to undermining others. In the cultural sphere, you participate (even just by giving your attention) in creating and maintaining some forms of art and culture, and dissolving others (even just by ignoring them). In the psychological sphere, you create mental constructs that represent and interpret select aspects of reality, become self-identified with them, and therefore invest energy in maintaining them—and you eventually see through them, allowing them to dissolve to make way for new, more effective belief structures. (We call the permanent cessation of this process of storymaking 'liberation'. More on that later.) In the realm of the physical, you create, maintain, and dissolve the various states of consciousness called waking, dreaming, and deep sleep.

I've discussed the first three Acts—what about the fourth and fifth? Well, in any of these spheres, you can either conceal to yourself the

* For a detailed explanation of these Five Acts of God, see page 111 of *Tantra Illuminated.*

fact of your agency as a creator (or co-creator) and dissolver of these realities, or you can reveal that fact to yourself through an expanded meta-awareness, something that is available to you at any moment through the simple act of slowing down for a moment of wordless introspection. (This will be discussed more fully in the chapters to come.)

Though we can contemplate how these Acts play out on many different scales, Kṣemarāja is most interested in bringing our attention to the smallest, most immediate scale of reality, the one that we are all experiencing all the time: our moment-to-moment perceptions, sensations, and cognitions. (Since 'cognition' can cover all three of these, we'll use that term—just remember that it can refer to *any* vibration of consciousness, not only thoughts.) In this he follows the Krama tradition (see *Tantra Illuminated*, pages 248–269)[3] in observing that each and every cognitive event is an expression of the Five Acts.*

Let's explore how this is true. First, any given cognition emerges out of the field of infinite potential (known variously as pure consciousness, spirit, and the timeless ground of being); then it is maintained for a moment, nourished and imbued with reality by your focused attention; then, when attention is withdrawn from it, it dissolves back into the timeless ground. These three phases are expressions of the first three of the Five Acts, on the microcosmic scale of your own mind. This process is easy to observe with the arising of a memory or thought, for a thought really seems to arise out of nowhere and dissolve into nothing. It is a little harder to see (but no less true) with an act of external perception.

Let's take an example. Notice how your gaze might fall on a beautiful flower, and you naturally give it your full attention—'flower-consciousness' arises (*sṛṣṭi*) and remains for a moment (*sthiti*), but when your attention turns elsewhere, such as to a memory or thought, the 'flower-consciousness' dissolves (*saṃhāra*), even though your eyes might still be focused on the flower. The flower fades into the background when you think about something else, and it is no longer experienced in its fullness. It has become the 'wallpaper' on the computer screen of your mind, and your inner state is now colored by the vibration of whatever thought holds your attention.

---

* To be more precise, each is an expression of four of the Five Acts, since the fourth and fifth are alternate possibilities.

Now, according to the Krama tradition, whose esoteric doctrine forms much of the subtext of *The Recognition Sūtras*, every cognition arises from, and subsides into, the timeless transpersonal ground of pure awareness. That is, at the terminus of any stream of cognition (or 'train of thought'), cognition dissolves into stillness, into simple openness—even if only for a second. At that moment, the ground of being, which is unconditioned and expanded awareness, is revealed. That unconditioned awareness, apparent after the dissolution of one cognition and before the emission of the next, is called 'the Nameless' (*anākhya*) in the Krama. It is not so much a separate moment or phase but the ground of the whole process of cognition. It is constantly present, pervading and supporting the three primary phases (or Acts) mentioned above. We are taught that it is most easily accessed in the 'space between thoughts'. In other words, we notice it most readily when being lost in thought gives way to 'coming back to oneself', which is a moment of awareness of your innate subjectivity: it is a tiny window of opportunity, in which you might recognize your true nature.

It is in this moment of touching down in the Awareness-ground that either the fourth or the fifth Act is expressed. If you open to the opportunity for self-recognition, that is an expression of the fifth Act, revelation or grace (*anugraha*); if you miss the opportunity, and remain on autopilot, unreflectively initiating another train of thought to get lost in immediately, then that is an expression of self-concealment or forgetting (*nigraha*). Not to worry, however: the opportunity of which we speak arises many times every single day.

Let's get a bit more specific about what 'opening to the opportunity for self-recognition' means. It refers to noticing that the Power of Awareness (*cit-śakti*) that empowers and englobes the whole process—the creation, maintenance, and dissolution of each cognitive experience—is nothing but your very own Self, your essential Being. (I capitalize Self and Being here to denote equivalence to the Divine.) In other words, you recognize that you, the real you, the conscious *knower* of the process of cognition, are also its *author*.* Furthermore, you see that this Awareness-self is the ground of the threefold process and is not separate from it; in fact, the act of creating, immersing in, and dissolving an experience is a *self-transformation* of Awareness.† It is not such a huge step from that to the realization that you—what you really are—are the creator, sustainer, and dissolver of the whole world of your experience, of the universe as you know it. You are not only a manifestation of God (as all beings are), you are *the* God of the universe as you know it, in the sense that the universe *as you know it* is a direct expression of what you are. Though I have described this revelatory moment of recognition in words, it is not a thought; rather, it is a flash of wordless insight, a moment of nonconceptual seeing. We will return to this teaching later in the book.

So much for *anugraha*, 'self-revelation'. By contrast, in *nigraha*, 'self-forgetting', you do not recognize your authorship of the threefold process of cognition, and so you do not notice the dynamic stillness, the nameless ground of the process, underlying the movement of cognition. This lack of recognition should not be seen as a failure on your part, for to judge yourself for it perpetuates the contraction of *nigraha*, and to love yourself for it opens you to *anugraha*. You can miss the window of opportunity a thousand times, and the same fullness is still available to you the next time. (Though it is also true that the more you visit the fullness, the fuller it somehow gets!) The moment passes; another stream of cognition arises, is maintained, and dissolves, to offer yet another window of opportunity, and so on, infinitely—the rhythmic flow of the waves of consciousness.[4]

*Anugraha* ('revelation'), then, manifests most fully as *pratyabhijñā* ('self-recognition'). The fundamental self-recognition upon which all other empowering acts of recognition are based is the deep, wordless, revelatory recognition that you are the source and author of all that you experience, and yet you are simultaneously something more, which

---

* But not in the sense of being in *control* of the process of cognition. The concept of control of the kind a puppeteer exerts is wholly inapplicable here; the aspect of mind that generates the illusion of that kind of control is *not* the true author of the threefold cognitive process as it imagines itself to be.

† Note that this teaching is therefore distinct from the Patañjalian or Vedāntic teaching of the Self as 'witness', a passive observer that stands apart from what it witnesses.

is eternally free of the conditions of those experiences (such as time and space). This, then, is what Kṣemarāja means when he says that by performing the Five Acts, Śiva reveals (*avabhāsin*) the ultimate reality (*paramārtha*) of His/your own Self (*svātma*): because Consciousness performs the Five Acts through and as you, you are given, again and again, the opportunity to recognize that you are that Consciousness. The Five 'Acts of God' are nothing other than what you yourself are doing constantly (*satatam*), so who could you be other than that One? And if that realization lands properly, it triggers a sense of humble awe, not egoic self-importance (because the socially constructed separate self is not the 'you' we're talking about).

Now, what is the nature of this Self that is revealed through recognition of one's authorship of the Five Acts? Kṣema tells us that this recognition reveals what is ultimately true (*paramārtha*) about the Self: the fact that it is *cid-ānanda-ghana*, 'nothing but the Joy of Awareness'. The phrase could also be translated as 'thick with the joy of being [fully] aware'. That is to say, when you truly recognize the Self that is the ground of every moment of experience, you realize that it is inherently blissful with a joy that derives from the very fact of being conscious, rather than from what you are conscious of. In fact, that quiet joy is a signal that indicates you have in fact accessed the true ground of your being. When awareness rests in itself (*viśrānti*), fully self-aware (*vimarśa*), it always accesses its intrinsic joy (ānanda) in some measure.

Finally, we may note that the phrase *cid-ānanda*, in Kṣema's usage, suggests the eternally conjoined pair of Śiva and Śakti. This is because *cit* (which becomes *cid* when combined with ānanda) denotes the Light of Awareness (*prakāśa*), and ānanda is the natural and invariable expression of the Power of Self-reflection (*vimarśa-śakti*) that is eternally conjoined with that Light. In the Recognition school, *prakāśa* and *vimarśa* are understood to be the non-theistic names of the principles denoted by Śiva and Śakti, respectively. Therefore, Kṣema is also saying that the Self is identical to God/dess.

We may, then, express the inner meaning of the opening verse, as intended by its author, as follows:

> *I allow my awareness to merge into my true divine Self, which, through constantly performing the Five Acts, reveals the ultimate reality of its own nature: that it is replete with, and nothing but, the*

*joy of being aware—of being the fundamental Awareness that is the author and the self-transforming dynamic ground of the process of cognition, identical to God/dess.*

Kṣemarāja's introduction to his text consists of the verse we have been discussing at length, a second verse stating the scope and purpose of the work and a brief prose section describing his intended audience. In the second verse, to which we now turn, he takes up his position as human author and professor of philosophy, while simultaneously implying that he will once again speak with that voice of authority that comes solely from being the recipient of, and vehicle for, lineage transmission.

*Second Introductory Verse*

*śāṅkaropaniṣat-sāra-pratyabhijñā-mahodadheḥ |*
*uddharāmi paraṃ sāraṃ saṃsāra-viṣa-śāntidam* || 2 ||

**I will** [here] **extract** [for you] **the ultimate essence from the great ocean of the Recognition philosophy, which is itself the essence of the esoteric teachings** *(upaniṣads)* **of the Auspicious One** *(Śaṅkara; = Śiva)*, **for it neutralizes the poison of the cycle of suffering** *(saṃsāra)*.

This verse identifies the present work as the *crème de la crème* of the Śaiva teachings, for it is the essence or core of the Recognition philosophy, which is itself declared to be the essence of the Śaiva scriptures. The latter, usually called *tantras*, are here identified as *upaniṣads*, literally 'esoteric teachings' or 'hidden connections', but the term *upaniṣad* is also meant to imply that the Śaiva tantras are equivalent in value to the earlier revelation of the Vedas (for the philosophical sections of those texts are always designated as *upaniṣads*). The Recognition philosophy is here described as a 'great ocean', a standard metaphor for a subject that is vast and as difficult to master as the ocean is to cross. But the use of that metaphor also allows Kṣema to subtly allude to the ancient story of "The Churning of the Ocean", in which the gods and Titans are said to have churned the primordial ocean to extract the Nectar of Immortality (*amṛta*), like milk is churned to make sweet butter. He implies, then, that the essence of the Recognition teachings presented in this text both is as delicious as the sweetest nectar and saves one from the repeated deaths of the cycle of suffering. Indeed, the second claim is explicit, for this 'ultimate essence' of the Śaiva teachings is said to 'neutralize the poison of *saṃsāra*'. There is an allusion here to the legendary poison called *kālakūṭa* (literally, 'the trick of Time'), which the churning of the ocean produced prior to producing the *amṛta*, and which only Śiva could neutralize, just as here only the philosophy based on the scriptures revealed by Śiva can liberate one from all bondage. There is also a secondary metaphor here, that of a poisonous snakebite, for when an antidote for snakebite is administered, it does not remove the poison from the system, but neutralizes its deadly effect. In the same way, the Tantrik teachings do not remove one from the challenges of worldly life, but eliminate the mental suffering that those challenges commonly entail. The *tāntrika* does not seek to escape the world, but to remain fully engaged with it while becoming free of the wrong understanding that causes him to see his life situations as anything but a blessing. This is Kṣema's explicit goal in writing the text.

*Introductory Prose*

**Here, the essential substance of the teachings on the Recognition of** [oneself as] **God will be gently and concisely opened up for the benefit of those rare devotees whose minds are childlike** *(sukumāra)*, **who have not labored in the science of rigorous** [philosophical] **reasoning, and whose longing for immersion** *(samāveśa)* **into the Highest Divinity continues to grow through the influence of their initial awakening experience** *(śaktipāta)*.

Kṣemarāja promises to give his audience the pith and marrow of the Recognition teachings, and then describes what sort of audience he has in mind: those who are devoted to the spiritual path (*bhakti-bhājaḥ*), and whose minds are 'childlike', that is to say, open and receptive, fresh and intuitive, but not scholastically trained, and thus easily put off by too much philosophical wrangling. This last point is reinforced by Kṣema's next statement, that he has written the present work for those who have not labored to master the Indian disciplines of logic and philosophical discourse, and are therefore not overly concerned with our author's ability to refute the arguments of the Buddhists and others. Here Kṣema specifically contrasts his work with its primary source, the *Stanzas on the Recognition of the Divine* by Utpala Deva, which certainly *is* concerned with extremely subtle and refined argumentation aimed at the refutation of the Buddhists and others in matters concerning the operation, function, and ontological status of the powers of consciousness. In other words, Kṣema implies that his work is especially for those whose hearts are open to learning but who cannot or will not read the extremely difficult and abstruse *Stanzas on the Recognition of the Divine.*

Kṣema adds a third, all-important criterion for his readers: he pictures them as having a longing for the experience of union with God, i.e., total immersion in the all-encompassing absolute reality that is the Highest Divinity (*pārameśvara-samāveśa*), an experience that becomes one's default state and fundamental reference point for existence through the teachings and practices of the spiritual path. This longing (*abhilāṣa*) drives you along the path, keeping you from settling for ordinary worldly happiness, beckoning you onward (or inward) with the promise of something infinitely greater: the possibility of becoming established in the truth of your fundamental being, and in your total connection to the whole field of life energy, with all the wisdom and joy that brings.

He tells us that this longing grows due to the lasting influence of *śaktipāta*, a term that denotes the initial awakening to the spiritual path (an awakening that the tradition would soon come to identify with the activation of the *kuṇḍalinī-śakti*, the innate intelligence of embodied consciousness). This awakening invariably has the effect of, first, opening up the inner realm, and second, making the path of inner growth the primary focus of a person's life. It is called the 'Descent of Power' or the 'Descent of Grace' (*śaktipāta*) because it often feels like a powerful, even life-changing, infusion of energy that was not earned or merited, but ultimately proves to be the greatest of blessings.*

This last criterion takes his text from the merely philosophical realm into the spiritual realm. He is expressly stating that his purpose is not only to educate, but to give devoted seekers the tools of

---

* For a thorough discussion of *śaktipāta*, see *Tantra Illuminated,* pages 152*ff* and 321*ff*.

understanding and practice that, if fully applied, will lead them to their goal of full immersion in divine reality. The present work, then, is classed not as a *śāstra* (work of philosophy or science), but as an *upadeśa* (wisdom-teaching) that serves as a direct means to liberation when put into practice.

We turn now to Sūtra One and its commentary. First we present Kṣemarāja's words alone, in literal translation, unadorned by any explanation of mine. Kṣema's words are presented in the original Sanskrit on left-hand pages and in translation on right-hand pages.*

Presenting Kṣema's original words on their own first allows for meditative contemplation. Don't try to have an intellectual understanding of what he says on the first reading; just let the words of the master percolate within. After that, Kṣemarāja's text appears again, this time in boldface type, interspersed with my thorough explanations, in roman type. Given the great cultural distance between you, the modern reader of English, and Kṣema's Sanskrit-reading audience of 1,000 years ago, my explanation is necessary to understand the text thoroughly, as you'll see (in Chapter Three, if not sooner!). I offer this explanatory material to engage the mind and senses to allow understanding to flesh out what your intuition has already glimpsed. Far from purely intellectual, the explanatory sections also include simple practices and contemplation exercises to help actualize your understanding on the level of holistic direct experience, which is always where we want to go with these teachings.

We will follow this structure throughout the book.

* But readers with knowledge of Sanskrit will need to refer to the appendix for the critical edition of the text, which is what is actually translated.

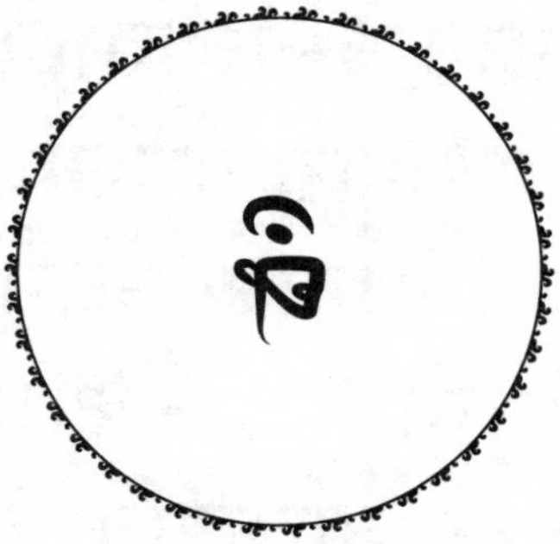

तत्र स्वात्मदेवताया एव सर्वत्र कारणत्वं सुखोपायप्राप्यत्वं महाफलत्वं च अभिव्यङ्क्तुमाह

चितिः स्वतन्त्रा विश्वसिद्धिहेतुः ॥ १ ॥

'विश्वस्य'—सदाशिवादेः भूम्यन्तस्य 'सिद्धौ'—निष्पत्तौ, प्रकाशने स्थित्यात्मनि, परप्रमातृविश्रान्त्यात्मनि च संहारे, पराशक्तिरूपा 'चितिः' एव भगवती 'स्वतन्त्रा'—अनुत्तरविमर्शमयी शिवभट्टारकाभिन्ना 'हेतुः'—कारणम्। अस्यां हि प्रसरन्त्यां जगत् उन्मिषति व्यवतिष्ठते च, निवृत्तप्रसरायां च निमिषति;—इति स्वानुभव एव अत्र साक्षी। अन्यस्य तु मायाप्रकृत्यादेः चित्प्रकाशभिन्नस्य अप्रकाशमानत्वेन असत्त्वात् न क्वचिदपि हेतुत्वम्; प्रकाशमानत्वे तु प्रकाशैकात्म्यात् प्रकाशरूपा चितिरेव हेतुः;

# CHAPTER ONE

*Kṣemarāja's original text*

To that end, to make it clear that the very Divinity that is one's own Self is the cause of everything, and can be reached through an easeful and direct path, and is the most worthwhile fulfillment possible, it is taught:

**Awareness, free and independent,**
**is the cause of the performance of everything.** || 1 ||

**Awareness** itself is the Goddess, the Supreme Power.

She is **free and independent**, meaning that she consists of absolute Self-awareness, and She is not different from Lord Śiva.

She **is the cause of the performance of everything**: 'everything' means all the Principles of Reality from Sadāśiva down to Earth; 'performance' means the creation [of all these Principles], their continued manifestation, and their dissolution, meaning their coming to rest within the Supreme Knower.

For when She is flowing, the world appears, and remains there; when her flow ceases, it disappears—your own experience is the witness of this.

Now anything else—such as *māyā*, *prakṛti*, and so on—could not be the cause of any object or aspect of reality because anything separate from the Light of Awareness would be unperceivable, and therefore cannot be said to exist. On the other hand, if something *is* manifest to perception, for that very reason it is inseparable from, and of one nature with, the Light of Manifestation, and the nature of this light is simply Awareness. So Awareness alone, and nothing else, must be considered the cause of anything that appears.

न त्वसौ कश्चित् । अत एव देशकालाकारा एतत्सृष्टा एतदनुप्राणिताश्च नैतत्स्वरूपं भेत्तुमलम्;—इति व्यापक-नित्योदित-परिपूर्णरूपा इयम् ।—इत्यर्थलभ्यमेव एतत् ।

ननु जगदपि चितो भिन्नं नैव किञ्चित्; अभेदे च कथं हेतुहेतुमद्भावः? उच्यते । चिदेव भगवती स्वच्छस्वतन्त्ररूपा तत्तदनन्तजगदात्मना स्फुरति,—इत्येतावत्परमार्थोऽयं कार्यकारणभावः । यतश्च इयमेव प्रमातृ-प्रमाण-प्रमेयमयस्य विश्वस्य सिद्धौ—प्रकाशने हेतुः, ततोऽस्याः स्वतन्त्रापरिच्छिन्नस्वप्रकाशरूपायाः

For this very reason place, time, and form are not able to divide the fundamental nature of Awareness, for they are emitted from it and are sustained & animated by it. Thus, this Awareness equally pervades all places, arises at all times, and encompasses all forms. Exactly this meaning is to be inferred from the sūtra.

Objection: I understand that the world cannot exist as something different from Awareness. However, if Awareness and the world are the same thing, how can one be the cause and the other an effect?

It is said in reply: It is the blessed Goddess who is nothing but Awareness, pure and free, who vibrates as the various infinite worlds—the condition of 'cause and effect' has only this much reality.

And the sūtra reads as it does to allow for this [second] interpretation: this Awareness alone is **the cause of the performance of everything**, which means the manifestation of knowers, the means of their knowing, and the objects they know.

The function of the ordinary, feeble means of knowledge is to make apparent some previously unknown fact. Therefore, they are neither useful for nor capable of establishing Awareness, which is **independent**, undivided, and continuously revealing itself.

सिद्धौ अभिनवार्थप्रकाशनरूपं न प्रमाणवराक-मुपयुक्तम् उपपन्नं वा[३]। तदुक्तं त्रिकसारे

> 'स्वपदा स्वशिरश्छायां यद्वल्लङ्घितुमीहते।
> पादोद्देशे शिरो न स्यात्तथेयं बैन्दवी कला[४] ॥'

इति।

यतश्च इयं विश्वस्य सिद्धौ पराद्वयसामरस्यापादनात्मनि च संहारे हेतुः, तत एव स्वतन्त्रा। प्रत्यभिज्ञातस्वातन्त्र्या सती, भोगमोक्षस्वरूपाणां विश्वसिद्धीनां हेतुः।—इति आवृत्त्या व्याख्येयम्।

अपि च 'विश्वं'—नील-सुख-देह-प्राणादि[५]; तस्य या 'सिद्धिः'—प्रमाणोपारोहक्रमेण विमर्शमयप्रमात्रावेशः, सैवं[६] 'हेतुः'—परिज्ञाने उपायो यस्याः।

As it is said in *The Essence of the Trinity*:

> If a person desires to step on the shadow of his head with his own foot, he will find his head will never be in the place of his foot. The power of the Point is similar. ||

And the sūtra reads as it does to allow for this [third] interpretation: This Goddess Awareness is the **cause of the completion of everything**, meaning its *reabsorption*; that is, She brings about the fusion of everything in complete nonduality, causing one to relish all things as a seamless unity. For this very reason, She is said to be **free and independent**.

[4] We can derive a further explanation by reading the sūtra in this way: when its **independence** is fully recognized, this Awareness becomes the **cause of all attainments**, i.e., both happiness and liberation.

[5] Furthermore, this Awareness can be **'caused'** through the **'attainment'** [i.e., the experience] of **anything.** That is, there is an opportunity to recognize Awareness whenever any object of perception—the color blue, the feeling of happiness, the body, the breath, etc.—enters and merges with any self-aware knower by ascending through the path of perception. Through this reading, the sūtra teaches that there is an easy means of realization.

अनेन च सुखोपायत्वमुक्तम्। यदुक्तं श्रीविज्ञान-भट्टारके

'ग्राह्यग्राहकसंवित्तिः सामान्या सर्वदेहिनाम् ।
योगिनां तु विशेषोऽयं संबन्धे सावधानता ॥'

इति।

'चितिः'-इति एकवचनं देशकालाद्यनवच्छिन्नताम् अभिदधत् समस्तभेदवादानाम् अवास्तवतां व्यनक्ति। 'स्वतन्त्र'-शब्दो ब्रह्मवादवैलक्षण्यम् आचक्षाणः चितो माहेश्वर्यसारतां ब्रूते। 'विश्व'-इत्यादिपदम् अशेषशक्तित्वं, सर्वकारणत्वं, सुखोपायत्वं महाफलं च आह ॥ १ ॥

As it is said in the sacred *Lord Vijñāna-Bhairava*:

> The awareness of knower and known is common to all
> embodied beings, but for yogīs there is this difference:
> they pay careful attention to the connection. ||

The word '**Awareness**' is in the singular, expressing that it is not limited by place, time, or form, and suggesting the falsity of all dualistic doctrines. The phrase '**free and independent**' denotes difference from the Vedānta by stating that Awareness has an unlimited power of action as its essence.

Thus the compound '**the cause of the performance of everything**' conveys that the Divinity that is one's own Self is infinitely powerful, is the cause of everything, is reachable through an easeful and direct path, and is the most worthwhile fulfillment possible. || 1 ||

# CHAPTER ONE

*with explanation*

Before each sūtra, Kṣemarāja writes a short introduction explaining its purpose and/or how it connects to the previous sūtra(s).

**To that end, to make it clear that the very Divinity that is one's own Self [1] is the cause of everything, [2] can be reached through an easeful and direct path, and [3] is the most worthwhile fulfillment possible...**

Right up front he tells us the purpose of Sūtra One, communicating clearly what he wants us to understand from it (the mark of a good teacher). Since he will unpack five main meanings from the sūtra, he highlights here the three teachings he thinks are most important: [1] above corresponds to the first and second interpretations below, [2] to the fifth interpretation, and [3] to the fourth. But the most significant element of this brief introduction is the phrase 'the Divinity that is one's own Self', since that corresponds to 'free and independent Awareness' in the sūtra below. He is indirectly telling us that Awareness, Divinity, and the Self are three different terms for one and the same thing in this system. That is to say, unbounded Awareness is the true identity of the Deity that is not different from one's own essential nature. Or to put it another way, the essential nature of all conscious beings is Awareness, and that is the Deity of this system.

Oh, and 'to that end' at the beginning of the introduction refers back to the prose paragraph of the prologue, so it means 'to begin to open up the essential substance of the Recognition teachings'.

**...it is taught:**

**|| CITIḤ SVATANTRĀ VIŚVA-SIDDHI-HETUḤ || 1 ||**

**Awareness, free and independent,**
**is the cause of the performance of everything.**

The first sūtra is the beginning and the end of the journey, and it pervades the whole. Full realization of the truth the sūtra points to is itself final liberation. The sūtra's scope ranges from the entire cosmos of time and space down to the most trivial and ordinary of human experiences; furthermore, it dissolves the apparent gulf between those two extremes. In light of this teaching, the ordinary becomes extraordinary, and the extraordinary becomes rather ordinary (or at least to be expected). In its light, the whole of reality is seen to be animated by conscious energy, pulsing in a dynamic dance of self-reflection, seemingly achieving ever-greater harmony with itself, yet paradoxically complete and perfect in each moment.

The word 'performance' rightly suggests that all activity is the artistic self-expression of the Absolute: sometimes a joyous dance, other times a tragic play, but like all art, always a conscious self-exploration that yields wondrous beauty as its fruit. Indeed, that beauty, that sense of expansive, awestruck wonder (*camatkāra*) that naturally arises upon truly seeing the exquisite pattern of the Whole, is the only consummation sought by divine Consciousness in all Her activities. In that state of true seeing, Awareness becomes fully itself. Since the joy of seeing and being seen in Her true nature is the only purpose to Her 'performance', anything whatsoever can contribute to that consummation.

Before we turn to Kṣema's detailed commentary on the first sūtra, let us contemplate some alternative translations of this all-important initial revelation of the text. All of these possibilities are allowed, even suggested, by the Sanskrit, and the first four are alternatives that Kṣema definitely has in mind, as we shall see. Take your time with these; savor them, feel their vibration, and ask yourself, "What experience of reality might give rise to these words?" Instead of answering that question with more words, simply explore the feeling that arises when you gently hold it in awareness.

### *Sūtra One Alternative Translations*

- » **Awareness, needing nothing outside itself, is the cause of the manifestation of all things.**
- » **Awareness, of its own accord, is the cause of the** [ultimate] **fulfillment of all things** [and beings].
- » **Autonomous awareness is the source of all attainments.**
- » **Autonomous awareness can be accessed through the experience of anything.**
- » **Awareness voluntarily causes all things to become what they are.**
- » **Awareness, free and independent, is the cause of the magic of the universe.**

Now we will turn to Kṣema's commentary. He begins, as usual, with a simple gloss of the sūtra. A gloss is a terse definition or rephrasing that provides one or two synonyms for each word in the sūtra. It is an important device a Sanskrit commentator uses to clarify the basic meaning. For these crucial phrases, I give both the English and the Sanskrit, bolding the Sanskrit words that occur in the original sūtra.

**Awareness itself is the Goddess** [we worship]**, the Supreme Power.** (*Parā-śakti-rūpā* ***citir*** *eva bhagavatī*)

The opening statement of Kṣema's commentary describes the first word of the first sūtra: *citi* (pronounced CHIT-ee), or 'Awareness'. He tells us that in his school of nondual Śaiva Tantra, awareness is the ultimate principle of reality, the highest goal to be attained, and that which is most worthy of worship. And the adherents of this school do worship awareness, quite literally, in the form of the lineage-goddess of the Trika, Parā Devī. Parā Devī ('Supreme Goddess'), also known as Parā Śakti ('Supreme Power') and Parā Vāk ('the Supreme Word'), is nothing but the personification of the power of fully expanded Awareness. As her name suggests, she is not so much a sectarian deity as a means of focusing devotion on the most fundamental power of reality as we know it. In Tantra, of course, every power or potency (śakti) is worshiped as a goddess, or rather as an aspect of *the* Goddess. So clearly, the Supreme Goddess is she who embodies the most fundamental power. Looking at it another way, we could say that equating

Parā Śakti with awareness constitutes an argument on the part of this school that awareness is indeed the fundamental power. The Sanskrit permits this alternate translation: **The blessed Goddess who is nothing but Awareness is the Supreme Power.** Imagine the cumulative impact on your life of worshiping 'Goddess Awareness' every day for years on end—for adherents of this school did just that.

Parā is a multivalent deity, associated not just with the power of awareness, but also with two of its specific features. The first of these is *pratibhā*, which simultaneously means intuitive insight, embodied instinct, and creative inspiration. The second is *icchā*, the urge to act on that inner wisdom—i.e., the movement of the unconditioned will. So worship of Parā is the veneration of these principles as well, both of which we shall return to in due course.

### She is free and independent, meaning that she consists of absolute Self-awareness. (*svatantrānuttara-vimarśa-mayī*)

Kṣema next addresses the second word of the sūtra, *svatantra*, which means independent, self-reliant, free, and autonomous. Following his teacher, he argues that the fundamental attribute of Awareness is its total autonomy, its unlimited freedom (*citiḥ svatantrā*). But here's where it gets interesting: he glosses *svatantrā* with 'consisting of absolute self-awareness' (*anuttara-vimarśa-mayī*). That is to say, Kṣema is telling us that to be completely self-aware is to be completely free. This is one of the most powerful teachings he has to offer us. We continually seek to experience freedom by manipulating our external circumstances; for example, most people believe if they have more money, they will be more free and independent. But what kind of independence is it that depends on money for its continuance? Kṣema tells us that freedom is an inner state that arises naturally once you know yourself completely. To know the whole of your real being is to know a freedom so limitless that it has to be directly experienced to be believed. The attainment of such self-awareness is made possible by clear and honest self-reflection. Let's engage in a little of that now.

*Contemplation Exercise*

Hold this question in awareness for a few minutes, without grasping toward an answer: *What is the connection between self-awareness and independent freedom?*

Now, think of a time when your self-understanding increased substantially. How did it result in greater independence and freedom?

Conversely, think of a time when you experienced a breakthrough in your sense of your independence. Can you see how it was linked to an increased self-awareness?

The most common misunderstanding here is to think that this freedom is something individual or personal. In fact, we are talking about the innate autonomy of awareness, and that awareness is one and the same for all beings. When you access this divine freedom, you recognize that no one could ever limit your experience but you. You see all beings in yourself and yourself in all beings, so this is not the sort of 'freedom' in which you try to take what you want at others' expense, which in reality is not freedom at all but another kind of bondage.

[and] **She is not different from Lord Śiva.** (*śiva-bhaṭṭārakābhinnā*)

Here we have an interesting ambiguity: did Kṣemarāja mean this phrase to stand on its own, or to be a further explanation of why Goddess Awareness is free and independent? If the latter, then he is letting us know that in this system, the Goddess is not considered subordinate to Śiva, as she is in some lineages. If the former, he is telling us that in this system, God is not different from or other than Awareness. Perhaps both are intended. At any rate, we can be sure that he intends us to understand that Śiva and the Goddess are just two names for the same principle.

Contrary to popular perception, in Tantra the ultimate reality is not commonly represented by the conjoined pair of Śiva and Śakti. More often, one or the other name/image will be used, for either the God or the Goddess can be taken to signify the whole of divine reality. Here, Kṣema tells us that he will use the image of the Goddess as the guiding metaphor in his teaching, while signaling to us that he doesn't mean anything different from what is signified by the name Śiva. Nondualist Tāntrikas have always preferred to focus on Śakti, because they are more interested in the ways consciousness flows in manifest reality than in the purely transcendent realms often denoted by the concept of Śiva. Having said that, we should acknowledge that these categories are fluid, and in nondual contexts, either name can denote the all-encompassing Divinity.

Note that in the bold phrase above we have the pronoun 'She'. But the Sanskrit is actually much more subtle than that. Remember that as a pure nondualist, Kṣema is *never* differentiating the Goddess from your very own power of awareness, the power you're using right now. Thus he can talk about the infinite field of divine consciousness and your individual experience in the same breath, with the same word (*citi*). One reason he can do this easily is that Sanskrit is a gendered language, and the word *citi* (awareness) is a feminine noun—so you see, the pronoun 'she' can simultaneously refer to the Goddess and awareness as such. In other words, the feminine pronoun can be translated as 'she' or 'it' interchangeably, depending on the context. Kṣemarāja takes advantage of this ambiguity at many points in the text. Unfortunately, this flexibility of the pronoun is impossible to translate, since in English we only use 'she' to refer to persons. But try to keep the flexibility of the original Sanskrit in mind when you see the word 'she'—it means *both* awareness and the Goddess.

So far he has explained the first two words of the sūtra. Now he goes on to gloss the rest of the sūtra—and note that this is only his first of five different explanations of its meaning.

**She/it is the cause** (*hetu*) **of the performance** (*siddhi*) **of everything** (*viśva*)**: 'everything' means** [all the Principles of Reality] **from Sadāśiva** (tattva #3) **down to Earth** (tattva #36)**; 'performance' means** [1] **the creation** [of all these Principles]**,** [2] [their continued] **manifestation, i.e.,** [their] **stasis, and** [3] [their] **dissolution, meaning** [their] **coming to rest within the Supreme Knower.**[5]

Kṣema tells us that this Power of Awareness is the cause of the creation, stasis, and dissolution of the whole of reality. He defines 'reality' in terms of the schema of the thirty-six *tattvas* (please see pages 124–149 of *Tantra Illuminated*, for without understanding the *tattvas*, you will be confused at a number of points in this book). This is significant, because the thirty-six *tattvas* are not a map of reality like one that a material scientist would draw; rather, they constitute a map of the total experience of reality had by conscious beings. A map of subjectivity, then: unlike the periodic table of the elements, *all* of the *tattvas* appear in and inform every moment of human experience (though you may not yet be aware of the more subtle among them).

As Kṣema indicates, thirty-four of the thirty-six *tattvas* are caused, that is, they emerge from the primal Cause, whether the latter is identified as Śiva (tattva #1) or Śakti (tattva #2), two sides of the same coin. That Cause, or Source, is not only the Creator, but also the Maintainer and Destroyer of every aspect of reality. Kṣema carefully chooses words for these three Acts that point to their real nature: thus 'creation' is really the *emergence* of what is eternally held in the Source as pure potentiality (*sṛṣṭi* = *niṣpatti*, and note that the latter word means 'consummation' as well as 'emergence'). The second Act, known as 'maintenance' or 'stasis', is not at all static, but rather a continually refreshed manifestation, he tells us (*sthiti* = *prakāśana*). And 'dissolution' is really the *reabsorption* of what has been manifested back into its Source, here named as 'the Supreme Knower' (*saṃhāra* = *para-pramātṛ-viśrānti*).

With that final phrase, Kṣema reminds us again that he is not differentiating here between divine Awareness and your apparently ordinary awareness, for the Supreme Knower is the essence and core of all beings whatsoever. This non-differentiation is easy to see in the original Sanskrit, where it is clear that this description of the creation and dissolution of the whole universe is equally a description of your individual creation and dissolution of your own experience of reality—for the latter process is nothing but the former reiterated on a smaller scale. Indeed, it is only in translating Kṣema's words into English that even the illusion of difference appears. He simply describes the one process, which operates on all scales. This point is driven home by what he says next:

**For when She** [i.e., Awareness] **is flowing forth, the world appears** (*unmiṣ*)**, and remains there; when Her flow ceases, it disappears—your own experience is the witness of this.**

Since reality is manifested by the power of awareness and has no existence apart from awareness, the world only appears when awareness is flowing. Kṣema tells us that our own experience is the witness (*sākṣī*) of this: a nice double meaning, for he suggests 'I' am nothing but the witness of all that arises and subsides in my moment-to-moment experience, and also implies that my daily experience of falling asleep repeatedly confirms that when my awareness does not flow toward it, the world truly ceases to exist for me. Similarly, the world of dreams ceases to exist the moment I awaken and reverse the flow of awareness.

As within, so without. As above, so below. The daily cycle of waking and sleeping is a microcosm of a vast cycle of creation and dissolution and re-creation of worlds. If the consensus reality I know in my waking state still exists while I am asleep, it is only because other beings are awake to witness it. Since all that exists exists solely within Awareness, there cannot be objects without subjects; in other words, without perceivers, there are no perceivables. This proposition reminds people of the old saw "If a tree falls in the forest, and no one is there to hear it, does it make a sound?" The answer, in fact, is indisputable: it cannot make a sound, because 'sound' denotes the experience a perceiver has when a vibration moving through the medium of air strikes the eardrum. It denotes the coming together of all those factors within the field of awareness. It is meaningless to talk of 'sound' otherwise. Similarly, it is meaningless to talk of the existence of the universe independent of our conscious perception of it (except as a theoretical construct wholly dependent on that very perception). Note, however, that this philosophy is not asserting simplistically that there was no universe before we were here to see it—rather, what is being said is that 'the universe' denotes the collection of perceivable objects *as they exist within our perceptions.* What we call 'the universe' is only the coming together of perceivers and things perceived, a coming together exclusively mediated by the means of perception (including ṃind and consciousness) possessed by those perceivers. We cannot know anything apart from this. One of the most widespread modern myths, produced by a superficial understanding of physics, is the notion of an unconscious universe that exists independently of conscious beings, vast and uncaring, against the backdrop of which our appearance is a meaningless and accidental blip. The fact is, such a universe exists only as a figment of our imagination. All that we have direct evidence of, all that can be properly called real, are the phenomena that arise from the union of perceivers and perceived. So it is literally true to say that the universe appears when awareness is flowing. Scientists and philosophers can all accept the main point being made here (provided they understand it)—but Kṣema takes it further, making a point that not all will accept without meditative investigation: that awareness is not only necessary for the appearance of reality, it is the *cause* of its appearance, its apparent consistency, and its disappearance too.

Though the universe has no existence apart from awareness, awareness can and does exist apart from the universe. You can verify this through your own experience as well, for example, in states of meditation where all percepts and concepts have dissolved, but awareness remains. Since it is the only constant in radically different states of experience, wholly divided from each other—the waking state, the dream state, and the *samādhi* state ('contentless meditation')—the tradition argues that awareness must be seen as the substratum of all these states. And in Indian philosophy, the substratum of anything is also the cause of its manifestation.

We will return to all these themes later, so don't feel you need to understand them completely now.

We can sum up everything we've learned so far quite easily: *Awareness brings about the emission, sustenance, and reabsorption of all subjects and objects of experience as an expression of itself. Awareness is therefore the ultimate principle of reality and that which is most worthy of reverence.* Of course, these propositions will only make sense if you grasp that the mind is one of the things produced by this all-encompassing Power of Awareness, not the other way around as materialists believe. This is why we use the phrase 'divine awareness'—not to denote the awareness that is possessed by some separate God, but to indicate an Awareness that is all-encompassing and fundamental to all that it can observe, including the mind and its contents, including time and space, and especially including your very sense of self.

Having established Awareness as the ultimate universal cause and source of all phenomena and the experiencers of those phenomena, Kṣema now seeks to refute some of the other principles put forward as the universal cause by other schools of Indian philosophy. He seeks to demonstrate, with a terse bit of logical argument, why these other principles (such as *māyā*, 'illusion', or *prakṛti*, 'primordial materiality') cannot possibly be the universal cause. To understand his argument here, we need to first understand the Sanskrit word *prakāśa.* There is no direct translation for *prakāśa* into English, as will become clear when you look at the meanings of the word below.

Some meanings of the word *prakāśa:*

(adjective) visible, shining, apparent, manifest; (out in the) open, public
(noun) light, splendor; manifestation; expansion, diffusion

The meanings here group around two distinct concepts in English: light, on the one hand, and appearance or manifestation on the other. We can understand the connection between them by considering the fact that only when something is illuminated does its existence become apparent (at least to our visual sense). The noun *prakāśa* derives from the verb *prakāś*; its meanings are 'to shine, to shine forth, to appear, to manifest, to come into being'. The Sanskrit language itself, then, has already predisposed our philosophers toward a certain line of thought, which is hardly a problem for them, because they consider Sanskrit a sacred, divinely revealed language. (Later we will explore a word often paired with *prakāśa*, the word *vimarśa*, 'reflection', which continues and deepens the metaphor of Awareness as Light.)

Light becomes, then, the central metaphor for Awareness in nondual Tantrik philosophy. This is a felicitous choice of metaphor, because it correctly implies that the whole of manifest reality consists of various forms of energy. We can translate *prakāśa* in the current context as 'the Light of Manifestation', 'the Light of Creation', or even 'the Light of Awareness', since we already understand that it is Awareness that manifests all things and states of being. But keep the more basic meanings in mind and you will understand the following paragraph better; for example, *aprakāśa* simultaneously means 'unmanifest', 'unperceivable', and 'not shining'. Let's turn now to Kṣemarāja's refutation of the other schools.

**Now anything else—such as *māyā*** ['the power of illusion']**, *prakṛti*** ['primordial materiality']**, and so on—could not be the cause of any object or aspect of reality because anything separate from the Light of Awareness** (*cit-prakāśa*) **would be** [by definition] **unperceivable** (*aprakāśa*)**, and therefore cannot be said to exist. On the other hand, if it *is* something manifest to perception** (*prakāśamāna*)**, for that very reason, it is inseparable from, and of one nature with, the Light of Manifestation** (*prakāśa*)**; and the nature of this light is simply Awareness** (*cit*)**. So Awareness alone, and nothing else,** [must be considered] **the cause** [of anything that appears].

Now let's break that down a bit. Kṣema specifically cites the causes of the manifestation of the universe that are posited by two of the popular philosophies of his day: *māyā*, 'the power of illusion', posited by Vedānta, and *prakṛti*, 'unconscious materiality', posited by Sāṅkhya. We cannot get into the details of these concepts here, though I will mention that *prakṛti* is not so very different from the modern concept of nature as an unconscious collection of matter-energy and the mechanical laws that govern it. What is important to realize is that in both of these philosophies, the cause of manifestation (whether *māyā* or *prakṛti*) is something distinct from Awareness or conscious Spirit. Sāṅkhya philosophy endorses a strong duality of matter and spirit, but sees both as real, whereas Vedānta argues that only divine consciousness (*brahman*) is real, and matter only appears to be so, like a convincing mirage of water in the desert. Note that both of these views derive from, and perpetuate, a fundamentally world-denying attitude. In these views, the world is basically a vale of tears, tainted by sin, and thus not to be associated with divine Consciousness, which is absolutely pure and couldn't possibly be sullied with the creation of a messy reality filled with dualities like pure and impure, good and bad, beautiful and ugly.

The Tantrik View, by contrast, refutes all duality, or rather argues that duality is only true as a level of perception that does not yet see the unity of the whole. It argues that everything is a direct expression of the Light of Awareness, which can assume any form without losing its fundamental nature.

Kṣemarāja's paragraph above is a condensation of an argument previously presented by his teacher, Abhinava Gupta. Abhinava Gupta's argument amounts to this: that to whatever cause the philosophical opponent proposes, we can respond, "Is this cause something separate from the Light of Awareness or not? If you say it is separate, we say then that anything separate from that Light is by definition unknown and unperceivable, in which case it cannot be said to exist except as a mental construct, which clearly *is* a vibration of the Light of Awareness. If you say it is not separate, but rather is indeed something manifest and perceptible, then you must allow that it is just another form of the Light of Awareness, whose nature is to manifest objects of experience. Therefore, the only possible cause of anything and everything is Awareness."[6]

(If this is a bit exhausting for you, take heart from the fact that this kind of philosophical argument is rather rare in Kṣemarāja's text. I can tell you that it is quite a bit easier to follow in the Sanskrit!)

In Western philosophical terminology, the nondual Tantrik View is considered 'idealism' (as opposed to 'realism'), since it argues that everything is internal to Awareness and is an expression of the same. Regardless of how it's labeled, the fundamental point here is undeniable: we can be sure that objects of experience are internal to awareness, but we cannot be sure that they have any existence external to awareness, and it is pointless to speculate anyway, since all we have access to are the contents of awareness. Some of the contents of awareness may allow us to construct speculative models of realities external to awareness (such as models of the workings of the subconscious mind), but they will necessarily always remain merely models—we will never be able to *prove* that anything exists external to awareness.

Having established that undeniable fact, in the Tantrik View it then follows that there is only *one* Awareness, not many, since we observe that we do not each live in our own private universe, but rather can communicate effectively about an obviously shared reality, divided only by our concepts of it. To put it more accurately, each instantiation of the one Awareness has both a private reality (such as your dream world) and a shared reality (what we call the physical universe, though of course it is made of nothing but consciousness). It's like a Venn diagram, except that the shared reality is considerably larger than the diagram depicts, and the 'private' realities exist only in relation to the shared reality.

In the Tantrik View, there is really only one Being, looking at the world that is its 'body' through countless pairs of eyes. This One Being, we could say, looks at itself from every possible angle. This is logically true as much as it is 'spiritually' true, but we will have to wait until later to see how that's so. Suffice to say for now that the only divisions that exist are mental constructs, that is, divisions created by the way we see and think about things. Therefore, they too are not different from the Light of Awareness, and hence cannot divide it. This is exactly what Kṣema declares next.

**For this very reason place, time, and form are not able to divide the fundamental nature of Awareness, for they are emitted from it and are sustained & animated by it. Thus, this Awareness** [equally] **pervades all places, arises at all times, and encompasses all forms. Exactly this meaning is to be inferred** [from the sūtra]**.**

Since Awareness is the only cause of everything, the primary apparent divisions of reality—place, time, and particular form—are themselves expressions of the one Light, and have their being solely within it. They are ways of experiencing reality, rather than absolute divisions. They seem absolute from the perspective of the mind, which is conditioned to notice difference, and to perceive as static form what is really a flux of interrelating and interdependent energies. As modern physics has shown, time and space are not fixed but relative: for example, time flows at a very different rate when space is different (e.g., altered by the presence of a massive body like a planet). Furthermore, in the equations of physics, which have now described the nature of the physical universe to quite a precise degree, there is no intrinsic difference between the past and the future (since nearly every equation in physics works the same in both 'directions')—which seems to support the Tantrik notion that past and future are mental constructs, or at least functions of the way our consciousness perceives.

According to the Tāntrikas, particular forms—people, trees, bugs, stars—which seem so absolutely different to our senses are really just various permutations of a single indivisible matter-energy field, animated by a single Awareness. Differences of name and form are significant to the conditioned mind, so it easily misses the fact that people, trees, stars, potatoes, etc. are all different forms *of the same thing,* in the same way that gold objects are all nothing but gold, whether we call them a necklace, an earring, a bracelet, a statue, or bullion. Everything we can name is not only made of the same 'stuff' (the fundamental particles and waves that, in this view, all express the one Light of Awareness), it also forms a *single interconnected matrix.* Everything in the universe is inseparably 'entangled' (to use the physics terminology) with everything else. Right now, you are constantly exchanging particles with your environment, and you are so intrinsically interconnected with it that if you were separated from it for even sixty seconds—if, for example, you were suddenly teleported to outer space—your body would immediately die and fall apart. That's how interconnected and interdependent reality is, and that's just one of countless examples we could give.

Rather than go on and on, let's sum up the main points here. Apparent divisions in the field of reality, whether of time, space, or form, are not absolute, but are categories with which the analytical mind carves up reality. These categories are not, on the other hand, pure imagination, for they are based on actual boundaries. And boundaries, properly understood, are the places we meet: the points where different aspects of the one field meet and trade information and/or share being. These boundaries are fluid and ever shifting with the currents of the one field of energy that constitutes the manifest form of the Light of Awareness. They are the ways in which Awareness interacts with itself, so they do not constitute actual divisions of the One. Therefore, Kṣemarāja argues, the Light of Awareness equally pervades all places (*vyāpaka*), is continuously arising in all times (*nityodita*), and expresses itself as all forms (*paripūrṇa-rūpa*).

Of course, this logical argument about the nature of reality doesn't change the quality of your life until and unless it becomes direct experience. The joy of that direct experience makes the pleasure of entertaining these concepts seem feeble and pale by comparison.

Whew! We are almost done with the dense philosophy stuff. Some people call it 'heady', but here it's just the opposite: we are trying to get beyond the limitations of the conditioned mind. These reflections can feel difficult for the mind because the mind's parameters are generally much narrower than the scope of what we are trying to look into here. In other words, in this section we are trying to use concepts to go beyond the mind! That's not easy, especially if you keep trying to figure out the concepts instead of intuitively looking in the direction they're pointing. Don't get bogged down by the philosophical arguments; they're really only for those people who need to see that a View has been thoroughly thought through before they can entrust themselves to it (I'm one of those people, but you may not be, and either way it's fine).

Now Kṣema starts to shift the discussion away from the terms of philosophy and toward those of theology. But one would be misunderstanding him to think he's saying something different: he's always just using different forms of discourse, different pedagogical strategies, to get at the same thing. If you experientially (nonconceptually) grasped a single one of his statements in its completeness, you wouldn't need any others.

In the next paragraph, he pictures a student raising a logical objection, and gives an answer that shows us that words and logic can only approximate the truth.

[A skeptical student asks:] **I understand that the world cannot exist as something different from Awareness. However, if Awareness and the world are the same thing, how can one be the cause and the other an effect?**

**It is said in reply: It is the blessed Goddess who is nothing but Awareness, pure and free, who vibrates as the various infinite worlds** [of experience]**: the condition of 'cause and effect' has only this much reality.**

It's significant that early in his text, Kṣema alludes to the importance of questioning. His hypothetical skeptical student, who reappears throughout the text, shows us that we are not supposed to accept these teachings as dogmas. We are supposed to interrogate them, wrestle with them, unpack them, and try to climb inside them, as it were. And Kṣema's answer to this first question is meant to show us the limits of words and concepts. In general, his language grows more poetic as he leans deeper toward truth, as indeed it must. Nor is it always directly translatable into English: for example, the word *sphurati*, here rendered as 'vibrates', simultaneously means 'scintillates, sparkles, shines' and 'bursts into view, becomes manifest, expands'. Try reading the sentence above again, substituting the various alternate meanings I've just mentioned. Slow down, get quiet, whisper it to yourself, and feel its deep power.

To explicate Kṣema's beautiful sentence, I can hardly do better than to quote the words of my primary academic teacher, the greatest living scholar of Śaiva Tantra, Alexis Sanderson of Oxford. He paraphrased Kṣemarāja in this way:

> Consciousness is that unique reality that can appear this way, i.e., as the substance of all our experiences; it is one thing that can appear as a plurality without losing its central identity.[7]

As Sanderson demonstrates, someone who is completely steeped in the teachings of these texts can spontaneously produce a sentence as worthy of contemplation as the original source itself.

We can summarize all we've learned so far with two sentences: *Goddess Awareness brings about the emission, sustenance, and reabsorption of all things as an expression of herself. Nothing else could be the cause because nothing exists separate from the divine Light of Awareness.* The second sentence summarizes the last five pages.

Now Kṣema introduces a second interpretation of the meaning of his sūtra, his second of five interpretations, in fact, each one more concise than the last. He wants to show us that the first sūtra is so richly layered with meanings that it contains in seed form the whole rest of his text.

**And the sūtra reads as it does to allow for this** [second] **interpretation: this Awareness alone is the cause of the performance of everything, which means the manifestation** (*prakāśa*) **of knowers, the means of their knowing, and the objects they know.**

**The function of the ordinary, feeble means of knowledge** [that is, sense-perception, reasoning, or authoritative testimony] **is to make apparent** (*prakāśa*) **some previously unknown fact. Therefore, these are neither useful nor capable of establishing** [the nature of] **Awareness, which is independent** (*svatantra*)**, undivided, and continuously revealing itself** (*sva-prakāśa*)**.**

Here Kṣemarāja introduces one of the primary triads for which his lineage (the Trika or 'trinity') is named: that of the knower, the means of knowing, and the object known. 'The performance of everything' or the 'universal accomplishment' (*viśva-siddhi*) of the sūtra here means manifesting the whole of reality as an expression of this triad. That is to say, everything that exists is either a knower, a means of knowledge, or an object of knowledge. These three categories exhaust the whole of reality. 'Knower' and 'knowledge' have become such intellectual terms in English, but the equivalent terms in Sanskrit (*pramātṛ/pramāṇa/prameya*) could be translated equally well as 'perceiver–perception–perceived' or 'cognizer–cognition–cognized'. These three are all seen as arising from a single ground, Awareness. One of the central arguments of the Trika, based on meditative experience wedded to logical reflection, is that the three are aspects of a single process, and it is erroneous to regard them as separate. It's like the case of a trident mostly immersed in the water—a viewer might think that there are three separate rods sticking out of the water, when if he just looked a bit deeper, he would see that there is only one object.

Ādyashānti, a contemporary meditation master and spiritual teacher, describes his final awakening in these terms. He tells us that he was sitting in his meditation room one morning, and he heard a bird chirp outside, and in that moment he clearly saw the nature of things: "I suddenly realized I was as much the sound and the bird as the one hearing the bird, that the [one] hearing and sound and bird were all manifestations of one thing. I cannot say what that one thing is, except to say *one* thing." This is exactly the insight of the Trika masters of 1,000 years ago (whose teachings Ādyashānti was wholly unaware of at the time of his awakening). They called the *one* thing *citi*, which we translate as Awareness or Consciousness.[8]

Kṣema next makes the point that the usual ways in which we figure out the nature of things don't apply when it comes to ascertaining the nature of Awareness. He alludes to the three most common ways of acquiring knowledge: direct perception with the senses, sound logical inference, and the testimony of a reliable, authoritative source. He scorns all three as 'feeble' in this case, for they are all ways that the mind comes to acquire some fact it didn't know before, and Awareness cannot be known in this way—it cannot be illuminated by the mind, for it is the very source of whatever light the mind possesses. The mind is a functional contraction within Awareness, dependent on it and limited; it is the moon to the sun of Awareness, luminous only because of its capacity to reflect light. Awareness, by contrast, is independent, unlimited, and self-luminous. It knows the mind, but the mind cannot know it. It is the prerequisite for the mind's activity, but it can see with or without the mind. The mind cannot grasp it, because grasping is a form of contraction, and Awareness is completely uncontracted. It remains, quietly illuminating itself, when the mind dissolves.

If you're not quite getting this, then perhaps you've understood perfectly. That's the whole point—the mind will never grasp Awareness. All it can do is surrender to that fact, and in surrendering, melt into the ever-present field of Awareness. Kṣemarāja conveys this truth with a quote from a scriptural text, the *Trikasāra*. In this text, Awareness is characterized as the absolute center of your being, the point from which all seeing is done. That point, by definition, is unobjectifiable. That is, it cannot be made into an object of perception, since it is the very center of your subjectivity. You cannot see the point from which all seeing is done—you can only *be* it. The text communicates this truth with a clever metaphor.

**As it is said in the *Trikasāra* ('The Essence of the Trinity'):**

> **If a person desires to step on the shadow of his head with his own foot, he will find his head will never be in the place of his foot. The power of the Point is similar. ||**

How can you see the seer? Just as you've never seen your own face directly, when you go looking for your innermost Self, you cannot find it. But you can be it—in fact, you've never stopped being it, and you'll notice that the moment you stop trying to become anything and everything *but* it. As a wise man once said, "The one you are looking for is the one who is looking." But if you are trying to *see* that one, to have an 'experience' of it, you can search forever, like someone searching high and low for the glasses on their own head. When you give up the search and relax into the fullness of your own being—there it was, all along. To be a 'seeker' presumes the absence of that which you seek. So ironically, to go searching for the truth, you must deny that it is here. And for most people, that denial is what makes the spiritual path take a long time.

If this teaching is at all frustrating or confusing for you, good. That's the mind being 'checkmated'. Don't worry; everything will become clear for you as we go along. For now, just breathe and be okay with where you're at now. That's the real beginning of the spiritual path.

We can sum up the second interpretation of the sūtra in this way: *Awareness is the ever-present and sole identity of you, your experience, and the objects of your experience, which are really three aspects of a single process.*

Now let's go on to Kṣemarāja's third interpretation of his own sūtra. This interpretation focuses on the ultimate consummation of the creative play of Awareness, a consummation sometimes characterized as the goal of spiritual life—but the term 'goal' implies a future point we want to get to, a point at which things will be more right and perfect and divine than they are now. That is not what is implied here. Rather, Kṣemarāja simply alludes to the inevitable culmination of the process. Is a river more beautiful and perfect when it merges with the sea? Surely its beauty is expressed in the whole of its length, and so it is for your process as well. Let's contemplate his words:

**And the sūtra reads as it does to allow for this interpretation: This Goddess Awareness is the cause of the completion (*siddhi*) of everything, meaning its *reabsorption*; that is, She brings about the fusion of everything in complete nonduality, causing one to relish all things as a seamless unity (*parādvaya-sāmarasya*).**[9] **For this very reason, She is** [said to be] **free and independent (*svatantrā*).**

The completion or fulfillment (yet another meaning of *siddhi*) of all things is their merging or reabsorption into the ground of being, the divine absolute. However, this does not refer to the dissolution of the universe at the end of time, but rather the true seeing had by awakened awareness: that all is one, a single field, a seamless whole. Now, since this oneness is always and ever the true nature of reality, what Kṣema is referring to here is the shift in perception had by one who transitions from the unawakened paradigm to the awakened paradigm. Subjectively speaking, it may seem as if that which was divided becomes undivided, that which was many merges into one. The advent of this state of true seeing is called *parādvaya-sāmarasya*, literally 'fusion into total unity'. The word *sāmarasya* ('fusion, unification, oneness') comes from *sama-rasa*, literally 'same taste', so the implication is that in this state, everything is imbued with the flavor of the Divine. That should not be taken to mean that every experience literally 'tastes' the same, which would of course be terribly boring, but rather that everything 'tastes like God', meaning it is seen as absolutely beautiful exactly as it is, as expressing divine perfection and wholeness. In this tradition, remember, the capacity to experience beauty and expansive wonder (*camatkāra*) is the highest nature of Awareness. And this is not some kind of Pollyanna-fantasy overlay onto reality. Rather, the masters of this tradition speak of the capacity to experience the terrifying, the disgusting, and the wrathful as beautiful, just as much as the astonishing, the compassionate, and the peaceful (see page 303 of *Tantra Illuminated*).

It is the Goddess Awareness, Kṣema tells us, that brings about the fusion into complete nonduality. This means that it is not the conditioned mind that accomplishes this. However much the everyday mind with which we are generally identified might want to bring about this divine state, it has no power in this realm. This consummation can only be effected by your deeper nature, the Goddess power within all things. For this reason, your primary responsibility on the spiritual path is to open to that deeper power within you, surrender your false sense of agency in the process, and simply allow it to unfold. Accepting that 'you' are not in control of this process doesn't mean resigning yourself to some sort of fatalism—on the contrary, if you want to see this process unfold in the present lifetime, it is your responsibility to give Goddess Awareness the space to do what she does best, if you only give her the chance. That is what a daily practice really is—giving Her the time and space to do Her work. Not a daily practice where you are just going through the motions or 'numbing out' with pleasurable meditation techniques, but one in which you listen deeply and seek to open fully to what is true for you in the present moment.

Kṣema ends this paragraph with: **For this very reason, she is free and independent** (*svatantrā*). Why does he say that? What's the connection? First, Goddess Awareness is independent in the sense just discussed, that she brings about the unfolding of the spiritual process that leads to total immersion in nondual reality with *or* without the understanding of the conditioned mind. Second, she is independent in the sense that she is also the ground of the whole process; she is the unified field, that which manifests everything in oneness with itself. Third, she retains her nature of absolute freedom regardless of whether individual beings perceive her correctly or not. That is, you are Awareness whether you see it or not; Awareness is free whether you sense that or not; oneness is true whether you perceive it or not; and the you you think you are is lovingly held by Awareness in every moment, whether you feel that or not.

To look at this key issue of the autonomy of Awareness from another perspective, we may observe that all objects of awareness are relative and dependent: they are created by your (and others') perception of them and don't exist independently of that perception. But Awareness is independent and absolute, not dependent on its objects or on your perspective—just like the speed of light is always the same, no matter how fast you are going.[10] Einstein declared that the speed of light has an absolute value, while all other motion is relative. This is a perfect parallel to the way the tradition understands Awareness as absolute, though its manifestations are relative. This is why your essence-nature, which is this very Awareness, remains as it is despite all the changes and traumas endured by the mind and body.

We may summarize the third interpretation in this way: *Awareness independently brings about the completion/fulfillment of all beings and things by causing you to experience their perfect unity.*

We now proceed to Kṣemarāja's fourth interpretation of his own sūtra, which is quite straightforward.

**We can derive a further explanation by reading the sūtra in this way: when its independence is** [fully] **recognized, this Awareness becomes the cause of all attainments** (*siddhi*), **i.e., both happiness** (*bhoga*) **and liberation** (*mokṣa*).

In the Tantrik View, there are two goals in human life: worldly success and spiritual liberation. The former consists of learning how to successfully negotiate the challenges of embodiment. Creating sufficient harmony and balance in relation to one's work, family, mental and physical health, and so on gives rise to worldly happiness, the ability to simply enjoy life (*bhoga*). Unlike all the pre-Tantrik forms of yoga, the Tantra does not reject this goal, but actually provides tools to achieve it. The second goal, or purpose, of human life is seemingly very different: to achieve a spiritual liberation that entails a deep and quiet joy that is utterly independent of one's life circumstances, a joy in simply existing, free from all mind-created suffering (*mokṣa*). Tantra does not see these goals as necessarily mutually exclusive: you can strive for greater happiness and success (*bhoga*) while at the same time cultivating a practice that will enable you to deeply love your life even if it doesn't go the way you want (*mokṣa*). It's a win–win proposition. But the tradition correctly points out that unless the former activity (*bhoga*) is subordinated to the latter (*mokṣa*), it is likely that pursuit of *bhoga* will take over. That outcome is potentially regrettable for two reasons: first, if you haven't cultivated *mokṣa* (spiritual liberation) and your carefully built house of cards collapses, as can happen to any of us at any time, you will have no inner 'safety net' to catch you. Second, even if everything goes your way, the greatest happiness that *bhoga* has to offer you is nothing compared to the infinite joy (*ānanda*) and freedom of *mokṣa*. (However, I must also say that this way of talking can be misleading, because the mind cannot imagine 'infinite joy' except as worldly happiness times infinity. That's not the nature of *ānanda*—it is indeed infinite in the sense of boundless and independent, but the word 'joy' is just a pseudonym, an approximation. This is a state impossible for the mind to encompass, as you can easily see if I tell you that in this state, one can experience agony or grief as an aspect of *ānanda*. The truth is, there is *nothing* about *mokṣa* that could satisfy the mind the way *bhoga* does, but since, as it turns out, the mind is a very small part of your real being, that ends up not mattering as much as you might think.)

Now, we tend to think that *bhoga* and *mokṣa* require very different skill sets, and in terms of techniques that is true. But, Kṣema tells us, both forms of development are propelled by the same fuel: the power of Awareness. It gives rise to both **when its independence is** [fully] **recognized**. That is, when the total autonomy of Awareness is seen, a profound shift takes place. You recognize that it is you who creates your experience of reality, and that nothing, not your karma and not even your own conditioning, can determine your inner state; therefore, you are the sole author of your destiny. Not, however, in the usual sense of that phrase, that you can make anything happen by dint of sufficient effort, that you can bend the world to your individual will. No, that is total delusion. Rather, you become the author of your own destiny when you recognize that there is only ever one real choice: whether to listen to your programming or to listen to your deeper wisdom, the intuitive sensing of your essence-nature. Awareness is so free it can choose to bind itself to the mind's conditioning and become nothing but an expression of that conditioning, with little to no hint of its deeper nature. And, in turn, it can melt into its expanded state and thereby access the unbounded wisdom of its intimacy with the pattern of the whole. You create your experience of reality through this choice, moment to moment.

The beauty of it is that choosing to act from your deeper wisdom, your innate inspiration (*pratibhā*), does not mean you must rid yourself of all your conditioning (which you couldn't do anyway). It means that the conditioned mind, which includes all learned behavior, becomes the servant of this wisdom that contains and expresses the pattern of the whole. Of course, discerning the difference between that wisdom and your subconscious layers of conditioning is only possible with an introspective, listening-based meditation practice, because the latter creates ever-increasing clarity of perspective. But the practice starts now, with the simple intention to listen more deeply, to see whatever needs to be seen, and to feel whatever needs to be felt.

Recognizing the freedom you have to choose—recognizing that no matter how challenging your circumstances, Awareness is never bound—is the key to both *bhoga* and *mokṣa*. Recognizing the innate autonomy of your real nature is profoundly inspiring. You always have the freedom to shift your inner stance, the perspective from which you're seeing a situation, and that shift makes all the difference: it will always unveil either a different way of approaching the situation or an opportunity to surrender more deeply to what is, or both.

*Contemplation Exercise*

Think of a situation in your own life that is challenging. Become aware of the stance you are adopting toward it. Then recognize that other stances are possible. Give yourself the freedom to adopt any stance, noticing that each creates a different experience of reality.

Now, recognizing your freedom to choose, tap into your deeper wisdom. Which perspective, which stance allows you to be in service to all beings involved (including yourself)?

Now surrender a little deeper, giving your heart's consent to things as they are, including your role in them. Let yourself fall into harmony with the situation by adopting the stance that is both true to you *and* in service.

Now we turn to Kṣemarāja's fifth and final interpretation of Sūtra One. It is both powerful and subtle, for here Kṣema begins to hint at the secret teachings of the Krama lineage, which he will delve into further in Sūtras Eight, Eleven, and Twelve. Both Kṣema and his guru, Abhinava Gupta, were initiates into the lineage called the Krama ('Sequence', referring to the phases of cognition), also known as the Mahārtha ('Great Truth'). They both present the Krama teachings as the inner core of the Trika and Pratyabhijñā teachings. In the following interpretation, Kṣema arrives at a very different reading of Sūtra One (by taking the sūtra as a *bahuvrīhi* compound, for you Sanskritists out there), which essentially amounts to this: *This Goddess Awareness can be recognized through any experience whatsoever.* With that orientation, carefully read through Kṣema's paragraph a couple of times.

**Furthermore, this Awareness can be 'caused' through the 'attainment'** [i.e., experience] **of anything. That is, there is an**

**opportunity to recognize Awareness whenever any object of perception—the color blue, the feeling of happiness, the body, the breath, etc.—enters and merges with any self-aware knower by ascending through the path of perception. Through this reading, the sūtra teaches that there is an easy means of realization** [taught as the Krama revelation].

The path to liberation was generally considered arduous, requiring incredible self-discipline and the cultivation of ever more refined states of consciousness through yogic meditation. The Krama, however, took a different approach, arguing that because we are never separate from our true nature, it must be accessible at any given moment, not only in the transcendental state. All that is required is careful attention to what happens in any given act of perception. This method, which is only briefly touched on here, is called the *sukhopāya*—the easy or pleasant method. Easy is a relative term, however, and 1,000 years ago life required quite a bit more hard physical labor than it does for many of us now. Compared to such labor, or to the privations and striving of *haṭha-yoga*, quiet contemplation is pleasant and easeful. Yet the 'easy means' Kṣema alludes to here is not really all that easy for us modern folks, because it requires both patience and an ability to slow down and become fairly quiet inside. Isn't it interesting that slowing down and getting quiet, so pleasant and easeful for a premodern person, is so difficult for an overstimulated, attention-deficit denizen of the twenty-first century? Yet for just that reason, it's even more powerful!

Let's briefly explore the method Kṣemarāja has in mind. The key term that differentiates what he is describing above from ordinary perception is the term 'self-aware' (*vimarśa*). Through the intensified awareness brought on by being clear, sharp, awake, and fully present, one may see the nature of reality more deeply and absorb the significance of what is seen more fully. What is it that Kṣema would like us to see clearly? In a nutshell, that everything you experience becomes a part of you. There is no actual separation between you and the object of your experience, because all that really exists is the energy of awareness, vibrating at the 'frequency' of each particular object of experience. The practice that leads to this realization is the simple tracking of each object as it transits from being an apparently objective phenomenon to merging with your innate subjectivity. First you notice an object (e.g., chocolate ice cream), then you become absorbed in perceiving it for a short length of time ("mmm ... *chocolate*"), then your attention shifts to the quality of your experience of the object ("I love chocolate!"), and finally it shifts to a wordless contemplation of your inner being, with a subtle remnant of the flavor of the experience lingering. These four phases of experience are what Kṣemarāja describes as "the process of the ascent of the object through the path of perception to merge with the self-aware knower" (here giving a slightly different translation from the one found above).

The fourth and last stage of this process is the one we move on from the quickest and savor the least, though it is actually the most crucial stage for a person developing self-awareness. When you follow through each experience completely, it leads to the center of your subjectivity, your innermost self. To put it in spiritual language, each object of perception attains union with God through your experience of it. To understand this, remember that God = Awareness in this system, and then contemplate that each thing you experience becomes one with Awareness through the simple act of being perceived: it rises through one of the sense-channels (vision, hearing, etc.) and dissolves within the space of pure subjectivity. Thus each act of perception is a mirror of the universal process by which all things are realized as an aspect of the One.*

Kṣemarāja gives this innovative teaching greater legitimacy by citing a scriptural verse that can be interpreted in a similar way:

**As it is said in the sacred *Lord Vijñāna-Bhairava*:**

> **The awareness of knower and known is common to all embodied beings, but for yogīs there is this difference: they pay careful attention to the connection.** || [verse 106]

The *Vijñāna-Bhairava*, itself an innovative text, here defines a *yogī* (which in general means 'meditator') as one who closely examines the relationship between subject and object, seer and seen. The pre-Tan-

* Indeed, as if to underscore this point, some manuscripts of our text read 'offering' (*upahāra*) where we have 'ascending' (*upāroha*), implying that each sense-experience is an offering to God within.

trik yogas (such as that of Patañjali) posited an absolute division between seer and seen, describing the innermost self as a witness that stands apart from everything it sees. Furthermore, in those systems this witnessing self (*puruṣa*) is qualitatively different from that which it perceives: it is conscious spirit, and everything that it perceives is unconscious matter. The Tantrik view alluded to in the above verse is radically different. It argues that every thing is the self-transformation of Awareness; therefore, that which is perceived is an aspect of the perceiver. In this context, 'paying careful attention to the connection' means, among other things, noticing that each and every phenomenon is simply a vibration in the field of your awareness, and that you are that which encompasses all that is perceived, and that you are that which unifies it into a single field. We will investigate this more later on—this is just a foretaste.

We have now explored the five different interpretations Kṣemarāja gives to his first sūtra, so we're ready to sit and meditate on the sūtra itself. Read it to yourself quietly, three to five times, and then just sit and absorb its vibration. There's no need to think about all you've learned, and no need to try to clear the mind either. Just take the vibration of the sūtra into the deepest part of your being that you can.

**Awareness, free and independent,**
**is the cause of the performance of everything.** || 1 ||

Kṣemarāja concludes his commentary on Sūtra One with some footnotes and a summary. The notes briefly indicate how this teaching differs from other forms of Indian philosophy and religion.

**The word 'Awareness'** [in the sūtra] **is in the singular** [i.e., not the plural], **expressing that it is not limited by place, time, or form, and suggesting the falsity of all dualistic doctrines. The phrase 'free and independent' denotes** [the] **difference** [of our View] **from the Vedānta by stating that Awareness has an unlimited power of action as its essence** (*māheśvarya-sāratā*)**.**

We already explored above (page 54) the teaching that Awareness is unlimited by place, time, and form, since those categories are all emitted and sustained by Awareness itself. Kṣemarāja briefly notes here that his system denies that any dualism is ultimately real. Dualism is simply the teaching that everything boils down to two or more irreducible essences, such as spirit *versus* matter. Though some forms of dualism are provisionally, partially, or temporarily real, none are ultimate, for as we have seen, everything is an expression of a single unified field, the Light of Awareness.

In his second point, Kṣema wants to make sure we're aware that his system is different from that of the Vedānta, which also asserts that 'everything is consciousness'. Despite that basic agreement, the two systems are very different indeed, because in Vedānta, all activity is an illusion. This must be so because in the Vedāntic view, the Absolute (*brahman*) has no *śakti* ('energy, power, dynamism')—specifically no *kriyā-śakti*, or 'power of action'.[11] This is why Kṣema makes the following point the one that sets his system apart: **Awareness has an unlimited power of action as its essence.** This crucial phrase, *cito māheśvarya-sāratāṃ* in the Sanskrit, admits more than one possible translation. Alternatives would be 'Awareness has boundless sovereign power as its essence', or, more vaguely, 'Awareness has Divinity as its essence'. For Kṣema, the use of the word *maheśvara* instead of *brahman* to denote the Divine is important, because the former, in Sanskrit grammar, implies an absolute capacity to act, a dynamic quality that the static Brahman of the Vedānta lacks.

Finally, like in any good college textbook, Kṣema sums up what his Sūtra One commentary has shown us.

**Thus the compound 'the cause of the performance of everything' conveys the fact that Awareness, the Divinity that is one's own Self, consists of all powers and potencies, is the cause of everything, is realizable through an easeful path, and constitutes the most worthwhile fulfillment possible.**

The astute student who compares this summary with Kṣema's introduction to Sūtra One (see page 42 above) will notice that something has been added: there are four points established in this conclusion, whereas only three points were stated in the introduction. Clearly, Kṣema feels that the various powers of Awareness were established along the way; he is perhaps thinking of the most recent discussion above, though he may also be alluding to the third interpretation of

Sūtra One (since that is the only interpretation of the five that doesn't correspond to one of the points of the introduction).

In these brief concluding points, Kṣemarāja is suggesting that if you were to fully see and know the reality of your essential nature, you would realize that it is the infinitely powerful cause of everything. For this to be true, of course, it must be the case that this Awareness is not personal to you, for it is clear that your individual personhood is not infinitely powerful. The ground of your being is the ground of all Being, and *that* is the infinitely powerful cause of everything. He also offers an assurance that since it *is* your essential nature, realization of the Awareness-ground can occur through an easeful and direct path (the *sukhopāya*, which will be elaborated further at the end of Chapter Eight and in Chapters Eleven, Seventeen, Eighteen, and Nineteen). And finally, he tells us that this realization is the most worthwhile fulfillment possible, literally the 'great fruit' (*mahā-phala*) that is the consummation of human life. It is the fullness of being (*pūrṇatva*) that all human striving is aimed at and which only the realization of one's true nature succeeds in reaching.

This completes our study of Sūtra One and its commentary.

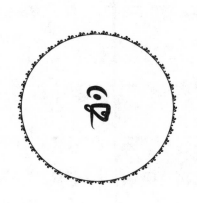

ननु विश्वस्य यदि चितिः हेतुः, तत् अस्या उपादानाद्यपेक्षायां भेदवादापरित्यागः स्यात्— इत्याशङ्क्य आह

स्वेच्छया स्वभित्तौ विश्वमुन्मी-
लयति ॥ २ ॥

'स्वेच्छया', न तु ब्रह्मादिवत् अन्येच्छया,

तयैव च, न तु उपादानाद्यपेक्षया,—एवं हि प्रागुक्तस्वातन्त्र्यहान्या चित्त्वमेव न घटेत—'स्व भित्तौ', न तु अन्यत्र क्वापि, प्राक् निर्णीतं 'विश्वं' दर्पणे नगरवत् अभिन्नमपि भिन्नमिव 'उन्मी-लयति'। उन्मीलनं च अवस्थितस्यैव प्रकटीकरणम् ।—इत्यनेन जगतः प्रकाशैकात्म्येन अवस्थानम् उक्तम् ॥ २ ॥

# CHAPTER TWO

*Kṣemarāja's original text*

Objection: "Surely, if Awareness is the Creator, it needs something to create *with*, in which case you have failed to avoid a dualistic doctrine."—To address this doubt, it is taught:

**Through Her own Will, Awareness unfolds the universe on the 'canvas' that is Herself.** || 2 ||

**'Through Her own Will'**, not through another's will, such as Brahmā's or anyone else's.

Through that Will alone, without relying on any external materials or causes—for if She were dependent in that way, she would not have the autonomy that we have described as inherent to Awareness; therefore, the very fact of *being* Awareness would be compromised.

**'On the canvas which is Herself'**, and not on anything else, She **unfolds the universe** as if it were separate and different from Herself, though in actuality it is not separate, just like the image of a city reflected in a mirror.

And this process of unfolding is simply the making manifest of what abides within Awareness as latent potential.

Therefore, it is taught here that the world exists in a state of oneness with the Light of Awareness. || 2 ||

# CHAPTER TWO

*with explanation*

Kṣemarāja opens Chapter Two with a possible objection to what we have learned so far, again showing us the importance of critical thinking in this tradition.

[Objection:] **"Surely, if Awareness is the Creator, it needs something to create *with*, in which case you have failed to avoid a dualistic doctrine."**

**To address this doubt, it is taught:**

|| SVECCHAYĀ SVABHITTAU VIŚVAM UNMĪLAYATI || 2 ||

**Through Her own Will, Awareness unfolds the universe on the 'canvas' that is Herself.**

In other words, the whole of reality is nothing but the creative self-expression of the Absolute. It is the articulation in tangible form of the myriad ways in which Goddess Awareness reflects on Her infinite Self. It is Her self-awareness flowing into form, coalescing into patterns of embodiment. The universe exists for no other reason than Her innate urge toward creative self-expression, and the medium of that expression is nothing other than Herself.

In contemplating this sūtra, remember, first of all, that this universal Awareness is not different or separate from your apparently individual awareness. The fact that Awareness is worshiped as divine in this system should not be taken to imply that it exists as a kind of cosmic 'person' separate from you. In this nondual view, Awareness is *always* simultaneously divine and ordinary, both all-encompassing and limiting itself to this very moment. (Note that the Sanskrit grammar allows us to translate this sūtra using either 'itself' *or* 'herself'.)

The Tantrik authors who flourished in Kashmīr in the tenth century were nearly as interested in the philosophy of aesthetics—which explores the question of what makes art beautiful—as they were in spiritual inquiry. It is not surprising, then, that Kṣemarāja chooses an artistic metaphor when he comes to describe how Awareness expresses itself as the tangible, sensual universe. Let's break down the words of the sūtra to deepen our understanding of the metaphor. The verb *unmīlaya*, 'unfold', or 'display, cause to appear', also means 'unfurl, open up, cause to blossom'. It is a word often used for the blossoming of a flower, the opening of the eyes, or the gentle and gradual unfolding of something previously hidden from view. The unfolding of the universe, or 'everything' (*viśva*) takes place **through Her own will**, where the word used for 'will' (*icchā*) also refers to creative impulse, the pre-cognitive urge toward self-expression. Though *icchā* in common parlance can mean 'desire', in nondual Śaiva Tantra it is used in this special sense. Ordinary desire arises in response to seeing or experiencing a desirable object, whereas *icchā* here designates a 'pre-cognitive' urge, an urge to express what lies latent and hidden within, without having to know exactly what that is before it is expressed. Ordinary desire seeks to grasp and obtain something not yet obtained, while *icchā* seeks to pour oneself forth into the world, to actualize one's essence-nature in action and expression.

The metaphorical substrate for this creative self-unfolding is likened to a canvas; in fact the word *bhitti* means 'a screen, a wall, or a plaster surface prepared for painting'. Kṣemarāja indicates that the metaphor only goes so far, since unlike in the normal state of affairs where an artist and her materials are separate, here the canvas is simply an aspect of **Herself**.

To sum up, then, *Awareness flows into form as a creative act, arising solely from its innate desire for self-expression, and the substrate or ground of this process is simply itself.* Note that in the mainstream Tantrik tradition, this substrate or ground is normally identified with the masculine deity Śiva, which is why you will see images of the Goddess sitting or standing on top of a prostrate Śiva. He is the symbolic ground for her dynamic, creative activity. But here, in the radical nondualism of the Recognition school, Kṣemarāja wants to avoid the implied dualism of the standard Śiva–Śakti paradigm, so both roles are depicted as aspects of one absolute Goddess power.[12]

So with a bit of poetic license, we could also translate Sūtra Two as:

**Through Her own Will, Awareness unfolds Herself as the fabric of the universe.***

Let's now explore Kṣemarāja's commentary on his own sūtra. The commentary here takes the form of a brief series of notes, which tells us that he views the sūtra as mostly self-explanatory.

**Through Her own Will (*icchā*), not through another's will, such as Brahmā's or anyone else's.**

Kṣema clarifies that unlike in some other systems, here the Goddess is absolutely autonomous, not the deputy of some other deity, such as Brahmā, who is the creator deity in some branches of Sanskrit literature.

**Through that** [will] **alone, without relying on any external materials or causes—for if She were dependent in this way, she would not have the autonomy (*svātantrya*) that we have described** [as inherent to Awareness]**, and therefore the very fact of *being* Awareness would be compromised.**

Kṣemarāja clarifies here that he does not picture Goddess Awareness as a traditional creator deity under some other name, as already mentioned above. Therefore 'She' does not require any materials outside of Herself with which to create—because all creation is a spontaneously arising self-expression of Awareness, and it all takes place *within* Awareness; nothing is ever separate from or external to Her/It at any time. Kṣema tells us that if it were otherwise, then that would mean that Awareness was dependent on something other than itself, not truly independent after all. And here we come to an important point, already touched upon above: Awareness's inherent nature is unbounded freedom.† This can easily be verified in your own experience. Notice that your awareness is infinitely malleable; though formless, it can adopt any form. It can easily imagine forms the senses have never encountered, in boundless variety. It can revise the past, take radically different perspectives on the present, and endlessly reimagine the future. Indeed, the Recognition teachings argue that *svātantrya*—free-

---

* This translation suggested by poet Alicia Frost.

† See the third interpretation of Sūtra One.

dom, independence, autonomy—is so central, so thoroughly inherent to awareness, that without it it simply would not *be* awareness, but "something like a pot".[13] Without its autonomy, awareness would be as absolutely predictable as any purely mechanistic process. It is self-reflective awareness that makes human beings creative and unpredictable where other life-forms are nearly always thoroughly predictable for one intimately acquainted with them.[14] Autonomous awareness is what defines sentient beings, and it is their very essence.

Think about the implications of this for your own life. If your awareness is by nature absolutely free, that means that your life circumstance cannot dictate your inner experience in a mechanistic, cause-and-effect manner. Awareness can, if it is aware of itself (more on that later), choose what perspective to have on any given situation, and the perspective determines the attitudes you can have, the stories you can tell, and your sense of what is possible. And all these together greatly influence your moment-to-moment experience. So, with some practice, awareness can choose what experience to have of life. Not in the sense of being able to choose what you feel or how you react in any given moment, but rather in the way you might patiently shape the walls and moat of a sand castle over hours, such that when the water arrives, it flows the way you want it to instead of every which way. Similarly, over months and years of practice, through the power of nonjudgmental self-reflection you can tap into awareness's natural freedom and access a different perspective, even a different paradigm you might not have thought possible. As we'll learn in the next chapter, different ways of seeing make possible different modes of being.

So anything is possible for you, but not in the way you've been told. Due to the reality of karmic limitations, you cannot manifest whatever you'd like in the material world. But you *can* learn to manifest any experience of reality you'd like, and that ends up being a much more effective path to fulfillment. As we will discover in Sūtra Four, you are a microcosm of the pattern of the whole, and therefore your *whole* life—as it is right now—is an authentic expression of what is within you, but not the whole of what is within you. The manifest world of your experience at any given moment is merely a fraction of the range of possibilities latent within Awareness. Furthermore, since Awareness needs nothing outside itself, you can trust that you have everything that you could possibility need inside of yourself to experience abiding fulfillment, to realize the full beauty of the unique expression of the divine that is you.

Fulfillment is a *mode of awareness*, not a state caused by external circumstance. (Note that external circumstances can *facilitate* happiness, but they can't cause it—more on this important distinction later.) If you think anything outside yourself (including intangible 'things' like romantic love or the recognition of your peers) is essential to accomplish that goal, you aren't seeing clearly yet.

*Contemplation Exercise*

Look at your total life situation clearly and without judgment, realizing that it is largely the expression of the various strata of your inner world. Take responsibility for what you have manifested, and how it has impacted others, without self-blame or self-praise. (It might be hard, but try.)

Then affirm to yourself that you have everything you could possibly need to experience abiding fulfillment within. How does that feel?

Now let's continue with Kṣemarāja's commentary. Here he wants to explain how diversity can appear within the context of a greater unity.

**On the 'canvas' which is Herself, and not on anything else, Awareness unfolds the universe previously described** [as consisting of knowers, ways of knowing, and things known] **as if it were separate and different from Herself, though in actuality it is not separate, just like the image of a city reflected in a mirror** [is inseparable from the mirror].

The Power of Awareness that you are manifests as all the interdependent activities of apparently distinct subjects and objects—the variegated patterns of light and color in the 'painting' of the universe. That same Power, in its unmanifest aspect, also forms the substrate for all that activity: the formless ground of all things, which is itself completely empty (like a blank screen or canvas), yet full of the potential for absolutely everything. To make it clear that the canvas/painting metaphor is just one possible analogy, in the above paragraph Kṣema offers another comparison, one that was fairly well-known in his time: that of the city in the mirror.

Imagine yourself standing on a hill overlooking a city in a valley below. You then turn your back on the city and look at its reflection in a relatively small mirror. All the citizens, all their activities and creations, are all contained within that single image, and the image is inseparable from its substrate, the mirror. Just as there is no painting without a canvas, there is no image without a mirror. Though the moving image in the mirror is what fascinates our senses, the unchanging substrate is what abides. In the same way, nondual Śaiva Tantra teaches, the whole of reality is held as a reflection in the sky of Awareness, inseparable from it.[15] It is difficult for the mind to grasp this, because the 'sky' that forms the substrate for the perceptible universe is nothing but intangible, formless, spacious Awareness (or aware spaciousness), a 'field' of absolute potential.

In this view, which those who are patient can verify in direct experience, what is unseen is more real, in a sense, than what is seen, if that which abides is more 'real' than that which is ever changing. Furthermore, the unseen is precisely what manifests as the seen. The formless manifests as form. So the 'city in a mirror' simile only extends so far, because there really is no 'city', only the 'reflection' and its substrate. Again, the 'reflection' here is the ever-changing field of manifest reality, and the source and ground of the reflection is the formless field of infinite potential, as Kṣema tells us next.

**And this process of unfolding is simply the making manifest of what abides** [within Awareness as latent potential]**.**

Everything that has ever been and everything that ever could be or will be exists in a latent state within the field of absolute potential—the implicate order that is said to be simultaneously empty yet 'pregnant' with the possibility of everything whatsoever. Everything that manifests emerges out of this field of potential, is sustained by it, and merges back into it once again. As mentioned above, this is where the metaphor Kṣema has been using breaks down, because though anything can be painted on a canvas, we cannot say that all possible paintings abide within it (except in a poetic sense), nor can we say that the canvas 'manifests' the painting. Nor is there a separate artist. Artist, canvas, and painting are all aspects of *one* thing: the Light of Awareness, which spontaneously spills itself again and again into creative manifestation, projecting the vastness of diversity within its own being.

**Therefore, it is taught here that the world exists in a state of oneness with the Light of Awareness (*prakāśa*).** ||

Just as there cannot be a painting without a surface that supports it, or a movie without a screen, the world exists in a state of oneness (*aikātmya*) with the Light of Awareness. Kṣema returns here to his fundamental teaching metaphor, that of light, for in the end it is the most apropos. What we were calling the substrate or canvas or ground of being above can be understood as pure white light in this analogy, whereas manifestation is the refraction of that light into a variety of colors. Unlike in the canvas example, all possible visible colors are literally contained within white light. This refraction into color is, as we shall see later, the Light's modes of reflecting on itself. Of course, there is never any separation of color and light; in the same way, what we call the world has always been, and always will be, a manifestation of the One. And you are that One. This is the simplest and briefest way to say what this whole chapter has been about:

Whatever appears is *what you are* appearing as that.

*Whatever* appears is what you are appearing as that.

Whatever appears is what you are appearing as *that.*

Whatever it is that's arising in your experience, in truth it's not a reward or a punishment, it's not deserved or undeserved, it wasn't ordained by some other being, it wasn't chosen by some earlier self of yours so that this self could learn a lesson, and it's not happening to fulfill a part in the story your mind wants to tell about your life: it's simply, beautifully, spontaneously, perfectly, and completely expressing *what you are.* It has no other reason for being and needs no other reason.

This completes our study of Sūtra Two and its commentary.

So you see, Chapters One and Two describe the ultimate nature of reality, which simply means 'that which is most completely true' (with the caveat that even the most accurate words are still only pointers toward, never adequate descriptors of, the Truth). If you could fully experientially grasp what has been said so far, no more need be said. For the vast majority, however, we need to go on a journey, a journey that explains how and why human delusion and self-limitation and suffering come about, and how the seeds of their resolution are already present within them. When we go on that journey, and come back full circle to where we began, we clearly see that beginning (and ending) point for the first time. This pattern is found in all the great myths of humanity through the ages, and it is found in this book. Come, let's push off...

अथ विश्वस्य स्वरूपं विभागेन प्रतिपादयितुमाह

तन्नाना अनुरूपग्राह्यग्राहक-
भेदात् ॥ ३ ॥

'तत्' विश्वं 'नाना'—अनेकप्रकारम् । कथं ? 'अनुरूपाणां'—परस्परौचित्यावस्थितीनां 'ग्राह्याणां ग्राहकाँणां' च 'भेदात्'—वैचित्र्यात् । तथा च

सदाशिवतत्त्वे अहन्ताच्छादित-अस्फुटेदन्तामयं यादृशं परापररूपं विश्वं ग्राह्यं, तादृगेव श्रीसदाशिवभट्टारकाधिष्ठितो मन्त्रमहेश्वराख्यः प्रमातृवर्गः परमेश्वरेच्छावकल्पिततथावस्थानः । ईश्वरतत्त्वे स्फुटेदन्ताहन्तासामानाधिकरण्यात्म यादृक् विश्वं ग्राह्यं, तथाविध एव ईश्वरभट्टारकाधिष्ठितो मन्त्रेश्वरवर्गः । विद्यापदे श्रीमदनन्तभट्टारकाधिष्ठिता बहुशाखावान्तरभेदभिन्ना यथाभूता मन्त्राः प्रमातारः, तथाभूतमेव भेदैकसारं विश्वमपि प्रमेयम् । मायोर्ध्वे यादृशा विज्ञानाकलाः कर्तृताशून्यशुद्धबोधात्मानः, तादृगेव तद्भेदसारं सकल-प्रलयाकलात्मक-पूर्वावस्थापरिचितम् एषां प्रमेयम् ।

# CHAPTER THREE

*Kṣemarāja's original text*

Now, to begin to explain the nature of the universe in terms of its various parts, it is taught:

**It is diverse because it is divided into mutually adapted subjects and objects.** || 3 ||

**It**, i.e., the universe, **is diverse**, i.e., has multiple aspects. In what way? **Because of its division**, i.e., its diversification, into '**graspers**' and '**grasped**', which are **mutually adapted**—i.e., existing in a state of mutual congruity.

To explain: on the level of Sadāśiva there exists the type of perceiver called the 'Great Lord of Mantra'—empowered by the revered Lord Sadāśiva—whose nature corresponds to that which they perceive: the universe as unified diversity, in which subjectivity predominates, enveloping an implicit and indistinct objectivity. They are in that state because they are expressions of the Will of the Supreme Lord.

On the level of Īśvara, there exists the type of perceiver called the 'Lord of Mantra'—empowered by Lord Īśvara—who are exactly appropriate to what they perceive: the universe, consisting of a clearly delineated objectivity and subjectivity in perfect balance.

In the domain of Gnosis, the perceivers are *Mantras*—empowered by the revered Lord Ananta—divided into subcategories with many branches. They perceive the universe exactly according to their nature: as completely diversified, yet retaining a single essence.

Above the level of Māyā, there are the *Vijñānākalas*, who are free of limitation due to their insight. Their nature is pure awareness without agency. In accordance with their nature, they perceive the universe—the same one known to them in their previous state of being *Sakalas* or *Pralayākalas*—as essentially non-different from themselves.

मायायां शून्यप्रमातॄणां प्रलयकेवलिनां स्वोचितं प्रलीनकल्पं प्रमेयम्। क्षितिपर्यन्तावस्थितानां तु सकलानां सर्वतो भिन्नानां परिमितानां तथाभूतमेव प्रमेयम्। तदुत्तीर्णशिवभट्टारकस्य प्रकाशैकवपुषः प्रकाशैकरूपा एव भावाः। श्रीमत्परमशिवस्य पुनः विश्वोत्तीर्ण-विश्वात्मक-परमानन्दमय-प्रकाशैकघनस्य एवंविधमेव शिवादि-धरण्यन्तम् अखिलम् अभेदेनैव स्फुरति; न तु वस्तुतः अन्यत् किंचित् ग्राह्यं ग्राहकं वा; अपि तु श्रीपरमशिवभट्टारक एव इत्थं नानावैचित्र्यसहस्रैः स्फुरति।—इत्यभिहितप्रायम्॥ ३॥

Within the realm of Māyā, there are those perceivers called the *Pralayākalas*, who are temporarily free of limitation due to dissolution: they know [only] the Void (*śūnya*). Appropriate to them, their object of perception is almost completely dissolved.

Situated in the realm of *tattvas* extending down to Earth, the embodied souls (*Sakalas*), completely divided and limited, perceive the world as exactly the same.

Transcending all those lower perceivers is Lord Śiva, whose substance and nature is solely the Light of Awareness. For Him, all beings and states have a single nature: that very Light.

However, Śrī-Paramaśiva, replete with the Light of Awareness that consists of absolute Bliss, simultaneously transcends the universe and embodies itself as the universe. From that perspective, all of existence from transcendent Śiva down to Earth vibrates into manifestation in that same way, without any duality whatsoever.

So in reality, there is no subject or object whatsoever that is other; rather, it is simply Śrī-Paramaśiva that is vibrating thus in thousands of various different forms. This is what is implied by the sūtra. || 3 ||

# CHAPTER THREE

*with explanation*

**Now, to begin to explain the nature of the universe in terms of its various parts, it is taught:**

|| TAN NĀNĀNURŪPA-GRĀHYA-GRĀHAKA-BHEDĀT || 3 ||

**It is diverse because it is divided into mutually adapted subjects and objects.**

[Gloss:] **It = the universe. Diverse = has multiple aspects. In what way? Because of its division, i.e., its diversification, into 'graspers'** [those who perceive]**, and 'grasped'** [that which is perceived]**, which are mutually adapted—that is, existing in a state of mutual congruity** [or 'fittedness'].

We now enter into one of the most difficult discussions in the entire text—difficult for us, that is, not for Kṣemarāja's original audience, since they were already familiar with many of the theological terms and concepts that he works with here. The reader new to Śaiva Tantrik philosophy should probably skip to Chapter Four (page 105) after reading the next four pages rather than risk getting bogged down in the philosophical subtlety of Chapter Three. You can always come back later.

To understand Kṣema's commentary, we will need some background. First let's come to grips with the argument that is the third sūtra itself, which was radical and innovative in its own time. Notice in the sūtra above that Kṣema has now shifted his primary referent (the subject of the sentence) from Awareness to 'the universe' (*viśva*, which we could equally translate as 'the Everything'), because he is now discussing manifestation as opposed to what lies behind manifestation (though in reality they are not different, as we learned in the last chapter). Now, as we have discussed, the fundamental dichotomy of manifest reality is this: there are things that perceive (which we call 'subjects') and things that are perceived ('objects', and this includes *any* perceivable, not just physical objects). Tellingly, the word Kṣemarāja uses for 'subject' in

Sūtra Three (*grāhaka*) literally means 'grasper', while the corresponding word for 'object' (*grāhya*) is literally 'graspable thing' (where 'grasp' means cognize or comprehend). While these terms in Sanskrit are more neutral than their English equivalents, there is still some suggestion of the fact that perceivers tend to compulsively grasp for what is perceived (where aversion counts as a kind of cognitive 'grasping' just as much as attraction). Since we tend to be obsessed in one way or another by the various objects of our consciousness, the relation of consciousness to what it perceives is of paramount importance.

In fact, much of Indian philosophy turns on the issues raised by the apparent dichotomy of perceiver versus perceived. For example, what exactly is the 'thing that perceives'? If the core self of a sentient being is that being's capacity to be conscious of something, where can we locate that capacity? Is it a side effect of having a physical body? Is it a mental function? If so, how is it that we can exist as a 'me' that watches the thought process or the body while remaining distinct from it?

In the extremely influential pre-Tantrik philosophy called Sāṅkhya, this line of questioning resolved itself into a doctrine that asserted an absolute dualism between Spirit and Matter, where 'spirit' means pure consciousness (*puruṣa*), also known as 'the perceiving witness' (*sākṣin*), and 'matter' (*prakṛti*; more precisely, 'matter/energy'), which is unconscious, is all that can be perceived. In this system, Spirit is thought to be unchanging and unaffected by Matter, incapable of acting on it or of wanting to act on it, and Matter is constantly changing, due to the constant combination and recombination of its three basic constituents (the *guṇa*s) which comprise twenty-three basic principles (*tattva*s). On this view, Spirit can see but not act, and Matter can act but not see (that is, not consciously). Furthermore, Sāṅkhya asserted that anything that can be objectified (i.e., made into an object of consciousness) is part of Matter—therefore, our bodies, our minds, our thoughts, and our emotions are all part of inert, insentient Matter. Our true self, on the other hand, is simply that conscious spirit that observes any aspect of matter. When enough consciousness is directed toward some aspect of inert Matter, such as the mind, it appears to take on the qualities of Spirit, like iron heated by fire starts to glow. Thus we come to wrongly see the mind as our locus of selfhood, when it is simply a mechanism that executes its programming, just like the body. In fact, Sāṅkhya says, conscious Spirit (*puruṣa*) and the mind (part of *prakṛti*) are absolutely distinct, and are not of the same nature. It's as if the Sāṅkhyas imagined a glass wall between consciousness and everything it can see (including thoughts). Thus they could assert that spirit was pure, untainted by the messy and degraded world, which it is ever content to merely witness.

It was this very Sāṅkhya philosophy that Patañjali espoused in his *Yoga-sūtra*. But if you think about this picture of things for long enough, you will doubtless see that it really doesn't work. You will probably see the same problem with it that the Tāntrikas saw: upon deeper reflection, it is impossible to draw a hard line between consciousness and its objects. If there were such a line, you would have to assert that the mind is never anything but an organic computer, making all decisions based on its programming, and unaffected by the consciousness that watches it. But this doesn't seem to fit our experience very well. How can the mind be totally separate from the consciousness that enlivens, animates, and powers it? And in the spiritual context, how could attaining self-realization and abiding in pure Spirit (*puruṣa*) cause any change in the behavior of the body-mind? It couldn't, in the Sāṅkhya view, and therefore the system cannot explain why its own sages exhibit such peaceful, stoic, and quietistic behavior after attaining 'the goal of the system' (*kaivalya*). Furthermore, though Sāṅkhya posits an absolute distinction between subjects and objects, any subject can objectify other conscious beings, thus apparently compromising their status as subjects ('perceiver' rather than 'perceived').

The only workable solution is to posit that the perceiver and the perceived are two aspects of one thing, a single process. This is the doctrine of nonduality that is fundamental to the tradition we are studying, already presented in Chapters One and Two. In this view, any subject can also be an object. But what are the implications of the assertion that one thing (Goddess Awareness) manifests as two (perceiver and perceived)? What it means, says Kṣemarāja, is that the perceiver and perceived must be understood as *anurūpa* (the key term of the sūtra): **mutually adapted, shaping one another in interdependence, conforming themselves each to the other**. In the act of perceiving, the perceiver is subtly changed by what s/he perceives, and what s/he perceives is changed as a result of being perceived, and this is constantly happening, moment to moment, in an endless flux—the infinite dance of Awareness.

For us, the radical argument here is this: as conscious beings, we are not the passive recipients of the data of some independent, objective reality flowing into us from the outside. Rather, the principle of *anurūpa* expressed in this sūtra is telling us that in any act of perception, the object perceived and the one perceiving it are *co-creators*, as it were, of the experience of reality being had. You are just as responsible for the way in which you experience any object as the intrinsic nature of the object itself. This is crucial to realize, since most of us tend to assume that we are encountering reality as it is. In fact, what you bring to any given experience (which, of course, is your entire history) profoundly shapes the nature of that experience. And it is also the case that the experience shapes you. It is what scholars call a dialectical process: the object affects your consciousness, and your consciousness affects the object, which then affects your consciousness, and on and on.

Let's look at that process in slightly more detail. You come at each experience with many preformed assumptions about how things are, conditioned interpretive thought-matrices (called *vikalpas* in Sanskrit) that shape and delimit your experience. On the other hand, the experience you have of any given object (or person) impacts you and shapes or reshapes your assumptions. Even incrementally altered assumptions lead to slightly different actions, which then lead to different experiences, which again slightly alter your assumptions—if you're paying attention. (In the Tantrik View, the power of awareness and the power of action cannot be separated, for the latter is an expression of the former—precisely the opposite of the Sāṅkhya view.) This intimate of a relationship between subject and object is only possible, the Tāntrikas argue, if they are two aspects of one reality, and therefore they sought, through awareness-cultivation techniques, to realize each object of experience in its true nature: as a vibration of Awareness.

The shift from the Sāṅkhya view to the Tantrik one is parallel in some ways to the shift in physics from the deterministic, mechanistic view of reality expressed by Newtonian physics to that of relativity and quantum mechanics. Heisenberg's uncertainty principle showed us that the act of observation affects that which is observed (and that we can never know to precisely what degree). More specifically, the *way* in which something is observed determines how it manifests. Nothing exists in a 'pure' state in which it is uninfluenced by the observer. There is no such thing as observer-independent reality. In other words, we cannot ever know the purely 'objective' or unobserved nature of a thing, *because it has no such nature.* The implications of this are tremendous. To put it in Kṣemarāja's terms, you can only see reality in the way that a being configured such as you are sees reality. If you wish to experience reality differently, you must radically reconfigure the way in which you perceive: you must become a different sort of perceiver. The good news is, the potential to perceive in six different ways from how you currently do already exists within you. That's the main point of Chapter Three.

Now before going on to the commentary, let's review the implications of Sūtra Three. Even though the teaching in this sūtra seems esoteric, it is simply a subtle and profound reflection on the most fundamental features of our everyday reality. We have learned that in any given experience, neither the object nor the subject can be said to wholly determine the nature of that experience. Rather, *the knower and the known are co-arising, interdependent, co-creating aspects of one reality.* If this is true with *any* object of consciousness, how much more is it true when the 'object' is another person? When two people are each perceivers and yet are each objects of perception to the other? They are both *actively* co-creating a reality and modifying each other's perception, with the result that they can create a whole world unto themselves, for in a relationship, each becomes a person that they would not be except in relation to that other being. As Anaïs Nin famously put it, "Each friend represents a world in us, a world possibly not born until they arrive; it is only by this meeting that a new world is born."

In his commentary, Kṣemarāja teaches the traditional Trika doctrine of the Seven Perceivers, the seven types of sentient beings that are, he argues, mirrored within each one of us *in potentia* as the seven ways we can see or experience reality. The reason he includes this esoteric teaching is that it was a doctrine commonly known to Trika practitioners in his community, who probably expected him to explain it.[16] However, he cleverly uses his exposition as an opportunity to make a point that the original text did not make (at least, not very explicitly): that the seven types of being in the traditional list are really seven levels or aspects of universal Awareness, i.e., seven ways of experiencing reality.

Of the seven, three are states of unliberated consciousness, and four are states of liberated awareness. Now as you delve into the subtleties of

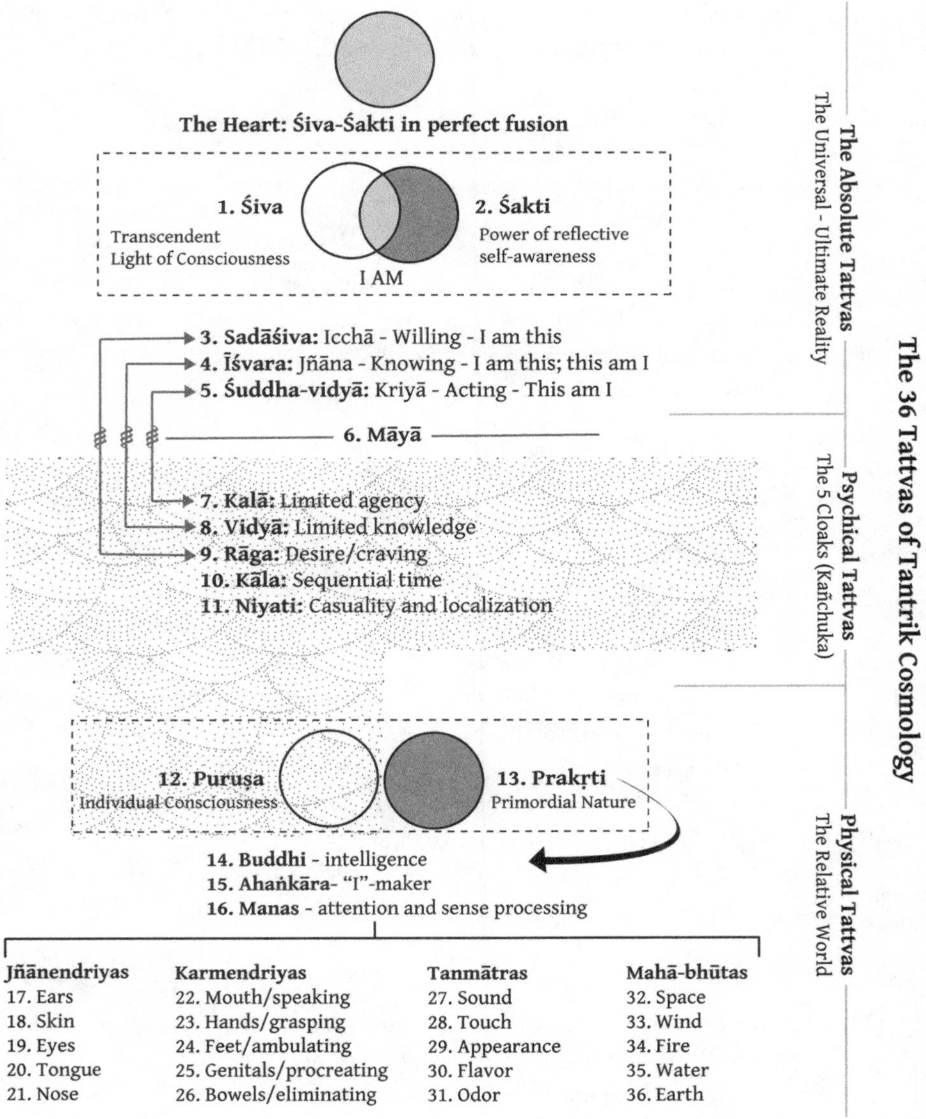


the doctrine of the Seven Perceivers, remember that Kṣemarāja is really just making the same point again and again: that each type of being (or level of Awareness) is constituted appropriately to the reality that they perceive, even in a sense *defined* by the level of reality that they are able to perceive. Once again, if you want to have a radically different experience of reality, instead of trying to change *reality* (a rather tall order demanding endless stress and struggle), reconfigure the mode of your perception: become the kind of being that sees reality that way. Or, as Swāmī Muktānanda put it simply and powerfully in the 1970s: "The world is as you see it. So change the prescription of your glasses."

*The Seven Perceivers*

Here is a summary of the Seven Perceivers; you certainly don't need to understand this list now. This is just the first iteration. From the most fundamental, universal, expanded, and unparticularized mode of perception to the most contracted and particularized:

1. **Śiva** – absolutely nondual Awareness
2. **Mantra-maheśvara** – the liberated perceiver of objectivity enveloped by a greater subjectivity (diversity within unity)
3. **Mantreśvara** – the liberated perceiver of subjectivity and objectivity as mirrors of each other, in appositional balance
4. **Mantra** – the liberated perceiver of diversified (and dominant) objectivity as an expression of underlying subjectivity
5. **Vijñānākala** – the unliberated perceiver who is almost free by virtue of his insight, but unwilling to surrender his separate identity
6. **Pralayākala** – the unliberated perceiver who is temporarily partially free by virtue of existing in the Void
7. **Sakala** – the unliberated perceiver who sees duality as the basic reality, perceiving himself as separate from the whole

Remember that in Kṣemarāja's nondual view, each of these perceivers exists within you, as a way you can experience reality.

In describing the Seven Perceivers, Kṣemarāja begins with the second, skipping over the first, probably because he has already presented the Śiva-perspective in Sūtra One, and because he wants to climax his discussion of the Seven Perceivers by coming back to Śiva at the end. But to proceed in a logical order, we'll just mention up front that the word 'Śiva' here refers to that type of perceiver that experiences reality in terms of the absolute nonduality of the supreme Subject. In other words, from the Śiva-perspective, there is only 'I', only the Light of

Awareness. There is no sense of any reality even slightly separate from the 'I'. (More on this near the end of the chapter.)

The first Perceiver encompasses both of the first two *tattvas* (see the tattva chart on page 91). As we step down to the third *tattva*, which is the plane of the second type of perceiver, we step into the barest beginnings of perceiving reality in terms of two separate aspects: 'I' (*aham*) and 'this' (*idam*). When seen in the context of an account of the emanation of the universe from Awareness, the movement from the first Perceiver to the second is the first movement toward the creation of manifest reality.

We must understand each level from two different angles, you see: the order of emanation or creation (*sṛṣṭi-krama*), to which I have just referred (and which is given in the table above), and the order of reabsorption or liberation (*saṃhāra-krama*), which is the reverse, being the stages you would follow to become (that is, embrace and embody) your absolute Śiva-nature. Kṣemarāja alludes to both *kramas* at each stage, though he is following the order of emanation. Confused yet? It will become clear as we proceed.

Now let's finally encounter Kṣemarāja's commentary.

**To explain: on the level (*tattva*) of Sadāśiva there exists the type of perceiver called the *Mantra-maheśvara*** ['Great Lord of Mantra'; the second Perceiver]**—empowered by the revered Lord Sadāśiva—whose nature corresponds to that which they perceive: the universe as unified diversity (*parāpara*), in which subjectivity predominates, enveloping an implicit and indistinct objectivity. They are in that state because** [they are expressions] **of the Will (*icchā*) of the Supreme Lord.**

In the earlier Tantrik tradition that Kṣemarāja inherited, the second, third, and fourth perceivers constituted something like the hierarchy of angels in the Judeo–Christian–Islamic tradition. The second type of perceiver, the 'Great Lord of Mantra', was similar to an archangel.[17] However, Kṣema pictures this as a level of awareness that exists in potential form within *all* sentient beings. Attaining liberation on the third *tattva* ('level of reality') means becoming a Mantra-maheśvara—but in Kṣema's nondualist teaching, the Mantra-maheśvara is not a being separate from God, but rather an aspect of the one Divine Awareness, specifically an emanation of God's Will (*icchā-śakti*).

But what defines the second Perceiver? Kṣemarāja tells us that their nature is expressed by how they see reality. Now, this *Sadāśiva-tattva* (tattva #3 in the chart) is the level at which the universe exists in its potential form, as a thought of its possibility, within the formless Divine. So this phase of Awareness perceives the nascent, inchoate universe entirely within itself. In other words, though the slightest subtle differentiation has begun between 'I' and 'this', the latter is experienced as totally enveloped by the former. This state of awareness is characterized by the phrase *idam aham*, 'This [potentiality] am I', or 'This [totality] is my very Self', but without any sense that the universe thus perceived exhausts its Being—indeed, it is a relatively small movement within infinite vastness. Now, since *all* beings who reach this level of liberation experience the same thing, that the universe is a single mass of energy within themselves, it must be the case that all such perceivers are aspects of one Perceiver, and nonduality is not compromised.

Note that since we are proceeding from the top down, the language here primarily reflects the *sṛṣṭi-krama*, or 'order of emanation'. We could equally well proceed from the bottom up, emphasizing the levels as successively higher states of awakening reached by conscious beings, but we are following the order Kṣemarāja has set.

**On the level of Īśvara, there exists the type of perceiver called the *Mantreśvara* ('Lord of Mantra')—empowered by Lord Īśvara—who are exactly appropriate to what they perceive: the universe, consisting of a clearly delineated objectivity and subjectivity in perfect balance.**

The third Perceiver (which is also the third-deepest layer of your awareness) is called Mantreśvara, 'Lord of Mantra'.[18] As beings, the Mantreśvaras exist at the level of the *Īśvara-tattva*, the personal Deity, of whom they are emanations. *Īśvara*, which simply means 'God' or 'the Lord', is that aspect of the Divine that is taken to be Supreme in the three Western monotheisms; in Shaivism it is allocated to the fourth level of the universal hierarchy.* Note that when we speak of 'levels'

* Having said that, in some Western mystical traditions, such as the teaching of Meister Eckhart, the personal God is subordinated to the formless and indescribable 'Godhead', an articulation that parallels the Śaiva teaching.

such as *Īśvara-tattva*, we are not talking about a *place*, such as another dimension. In fact, all of the higher *tattvas* pervade all of the lower *tattvas*, so each of them represents a way of experiencing reality. (While the dualistic tradition asserted that you could not attain the higher *tattvas* while in the physical body, nondualists like Kṣemarāja held the opposite view.)

From the top-down perspective, at *Īśvara-tattva* the universe has grown toward explicit expression within Awareness, and is as prominent as its awareness of itself. Thus the phrase that expresses the experience of this level is said to be 'I am this; This am I' (*aham idam idam aham*).[19] As an interesting footnote, we may observe that in the Torah and the Bible, this is expressed in an extremely similar manner: when asked for his name, the personal Deity declares, "I am That am I" (*ehyeh ašer ehyeh*).

As a level of awakened consciousness, the Mantreśvara-perceiver is one who sees the universe as a total expression of the Self. Neither 'I' nor 'this' has predominance; they are perfectly balanced mirrors of each other. The Mantreśvara-perceiver has knowledge of the pattern of the Whole, but is not yet aware that his total Being is far 'vaster' than even the whole of the currently manifest universe.

**In the domain of Gnosis [= *śuddhavidyā-tattva*], the perceivers are *Mantras*—empowered by the revered Lord Ananta—divided into subcategories with many branches. They perceive the universe exactly according to their nature: as completely diversified, yet retaining a single essence.**

The fourth Perceiver is known as Mantra. Mantra-beings exist 'at' *Śuddhavidyā-tattva*, the lowest level of the so-called Pure Realm. The latter is just a term that refers to the 'domain' of spiritual liberation—it is not a world separate from this one. *Śuddhavidyā-tattva* is the lowest 'level' of full awakening to reality as it is. Just as *icchā-śakti* ('the Power of Will') was dominant at the Sadāśiva level, and *jñāna-śakti* ('the Power of Knowing') was dominant at the Īśvara level, here at the Śuddhavidyā level, *kriyā-śakti* ('the Power of Acting') is dominant. (See *Tantra Illuminated*, pages 101–109, for more on the Powers.) And indeed, Mantra-beings are devoted to acting to uplift beings in the unliberated state (more on that below). As on the previous levels, Mantra-beings are not separate from the Divine; they are emanations of Śiva's

Awareness. Though they are in a state of oneness, there is still diversity on this level, because all the Mantra-beings are all *different* vibrations of the One.

Mantra-beings, like all beings, see the universe in a form consonant with their own nature. That is, they see all reality as variegated pulsations of energy, as interacting patterns of vibration flashing into view. The phrase that expresses the experience of a Mantra-being is *idam aham*, 'I am this', for in this liberated state all things are seen as an expression of one's own nature. But on this level, there is more attention on the object than the subject; that is, the 'this' is predominant in experience, rather than the 'I'; that is, 'I am *this*'.

To understand this level, remember once again that the doctrine of the Seven Perceivers has two aspects: it tells us about the seven types of beings in this universe *and* about the seven layers of our own consciousness. This makes perfect sense in this system, for each individual part of the whole contains the pattern of the whole. If there is a type of being out there in the universe, it will be reflected within us as a part of ourselves, and *vice versa*. So why are the beings on this level called Mantra?

A unique doctrine of Śaiva Tantra is that mantras are not just sound vibrations or sentences; they are considered as conscious beings, emanations of the One Being but expressing a distinct flavor of Awareness, as it were. Some of these Mantra-beings are what we usually refer to as the gods and goddesses of the mainstream Indian tradition. That is, in the Tantra, the true form of any god/dess is in fact a sound vibration: its mantra. For example, the true form of the Goddess Lakṣmī is her mantra, her sonic form, OṂ ŚRĪṂ MAHĀLAKṢMYAI NAMAḤ. So Lakṣmī is a Mantra-being as well as a goddess: an emanation of the Divine that serves to help embodied beings experience abundance and beauty. (Of course, since the Mantras are one with God, and so is your essence-nature, all the Mantras, i.e., all the gods and goddesses, exist within you. See Chapter Four.) However, there are said to be seventy million Mantra-beings in total, and so not *all* of them are what we call gods and goddesses.

Mantra-beings are said to be synesthetic in nature, that is, they are beings of light as much as they are beings of sound, refractions of the One Light. If we ponder the description of these Mantra-beings as structures of light, sonic emanations of God, complexifications of Awareness that serve to uplift limited beings, then perhaps we will call them by another name: angels.* In the context of Śaiva Tantra, I argue, 'angel' is an accurate translation of 'mantra', taking into account exactly what *mantra* actually means to the Tantrik users of the term.

To sum up, in this doctrine the term *mantra* refers both to these Mantra-beings, who exist at the level of the *śuddhavidyā-tattva*, *and* as the fourth layer of our own consciousness, that is, our 'angelic' layer of being, the layer of divine sound vibration.

[Below the Pure Realm, but] **above the level of Māyā, there are the *Vijñānākalas*, who are free of limitation due to their insight. Their nature is pure awareness without agency** [or autonomy]. **In accordance with their nature, they perceive the universe—the same one known to them in their previous state of being *Sakalas* or *Pralayākalas*** [see below]**—as essentially non-different from themselves.**

The fifth type of Perceiver, pictured in the *tattva-schema* as existing in the space between Māyā (tattva #6) and the Pure Realm above, are the Vijñānākalas, those beings who through insight have become free of every limitation but the belief in their own separate individuality. In other words, they are free of *kārma-mala* (the Impurity of Karma), and *māyīya-mala* (the Impurity of subject–object Differentiation), but not free of *āṇava-mala* (the Impurity of Individuality). (See Chapter Nine of this book and *Tantra Illuminated*, page 150, and following.) In other words, they do not see themselves as separate from the objects of their perception, but *do* see themselves as separate from God (and other perceivers). Such beings have gone as far as they can without the power of grace, and are stuck at the gates of heaven, as it were, for only through surrender of their final attachment to their own individual identity can they rise into the 'Pure Realm' (= liberation) and become what they really are, an aspect of the One Light.

---

* In the early Christian tradition, St. Augustine wrote, "Angel is the name of their office, not of their nature. If you seek the name of their nature, it is spirit; if you seek the name of their office, it is angel." This parallels the Śaiva doctrine, in which Mantras are one with God, yet carry out different functions.

As before, the Vijñānākala-perceiver also represents a layer of our own being. People stuck on this level identify their true nature as 'pure consciousness' over and against any other aspect of their being, which they reject as not-self. In other words, they reject the body, the mind, the emotions as not-self, and enjoy escaping the world by entering the transcendent Void (*śūnya*) in deep meditation.* The Tantrik tradition criticizes such 'transcendentalists' as unintegrated escapists. Because they reject all aspects of their being apart from pure (i.e., empty) consciousness, they are devoid (*śūnya*) of the power of action, since that expresses through mind and body. Thus they are entirely passive and detached, unable to tap into the dynamic autonomy of unbounded Awareness and its power of active manifestation. Ironically, those stuck at the Vijñānākala level often believe themselves superior to other people by virtue of their ability to enter the Void in meditation. Their very sense of themselves as a highly evolved being keeps them from realizing their identity with all other beings.

Note that these Vijñānākala types attain a state very similar to the adherents of the Sāṅkhya system described above, so the present critique is implicitly a critique of Sāṅkhya as well. The Sāṅkhyas (including Patañjali) describe their state of liberation as *kaivalya*, which means 'isolation' or 'standing apart', which refers to separating from all aspects of being other than 'pure consciousness'.†

**Within** [the realm of] **Māyā, there are** [those perceivers called] **the Pralayākalas, who are** [temporarily] **free of limitation due to dissolution: they know** [only] **the Void (*śūnya*). Appropriate to them, their object of perception is** [the universe,] **almost completely dissolved.**

The sixth Perceiver is called the Pralayākala, 'one free of limitation due to dissolution'. In ancient Shaivism, this was the name of beings who had not attained liberation by the time of the dissolution of the uni-

---

* Jayaratha comments, "The Pralayākalas and Vijñānākalas are essentially synonymous with yogīs in the void-trance (*śūnya-samādhi*); they are like sleeping serpents" (introduction to *Tantrāloka* 10.133cd–135ab).

† Not coincidentally, Vijñānākalas are also called Vijñāna-kevalins, 'those isolated by their insight', where *kevalin* comes from the same word as does *kaivalya* (that being *kevala*, which means alone or isolated).

verse (*pralaya*), and who therefore existed in a kind of limbo until the next universe was created, that they may have bodies again and continue working out their karma. But in Kṣemarāja's usage, *Pralayākala* refers to the second layer of consciousness within each one of us: the mode of nondual perception that we access every night in deep sleep. Deep sleep is a state in which we are free of limitation, but not conscious of that freedom. It is a nondual state, but it is the nonduality of nothingness, for it is void of conscious awareness. It is a state accessed by meditators as well: an almost completely insensate, restful state similar to sleep but with a trace of awareness that makes it less *tamasic* than sleep (Swāmī Muktānanda called it *tandrā*, Satyānanda called it *nidrā*). It is a lovely state, but hardly very advanced, and an easy place for your meditations to get stuck in a rut.

However, if you pass through the sensationless Void (*śūnya*) in completely wakeful meditation, that is considered a very high attainment—it requires you to surrender your sense of self, becoming nothing by passing through this non-state of complete emptiness, which is, for most, utterly terrifying. Successfully surrendering to it and 'coming out the other side' usually means attaining liberation at some level. Swāmī Lakṣman-jū compared this experience to "passing through the eye of a needle", in the sense that it is difficult to traverse and requires you to surrender everything. If you do not surrender your individuality and thereby fully pass through the eye of the needle, you become stuck on the level of the Vijñānākala mentioned above.

**Situated in the realm of *tattvas* extending down to Earth, the embodied souls (*Sakalas*), completely divided** [from each other and from the objects of their perception] **and limited** [in their powers of cognition and action], **perceive the world as exactly the same** [i.e., divided and limited].

Perceiver number seven is the Sakala, which refers to (most of) us: embodied souls in their ordinary waking state of limited awareness. *Sakala* literally means 'with (*sa-*) limited powers (*kalā*)' of knowing and acting. Sakalas experience themselves as completely differentiated from each other and from objects they know, and they experience limitation in terms of place, time, and form. They live, in other words, in a world of differentiation.

Since all beings perceive the universe in a manner defined by how they are constituted, Sakalas see the world as they see themselves: differentiated, limited and circumscribed. Once again, the world is as you see it—or more precisely, you see the world in terms determined by how you see yourself. Until you awaken to a wider reality, you tend to gaze at the horizon of your own knowledge and assume you see, more or less, the horizon of reality itself. This is precisely the definition of ignorance in nondual Tantra. Until a Sakala-being touches a deeper layer of his own consciousness, he will find it very difficult to believe that there is another reality to be experienced at all.

Having said all that, we should also acknowledge that a Sakala is an amazing thing: a self-aware being. Such a being can not only perceive an object, like all animals can, but can also be aware of itself as the perceiver of the object. That is, a Sakala has the basic capacity to *know that she knows.* Yet it is this very self-awareness that causes the Sakala to believe in her own separateness: since she knows herself as a knower, she believes herself to be separate from that which she knows. Only an earnest and faithful application of the spiritual practices directly reveals the reality of deeper layers of consciousness, whereby the former Sakala sees that knower, knowing, and known are three aspects of one dynamic reality.

**Transcending all those lower perceivers is Lord Śiva, whose substance and nature is solely the Light of Awareness (*prakāśa*). For Him, all beings and states have a single nature: that very Light.**

Kṣemarāja, having summarized the perspectives of Perceivers two to seven, now jumps to Perceiver one, the Supreme Subject, known in this tradition as Śiva, 'the Benevolent One'. Śiva is the ultimate and fundamental nature of all conscious beings, the root of every 'self'. From the totally transcendent Śiva-perspective, only the single Light of Awareness exists; in other words, as mentioned above (page 93), here there is no sense of any reality even slightly separate from the 'I'. The whole of reality is a single consciousness: one without a second. This is a state impossible to think ourselves into, impossible for Sakalas to even imagine, because the mind necessarily thinks in dualistic categories. Yet it is possible to directly experience this absolute nonduality of the supreme Subject: it is the level of realization in which all separation has been completely dissolved, and everything that ever was, everything that could ever be throughout all time and space, is simply the vibration of a single word, the *mahā-mantra* AHAM ('I').

Though the level of Śiva is the level of absolute nonduality, it is not the principle most venerated in the Recognition school. For these masters, the ultimate principle is not the one that tops any hierarchy, not that which is the most transcendental. Rather, it is that which is *simultaneously transcendent and immanent*, that all-pervasive Power that is equally present in the experience of the most sublime meditation and the experience of the putrid smell of a rotting corpse. This undefinable, incomprehensible, all-pervasive Power, naturally and eternally endowed with love for itself in any and every possible form, is here called Śrī-Paramaśiva. In fact, it goes by many names in the tradition, for it cannot be named.

**However, Śrī-Paramaśiva, replete solely with the Light of Awareness that consists of supreme Bliss, simultaneously transcends the universe and** [yet] ***is*** **the universe. From that 'perspective', all of existence from** [transcendent] **Śiva down to Earth vibrates into manifestation** (*sphurati*) **as an expression of That, without any duality whatsoever. So in reality, there is no subject or object whatsoever that is other; rather, it is simply the revered Śrī-Paramaśiva that is vibrating thus in thousands of various different forms. This is what is implied** [by the sūtra]. || 3 ||

Śrī-Paramaśiva is not one of the Seven Perceivers, for it is that all-encompassing Consciousness that is 'beyond' any kind of subjectivity, any kind of 'I'-ness. Yet Śrī-Paramaśiva manifests as all of the Seven Perceivers.

Let us note that *Śrī* is one of the commonest names of the divine feminine. So the name Śrī-Paramaśiva implies the inseparable union of Śiva with Śakti, that is to say, Awareness with Bliss (*cid-ānanda*), Manifestation conjoined with Reflection (*prakāśa-vimarśa*). Here Kṣemarāja has carefully chosen a designation that suggests this perfect union, for *śrī* is also commonly used as an honorific prefix (almost like Mr./Ms. in English), and therefore Śrī-Paramaśiva clearly designates a single 'being' while simultaneously signaling to us that this being is the perfect fusion of the principles that, when difference is discernible, we call Śiva and Śakti. He drives the point home by describing

Śrī-Paramaśiva as *paramānanda-maya-prakāśaika-ghana*, 'replete solely with the Light of Awareness (*prakāśa*) that consists of supreme Bliss'.[20]

A word or two is necessary about the meaning of *paramānanda*, here translated as 'supreme Bliss'. We could also translate 'unconditioned joy' or even 'unimpeded wonder'. *Paramānanda* spontaneously arises when Awareness is full and complete, and furthermore is aware that whatever it is aware of is itself (i.e., *vimarśa*). *Paramānanda* is awareness savoring the given expression of itself. It is what makes Awareness not sterile, but juicy-sweet, full of wonder and delight. It is the inherent Power (*śakti*) of Śiva, which means that it cannot fail to arise when awareness is fully experienced.

*Contemplation Exercise*

Think of the times in your life when you have felt spontaneous joy, a sense of freedom and lightness and that 'all is right with the world'. This is *ānanda*. What do you think was the cause of these experiences of *ānanda*? Did all these experiences have any objective feature in common?

You may notice that you can't identify any external element that is the same in all the experiences. The only thing they have in common, probably, is the fact that you were fully present and in harmony with yourself (however briefly) in each case. Tantrik philosophy argues that the sole cause of true *ānanda* is this fullness (*pūrṇatā*) of awareness. When the fullness of the Light of Awareness manifests, Bliss automatically manifests with it. When the fullness is not manifest, it is always because you are internally divided, and are identifying with a part of yourself instead of the whole. The path to joy is that of seeing the truth of the whole of your being.

Let's return to Kṣemarāja's final paragraph above. He tells us that Śrī-Paramaśiva (= Awareness-Bliss) simultaneously transcends all things (*viśvottīrṇa*) and yet is the very substance of all things (*viśvātmaka*). This is why Śrī-Paramaśiva does not top the hierarchy of the Perceivers or of the Principles (*tattvas*)—the top of any hierarchy is the most transcendent thing, but Śrī-Paramaśiva is equally the most immanent thing *and* the most transcendent thing. It vibrates as the whole field of the thirty-six *tattvas*, from the most transcendent to the most earthy, from the most refined to the most vulgar, 'without any duality whatsoever'. The great Krama master Prabodha summed up this teaching in his beautiful verse,

> *Whatever form I conceive, however transcendent, is lower than You!*
> *Yet nor can I conceive of anything, however low, in which You are*
> *not completely present!*

It is important to note, however, that saying duality is absent from this perspective is not the same as saying that diversity is unreal. Rather, the completely full consciousness of Śrī-Paramaśiva allows for diversity as an expression of the One, unlike the perspective of the first Perceiver, Śiva, which denies diversity. The implications of this for real-world spirituality are huge. For this tradition, the 'highest state', if there is one, is that of coming back down to earth after experiencing transcendence, and seeing that the ordinary is no less divine than the transcendent.

Kṣemarāja concludes with the central teaching of the sūtra: that the division into subject and object, grasper and grasped, while fundamental, is not ultimate. It is one consciousness that becomes both, and thus liberation in this system entails the end of all grasping, because it entails the end of the false perception that there is a 'grasper' or anything separate from him that could be grasped. There is only the One vibrating and shining in thousands of different forms, so what could be the point of grasping? Of course, there is a considerable gap between understanding this truth and the abiding experience of it, which is why there are seventeen more sūtras.

This concludes our study of Sūtra Three and its commentary.

यथा च भगवान् विश्वशरीरः, तथा

चितिसंकोचात्मा चेतनोऽपि

संकुचितविश्वमयः ॥ ४ ॥

श्रीपरमशिवः स्वात्मैक्येन स्थितं विश्वं सदाशिवाद्युचितेन रूपेण अवबिभासयिषुः पूर्वं चिदैक्याख्यातिमयानाश्रिताशिवपर्याय-शून्यातिशून्यात्मतया प्रकाशाभेदेन प्रकाशमानतया स्फुरति; ततः चिद्रसाश्यानतारूपाशेषतत्त्वभुवन-भाव-तत्तत्प्रमात्राद्यात्मतयापि प्रथते । यथा च एवं भगवान् विश्वशरीरः, तथा 'चितिसंकोचात्मा' संकुचितचिद्रूपः 'चेतनो' ग्राहकोऽपि वटधानिकावत् संकुचिताशेषविश्वरूपः । तथा च सिद्धान्तवचनम्

'विग्रहो विग्रही चैव सर्वविग्रहविग्रही ।'

इति । त्रिशिरोमतेऽपि

'सर्वदेवमयः कायस्तं चेदानीं शृणु प्रिये ।
पृथिवी कठिनत्वेन द्रवत्वेऽम्भः प्रकीर्तितम् ॥'

# CHAPTER FOUR

*Kṣemarāja's original text*

Just as God has the whole universe for his body, in the same way,

**The individual conscious being,**
**as a contraction of universal Awareness,**
**consists of the entire universe in a microcosmic form.** || 4 ||

Śrī-Paramaśiva desires to make manifest the universe—abiding in oneness with itself—in forms that express all the aspects of its being, from Sadāśiva to Earth. So S/he first vibrates as a manifestation that is not different from the Light of Awareness, that is 'more void than the void'—a synonym for Transcendent Śiva, consisting only of the expression of the unity of Awareness.

Only then does S/he appear also as all the other Principles of Reality, the 118 Worlds, all existent things and states of being, various Knowers, and so on—all of which are simply the crystallization into form of the dynamic flowing essence of Awareness.

Thus, in the same way that God has the entire universe for his body, **the individual conscious being**, i.e., the knowing subject, **as a contraction of universal Awareness**, embodies the **entire universe in a microcosmic form,** like the seed of a banyan tree. As it is said in a sacred text of the Siddhānta school:

> He is the body *and* He is the embodied one; He is the soul in all bodies.

In *The Doctrine of the Three-Headed Bhairava*, Śiva gave this [same] teaching, that the perceiver consists of the entire universe in a contracted form, in the passage beginning:

> The body is composed of all the deities; listen to this now, Beloved. It is said to be earth in its solidity; it is water in its fluidity...

इत्युपक्रम्य

'त्रिशिरोभैरवः साक्षाद्व्याप्य विश्वं व्यवस्थितः ॥'

इत्यन्तेन ग्रन्थेन ग्राहकस्य संकुचितविश्वमयत्वमेव व्याहरति ।

अयं च अत्राशयः—ग्राहकोऽपि अयं प्रकाशैकात्म्येन उक्तागमयुक्त्या च विश्वशरीरशिवैकरूप एव, केवलं तन्मायाशक्त्या अनभिव्यक्तस्वरूपत्वात् संकुचित इव आभाति; संकोचोऽपि विचार्यमाणः चिदैकात्म्येन प्रथमानत्वात् चिन्मय एव, अन्यथा तु न किंचित् ।—इति सर्वो ग्राहको विश्वशरीरः शिवभट्टारक एव । तदुक्तं मयैव

'अख्यातिर्यदि न ख्याति ख्यातिरेवावशिष्यते ।
ख्याति चेत् ख्यातिरूपत्वात् ख्यातिरेवावशिष्यते ॥'

इति । अनेनैव आशयेन श्रीस्पन्दशास्त्रेषु

'यस्मात्सर्वमयो जीवः........................ ।'

इत्युपक्रम्य

'तेन शब्दार्थचिन्तासु न सावस्था न यः शिवः ॥'

इत्यादिना शिवजीवयोरभेद एव उक्तः । एतत्तत्त्वपरिज्ञानमेव मुक्तिः, एतत्तत्त्वापरिज्ञानमेव च बन्धः;—इति भविष्यति एव एतत् ॥ ४ ॥

and ending:

> ...thus the Divine stands before your very eyes, directly pervading the totality of things.

This is the point: though a limited perceiver, because you are one with the Light of Awareness, and because of the reasoning given in the scriptures, you must be entirely of one nature with all-embodying Śiva. You merely *appear* as if contracted because your essential nature is not fully manifest, due to the power of His *māyā*. And upon contemplating that state of contraction, we realize that even *it* is nothing but Awareness, because it can only exist as an aspect of Awareness; otherwise it would be nothing whatever. Thus every perceiver is the all-embodying Lord Śiva himself.

As I have taught:

> If ignorance is unknown, knowing alone remains. If it is known, then because it is a part of our knowing, knowing alone remains.

The sacred *Spanda* scripture makes the very same point:

> Because the embodied soul is made up of all things, and perceives its oneness with the awareness it has of all things that arise, the state that is not Śiva does not exist in word, thing, or thought.

Thus, it states that there is no difference at all between Śiva and the embodied soul (*jīva*). Thorough insight into this Truth itself is liberation, and thorough ignorance of this Truth itself is bondage. This will be explained later. || 4 ||

# CHAPTER FOUR

*with explanation*

**Just as God has the whole universe for his body, in the same way,**

**|| CITI-SAṄKOCĀTMĀ CETANO 'PI SAṄKUCITA-VIŚVA-MAYAḤ || 4 ||**

**The individual conscious being,**
**as a contraction of universal Awareness,**
**consists of the entire universe in a microcosmic form.**

It is a traditional teaching in Shaivism that God is that being whose body is the entire universe and whose soul is Consciousness. Kṣemarāja uses that well-known language here to convey a central Tantrik teaching: since the individual's awareness is simply a contracted form of divine Awareness, the individual's body-mind likewise must be a microcosm of the whole universe. The implications of this are considerable, and will be explored more fully below. First Kṣemarāja wants to present a brief sketch of the Tantrik theory of creation as the *emanation*, or self-expression, of the Absolute.

**Śrī-Paramaśiva** [tattva #0] **desires to make manifest the universe—abiding in oneness with itself—in forms that express** [all the aspects of its being,] **from Sadāśiva to Earth. So S/he first vibrates as a manifestation** [tattva #1] **that is not different from the Light of Awareness** *(prakāśa)*, **'more void than the void'—a synonym for Transcendent Śiva, consisting** [only] **of the expression of the unity of Awareness.**

In most Indian philosophy, the Absolute is free of all desire, desire being seen as a base or vulgar thing, so it is telling that here, the Absolute is pictured as having an innate desire to manifest that which is within it. The universe is a latent potentiality within the awareness of the One, and it desires to actualize that potential, out of love for itself. The first step in that manifestation is to tease apart Śiva and Śakti—not that they ever truly separate, but they pull apart somewhat, as it were, to dance together. The prerequisite and ground of the manifestation that is to come is 'transcendent divinity' (*anāśrita-śiva*), the supreme Void, the pure Light of Awareness, untouched by any difference. This is the first *tattva*: the silence that lies behind all sound, the stillness that is the ground of all action. It is absolutely quiescent, unmanifest to the senses, yet constantly present and all-pervading.

Yet the phrase ending Kṣema's paragraph above, describing Transcendent Śiva and here translated as 'an expression of the unity of Awareness' (*cidaikyākhyāti*), could also be translated as 'not expressing the totality of Awareness'.[21] That is, the transcendent emptiness of 'pure' unity-awareness does not express the whole of the potentiality that is latent within Awareness. Not only because there is form as well as formlessness latent within Awareness, but also because Transcendent Śiva is still, and there is also the Śakti aspect, i.e., *dynamism*, which must be expressed.

**Only then does S/he appear also as all the other Principles of Reality (*tattvas*), the 118 Worlds, all existent things and states of being, various Knowers, and so on—all of which are simply the crystallization into form of the dynamic flowing essence of Awareness (*cid-rasa*).**

With transcendent Śiva—identical to what the Buddhists call Emptiness[22]—as the formless ground, the whole of manifest reality spills forth into being: the thirty-four other *tattvas* (Śakti, tattva #2, is the very dynamism of their spilling forth), the 118 dimensions on which beings may exist (*bhuvanas*), all existent things and states (*bhāvas*), and the six other classes of conscious perceivers detailed above in Chapter Three (*pramātṛs*). All of these are said to be the coagulation, or crystallization, or thickening into form (*aśyānatā*) of the *rasa*, or dynamic flowing essence, of Awareness. In this evocative image, Kṣemarāja pictures divine Awareness as a flowing liquid that congeals into solid form (like a sap that crystallizes) and then melts once again, dissolving its form into the dynamism of pure energy, only to assume yet another form, and another, in an endless series. He sees the whole universe as the enactment of this rhythmic pulse (*spanda*), as interrelated patterns of the freezing and melting of the endless unimpeded flow of the power of Awareness, delighting in its ability to assume ever-new forms and relinquish them again.

Let's apply this teaching to our human lives as well. Consciousness, out of its own free will, chooses particular roles to play out of the nearly infinite possibilities—and then naturally seeks to relinquish those roles to make space for new possibility. Adult humans tend to be afraid of letting go of a self-image that matches a role they understand, despite how stale it has become, unless a new prospect is already being offered. But Awareness doesn't work that way: it seeks to melt into flowing possibility before reforming in organic response to its situation.

*Contemplation Exercise*

Reflect on your own life, and the many roles you have adopted. Are you 'the party girl', or 'the successful guy', or 'the know-it-all', or 'the one whose relationships never work out', or 'the spiritual seeker', or 'the damaged victim', or the 'good daughter/son', or the 'rebel'? Make an inventory of all your roles, all your self-images.

When you survey them, which ones still feel really 'right', such that you are delighting in them and learning from them, and which ones no longer feel true to you, and have become stale and dry, past their natural expiration date?

Usually, we hang on to the latter type of roles out of fear. Who will you be if you're not (fill in the blank)? Realize that everyone is afraid of letting go without knowing what comes next, and that courage means doing it anyway, despite the fear. If, in the space of openness left by the letting go, you drop deep inside, with an attitude of being open to whatever may come, a new inspiration will start to make itself felt.

Now, Kṣemarāja has established that the whole of reality, all the worlds and all the beings living in them and all the states that they pass through, are all the self-expression of the One, the single underlying consciousness sometimes called the Blessed Lord (*bhagavān*) or God.

**Thus, in the same way that God has the entire universe for his body, the individual conscious being (*cetana**), i.e., the knowing subject, as a contraction of universal Awareness (*citi*), embodies the entire universe in a microcosmic form, like the seed of a banyan tree** [contains the pattern of the whole tree].

Here we get a clear statement of the primary thesis of Chapter Four, which relates to what might be called the 'holographic' vision of reality in nondual Śaiva Tantra. If you have a piece of real holographic film, when you shine a laser through it, you get a three-dimensional image. If the film records the image of a toy truck, say, then if you cut the piece of film in half and shine a laser through each half, what do you see? Not two halves of a truck, but two complete smaller toy trucks. This is because the information of the image is a pattern recorded everywhere on the film. Thus, something can be said to be 'holographic' when *the pattern of the whole is contained in each of its parts* in a smaller iteration (we see this phenomenon in fractals as well). When Kṣemarāja tells us that each individual conscious being embodies the entire universe in microcosm, he is telling us that each part contains the pattern of the whole. He managed to explain holographic information encoding nearly 1,000 years before it existed.

Though he did not have the perfect analogy of a hologram or a fractal, he is clearly groping in that direction when he cites the example of the seed of the banyan tree. The banyan fig tree is the largest tree in the world; a single tree can cover several acres due to its aerial roots that become supplementary trunks. However, the seeds inside its fruit are very tiny, and yet from that tiny seed, a vast tree can grow, because (as we *now* know) each seed contains the DNA pattern of the whole. Indian philosophers had long intuited the existence of DNA, supposing that all the information necessary to produce the tree must somehow exist within the seed, in a tightly packed form.† In Kṣema's formulation, then, just as each of our cells contain the DNA that describes our whole body-mind, our body-mind itself is like a 'cell' of the universe, containing its entire pattern in contracted form.

---

* *Cetana* is literally 'the agent of consciousness', that is, the one who does the act of being conscious. In this text it refers to the individuated conscious being, as opposed to *citi,* which is not individuated.

† Cf. *Chāndogya Upaniṣad* 6.12.

Okay, now having established the model of reality being presented here, what are the real-world implications? They are considerable. First, there is no state experienced by anyone ever that *you* cannot experience in this very body. It is literally all within you, and should you choose to plumb the depths of your being, you will directly know that that is true—without having to actually experience the entire range. On the spiritual path, everyone discovers sooner or later that the sense they have of themselves, of who and what they think they are, is grossly limited and small compared to the reality of the vastness of their being. The capacity to be the holiest of saints and the most heartless of killers exists within each of us. You may have heard this before, but take a moment to actually feel the truth of it within yourself. Such a feeling inspires us to embrace our own greatness on the one hand, yet also gives us greater compassion for the wicked on the other hand—for we know that "there, but for the grace of God, go I".

When you can really feel the full range of human possibility within yourself, it also gives rise to reverent wonder at the manifestation of the unique selection of that range called 'me'—a selection that is never static, but ever fresh and new, if we let it be. A sense of humbled awe arises when you realize that of all the things God could have chosen to be, she has chosen to become *you*—and chooses it again, afresh, now, and each moment. For the Tāntrika, or any awakened being, there really is no greater joy than simply seeing which part of the infinite pattern will manifest next. "What will God do—and be—through me today?" spoken with a soft smile, roughly approximates this experience.

Tantra teaches that all the sacred sites, all the places of pilgrimage, and all the deities are within. In fact, the Tāntrikas went so far as to map the sacred sites of India onto the human body, implying that anything you can experience by going to a sacred site can be experienced within. As beautiful as this world can be, the inner landscape is just as varied and just as beautiful. This can be hard for many people to believe, because what you experience when you first turn within is usually just the spinning of your own mind, or else boring nothingness. But if you are patient, just when you've given up on seeing anything, a subtle depth starts to open up, a vastness filled with quiet presence, and in that vastness, little by little, something indescribable starts to be revealed—but never when you're specifically looking for it.

Now Kṣemarāja proves his point by citing scriptural authority, as is traditional. In his context, it was believed that if you couldn't cite a scripture to support your point, your point was suspect. Originality is suspect in the spiritual sphere, because something only has the weight of real truth if it's been divinely revealed and/or tested over generations. A new idea, however attractive, cannot be called truth until it has stood the test of time, and been examined over and over again in the light of a broad range of human experience.

Here Kṣema first cites a text from the broad base of the tradition, the most universally accepted layer of scripture, called the Siddhānta, and then cites a Trika text immediately afterward, thus covering both the orthodox Śaiva side and the more heterodox Śākta side, implying that they both agree on this key point.

**As it is said in a sacred text of the Siddhānta school:**

> **He is the body *and* He is the embodied one; He is the soul in all bodies.**

**In the *Triśiro-mata* (*The Doctrine of the Three-Headed Bhairava*), Śiva gave this** [same] **teaching, that the perceiver consists of the entire universe in a contracted form, in the passage beginning:**

> **The body is composed of all the deities;[23] listen to this now, Beloved. It is said to be Earth in** [terms of] **its solidity; it is Water in its fluidity...**

**and ending:**

> **...thus the Divine stands before your very eyes, directly pervading the totality of things.**

The *Triśiro-mata* is a lost text of the Trika, teaching the three Trika Goddesses (Parā, Parāparā, and Aparā: see page 236 of *Tantra Illuminated*) as the 'three heads' of Bhairava (which is the preferred Śākta term for Śiva, or God), to emphasize that the three are aspects of one Consciousness. In the quote given above, we see the divinization of the body in Tantra, for it is only in physical embodiment that all thirty-six *tattvas* are fully expressed. Note that here the *tattvas* are called 'deities', an unusual usage. The quote must have continued with all the other *tattvas*, saying "It is Fire in its warmth; it is Wind in its mobility;

it is Space in its extension" and so on. Since all the *tattvas* are expressions of the Divine, the culminating quote makes sense. In this (Trika) tradition, then, the Divine is hardly something far removed in a distant heaven; it is the very substance of all that we experience.

**This is the point: though a limited perceiver, because you are one with the Light of Awareness, and because of the** [other] **reasoning given in the scriptures** [and taught above]**, you must be entirely of one nature with all-embodying Śiva. You** [merely] ***appear*** **as if contracted, because your essential nature is not** [fully] **manifest, due to the power of His *māyā*** [by which differentiation appears ultimately real]**. And upon contemplating that** [state of] **contraction, we realize that even *it* is nothing but Awareness, because it can only exist as an aspect of Awareness; otherwise it would be nothing whatever. Thus every perceiver is the all-embodying Lord Śiva himself.**

Here Kṣemarāja hits a kind of crescendo in his argument. "You must be entirely of one nature with all-embodying Śiva" could also be translated as "You can't be anything but a form of the one, the Deity whose body is the whole universe." (*viśva-śarīra-śivaika-rūpa eva kevalam.*) He goes on to say that contraction is but an appearance, not ultimately real. This does not belittle the sometimes painful reality of contraction, because in the Recognition philosophy, *everything* is termed an 'appearance' (*ābhāsa*) insofar as it is, in reality, a shining of the One Light that merely appears to have its own separate being. The Power called *māyā* is, in this system, the power of creative diversification by which things appear to have separate, individual, independent existence. (Note that individuality in the sense of diversity *is* accepted in this system, while individuality in the sense of separate existence is not.[24]) But contraction falls away when your essential nature (*svabhāva*) becomes fully manifest, meaning you will experience the expansive state of your own divinity even in the midst of those states others would call contraction. For even contraction itself is nothing but a form of Awareness; after all, that which is not part of Awareness cannot be said to exist, as we have seen. Therefore, in this system, there is no demonizing of contraction; it is part of the One Light, and every conscious being, in whatever state of mind, is none other than Lord Śiva, he who embodies all things. Some are Lord Śiva in his divine state of concealment, others are Lord Śiva in his equally divine state of self-revelation. (More on this later.)

**As I have taught** [elsewhere]:

> **If ignorance is unknown, knowing alone remains. If it is known, then because it is a part of our knowing, knowing alone remains.**

On the topic of whether contraction is something separate from divine Awareness, Kṣemarāja cites a parallel passage from another work of his. Here we see an important difference of this philosophy from the Vedānta. In the latter view, ignorance cannot be said to be a part of the Absolute (*brahman*), nor can it be said to have a separate existence: its status is simply said to be 'unexplainable'. However, here there simply is no ignorance, except in the sense of 'that which has not yet been seen'. There is no badness or wrongness, just knowing that is incomplete (which can of course be very painful at times).

Let's try to understand the riddle-like statement Kṣema makes above. We can rephrase the same thing in different ways, such as: if the state of unconsciousness is not known to us, then we experience only consciousness; if it *is* known to us, then because we are aware of it, again, we are left with consciousness alone.

To put it another way, is the state of separation from the Light of Awareness something that is manifest or not? If not, we are left only with what is manifest (the Light of Awareness); if the state of separation is manifest, it is simply another aspect of that Light, because it is by that one Light that all things are known. Therefore, there is no 'darkness' in your being—if you see it, it is part of your light. The only absolute darkness would be nonexistence, which by definition does not exist. What really exists, then, is not ignorance but partial knowledge that can be expanded; a partial aperture for the passage of light that can be further opened. Thus we can start from any being's knowledge of their reality and work from there to knowledge of the ultimate, and this is exactly what a master teacher does.

Note an important implication of this teaching: it problematizes the common Western articulation of challenging personality traits as 'the shadow', as in, "I'm working with my shadow." All too often this is just a euphemism for 'my dark side', and as such reinforces a false dichotomy between the light and dark within, the apparent struggle between the angelic and demonic natures. From the Tantrik perspective, this view of things is wrong, and more importantly, it does not lead to a successful outcome, because it precludes loving the whole of your being, and it is only through love that real healing and integration can occur. Demonizing your anger, or desire, or whatever, does not lead to healing—unless of course you are following the Tantrik practice of *feeding* your demons instead of fighting them.* The affirmation that there is no darkness within, only light unseen, or light that is stagnant, reorients us to do our work with greater courage, confidence, and love.

Another way of saying the same thing is the assertion that only Truth exists; untruth only seems to exist because we're not seeing the Truth clearly (this is the line of argument that nondualist Jed McKenna takes).†

Lastly, we might note that the language of Kṣemarāja's verse above recalls the beautiful and very ancient Upaniṣadic verse:

> *Oṃ pūrṇam adaḥ pūrṇam idaṃ pūrṇāt pūrṇam udacyate* |
> *pūrṇasya pūrṇam ādāya pūrṇam evāvaśiṣyate* ||

> **Om. That [what is external] is perfect, whole, complete. This [what is internal] is perfect, whole, complete. From perfect wholeness, perfect wholeness proceeds. If the whole is taken from the whole, what remains is still perfectly whole.**

When you see yourself as complete just as you are, you realize that spiritual work involves neither getting rid of what is 'bad' within you nor acquiring something that is lacking; rather, it centers on learning to work with old energy in new ways, creating more alignment throughout the system, and moving that which is stagnant. In this scenario, everything naturally finds its place: you allow that which 'wants' to depart to flow out (and when it does, you are somehow still perfectly whole), and allow that which 'wants' to enter to flow in and through, without grasping at it. When you see with the eyes of truth, you see

---

* See Tsultrim Allione's masterful book *Feeding Your Demons*, which is a modern and accessible interpretation of ancient *chöd* practice.

† See his *Theory of Everything*.

that nothing could be added to, or subtracted from, this moment to make it any more perfect.

Kṣema now cites one more scriptural source, the most subtle and powerful of the citations in this chapter.

**The sacred *Spanda* scripture makes the very same point:**

> **Because the embodied soul is made up of all things** [that arise in its field of experience]**, and perceives its oneness with the awareness it has of all things, the state that is not Śiva does not exist in word, thing, or thought.**[25]

**Thus, it states that there is no difference at all between Śiva and the embodied soul (*jīva*).**

Kṣemarāja cites a verse and a half from the *Stanzas on Vibration*,[26] which summarize an argument that we can spell out more clearly here. This is, perhaps, one of the more 'watertight' arguments in this philosophy, provided of course that you accept the first axiom, which can only be demonstrated through direct (spiritual) experience, but which can hardly be doubted by anyone who has had that experience. (Of course, for the original audience, scripture was a valid means of knowledge, in fact the most reliable means of knowledge.) Here is the argument:

(A) It is known from scripture that God/dess comprises all things, i.e., has the universe for its body (axiom).

(B) No object is ever manifest without a simultaneously manifesting awareness of that object, and therefore, by the principle of invariable concomitance (which states that two things that *always* arise together must in fact be two aspects of one thing),

(C) any object and one's awareness of it are two aspects of one thing.

(D) The knowing subject (e.g., you) in which manifests the awareness of any thing is, clearly, not something separate from the awareness she has of that thing. So, combining (C) and (D), we must conclude that

(E) the individual being is comprised of all things (in his realm of experience), and therefore, combining (A) and (E),

(F) the individual and God are one and the same (in nature, though not in scope).

The only difference between the individual and God, by this argument, is the one already mentioned in the sūtra that began this chapter: the individual's awareness is, generally speaking, contracted (indeed, it is by virtue of that fact that we call him an individual), and thus the scope of his awareness is usually limited to a narrower field, that of his individual experience. 'God' is nothing but a name for the total, transindividual field of Awareness (by virtue of participating in which each individual has whatever degree of awareness he does), and thus God's consciousness is only different in scope, not in nature. Even that difference disappears at certain moments for certain people, and it is this that we tend to call a 'spiritual experience' (*samāveśa* in Sanskrit).

Kṣemarāja comments further on this *Spanda* verse in his work called *An Investigation into the Doctrine of Vibration* (*Spanda-nirṇaya*). There he writes:

> The individual soul is a cognizer, who, like Śiva, consists of everything [that arises in his sphere of experience]; therefore, the state that is not Śiva does not exist in words, things, or thoughts (whether discursive or otherwise), whether past, present, or future. The real meaning of this verse is that *everything* has Śiva as its real nature. [Next Kṣema comments on the second half of verse 4, not cited above:]
>
> And since it is so, the conscious perceiver is an active experient who exists as the feeling-state of the given object of experience, [yet] remains the same, i.e., neither lessened nor increased, at all times and in all loci [of experience], such as the various *tattva*s and worlds. Nor can any object of experience whatsoever be [known as] something separate from its experiencer.
>
> So the passage [above] establishes that in actuality there is no difference whatsoever between Śiva and the individual soul. Thus, one should not think oneself incomplete or imperfect with regard to any state of the body, mind, etc. On the contrary, one should know "My essence-nature is Śiva, undivided Awareness [in the form of this state]."

This passage is quite astonishing for those used to the mainstream teaching in Indian spirituality, that the innermost self is a witness (*sākṣī*), detached from and untouched by all that it experiences. Here, by contrast, the self is said to be an engaged, active experient (*bhoktā*), not separate from the feeling-state it experiences. That is, in this view the inner self is not a detached witness of some state like 'cold' experienced by the body; the self-which-is-consciousness actually *becomes* the 'felt-sense' of cold, just as Śiva (universal consciousness) has really become this manifest universe, which is not at all an illusion.[27] But, and here's the interesting part, the self-which-is-consciousness, the soul, is not depleted or enlarged by any experience whatsoever, or divided or fragmented either—just like Śiva retains his undivided and complete nature even as he becomes this whole reality. Feeling depleted or enlarged is something that happens on the level of the *prāṇa*, and the soul is even more fundamental than *prāṇa*; it is unbounded Awareness. By definition, Awareness can adopt any form, have any experience, and it remains simply what it is: something like pure radiance, a conscious field that is like gold in that it is soft, malleable, and shining.* It does not become incomplete or imperfect due to any alteration in mind or body.

The significance of this teaching is huge, for it is a decisive turn against the dissociative consequences of the 'detached witness' teaching still prevalent throughout the world of yoga today. Tantra teaches that no detachment is ultimately necessary to be healthily centered in your innermost being. *Both* detachment and attachment result in suffering. Since attachment occurs through identification with body and mind (see Chapter Seven), the solution in that case is the same: know your soul, your essence-nature, divine Awareness, and become centered in it.

Kṣema finishes with:

**Thorough insight into this Truth** [that Śiva and *jīva* are of one nature] **itself *is* liberation, and thorough ignorance of this Truth itself is bondage. This will be explained later.**

Liberation (*mukti*) is nothing but your natural state when you are seeing the whole truth clearly (*parijñāna*). Bondage is your natural state

---

* To borrow a beautifully apropos simile first articulated by the Buddha.

when you have not yet seen the whole truth clearly. He will explain this further in Chapters Twelve and Thirteen. Let's end this chapter with a contemplation.

*Contemplation Exercise*

"The state that is not Śiva does not exist in word, thing, or thought." Take in this powerful statement, remembering that *Śiva* means both 'God' (or 'the Divine') and 'a blessing'. What might it be like to experience the state of being from which this statement arose? What might it be like to feel that your every thought, however exalted or base, is a vibration of the one divine energy?

Notice the way in which you almost unconsciously categorize your thoughts, words, and actions as high versus low, worthy versus unworthy, divine versus mundane—fundamentally, as 'that which should be' versus 'that which should not be'. Right now, take a deep breath, and allow everything to be, just as it is.

Realize that every thought and action, however seemingly misguided, springs from seeking love, bliss, or insight, and these are the primary characteristics of the Divine. So every action is nothing but the Divine seeking to know itself, sometimes gracefully, sometimes clumsily. Realizing this, be gentle with yourself.

This concludes our study of Sūtra Four and its commentary.

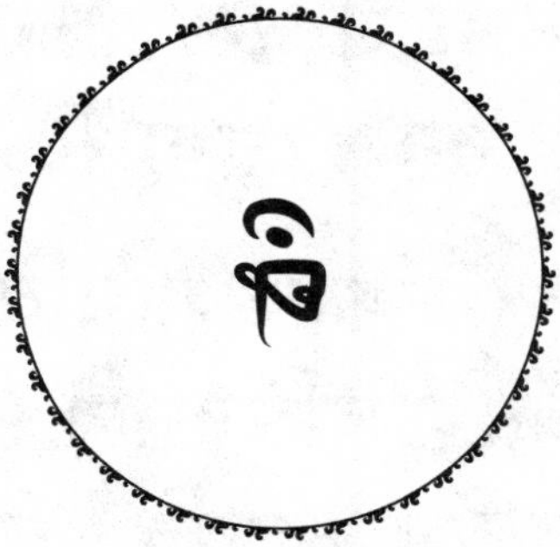

ननु ग्राहकोऽयं विकल्पमयः, विकल्पनं च चित्तहेतुकं; सति च चित्ते, कथमस्य शिवात्मकत्वम्?—इति शङ्कित्वा चित्तमेव निर्णेतुमाह

**चितिरेव चेतनपदादवरूढा चेत्य-**
**संकोचिनी चित्तम् ॥ ५ ॥**

न चित्तं नाम अन्यत् किंचित्, अपि तु सैव भगवती तत् । तथा हि सा स्वं स्वरूपं गोपयित्वा यदा संकोचं गृह्णाति, तदा द्वयी गतिः; कदाचित् उल्लसितमपि संकोचं गुणीकृत्य चित्प्राधान्येन स्फुरति, कदाचित् संकोचप्रधानतया । चित्प्राधान्यपक्षे सहजे प्रकाशमात्रप्रधानत्वे विज्ञानाकलता; प्रकाशपरामर्शप्रधानत्वे तु विद्याप्रमातृता । तत्रापि क्रमेण संकोचस्य तनुतायाम्, ईश-सदाशिवानाश्रितरूपता । समाधिप्रयत्नोपार्जिते तु चित्प्रधानत्वे शुद्धाध्वप्रमातृता क्रमात्क्रमं प्रकर्षवती । संको-

# CHAPTER FIVE

*Kṣemarāja's original text*

Objection: "Surely, the individual perceiver is made up of dualistic mental constructs, and the mind is the basis of these mental constructs. So, if the perceiver is the mind, how can it be God?"

Addressing this doubt, in order to explain the mind, it is taught:

**Awareness itself, descending from its state of pure consciousness, becomes contracted by the object perceived: this is** [called] **the mind.** || 5 ||

The mind is nothing other than this very Goddess Awareness. To explain: when She conceals Her true nature and takes on contraction, there are two modes in which She does so.

Sometimes, She vibrates predominantly as Awareness, subordinating contraction, even though it is still present. Other times, contraction is predominant.

In the case of Awareness being predominant,

» If it predominates exclusively as the innate Light of Awareness, that is the state of the Vijñānākala.

» However, when the Light's capacity for Self-reflection is predominant, that is the state of being a Wisdom-perceiver. In that state, through the progressive diminution of contraction, one ascends through successively higher layers: the states of Īśvara, Sadāśiva, and Transcendent Śiva.

» And when the predominance of Awareness is achieved through effort in meditation, the state of being a knower of the Pure Realm keeps gradually becoming greater.

चप्राधान्ये तु शून्यादिप्रमातृता । एवमव-
स्थिते सति, 'चितिरेव' संकुचितग्राहकरूपा 'चेतनपदात् अवरूढा'–अर्थग्रहणोन्मुखी सती 'चेत्येन'–नील-सुखादिना 'संकोचिनी' उभयसंकोचसंकुचितैव चित्तम् । तथा च

'स्वाङ्गरूपेषु भावेषु पत्युर्ज्ञानं क्रिया च या ।
मायातृतीये ते एव पशोः सत्त्वं रजस्तमः ॥'

इत्यादिना स्वातन्त्र्यात्मा चितिशक्तिरेव ज्ञान-क्रिया-मायाशक्तिरूपा पशुदशायां संकोचप्रकर्षात् सत्त्व-रजस्तमःस्वभावचित्तात्मतया स्फुरति;–इति श्रीप्रत्यभिज्ञायामुक्तम् । अत एव श्रीतत्त्वगर्भस्तोत्रे विकल्पदशायामपि तात्त्विकस्वरूपसद्भावात् तदनुसरणाभिप्रायेण उक्तम्

'अत एव तु ये केचित्परमार्थानुसारिणः ।
तेषां तत्र स्वरूपस्य स्वज्योतिष्ट्वं न लुप्यते ॥'

इति ॥ ५ ॥

However, when contraction predominates, then one is merely a knower of the peripheral layers of one's being: the void, the life force, the mind, and the body.

This being the case, **Awareness itself,** in taking the form of the contracted perceiver, **descends from its state of pure consciousness**—being eager to grasp the objects of perception—and **becomes contracted by a perceived object**, such as 'blue' or 'pleasure'. She is contracted by a double contraction: **this is the mind.**

It is taught in the sacred *Recognition* scripture:

> The Lord's powers of Knowing, Acting, and Differentiation, in the case of the beings that are forms of His own body, become the *sattva*, *rajas*, and *tamas* of the bound soul. ||

The sacred *Recognition* scripture is here teaching that the Power of Awareness, which is absolutely free, has three primary forms: the Powers of Knowing, Acting, and Self-concealment-in-plurality. In the state of the bound soul, due to the increase of contraction, that same Power of Awareness vibrates as the mind, with its intrinsic qualities of *sattva*, *rajas*, and *tamas*.

For this very reason, the sacred *Hymn on the Core of Reality* teaches that because one's real nature as Awareness continues to exist even in the state of dualistic thought, it is possible to maintain awareness of it at all times. It says:

> For those rare people who maintain close awareness of ultimate reality, the self-illumination of their true nature is not interrupted in that state.

|| 5 ||

# CHAPTER FIVE

*with explanation*

[Objection:] **"Surely, the individual perceiver (*grāhaka*) is made up of dualistic mental constructs (*vikalpa*), and the mind (*citta*) is the basis of these mental constructs. So, if the perceiver is the mind, how can it be God?"**

In pre-Tantrik yoga (such as that of Patañjali), divine spirit is thought to be completely different from matter: spirit (*puruṣa*) and matter-energy (*prakṛti*) are two separate, co-eternal, irreducible things, and should not be confused with each other. In fact, confusing the two is thought to be the source of all suffering. Mind is part of matter, of course, and so cannot be divine. This is the basis of the objection raised here. The objectioner argues that what defines an individual perceiver is a flow of thoughts—specifically *vikalpas*, which are language-based, inherently dualistic thought-forms (Kṣemarāja will later disagree that this is what defines the individual perceiver). And these thoughts have the mind for their basis, and hence subjective awareness is really nothing but the mind, and therefore cannot be God. Kṣema has something rather important to tell us about this, a radically different perspective that is very much at the heart of what makes the Tantra distinct from other philosophies of mind and personhood.

**Addressing this doubt, in order to explain the mind, it is taught:**

**|| CITIR EVA CETANA-PADĀD AVARŪḌHĀ CETYA-SAṄKOCINĪ CITTAM || 5 ||**

**Awareness (*citi*) itself, descending from its state of pure consciousness (*cetana*), becomes contracted by the object perceived: this is** [called] **the mind (*citta*).**

Far from teaching an absolute distinction of divine spirit and mundane matter, Tantra teaches that they are in fact different phases of one thing, i.e., Awareness. Take the example of $H_2O$: in one phase, we call it steam, in another, water, in another, ice. These three states are very different from one another, and we necessarily interact with each of them in very different ways. This is a perfect analogy for what Kṣemarāja intends here: there are three different states or phases of one 'thing'—in one state, we call it God, in another, pure consciousness, in another, the mind.

The implications of this are of course huge. First, though, let's explore the specific three terms that Kṣemarāja is using here for these three states of the One. First we have *citi*, introduced in the first sūtra, which we translate (imperfectly) as Awareness. *Citi* (pronounced CHIT-ee) is the state in which Awareness is fully expanded, that is to say, untouched by any trace of contraction, including that of subjectivity or selfhood. In other words, there is no concealment whatsoever operative on the *citi* level (not that it's really a level, of course). When *citi* manifests as an individuated subject, then that is the phase called *cetana*, here translated as 'pure consciousness'.

We have to define this second phase, *cetana*, more carefully so that we don't confuse it with the third phase (the mind). *Cetana* (CHAY-tuh-nuh) is the state of being the conscious knower or agent of consciousness. We experience *cetana* in the space between trains of thought, a space of awareness momentarily devoid of thought-forms (*vikalpas*). That's why I translate it as 'pure consciousness'. We experience it dozens of times a day, but usually only for a second, and usually without the reflective self-awareness (*vimarśa*) by which we can know that we are experiencing *cetana*. (This 'knowing', when it does occur, does not take the form of a thought, or else it is no longer the *cetana* state.) The *cetana* state is open and expansive awareness; in fact, it is as expanded as awareness can be while still having a subtle 'sense of self'.

The third phase is *citta*, which we translate as 'mind'. If, in our $H_2O$ metaphor, *citi* is steam, and *cetana* is water, then *citta* is ice. *Cetana* contracts and solidifies, as it were, into the mind, that is, the cognitive apparatus that knows and thinks about specific objects. It is only on this level that specific thought-constructs are operative, the cognitions by which awareness interprets or represents reality to itself. This is the phase of awareness with which we are most familiar, because it is the phase that we are most identified with.

Now let's look at the sūtra again. Kṣemarāja tells us that it is Awareness (*citi*) that is the mind (*citta*), and that it enters its mind-phase by descending or stepping down (*avarūḍhā*) from its *cetana* phase and becoming contracted (*saṅkocinī*) by a perceivable object (*cetya*).

Notice that all the different phases have a common root in Sanskrit, that is, √*cit*. It would be a normal Tantrik argument, though Kṣema does not make it here, that the Sanskrit language itself encodes the true nature of reality, demonstrating that all the phases here examined, including even that of the perceivable object, are all permutations of the same fundamental thing (√*cit*→ *citi, cetana, citta, cetya*).[28] Like steam that condenses into water yet is still $H_2O$, when *citi* appears as *cetana* or *citta*, it does not relinquish its true nature in any measure but remains complete, perfect, divine, fully itself. Realizing this clearly and fully is what we call awakening to the truth.

Now, having said all that, we must realize that the question of what state *citi* is in is not all that important to the Recognition philosophy. In this tradition, to try to silence the mind and remain solely in 'pure consciousness' is seen as a frustrating and largely fruitless task (as anyone who's tried it will probably agree!). That is the transcendentalist, escapist path that nondual Tantra rejects. What really matters, then, is not the presence or absence of contraction, but rather whether Awareness or contraction is *predominant*. Let's turn now to Kṣemarāja's commentary on Sūtra Five, where he explains this.

**The mind is nothing other than this very Goddess** [Awareness]. **To explain: when She conceals Her true nature and takes on contraction, there are two modes** [in which She does so]:

1) **Sometimes, She vibrates (*sphurati*) predominantly as Awareness, subordinating contraction, even though it is still present.**
2) **Other times, contraction is predominant.**

The central issue here is one of identification. If you are more identified with the fact of *being aware* than with what you happen to be aware *of*, Awareness will naturally be predominant, which is subjectively experienced as rather more blissful, expanded, and/or nondual than when contraction is predominant. On the other hand, contraction will inevitably be predominant when we are identified with it, that is, when we are constructing a self out of our thoughts and feelings, or our moods, or our bodily condition.

Notice that Kṣema implies that we need not banish contraction altogether to experience the Joy of Awareness. The latter simply needs to gain the upper hand, as it were, and become predominant. The thing is, the fact of being aware doesn't grab at our attention the way the objects of awareness do. We have to bring our attention to it, and then it starts to reveal itself as the very ground of all our experience.

Next he explains the other significant feature in this schema, which was already mentioned in passing above: the presence or absence of *vimarśa*, the self-reflective awareness by which we can look at ourselves, by which we know that we know, or are aware that we are aware. Without *vimarśa*, the power of self-reflection, full awakening is not possible. Now, *vimarśa* is almost never completely absent in humans, but again, at issue is whether it is 'predominant' or not. Here is an outline that organizes the information in Kṣemarāja's next comments. It is explained in the following paragraphs.

1) Awareness predominant, subordinating contraction
   a) *prakāśa** alone predominant = the state of a Vijñānākala (on the threshold of full awakening)
   b) both *prakāśa* and *vimarśa* predominant = the state of a *vidyā-pramātā* (an awakened and liberated being)
   c) both *prakāśa* and *vimarśa* predominant, but initially incomplete; they increase by stages, through *sādhanā* (gradual awakening through spiritual practice)
2) Contraction predominant = *māyā-pramātā* (the standard human condition of body-identification, mind-identification, etc.)

**In the** [first] **case,** [that] **of Awareness being predominant,** (1a above) **if there is a spontaneous predominance of the Light of Awareness** (*prakāśa*) **alone, that is the state of the *Vijñānākala*** [fifth Perceiver].

As we have already seen, the Vijñānākala is one who has embraced the true Self as pure 'witness-consciousness', and therefore has relinquished agency, believing that the Self does nothing eternally but observe. By holding to that view, such a person relinquishes the inherent freedom of Awareness by which it purposefully takes on agency and plays various roles. Lacking the *vimarśa-śakti* (power of self-reflection) by which s/he would realize that this is not the highest state, such a person is stuck, as it were, on the threshold of real liberation. Such a

* For *prakāśa*, see above, page 51.

person might become a 'spiritual by-passer', denying that any work on the level of body/mind/psyche is necessary, because s/he knows that the Self is already perfect and the body-mind will never be. Still, since for such a person, awareness persistently predominates over contraction, they exist in a state that looks a lot like the fully awakened state, and so the Vijñānākala may convince himself that he is 'done', and likewise convince others of the same, others who may then take him as a guru, bringing inevitable suffering to both parties.

Note that Kṣema uses the word 'spontaneous' (*sahaja*) above, perhaps implying that this state can be attained through a 'sudden enlightenment'-type awakening. If so, the subtly implied critique here is that most who attain so-called 'sudden enlightenment' do not possess the predominance of *vimarśa-śakti* that is necessary for full awakening.[29]

**1b) However, when the Light's capacity for Self-reflection** (*vimarśa*) **is predominant, that is the state of being a Wisdom-perceiver** [i.e., full awakening, on the level of the fourth Perceiver]**. In that state, through the progressive diminution of contraction,** [one ascends through successively higher layers]**: the states of Īśvara, Sadāśiva, and Transcendent Śiva** [Perceivers three, two, and one, respectively]**.**

When the self-reflective power of Awareness (the *vimarśa* of *prakāśa*) is fully present, then one enters the Pure Realm (the 'domain' of liberation), fully liberated and fully awake. Kṣemarāja calls the fully awakened state that of being a *Wisdom-perceiver*.[30] Once one has crossed that final threshold (which some Buddhist lineages call 'the Gateless Gate'), there is a natural, continual, effortless diminution of contraction, whereby one rises in stages through the remaining *tattvas* (or Perceiver-levels, depending on which model you're using).

Kṣemarāja's next comment seems to suggest that the process described above can unfold through the cultivation of insight alone, for all that has been said under the headings of 1a) and 1b) is now contrasted to a meditative process.

**1c) When the predominance of Awareness** (*cit*) **is achieved through effort in meditation** (*samādhi*)**, the state of being a knower of the Pure Realm keeps gradually becoming greater.**

He seems to suggest that the path of meditation, or rather the conscious cultivation of unitive states of awareness (for that is the more precise meaning of *samādhi*) is both more gradual and yet more sure than the process described above. Here there is no possibility of *prakāśa* without *vimarśa*; the path leads inevitably to full awakening. This, at least, is my reading; in this section of our text it is considerably more difficult to discern authorial intent than in any section previous. The lack of any static final state is, however, clearly emphasized in the language here; literally, we have 'Pure Realm-knower-ness becoming [ever] greater, step by step'.[31]

Finally, Kṣema contrasts the Wisdom-perceiver (*vidyā-pramātā*) he has been discussing with the normal, unliberated state of awareness, that of the *māyā-pramātā* or 'one who sees duality as ultimately real'. Here he is returning to the basic twofold division he introduced at the beginning of his commentary on this sūtra.

**2) However, when contraction predominates, then one is** [merely] **a knower of** [the more peripheral layers of one's being:] **the void, the life force, the mind, and the body.**

Here our author alludes to the Tantrik theory of the five-layered self, which we will discuss in Chapter Seven. Right now it is important to understand that contraction predominates because of wrongly identifying one of the peripheral layers of one's being as the center of selfhood. That is, identification with the body, the mind, the *prāṇa*, or the inner void rather than the dynamic nondual Awareness that is one's true core leads to (or rather, *is*) the predominance of contraction.

One of the most basic forms of contraction, which can give rise to much suffering, is the identification with one's mind. Now Kṣema reiterates the basic thesis of Sūtra Five, expanding it slightly.

**This being the case, Awareness itself, in taking the form of the contracted perceiver, descends from its state of pure consciousness** (*cetana*)**—being eager to grasp the objects of perception—and becomes contracted by a perceived object, such as 'blue' or 'pleasure'. She is contracted by a double contraction: this is** [called] **the mind.**

Awareness innately desires to experience itself in the form of particular objects,* and thus willingly descends from the expanded subjectivity of the *cetana* state. In the act of perceiving a particular object, whether an

* Unlike in Vedānta philosophy.

external sensory perception (like the color blue), or an internal feeling-state (like pleasure), awareness partially takes on the qualities of that object, vibrating with its frequency, as it were. This is what we call the mind. We could translate Kṣema in another way, saying *Mind is nothing but Awareness contracted in accordance with the object perceived.*

When Kṣema refers to a 'double contraction' in his last line above, I think he means that the mind is contracted both in the sense that it is no longer an open space of pure subjective awareness, and in the sense that it has temporarily taken on the qualities of that which it perceives. But the phrase is unclear to me.

Since we tend to locate our sense of self in the mind, when the mind takes on the qualities of that which it perceives, we tend to construct a self out of those objects of experience, and say (for example), "*I* am happy," or "*I* am sad." We do this even in relation to external objects: identifying your preferences with your self, you feel good when others agree that whatever *you* like is good, or lovely, or tasteful, and whatever you don't like is bad, or ugly, or tasteless (we call this 'feeling validated', which really means 'experiencing the pleasure of believing oneself right, and that one's limited sense of self is therefore justified'). The important thing to realize here is that the mind will *always* by colored by the qualities of whatever it perceives, and if there is identification with that mind-state, or resistance to it, it becomes 'sticky' and leaves an impression. The collection of these impressions forms our constructed sense of self. However, if there is no identification, and no resistance, then when any given object has been fully experienced, the mind releases it and dissolves back into pure awareness (if only for a moment). That is its nature, to always return to its source.

The picture of internal reality presented here is a *spanda*: a pulsing oscillation, in this case, between expanded awareness and the contracted mind-perceiver. Awareness contracts in order to perceive an object, and contracts in precise accordance with the nature of that object, becoming a 'blue-mind' or a 'pleasure-mind'. Then, each mind (for, in a sense, each object of perception produces a different mind), having run its course with that experience, will, if it is allowed to, dissolve completely back into the formless open space of pure awareness, before beginning the process again. If it is not allowed to—that is to say, if there is resistance to completely releasing an experience as it comes to an end—it leaves an impression of the experience in the psyche or emotional body. This is the natural, endless process of embodied consciousness. What gums up the works, then, is the inability to let a given mind-state dissolve due to attachment or aversion regarding its object.

Pre-Tantrik yogīs thought the solution was to rid themselves of all attachment or aversion. Those who take this path usually wind up in repression and denial, often with disastrous results. There is, however, a more effective (if subtler) method: release the object-cognition when it starts to dissolve, and let the attachment or aversion you are feeling (if any) become the new object of cognition, without mistakenly thinking that it is an energy coming from the object itself. If you give complete, open, and nonjudgmental attention to the attachment-mind or aversion-mind, it will naturally dissolve into its ground, leaving no impression. Simple, subtle, and incredibly effective, once you get the hang of it.

Kṣema then adduces supporting evidence from his primary source text, the *Stanzas on the Recognition of [Oneself as] the Divine*, the foundational text of the Recognition school, written by his guru's guru's guru, Utpala Deva. This verse, found in the fourth (and most accessible) portion of that text, articulates the notion that the Powers of God exist in a contracted form within every bound soul (*paśu*, the traditional Śaiva term for an unliberated being, deriving from the word for a domesticated animal). Kṣema follows the quotation with an explanation of its meaning.

> **The Lord's powers of Knowing, Acting, and Self-concealment-in-plurality, in the case of the** [human] **beings that are forms of His own body, become the *sattva*, *rajas*, and *tamas* of the bound soul.** || [*Īśvara-pratyabhijñā-kārikā* IV.4]

**The sacred *Recognition* scripture is here teaching that the Power of Awareness** (*citi-śakti*)**, which is absolutely free** (or autonomous, *svātantrya*)**, has** [three primary] **forms: the Powers of Knowing** (*jñāna-śakti*)**, Acting** (*kriyā-śakti*)**, and Self-concealment-in-plurality** (*māyā-śakti*)**. In the state of the bound soul, due to the increase of contraction** [there]**, that same Power of Awareness vibrates as the mind, with its intrinsic qualities of *sattva*** (lightness, purity, clarity), ***rajas*** (passion, energy)**, and *tamas*** (heaviness, darkness, inertia)**.**

To spell it out, in the contracted state of the bound soul, the Power of Knowing becomes *sattva*, Acting becomes *rajas*, and Self-concealment-in-plurality becomes *tamas*. Kṣemarāja adds something not explicitly stated in the verse, but very much in its spirit, i.e., that the fundamental Power of Awareness becomes the mind. The mind is the substrate of those three qualities (*guṇas*), which are intrinsic to it.

Yogīs tend to glorify *sattva*, alternately glorify and denigrate *rajas*, and denigrate *tamas* (which is often associated with 'negativity'). There is some reason to this, because a predominance of *tamas*, and sometimes *rajas*, makes a clear vision of one's essential nature much more difficult to have. However, here all three are equally seen as contractions of divine Powers. In the Tantrik view, one does not need to reject or demonize any of one's innate qualities to realize that letting them get out of balance will likely preclude the attainment of one's spiritual goal. Even *māyā* is not seen negatively in this system, for through it, each individual facet of the One is expressed in embodied form. Similarly, by wisely utilizing the grounding and rooting nature of *tamas*, one can come more fully into one's embodiment.

Having established his thesis, Kṣema now gives us its most significant implication. It is this teaching that clearly marks out the difference between the Tantrik view and that of the Classical Yoga of Patañjali. The mind is merely a contracted form of universal Awareness, so—

**For this very reason, the sacred *Hymn on the Core of Reality* teaches that because one's real nature** [as Awareness] **continues to exist even in the state of dualistic thought (*vikalpa*), it is possible to maintain awareness of it** [at all times]**. It says:**

> **For those rare people who maintain close awareness of ultimate reality, the self-illumination of their true nature is not interrupted in that** [thinking state]**.**[32]

This is in direct opposition to the famous definition of yoga found in the *Yoga-sūtra*, "Yoga is the stilling of the mind's fluctuations", where the word translated as 'stilling' (*nirodha*) could equally be translated as suppression, restriction, or cessation. Here, by contrast, for one who habitually focuses on her ultimate nature as the all-encompassing field of Awareness (instead of habitually identifying with the objects of awareness), the innate luminosity (*sva-jyotis*) of that nature remains unconcealed, even in the presence of various thoughts.

To put it another way, since this philosophy denies the division of spirit and matter that is central to pre-Tantrik philosophy, it is not necessary for the mind (which is part of matter) to become entirely silent to access one's essence-nature. Your real nature (*svarūpa*) is never not present; it both encompasses and expresses as all thoughts and feelings. However, to have a direct experience of that truth, you need to become what the scripture calls a *paramārthānusārin*, one who 'maintains a close awareness of ultimate reality'. This essentially means identifying more fundamentally with awareness itself than with any of its objects (including your thoughts and feelings). This happens through a moment-by-moment practice of bringing your attention to the field in which all thoughts, feelings, sensations, and perceptions are vibrating.

*Awareness Cultivation Exercise*

Exhale long, and then breathe in deep. Release the jaw, and soften the muscles of the face. Now let the base of your heart be the center point of an expanded field of awareness that includes everything that is present. If you tend to be externally focused, bring a little more attention to the vibrations of sensation, feeling, and thought; if you tend to be internally focused, bring a little more attention to subtle sounds in your environment, and the quality of the light. Become aware that everything you are perceiving and feeling is a vibration within a single field. Pay attention to the whole field; don't get fixated on any one feature of it. If you do, take another breath and return your attention to the whole field.

Eventually, you may start to experience a presence underlying the whole field, permeating all of it, but undisturbed by any of it. This presence is the Ground of Being; the ground of *your* being.

This concludes our study of Sūtra Five and its commentary.

चित्तमेव तु मायाप्रमातुः स्वरूपम्,–इत्याह

**तन्मयो मायाप्रमाता ॥ ६ ॥**

देहप्राणपदं तावत् चित्तप्रधानमेव; शून्य-

भूमिरपि चित्तसंस्कारवत्येव; अन्यथा ततो व्युत्थितस्य स्वकर्तव्यानुधावनाभावः स्यात्;– इति चित्तमय एव मायीयः प्रमाता। अमुनैव आशयेन शिवसूत्रेषु वस्तुवृत्तानुसारेण

'चैतन्यमात्मा' (१–१)

इत्यभिधाय, मायाप्रमातृलक्षणावसरे पुनः

'चित्तमात्मा' (३–१)

इत्युक्तम् ॥ ६ ॥

# CHAPTER SIX

*Kṣemarāja's original text*

Now it is this mind that constitutes the selfhood of one who sees plurality as ultimately real. Thus it is taught:

**One who consists of the mind perceives duality.** || 6 ||

Clearly, it is the mind that predominates in the domain of body and *prāṇa*. Even the level of the Void retains a subtle trace of the mind. Otherwise, one would not continue with one's duties or pursue one's aims upon emerging from that state [of immersion in the Void]. Therefore, **the perceiver** in the domain **of differentiation is** simply **the mind.**

On this point, the *Aphorisms of Śiva* state, in accordance with the true nature of reality, that 'Awareness is the self', but by contrast, when characterizing the *māyā*-perceiver, they say that 'The mind is the self'. || 6 ||

# CHAPTER SIX

*with explanation*

**Now it is this mind that constitutes the selfhood of one who sees plurality as ultimately real (*māyā-pramātā*). Thus it is taught:**

### || TAN-MAYO MĀYĀ-PRAMĀTĀ || 6 ||

### One who consists of the mind perceives duality.

In Chapter Five, Kṣemarāja discussed a twofold division of experience, that of Awareness-predominant versus contraction-predominant. When the former is steady and abiding, that being is known as a Wisdom-perceiver; when the latter is more usually the case, that being is known as a *māyā*-perceiver (one who sees duality and separation as ultimately real). The latter is characterized, he told us, by identification with body, mind, life force, or the void. Now he wants to single out and emphasize the mind among those four, saying that the primary locus of identity of any *māyā*-perceiver is the mind. Another way of saying the same thing is that it is the mind that perceives duality (or plurality), and therefore anyone who is mind-identified will naturally be a duality-perceiver.

Now, *citta* is a word that we translate as 'mind' but is more accurately rendered 'heart-mind' in English because it is the locus of both thought and emotion, these being inextricably linked. It is therefore no surprise that Kṣema argues that the *citta* is the primary locus of our limited sense of self, our sense of our separate, different, and independent identity. This heart-mind is a *māyā*-perceiver because the primary meaning of *māyā* in this system is not 'illusion' but 'Self-concealment in plurality'. That is, *māyā* is the Power of Differentiation, and it is through differentiation that Oneness becomes concealed (though it remains just as present).

The mind sees reality through the lens of *māyā* (that is, it sees things as fundamentally separate and differentiated) because its primary function is to produce discursive thought-forms, or *vikalpa*s. *Vikalpa*s are mental constructs or interpretive filters that divide up (*vi-kḷp*) the world into discrete chunks for analysis (e.g., "Dangerous to me or not?" "Source of food or not?" "Potential mate or not?"). This function of the mind was very useful and important in our evolution, but has led to a problematic situation in which our interpretive lenses are constantly interposed between awareness and the rest of reality, such that it's very easy to mistake the *lens* for reality. (To be more precise, we take the modified image that appears in the lens or filter as being accurate, when in fact it's distorted to an unknown degree, until you learn how to remove the lens, at least temporarily). This is one definition of the 'unawake' state or dreamstate.

We often translate *vikalpa* as 'differential thought-construct', which indicates two things: first, the fabricated nature of *vikalpa*s, which after all are not reflections but *interpretations* of reality, and second, the fact that all *vikalpa*s are based in perception of difference and articulated in terms of difference (with the most basic difference being self versus other). By its very nature, the mind is a perceiver of differentiation, not unity. Pleasant *versus* unpleasant, good *versus* bad, the way things should be *versus* the way things are. That's no fault of the mind. Its function is to see difference, without which we couldn't survive. But to what extent has that function come to dominate? The price we have paid is the increasing loss of the ability to see the greater unity which subsumes all difference. The mind is, in its natural state, a useful tool, not a locus of selfhood. A servant, not a master. And certainly not the aspect of our being that has the last word on what is ultimately real, and ultimately significant.

*Vikalpa*s are primarily a left-brain phenomenon, associated with the active mode of the brain rather than the receptive mode. Because they are concerned with contrast and hierarchy, this *versus* that, *vikalpa*s are often linked to behaviors of fear and aggression. When a whole group of people have come to agree on a particularly distorted *vikalpa*, the result is anything up to and including genocide. Some *vikalpa*s (like fundamentalist dogmas) function much like mental viruses in the way they spread and the harm they can cause. We could write a history of the human species in terms of the increasing dominance of *vikalpa* in human life.

◇◇◇◇◇◇◇◇◇◇◇◇◇◇◇◇◇◇◇◇◇◇◇◇◇◇◇◇◇◇◇◇◇◇◇◇◇◇◇◇◇◇◇◇◇◇◇◇◇◇◇◇◇◇◇◇◇◇◇◇◇◇◇◇◇◇◇◇

### *Brief Opinionated Excursus*

To hint toward that history in a single paragraph, we may observe that with the advent of agriculture, *vikalpa*s (and thus the part of the mind that manufactures them and chooses among them) became more significant, as agriculture necessitated the new concept of ownership of land and resources, mine *versus* yours. Not coincidentally, the primary crops that came to be cultivated were ones that break down easily into glucose (e.g., rice and wheat). Glucose is the food for the brain. So the more it gets overfed with glucose, the more it becomes overactive, and then it uses that extra thought-energy to get hold of more glucose, in a feedback loop. Not only that, but it constructs elaborate narratives that justify hoarding resources ('wealth') that represent the ability to obtain unlimited glucose. This is no doubt an oversimplification, but it remains a fascinating hypothesis: that the history of modern man is one in which the brain has effectively 'taken over' the body, prioritizing its glucose needs over the nutrients needed by all the other organs, with disastrous results, not least because they are not only physical (rampant obesity, diabetes, etc.) but mental. The overfed brain has produced bloated, sickly, distended vikalpas as well: nationalism, dogmatism, religion, fundamentalism, science divorced from morality, financial markets, escape into fantasy worlds (such as video games, online communities, sexual fantasy, sterile intellectuality)—the list is endless. And these are the features that dominate our modern landscape.[33] With the advent of the Internet, we can now spend more and more of our waking hours in a dimension entirely shaped by vikalpas, a mental landscape of the human race undergirded and shot through with largely unexamined charged emotional states (revolving primarily around desire and/or fear) articulated as opinions.

◇◇◇◇◇◇◇◇◇◇◇◇◇◇◇◇◇◇◇◇◇◇◇◇◇◇◇◇◇◇◇◇◇◇◇◇◇◇◇◇◇◇◇◇◇◇◇◇◇◇◇◇◇◇◇◇◇◇◇◇◇◇◇◇◇◇◇◇

We could say that the aim of a Tantrik *sādhanā* is 'letting everything adopt its proper place'. Any feature of our being, however benign normally, becomes swollen and distorted when it is the sole locus of our identity. When we are slaves of the mind, it becomes a tyrannical master. You are its slave insofar as you are constantly trying to please it, to make it happy. If you think the goal of life (or, even worse, the spiritual path) is to feel good all the time, then you are a slave of the mind. If you think happiness is the result of maximizing everything you like and minimizing everything you don't like, then you are a slave of the mind, and you run around doing its bidding every day.

A student in my online course on this text asked me this thoughtful question: "Should the sūtra be read as stating that there is no *māyā* (by which I'd understand the differentiated universe) without mind? That is, that these trees, mountains, potatoes, galaxies, etc. we all see around us only have whatever existence they have if they exist alongside the minds that perceive them? In a sense then an integral part of manifesting the diversity of the universe is manifesting minds to grasp that diversity, and neither exists independent of the other."

I replied as follows: "Absolutely correct! There is no *māyā* without mind on two levels. Without Mind, i.e., Awareness (which is the essence of mind), there would be no mountains, potatoes, etc.—no observed without observer. But also, without the conditioned mind, there are no analytical categories, no divisions, no separation in anything, since it is solely the discursive conditioned mind that creates division. This second sense is the primary one intended by Kṣemarāja in Chapter Six. Clearly, there are both advantages and disadvantages to the ability to carve up the world into categories; the primary advantages being cultural and technological, and the primary disadvantages being spiritual—we get so invested in our minds' brilliant categorization (example: the taxonomy of species) that we come to see difference as fundamental, when in reality it is unity that is fundamental. Through this unconscious investment, we feel separate from all that we perceive to some degree, leading us to strive desperately to *belong* and to merge into a greater whole (whether through romantic relationships, political parties, religious identities, etc.) while never managing to lose the fundamental sense of separation created by the apparent division of subject and objects."*

---

* See Chapter Nine for more on this.

Kṣemarāja's commentary further clarifies his reasons for the assertion of the sūtra:

**Clearly, it is the mind that predominates in the domain of body and *prāṇa*. Even the level of the Void retains a subtle trace *(saṃskāra)* of the mind. Otherwise, one would not continue with one's duties or pursue one's aims upon emerging from that state** [of immersion in the Void]**. Therefore, the perceiver in the domain of differentiation (*māyā*) is simply the mind.**

You might be surprised that Kṣema thinks it clearly obvious that the mind predominates in the domain of both body and *prāṇa* (life force, breath). A little contemplation shows that this is true. The mind directs the activity of the body, and in its ego-function (*ahaṃkāra*) constructs self-images on the basis of the body ("I am attractive/ugly," etc.). Body-consciousness and shame or pride in one's body are clearly functions of the mind, not the body itself. Most people's bodily activities are executed in pursuit of the mind's aims and desires. (It is possible to allow the body to act on the basis of its own instinctual wisdom or playfulness without any mind direction, but this is very rare in our society.)

Though *prāṇa* is more fundamental than mind, for most people, mind is dominant on this level as well. For example, your mind-state directly impacts the way you breathe moment to moment. The chronic low-level anxiety that more than half the population now suffers from causes shallow and irregular breathing. In teaching people *prāṇāyāma*, I have learned that most people don't really know what it means to breathe deeply; the natural movement of the breath has been disturbed by the mind's disturbance. And we need the mind to retrain the breath to move more deeply, evenly, and rhythmically once again (this is what *prāṇāyāma* is, of course).

Traces of the mind exist even on the level of the formless Void within, in the form of *saṃskāra*s (subtle impressions of past painful or pleasurable experience). Otherwise, when the mind completely dissolves in that state of meditation in which we spontaneously enter into the inner Void of absolute quiescence, you wouldn't still be you upon emerging from meditation, with your particular attachments and goals; you would be a blank slate. Upon what basis would the mind, having dissolved, re-form? The answer is that there is an aspect of mind (now known as the subconscious) that does not dissolve even in the absolute nothingness of the Void.[34]

Therefore, Kṣemarāja tells us, the 'māyic' perceiver (he uses the adjective form at this point) consists of the mind; that is, the mind is the center of gravity for our limited, constructed, separate sense of self. Joining this sūtra with the previous chapter's discussion, we can say, *When contraction predominates, one experiences oneself to be (nothing but) the mind.* And mind-identification perpetuates contraction, in a cycle of suffering (*saṃsāra*).

Kṣemarāja underscores his main point and concludes his discussion by juxtaposing two sūtras from the *Śiva-sūtra*, describing the two primary modes of the self:

**On this point, the *Aphorisms of Śiva* state, in accordance with the true nature of reality, that "Awareness is the self"** (*caitanyam ātmā*)**, but by contrast, when characterizing the *māyā*-perceiver, they say that "The mind is the self".** (*cittam ātmā*)**.**

The *Śiva-sūtra* is a rather mysterious nonsectarian text received by the sage Vasugupta as a divine inspiration, or in other accounts, in oral transmission from a *siddha* and *yoginī*. Kṣema implies that such a divinely infallible source cannot contradict itself, and that therefore Sūtras 1.1 and 3.1 (cited above) must both be true. The only way that this is possible is if both Awareness and the mind constitute the self, in different phases (as in the water and ice example in Chapter Five). Kṣema clarifies that in the first instance, the scripture is speaking in terms of ultimate truth, and in the second, in terms of the contracted perceiver within the field of *māyā*. We are invited to awaken to the nature of the mind-self as a contracted form of the Awareness-self, one which perceives in a limited and distorted way. Realization of this truth compels us to look more deeply and discover the nature of that Awareness-self, our essential being.

This concludes our study of Sūtra Six and its commentary.

अस्यैव सम्यक् स्वरूपज्ञानात् यतो मुक्तिः, असम्यक् तु संसारः, ततः तिलश एतत्स्वरूपं निर्भङ्क्तुमाह

स चैको द्विरूपस्त्रिमयश्चतुरात्मा
सप्तपञ्चकस्वभावः ॥ ७ ॥

निर्णीतदृशा चिदात्मा शिवभट्टारक एव 'एक' आत्मा, न तु अन्यः कश्चित्; प्रकाशस्य देशकालादिभिः भेदायोगात्; जडस्य तु ग्राहकत्वानुपपत्तेः। प्रकाश एव यतः स्वातन्त्र्यात् गृहीतप्राणादिसंकोचः संकुचितार्थग्राहकतामश्नुते, ततः असौ प्रकाशरूपत्व-संकोचावभासवत्त्वाभ्यां 'द्विरूपः'। आणव-मायीय-कार्ममलावृतत्वात् 'त्रिमयः'। शून्य-प्राण-पुर्यष्टक-

# CHAPTER SEVEN

*Kṣemarāja's original text*

Since liberation results from correct insight into one's essential nature, while the cycle of suffering (*saṃsāra*) results from wrong understanding of it, its nature is explained in greater detail:

> **It is one, and yet it is two; it consists of three, has a quadruple being,** and **is seven, five, and seven times five in its nature.** || 7 ||

In accordance with the view explained earlier, there is only **one** being—called Lord Śiva, or Awareness—and nothing else. This must be so because it is impossible that the Light of Awareness could be divided by place, time, or form, and also because it is impossible that anything unconscious could be a knower.

This very Light, freely taking on the contraction of embodiment, becomes a perceiver of contracted objects; therefore:

» **It is two**, because it is the Light of Awareness, and yet it possesses the appearance of contraction.

» **It consists of three** because it is covered by the three Impurities: that of contracted individuality, that of differentiated perception, and that of *karma*.

शरीरस्वभावत्वात् 'चतुरात्मा'।'सप्तपञ्चकानि'—शिवादिपृथिव्यन्तानि पञ्चत्रिंशत्तत्त्वानि 'तत्स्वभावः'। तथा शिवादि-सकलान्त-प्रमातृसप्तक-स्वरूपः; चिदानन्देच्छा-ज्ञान-क्रियाशक्तिरूपत्वेऽपि अख्यातिवशात् कला-विद्या-राग-काल-नियतिकञ्चुकवलितत्वात् पञ्चकस्वरूपः। एवं च शिवैकरूपत्वेन, पञ्चत्रिंशत्तत्त्वमयत्वेन, प्रमातृसप्तकस्वभावत्वेन चिदादिशक्तिपञ्चकात्मकत्वेन च अयं प्रत्यभिज्ञायमानो मुक्तिदः; अन्यथा तु संसारहेतुः ॥ ७ ॥

» It **has a quadruple being** because its embodied nature consists of the Void, *prāṇa*, the eightfold subtle body, and the physical body.
» It **is seven times five in its nature**, i.e., the thirty-five *tattvas*, from Śiva/Śivā down to Earth.
» Further, **its nature is sevenfold**, i.e., that of the Seven Perceivers, from Śiva/Śivā to the Sakala.
» **Its nature is fivefold**, because, though in reality it consists of the Powers of Consciousness, Bliss, Willing, Knowing, and Acting, due to the influence of concealment, it is enclosed by the five 'armors': the limited power of action, the limited power of knowing, craving, limited time, and causal law.

Thus, liberation is simply recognizing that you are one with Śiva: made up of the thirty-five tattvas, having the nature of all Seven Perceivers, consisting of the five Powers of Consciousness, etc. Otherwise, seeing yourself solely in terms of the three impurities, five armors, etc., you perpetuate the cycle of suffering (*saṃsāra*). || 7 ||

# CHAPTER SEVEN

*with explanation*

**Since liberation (*mukti*) results from correct insight into one's essential nature, while the cycle of suffering (*saṃsāra*) results from wrong understanding of it, its nature is explained in greater detail.**

The spiritual goal of this system is *mukti* (also known as *mokṣa*), commonly translated as 'liberation' but perhaps better rendered 'freedom' or 'release'. In both India and the West, *mukti* has frequently been objectified, made into a 'thing' to be attained, imagined as a kind of divinely elevated state of constant bliss. This is not correct. We can understand *mukti* better with reference to a more basic meaning of the word: the opposite of imprisonment. One who has been freed (*mukta*) from imprisonment is not constantly in the same state of mind as a result, yet his daily life experience is very different from when he was imprisoned. In one sense, he is the same person as before; in another, his experience of life is radically different, filled with possibility, and with a deeper appreciation for things others might take for granted. This, then, is closer to what is envisioned as the goal of the path: a state of release from the cycles of mind-created suffering, a feeling of freedom and natural appreciation for the simple things of life.

Kṣemarāja tells us that this freedom is the natural and inevitable result of "correct insight into one's essential nature (*svarūpa-jñāna*)".* When you see yourself as you really are, free from the impressions of your mind's conditioning, you access your natural state of freedom. By contrast, when your idea of your essential nature is misaligned with reality, the cycles of suffering run on and on (the literal meaning of *saṃsāra*). Therefore, Kṣema offers us a more minute analysis of the nature of our embodied consciousness.

---

* Here he follows the teaching of his guru, Abhinava Gupta, who begins his *Essence of the Tantras* with the statement "In our way, insight is the [sole] cause of liberation, because it is the opposite of ignorance, the cause of bondage." Here, ignorance means possessing 'knowledge' (e.g., beliefs) that does not accurately correspond (*asamyak*) to the true nature of reality.

|| SA CAIKO DVI-RŪPAS TRI-MAYAŚ CATUR-ĀTMĀ SAPTA-PAÑCAKA-SVABHĀVAḤ || 7 ||

**It is one, and** [yet] **it is two; it consists of three, has a quadruple being,** [and also] **is seven, five, and seven times five in its nature.** || 7 ||

Like light passed through a prism refracts into all the colors of the rainbow, the One is also two, and three, and four, and five, and seven, and thirty-five. Each of these numbers corresponds to a doctrinal list, each list being a different 'angle of analysis' of the nature of embodied consciousness.

**In accordance with the view explained earlier, there is only one being—**[who we call] **Lord Śiva, or Awareness—and nothing else. This must be so because it is impossible that the Light of Awareness** (*prakāśa*) **could be divided by place, time, or form, and also because it is impossible that anything unconscious could be a knower.**

Simply put, reality is one because it is a single interconnected matrix. There are no divisions, no impermeable barriers in our universe; even black holes, formerly thought to be cut off from the rest of reality, are now known to slowly evaporate, offering the energy inside them back into the rest of the universe from which it came. Analytical divisions within time as well as space are purely mind-created. Physics equations need not specify 'past' or 'future' to work; they work equally well in both directions.[35] In fact, physicists have a hard time explaining the difference between past and future (one of the puzzles of physics is why we remember the past and not the future, since we can't find an intrinsic difference between them).[36] So Kṣemarāja is entirely correct when he argues that the divisions that seem fundamental to the mind—distinct place, time, and form—are actually functions of how our mind operates. Just as no place or time is inherently different from any other (since the same physical laws apply), no form is inherently different from any other (since all forms are simply different arrangements of the same fundamental particles bound by the same forces, and all such arrangements are impermanent). The reader may think I project present-day ideas onto the past when I use physics as a tool of understanding here, but note the key word that Kṣemarāja uses: "It is impossible that *prakāśa* could be divided," he says. Though *prakāśa* is translated as 'Light of Awareness' here, it could equally be rendered as simply 'manifestation',* for it refers to the entirety of manifestation conceived as a single field of energy (hence the metaphor of light). In the entire Sanskrit language, *prakāśa* is the word that most closely hints toward the understanding that modern physics has of reality.

But what about the element of awareness here? The whole of reality is a manifestation of the Light of Awareness—surely that is a mystical assertion, not a scientifically verifiable one. Yet we have already seen that the universe is inseparably continuous, and we can hardly deny that awareness is a feature of reality, and since we cannot separate out awareness any more than we can separate out anything else, it is most accurate to speak of a *self-aware universe*. It is a reality that has the capacity to know itself. (Some physicists, such as Erwin Schrödinger, have realized and addressed the implications of this.) The Tantrik tradition argues that awareness is 'non-local' (*nirniketa*), in the sense that its source cannot be pinpointed in space and time, and in the sense that it pervades all things, because nothing can be proven to exist separate from it or outside of it, as discussed in Chapter One. Hence, it is valid to characterize the 'one thing' that exists in terms of awareness (= Śiva) and/or energy (= Śakti), depending on which aspect one is emphasizing.

Kṣemarāja closely follows his guru on the wording of these philosophical points, as we can see from quoting a parallel passage in Abhinava Gupta's *Essence of the Tantras*:

> The Light of Creation (*prakāśa*) is not multiple, because there can never be any division of its essential nature, since it is not possible for anything having a nature different from it to enter it. Even space and time do not divide it, because both have that very Light as their real nature. ...
>
> Insofar as the very nature of the Highest Divinity is the fact that s/he consists of the whole [universe], he is not unaware of [that universe], because it is impossible that one whose very essence is Awareness could be unaware of his own nature. For if he were unaware of his own form, he would necessarily be insentient and inert. [Therefore, the universe is pervaded by awareness.]

* Refer to page 51 for the various meanings of *prakāśa*.

Abhinava Gupta's formulation is even subtler than his student's, and in-depth exploration of it will have to wait for my forthcoming book, *The Essence of Tantra.*

To summarize, there is one thing that exists, and we may call it God if we seek to emphasize that it is worthy of veneration and appreciation, or Awareness, if we seek to emphasize its most universal quality, or the Light of Creation, if we seek to emphasize that it is a single dynamic field of energy.

**This very Light (*prakāśa*), freely taking on the contraction of embodiment, becomes a perceiver of contracted objects; therefore, it is two, because it is the Light of Awareness, and** [yet] **it possesses the appearance of contraction.**

This twofold division was already addressed in Chapter Five. Here again, Kṣema emphasizes that the Light only has the *appearance* of contraction; that is, particularized subjects and objects are ways in which the one Light shines. We can think of this twofold division in terms of the metaphor of white light, which contains all colors, and the rainbow of particularized colors, which is another way the same light can appear.

**It consists of three because it is covered by the three Impurities: that of contracted individuality (*āṇava-mala*), that of differentiated perception (*māyīya-mala*), and that of *karma* (*kārma-mala*).**

The three Impurities, which are not actual impurities but fundamental forms of misperception, are covered in Chapter Nine, and in pages 150–162 of *Tantra Illuminated.*

**It has a quadruple being because its** [embodied] **nature consists of the Void, *prāṇa*, the eightfold subtle body, and the physical body.**

The Tantrik quadripartite self is detailed in *Tantra Illuminated* (pages 92–101), where it is called the 'five-layered self', because the latter explanation counts Awareness as a layer, though of course it in fact permeates the whole. We can briefly summarize the other four aspects of selfhood, moving from subtle to coarse, from core to periphery. As already briefly discussed in Chapter Six, overidentification with any of these four layers results in misalignments that inevitably bring suffering.

The deepest layer of a human being other than dynamic nondual Awareness is that of the Void (*śūnya*). It is transcendent, completely empty of all form and energy, absolutely still and silent. It is, in a sense, Śiva without Śakti, or rather with Her existing as unexpressed potentiality. Everyone accesses this layer in deep dreamless sleep, but we can also touch it while awake in meditation. To some people, it feels like terrifying nothingness, and they pull back from it immediately; to others, it feels like blessed peace, and they love immersing in it, even to the point of escapism. Some meditators identify with it to the point of denying selfhood to any other layer of their being, feeling "I am not of this world; my true self transcends all things." Now we know that exclusive identification with any layer of your being is a misalignment that brings suffering. In this case, those identified with the Void-level tend to renounce the material world, body, and mind, becoming transcendentalists. They can attain deep states of peace, but cannot integrate them into daily life, sometimes losing their ability to relate to others or to their own body. This is not the Tantrik path. (Note that it is easy to cite more extreme cases to make the point, but this should not prevent you from reflecting on whether you have this tendency, or any that follow, in a lesser degree.)

The next layer of the self is that of the *prāṇa*, which is usually translated as 'vital energy' or 'life force', something we share with all living things. The movement of *prāṇa*, which is intimately connected to (but not identical to) the breath, is vital for life to continue. In fact, it serves as the interface between the physical body and the mind, and is key to the mind–body connection, though it is subtler and more fundamental than either. The amplification and depletion of *prāṇa*, which is connected to diet, exercise, sleep, and thought-patterns, is responsible for our general energy level and many of our moods as well. Identification with the *prāṇa*-layer is expressed in such statements as "I'm energized," "I'm drained," "I feel alive!" or "I feel *blah*." Overidentification with the *prāṇa* leads us to stake too much significance on our moods, and to form or modify self-images on the basis of our mood or energy level.

The next layer is that of the eightfold subtle body (*puryaṣṭaka*). The subtle body, often known in the West as the 'energy body', consists of the three aspects of the mind (*manas*, attention; *ahaṃkāra*, ego; and *buddhi*, discernment) and the five subtle elements (*tanmātras*), which in this context denote the impressions left by things we have heard, touched, seen, tasted, and smelled. The subtle body, then, is essentially the mind or psyche, though the Tantrik understanding of mind is broader and deeper than the Western one. The subtle body can be understood as the way in which the mind *extends itself throughout the physical body* and interfaces with it. For example, it is the means by which mental and emotional states impact and shape the physical body. Dis-ease on the mental-emotional level creates corresponding disease on the physical level through the mechanism of the subtle body. From the yogic perspective, the subtle level, while intangible, is more fundamental than the physical, and sets the pattern for it.

Overidentification with the subtle body layer takes many forms: inability to be okay with certain emotional states, belief that your stories about reality *are* reality, clinging to old wounds or past glories and defining yourself in their terms, pursuing pleasure and avoiding pain as the way to happiness, and so on. We express our identification with the subtle body layer in thoughts or statements such as "I am smart/stupid," "I am competent/incompetent," "I am sad/happy," and so on. From these statements, you can see that identification with this layer is almost universal, as discussed in the last chapter. It may seem that no one is free from such identification, but an awake person might use a phrase like "I'm sad/happy" as a matter of verbal convention, without actually experiencing that the 'I' is conditioned by these states or defined in these terms.

Identification with the physical body layer is expressed in thoughts or statements like "I am fat/thin," "I am young/old," "I'm pretty/ugly," and so on. Statements such as these indicate a belief that your identity is defined by your physicality. If you are identified with the body to the exclusion of the deeper layers of your being, then you will necessarily base your self-worth on your own and others' opinions of your body. In this case, you are setting yourself up for considerable suffering, for the one universal truth of the body is that it will break down, age, decay, and die. If you believe you are this body and nothing more, that truth is terrifying.

This line of thought is beginning to sound like that of a renunciate tradition, isn't it? But the Tantrik teaching is not that identification with these four layers is wrong, but rather that overidentification or exclusive identification with one or more of them causes suffering. The Tāntrika identifies with *all* of these layers and none of them, seeing them all as expressions of dynamic nondual divine Awareness. To put it another way, Awareness vibrates forth into manifestation as all the layers of your being, from the Void outward. The goal here is to let everything adopt its proper place, to know the difference between what is core and what is peripheral, what is eternal and what is impermanent. We seek to honor all four layers of our being while realizing that none of them is our essence-nature. We might express this truth with the statement "I am all of these layers of being and yet inexpressibly more than that!"

Kṣemarāja's guru's guru's guru, Utpala Deva, defined spiritual experience in precisely these terms, writing:

> 'Immersion into reality' is experientially realizing the primacy of the Conscious Self as the true Knower and the one Doer, and that the other layers of individuality—from the Void to the body—are [mere] attributes of it. [*Stanzas on the Recognition of the Divine* III.2.12]

'Immersion into reality' (*samāveśa*) is the technical term in this tradition for spiritual experience. The description above is an attempt to explain what it is that happens in spiritual experience that demarcates it as different from other kinds of experience.

**It is seven times five in its nature, i.e., the thirty-five *tattvas*, from Śiva/Śivā down to Earth.**

The *tattvas*, or Principles of Reality, are covered in detail in pages 124–149 of *Tantra Illuminated.* They are usually reckoned as thirty-six in number, but here Kṣemarāja gets thirty-five by combining Śiva and Śakti (tattvas #1 and #2) into a single Principle, emphasizing the nonduality of his system. He does this with a clever Sanskrit device: in the compound *śivādi-*, the gender of the word *śiva* is intentionally ambiguous: it can be either masculine *Śiva* or feminine *Śivā*, which is a name for Śakti. In this case, it is both in one.

**Further, its nature is sevenfold, i.e., that of the Seven Perceivers, from Śiva/Śivā to the Sakala.**

These were covered in detail in Chapter Three. Kṣemarāja has again used the same grammatical ambiguity (Śiva/Śivā) to avoid excluding Śakti from the list of the Seven Perceivers,[37] and to emphasize Her inseparable union with Śiva.

**Its nature is fivefold, because, though** [in reality] **it consists of the Powers of Awareness, Bliss, Willing, Knowing, and Acting, due to the influence of concealment** (*akhyāti*)**, it is enclosed by the five 'armors'** (*kañcuka*)**: the limited power of action, the limited power of knowing, craving, limited time, and causal law.**

The five Powers of God are discussed on pages 101–109 of *Tantra Illuminated*, while the five *kañcuka*s are found on pages 134–139. While the *kañcuka*s are often interpreted negatively as 'veils', the original tradition understood them as the protective 'armors' that allowed the contracted individual soul to function in the world. Though they are limited powers, they are still powers. They flow forth from the Power of Māyā (note that the word *akhyāti* in the passage above is a synonym for *māyā*, though it also means ignorance or concealment). But, just like literal armor, even as they protect the vulnerable soul, they separate it from the rest of the world.

**Thus, liberation is** [simply] **recognizing that you are one with Śiva: made up of the thirty-five tattvas, having the nature of** [all] **Seven Perceivers, consisting of the five Powers of Consciousness, etc. Otherwise** [seeing yourself solely in terms of the three *mala*s, five *kañcuka*s, etc.]**, you perpetuate the cycle of suffering** (*saṃsāra*)**.** || 7 ||

We began this chapter with a discussion of the term *mukti* or liberation. Here, Kṣemarāja defines it as recognition (*pratyabhijñā*) of what is always already true: you are Śiva embodied, divine reality made manifest, and have never been otherwise. Significantly, he uses the present participle here (*recognizing*), not the noun, implying that liberation is a continuous act (even if it becomes an effortless one), not a thing or state. The other point worthy of note in this paragraph is its nondual language: if you do not recognize the full scope of who and what you are, it is you who perpetuates the cycle of suffering. There is no one else to blame. Though each conscious being expresses free and autonomous agency, there is only one agent, one performer of all action, and from your perspective, that One is you.

This concludes our study of Sūtra Seven and its commentary.

एवं च

तद्भूमिकाः सर्वदर्शनस्थितयः ॥८॥

'सर्वेषां' चार्वाकादिदर्शनानां 'स्थितयः'—सिद्धान्ताः 'तस्य' एतस्य आत्मनो नटस्येव स्वेच्छावगृहीताः कृत्रिमा 'भूमिकाः'। तथा च

'चैतन्यविशिष्टं शरीरमात्मा।'

इति चार्वाकाः।

नैयायिकादयो ज्ञानादिगुणगणाश्रयं बुद्धितत्त्वप्रायमेव आत्मानं संसृतौ मन्यन्ते, अपवर्गे तु तदुच्छेदे शून्यप्रायम्।

अहं-प्रतीतिप्रत्येयः सुखदुःखाद्युपाधिभिः तिरस्कृतः आत्मा—इति मन्वाना मीमांसका अपि बुद्धावेव निविष्टाः।

ज्ञानसंतान एव तत्त्वम्—इति सौगता बुद्धिवृत्तिषु एव पर्यवसिताः।

प्राण एव आत्मा—इति केचित् श्रुत्यन्तविदः।

असदेव इदमासीत्—इत्यभावब्रह्मवादिनः शून्यभुवमवगाह्य स्थिताः।

# CHAPTER EIGHT

*Kṣemarāja's original text*

**The positions held by all the philosophical Views are Its** various **roles, the levels of Its** self-expression. || 8 ||

The **positions**, i.e., the fixed doctrines, **of all the philosophical Views**—from the Materialists on—are the crafted roles that **It**, i.e., this Self, freely adopts, like an actor. To explain:

The Materialists say: "The self is just this body, qualified by [the accidental fact of] consciousness."

The Logicians and Atomists hold that the self as it exists in the course of mundane existence is nothing more than the substrate of the collection of the nine qualities of cognition, etc.—this is synonymous with what we call the principle of the mind (*buddhi*). But in the state of what they call liberation, when those qualities have been cut away, the self is synonymous with what we call the Void.

The Exegetes are also stuck in the mind alone, believing that the self, inferable on the basis of the cognition 'I', is concealed by limiting factors, adventitious conditions such as pleasure and pain.

The Buddhists only reach up to the activities of the mind, holding as they do that the sequential stream of cognitions are the only reality [to the notion of self].

Some Vedāntins say that it is just *prāṇa* that is the self.

Those who claim that *brahman* is nonexistence, citing the passage "In the beginning, all this was nonexistence", immerse themselves in the level of the Void and remain there.

माध्यमिका अपि एवमेव ।

परा प्रकृतिः भगवान् वासुदेवः तद्विस्फुलिङ्गप्राया एव जीवाः—इति पाञ्चरात्राः परस्याः प्रकृतेः परिणामाभ्युपगमात् अव्यक्ते एव अभिनिविष्टाः ।

सांख्यादयस्तु विज्ञानाकलप्रायां भूमिम् अवलम्बन्ते ।

सदेव इदमग्र आसीत्—इति ईश्वरतत्त्वपदमाश्रिता अपरे श्रुत्यन्तविदः ।

शब्दब्रह्ममयं पश्यन्तीरूपम् आत्मतत्त्वम्—इति वैयाकरणाः श्रीसदाशिवपदमध्यासिताः । एवमन्यदपि अनुमन्तव्यम् । एतच्च आगमेषु

'बुद्धितत्त्वे स्थिता बौद्धा गुणेष्वेवार्हताः स्थिताः ।
स्थिता वेदविदः पुंसि अव्यक्ते पाञ्चरात्रिकाः ॥'

इत्यादिना निरूपितम् ।

विश्वोत्तीर्णमात्मतत्त्वम्—इति तान्त्रिकाः ।

विश्वमयम्—इति कुलाद्याम्नायनिविष्टाः ।

विश्वोत्तीर्णं विश्वमयं च—इति त्रिकादिदर्शनविदः ।

The Mādhyamika Buddhists are just the same.

The Vaiṣṇava Pāñcarātrikas are stuck solely on the level of Physical Nature, because they accept that everything (including the self) is a material transformation of Supreme Nature, saying, "Supreme Nature is the Lord Vāsudeva, and souls are exactly like sparks of that fire."

The Sāṅkhyas and Pātañjala Yogins cling to a level equivalent to that of the Vijñānākalas.

There are other Vedāntins who reach the level of Īśvara-tattva, for they say, "In the beginning, all this was solely the Existent."

The Grammarians have settled upon the level of revered Sadāśiva, for they hold revered that the reality of the Self consists of the Word-absolute, which has the Visionary level of Speech as its nature.

Thus the position of other [Views] may be inferred as well. This is taught in scripture with such verses as:

> The Buddhists remain in Buddhi-tattva; the Jains remain in the three guṇas, the Vedāntins remain in Puruṣa-tattva, and the Pāñcarātrikas in Formless Nature. ||

Some Tāntrikas hold that the reality of the Self transcends all. Those devoted to the traditions of the Kula and Kaula say it is immanent in all. The knowers of the View of the Trika and the Krama hold that it is simultaneously all-transcending and all-embodying.

एवम् एकस्यैव चिदात्मनो भगवतः स्वातन्त्र्यावभासिताः सर्वा इमा भूमिकाः स्वातन्त्र्यप्रच्छादनोन्मीलनतारतम्यभेदिताः; अत एक एव एतावद्व्याप्तिक आत्मा । मितदृष्टयस्तु अंशांशिकासु तदिच्छयैव अभिमानं ग्राहिताः, येन देहादिषु भूमिषु पूर्वपूर्वप्रमातृव्याप्तिसारताप्रथायामपि उक्तरूपां महाव्याप्तिं परशक्तिपातं विना न लभन्ते । यथोक्तम्

'वैष्णवाद्यास्तु ये केचिद्विद्यारागेण रञ्जिताः ।
न विदन्ति परं देवं सर्वज्ञं ज्ञानशालिनम् ॥'

इति । तथा

'भ्रमयत्येव तान्माया ह्यमोक्षे मोक्षलिप्सया ।'

इति ।

'त आत्मोपासकाः शैवं न गच्छन्ति परं पदम् ॥'

इति च ।

Thus, all these levels or roles of the Blessed Lord—i.e., the singular Awareness-Self—manifested through His autonomy, are differentiated by degrees of revelation or concealment of that autonomy. Hence, there is only One Self that pervades all of this.

As for those of limited views, they have been caused to adopt egoic identification with various limited aspects of that One through the spontaneous play that expresses its Will. As a result, lacking the highest Descent of Power, they do not attain the experience of the Great Pervasion in the four levels of embodiment, though it is clear that the very essence of each of those levels is the fact of its pervasion by all the loci of perception more fundamental than it.

As it is said in the *Pauṣkara-Pārameśvara*:

> But some, stained by attachment (*rāga*) to their [incomplete] knowledge, do not yet know the omniscient supreme Divinity, endowed with all wisdom.

Similarly (in the *Svacchanda-tantra* and *Netra-tantra*):

> Though those who are addicted to dry, fruitless argument wish to gain liberation, Māyā causes them to wander in non-liberation.
>
> They who are worshippers [only] of the self do not go to the highest level spoken of in the scriptures of Śiva.

अपि च 'सर्वेषां दर्शनानां'—समस्तानां नीलसुखादिज्ञानानां याः 'स्थितयः'—अन्तर्मुखरूपा विश्रान्तयः ताः 'तद्भूमिकाः'—चिदानन्दघनस्वात्मस्वरूपाभिव्यक्त्युपायाः । तथा हि यदा यदा बहिर्मुखं रूपं स्वरूपे विश्राम्यति, तदा तदा बाह्यवस्तूपसंहारः; अन्तःप्रशान्तपदावस्थितिः; तत्तदुदेष्यत्संवित्संतत्यासूत्रणम्;—इति सृष्टि-स्थिति-संहारमेलनारूपा इयं तुरीया संविद्भट्टारिका तत्तत्सृष्ट्यादिभेदान् उद्वमन्ती संहरन्ती च, सदा पूर्णा च, कृशा च, उभयरूपा च, अनुभयात्मा च, अक्रममेव स्फुरन्ती स्थिता । उक्तं च श्रीप्रत्यभिज्ञाटीकायाम्

'तावदर्थावलेहेन उत्तिष्ठति, पूर्णा च भवति'

इति । एषा च भट्टारिका क्रमात्क्रमम् अधिकमनुशील्यमाना स्वात्मसात्करोत्येव भक्तजनम् ॥ ८ ॥

And another reading of the sūtra would be:

**The positions of all views are opportunities for That.** || 8 ||

meaning the inward points of repose of all cognitions—such as blue, pleasure, etc.—are the means for revealing the true nature of one's Self, overflowing with the undiluted Joy of Awareness.

To explain: whenever the outward form of a cognition comes to rest in oneself, there is a withdrawal of focus from the external object; then, a momentary holding of a point of internal stillness; then, the intimation of the stream of various cognitions that are about to arise. The Lady Awareness, known as the Fourth (*turya*), is the ground and unified flow of this process of withdrawal, stasis, and creation; she is constantly pouring forth and reabsorbing the differentiated realities of the threefold process. She remains constantly full and constantly empty, both and neither, vibrating in absolute simultaneity.

As it is said in Utpala's commentary on his sacred *Recognition* text,

> By devouring all the objects of consciousness, she is intensified and becomes replete.

And this noble Lady, being cultivated, served, attended to & contemplated progressively more and more, actually makes her devotee one with herself. || 8 ||

# CHAPTER EIGHT

*with explanation*

**|| TAD-BHŪMIKĀḤ SARVA-DARŚANA-STHITAYAḤ || 8 ||**

**The positions held by all the philosophical Views are Its** [various] **roles, the levels of Its** [self-expression]**.**

First, a warning: this chapter, like Chapter Three, contains a lot of discussion of ideas and doctrines current in Kṣemarāja's time, and not in ours. So readers interested in the more universal teachings may wish to skip ahead. However, unusally, Sūtra Eight receives two distinct interpretations, and the second of these is a universal teaching. If you wish to skip ahead, that second interpretation begins on page 190.

Now Kṣemarāja glosses his own sūtra, adding some details:

**The positions, i.e., the fixed doctrines, of all the philosophical Views—from the Materialists on—are the crafted roles that 'It', i.e., this Self** [= nondual Awareness]**, freely adopts, like an actor.**

For the first time, Kṣemarāja uses 'the Self' (*ātman*) to refer to the ultimate reality, which he previously described as nondual Awareness. In fact, this chapter is largely an exploration of the various views on what constitutes selfhood in Indian philosophy. By using this term, Kṣema signals to us that however close he seems to Buddhism at times, his tradition does not wish to relinquish agency (the notion of an 'actor') at the ultimate level. In other words, though personal/individual agency is seen as an illusion, there is a divine Actor behind all actions in this view: the Self that constitutes all selves. It is this strain of theism in the tradition, even if it is a nonpersonal and nondual theism, that is the main difference between Shaivism and Buddhism.

Since his tradition teaches that agency is singular, i.e., that there is only One performer of every action,[38] he argues in Sūtra Eight that all the different schools of spiritual philosophy (*darśanas*) are like different parts played by one actor. Kṣema is indirectly echoing *Śiva-sūtra* 3.9, which says "The Self is an actor."* One Consciousness, one Being adopts every possible viewpoint by taking on all the roles played by sentient beings throughout time and space. We might call this One 'transindividual awareness' if that resonates more than 'divine consciousness'.

I am reminded here of a story that Swāmī Muktānanda used to love to tell, the story of "The Lords' Club." According to this story, there was once a group of lords, members of the aristocracy, who decided to form a club. But, being an exclusivist sort of group, they didn't want anyone to set foot in the club who wasn't a lord. "Then who shall do all the menial tasks, such as cooking and cleaning and so on?" one of them asked. "We all will!" said another. "We'll take it in turns. Each week, we'll put all the different jobs on slips of paper, put them in a hat, and each member will draw out a job, and perform that job for that week." Which is what they did. The president of the club one week would be the cook the next, the sweeper one week would be the master of ceremonies the next, and so on. Swāmī Muktānanda would get very excited at this point, proclaiming, "You see? Whatever task they performed, whatever role they played, they enjoyed it, because they never forgot that they were lords! In the same way, whatever is your role in life, you play it to the best of your ability, without believing it defines you, when you know that you are really the Lord." And he would laugh with delight.

In a parallel metaphor, an actor who is playing a part on stage, even a very tragic one, derives a profound joy from playing it well. However much he loses himself in the part, feeling the pain of the character, there is still that undercurrent of joy, because he never totally loses touch with the fact that he is an actor who can play virtually any part he is called upon to play. Similarly, when you are actually in touch with your deepest Self, you can sense the fluidity of awareness, its capacity to play a seemingly infinite range of parts when called upon to do so by life. There is a unique kind of joy in simply playing well the part given to you in this moment, and releasing all the parts when none are called for.

But let us return to the specific topic here, which makes a somewhat different point than the general one of 'The Self is an actor'. Kṣema is postulating that the different philosophical schools or spiritual

---

* Note that the same Sanskrit words that mean 'actor' also mean 'dancer' (*nartak* or *naṭa*).

viewpoints that persist over centuries are like roles (*bhūmika*) played by the one Self on the stage of the history of human thought, as it were. Now, the word *bhūmika* in the sūtra means both 'performance parts' and 'levels' (as on a terraced hillside), so it is translated twice here, to bring out its suggestive quality. For it is not the case that Kṣema thinks all these different schools of thought are equally true (that is a philosophically incoherent position known as 'relativism'); rather, he ranks them in a hierarchy of levels, according to the degree of revelation or concealment of the true autonomy of Awareness that is displayed in each. (More on that later.) In the commentary immediately following the sūtra (see page 181), Kṣema adds an adjective modifying 'roles', and that is the word *kṛtrima*, which means crafted, constructed, or artificial. Thus, *kṛtrimā bhūmikāḥ* means 'crafted roles/scripted parts' or 'constructed levels'. This implies that each philosophy constitutes a fixed doctrine that is a product of the (collective) intellect, and as such can only partially represent the true nature of reality, which is organic, spontaneous, and multiform. Nonetheless, reality does have order and pattern, a given part of which can be represented by any given philosophy—and some fall short in their representation a little less than others (though they all necessarily fall short to some degree).

While Kṣemarāja does present a hierarchy of philosophies, it is still an inclusivist model, something rarely found in the premodern world. That is, he is not simply saying that the other schools of thought are wrong. He is saying that the followers of each school do indeed reach the goal promised by their system; the question is, what do they conceive as the ultimate goal? One can hardly argue with his thesis here, which is that *followers of each philosophy can access a level of reality no higher than the one they postulate as ultimate.* (Note that the tradition uses words like 'higher' and 'ultimate' in the sense of 'more complete' and 'most all-encompassing', respectively. There are 'levels' of reality only in the same sense that climbing higher up a mountain gives you a wider view of the landscape.) If you don't believe there is anything higher than the level you have reached, you will not be open to realizing anything more, and without that openness and that intention, it is very unlikely that you will realize anything more. (Nonetheless, it can sometimes happen, and this what we call 'the power of grace', which refers to the capacity of awareness to open to a perspective to which your conditioned mind is closed.)

Some modern readers might be turned off by a philosopher ranking philosophies in a hierarchy with his own philosophy at the top. I would argue that this attitude is hypocritical, since that is in fact what we *all* do, consciously or unconsciously. While paying lip service to the modern relativist idea that every point of view is equally valid, in reality most of us believe that some perspectives are truer than others (and rightly so), and we tend to think that our own interpretation of reality is the truest, and others are true precisely to the degree that they approach our own. You may not be conscious of that conviction, but you have it, because you could not act decisively in any matter without believing that your interpretation of reality is correct.* You couldn't form coherent thought-structures without believing that some things are truer than others. So what Kṣemarāja is doing here is simply demonstrating *intellectual honesty*. All the more honest because he has an argument to make that, if accepted, justifies his whole project.

There is no philosopher, of any time or culture, who accepts the relativist maxims that 'everyone's point of view is equally valid' or 'everyone's entitled to his own opinion'. Rather, philosophers examine the reasons for holding different opinions and make arguments about the validity of those reasons (or lack thereof). In the context of philosophy, if you cannot explain your reasons for holding your opinion, and demonstrate that they might be good reasons, you have no business holding that opinion.[39] Kṣemarāja displays intellectual integrity by making a coherent argument, explaining *why* he thinks as he does.

Furthermore, Kṣema displays innovative open-mindedness in his hierarchy of philosophies. None of his predecessors, except perhaps his guru, allowed for the possibility that non-Śaivas could attain full liberation. But Kṣema argues (as we shall see) that some members of other groups do indeed enter the 'Pure Realm'. This is another example of intellectual integrity on his part, for he argues that "if they see the same truth we see, they must be liberated to the same extent." No one else of Kṣemarāja's era displayed this level of inclusiveness.

---

* Unless, of course, you are a liberated being who can act decisively through a subtle sensitivity to the pattern of the whole, without the need to form a mental construct about it. In fact, long before the final awakening, we all have moments of such spontaneous action, but for most of us, they are rare.

With that orientation in mind, let's turn to Kṣema's ranking of the philosophies of his time. This is more relevant to your world than you might think, because some of these same views persist today under different names. To understand what follows, you need to be familiar with the teaching of the 'quadripartite self' (see Chapter Seven) and the chart of the thirty-six *tattva*s (see page 91). These are the two maps that Kṣema uses to assign the different schools of philosophy to different levels of reality, according to what each school takes to be the ultimate principle. He proceeds from the bottom up, as it were. And by the way, as you will see, we need not understand this hierarchy as a simplistic vertical structure; rather, we see that the schools ranked 'higher' are in fact more all-encompassing in their view. That is, they accept principles of reality that the 'lower' schools do not, principles that provide a broader context for human experience.

**To explain: The Materialists (*Cārvāka*s) say: "The self is just this body, qualified by** [the accidental fact of] **consciousness."**

Despite being one of the oldest schools of thought in India, this school corresponds closely to modern 'scientific materialism', for it holds that only the physical world we can measure is real, and that consciousness is produced by physical matter (electrical activity in the cells of the brain). The ancient Indian Materialists accepted only the tangible elements (the bottom four *tattva*s in the *tattva*-chart) as real. They argued that consciousness is not a self-existent or integral attribute, but is purely an epiphenomenal by-product of brain activity, just like alcohol is produced as a by-product of fermenting fruit or grain. It evolved by chance, has no deeper meaning, and dies along with the body. Therefore, they take the word 'self' to denote nothing more than the body (*śarīram ātmā*). Their philosophy prevents them from attaining knowledge of the other four layers of the self (heart-mind/subtle body, *prāṇa*, Void, and Awareness).

Kṣemarāja is not criticizing the Materialists as a specific group, he is criticizing their view. Therefore, anyone who implicitly or explicitly holds the same view today can 'ascend' no further than the body level in their understanding. That is, even if a modern Materialist were to study consciousness (and many do), he will study it as a function of the body, and therefore not be open to an understanding that goes beyond his mechanistic, materialistic view. If he is not open to it, he will not see it (unless grace intervenes), and will confidently deny its existence.

**The Logicians (*Naiyāyika*s) and Atomists (*Vaiśeṣika*s) hold that the self as it exists in the course of mundane existence (*saṃsṛti*) is** [nothing more than] **the substrate of the collection of the nine qualities of cognition, etc.—this is synonymous with** [what we call] **the principle of the mind (*buddhi-tattva*). But in the state of** [what they call] **liberation, when those qualities have been cut away, the self is synonymous with** [what we call] **the Void.**

The Logicians and the Atomists are two important schools of Indian philosophy, dating from the Gupta period onward, and they are still studied by Indologist scholars today. They are grouped together here because they are both realist and pluralist; that is, they accept the world as real, and do not believe that it is ultimately one thing, or two, but rather is composed of a number of irreducible elements. Their teaching on the self holds that it can exist in two different states: that of the cycle of bondage (*saṃsāra*) and that of liberation (*apavarga*).

In the first case, the self is described as the substrate of the 'nine qualities', which are: cognition, pleasure (*sukha*), suffering (*duḥkha*), desire (*rāga*), hatred (*dveṣa*), effort (of the will), *dharma*, *adharma*, and latent traces or subliminal impressions (*saṃskāra*s). In our tradition, these are all qualities that reside in the mind and the subtle body (which, recall, is really just the extended mind), so Kṣemarāja argues that since the Logicians and Atomists wrongly identify the self with the mind, they can 'ascend' in awareness no higher than the *buddhi-tattva* (tattva #14), which is equivalent to the highest aspect of the 'heart-mind' layer of selfhood in the 'five-layered self' model.

However, the Logician/Atomist school also teaches a doctrine of liberation from *saṃsāra*, in which all of the nine qualities listed above have been obliterated. They argue that even cognition (conscious perception and reflection) can be obliterated, because it is not an essential attribute of the self. All cognitions are cognitions of something, so there is no 'pure consciousness', they say (this view is held by some modern philosophers as well). Furthermore, all cognitions (and pleasure, and pain, etc.) arise due to *karma*, so when karma is destroyed through liberating insight, there will be no more cognitions (or pleasure, or pain, etc.). So liberation in this system is existing in a state of complete nothingness; no wonder we don't have examples of people claiming liberation through the systems of Logic or Atomism! Needless to say, their version of liberation is indistinguishable with the Void as taught in the Tantra, so the Tāntrikas reject the notion that it is liberation.

As I explained earlier in this chapter, at no point is Kṣemarāja misrepresenting the schools he criticizes. He grants that adherents of the school attain the goal of their school as described, then leaves the reader to agree (or not) with his implicit view that that goal is not, in fact, the real goal or essence of reality.

**The Exegetes (*Mīmāṃsakas*) are also stuck in the mind alone, believing that the self, inferable on the basis of the 'I'-cognition, is concealed by limiting factors & adventitious conditions such as pleasure and pain.**

The Exegetes are a school of orthodox brāhminical interpreters of the Vedic scriptures with very old roots. They started to flourish in the Gupta period, and the most intelligent proponent of their view was Kumārila (seventh century). Unlike the Vedāntins (see below), they focused on the ritual portion of the Veda, not the philosophical portion known as the *upaniṣads* ('hidden connections'). In fact, they argued that the only purpose of the Veda is injunction to ritual action, and that all non-ritual passages (stories, myths, philosophy) have no purpose except to convince the reader to perform the Vedic rituals. The Exegetes were often atheists (though some were polytheists), arguing that there is no reality to the gods apart from their names expressed in Vedic mantras. Finally, they argued that perfect ritual performance entails doing the ritual for no other reason than that the Veda tells you to. What an interesting reversal, from the Western perspective: the most orthodox religious authorities in premodern India were utterly practical, deterministic, and atheistic—though of course, like orthodoxy in the West, they were also socially conservative and believed in divinely revealed scripture (i.e., the Veda).[40]

Since their philosophy is closely linked to Sanskrit grammar, the Exegetes taught that there must be a self, because there is a word-concept that denotes it, the word 'I' or 'me'. (The Buddhists found this reasoning laughable, of course.) This self is ordinarily concealed or occluded by a variety of limiting factors (*upādhi*), such as pleasure and pain. In other words, they held much the same conception as we saw above with the Logicians and Atomists. Exegete Kumārila wrote that the self is somehow both eternal and non-eternal, like a snake that is constantly changing its configuration but remains always a snake. It is eternally the same in terms of the immediate intuition of its 'I'-ness, but ever changing in terms of its limiting factors.[41] Without those limiting factors, the self is free of all cognition and therefore free of all experience. As with the Logicians and Atomists, the Exegetes' self in the state of liberation exists in a sensationless void, possessed of no more experience than a stone; though it retains a latent trace of the ability to know, that ability is never exercised. Therefore, their view of the nature of the self is very different from that of the Śaivas, for whom the self can experience liberation while still engaged with the world, cognition, and experience.

**The Buddhists only reach up to the activities of the mind, holding as they do that the sequential stream of cognitions are the only reality** [that compares to the notion of self]**.**

The Buddhists' fairly sophisticated arguments regarding the nature of cognition are dismissed too easily here, though Kṣemarāja knew well that they had been thoroughly engaged already by some of his predecessors.[42] It is true, though, that the Buddhists he is thinking of (mainly the Sautrāntika school) argue that what others call a 'self' is merely a stream of cognitions, each one caused by the one before. In other words, they deny that there is any abiding self distinct from the thought-stream with which most people identify themselves. Because this thought-stream includes memory, the Buddhists argue, we imagine that there is a constant self that has these cognitions, but there is no such being. There is only an aggregation of five qualities, each of them ever in flux: form (the body), sensation, cognition (reflection on what is sensed), mental formations (including emotionṣ), and consciousness (*vijñāna*, which is not a constant, but always consciousness *of* something in particular). None of these can be called a self, not separately, nor all together.[43] As the Buddhist scripture called *The Pure Path* (*Visuddhi-magga*) declares:

> No doer is there does the deed
> Nor is there one who experiences its result;
> Constituent parts alone roll on;
> Only this view is orthodox.

And thus the deed, and thus the result
Roll on and on, each from its cause;
As of the round of tree and seed,
No one can tell when they began.

Thus, in this doctrine, the (Sautrāntika) Buddhists ascend no higher than the activities of the mind (*buddhi-vṛtti*), since that is what approximates selfhood for them. But these are non-yoga-practicing Buddhists. Kṣema's guru, Abhinava Gupta, said that the Buddhists who practice the inner yoga, the Yogācārins, reach right up to the edge of the Pure Realm, and it is unlikely his primary disciple disagreed with him. The Yogācārins cannot enter the Pure Realm without *svātantrya-śakti*, the autonomy of Awareness, which their doctrine does not teach. The Yogācāra teaching, also known as *Vijñānavāda*, 'the Way of Consciousness', is very close to our nondual Śaiva teaching, for it also argues that everything is a form of consciousness—but not a single consciousness. Without the doctrine of the unimpeded autonomy of Awareness, there is nothing to unite all the subjects into a single Subject, because that doctrine teaches that it is through the power of Autonomous Freedom (*svātantrya-śakti*) that the one Consciousness embodies itself in countless forms. But in the *Tantrāloka*, Abhinava Gupta goes even further and implies that Yogācārins who practice in the higher Tantra *do* in fact access the power of Autonomous Freedom, whether they call it that or not, and thereby achieve true and final liberation.[44]

Here we see, and there are more examples below, that these philosophers are not as rigidly sectarian as most in their day; they submit themselves to rationality over dogma, and argue that if others, even non-Śaivas, have the same realization, they must thereby be liberated to the same degree. This is a necessary consequence of the teaching that it is insight, not ritual action, which liberates.

### Some Vedāntins say that it is just *prāṇa* that is the self.

Vedānta is the sister philosophy to the Exegesis school (*mīmāṃsā*) described above—except instead of focusing on the ritual portion of the Vedic scriptures, Vedānta focuses on the philosophical portion, the Upaniṣads, which are the end (*-anta*) of the Veda, thus *vedānta.*

As we have seen, *prāṇa* means life force or vital energy, that which is shared in common with all living things. Here Kṣemarāja has explicitly shifted from the *tattva* hierarchy to the five-layered-self model, telling us that these Vedāntins who believe that *prāṇa* is the self reach only to layer three out of five. Though we know of no specific school of Vedānta that teaches this, Kṣemarāja is doubtless thinking of statements that can be found in the Upaniṣads to this effect. For example, the *Kauṣītaki Upaniṣad* says, "It is *prāṇa* that is *brahman* [the Absolute]." (2.1–2) In the *Bṛhad-āraṇyaka Upaniṣad* 4.1.3, the same doctrine is presented, and this teaching is given: "Clearly, the highest *brahman* is *prāṇa*. When a man knows and venerates it as such, breath never abandons him."[45]

**Those** [Vedāntins] **who claim that *brahman* is nonexistence, citing the** [Upaniṣadic] **passage "In the beginning, all this was nonexistence", immerse themselves in the level of the Void and remain there.**

There may have been a subsect of Vedānta that taught this in the early days before the standardization of Vedāntic doctrine, which began a little before Kṣemarāja's time. Certainly there were early Advaita Vedānta authors who described their goal as a *samādhi* state that is completely devoid of cognition and action (similar to the Logicians, Atomists, and Exegetes above). And we do indeed find the passage that Kṣemarāja cites here (*asad vā idam agra āsīt*) in the Upaniṣads.[46] Since such thinkers believe that the universe arose from nothingness and will return to nothingness, nothingness is their Absolute and thus the highest (or deepest) level they can attain. The Void, recall, is layer four of the five-layered self (from the liberationist perspective; it's layer two from the emanationist perspective).

**The Mādhyamika** [Buddhists] **are just the same.**

This may be the only time in the history of Sanskrit literature that the rigorously argumentative Mādhyamika school was dismissed with just four words (*mādhyamikā apy evam eva*)! But it is not so absurd, for the Mādhyamikas were not metaphysicians like the other schools considered here. We might call them dialecticians, or even deconstructionists, for they were concerned to show that whatever proposition you might make about the nature of reality, it can be shown to be no more true than its opposite. Thus all propositions are merely mental constructs, even the most basic, and truth cannot be stated in words. The only purpose to a verbal or mental construct, then, is its usefulness in destroying another verbal or mental construct. They also denied that anything can definitively be called 'real'—that all things were *śūnya*, empty of intrinsic reality, empty of independent existence, and empty of everything we might think about them. *Śūnya* means void, so that is the 'level' that they reach.

**The** [Vaiṣṇava] **Pāñcarātrikas are stuck solely on the level of Physical Nature (*prakṛti*), because they accept that everything** [including the self] **is a material transformation of Supreme Nature (*parā prakṛti*), saying, "Supreme Nature is the Lord Vāsudeva, and souls are exactly like sparks of that** ['fire']**."**

Here an early form of the Vaiṣṇava Tantra tradition known as the Pāñcarātra is addressed (quite different from the later south Indian form that survives to this day).[47] This early Pāñcarātra is what we might call a pantheist view; it is rejected by the Śaivas because in it, there is no possibility of individual souls accessing any transcendent reality. In fact, in this view the soul is not divine, since it is just a temporary transformation of matter, not an eternal form of conscious spirit. Furthermore, God (called Vāsudeva) is precisely equated with material Nature; that is, he/it is the whole of the universe, and the primal insubstantial stuff out of which it evolved, but he has no being beyond that. That, combined with the standard Vaiṣṇava view that the devotee is nothing and God is everything, leads to the conclusion that individual souls are transient permutations of deified, yet still material, nature—they are just sparks of its fire, that flare briefly and die out. However, the main criticism in Kṣemarāja's mind here is not of the doctrine that souls are transient, but rather of the teaching that the Divine is *only* Nature and nothing more. Needless to say, this teaching causes Kṣemarāja to assign the Pāñcarātrikas to the level of *prakṛti* (material nature) in the *tattva* schema (obviously discounting their attempt to deify their version of *prakṛti* by calling it 'Supreme Nature'), since no one can progress beyond the level they have conceptualized as the highest.

**The Sāṅkhyas and Pātañjala Yogins cling to a level equivalent to that of the Vijñānākalas** [above Māyā but still outside the Pure Realm]**.**

For the school of Classical Yoga, based on Patañjali's *Yoga-sūtra*, and for the very closely allied Sāṅkhya school, the ultimate principle of reality is the *puruṣa-tattva*, the inactive witness-consciousness or pure Knower. The goal of both schools is to realize the eternal distinction between Spirit (*puruṣa*) and Matter (*prakṛti*); that is, to disentangle pure consciousness (one's real nature) from its objects, for it is that entanglement that generates ignorance, attachment, aversion, egoism, and fear of death. Thus, one would think that Kṣemarāja would assign the followers of both schools to *puruṣa-tattva*, the goal to which they aim. However, out of respect for the Sāṅkhyas and the Yogins, who as the Śaivas were aware contributed much to the formation of their own system, Kṣemarāja assigns their liberated souls to the pinnacle of the Impure Realm, six tattvas *above* that of *puruṣa*. This, then, appears to be an exception to the general rule that each school attains exactly the liberation it aims for. But it is a rational one, for if it is the case that a soul has truly discerned the difference between *puruṣa* and *prakṛti*, then it has indeed seen through the five veils or *kañcuka*s (= tattvas #7 through #11), despite the fact that their philosophy does not enumerate those tattvas.

The highest attainment possible for the Sāṅkhyas and Yogins is here understood to be equivalent to that of the Vijñānākalas (the fifth of the Seven Perceivers; see Chapter Three). This makes sense, for the Sāṅkhya/Yoga schools are transcendentalist in their orientation, frequently atheistic, and do not teach nonduality, and as you will recall, the Vijñānākalas have realized their oneness with the transcendent, but not the immanent, for they still cling to their individuality, not being open to divine grace. Thus they stand at the gates of heaven, as it were, but cannot (yet) enter.[48]

**There are other Vedāntins who reach** [liberation on] **the level of *Īśvara-tattva*, for they say, "In the beginning, all this was solely the Existent."**

Here we see Kṣemarāja's unusually liberal view. Most religions declare that only the members of their religion attain salvation or liberation, but here the members of a different religion entirely are explicitly said to achieve full liberation. It is difficult for a historian of this period to explain why Kṣemarāja should be so inclusive. What was at stake that he should make the effort to include certain (unnamed) Vedāntins? It's not clear.

At any rate, Kṣema tells us that those Vedāntins who declare, "In the beginning, all this was solely the Existent" (*sad evedam agra āsīd*) attain as their goal tattva #4, that of Īśvara. He seems to be saying this because, as we have seen above, at that level Awareness equates the whole of the as yet undifferentiated universe with itself, saying, "I am this; this am I." In other words, this view says that at the beginning of the universe there was only a dimensionless homogenous mass of undifferentiated matter-energy-time-space-consciousness,[49] in which the consciousness part pervaded and was exactly equal to the matter-energy-time-space part, and saw the latter as an expression of itself (and *vice versa*). (This, incidentally, matches the Big Bang Theory in physics, with the exception that physics does not postulate any consciousness at the beginning.) This is also the experience that Awareness has of reality at the level of tattva #4. Even though the primordial homogenous mass of the universe has become greatly expanded and internally differentiated, it's still precisely the same mass of matter-energy-time-space as it was at the beginning, and someone at the Īśvara level sees that truth and also sees that the universe is the expression of Awareness, that they are not different. (As the Heart Sūtra says, "Emptiness is Form, and Form is Emptiness," where Emptiness means the formless transcendent Awareness-ground of reality.)

As for Kṣema's source for this Vedāntic teaching, he is probably thinking of *Chāndogya Upaniṣad* 6.2.1: "O Somya, in the beginning all this was solely the Existent, one without a second."

**The Grammarians have settled upon the level of revered Sadāśiva, for they hold that the reality of the Self consists of the Word-absolute (*śabda-brahman*), which has the Visionary level of Speech (*paśyantī*) as its nature.**

By 'the Grammarians' Kṣemarāja means the followers of the school of Bhartṛhari, an influential fifth-century linguist and philosopher whose intriguing ideas about language were inextricably linked to spiritual ideas about the nature of ultimate reality. Bhartṛhari had a strong influence on some schools of Vedānta as well as Śaiva nondualism. Perhaps because of his significant influence on the Recognition school, Kṣema tells us that those who directly realize Bhartṛhari's teaching of the Word-absolute attain full awakening at the level of tattva #3.

Let's explore the connection between Bhartṛhari's teaching and the *Sadāśiva-tattva*.

Bhartṛhari tells us that the fundamental nature of reality consists of a kind of patterned vibration of consciousness that he called 'the Word-absolute' (*śabda-brahman*). It is this vibration that makes up thoughts, sentences, and indeed the whole of reality, since in his view reality cannot be considered as something separate from our experience of it, and that experience is largely shaped by language.[50] In a doctrine later incorporated by the Śaiva nondualists, Bhartṛhari describes three levels of the Word: spoken words, thought-structures, and a deeper level that he called 'the visionary'. This is a level of the Word prior to language as we understand it—a subconscious, precognitive, intuitive reality that informs language, for though it is undifferentiated it compresses within itself the potential for any thought or utterance. (See *Tantra Illuminated*, page 170.) It corresponds to the theory in Western cognitive psychology that the human brain is hardwired for language, that the fundamental structures of human expression are bound up with the very fact of consciousness itself.[51] But for Bhartṛhari, the Visionary is something even more mystical, something that goes beyond the human since it shares, at bottom, in the fundamental structures of reality itself. We can cite a verse of Bhartṛhari's *Vākyapadīya* that tells us about the Visionary, touching upon the points made above:

> The Visionary is an undivided, subtle form of the Word that completely withdraws within itself the temporal and spatial sequentiality [that characterizes ordinary speech]. It has an intrinsic power to illuminate. It is internal to consciousness and never departs from it."[52]

Śaiva nondualist Utpala Deva comments on this verse, saying, "The Absolute in the form of the Visionary is prior to the division into subject and object," or rather, that division is indistinct. Now, as we saw in Chapter Three, from the perspective of the Sadāśiva level of Awareness, all objectivity is subsumed within subjectivity, which is predominant. To put it another way, the sense of 'this'-ness is absorbed within the dominant sense of 'I'-ness, and the experience that Awareness has of reality at this level of perception is alluded to by the phrase 'All this is myself alone'. This level of Awareness is, then, precisely analogous to the level of the Word that Bhartṛhari calls the Visionary. Therefore, Kṣemarāja reasons, those who realize that to which Bhartṛhari's teachings point must achieve the perspective of Sadāśiva, which is of course a variant of full awakening.

This brings to an end Kṣemarāja's enumeration of other schools of thought and the positions they hold in the maps of reality that the Śaivas came up with (specifically, the *tattva* schema and the five-layered self model). Remember that for him, all these different philosophical Views are the levels of self-expression of the universal Awareness; they are roles played by the one Self. He sums up this section with the following.

**Thus the position of other** [Views] **may be inferred as well. This is taught in scripture with such verses as:**

> **The Buddhists remain in Buddhi-tattva; the Jains remain in the three guṇas** [of *Prakṛti*]**, the Vedāntins remain in Puruṣa-tattva, and the Pāñcarātrikas in Formless Nature** (*Prakṛti*)**.** ||

Notice that Kṣema wishes to stress here that this allocation of schools has been logical, not arbitrary, and therefore the reader can infer the position of any Views not mentioned here by applying the same logic concerning the highest level of Awareness known by that View. He then rightly points out that this practice of allocating spiritual Views to appropriate levels in the cosmic hierarchy has scriptural support. In fact, there are many such passages in the original Śaiva scriptures apart from the one he cites here, which comes from an unknown source.

Next Kṣema climaxes his discussion by telling us what distinguishes his View from others and why it is more all-encompassing and integrative.

**The Tāntrikas** [e.g., the Saiddhāntikas and others] **hold that the reality of the Self** (*ātma-tattva*) **transcends all. Those devoted to the traditions** (*āmnāyas*) **of the Kula and** [Kaula] **say it is immanent in all. The knowers of the View of the Trika and** [the Krama] **hold that it is simultaneously all-transcending and all-embodying.**

This is Kṣemarāja's key paragraph, that defines his View in the most succinct way possible. As explained in my previous book, when the word *tāntrika* is used in contrast to *kaula*, as it is here, it refers to dualist Tāntrikas (like the Saiddhāntikas) who worship Śiva without Śakti and who believe that both God and the divine soul are separate from the manifest world—that they transcend base matter and everything connected with it. By contrast, the followers of the Kulamārga, often known as Kaulas, who (sometimes) worship Śakti without Śiva, focus on the divinity of embodiment, and argue that supreme Consciousness is fully expressed in the world that we can access with our bodies and senses, and therefore we need not seek it in some transcendent Void of 'pure awareness'. Note that Kṣema uses the word *āmnāya*, which means 'tradition' or 'transmission' but specifically refers to the four Āmnāyas of the Kulamārga.[53]

Kṣema, like his Guru before him, defines his View as occupying a kind of middle path between the extremes of transcendentalism (the 'Tāntrikas') and pantheism (the Kaulas). His lineage teaches something that in my view is both more powerful and more liberating than the alternatives: that the Divine utterly transcends all that you can see, touch, taste, smell, hear, or think about, and yet it is directly manifest as *everything* that you can see, touch, taste, smell, hear, or think about. Both simultaneously. In the apropos phrase of Douglas Brooks, "The Divine is more than meets the eye, and yet it is everything the eye can meet." Now, it is relatively easy to imagine there's a transcendent part to the Divine and an immanent part—but that is not correct, for Awareness is undivided, one without a second, partless. So somehow, in a way that our minds cannot fathom, the One Divine Consciousness is simultaneously the changeless ground of all that is, providing the basis for the activity of the whole universe, yet completely untouched by it, *and* it is that constantly changing flux of activity itself. It becomes everything without compromising its integrity. It expresses as all form while never losing its formless essence. Pure Awareness manifests as Energy; Energy dances within Awareness. Emptiness is form, and form is emptiness. Śakti and Śiva, never separate but ever delighting in the play of their union.

This doctrine is easy enough to articulate, but the direct realization of the Divine as *simultaneously* transcendent and immanent is mind-blowing and life-changing. It resolves the dichotomy found in most religions whereby transcendent awareness is privileged over and above forms of embodied energy (like desire), which are judged as sinful or at least problematic. To realize that the same Divine is *equally* transcendent and immanent is to step into a whole new realm of spiritual maturity, one in which your embodied energies are no longer a problem to be solved, but nor are you lost in them.

If you feel intuitively that this View is correct (as far as words can approximate) it is important, then, to take a look at your practice and see if it actually aligns with your View. If we oversimplify a little bit, we can say that Śakti practices are those dynamic practices that emphasize Energy, such as yoga *āsana*, energy-body practices, *prāṇāyāma*, mantra, working with thought-constructs, and so on—while Śiva practices are those that emphasize pure Awareness, i.e., meditation, mindfulness, witness-consciousness, cultivating spacious awareness, and so on. In brief, the former are practices in which we do something, the latter are practices in which we learn to stop doing and just open. The former are practices that help us realize the Divine in this body, in this world, and the latter are those practices that help us realize that behind all appearances and all temporary bodies, the Divine exists as the changeless ground of all change. When we have both sorts of practices, we realize that they support each other, because *awareness clarifies and refines energy* and *energy enlivens awareness*. When we have both, we are able to rest completely in the core of our being, while being immediately available for whatever arises. We are able to deal with challenges far better, because we are grounded in our Śiva-nature, where we know that everything is always okay, yet we have no need to escape into the transcendent, because we intuitively understand the patterns of energy (Śakti) in this world, especially in human beings.

When our practice focuses one-sidedly on the Śakti aspect, we don't get to rest in the absolute ground, the core of our being, and we become burned out by overdoing. Energy without Awareness becomes ungrounded, misdirected, and frazzled. On the other hand, when our practice focuses one-sidedly on the Śiva aspect, we become transcendentalists, only happy in a peaceful retreat-type environment and unable to cope with challenging people (whom we judge as 'negative') or, for that matter, with environmental conditions (e.g., food, lighting, noises) that are not completely peaceful and *sattvik*. Awareness without Energy lacks strength, resilience, and adaptability; though spacious and peaceful, it becomes stagnant, dry, or unemotional (flat).

So you can see how important it is to balance our practice, and relate fully to both Śiva and Śakti aspects of the One. And, believe me, the list above of advantages to balancing your practice, and the pitfalls of not doing so, is far shorter than it could be.

*Contemplation Exercise*

Take stock of your practices. Take out your journal, and make a column headed "Śiva" for awareness-based practices and another headed "Śakti" for energy-based practices. List the practices you do in each category, approximately how many times a week you do them, and for how long. We are not interested in which list is longer (it is probably the Śakti list, if only because there are many more Śakti practices to choose from), but we are very interested in your intuitive sense of whether you are in balance or not. So it's *not* an issue of quantity at all—making the list just organizes the information. Then you need to go inside and ask your intuitive wisdom if you need more Śakti-type practice or more Śiva-type practice to be in balance.

To return to the text, Kṣema now presents the teaching that every philosophy, every interpretation of the nature of reality, reveals the nature of Awareness to some degree or another.

**Thus, all these levels or roles of the Blessed Lord—i.e., the singular Awareness-Self—manifested through His autonomy** (*svātantrya*) **are differentiated by degrees of revelation or concealment of that autonomy. Hence, there is only One Self that pervades all of this.**

If, as Kṣemarāja has said, the different Views are roles played by the one Actor on different levels (or stages), then what is it exactly that differentiates them? What is the factor that allows us to put them on different levels relative to each other? He answers that the differentiating factor is the degree of revelation of the absolute freedom or autonomy of Awareness, which is the very power by which all these Views are manifested. In other words, the singular Awareness-Self (*cid-ātman*), though equally present in and as all things, 'plays' by partially concealing its real nature to different degrees. We all experience this in daily life in the simple fact that it is easy to see God in some people and not so easy in others. But the Divine is equally present in all beings, so the awakened one delights in seeing the One playing the game of concealing itself here and revealing itself there, while never being less or more of itself. In the same way, some Views conceal and others reveal the power of autonomy by which Awareness freely takes on the roles of *all* the Views without ever becoming less of itself. For example, Views that are more rigid, fixed, dogmatic, and attached to formulae display less of the natural autonomy of Awareness, while others exhibit situationally sensitive fluidity in their principles and thus display more of that autonomy. By this same principle, we could say that a View that asserts that only itself is correct and all others are simply false is one in which there is more concealment of the true autonomy of Awareness, while a View that includes all other Views as valid (to some degree) is one in which there is a greater degree of revelation of that autonomy.

At any rate, the vast diversity of Views displays the incredible freedom with which Awareness formulates self-representations. Since that autonomy underlies all Views, this permits Kṣemarāja to say that only one divine Self pervades all of them—the Being to whom that autonomy belongs. In more religious language, we could say that there is only one God behind all religions—*without* having to say that all religions are equally true, which is of course logically impossible.

**As for those of limited Views, they have been caused to adopt egoic identification with various limited aspects** [of that One] **through the spontaneous play that expresses its Will** (*icchā*)**.**

As we have seen, there is only one Actor, one cause of all phenomena. Therefore, the process by which limited conscious beings identify with limited Views is a part of the spontaneous play that expresses the Will of that One. In other words, nothing has gone wrong here. All beings will naturally adopt limited and limiting Views when those Views accord with their conditioning and serve their agendas. Anyone whose consciousness starts to wake up to itself begins to adopt an attitude of open exploration, relinquishing the conviction that their knowledge is complete. Anyone who has such an attitude is led, step by step, from a more narrow View to a more all-encompassing one.

When your vision of reality has begun to open up and become more inclusive, then it's natural at first to judge those with narrow or exclusive Views, thinking that it's wrong for them to hold these Views, since you see how exclusive Views cause suffering. Therefore, you might argue with them and try to change their View. If you do this out of a sense of their wrongness, you are only demonstrating that your own View has not yet become all-inclusive. Just as they judge others, you too are judging them for judging. When your View opens up more, it becomes natural to grant all beings their freedom to be exactly as they are and to hold the Views they do. This doesn't necessarily mean that you don't argue with them, but it's with a different attitude: openness to the meaningful exchange of ideas motivated by a curiosity as to how that other person came to hold the View they do, rather than a conviction of wrongness in them that ought to be corrected (I need hardly point out the egoic arrogance in the latter stance).

But, you might object, some Views of reality make the people who hold them suffer, so they can't be okay. With this objection, you have assumed that suffering is not okay, when in fact it is the only way that anyone gets shown that their View is out of alignment with reality. (Of course, this should not be taken to imply that all suffering is a result of conceptual or spiritual misalignment!) This kind of suffering is a necessary part of the awakening process. Someone has to see for themselves how their View causes them suffering before they can wake up out of it. When the 'someone' is a loved one, this can certainly be hard to accept. However, shifting from a position in which you think it is your duty to change peoples' minds (especially those you care about) to a position in which you grant to all beings their freedom to think what they like, while still playfully challenging them when it feels right to do so, lifts a tremendous burden and opens you up to a world of ease and flow in your relationships. It is a shift from an exhausting battle against the reality of inexorable historical and psychological processes to one in which you experience the endless joy of granting all beings their freedom to be exactly as they are. (And this must include granting *yourself* your freedom to be as you are, which is precisely why you still challenge others when it feels right and natural to do so.) As Kṣemarāja indicates to us, this shift is supported by the contemplation that the part played by each form of consciousness in the vast drama is a part that expresses the spontaneous play of the one Consciousness that we all embody.

When we have this realization, we accept the reality of people holding limited Views, for we understand that those Views will tend to shift and give way as a part of the process by which life relentlessly chafes against any misaligned View. (Sometimes this shift doesn't happen until the moment of death or a subsequent lifetime. That's okay too.) If another person's View causes you suffering directly, please do share that with them if you think they might be open to hearing it, because sharing *your* truth is a natural part of accepting reality as it is. However, you need not sustain any illusions that sharing your truth will 'enlighten' the person with limited View, or that they need you to enlighten them (which would indicate a false view that you are 'above' them somehow). In other words, we start to access the joy and freedom of deep acceptance when we realize that every individual expresses a different point in the universal process by which Consciousness wakes up to itself and sheds all its self-created illusions. (In some people, this process appears completely frozen, but just as pressure builds up in a tectonic plate that hasn't budged in centuries, the pressure of angst, ennui, or suffering builds up in those who have not taken the first step of awakening.)

But, some object here, I *can't* accept the reality of systemic racism or sexism (for example), and I can't accept the Views that sustain them, and I think we must fight against them. To which of course I say, great! If that is your View, go to it, and may it do good for you and others. However, to those who are open to hearing it, I offer a subtle reframing that makes a huge difference in the long run. If you demonize those who unconsciously perpetuate systemic racism and sexism, you are decreasing the possibility that you will make any positive change, because hatred drains life-force energy. In this View, hatred begets hatred and love begets love, so if you are motivated to work for social justice, do so out of love for the people you wish to benefit, not out of anger against whoever you imagine is responsible for social and economic inequality.

I propose that it is possible for you to accept reality as it is and still work for social change and social justice if that is what you are truly inspired to do. I entreat you to consider the long-term emotional impact of acting for a negative reason ("Something's not as it should be and we must fix it!") versus a positive reason ("I long to be a part of the gradual process of creating a world of equal opportunity for all").

I submit that acting for a negative reason, however well-intentioned, is exhausting, unsustainable, and leads to burnout. (The very fact that it doesn't work very well over the long term demonstrates that the View is misaligned.) By contrast, acting for a positive reason is sustainable, for it provides long-term inspiration and energy. A positive reason is one linked to a desire to serve and uplift rather than linked to exhausting emotions like outrage, anger, or fear. If that positive reason is coupled to a well-contemplated acceptance of large-scale historical processes and the time-frames that they involve, it can bring you profound contentment to be a small part of a long-term change, even though you may not live to see its full fruit.

Ultimately, you discover that there is a way to work for change *while* accepting reality exactly as it is—when working for change in a particular area is an authentic expression of your real nature. When it is such an expression, you require no view about the wrongness of things to offer your energies toward the benefit of all. You learn to simply, lovingly, make the small contribution you can make because it is your nature to do so. Acceptance of this kind is true contentment, as is well known to all who have achieved it.

*Contemplation Exercise*

Consider someone you greatly disagree with, anyone from the president to your next-door neighbor. If you open to the possibility that they are a necessary part of the pattern, can you intuitively sense the function of the role they play? Can you even feel the 'rightness' of their existing, without needing to relinquish your opposition to their View?

To return now to the text, Kṣemarāja addresses "those of limited Views" mentioned in his previous paragraph, saying that what defines such limitation is the inability to perceive that which undergirds the whole range of human experience. By definition, then, a limited view is one that fails in some degree to recognize that which unites us all, and that fails to recognize that what unites us is far more fundamental and enduring than what divides us.

**As a result, lacking the highest Descent of Power (*śaktipāta*), they do not attain** [the experience of] **the Great Pervasion (*mahā-vyāpti*) in the** [four] **levels of embodiment, though it is clear that the very essence of each of those levels is the fact of its pervasion by all the loci of perception more fundamental than it.**

In this dense statement, we get a better idea of the experience of reality that Kṣemarāja believes goes beyond all the limited Views discussed above. We'll need to unpack it step by step. First, he implies that the result of clinging tightly to limited Views is a lack of openness. By contrast, knowing that your knowledge of reality is incomplete, in fact covers only a tiny sliver of the infinite possibilities of the human experience, means that you are always open to seeing, open to being shown more. This openness is a prerequisite, he suggests, to receiving a Descent of Power sufficiently strong to trigger the experience of the Great Pervasion. These terms need some explaining. We have already briefly addressed the key doctrine of the Descent of Power or Grace (*śaktipāta*) above, and it is also discussed in detail in *Tantra Illuminated* (pages 152–155 and 321–331). Recall that this 'Descent' (a metaphorical term) basically refers to the initial awakening that brings one to the spiritual path. By the 'highest' Descent of Power, Kṣemarāja means one of the three strongest grades of *śaktipāta* awakening (out of nine total: see *Tantra Illuminated*, pages 328–330). These grant the experience, however briefly, of the Great Pervasion (*mahā-vyāpti*), which is a near synonym for *samāveśa*, immersion into one's ultimate essence-nature, which is the essence-nature of all beings.

The great master Utpala Deva describes the spiritual experience of *samāveśa*—which is simply merging into our natural state—in terms of the five-layered self we have discussed above:

> *Samāveśa* is experientially realizing the primacy of the Awareness-self as the true Knower and Actor, and that the other layers of individuality—from the Void to the body—are mere attributes of it. [Stanzas on the Recognition of the Divine III.2.12] [54]

In other words, the deepest and truest experience of your own being consists of the experiential realization that transindividual Awareness is your real essence, and that that Awareness vibrates forth into manifestation as all the more peripheral layers of your being, from the Void outward. Those other layers are epiphenomenal expressions of the core Awareness, not the other way around. Now, above I said that the Great Pervasion is a *near* synonym for *samāveśa*, because it connotes not only the realization just described, but also the further realization that each layer of the five layers is defined by the fact of its pervasion by all the layers more fundamental than it. In other words, the Void is permeated by Awareness, the *prāṇa* layer is permeated by Awareness and Voidness, the heart-mind layer is permeated by Awareness, Voidness, and *prāṇa*, and the body is permeated by Awareness, Voidness, *prāṇa*, and the heart-mind. A living human body is nothing but flesh permeated by those four. And it is its pervasion by those four that defines it, that makes it what it is. In other words, the body is the physical vehicle for conscious experience of reality precisely because it is permeated by those four.

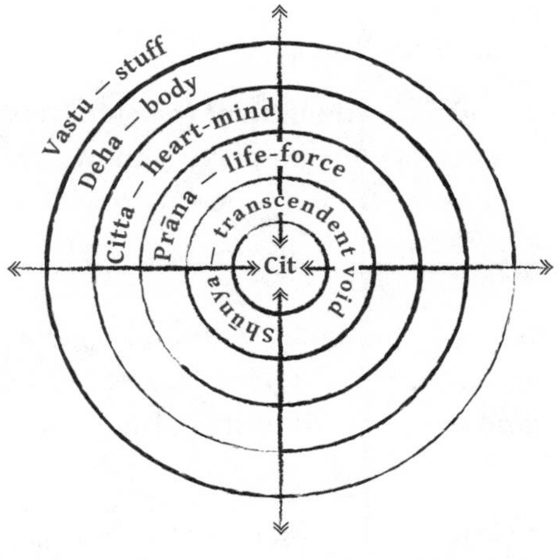


Direct, nonconceptual realization of this truth is what Kṣema is calling the Great Pervasion. When this realization is stabilized, it matures into abiding awakeness, and it instigates a process of profound integration of the parts of one's being—the complete dissolution of internal dividedness, also known as liberation.

There is one more detail to account for in Kṣema's description above. He takes the innovative step of describing each of the layers of the five-layered self as a 'locus of perception' (*pramātṛ*). Each of the layers, then, can be understood as a potential 'individual identity assemblage point' (to use Paul Muller-Ortega's felicitous phrase), and a place from which reality can be perceived. The shift entailed by the

'Great Pervasion', then, is a shift of the fundamental place from which we see the world. Since Awareness pervades not only the four layers of embodiment, but the whole of reality, when your locus of identity and perception shifts into identification with it, you actually experience *yourself as all-pervasive*. This is a very familiar experience to those who have walked the yogic path for some distance, but having it does not mean you have reached the end of the path. Rather, it means that the central point of your sense of being has begun shifting. When it is permanently established in dynamic Awareness, which realizes itself as independent of the other layers and yet constantly expressing itself *as* those layers, that is the culmination of the path.

Next Kṣema offers some scriptural proof-texts that support his argument. Remember how important scriptural evidence was in his cultural framework.

**As it is said** [in the *Pauṣkara-Pārameśvara*]:

> **But some, stained by attachment** (*rāga*) **to their** [incomplete] **knowledge, do not** [yet] **know the omniscient supreme Divinity, endowed with all wisdom.**

**Similarly** [in the *Svacchanda-tantra*]:

> Though those addicted to dry, fruitless argument **wish to gain liberation, Māyā** [dualistic perception] **causes them to wander in non-liberation** [for what they think is liberation is not]**.**[55]

These scriptural quotes reinforce the point already made: that attachment to one's view of reality, which is always more limited than you think it to be, can inhibit your progress on the path. Opening up to the truth that you don't know far more than you know, and that there are unguessed-at possibilities in every human being and in every corner of the universe, gives room for an influx of insight, grace, and wonder.

**And** [in the *Netra-tantra*]:

> **They who are worshippers** [only] **of the self** [i.e., individuated consciousness] **do not go to the highest state spoken of in the scriptures of Śiva.**[56]

This quote is important because it shows that in this View, the self or soul or *ātman*, though it is identical to the Divine, is not the ultimate principle. Though the nature of the self is not different from Śiva, it is a contracted form of the universal Principle, and like all contractions, it must eventually give way to expansion. Therefore, at some point on the journey, individuality is relinquished, that seamless unity may be realized. Even the word 'unity' is inappropriate here, because it implies two things that have become one. But the 'highest' state is that in which it is impossible to say "I am one with God (or the universe)," because all sense of separation has been so utterly stripped away that the term 'I' has no real meaning, and thus the statement itself becomes absurd. There is only One.[57]

What a rich feast of contemplations Chapter Eight has offered us already! And it's not over. Kṣemarāja offers as a coda to this chapter a wholly different way of reading the sūtra. We saw in Chapter One that Sūtra One could be read in five different ways; here, too, Kṣema uses alternate meanings of the Sanskrit words in Sūtra Eight to convey a very different teaching. The teaching is drawn from the esoteric left-current lineage known as the Krama. A poor understanding of the Krama teachings in twentieth-century scholarship meant that this interpretation of Sūtra Eight (as well as the whole of Chapter Eleven, which it foreshadows) has never before been published in an accurate translation.

This second reading seeks to show that the nature of Consciousness can be realized by reflecting on the process of cognition—specifically, how thoughts, feelings, and perceptions arise and dissolve within awareness. This reflection, we learn, can be done on the basis of *any* cognition. Such profound and careful self-reflection (*vimarśa*) leads one beyond philosophy to a direct contemplation of the nature of fundamental Awareness itself. This contemplative process, if properly directed, results in awakening to your true nature.

In translating Kṣema's alternate reading of his own sūtra, we have a couple of options:

**The positions of all 'views' are opportunities for That.** ||

*or,*

**The 'landing-points' of all cognitions are opportunities for That.** ||

These are simply two different ways of saying the same thing. He goes on to explain:

**And another** [reading of the sūtra would be]**: The 'positions of all views are opportunities for That', meaning the inward point of repose of all cognitions—such as blue, pleasure, etc.—is the means for revealing the true nature of one's Self, overflowing with the undiluted Joy of Awareness.**

Here Kṣemarāja provides an alternate gloss of the words of the Sūtra that creates an entirely different meaning, one that allows him to give us the key Krama teaching that he wants to convey. Below I present the Sanskrit terms of the Sūtra, with their meaning in both the first interpretation that we have discussed at length above and the second interpretation that we are discussing now. I also give the alternate glosses that Kṣema uses to further define his terms (this is what follows the 'i.e.'):

| Sanskrit | First Interpretation | Second Interpretation |
|---|---|---|
| *sthitayaḥ* | positions, i.e., doctrines | positions, i.e., points of repose |
| *darśana* | philosophical Views | literal views, i.e., cognitions |
| *bhūmikāḥ* | roles, levels | opportunities |
| *tad* | Its | That |

Now I'll explain what he's talking about in the bold paragraph above.

The Krama (also known as the Mahārtha) was a practice tradition and a school of thought (see pages 248–269 of *Tantra Illuminated*) which was primarily concerned with the nature of consciousness and the cycles of cognition through which it moves. A central doctrine of the Krama is that by following the cycle of any cognition back to its source, we can access our essence-nature. This radical teaching moves us past concern about the content of our thoughts and feelings and brings our attention to the process of their arising and subsiding, as well the ground of the process, which is our innate being or essence-nature. Here we are concerned with thoughts and feelings as movements of energy alone, and the practice of observing their movement and the quality of their vibration not only helps us become free of attachment or aversion *vis-à-vis* their content, but also has a curiously empowering effect on our energy body (more on that later).

The standard examples of cognition in Indian philosophy are 'the color blue' and 'the feeling of pleasure', the former exemplifying outward-focused cognitions we can share with others, and the latter exemplifying inwardly experienced cognitions not directly knowable by others. We can also see from the examples that 'cognitions' here means anything perceived (such as a color or feeling) as well as anything conceived (such as a thought).

Kṣemarāja tells us that the practice of paying attention to where each cognition comes to rest is a subtle but powerful means for revealing the true nature of one's innate being (*svātma-svarūpa*). Of course, there isn't exactly a *place* that each cognition comes to rest, but by staying with a given thought or feeling (without prolonging it) we can carefully track how it loses energy and dissolves. What does it dissolve into, exactly? Like listening to a sound die away into nothingness, if we stay with the cognition as it attenuates and dissolves, we can repose for a timeless moment in the ground of our being, the field of pure potential that makes all cognitions possible.

Even though it is actually indescribable, Kṣemarāja gives us some hint about the nature of this ground of being, so that we might know whether we have indeed fully arrived there (not that it's a 'there'). He says it is the "undiluted joy of awareness" (*cid-ānanda-ghana*). The attentive reader will recall that this is a key phrase from the invocation verse with which Kṣemarāja opened the entire work (see page 22). This fact implies that the present teaching is one that he regards as among the most important he has to convey. The main point here is that when we learn to be very present with the process and ground of cognition, rather than getting caught up in the content, we realize that Awareness—our fundamental nature—has the capacity to experience a kind of quiet joy and wonder (*camatkāra*) in relation to any experience whatsoever.* We usually are not in touch with that capacity except with regard to experiences that the mind judges as positive. This is because we *open* to those experiences, whereas we resist experiences that the mind judges as negative, and this resistance impedes our ability to access our natural capacity for wonder, while openness does not. This is a natural law of consciousness.

The implications of this teaching are huge, for it completely reconfigures our sense of how to be happy. Instead of chasing after and maximizing the 'positive' experiences that we believe will make us happy, we orient to the possibility of discovering that when we are in touch with our essence-nature, *any and every cognition* can be a source of joy, wonder, and fascination—*camatkāra*. (For more on this, see Chapter Eleven.) It is important to note here that the Sanskrit words *ānanda* (joy) and *camatkāra* (wonder, fascination, sense of beauty or awe) do not imply a feeling of happiness as opposed to unhappiness. If they did, it would be impossible to experience *ānanda* or *camatkāra* while sad, for example. But this is a kind of joy that has no opposite—a capacity to perceive beauty in *what is*, whether that be sadness, happiness, a grey day, or a blue sky. Essence-nature not only experiences beauty in what is, but can experience *just as much* beauty and wonder in what the mind doesn't like as in what it does.

Let this sink in, because if you do, it is world-rocking and life-changing. Not as a concept, of course, but as a real possibility for *your* life.

*Contemplation Exercise*

Can you remember a time in your life when you were sad or grieving and yet felt an undercurrent of inexplicable joy? That is *ānanda*. Perhaps you felt it as profound gratitude to be alive to experience sad moments in the first place. Perhaps you could feel that heartbreak is a gift that bestows blessings, such as increased compassion. The brain

* Even the skeptical rationalist meditator Sam Harris argues that, against rationalist expectations, "there is a feeling tone to consciousness, and once realized, it can be felt to permeate every aspect of experience" (*Waking Up*, Chapter 3, Endnote 2).

doesn't do very well at remembering things that don't fit in with our picture of reality, but dig a little deeper and see if you can find examples of times in your life that you felt this undercurrent of quiet joy/aliveness/wonder, regardless of whether you also felt sad, bored, angry, or happy.

Actualizing your capacity to experience *ānanda* in all life circumstances requires the ability to cultivate your sense of curiosity and wonder. The sense of curiosity is needed to give you the patience to track your thoughts and feelings as movements of energy—paying more attention to form and quality than content. For example, instead of taking seriously the words of a thought like "I'm not good enough," or "I'm better than her," you become curious about: (a) how it feels to have that thought, its quality or 'flavor'; (b) where it comes from, not so much psychologically but more like where it *arises from* in your body and what want or need it fulfills; and (c) where it moves to, what its trajectory is, and what kind of destiny it creates. The subtle practice here involves an exploration very different from the kind of analytical dissection and psychological evaluation to which we have all become accustomed in our culture. Rather, this involves taking a bird's-eye view and intimately looking into the nature of the cognition. You notice its arc, where it arises from and where it subsides, in a subtle 'energetic' way, not in terms of another series of thoughts (though those inevitably appear).

In this way, in time, you start to notice the 'ground' of the process of cognition, and when you relax into that ground, you naturally begin to access the inherent Joy of Awareness—your capacity to experience wonder and awe because of the miraculous fact of awareness itself. You are no longer dependent on gathering to yourself only pleasurable sense-objects (an impossible endeavor anyway) or having the 'right' experience. You feel radically free, because now you have access to a joy that is not dependent on external circumstance, without requiring you to distance yourself from reality in the slightest. This is called becoming *nirālamba* in Sanskrit—a joy that is free from any need for external support. It is not an attainment that comes easily, but in this View, there is nothing more worth working toward.

If you go back and read the bold paragraph above that I have been explaining, you should find that you understand it much better now.

Kṣemarāja furthers explains what he has in mind here in the paragraph below, but note that this is a foreshadowing of teachings he will reveal in Chapter Eleven, so don't worry too much if you don't get it all right now.

**To explain: whenever the outward form** [of a cognition] **comes to rest in oneself, there is** [1] **a withdrawal** [of focus] **from the external object; then,** [2] **a momentary holding of a point of internal stillness; then,** [3] **the intimation of the stream of various cognitions that are about to arise.**

Now Kṣemarāja talks about the process of cognition in terms of the divine Acts of creation/emission (*sṛṣṭi*), stasis (*sthiti*), and dissolution/withdrawal (*saṃhāra*) that we have discussed already (in the commentary on the Prologue). Here the relevant order is actually (1) withdrawal, (2) stasis, and (3) creation (also numbered in the bold paragraph above). But in fact, if we fill out the picture a little bit, to make it easier to understand, there are five stages: creation→stasis→withdrawal→stasis→creation, of which Kṣema here mentions the last three. (The full teaching is given in Chapter Eleven.) If you're confused, that's only to be expected, since this is an esoteric doctrine that Kṣema alludes to obliquely—he doesn't want you to understand it without access to a teacher who knows the Krama.

Let's take a simple example to understand what he's talking about. Imagine you're sitting in a great restaurant with a good friend, and you decide to order some chocolate mousse. The mousse arrives (initial creation of the experience), and it is unexpectedly delightful, so you pause the conversation for a moment and just savor it (stasis). The chocolateyness slowly dissolves on your tongue, the moment passes, and you become aware of yourself as the experiencer (withdrawal phase). Then stasis again: a momentary pause, a repose in a point of internal stillness, as Kṣema puts it. This silent moment of self-awareness is extremely brief for most people; yogīs seek to prolong it, for in this moment one can sense *camatkāra*, the aesthetic rapture that we will learn about in Chapter Eleven.

This wordless moment of internal awareness makes possible the creation that follows: in this case the creation of a cognition expressing the experience you just had, like "This mousse is amazing!" With practice, Kṣema implies, you can actually feel the energy of this discursive thought moving toward the surface of consciousness even before it breaks into words. If you practice tuning into the quality of the vibration of a thought before it takes the form of words, then you begin to notice other possibilities for expressing that thought-energy. In the example given above, you might realize that the expression "This mousse is amazing!" is a representation of a cognition more accurately depicted as "I am enjoying this flavor of experience"—that is, it is a cognition with which consciousness is representing itself and the quality of its experience. With subtler perception, you begin to notice the tendency to represent your inner experience as an evaluation or judgment of the person or thing you credit or blame for that experience (as if amazingness were an objective quality the mousse had that caused your experience, which is proven false with just a little reflection). Understanding how this linguistic objectivization of experience distorts its representation is just one of many benefits to becoming aware that words are the 'clothing' on the 'body' of a thought-vibration that fundamentally is the expression of an internal state. When you realize the only true statement that you can validly make is an expression of your internal state (since you don't have access to anyone else's inner world),[58] *you are also alerted to the one element that runs through all your experiences*: the sense of 'I am', vibrating in countless different forms (such as "I am the enjoyer of this flavor").

This realization draws you inevitably to meditate on the nature of that 'I am', that constant. What is the ground of the cognitive process, that which gives it its cohesion and imparts the sense of 'I am'? Is it, as some Buddhists argue, an illusion, the 'I' being different in each case, its continuity a mere mental construct? The nondual Śaivas say otherwise: that in each different experience of 'I am' (such as "I am an enjoyer" and "I am a sufferer"), the same fundamental Awareness-principle vibrates at a different frequency, as it were. In the Krama school, that principle is worshiped as the Goddess, alluding to the fact that the real 'I' is not personal but universal. That most intimate wordless sense of yourself is felt in exactly the same way by all sentient beings, because it *is* the same: Awareness is one and undifferentiated, so its deification is logical. It is also called 'the Fourth' because it is the source and ground of the threefold process of emission, stasis, and retraction discussed above. In it the three are fused as absolute potential. Therefore, Kṣema says:

**The Lady Awareness,** [known as] **the Fourth** (*turya*)**, is the ground and unified flow** (*melana*) **of this process of withdrawal, stasis, and creation;** [she is constantly] **pouring forth and reabsorbing the differentiated realities of the threefold process. She remains constantly full** (*pūrṇa*) **and constantly empty** (*kṛśa*)**, both and neither, vibrating in absolute simultaneity.**

Kṣema's resonant language here alludes to the different forms of the Goddess known in Indian tradition. All such forms express one of two basic classes: first, the sweet, abundant, full-bodied (*pūrṇa*) forms such as Lakṣmī and Parvatī, and second, the wrathful, intense, emaciated (*kṛśa*) forms like Kālī and Cāmuṇḍā. The first type is more associated with creation, the second with dissolution/withdrawal. Paradoxically, Kṣema tells us, both these aspects of the Goddess express the nature of divine Awareness: She is 'full' because whatever appears is appearing *inside* her, for all knowable phenomena are internal to Awareness, and She is 'empty' because she is literally insatiable, for She infinitely devours the objects of experience and the contents of consciousness (in the sense that they all dissolve into her) and always has room to spare. But She is also neither of these aspects, for Her nature is not exhausted by the fullness of phenomenal experience or by the emptiness of infinite potential. In Her ultimate nature She is beyond existence and nonexistence, which is why Awareness cannot be destroyed with the death of the physical body or created with its birth. Finally, Kṣema tells us, our limited perception that these aspects of the Goddess must be successive is not accurate: She 'vibrates in absolute simultaneity', meaning She is simultaneously full and empty, simultaneously both and neither. The language here is similar to that used when physicists describe the mysteries of quantum mechanics (such as light being simultaneously wave and particle), which likewise escape the mind's limited capacity of comprehension.

Next Kṣema quotes his teacher's teacher:

**As it is said in Utpala's commentary* on his sacred *Recognition* text:**

> **By devouring all the objects [of consciousness], She is intensified and becomes replete (*pūrṇā*).**[59]

This line is fascinating, for it is an example of how Kṣemarāja's lineage repurposed the ancient imagery of goddess worship to describe the nature of consciousness itself. Without making it explicit, the language here subtly suggests the image of a ferocious goddess licking up the blood offerings presented by her devotee, offerings that intensify her power until she rises up, satiated (*pūrṇā*), and confers a blessing upon her worshiper. This image was a central one for the ancient tradition that Kṣemarāja's gurus inherited. Over time, it came to be seen as a metaphor. For example, in his *Essence of Spanda* (discussed in Chapter Ten below), Kṣemarāja cites a verse from a scripture called *The Kaula Ocean of Waves*, a verse that shows the transformation of the meaning of this goddess imagery already in progress:

> Lelihānā ('She who Licks up and Devours the World'), the eternal Goddess, eternally shines in fullness (*pūrṇā*), containing all things. This wave of the Ocean of Consciousness is the Lord's Power of Will (*icchā-śakti*).[60]

The common theme here involves the metaphor of devouring and becoming full. When this is interpreted in terms of spiritual experience (as Kṣemarāja's lineage loved to do), we can understand it in terms of a meditative process of expanding consciousness until it embraces its natural fullness. In other words, Awareness achieves its fullest expression when, instead of engaging attention selectively according to the preferences of the conditioned mind, it expands to encompass the whole field of objectivity—embracing all that can be perceived in a given moment simultaneously. This act intensifies Awareness and lets it access its natural state of fullness, completeness, wholeness (*pūrṇa*). This is a meditative practice; it cannot be achieved through thinking about it.

* Now lost.

*Awareness Cultivation Exercise*

*Tattva-bhāvanā:* meditation on reality

(Make a recording of this text, or take turns with a friend slowly reading it to each other.) Sit in a comfortable posture and take some deep, slow breaths and let the energy of the body settle. Keep relaxing until the body becomes still. With the eyes open but still, soften your gaze, letting things go out of focus a bit, and become aware of the whole visual field.

Then notice the field of touch—all the sensations your skin can feel, such as the feeling of the clothes against your skin and the temperature of the air, as well as internal sensations, such as the sensation of breathing. Notice all touch sensations simultaneously—the whole field of touch.

After a little while, bring your attention to the whole field of sound—all the sounds you can hear, tiny ones as well as louder ones. Don't think about what they are, just notice them all equally. Give them all equal attention as best you can.

Then become aware of *all* the objects of consciousness simultaneously and equally—visuals, sensations, sounds, thoughts, and feelings. (This takes practice, for you need to let go of the compulsion to focus in on one thing in particular, and soften your awareness to encompass everything.) Let yourself melt into the whole field of awareness; notice everything, while fixating on nothing. Become the whole field.

When something grabs your attention (like a sound or a thought), deepen the breath a little bit and return to the whole field of awareness. Be with the whole; become the whole.

Finally, notice that which underlies, unites, and embraces the whole field of perception: Awareness itself. Can you sense that which subtly pervades everything you feel, hear, and sense?

With some practice of the above meditation, you will have the experience that Utpala was referring to: an intensification or heightening of awareness and a feeling of profound fullness or completeness. In time, you will become more and more aware of Awareness itself, until it is as palpable and present as any object within its field. Furthermore, if you do this *tattva-bhāvanā* practice regularly, you will be much better prepared to do the 'expansion of energy' (*śakti-vikāsa*) practice given in Chapter Eighteen.

**And this noble Lady, being cultivated, served, attended to & contemplated progressively more and more, actually makes her devotee one with herself.** || 8 ||

To conclude, Kṣema invokes a feudal metaphor more appropriate to his medieval culture than to ours, yet still beautiful: that of a devoted servant serving his Lady so well that he wins her favor. He uses a rich word, *anuśīlyamāna*, which means cultivating, serving, attending to, and contemplating all at once. But the Lady here is simply Awareness itself; we are encouraged to attend to our own awareness, notice how everything we perceive arises and subsides within it, and let our awe and reverence for it grow. In time, you will become at least as fascinated by awareness itself as by anything that you are aware of. Then you will enter your natural state of fullness and completeness.

This concludes our study of Sūtra Eight and its commentary.

यदि एवंभूतस्य आत्मनो विभूतिः, तत् कथम् अयं मलावृतः अणुः कलादिवलितः संसारी अभिधीयते ?–इत्याह

चिद्वत्तच्छक्तिसंकोचात् मलावृतः संसारी ॥ ९ ॥

यदा 'चिदात्मा' परमेश्वरः स्वस्वातन्त्र्यात् अभेदव्याप्तिं निमज्ज्य भेदव्याप्तिम् अवलम्बते, तदा 'तदीया इच्छादिशक्तयः' असंकुचिता अपि 'संकोचवत्यो' भान्ति; तदानीमेव च अयं 'मलावृतः संसारी' भवति । तथा च अप्रतिहतस्वातन्त्र्यरूपा इच्छाशक्तिः संकुचिता सती अपूर्णमन्यतारूपम् आणवं मलम्; ज्ञानशक्तिः क्रमेण संकोचात् भेदे सर्वज्ञत्वस्य किंचिज्ज्ञत्वाप्तेः अन्तःकरण-बुद्धीन्द्रियतापत्ति-पूर्वम् अत्यन्तं संकोचग्रहणेन भिन्नवेद्यप्रथा-रूपं मायीयं मलम्; क्रियाशक्तिः क्रमेण भेदे

## CHAPTER NINE

*Kṣemarāja's original text*

If this self possesses such divine majesty, then how is it that this person is referred to in the scriptures as a tiny spark of consciousness, veiled by 'impurity', enclosed by the 'armors' of limited action and so on, in other words a *saṃsārin* (a mundane creature bound to the cycle of suffering)? With this objection in mind, it is taught:

**Due to the contraction of those Powers belonging to Awareness,**
**It becomes a *saṃsārin*, veiled by Impurity.** || 9 ||

When the Highest Divinity, which is **Awareness**, submerges the pervasion of nonduality out of Its own spontaneous freedom, and thereby has recourse to the pervasion of duality, then **its Powers**—Willing, Knowing, and Acting—though uncontracted, appear to take on contraction. And at that very moment, **It becomes a *saṃsārin*, veiled by Impurity**.

To explain: the Power of Will, whose nature is unimpeded freedom and spontaneity, in contracted form is the Impurity of Individuality, the state in which one thinks oneself incomplete and imperfect.

The Power of Knowing, through gradually increasing contraction, becomes, in descending order: omniscience-in-duality, the acquisition of partial knowledge, the mind-ego-intellect, and the five cognitive senses. Subsequently, by taking hold of complete contraction, it becomes the Impurity of Differentiation, whose nature is the manifestation of knowable objects apparently distinct from oneself.

सर्वकर्तृत्वस्य किंचित्कर्तृत्वाप्तेः कर्मेन्द्रियरूप-
संकोचग्रहणपूर्वम् अत्यन्तं परिमिततां प्राप्ता
शुभाशुभानुष्ठानमयं कार्मं मलम् । तथा सर्व-
कर्तृत्व-सर्वज्ञत्व-पूर्णत्व-नित्यत्व-व्यापकत्वशक्त-
यः संकोचं गृह्णाना यथाक्रमं कला-विद्या-
राग-काल-नियतिरूपतया भान्ति । तथाविधश्च
अयं शक्तिदरिद्रः संसारी उच्यते; स्वशक्ति-
विकासे तु शिव एव ॥ ९ ॥

The Power of Action similarly takes on contraction, successively becoming omnipotence-in-duality, the acquisition of partial agency, and the five faculties of action. Subsequently, taking on complete limitation, it becomes the Impurity of Action, consisting of the performance of actions viewed as meritorious and demeritorious.

| In the same way, the powers of: | | taking on contraction, appear as: |
|---|---|---|
| total agency | → | limited power of acting (*kalā*), |
| complete knowing | → | limited power of knowing (*vidyā*), |
| all-encompassing fullness | → | craving (*rāga*), |
| eternality/simultaneity, and | → | limited time (*kāla*), and |
| all-pervasiveness/nonlocality | → | causality/localization (*niyati*). |

And a person of such a nature, impoverished in these Powers, is called a *saṃsārin*, but when his powers are fully expanded, he is revealed as God Himself. || 9 ||

# CHAPTER NINE

*with explanation*

**If this self possesses such divine majesty** (*vibhūti*)**, then how is it that this person is referred to** [in the scriptures] **as a tiny spark of consciousness** (*aṇu*)**, veiled by 'impurity', enclosed by** [the 'armors' of] **limited action, and so on, in other words a *saṃsārin*?**

In Chapter Eight, we learned that the Self-that-is-awareness (*cid-ātmā*), like an actor, takes on the 'roles' of the various philosophies and spiritual views, each a more or less limited level of its self-expression. Since here the Self of all beings is equated with the highest Divinity (*parameśvara*), an objection naturally arises in light of the scriptural references to the human being as a contracted form of consciousness severely limited by the five 'armors' (*kañcukas*) and the three 'impurities' (*malas*), a condition summed up by the term *saṃsārin*, one who wanders aimlessly and haplessly through *saṃsāra*, the cycles of suffering, in life after life and death after death. It seems, *prima facie*, that a *saṃsārin* is the very opposite of what most people mean by God or the Divine Self. Yet it has been taught here that the Divine Self is one and the same as the everyday embodied self. How can this be?

**With this objection in mind, it is taught:**

**|| CIDVAT-TACCHAKTI-SAṄKOCĀN MALĀVṚTAḤ SAṂSĀRĪ || 9 ||**

**Due to the contraction of those Powers belonging to Awareness, It becomes a *saṃsārin*, veiled by Impurity.**

The key term here is 'contraction'. The apparently great difference between divine Consciousness and the *saṃsārin* or bound soul is due to the contraction of the innate Powers of the former. When those Powers are in their most contracted form, they appear as the so-called Impurities of Consciousness. But as we will see, these Impurities are actually forms of ignorance or misunderstanding. Though veiled, the

Powers retain their essential nature, making possible the return to their fully expanded state. The first step in this return is seeing that the Impurities that seem to stain one's very soul are in fact deeply held belief structures that can be shed. Even partially peeling back these 'veils' initiates the process of re-expansion into one's true nature, which once initiated cannot be stopped. But before discussing that, Kṣemarāja explains how the process of contraction happens in the first place.

**When the Highest Divinity, which is Awareness, submerges the pervasion of nonduality out of Its own spontaneous freedom, and** [thereby] **has recourse to the pervasion of duality, then its Powers—Willing, Knowing, and Acting—though uncontracted, appear to take on contraction. And at that very moment, It becomes a *saṃsārin*, veiled by Impurity.**

Why would the Highest Divinity (*parameśvara*) choose to become a *saṃsārin*? To explain, we must use a quasi-mythological narrative. Kṣemarāja here refers to the primordial state of things as the 'pervasion of nonduality'. This is a state of absolute potential in which every possibility for being exists—but nothing is expressed or actualized. Therefore, it is a homogenous state of perfect equilibrium. Divine Consciousness, which is not yet a cognitive entity (for it is not embodied), 'senses' the infinite potential of its own being and 'desires' to make manifest that which is latent within it. Therefore, it 'submerges' its nondual aspect and manifests its capacity to appear as a plurality of things. It does this out of its own free will, out of its spontaneous urge to express itself in form. Consciousness now has recourse to the 'pervasion of duality'—that is to say, the appearance of distinction between things, especially between subjects and objects. This is the foundation for the world of manifestation. Now, I called this a 'quasi-mythological' narrative because this is not really a description of what happened at the beginning of time, but rather what is happening in every moment.

Since everything is in reality an expression of Consciousness, that is, a coalescence into form of the primordial formless Absolute, duality must be only an appearance, not ultimately true. Thus the Powers of Consciousness only *appear* to take on contraction. The three primary Powers of Willing, Knowing, and Acting appear as the three Impurities explained below. This is what it means to be a *saṃsārin*, one who wanders aimlessly through the world, helplessly bound to the cycles of pain and pleasure, life, and death. (This is of course 99.99% of humanity at present.)

The three Impurities are covered in some detail on pages 150–162 of *Tantra Illuminated*. In the dualistic form of Shaivism, these were considered actual impurities, real metaphysical bonds that stain the soul and can only be removed through prescribed ritual action. In nondual Śaiva Tantra, however, these 'Impurities' are understood as forms of *ignorance*, that is, mostly unconscious cognitive errors that can be uprooted through the cultivation of insight and clear seeing. When they are uprooted, the Powers of Awareness automatically expand into their full expression.

With the Powers of Awareness contracted, it appears that one is a tiny part of the world. When those same Powers are expanded, it becomes clear that the world is a tiny part of oneself.

**To explain: the Power of Will, whose nature is unimpeded freedom and spontaneity (*svātantrya*), in contracted form is the Impurity of Individuality (*āṇava-mala*), the state in which one thinks oneself incomplete and imperfect (*apūrṇa*).**[61]

The Impurity of Individuality, by which one sees oneself as a tiny and insignificant part of the whole, unfulfilled and incomplete (*apūrṇa*), is here revealed as none other than a contracted form of the Power of Will (*icchā-śakti*). This makes sense because the more we feel unfulfilled and incomplete, the more we feel the desire to fill the inner void with external objects and experiences (such as wealth, food, sex, family, recognition, fame, etc.). This grasping desire is clearly a contracted form of the Power of Will.

Here is the key teaching that Kṣemarāja is alluding to: when we feel full and complete, the Will flows from the inside outward, due to a natural impulse to self-express and share that fullness in various ways with other beings. When we feel unfulfilled and incomplete, on the other hand, desire grasps for external things (or people), and seeks to pull them inward in a vain attempt to fill the inner emptiness. Thus the contracted form of the energy moves in the opposite direction from the expanded form. Where fullness translates to a desire to share (the fullness overflows), emptiness translates to a desire to grasp and hold and pull close (the vacuum sucks). The latter perpetuates emptiness in a vicious cycle (since the void cannot be filled by anything impermanent or external or experiential, yet pleasure gives a partial and temporary respite from it), whereas the former perpetuates fulfillment in a virtuous cycle (since to express and share your fullness is gratifying). The uncontracted Power of Will is free, open, and spontaneous (*svātantrya*): it intuitively recognizes that there are countless ways to share one's fullness and love, all of them beneficial. By contrast, the contracted Power, in the form of desire, grasps after the specific thing it thinks it needs in any given moment to be happy.[62] Since grasping is contractive in and of itself, it can never result in fulfillment. The awakening that shows the way out of the vicious cycle is called *śaktipāta*, the Descent of Grace.

**The Power of Knowing, through gradually increasing contraction, becomes, in** [descending] **order: omniscience-in-plurality, the acquisition of partial knowledge, the mind-ego-intellect** (*antaḥkaraṇa*)**, and the five cognitive senses. Subsequently, by taking hold of complete contraction, it becomes the Impurity of Differentiation** (*māyīya-mala*)**, whose nature is the manifestation of knowable objects** [apparently] **distinct from oneself.**

When the Power of Knowing (*jñāna-śakti*) contracts in conformity with the movement from nonduality into apparent duality, it does so in four stages (speaking theoretically and quasi-metaphorically). To understand this better, refer to the chart of the thirty-six Tattvas on page 91. The first stage is complete knowing, but in the context of the plurality of subjects and objects that are emerging from the formless Absolute (this corresponds to tattva #4). At this stage, objects of consciousness are still recognized as forms of one's own consciousness ('This am I'). The second stage (corresponding to tattva #8, *vidyā*) is a greatly reduced capacity of knowing in the emergent context of Māyā (defined as the creative power of divine Awareness by which it projects an apparently differentiated universe). All knowing in the domain of Māyā is necessarily partial knowing—the only problem being that the knower usually thinks his knowledge is more or less complete when in fact it encompasses merely a sliver of reality. The third stage is the contraction of *jñāna-śakti* into the form of the mind—more specifically, the three aspects of mind, being the faculty of attention, the ego, and the intellect or power of discernment (tattvas #14 to #16, about which see pages 129–132 of *Tantra Illuminated*). Finally, the fourth stage in this model is the manifestation of the cognitive senses, namely hearing, touching, seeing, tasting, and smelling (tattvas #17 to #21).

It is obvious that these four stages all express the Power of Knowing that inheres within Awareness. Despite the language used here, there is not much utility to regarding this as a temporal sequence; rather, it is simply a model that seeks to map the manifestations of that Power in terms of levels of increasing specificity and concreteness.

More importantly for our purposes is the assertion that the fifth and most contracted form of the Power of Knowing is the Impurity of Differentiation (*māyīya-mala*, the name being derived from *māyā*). This refers to the cognitive error by which the objects of consciousness (including other people) are seen as separate from oneself. It is, in a nutshell, subject–object duality. Due to seeing things in this way, we can perform a variety of mental operations such as analysis and categorization. But if we take subject–object duality as primary and fundamental instead of an appearance within a greater unity, the consequences can be dire indeed, including using other people as means to an end (instead of seeing them as ends in themselves) and destructively exploiting the environment. Such things are not natural when you see and feel that everything you can see and feel is a part of you, indeed *is* you. For more on the Impurity of Differentiation, see page 157 of *Tantra Illuminated*.

As noted, we have here been given a map of the stages by which the Power of Knowing contracts into the Impurity of Differentiation, each stage a kind of stepping down into greater specificity, narrowness, concreteness, and apparent limitation. In Tantrik philosophy, all such models are, when reversed, maps of the spiritual journey to freedom. Therefore, Kṣemarāja implies that we can access the fully expanded Power of Knowing by reversing the stages described: first, shifting out of the default belief in subject–object duality (i.e., seeing in terms of self versus other) by meditating on raw sensual experience (the totality of what you're hearing, feeling, seeing, etc.); then by carefully observing the contents of the mind; then by becoming aware that all you think you know constitutes a tiny fraction of a fraction of all possible knowledge, thereby opening up to the sense of wonder. When the openness, humility, and wonder of knowing how little you know is sustained (and when supported by other practices described elsewhere in our text), it opens up further into omniscience-in-plurality, an aspect of the awakened and liberated state. Now, the word omniscience (*sarvajña*) is here used in a spiritual context, so it does not mean 'knowing everything' in the sense of knowing every fact; rather, it refers to the calm conviction that you know everything you *need* to know. As one spiritual master put it, in the liberated state you "know whatever you need to know when you need to know it and not a moment sooner". It is in this sense that your knowing is complete (indeed, this is the only sense in which knowing could ever be complete).

Though he did not know this Tantrik doctrine, the author Alan Watts, on the basis of his own insight, fifty years ago perfectly summarized the Impurities of Individuality and Differentiation in this way:

> It is our firm conviction that beyond this 'wall of flesh' lies an alien world only slightly concerned with us, so that much energy is required to command or attract its attention, or to change its behaviour. It was there before we were born, and it will continue after we die. We live in it temporarily as rather unimportant fragments, disconnected and alone. ... This whole illusion has its history in ways of thinking; in the images, models, myths, and language systems which we have used for thousands of years to make sense of the world. These have had an effect on our perceptions which seems to be strictly hypnotic.

Breaking free of this hypnosis, shaking off our mental conditioning, and seeing the illusion as illusion is the process we call awakening.

**The Power of Action similarly takes on contraction, successively becoming omnipotence-in-plurality, the acquisition of partial agency, and the five faculties of action. Subsequently, taking on complete limitation, it becomes the Impurity of Action (*kārma-mala*), consisting of the performance of actions viewed as meritorious and demeritorious.**

The Power of Action (*kriyā-śakti*) is described in terms of the same stepping-down metaphor. As before, in the first stage the Power is complete, but operating in the sphere of plurality.* Then, in the domain of Māyā, the full freedom of action is lost and a merely partial agency is acquired (corresponding to tattva #7). This limited agency is expressed primarily in terms of the five faculties of action (tattvas #22 to #26): communication, manipulation, locomotion, copulation, and excretion (i.e., the faculties utilizing the mouth, hand, feet, genitals, and bowels). These five actions are highlighted by the tradition over all others because they are central to the strategies we use to sustain and perpetuate life. Finally, the most contracted form of the Power of Action is the Impurity of Action (*kārma-mala*). Like the other Impurities, this consists of a cognitive error. In this case, it is the error whereby some actions are viewed as good (*śubha*) and others as bad (*aśubha*). This requires some explanation.

A person under the influence of the Impurity of Action regards some actions as *śubha*, which means good, pure, honest, virtuous, or pleasant, and other actions as *aśubha*, which means the opposite of all those things. Such a person not only consciously and subconsciously labels actions with these value judgments, but—and this is the important part—he performs some actions and tries to avoid others *because* of those value judgments. That is to say, his social and cultural programming tells him which actions are good and which are bad, and he tries to act in accordance with that programming instead of in accordance with his deeper spiritual intuition about what feels right in any given real-life situation. This is problematic, because 'good' and 'bad' are of course mental constructs, not qualities that inhere in reality itself.

Tantrik philosophy argues that it's a problem when belief in 'good' and 'bad' takes the place of beneficial personal contemplation as to the best course of action, because such beliefs encourage us to follow social prescriptions that may not in fact be truly beneficial in a given situation. That is to say, benefit is always contextual, so it must always be situationally determined, and no single action is either always beneficial or always harmful in every circumstance. Contemplate this for yourself: is there *any* circumstance in which a 'bad' action (up to and including killing) might actually be the right thing to do? Is there *any*

* This corresponds to tattva #5 (the *śuddhavidyā-tattva*; see *Tantra Illuminated*, pages 141–142) as well as the fourth Perceiver in the Seven Perceivers schema (see above, page 92).

circumstance in which an action usually labeled 'good' (such as telling the truth when asked) might actually be harmful? If you can think of even one example in each case, the point is proven. Our best guide to right action is not through our conditioned judgments, but rather to gather information from all sides, invoke our intention to benefit all beings, become centered and still, and then trust the deepest intuition that arises.*

If you still doubt, consider this: human history is littered with examples of men who caused great harm while believing they were doing the right thing. If virtually everyone guilty of genocide, from Columbus to Hitler, *thought* he was doing the right thing (and they did), even thought that God was on his side, then we can be sure that many who committed lesser crimes also thought they were doing the right thing. Still others perform actions while believing them to be wrong, but think they are doing 'what has to be done'. This too is a mental construct that leads to harm and suffering. Of course *you* think you are different from those deluded people, that *your* mental constructs of what is right and wrong are somehow correct, though you allow that millions of others have been incorrect. Aside from the arrogance of such a view, how would you know? All those others were similarly convinced. That is why in the Tantrik way, we release mental constructs of both good and bad, right and wrong, and try to carefully feel into the most beneficial course of action unique to a given situation, as described in the previous paragraph. To be clear, this method does not dispense with thinking at all: on the contrary, we need the mind to deconstruct our conditioned ideas of right and wrong, and then we need it to gather data about the situation (this can be done intuitively as well as analytically), and then we need it to notice our bias and correct for it to properly assess the data. Only after having done all that do we become quiet and still, clear and empty, and feel intuitively which course of action is the most beneficial. Your ability to do this is to some extent

* This method only fails when incipient mental illness of certain kinds is present. To forestall this possibility, we accept reflection from others; for example, if you are following this method, but consistently receive feedback from others that you are causing harm, I recommend that you seek professional help.

predicated on your meditation practice, because without the ability to become still and quiet, clear insight usually cannot arise.

As before, the stages Kṣemarāja presents are also a map for practice toward liberation. We can move past our limiting mental constructs by first doing mindfulness practice in which we are fully present with our ordinary daily actions (walking, talking, eating, etc.). Then we contemplate the limitation of our agency by seeing that we are not in control of anything of significance. That is to say, no matter how you try, you cannot determine any outcome with certainty. Realizing this, you begin to surrender to reality as it is. To use a religious metaphor, you "do the best you can, and leave the rest to God." That is, you contentedly accept that you cannot determine the final outcome, and that even your best effort often plays only a small part in that outcome. Upon attaining spiritual liberation, you finally realize that you can do everything that you *need* to do. This is what 'omnipotence-in-plurality' means: the direct experience that you have the power to do whatever is actually required of you in a given situation, and the certain knowledge that whatever you cannot do (for whatever apparent reason) need not be done, at least not by you.

Finally, Kṣemarāja wants to show us that the five 'armors' or *kañcuka*s (tattvas #7 to #11) are also contracted forms of the powers of Divine Consciousness. The list on the right below is the traditional list of the *kañcuka*s (see also page 134 of *Tantra Illuminated*), whereas the list on the left comprises the powers (*śakti*s) that Kṣema sees as corresponding to them.

| **In the same way, the powers of:** | | **taking on contraction,** |
|---|---|---|
| **appear as:** | | |
| **total agency** | → | **limited power of acting (*kalā*),** |
| **complete knowing** | → | **limited power of knowing (*vidyā*),** |
| **all-encompassing fullness** | → | **craving (*rāga*),** |
| **eternality/simultaneity, and** | → | **limited time (*kāla*), and** |
| **all-pervasiveness/nonlocality,** | → | **causality/localization (*niyati*).** |

There is some overlap here, because the first three lines are identical to the three principles we just discussed, only in reverse order.[63] 'Total agency' translates the same word as does 'omnipotence' (*sarva-kartṛtva*), i.e., the unimpeded Power of Action; 'complete knowing' translates the same word as 'omniscience' (*sarvajñatva*), i.e., the unimpeded Power of Knowing, and 'all-encompassing fullness' (*pūrṇatva*) is the state in which the Power of Will naturally overflows, and one accesses the ability to want what is. The opposite of the latter is the Impurity of Individuality, in which a sense of lack or incompleteness (*apūrṇa*) in oneself gives rise to craving or grasping desire (*rāga*).

Two more powers are added here, so that we can understand that all five traditional *kañcuka*s are contractions of aspects of the Divine. The fourth, *nityatva*, refers to the fact that Awareness, as the meta-principle, is eternal—and yet, because it transcends time, we could equally say that it is simultaneous, that in which all times exist at once. When this power takes on contraction, it appears as linear sequential time (*kāla*), time as we usually experience it. The fifth and final power is *vyāpakatva*, which means both all-pervasiveness and nonlocality, meaning that Awareness as the meta-principle is prior to all divisions of space and thus pervades everything equally (since everything is equally an appearance within Awareness). The contracted form of this power is *niyati*, which refers to the power that binds our *karma*s to us according to an apparent law of cause and effect. *Niyati* in a narrower sense means localization, that is, your karmically determined location in space. Full awakening brings the realization that Awareness is all-pervasive and that localization is merely an appearance within it. That is, instead of the belief that you are a tiny speck limited to a tiny location in a vast universe, you see directly that the idea of a vast universe (and you having a specific location within it) is itself a tiny speck within the infinite potentiality of your own Awareness.

Thus the last two lines above teach us that Awareness is prior to, and more fundamental than, spacetime; that space and time are appearances within Awareness, functions of how it chooses to see itself.[64] Lest you think that this perhaps startling idea is merely a fantasy born of the mind of a medieval philosopher addled by too much meditation, you should know that there are respected scientists and philosophers of our own time who argue the same. One example is the cognitive scientist Donald Hoffman, who said in a *New York Times* interview: "I believe that consciousness and its contents are all that exists. Spacetime, matter and fields never were the fundamental denizens of the universe but have always been, from their beginning, among the humbler contents of consciousness, dependent on it for their very being."[65]

**And a person of such a nature, impoverished in these Powers, is called a *saṃsārin*, but when his powers are fully expanded, he is** [revealed as] **God Himself** (śiva eva). **||**

According to this view, '*saṃsārin*' and 'God' are simply two names for the same Awareness in two different states, in the same way that 'water' and 'ice' refer to the same substance in different states, though we would never confuse the two labels. (See Chapter Five.) In this case, we use the two labels to denote the same Awareness-entity with powers contracted and expanded respectively. In the expanded state, they manifest as the five divine capacities listed in the left column a couple pages above, and in the contracted state, they manifest as the five 'veils'/'armors' (*kañcuka*s) in the right column. But if God is that Consciousness whose powers are unimpeded, in what sense can we say that a being with contracted powers is a manifestation of the Divine? That forms the subject of the next chapter.

This concludes our study of Sūtra Nine and its commentary.

ननु संसार्यवस्थायाम् अस्य किंचित् शिवतोचितम् अभिज्ञानमस्ति येन शिव एव तथावस्थितः?—इत्युद्घोष्यते । अस्ति ।—इत्याह

तथापि तद्वत् पञ्चकृत्यानि
करोति ॥ १० ॥

इह ईश्वराद्वयदर्शनस्य ब्रह्मवादिभ्यः अयमेव विशेषः, यत्

'सृष्टिसंहारकर्तारं विलयस्थितिकारकम् ।
अनुग्रहकरं देवं प्रणतार्तिविनाशनम् ॥'

इति श्रीमत्स्वच्छन्दादिशासनोक्तनीत्या सदा पञ्चविधकृत्यकारित्वं चिदात्मनो भगवतः । यथा च भगवान् शुद्धेतराध्वस्फारणक्रमेण स्वरूपविकासरूपाणि सृष्ट्यादीनि करोति, 'तथा' संकुचितचिच्छक्तितया संसारभूमिकायामपि 'पञ्चकृत्यानि' विधत्ते । तथा हि

'तदेवं व्यवहारेऽपि प्रभुर्देहादिमाविशन् ।
भान्तमेवान्तरर्थौघमिच्छया भासयेद्बहिः ॥'

# CHAPTER TEN

*Kṣemarāja's original text*

One might now ask, is there some recognizable clue that indicates a person's Divinity such that, even with reference to the condition of being a *saṃsārin*, one may confidently proclaim, "S/he is really God in that state!"? There is. Thus it is taught:

**Even then s/he performs the Five Acts in the same way.** || 10 ||

Here we see the specific distinction between our View of the Nonduality of the Divine and that of the Vedāntins. For in our View, the Lord who is none other than the Self-that-is-awareness constantly performs the Fivefold Act, as exemplified in the teaching expressed in scriptures such as the sacred *Svacchanda-tantra*:

> He is the agent of creation and dissolution, the cause
> of concealment and stasis, and the bestower of grace:
> the Deity who destroys the suffering of those who bow
> [to Him].

Just as the Blessed Lord performs creation, etc.—which is simply the unfolding of His own nature—through the process of expanding the Pure and Impure Realms, **in the same way, He performs the Five Acts even** on the level of *saṃsāra*, in the form of one whose Power of Awareness is contracted. To explain:

> Thus the Lord, even in everyday life, out of his own free
> Will, manifests 'externally' the multitude of objects that
> are actually appearing within him by infusing himself
> into the levels of the body, mind, etc. ||

इति प्रत्यभिज्ञाकारिकोक्तार्थदृष्ट्या देहप्राणादिपदम् आविशन् चिद्रूपो महेश्वरो बहिर्मुखीभावावसरे नीलादिकमर्थं नियतदेशकालादितया यदा आभासयति, तदा नियतदेशकालाद्याभासांशे अस्य स्रष्टृता; अन्यदेशकालाद्याभासांशे अस्य संहर्तृता; नीलाद्याभासांशे स्थापकता; भेदेन आभासांशे विलयकारिता; प्रकाशैक्येन प्रकाशने अनुग्रहीतृता। यथा च

सदा पञ्चविधकृत्यकारित्वं भगवतः, तथा मया वितत्य स्पन्दसंदोहे निर्णीतम्।

एवमिदं पञ्चविधकृत्यकारित्वम् आत्मीयं सदा दृढप्रतिपत्त्या परिशील्यमानं माहेश्वर्यम् उन्मीलयत्येव भक्तिभाजाम्। अत एव ये सदा एतत् परिशीलयन्ति, ते स्वरूपविकासमयं विश्वं जानाना जीवन्मुक्ता—इत्याम्नाताः। ये तु न तथा, ते सर्वतो विभिन्नं मेयजातं पश्यन्तो बद्धात्मानः ॥ १० ॥

In accordance with the perspective taught in the *Stanzas on Recognition*, when the Great Lord, who is simply Awareness, 'externalizes' Himself, he enters into the levels of the body, *prāṇa*, etc., and manifests an object of awareness—e.g., the color blue—in a particular place, time, and form. When He does so, then He is a creator with respect to the aspects that are manifest, i.e., its specific place, time, and form. At the same time, by doing so, He is necessarily also a 'withdrawer' with respect to other places, times, and forms. He is a maintainer in terms of whatever aspects of the manifestation continue to be present. He is an agent of concealment when He manifests the object as something apparently separate. He is a bestower of grace when He manifests that same object as one with the universal Light of Consciousness. I have explained the way in which the Blessed Lord constantly performs the Fivefold Act in detail in my work *The Essence of Spanda*.

Thus, if those with devotion constantly contemplate with firm determination the fact of their own authorship of the Five Acts, it actually reveals their Divinity. For this very reason, those who constantly cultivate and practice this come to know that all things are the expansion of their own nature; they are called 'liberated-in-life' by our tradition.

But those who do not know this are bound souls, because they perceive the whole collection of knowable objects as completely differentiated. || 10 ||

# CHAPTER TEN

*with explanation*

**One might now ask, is there some recognizable clue that indicates a person's Divinity such that,** [even] **with reference to the condition of being a *saṃsārin*, one may confidently proclaim, "S/he is really God in that state!"? There is. Thus it is taught:**

**|| TATHĀPI TADVAT PAÑCA-KṚTYĀNI KAROTI || 10 ||**

**Even then s/he performs the Five Acts in the same way.**

With Sūtra Ten, Kṣemarāja offers us a teaching that is perhaps as surprising as it is beautiful: that even one who is thoroughly bound, deluded, and ignorant of his true nature is just as Divine as one who is free, awake, and self-realized. The evidence of this is the fact that the former type of person is also constantly performing the self-same Five Acts of God, though without recognizing that that is the case. The difference is one of awareness versus lack thereof; there is no difference in essential nature.

Therefore, a hallmark of the truly awake state (*bodhastha*) is that one does not think or feel that one is superior to others, more divine, or even more evolved. Being more aware doesn't make you a superior kind of human being; it just makes you more aware. Of course, having said that, a spiritually awake person has a clarity of view that often allows them to perform much more effective service to others, whether in the awakening process or in negotiating the challenges of everyday life.

In his commentary on his own sūtra, Kṣema wants to explain first how the View of nondual Śaiva Tantra is different from the other popular nondual View emerging from medieval India, Advaita Vedānta (which today is better known, but only in a form influenced by nondual Śaiva Tantra).

**Here we see the specific distinction between our View *(darśana)* of the Nonduality of the Divine[66] and that of the Vedāntins. For in our View, the Lord who is none other than the Conscious Self constantly performs the Fivefold Act, as exemplified in the teaching expressed in scriptures such as the sacred *Svacchanda-tantra*:**

> *sṛṣṭi-saṃhāra-karttāraṃ vilaya-sthiti-kārakam* |
> *anugraha-kāraṃ devaṃ praṇatārti-vināśanam* || 1.3
>
> **He is the agent of creation and dissolution, the cause of concealment and stasis, and the bestower of grace: the Deity who destroys the suffering of those who bow** [to Him]**.**

That is to say, the distinction between the views of nondual Śaiva Tantra and Vedānta (both of which propose an idealist monism in which all that exists is Consciousness) is that in Vedānta, Consciousness possesses no dynamism, no activity, no *śakti*—for according to that school, Consciousness is completely still, static, and peaceful, and therefore nothing has ever actually happened and the creation–dissolution cycle is illusory.

In Vedānta, then, the world exists only in the sense that a mirage exists. Or rather, not even in that sense, since the perception of diversity is said to be a cognitive error, like mistaking mother-of-pearl for silver, whereas a mirage (of water in the desert, say) is real enough to be captured on film. The main point here is that, according to the classical form of Vedānta that Kṣemarāja is here criticizing, everything you think is real and important is nothing but insubstantial dream-stuff; the quiescent Absolute Consciousness (*brahman*) alone exists, and life is but a dream. By contrast, nondual Śaiva Tantra is primarily distinguished by its doctrine of the *dynamism* of Awareness, whereby it actually self-transforms into diverse tangible and intangible expressions of its essential nature. As a consequence, in nondual Śaiva Tantra the universe we experience is regarded as real, not illusory, though it is entirely internal to Awareness. In other words, everything that you touch, taste, feel, etc. is a *real* form of divine Consciousness. This means diversity is real, even though everything you perceive is a different form of the One, as already discussed in Chapter One. In nondual Śaiva Tantra, then, diversity can and ought to be celebrated, whereas in Vedānta, acknowledging diversity could be seen as evidence of your unenlightened condition.[67]

The practical consequences of these different views were and are considerable. Since Vedānta regarded the world as illusory, it advocated renunciation (why engage with an illusion?), and both teachers and serious practitioners of that tradition were expected to takes vows of monkhood, and still are today (such people are called *swāmīs* and usually wear orange or saffron robes). By contrast, since Tantra taught the world was a tangible expression of God, it did not advocate renunciation, and its teachers and practitioners were expected to be householders with families and jobs, engaged in the world. In fact, a renunciate was specifically not allowed to be a guru or teacher of Tantra! In Tantra, it was considered inappropriate for renunciate swāmīs to teach nonrenunciate householders—which has become the normal state of affairs in Indian religion and yoga today.

Finally, Vedānta philosophy was always 'transcendentalist' in the sense that it sought to go beyond the mirage of this world and attain some higher state of consciousness; thus spiritual attainment involves in some sense leaving the ordinary sensual world behind. Therefore, this philosophy easily lends itself to 'spiritual bypassing', a (sometimes unconscious) tendency to avoid dealing with the human world, your ego, or others' pain because "they're not really real". By contrast, nondual Śaiva Tantra teaches that this whole world and everything in it is a form of divine Consciousness, and therefore we are called to respect, honor, and respond with sensitivity and care to whatever presents itself (insofar as we are able). We are called to greater intimacy with what is, not to greater dissociation.* Of course, greater intimacy with what is requires you to dissolve your mental constructs—your 'stories' about what is—since they interpose themselves between you and reality and distort your perception. (For more on this, see Chapter Eighteen.) This is a practice shared by the two traditions. But many other practices are not shared. Classical Vedānta is austere, frowning on devotional expressions (*bhakti* and *kīrtan*) as well as dismissing the value of ritual

* This is why cultivating 'witness-consciousness' is considered something of a beginner's technique in nondual Śaiva Tantra; for most people, it results in a kind of dissociation that can help one get a bit of perspective and breathing room, but is explicitly not the goal.

performance (originally, swāmīs were absolutely forbidden to kindle a ritual fire). By contrast, nondual Śaiva Tantra embraced a wide range of practices that worked for different kinds of people, including devotional poetry, music meditations, and ceremonies of all kinds, giving rise to a vibrant and highly aesthetic culture, similar in some ways to Tibetan Buddhism today.*

There are too many differences between Vedānta and nondual Śaiva Tantra to list here, but their divergence is obscured by the fact that in the last eight centuries or so Vedānta became heavily influenced by Śaiva Tantra, such that nearly all forms of Vedānta taught today are deeply 'tantricized'. However, it's fair to say that the many historical differences between the two Views all boil down to one, the one Kṣemarāja points out here: for Vedānta, Divine Consciousness is absolutely still and inactive, whereas for Tantra it is dynamic, pulsing with potential energy that spills forth into manifestation, into cycles of creation and dissolution metaphorically conceived as a vigorous cosmic dance (as in the image of the Naṭarāj).

Indeed, in nondual Śaiva Tantra, all reality can be described as countless forms and phases of one dynamic energy of Consciousness—though of course that energy exists in constant relationship with profound stillness, and its cycles return at regular intervals to that stillness. Thus, where Vedāntic meditation is always quietistic, Tantrik meditations can be energetic or sensual as well as quietistic. In short: for Tantra, the Absolute has *śakti*, while for classical Vedānta, it does not.

**Just as the Blessed Lord performs creation, etc.—which is simply the unfolding of His own nature—through the process of expanding the Pure and Impure Realms, in the same way, He performs the Five Acts even on the level of *saṃsāra*, in the form of one whose Power of Awareness is contracted.**

The dynamic energy of Awareness is expressed in terms of the Five Acts, already described in some detail in the commentary on the first Introductory Verse (page 22 and following). Creation, stasis, dissolu-

* The vibrancy and exuberant aesthetics of Tibetan Buddhism owe much to Śaiva Tantra (for example, the vivid cosmic maps called *maṇḍalas*, made with colored sand, were originally borrowed from Shaivism), but the traditions are also different since Tibetan Buddhism is largely monastic.

tion, concealment, and revelation all constitute the self-expression of the One, and they are all simultaneous and interdependent. Kṣemarāja refers to the manifestation of the so-called Pure Realm and Impure Realm, ancient terms he inherited from tradition that respectively denote tattvas #1 to #5 and #6 to #36. The Pure Realm is reality as experienced by awakened consciousness, and the Impure Realm denotes the bondage of the dreamstate. The point here is that the manifestation of the awakened consciousness characteristic of the Pure Realm is simultaneously the dissolution of delusion, and the manifestation of the Impure Realm is simultaneously the dissolution of clear seeing. Every expansion is simultaneously a contraction, and *vice versa.* When Awareness conceals (or forgets) its unitary nature, it reveals itself in the form of diversity and particularity. When it conceals its capacity to appear as separate, it reveals its unity. Thus all Five Acts are happening all the time at every conceivable level. They are happening on the largest scale, where all sentient beings co-create the experience of a shared reality, and they are happening on the smallest scale, in your moment-to-moment individual experience. This is the level of *saṃsāra*, which literally means 'running on', like the way the mind runs on and on, or the way your consciousness creates one experience after another, some pleasant and some unpleasant, in an endless cycle. The 'one whose Power of Awareness is contracted' is of course the ordinary embodied human being. How can we see and understand that each of us is creating, sustaining, and dissolving our experience of reality moment to moment? The world certainly seems to confront us from without—we seem to have been thrust into a world we didn't choose, one that exists as it does regardless of whether we exist or how we choose to see it. How can you *experientially* realize that the one infinite divine Consciousness actually creates and dissolves the very substance of reality *through you*?

**To explain:**

> **Thus the Lord, even in everyday life, out of his own free Will,** [seems to] **manifest 'externally' the multitude of objects that are actually appearing within him by infusing himself into the levels of the body,** [mind, *prāṇa*,] **etc.** || [*Īśvara-pratyabhijñā-kārikā* I.6.7]

Kṣemarāja now quotes his primary source text, the *Stanzas on the Recognition of [Oneself as] the Divine* by his guru's guru's guru, Utpala Deva, which explains that the manifestation of a variety of objects of experience is linked to, and dependent on, the process by which divine Awareness embodies itself in successfully denser and more tangible layers: the void, *prāṇa* (life force), mind, and body (see pages 92–101 of *Tantra Illuminated* and Chapters Seven and Eight above). Each of these levels is appropriate to different kinds of objects of experience, such as quiet nothingness, breath, thoughts and feelings, and sensations respectively. The verse implies that by entering into each of these levels, Divine Awareness is able to manifest the multitude of experiences appropriate to those levels (this corroborates our discussion back in Chapter Three). That is, though you have been conditioned to think that you are passively receiving the data of experience from without, very little of it created by you, in reality that which you experience is *flowing forth from you.* You are the portal through which Awareness spills forth into manifestation. If you sit quietly with your moment-to-moment experience, you will see that nothing contradicts this way of seeing things, which should at least cause you to open to the possibility that it might be true. But this is only the beginning of the explanation.

**In accordance with the perspective taught in the *Stanzas on Recognition* above, when the Great Lord, who is simply Awareness, 'externalizes' Himself, He enters into the levels of the body,** [mind, prāṇa,] **etc., and manifests an object of awareness—e.g., the color blue—in a particular place, time, and form. When He does so, then He is a creator with respect to the aspects** [of that phenomenon] **that are manifest, i.e., its specific place, time, and form.** [At the same time, by doing so]**, He is necessarily also a withdrawer with respect to other places, times, and forms. He is a maintainer in terms of whatever aspects of the manifestation continue to be present. He is an agent of concealment when He manifests the object as something apparently separate. He is a bestower of grace when He manifests that same object as one with the universal Light of Awareness (*prakāśa*).**

In other words, in every single cognitive event, four of the Five Acts are in play. The perception of a round blue pot is in fact its creation—its manifestation as an expression of Awareness itself. Awareness functions as a 'creator' with respect to the features 'round', 'blue', 'made-of-clay', 'in this room', and so on, and therefore simultaneously functions as a 'withdrawer' with respect to 'square', 'red', 'made-of-plastic', and 'in the other room', for all of these qualities (and infinitely more) exist *in potentia* within Awareness but are not part of the current experience.[68] Whatever phenomena are perceived are then maintained through the faculty of conscious attention, which as it were imparts energy and vividness to what is perceived, causing it to persist.

The upshot of all this is not only a profound reevaluation of your role in relation to phenomenal experience, but also a reevaluation of the nature of reality as dependent on, and inseparable from, consciousness. I need hardly point out that the developments in quantum physics in the last seventy years lend support to this view. To put it briefly, experiments in quantum mechanics (especially those of John Clauser, Alain Aspect, et al.) have shown that reality cannot be both objective and separable, and is probably neither. Let's briefly define these terms: some aspect of reality is 'objective' if it exists independent of observation, and reality is 'separable' if I can act on one part of it without affecting another part arbitrarily far away.[69] Now let this sink in: quantum physicists who have zero philosophical or spiritual agenda have demonstrated that reality *cannot* be both objective and separable, and is probably neither. Tantrik philosophy, of course, argues that it is definitely neither. But either one of these propositions radically undermines our conventional conditioned view of reality. For this reason, as Lama Yeshe said, we must "overthrow the tyranny of ordinary appearances". Your assumption that things exist without a perceiver to perceive them is just that: an assumption. It cannot be proven. The grade-school version of this proposition is the absurd claim that (for example) the moon does not exist when no one is looking at it. But we are not claiming that individual things magically disappear when you don't look at them; it is much more accurate to say that it is simply meaningless to talk of phenomena in the absence of an observer, since the manner in which anything manifests is dependent on the nature of the observer and the manner of his observation—and clearly, whether something can manifest in some other way in the absence of an observer is not only unknown but unknowable.[70] In other words, not just the moon but the whole universe is dependent on a conscious perceiver, as well as *vice versa*. To put it another way, there is no known or knowable universe apart from the universe of conscious experience, and the medium of conscious experience, clearly, is you.[71]

But let's cover the fourth and fifth of the Five Acts. At any given moment, Kṣemarāja tells us, Awareness may act as the agent of concealment, insofar as it views the object of experience as something separate from itself, or the agent of revelation, insofar as it views the object as one with itself. The former is an act of forgetting; the latter an act of remembering (and the latter word can also be read as *re*membering, the opposite of *dis*membering). The word here translated as concealment can also mean 'corrosion', for seeing the objects of your experience as separate from yourself has a corrosive effect in that it degrades the integrity and intrinsic equality of Awareness. It is countered by the act of revelation (*anugraha*), also known as grace, by which Awareness manifests the object as one with itself; that is, it reveals to itself the seamless unity of experience, and sees clearly the truth that the object is inseparable from consciousness. Kṣemarāja plays with words here, because he says Awareness is the bestower of grace when manifesting (*prakāśana*) the object as one with the Light of Awareness (*prakāśa*). In other words, the very fact that it is manifest within Awareness and known only through being illuminated by Awareness demonstrates that it can be nothing but Awareness. Grace, then, is the revelation by which this truth is directly (nonconceptually) *seen*. You are not part of the whole. You are the whole.

The great quantum physicist Erwin Schrödinger put it this way in his book *My View of the World*: "Inconceivable as it seems to ordinary reason, you—and all other conscious beings as such—are all in all. Hence this life of yours that you are living is not merely a piece of the entire existence, but is in a certain sense the *whole*; only this whole is not so constituted that it can be surveyed in one single glance."

In summary, then, each and every cognitive act simultaneously expresses four of the Five Acts of God (one, two, three, and four or five).[72] In the simple act denoted by the phrase "I see a pot," the integral potencies that lie at the very heart of Consciousness are expressed. *Every* act of perception, contemplation, or imagination utilizes these powers in equal measure, and thus all acts of Awareness are equally miraculous, equally divine. Every cognitive act is unique, but none are special. Each and every perception gives you the same opportunity to contemplate the nature of reality: that perception *is* creation, and that you—what you really are—are the creator (and sustainer and dissolver) of everything you experience.

**I have explained the way in which the Blessed Lord constantly performs the Fivefold Act in detail in my work *The Essence of Spanda.***

In the work to which he refers, Kṣemarāja seeks to extract the essence of the *Stanzas on Vibration* (*Spanda-kārikā*), just as in the present work he seeks to extract the essence of the Recognition philosophy. Kṣemarāja wrote two commentaries on the *Stanzas on Vibration*; in the shorter one, *The Essence of Spanda* (*Spanda-sandoha*), he shows that virtually all the teachings of the text are implicit in the first verse, which is as follows:

> We praise the Beneficent Source of the activity of the Wheel of Powers [of Consciousness], the expansion (*unmeṣa*) of which is the arising of the universe and the contraction (*nimeṣa*) of which is its dissolution. || 1 ||

In the course of expounding the verse, Kṣema does indeed explain the Five Acts in terms very similar to those in the present chapter. However, he is keen to show, in accordance with the Spanda doctrine, that every creation is simultaneously a dissolution and *vice versa*, since every kind of expansion can also be seen as a contraction of the opposite thing and *vice versa*. For example, he says, "'Creation' is an unfolding (*unmeṣa*) of an innate potential that is simultaneously the concealing or infolding (*nimeṣa*) of the true nature of something as nothing but Consciousness." By the same token, he says, "'Dissolution' is a concealing of differentiation, which is simultaneously an opening upward that touches into the nondual nature of whatever is dissolved." Similarly, the fourth Act of self-concealment is simultaneously a contraction into limitation and an expansion of identification with the body, etc. Revelation or grace, defined as 'a complete unfolding or opening up as the whole self once again' can also be seen as the contraction of duality. In this way, all processes can be seen in terms of a complementarity of balanced forces.

In this passage from *The Essence of Spanda*, Kṣema goes on to explain that the Light of Consciousness remains the author of the Fivefold Act on the level of the 'ordinary' embodied human being, as we have seen above. He repeats much information we have already seen, adding that an object of experience has greater persistence when it is co-created, that is, when it is an experience shared by multiple conscious entities.

He concludes the passage in this way: "This alone is sovereignty over the Wheel of Powers: being constantly established in one's own nature as the Awareness that performs the Fivefold Act." However, it should be understood that in the experience of sovereignty that he describes, there is no sense of personal agency; the self that performs the Five Acts is the universal Self, as explained in the next section.

**Thus, if those with devotion** [to this path] **constantly contemplate with firm determination the fact of their own authorship of the Five Acts,** [such contemplation] **will actually reveal their Divinity.**

The teaching that in your real nature you are the author of the Five Acts, and therefore identical to God, is useless (or even dangerous) as a mere concept. It must be directly and nonconceptually realized through contemplation and practice. Kṣema uses the word 'constantly' to encourage you to contemplate many times each day that whatever you are experiencing is flowing forth from what you are, for your own sake, and is dissolved by you and into you as well. Contemplating this does not mean thinking about it (which rapidly grows stale) but opening toward the feeling of it. It is not the conditioned thinking mind that performs these Five Acts, but your essence-nature of unlimited Awareness. That is why you cannot change reality at a whim: such whims arise from the limited ego-mind, which is *not* the agent of the Five Acts. In fact, the ego-mind is not the locus of subjectivity as it believes itself to be, but just one of the many objects of experience created, sustained, and dissolved by the Divine Awareness that you are. In other words, the self you think you are has no control over reality because it itself is merely a thought-form emanated by Awareness along with all other phenomena. (If the mind were subject and not object, you could neither scrutinize it nor dissolve it!) This leads to the inevitable conclusion that your fundamental being is not unique to you; it is no more yours than anyone else's. Yet it is the most intimate core of what you are. It is this universal Self (if Self is even the right word) that performs the Five Acts.

Kṣemarāja tells us that we need firm determination and devotion for this contemplative practice to be effective. Intellectual curiosity is not enough; you must get in touch with the heart's longing to know the truth of Being in order to generate enough energy to make the practice successful. The practice is more likely to bear fruit if the contemplation of your moment-to-moment experience becomes a beneficial obsession. For example, with each new experience that arises, internal or external, pleasant or unpleasant, you can remind yourself, "What I am created this and freely chose to experience this."* But try to move past the thought and into the feeling toward which it points. This contemplation can give rise to a sense of wonder, or amusement, or bemusement—or anger and denial if the experience in question is a 'negative' one. The latter reaction passes in time, and gives way to gentle acceptance of pain as part of the beauty of life.

One should not begin this contemplative practice in relation to external things (as in affirming "I created this person in front of me"), because that can easily lead to delusion through a wrong understanding of what is in reality a very subtle teaching. To avoid this pitfall, focus the practice first on your internal state(s). Affirm your authorship of your own inner experience: "This feeling (whatever it is) arose from me as a spontaneous expression of what I am and will dissolve back into that same ground of being." Try to feel it as you affirm it. In this way, you cease to be a victim of your own emotions and thoughts. In this contemplation, it doesn't really matter that some (most) thoughts point away from your essence-nature while others point toward it. They *all* arise out of what you are, so you are equal to each experience. If you do not resist it or seek to own it or deny it, you find that each experience dissolves at just the right moment and makes way for the next creation of Awareness. In this way, you go beyond the preferences of the mind and begin to sense the irreducible uniqueness and completeness of each moment as well as how perfectly integrated into the energetic flow of reality it is—and you are. You see that everything that arises within you is pure energy in the form of thoughts, feelings, and sensations, and that you are the timeless spacious ground out of which it all arises and into which it dissolves—and you are the constantly shifting play of energy as well. In this way, little by little, punctuated by sudden flashes of recognition, you realize your divinity. A day comes when the recognition is so complete that what has been seen cannot be

* I strongly recommend that you do the practice only with firsthand experiences, not secondhand ones mediated by television or Internet, because the way you experience an event through the selective (and therefore distortive) lens of the news media is not how you would experience it in person.

unseen, can no longer be forgotten. This is abiding nondual awareness, or full awakeness.

**For this very reason, those who constantly cultivate and practice this** [come to] **know that all things are the expansion** (*vikāsa*) **of their own nature; they are called 'liberated-in-life' by** [our] **tradition. But those who do not know this are bound souls, because they perceive the whole collection of knowable objects as completely differentiated.**

The fruit of this process is the direct knowing that all things—*everything* in the universe of your experience—is the expansion, the blossoming, the unfolding (*vikāsa*) of your real nature (*svarūpa*).* The beautiful Sanskrit word *vikāsa* also refers to growth, development, the opening of the heart, and the serenity resulting from an open heart. Therefore, it is untranslatable; it suggests that not only is everything in your experience an expression of your innate nature, it is the natural evolution of that nature, and is perfectly tuned to give you the opportunity to further open your heart and experience the serenity of that nature.

Directly knowing, without concepts or effort, that everything in the universe of your experience is the expression and expansion of your own nature is the state of being a *jīvanmukta*, one who is liberated in this very life, in this very body. Knowing that you are the whole, you know that you are unborn and undying. You are freed from fear and pettiness and delusion of all kinds. You know everything you *need* to know (which turns out to be not much, on the level of concept, anyway) and in that sense are 'omniscient'. You can do whatever needs to be done, and feel no need to do anything that you cannot do, and in that sense are 'omnipotent'. You feel as humble as the tiniest creature and as vast as the sky, and in that sense you are God. And—by this you know the experience is real—you viscerally feel that any attempt to put this into words is laughable, or awkward, or somehow just barely completely misses the point—including the words I write here.

---

* The word translated as 'all things' here—*viśva*—is also commonly translated as 'the universe'. But we must remember that it is not here claimed that the objective universe is the expansion of your true nature, because in this View there *is* no objective universe. Therefore in this philosophy, *viśva* can only mean 'the universe of one's direct experience'.

Not seeing this truth—which is the condition we all are in until we're not—is the state of bondage, characterized by the vision of reality as fundamentally differentiated and separable. In this state, you imagine yourself separate from the whole, which consists of a vast collection of distinct things (including people) that you can act on and that can act on you, for better and for worse. This is a world of fear and desire and delusion that subtly disguises itself as correct perception or well-founded conviction. In this state, you mistake the mind's ability to analyze experience into discrete things and categories and events for accurate perception. You see everything through the lens of a mind conditioned by language, which is inherently dualistic ('me' versus 'you', 'mine' versus 'yours', 'good' versus 'bad', and so on), and thus you see distinction as fundamental instead of what it is—a mental filter, a feature of the instrument you are using for measurement. Since you almost never stop using that instrument, you are unaware that there is a whole different mode of perception, and even scoff at those who allude to it, cynically doubting that there could actually be another paradigm for human existence. In this way you almost revel in your contraction, your certain sense that you know, more or less, how the world is, and you keep seeking ways to gain strategic advantage in this world of hard edges—only occasionally glimpsing that your true fulfillment lies in giving up the constant angling for advantage and melting yourself into the *real* world, which is all curves and fluidity, and which softly bends to embrace and accept your self-surrender the moment it is offered. These glimpses are occasional until the day comes that you have finally suffered enough in the hard-edged world, and one of those glimpses looks to you like an exit door, and you leap at the chance, even if it means that your life as you've known it up to that moment falls apart like the house of cards it was.

Pause and take a few breaths now.

We will conclude this crucial chapter, in which Kṣemarāja demonstrates that even the most ordinary or deluded of beings is constantly expressing their Divinity, with this contemplation. Since you already are That, but aren't fully awake to what you are, you can gain insight into the difference between who you are and who you *think* you are by comparing *what is* with what you think you want. In other words, as unbelievable as it might seem to you now, what you really are always loves and wants what *is* in any given circumstance (including the ever-changing nature of what is), and the tension generated by the belief that you want things to be different is the suffering that points out to you the presence of untruth.

If you really want to know what kind of person you are, look at the *whole world of your experience*, everything that you see and think and feel and know, because you—what you really are—creates and sustains it. Śiva gets what Śiva wants, always. And you are Śiva.

Even the barest beginning of realizing this truth causes the pattern of your life to start to shift. You are capable of astonishing beauty and terrible ugliness and everything in between, and somehow simply opening to the whole of what you are and allowing yourself to love the whole shifts the character of what manifests through you. Why? It's a divine mystery. You are unlimited in your real nature, so much so that you chose limitation in order to have a more specifically defined experience. We could say that you are so free, you chose to experience bondage to better appreciate your freedom, but it's even deeper and harder to define than that. This seeming paradox will resolve as we proceed.

This concludes our study of Sūtra Ten and its commentary.

न च अयमेव प्रकारः पञ्चविधकृत्यका-
रित्वे, यावत् अन्योऽपि कश्चित् रहस्यरूपो-
ऽस्ति ।—इत्याह

आभासन-रक्ति-विमर्शन-बीजावस्था-
पन-विलापनतस्तानि ॥ ११ ॥

'पञ्चविधकृत्यानि करोति'—इति पूर्वतः सं-
बध्यते। श्रीमन्महार्थदृष्ट्या दृगादिदेवीप्रसरण-
क्रमेण यत् यत् आभाति, तत् तत् सृज्यते;
तथा सृष्टे पदे तत्र यदा प्रशान्तनिमेषं कंचित्
कालं रज्यति, तदा स्थितिदेव्या तत् स्थाप्यते;
चमत्कारापरपर्यायविमर्शनसमये तु संह्रियते ।
यथोक्तं श्रीरामेण

'समाधिवज्रेणाप्यन्यैरभेद्यो भेदभूधरः ।
परामृष्टश्च नष्टश्च त्वद्भक्तिबलशालिभिः ॥'

# CHAPTER ELEVEN

*Kṣemarāja's original text*

Nor is this the only mode in which s/he performs the Fivefold Act, as there is also another, special mode, which is esoteric. Thus it is taught:

**S/he performs those Five Acts through manifestation, attachment, subjective awareness, laying down the 'seed', and dissolving it.** || 11 ||

The words 's/he performs the Five Acts' from the previous sūtra should be supplied here as well. According to the View of the sacred lineage of the Great Truth, whatever manifests through the process of the flowing forth of the sense-goddesses is said to be 'created'. Similarly, the object is [said to be] 'sustained' when one is, for some time, attached to the object that has been emitted, with the dissolution of one's sense faculties stalled. Then the object is 'dissolved' at the moment of subjective awareness, which is a synonym for aesthetic rapture (*camatkāra*). As it was said by the venerable Rāma:

> The mountain of duality cannot be shattered by others, even with the thunderbolt of deep meditation—but, by those who are endowed with the strength deriving from devotion to You, Goddess Awareness, as soon as it is recognized as an aspect of themselves, it is dissolved. ||

इति । यदा तु संह्रियमाणमपि एतत् अन्तः विचित्राशङ्कादिसंस्कारम् आधत्ते, तदा तत् पुनः उद्भविष्यत्संसारबीजभावमापन्नं विलयपदम् अध्यारोपितम् । यदा पुनः तत् तथा अन्तः स्थापितम् अन्यत् वा अनुभूयमानमेव हठपाकक्रमेण अलंग्रासयुक्त्या चिदग्निसाद्भावम् आपद्यते, तदा पूर्णतापादनेन अनुगृह्यते एव । ईदृशं च पञ्चविधकृत्यकारित्वं सर्वस्य सदा संनिहितमपि सद्गुरूपदेशं विना न प्रकाशते, इति सद्गुरुसपर्यैव एतत्प्रथार्थम् अनुसर्तव्या ॥ ११ ॥

But when, despite being dissolved, the experience of the object deposits internally various impressions (*saṃskāras*) such as anxiety and so on, then it is established in the state of concealment, becoming a 'seed' of worldly experience (*saṃsāra*) that will arise again. However, when something that has been internally deposited in this way, or even something that is actually being experienced now, becomes one with the Fire of Consciousness through the process of 'sudden digestion', also known as the method of 'total devouring', then it is said to be *graced*, because it has been integrated into the state of complete fullness.

Though this fact of being the performer of the Five Acts is present to everyone all the time, it is not revealed without the instruction of a true Master. Thus the propitiation of a true Master ought to be pursued by those whose goal is this revelation. || 11 ||

# CHAPTER ELEVEN

*with explanation*

**Nor is this the only mode in which He performs the Fivefold Act, as there is also another, special mode, which is esoteric (*rahasya*).**

Kṣemarāja here refers to the teaching of the Krama or Mahārtha ('Great Truth'), which is also known as 'the Secret Transmission'. (See *Tantra Illuminated*, pages 248–269.) This most radical and sophisticated of all the Tantrik traditions is focused on the veneration of the Goddess Kālī and the forms of consciousness that she embodies. Kṣemarāja subtly weaves Krama teachings in throughout this work; for example, the fifth interpretation of Sūtra One and the second interpretation of Sūtra Eight foreshadow the main teaching here in Chapter Eleven. In the introduction to the chapter above, he tells us that there is another way in which we can understand the Five Acts, a teaching revealed only in the Krama. We might almost say that Chapter Ten teaches us how Śiva performs the Five Acts, and Chapter Eleven teaches how his *alter ego* Kālī performs them.

**Thus it is taught:**

**|| ĀBHĀSANA-RAKTI-VIMARŚANA-BĪJĀVASTHĀPANA-VILĀPANATAS TĀNI || 11 ||**

[S/he performs those Five Acts] **through manifestation, attachment, subjective awareness, laying down the 'seed', and dissolving it.**

To make the correspondence clear, we can compare the original Five Acts with the new names they are being given here:

| | | |
|---|---|---|
| creation | → | manifestation |
| stasis | → | attachment |
| dissolution | → | subjective awareness |
| concealment | → | laying down the 'seed' |
| revelation | → | dissolving the 'seed' |

He now explains this new reading of the Five Acts, a teaching that holds incredible potential for your liberation, perhaps more than any other in this book.

**According to the View of the sacred** [lineage of the] **Great Truth** (Mahārtha)**, whatever manifests through the process of the flowing forth of the sense-goddesses is said to be 'created'.**

As we discussed in Chapter Ten, it's not the case that an external world flows in through the senses and is registered in your brain; rather, the Source-consciousness within you flows forth and manifests as everything you experience (including a brain that has electrochemical states that correspond to the phenomena perceived as external). In other words, the experience of reality doesn't flow in from the outside, it flows out from the Center that is your essence-nature, becoming all the phenomena of your experience. If you really contemplate it, you'll see that there is no reason to believe the first, more common view is correct other than deep conditioning. The second view, as strange as it might seem to your mind, is at *least* as possible, if our evidence is simply your direct experience.

So all creation is the *manifestation* of the infinite potential within you, which flows forth and appears in the form of sensual experience through the power of the 'sense-goddesses' or the capacities of consciousness to appear with form, shape, smell, etc. When consciousness focuses in on any object (whether a blue jar or the feeling of love), it becomes more vivid and more detailed. When we focus on something else, the previous object becomes vague, a kind of peripheral smudge. We assume that the object still has all its detail simply because that detail reappears when we focus on the object again. But if consciousness is everything, there is no static independently existing object waiting to be looked at. There is only your consciousness manifesting the various qualia of your experience. Thus, focusing on something is actually manifesting it in more detail. (When physicists look inside atoms, they find electrons and even smaller particles called quarks. Were those particles there before the physicists looked? Even they are forced by the evidence to respond with, "That question is meaningless."[73]) What happens when one gets absorbed in an object of awareness?

**Similarly, the object is** [said to be] **'sustained' when one is, for some time, attached to the object that has been emitted, with the dissolution of one's sense faculties stalled.**

An object is sustained (i.e., exists in the same way for a brief duration) when one's attention is absorbed in it, when one 'attaches' to it. The word *rakti* means attachment, but also 'dyed', as cloth is dyed with color. It's as if consciousness is temporarily 'dyed' with the object it becomes fascinated with. Thus the natural dissolution is momentarily stalled as consciousness is immersed in what it is like to experience itself as that object—the taste of melting chocolate, the smell of a rose, a beautiful image, the sound of captivating music, or an inner emotion. Within a short time, however, awareness reverts back to itself.

**Then the object is 'dissolved' at the moment of subjective awareness** (*vimarśana*)**, which is a synonym for aesthetic rapture** (*camatkāra*)**.**

When awareness reverts back to itself, it shifts from being primarily objective to primarily subjective, and the vividness of the object dissolves, and it becomes merely the background 'wallpaper' of consciousness. At this moment one becomes aware of oneself as the experiencer; this is the moment at which one can experience *camatkāra* or aesthetic rapture, the joy of being the kind of being that can experience the beauty of being aware.

In Chapter Eight we encountered this teaching of the Great Truth in abbreviated form. Here it appears in a more complete version (and an even more complete version will appear in Chapter Twelve). As before, let's unpack what Kṣemarāja is talking about by way of example.

Let's say you're at a music concert with a good friend. It's a band that's supposed to be really great, but you are not so familiar with them, and so you're drawn to catch up with your friend while sipping your drink with the music playing (rather loudly) in the background. Then, the band enters an improvisational section (it's that kind of band), and the music gets more and more inspired until it finally catches your attention when your conversation reaches a natural pause. This is the phase called 'manifestation' (*ābhāsana*): suddenly, a reality that had been vague and peripheral becomes central, and the whole quality of your awareness changes. (Of course, the manifestation of this music-consciousness is coterminous with the dissolution of the conversation-consciousness you were previously experiencing.)

Your attention is drawn toward the stage and the complex interplay of the musicians, and you become completely focused on their spontaneous group creation. Other thoughts fall away as you become absorbed in the play of light and sound on the stage. Your consciousness is now profoundly 'colored' by the music; or more accurately, it forms itself into a musical experience. It is suffused with the music, which takes on greater depth and nuance than before. This is the phase called 'attachment' in the sūtra (but note that we could also translate *rakti* as 'enjoyment' or 'devotion'). In this phase, you are not even aware of yourself, you are so immersed in your perception.

Then, perhaps when the song starts to draw to a close, awareness spontaneously reverts inward, and you become *aware of yourself as the one who has been absorbed* in the music. This is the phase called 'subjective awareness' (*vimarśana*) in the sūtra. You pause for a second in pure wordless apprehension of your experience (*camatkāra* moment), and then a thought-form rises like a bubble to the surface of consciousness, and then you turn to your friend and say, "Wow! These guys are really good!"—which of course is just a way of saying *I like this*, which in its essence is actually an acknowlegement of yourself as the conscious agent of the experience, i.e., "*I am the enjoyer* [of the current reality]." Kṣemarāja tells us that the preverbal moment of subjective awareness is, or can be, a moment of *camatkāra*—sweet savoring, aesthetic rapture, or pure wonder. The articulation of the thought is the bursting of the bubble, the anticlimax after the ineffable moment of aesthetic rapture. It is the transition from experience to representation of experience, and thus it is also the manifestation that initiates the next cycle (which, since it began with a thought, is likely to be a mental one).[74] If we don't learn how to rest in subjective awareness, we usually miss the opportunity to experience *camatkāra*. And that opportunity arises with the internalization of *each and every experience.*

We have used the example of a music concert, which you may or may not relate to. But we equally could have used the example of a fragrant bouquet of flowers, or delicious food, or a disgusting smell, or a loving caress, or witnessing a street fight, or anything else that absorbs your attention. If you like, compare this passage with the parallel ones near the end of Chapter One and Chapter Eight to see how Kṣema is emphasizing different things each time, changing the angle of the light he sheds as it were.

Before we go on to the fourth and fifth of the Five Acts of awareness, let me say a little more about *camatkāra*, or aesthetic rapture. 'Rapture' does not mean excitement or ecstasy; here it refers to being raised out of one's habitual consciousness in an intensified moment of awareness that results from internalizing an experience of beauty. But here we have a terminological problem, because the word 'beauty' does not suggest the range of experiences that these philosophers have in mind. *Camatkāra* is a term from aesthetic philosophy that refers to the sheer wonder of being that one accesses in connection with any experience that intensifies and absorbs awareness. So this includes things we find erotic, amusing, terrifying, disgusting, outrageous, inspiring, astonishing, or peaceful, as well as the traditionally beautiful.* Any of these can be an aesthetic experience.[75] Indeed, according to Tantrik philosophy, virtually *any* cognition can have a *camatkāra* moment, a moment of experiencing the pure wonder and beauty of being. In other words, the Tāntrika learns to access the beauty of being in the context of any given experience.

Kṣemarāja tells us that the *camatkāra* moment results from the dissolution of object-consciousness (which is focused on the music, the flower, or whatever) *into* one's innate subjective presence. It is the moment just after the conclusion of a moving poem and before one has a thought about the poem. For that moment, you simply abide in awareness, in your own presence, suffused with the beauty of the poem. You experience an ineffable 'poem-flavored' consciousness. If you learn to see everything, not just poetry, as beautiful, then you can have countless such moments every day. For this, we must go beyond our conditioned ideas of beauty; we must go beyond what the mind is conditioned to 'like'. We must thoroughly let go our resistance to what we don't like to see the beauty in it. Resistance is nothing but commitment to your conditioning. If you want wonder, beauty, and joy to become the leitmotifs of your life, you must become willing to allow the experience, whatever it is, to totally dissolve into the silent presence that you truly are.

---

* The list I give here is a traditional one; see *Tantra Illuminated*, page 303.

Then you discover that Awareness is fascinated by everything, by the whole range of experience. It's fascinated by an attractive form, and by the body-mind's pull toward that form. But it's also fascinated by the repulsive. It's fascinated by stillness and by activity, by emptiness and by fullness, and by grief as much as by joy. This is apparent to everyone who really gets to know the most intimate part of themselves. It's kind of in love with everything.

This kind of intimacy with our deepest nature is not really possible as long as we are viewing the object/person/experience as distinct from ourselves. Kṣemarāja then quotes a verse on this point from a Tantrik poet called Śrī Rāma, whose work has now been lost.

**As it was said by the venerable Rāma,**

> **The mountain of duality cannot be shattered by others, even with the thunderbolt** (*vajra*) **of deep meditation** (*samādhi*)**—but, by those who are endowed with the strength deriving from devotion to You,** [Goddess Awareness,] **as soon as it is recognized as an aspect of themselves** (*parāmṛṣṭa*)**, it is dissolved.** ||

Just as a lightning bolt cannot shatter a mountain, even achieving the *samādhi* state of deep meditation does not overcome duality; of this we have countless examples. However, those who are devoted to Goddess Awareness, to seeing everything as a form of consciousness, are nourished with a powerful strength, by virtue of which they can (in time) recognize anything as an aspect of the one true Self that they are. The moment they do, it dissolves into them, unleashing the joy of *camatkāra*.

This verse is inspired by an old Kashmiri *chummā*, or mystic saying, in the oral tradition of the Siddhas: "No sooner seen than gone" (*diṭṭo niṭṭo*). The moment something is seen for what it truly is, its separateness dissolves. But instead of the simple word 'seen', Śrī Rāma uses the technical term *parāmṛṣṭa*, which means to become intimately aware of, to recognize (something) as an aspect of oneself. It is both beautiful and significant that the root of this word is *mṛś*, 'to touch'. To touch in deeply to anything is to recognize oneself in it, and it in oneself. For this to happen, we must be devoted to Goddess Awareness; such devotion expands our sense of self until it encompasses everything. Such devotion is mightier than a thunderbolt and softer than silk. It brings such openness of heart that anything and everything is allowed in, all the way in. When anything is fully allowed in, the beauty of being reveals itself.

What happens, then, when resistance is our normal mode of being? When we are invested in the illusion of control, and try to manage our experience? What happens when we push away pain and grip onto pleasure? When experiences are not fully allowed in, just as they are? These questions lead us to the fourth phase, that of concealment, or 'laying down the seed'.

**But when, despite being dissolved** [into oneself]**, the experience of the object deposits internally various impressions** (*saṃskāra*) **such as anxiety** (*śaṅkā*) **and so on, then it is established in the state of concealment, becoming a 'seed' of worldly experience** (*saṃsāra*) **that will arise again.**

When something is pleasurable, we get anxious it won't last, and when something is painful, we get anxious it won't go away. This anxiety is an expression of resistance to reality. When any experience is resisted, it does not dissolve completely, but leaves behind a trace of itself called a *saṃskāra*, which literally means 'impression'. Before we discuss the nature of *saṃskāra*s in more depth, let us look at the movement of consciousness that creates them. Whenever we turn away, even partially, from what is happening in the present moment because it is too uncomfortable, too painful, or even too wonderful, it creates a *saṃskāra*. When we resist reality, don't show up, go unconscious, or 'check out', then we don't fully receive the experience, we don't allow it to fully pass through our being, and that is why it leaves an impression.

Have you ever turned away from what someone was trying to share with you because you didn't want to deal with it? Have you ever pushed your pain or loneliness away with alcohol, television, or anything else? Have you ever met someone's eyes and saw such intense love there that you had to look away? All these incidents, and many others like them, leave behind the impressions called *saṃskāra*s, which we could also call 'unfinished energy patterns'. It's almost as if *everything* wants to be fully seen; everything seeks the light of awareness, so if you turn the light down, if you go partially unconscious, an impression is formed in your energy body that will need to be seen and resolved later.[76]

In Tantrik theory, we each have a 'subtle body', also known as an energy body or emotional body, already mentioned above on page 152. Each experience we have is a kind of energy pattern that passes through our subtle body, so it stands to reason that only those experiences that are resisted in some way leave an impression. These impressions are of two basic varieties. Experiences that we turn away from because they are uncomfortable or painful leave *saṃskāra*s of aversion, and those we resist by clinging to them leave *saṃskāra*s of attachment. The second variety might need more explanation. If an experience is very pleasurable, we instinctively cling to it, thinking something like "I don't want this to end." Because of this clinging, the 'energy pattern' of the experience cannot freely pass through your being, so it leaves an impression. On the other hand, if the experience is quite pleasurable but not as wonderful as you want it to be, you might think, "If only it were more like *this* or less like *that*," and in this way you don't fully show up for *what is*, and therefore the unresolved experience leaves an impression. Each impression has a kind of energetic charge that will express when the *saṃskāra* is later activated, as discussed below.

The example of emotional charge Kṣemarāja gives is carefully chosen: *śaṅkā*, meaning anxiety, doubt, or inhibition, can characterize almost any type of impression. Impressions of painful experiences are charged with the fear of possibly having similar experiences in the future, while those of pleasurable experiences can be laced with anxiety about the transient nature of all feelings of happiness. The first causes aversion when activated, and the second, grasping. These *saṃskāra*s are metaphorically called 'seeds' because, like real seeds, they can lay dormant for a short or long time until the conditions are right, and then they sprout. That is, when along comes a situation that even superficially resembles that in which the *saṃskāra* was implanted, it is activated and surfaces in the form of aversion, attachment, or emotional reactivity.

For example, if your parent(s) yelled at you when you were young, someone yelling at you in a similar way now will trigger far more aversion in your being than it would for someone else who didn't have a yelling parent. The earlier experience that wasn't digested is now triggered and amplifies the unpleasantness of the present-moment experience. Likewise, if you meet someone who resembles a former infatuation, the 'one who got away', you'll feel an attraction that is amplified by the unresolved impressions of the previous love affair. Thus you end up having reactions that are disproportionate to the present-moment reality, because you are simultaneously reacting to what is present *and* to the unresolved past experiences hanging out in your system. In more extreme examples (which are actually very common), you are reacting much *more* to the past than to the present, and the *saṃskāra*s obscure your vision so much that you can't correctly gauge their distorting effect. It is crucial to understand that prior to substantial psychological work and/or spiritual practice, you are frequently projecting the past onto the present without even knowing it.

To sum up, not fully showing up for painful experiences creates *saṃskāra*s that, when later triggered, give rise to aversion in your body-mind; while not fully showing up for pleasurable experiences *as they are* creates *saṃskāra*s that, when later triggered, create grasping attachment in your body-mind. If you always act on your aversion and grasping, the samskāric patterns will deepen in a vicious cycle, creating fear-based behavior patterns in the first instance and addictive behavior patterns in the second. These *saṃskāra*s are concealed within the subtle body and can even block the flow of *prāṇa*, life-force energy. They are, Kṣema tells us, "seeds of *saṃsāra* that will sprout again". (*Saṃsāra* means both 'worldly experience' and 'the cycle of suffering'.) Inevitably, all your *saṃskāra*s will be triggered by your various life experiences. But that is your golden opportunity: when a *saṃskāra* is triggered, it can be healed, resolved, dissolved, and/or released. That is the fifth phase, the phase of revelation, resolution, and grace, to which we now turn.

**However, when something that has been internally deposited in this way, or even something that is actually being experienced now, becomes one with the Fire of Consciousness through the process of 'sudden digestion' (*haṭha-pāka*), also known as the method of 'total devouring' (*alaṅgrāsa*), then it is said to be *graced*, because it has been integrated into the state of complete fullness (*pūrṇatā*).**

Whenever a *saṃskāra* is triggered, you have an opportunity to resolve it, at least partially. Such resolution is characterized by Kṣemarāja as "becoming one with the Fire of Consciousness [*cid-agni*]". Consciousness is here compared to a fire because, like fire, it devours the fuel of emotions, thoughts, and experiences, releasing energy. The process by which this occurs is called *haṭha-pāka*, 'sudden digestion'. This special term comes from the Krama tradition,[77] which teaches that when the emotional energy of a *saṃskāra* is activated, if we are able to hold it gently, seeing that it is nothing but another form of the same divine Awareness that manifests as all things, then that energy is suddenly 'digested' rather than simply getting buried again. The key word in the last sentence, 'seeing', does not denote a cognitive operation but something much subtler. When the energy contained within the *saṃskāra* arises, we can choose to simply be fully present with it, relax into it, and even embrace it (without identifying with it and without making a story about it), and in this way we open the door to experiencing it as a form of divine Consciousness. Why use the term 'digestion', though? Because the energy of the *saṃskāra*, which had been partitioned off within one's being, now merges with the greater whole. Since the *saṃskāra* was deposited due to nonacceptance of reality, when its energy is fully accepted, it releases that energy and your whole being is subtly enhanced and magnified by it. If you are in a process of digesting a lot of *saṃskāra*s, as happens at a certain stage of the spiritual life, then you can palpably feel the enlargement and enhancement of your energetic being.

A popular phrase in many spiritual scenes these days is "Let go of that which doesn't serve you." But in Tantrik Yoga, we don't want or need to let go of our energy—we want to absorb and digest it, so that we can serve all beings with greater vitality and love. Besides, if you even can let go of your energy of anger, fear, or sadness, where is it going to go? Energy cannot be destroyed; you can only push it back down inside you or dump it on others. But there is something that needs to be released: to digest the energy, you need to let go of the story associated with it.* For example, if you are angry because you believe someone wronged you, you need to see that story *as* story, as a thought in the mind that arbitrarily labels experience on the basis of past conditioning, and then release it so that you can be intimate with the feeling of anger itself. When you release the story, sometimes that will change the emotion. For example, some anger is actually story-generated, and when the story is released, the anger will morph into sadness. We are always trying to access the underlying energy; that is what we want to digest. Those who believe sadness is a 'negative emotion' will be surprised to learn (and even more surprised to experience) that if you actually digest the sadness, it adds to your feeling of aliveness—like all forms of energy, when digested it increases your vitality and enhances your capacity to love. There is no such thing as a negative emotion, for if there was, digesting the emotion would deplete you. If you ever feel depleted by the digestion process, it's because you were unable to separate the story from the emotion. With time, delinking stories from emotions becomes easy, but at first it can be very difficult. One of the most effective (though oversimplified) teachings about how to do this is The Work by Byron Katie. You can learn the teaching from her website (thework.com), which has all the tools you need to do The Work. But any method that is effective for you is fine; there is no one way.

Some people get the idea that *saṃskāras* are something bad, that you have them only if you failed to properly process your experience, because you were psychically weak. This is not really the case; or rather, it's close to the truth, but there is no self-denigration necessary because we *all* start out with a weak energy body just as we all start out with a weak physical body. We all carry childhood wounds because children by definition cannot fully process a painful experi-

* To be more accurate, certain kinds of stories get released and instantly dissolve (because they were so unrelated to the truth of the situation), while other stories need to be seen as stories and then digested (because they have an element of truth in them). Another example of this difference is that stories taken on from others (internalization of someone else's story about reality) can simply be released, while stories that you built up yourself need to be digested. The latter often need to be worked through and deconstructed some before they can be digested; this is like the chewing of your food that makes it easier for the body to digest.

ence; their energy bodies are just not mature enough. Therefore, the unprocessed pain is stored in *saṃskāras* to be digested later when the energy body has matured. This is indeed a mercy and a miracle, this capacity we have to move through a difficult experience by storing some of it for later resolution. However, a yogī must eventually digest these *saṃskāras*, even if she has already become a fully functional adult, because on this path we seek not just functionality but integration and deep fulfillment. Without digesting and resolving these past experiences, we remain fragmented, partial versions of ourselves.

Kṣemarāja tells us that the method for digesting a *saṃskāra* and that for digesting a new experience that is happening to you is exactly the same. If you digest a present-moment experience, it will not deposit a *saṃskāra*. In other words, if you can be fully present to what you are feeling in the moment, without judging it or making a story about it, then you will 'devour' the energy. Just as with physical food, the excess energy will pass through you, and the rest will merge into the Fire of Consciousness and amplify your total being. Now here is another clue about how you can facilitate this: there is an inner attitude that will make 'total devouring' of the energy much more possible for you. That attitude is *camatkāra* (amazement or wonder), a term that was introduced earlier in this chapter. When one is experiencing an intense energy, whether it be sadness, anger, joy, boredom, or whatever, you can let yourself become fascinated by this particular appearance of consciousness. Let your attitude be one of wonder and curiosity: "Wow! My mind is totally freaking out right now! That's amazing! I wonder why it's reacting so strongly when everything's actually okay?" or something similar. This attitude cannot be forced, but it can be cultivated. You can let yourself become fascinated by your own emotional reactions in the same way that you get fascinated by a brilliant street performer or, for that matter, a raving crazy person. You can learn to watch the energy surging up inside and the stories the mind tells about it, without believing or disbelieving them, but being curious about where it's all coming from (without needing to analyze it mentally). In this way, you see the play of thoughts and feelings as patterns of energy, and therefore you're better able to digest them. This is called riding the wave of *camatkāra* to enter into the *alaṅgrāsa* process.[78]

So *haṭha-pāka* (sudden digestion) and *alaṅgrāsa* (total devouring) are synonyms, both being technical terms of the Krama. These terms were unintentionally echoed by the great twentieth-century nondualist Nisargadatta Mahārāj, who was unfamiliar with the Tantrik literature but reached the same conclusions about the nature of reality as a result of his awakening. He once said:

> Knowing the world to be a part of myself, I pay it no more attention than you pay to the food you have eaten. While being prepared and eaten, the food is separate from you, and your mind is on it; once swallowed, you become unconscious of it. I have eaten up the world, and I need not think of it anymore.
>
> Questioner: Don't you become completely irresponsible?
>
> How could I? How could I hurt something that is one with me? On the contrary, without thinking about the world, whatever I do will be of benefit to it. Just as the body sets itself right unconsciously, so am I [and all awakened beings] ceaselessly active in setting the world right.

We see similar language in the 900-year-old Krama/Mahārtha text called *Mahānaya-prakāśa* ('Illumination of the Great Way'), a primary source for the teaching on sudden digestion, which says that through *haṭha-pāka*, the whole world seems to dissolve, because its dependence on consciousness—indeed the fact that it is nothing but [different forms of one] consciousness—is revealed.[79]

This process instantiates the fifth of the Five Acts: grace, revelation, remembering, reintegrating, revealing. Kṣema tells us that a *saṃskāra* or current experience that is digested in this way and thus becomes one with the Fire of Consciousness is thereby said to be *graced*, "because it has been integrated into the state of complete fullness". When we saw it as other than ourselves (because we didn't like it and wanted to get rid of it or because we did like it but saw it as external or impermanent and therefore grasped at it), its energy was largely unavailable to us. When we welcome it, whatever it is, into the heart, jettisoning our mental projections about it and letting ourselves be intimate with it exactly as it is, then its energy merges with our own and the Fire of Consciousness blazes brighter. We then experience our natural fullness, and perhaps glimpse the truth that the experience arose within us simply because everything seeks the Light of Consciousness;

everything seeks to be bathed in the loving light of true awareness, and when it is, it integrates, melting into the light, and you experience sheer wonder at the realization that *you* are the means by which different forms of energy return to their source. You only need to learn to allow what naturally wants to happen.

**Though this fact of being the performer of the Five Acts is present to everyone all the time, it is not revealed without the instruction of a true Master. Thus the propitiation of a true Master ought to be pursued by those whose goal is this revelation. ||**

These Five Acts—manifestation, attachment, subjective awareness, laying down the 'seed', and (sooner or later) dissolving it—are just what we are all doing all the time. But the dynamics of the process and its significance are not readily apparent to all. This powerful Krama teaching suggests that our liberation is in the palm of our hand, and it unfolds through developing a deep understanding of the fundamental processes that consciousness is constantly cycling through. To develop this understanding, it is crucial at the outset to have a teacher who can point it out to you.

Let us remember that in ancient times, this teaching was esoteric, held by awakened masters who communicated it only in person to those who were deemed ready to receive it. This is why Kṣemarāja advises us to propitiate a true Master (*sad-guru*). Of course, Rājānaka Kṣemarāja was himself such a Master, and therefore the book you are holding is itself an example of the transmission he speaks of. We are fortunate indeed to live in a time when these teachings are finally accessible to all.

However, no book can replace the transformative power of relationship with a teacher who has integrity and clarity of view. While the path can unfold without a teacher, it happens only rarely, because there are stages of the journey that are very difficult to traverse without expert guidance and support. It is thus highly beneficial to position yourself as a student with regard to anyone you meet who has walked more of the path than you have *and* is able to clearly transmit teachings that help you get unstuck and reveal where you are holding yourself back. The traditional Tantrik path assumes that a several-year relationship with one or more qualified teachers is an absolute necessity on your journey.

Now, most people think that the ideal teacher or *guru* is 'enlightened' or fully awake. And the tradition does say that if you are lucky enough to meet someone who has actually completed the journey, then such a being's very presence is itself the highest teaching and transmission. The problem is that you cannot accurately assess whether someone has completed the journey unless you have yourself—but this is not such an important problem, because (thank goodness) your awakening process is not dependent on your teacher's. To think otherwise is to disempower yourself. A teacher who can transmit a taste of their inner state is helpful, but not required. Remember that the role of the teacher is not to do the work for you, but simply to point you in the right direction. (This is crucial because no matter how fast you run, it won't make a difference if you're facing the wrong direction!)

It also must be said that Western yoga practitioners have to date had a very distorted and/or incomplete understanding of what a Master is, and these wrong understandings have led some to reject discipleship as a part of the path. But in reality, someone is called a Master because he (or she) has mastered *himself*, not because you are expected to blindly obey such a being. In fact, a true Master doesn't give orders, and constantly seeks to make you more independent, not more dependent. In other words, a true teacher is always trying to put himself out of a job! He wants to give you all the help you need to graduate from student to friend and peer. Needless to say, any teacher who takes advantage of his students, deceives and manipulates, or cannot control his impulse to grope a woman is not a true Master (*sad-guru*). A real teacher is your ally and friend on the path. You can read more about the traditional understanding of the teacher in *Tantra Illuminated* (pages 341*ff*).

In conclusion, I invite you into the awareness that resolving your *saṃskāras* and integrating your experiences is a process that serves all sentient beings. Though the mind cannot begin to understand this, every experience you integrate makes it more possible for other beings to do the same. It is a great service.

*Contemplation Exercise*

Inspired by the possibility of liberating all beings, resolve now to allow yourself to be with and accept whatever arises within you. You don't need to go looking for things to accept—just resolve, "Whatever Goddess Awareness shows to me for my acceptance, I will receive it with loving (or at least nonjudgmental) awareness. I will allow it to be, I will affirm my capacity to digest it, and I will allow it to integrate."

Now very briefly visualize the *saṃskāra*s lodged in your subtle body dissolving one by one. With each integration visualize the light of the central channel growing brighter and brighter. Visualize that through the course of your practice your *saṃskāra*s are being absorbed into the central channel. The central channel is getting bigger and brighter until that light of the central channel penetrates your whole being. Your whole being is the center. That light pours out to bless others. All the love you have in your heart pours out to bless others.

This concludes our study of Sūtra Eleven and its commentary.

यस्य पुनः सद्गुरूपदेशं विना एतत्परिज्ञानं नास्ति,तस्य अवच्छादितस्वस्वरूपाभिः निजाभिः शक्तिभिः व्यामोहितत्वं भवति ।–इत्याह

तदपरिज्ञाने स्वशक्तिभिर्व्यामोहि-
तता संसारित्वम् ॥ १२॥

'तस्य' एतस्य सदा संभवतः पञ्चविधकृत्य-कारित्वस्य 'अपरिज्ञाने'–शक्तिपातहेतुकस्वबलोन्मीलनाभावात् अप्रकाशने 'स्वाभिः शक्तिभिः व्यामोहितत्वं'–विविधलौकिकशास्त्रीयशङ्काशङ्कुकीलितत्वं यत्, इदमेव 'संसारित्वम्'। तदुक्तं श्रीसर्ववीरभट्टारके

'अज्ञानाच्छङ्कते लोकस्ततः सृष्टिश्च संहृतिः ॥'

इति ।

'मन्त्रा वर्णात्मकाः सर्वे सर्वे वर्णाः शिवात्मकाः॥'

इति च । तथा हि–चित्प्रकाशात् अव्यतिरिक्ता नित्योदितमहामन्त्ररूपा पूर्णाहंविमर्शमयी या इयं परा वाक्शक्तिः आदि-क्षान्तरूपाशेषशक्तिचक्रगर्भिणी, सा तावत् पश्यन्ती-मध्यमादिक्रमेण ग्राहकभूमिकां भासयति । तत्र च पराारूपत्वेन स्वरूपम् अप्रथयन्ती मायाप्रमातुः अस्फुटासाधारणार्थावभासरूपां प्रतिक्षणं नवनवां विकल्पक्रियामुल्लासयति, शुद्धामपि च अविकल्पभूमिं तदाच्छादितामेव

# CHAPTER TWELVE

*Kṣemarāja's original text*

However, one who does not have the teaching of a true teacher and therefore does not have full understanding of this is thoroughly deluded by his own powers, because their true nature is concealed. Thus it is taught:

**When one lacks realization of this,**
**one exists in the state of a *saṃsārin*:**
**that of being deluded by one's own powers.** || 12 ||

**When one lacks realization** of the fact that one is constantly performing the Five Acts, i.e., when that fact is not apparent to you because the unfolding of your inner strength, brought about by the Descent of Power, has not yet occurred, then you **exist in the state of being deluded by your own powers.** This state of delusion is one of being nailed down by the 'spikes' of various anxieties, doubts, and inhibitions, both worldly and religious. It is *this* that constitutes the state of being a *saṃsārin.*

As it is said in the sacred and venerable [scripture called] *Union of All Heroes,*

> People are anxiously inhibited out of ignorance; because of it, there is creation and destruction [of limited realms of experience]...
> All mantras are sounds, and all sounds are Śiva. |

To explain: the Supreme Power that is the Word is not different from the Light of Awareness, has the nature of the continuously arising Great Mantra, consists of fully expanded 'I'-consciousness, and is pregnant with the entire circle of fifty powers from *a* to *kṣa.*

That same Power manifests the role of the limited perceiver through the Visionary, Intermediate, and Corporeal stages of the articulation of the Word. In that process, by not manifesting Herself in Her highest nature, She brings into play the differentiating cognitive activity of the limited perceiver. This activity changes moment-to-moment, and creates pictures of reality that are unclear and unshared. Moreover, this causes the prediscursive level—though it is always pure—to appear concealed by that cognitive activity.

दर्शयति। तत्र च ब्राह्म्यादिदेवताधिष्ठितककारादिविचित्रशक्तिभिः व्यामोहितो देहप्राणादिमेव परिमितम् अवशम् आत्मानं मन्यते मूढजनः। ब्राह्म्यादिदेव्यः पशुदशायां भेदविषये सृष्टिस्थिती, अभेदविषये च संहारं प्रथयन्त्यः, परिमितविकल्पपात्रतामेव संपादयन्ति; पतिदशायां तु भेदे संहारम्, अभेदे च सर्गस्थिती प्रकटयन्त्यः, क्रमात्क्रमं विकल्पनिर्ह्रासनेन श्रीमद्भैरवमुद्रानुप्रवेशमयीं महतीम् अविकल्पभूमिमेव उन्मीलयन्ति।

> '[22]सर्वो ममायं विभव इत्येवं परिजानतः।
> विश्वात्मनो विकल्पानां प्रसरेऽपि महेशता॥'

इत्यादिरूपां चिदानन्दावेशमग्नां शुद्धविकल्पशक्तिम् उल्लासयन्ति। ततः उक्तनीत्या स्वशक्तिव्यामोहिततैव संसारित्वम्।

किंच चितिशक्तिरेव भगवती विश्ववमनात् संसारवामाचारत्वाच्च वामेश्वर्याख्या सती, खेचरी-गोचरी-दिक्चरी-भूचरीरूपैः अशेषैः प्रमातृ-अन्तःकरण-बहिष्करण-भावस्वभावैः परिस्फुरन्ती, पशुभूमिकायां शून्यपदविश्रान्ता

And in this context, unaware people—who are deluded by the various powers of the classes of phonemes, which are animated by the Mother goddesses—identify themselves only with limited aspects of the Self (the body, *prāṇa*, etc.), because they are powerless to do otherwise.

In the state of the bound soul, these goddesses manifest emission and stasis of the sphere of duality and retraction of the sphere of nonduality, and thereby make a person into a vessel for limited dualistic cognitions (*vikalpas*).

However, in the state of the Lord, they manifest retraction of duality and the emission and stasis of nonduality. By the gradual diminishing of *vikalpas*, they cause the great Unconstructed Domain to open up; which is synonymous with entry into the sacred *Bhairava-mudrā*.

> One whose self is the whole, knowing fully that "All this
> is the expansion of what I am," experiences the divine
> state even in the flow of differential cognitions. ||

As taught in statements such as this, the goddesses of one's own awareness bring into play the power of 'pure' mental constructs: a power that is utterly saturated with the Joy of Awareness.

Therefore, by the principle taught here, **the state of being a *saṃsārin*** is nothing other than **that of being deluded by one's own powers.**

Moreover, the Supreme Goddess, who is simply the Power of Awareness, is called Vāmeśvarī because She pours forth (*vam*) the universe and because Her flow counters (*vāma*) the cycles of suffering.

She vibrates as the totality, in the form of the goddesses Khecarī, Gocarī, Dikcarī, and Bhūcarī, who respectively are the inner nature of the subjective knower, the mental faculties, the outer faculties, and the objects of awareness.

On the level of the bound soul, first reposing in the state of the Void:

2) She shines forth as the Khecarī-circle, consisting of the powers of the five '*armors*' (limited agency etc.), thereby concealing Her ultimate nature, which is to move freely in the sky of Awareness.

किंचित्कर्तृत्वाद्यात्मक-कलादिशक्त्यात्मना खेचरीचक्रेण गोपितपारमार्थिकचिद्गगनचरीत्वस्वरूपेण चकास्ति; भेदनिश्चयाभिमान-विकल्पनप्रधानान्तःकरणदेवीरूपेण गोचरीचक्रेण गोपिताभेदनिश्चयाद्यात्मकपारमार्थिकस्वरूपेण प्रकाशते; भेदालोचनादिप्रधानबहिष्करणदेवतात्मना च दिक्चरीचक्रेण गोपिताभेदप्रथात्मकपारमार्थिकस्वरूपेण स्फुरति; सर्वतो व्यवच्छिन्नाभासस्वभावप्रमेयात्मना च भूचरीचक्रेण गोपितसार्वात्म्यस्वरूपेण पशुहृदयव्यामोहिना भाति। पतिभूमिकायां तु सर्वकर्तृत्वादिशक्त्यात्मकचिद्गगनचरीत्वेन, अभेदनिश्चयाद्यात्मना गोचरीत्वेन, अभेदालोचनाद्यात्मना दिक्चरीत्वेन, स्वाङ्गकल्पाद्वयप्रथासारप्रमेयात्मना च भूचरीत्वेन पतिहृदयविकासिना स्फुरति। तथा च उक्तं सहजचमत्कारपरिजनिताकृतकादरेण भट्टदामोदरेण विमुक्तकेषु

> 'पूर्णावच्छिन्नमात्रन्तर्बहिष्करणभावगाः।
> वामेशाद्याः परिज्ञानाज्ञानात्स्युर्मुक्तिबन्धदाः॥'

इति। एवं च निजशक्तिव्यामोहिततैव संसारित्वम्।

3) She manifests as the Gocarī-circle, consisting of the goddesses of the three mental faculties, i.e., those predominantly concerned with dualistic judgment, egoic identification, and selective differentiating attention; thereby concealing her ultimate nature, which is to manifest a nondual mode of judgment, nondual ego, and undivided attentiveness to the whole field of perception.
4) She vibrates as the Dikcarī-circle, consisting of the divinities of the ten external faculties, which predominantly see dualistically, hear dualistically, and so on; thereby concealing her ultimate nature, which is to manifest these sense-fields in a nondual mode.
5) She shines as the Bhūcarī-circle, consisting of objects of awareness that appear thoroughly differentiated, thereby concealing the fact that Her/your true nature is one with everything,

thus deluding the heart of the bound soul.

But on the level of the Lord, She vibrates:
2) as Khecarī, moving in the Sky of Awareness, with her powers of total agency and the rest;
3) as Gocarī, whose nature is nondual judgment, nondual ego, and holistic attention;
4) as Dikcarī, whose nature is nondualistic vision, hearing, and so on; and
5) as Bhūcarī, whose nature is to manifest objects of awareness in their nondual essence, as if part of one's own body;

thus revealing the Heart of the Lord.

A similar idea is taught by Bhaṭṭa Dāmodara—who had a genuine enthusiastic devotion created by spontaneous aesthetic rapture—in his *Pearls of Liberation*:

> The five goddesses, Vāmeśvarī and the rest—manifesting as the expanded and limited knowers, the inner and outer faculties, and objects of experience—bestow liberation or bondage, depending on whether they are recognized or not. ||

In this way as well, **the state of being a *saṃsārin* is** nothing but **that of being deluded by one's own powers.**

अपि च चिदात्मनः परमेश्वरस्य स्वा अनपायिनी एकैव स्फुरत्तासारकर्तृतात्मा ऐश्वर्यशक्तिः। सा यदा स्वरूपं गोपयित्वा पाशवे पदे प्राणापान-समान-शक्तिदशाभिः जाग्रत्स्वप्न-सुषुप्तभूमिभिः देह-प्राण-पुर्यष्टककलाभिश्च व्यामोहयति, तदा तद्व्यामोहितता संसारित्वम्; यदा तु मध्यधामोल्लासाम् उदानशक्तिं, विश्वव्याप्तिसारां च व्यानशक्तिं, तुर्यदशारूपां तुर्यातीतदशारूपां च चिदानन्दघनाम् उन्मीलयति, तदा देहाद्यवस्थायामपि पतिदशात्मा जीवन्मुक्तिर्भवति। एवं त्रिधा स्वशक्तिव्यामोहितता व्याख्याता। 'चिद्वत्' इति (९) सूत्रे चित्प्रकाशो गृहीतसंकोचः संसारी इत्युक्तम्, इह तु स्वशक्तिव्यामोहितत्वेन अस्य संसारित्वं भवति,—इति भङ्ग्यन्तरेण उक्तम्। एवं संकुचितशक्तिः प्राणादिमानपि यदा स्वशक्तिव्यामोहितो न भवति, तदा अयम्

'...............शरीरी परमेश्वरः।'

इत्याम्नायस्थित्या शिवभट्टारक एव,—इति भङ्ग्या निरूपितं भवति। यदागमः

'मनुष्यदेहमास्थाय छन्नास्ते परमेश्वराः।'

इति। उक्तं च प्रत्यभिज्ञाटीकायाम्

'शरीरमेव घटाद्यपि वा ये षट्त्रिंशत्तत्त्वमयं
शिवरूपतया पश्यन्ति तेऽपि सिध्यन्ति'

इति॥ १२॥

Moreover, the Highest Divinity which is Awareness has an innate, constant, unitary Power of Sovereignty, consisting of an agency whose essence is vibrant dynamism.

When that Power, concealing its true nature, functions delusively on the level of the bound soul, it does so through the various states of the energies of *prāṇa*, *apāna*, and *samāna*; through the levels of waking, dreaming, and deep sleep, and through the limited powers of the body, subtle body, and Prāṇa. In that context, one exists in the state of a *saṃsārin*, i.e., that of being deluded by identification with those [states, levels, and powers].

But when she unfolds the energy of *udāna*, which activates the central Radiant Abode, and the energy of *vyāna*, whose essence is its capacity to pervade everything—corresponding to the state of the transcendent Fourth and Beyond the Fourth respectively, both replete with the Joy of Awareness—then arises liberation-while-living, the state of the Lord, even under the conditions [imposed by] the body, mind, etc.

Thus, the state of delusion by one's own powers has been explained in three ways. In the Ninth Sūtra, it was stated that the *saṃsārin* is none other than the Light of Awareness having taken on contraction; here, the same thing is said from another angle, i.e., that one enters the state of a *saṃsārin* by means of delusion by one's own powers.

Thus, I have indirectly taught that when one whose powers are contracted—because s/he has *prāṇa*, a body, etc.—is not deluded by those powers, that person is Lord Śiva himself. This is affirmed by scriptural tradition, e.g.:

> He is the Highest Divinity in bodily form.

Also in scripture:

> They are the Highest Divinity in disguise, having taken on human bodies.

And, in my *parameṣṭhī guru* Utpala's commentary on his own *Stanzas on the Recognition of the Divine*:

> They are perfected who see their very body, or even pots and other objects, as the form of God, composed of all thirty-six *tattvas*. ||

## CHAPTER TWELVE

*with explanation*

**However, one who does not have the teaching of a true teacher and therefore does not have full understanding of this is thoroughly deluded by his own powers, because their true nature is concealed.**

In this tradition, there is no outside agency (like the Devil or Māra) responsible for your delusion or your suffering. When you do not understand the nature of the powers and capacities of your own consciousness, they function to delude you rather than liberate you. But as soon as you truly understand your own innate capacities, and the way in which you (the real you) are constantly performing the Five Acts, then the very powers that previously effected your bondage now liberate you.

**Thus it is taught:**

|| TAD-APARIJÑĀNE SVA-ŚAKTI-VYĀMOHITATĀ SAṂSĀRITVAM || 12 ||

**When one lacks realization of this** [truth],
**one exists in the state of a *saṃsārin*:**
**that of being deluded by one's own powers.**

**When one lacks realization of the fact that one is constantly performing the Five Acts, i.e., when that fact is not apparent to you because the unfolding of your inner strength, brought about by the Descent of Power (*śaktipāta*), has not yet occurred, then you exist in the state of being deluded by your own powers.**

Remember that the Descent of Power (specifically, the Power of Grace) is the spontaneous awakening that inaugurates the spiritual path. Once this *śaktipāta* has taken place, the spiritual path naturally and inevitably unfolds, while you assist its unfolding through some actions (like spiritual practice and awareness cultivation) and hinder its unfolding through others (like indulging in addictions, believing your stories, and clinging to your self-images). However much you hinder it, the process initiated by *śaktipāta* will inevitably complete itself (though not necessarily in this lifetime).

Awakening assisted by spiritual practice grounded in 'right View' (understandings aligned with the nature of Reality) brings about the 'unfolding of your inner strength' (*svabala-unmīlana*), also known as your 'soul power' (*ātma-śakti*). With this inner strength, which is also an inner *maturity*, you become willing and able to see how you create your moment-to-moment experience, including all your suffering and all your boredom and all your joy. You have matured beyond the tendency to externalize and project, to blame others and thus assume the stance of a victim. When you see that you alone are the author of your own inner experience, that in turn strengthens your 'soul power' further, in a positive feedback loop that grants you radical autonomy, empowerment, and self-determination. If you use that power to reinforce your ego, you become what we call the oral tradition calls a 'sorcerer', a path that has considerable karmic consequences, not least of which is alienation and the inability to access the natural joy that comes from loving connection to all other beings. However, if you use that power to surrender your ego forever into the Fire of Consciousness, that joy beyond measure suffuses your being and you can never be deluded again. Yes—it's really possible to reach a point of no return, to pass through the 'Gateless Gate' beyond which the ego does not have the ability to resurrect itself. Then you fall in love with the whole of reality, experiencing everything as your very own blessed Self.

In our time, very few humans have gone through the whole process just described. Most are deluded about the source of their suffering and the possibility of their liberation, almost constantly playing the game of blame and shame, without realizing that the difference between bondage and liberation lies in understanding (or rather grokking) the innate potencies of their very own awareness.

Now let's take stock of where we are in the arc of the text. Chapters One and Two described the absolute nature of reality, then we went through a gradual stepping down process describing how universal consciousness contracts (see especially Chapters Five and Six) until we reached the central core of the text. That core is Chapters Nine through Twelve. Chapters Nine and Twelve describe the ordinary human condition, prior to awakening (*saṃsāritva*)—yet nestled between them are Chapters Ten and Eleven, which show how even in the state of suffering and delusion and ego, Awareness never relinquishes its essential nature and is still constantly performing the Five Acts. Therefore, anyone given the proper tools can start from wherever they are, and, on the basis of careful introspection, can, with patience and courage, unravel their false views and find their way to a fully expanded experience of their real nature. Chapters Thirteen to Twenty will chart this process with breathtaking precision and brevity, until we arrive back where we started, at the absolute nature of reality—except this time it will be *integrated* and *embodied*. We will come full circle, and when we do, we will fully *know* and abide in that eternal starting and ending point.

Now Kṣemarāja takes a moment to describe the effect of the state of delusion (i.e., the state that most of us dwell in most of the time):

**This state of delusion is one of being nailed down** [and thus paralyzed] **by the 'spikes' of various anxieties, doubts, and inhibitions (*śaṅkā*), both worldly and religious. It is *this* that constitutes the state of being a *saṃsārin*.**

Those people who don't yet sense their innate freedom and power to determine their own inner state (because they are not yet in touch with the inner strength by which they would sense it) tend to view themselves as a victim of karma, fate, circumstance, others, or 'the system'. Because they believe the world of their experience is determined from without, not from within, they are fraught with mostly subconscious anxiety about how to behave and how not to behave, seeing these 'shoulds' and 'shouldn'ts' as the rules of the game they must abide by or else suffer. This leads to a state of anxious inhibition concerning what ought to be done and ought not to be done.

In the original Indian context, this situation was much more severe than modern Westerners can imagine. There was an endless litany of things that you were supposed to do (injunctions) and not supposed to do (prohibitions) based on (a) your caste; (b) your stage in life (e.g., student, married householder, renunciate); (c) the time of day, month, or year; and (d) the place (village, home, temple, ritual arena, wilderness, etc.). Based on these four factors, there were rules about what is permissible to eat and what is not, what is permissible to look at and what is not, what is permissible to touch and what is not, and so on. Those members of mainstream society who contemplated entering the Tantrik path of freedom and awakening from one's cultural conditioning were beset by the fear of losing their habitual sense of self (*ātma-śaṅkā*), anxiety about practicing with non-Vedic mantras (*mantra-śaṅkā*), inhibition concerning mingling with people from other castes or classes of society (*jāti-śaṅkā*), and fear or doubt in exposing themselves to a radically different vision of reality (*tattva-śaṅkā*).[80] No wonder Kṣemarāja characterizes the average person in his society as virtually paralyzed by the 'nails' of inhibition, doubt, and fear (*śaṅkā*).

However, is our situation really so very different? We assume that we're better off for having far fewer rules—when in fact this creates *more* anxiety. Without a set of agreed-upon guidelines, we aren't sure how to behave in many situations and are beset by anxiety concerning what others will think of us in our awkwardness (or our false bravado). Well over half of all Americans are said to suffer from 'chronic low-level anxiety' as a default state of being. Most of us try to orient ourselves and generate a sense of security by attaching to a self-image that defines a code of behavior. When inhibition gets tied to self-image, it extends into all the domains that Kṣemarāja alludes to: I'm a vegan, I can't eat that (animal); I'm a red-blooded American, I don't eat ('rabbit food'); I'm spiritual, I don't look at (TV); I'm a down-to-earth person, I don't listen to that (hippy-dippy spiritual stuff); and so on. In this way, a deep undercurrent of fear and inhibition is translated into a prideful self-image, which serves to conceal how very frightened we are about how to navigate the currents of an overwhelming world. Sometimes this self-image is more subtle, sometimes less—but in any case, its self-righteousness always conceals anxiety. How amazing!

Furthermore, there are both culturally and religiously programmed forms of anxiety and inhibition, as Kṣemarāja points out. We have just seen examples of the former; examples of the latter might be: I'm a yogī, so I can't eat meat or onions or garlic; I'm a Christian scientist, so I can't take medicine; I'm psychically sensitive, so I can't be under fluorescent lights or near electromagnetic fields; I'm spiritual, so I wouldn't go to a Super Bowl party; I'm Jewish, I couldn't marry a Gentile; I'm a Christian, I can't do yoga; and on and on. When we consider both cultural and religious forms of inhibition in our society, you begin to see that our situation isn't so very different from that of

India 1,000 years ago, except that we don't have the security of always knowing what's expected of us and what others will be comfortable with, and therefore we frequently find ourselves defending our identity or feeling ashamed of it. What madness, when all such identities are mental constructs! We can acquire so many inhibitions that we paint ourselves into a corner and might become increasingly averse to leaving the house at all, or straying outside of very familiar territory (physically or emotionally). In another example, I have known people who forbid themselves to eat anything that might be unhealthy or that comes from a morally dubious source, and they end up anxious and inhibited, not able to share a meal with friends, and eating within an increasingly restricted range until they begin to waste away, surviving it seems only on their self-righteousness as they down their blue-green algae, pale and wan.

This is not the Kaula way. On this path, we seek to strengthen the energy body through yoga so that we have the power to digest *any* experience (or, for that matter, any food). Though we do not choose to eat processed food or seek out the company of those who frequently speak negatively, we want to be able to digest the experience when we are in those contexts, without judging others or setting ourselves apart. Since we know that it is habitual not occasional action that shapes our emotional and physical health, once that robust health is established we need not rigidly cling to *always* and *never*. While we default to choosing heathful and sustainable modes of eating and behaving, we don't want to be anxious or obsessed; we want to be able to move through the world freely, without needing to close down or cringe away from whatever presents itself. Kaula Tantriks like Kṣemarāja taught that those who 'starve' the goddesses of the senses by needlessly restricting their intake (on the basis of self-image or conditioning) become enslaved by those very goddesses, by those powers of awareness. Instead we are invited to learn to see a wider and wider range of our experiences as an expression of divine beauty, and to lovingly feed that beauty to the sense-goddesses, that they may bestow their blessing of an ever-increasing capacity to experience the beautiful. (Of course, this is a teaching not generally given to hedonists, because it can be grossly misused in their case to justify addictive or compulsive behavior.)

Kṣema next quotes a Kaula scripture to support his case. This scripture is now lost to us, but we can add a little bit to the quote that he gives us, since a fuller version of it is cited in other sources—and he probably assumed that his readers knew this quote, and he need only remind them of the first couple of lines.

**As it is said in the sacred and venerable** [scripture called] ***Union of All Heroes*** (*Sarva-vīra-samāyoga*)**,**

> **People are anxiously inhibited out of ignorance; because of it, there is creation and destruction** [of limited realms of experience].
>
> [*For example, why this orthodox inhibition against practicing Tantrik mantras? After all,*]
>
> **All mantras are sounds, and all sounds are Śiva.**
>
> [The quote continues:] All beverages, whether they 'ought to be drunk' or 'ought not to be drunk' are equally forms of the element Water; whatever 'ought to be eaten' or 'ought not to be eaten', it is all Earth; whatever is beautiful or ugly, it is all visible Light; whatever 'ought to be touched' and 'ought not to be touched', understand it to be nothing but the element Wind, and every bodily aperture or opening is merely Space. One who offers food to the Deity, [whatever it is,] receives blessed food. Everything [in the sensual world] without exception consists of the five [Elements]. The self generates desire [freely]; why should it be inhibited? ||[81]

This quote has already been adequately explained above, apart from the traditional associations of the five Elements with the sense-faculties (Wind with touch, Fire with visible appearance, and so on). Note that though Kṣema expects his readers to be familiar with the full quote that I have given here, he only explicitly quotes the line "all mantras are sounds, and all sounds are Śiva"—which gives him a perfect lead-in to the next section.

Kṣema's prose up to this point has merely been the preamble to this, the longest chapter in his work. He now explains Sūtra Twelve in three ways: according to the linguistic mysticism of the Kaula Trika, according to the Krama's teaching of the five Flow Goddesses, and according to the Recognition (*pratyabhijñā*) school's teachings on yoga. This will be a bit heavy going for those who are not serious students of Śaiva Tantra, and you can no doubt safely skip ahead to Chapter Thirteen and read the rest of this chapter on your second go-through of the book.

The Kaula Trika Reading

**To explain: the Supreme Power that is the Word** (*parā vāk śakti*) [a] **is not separate from the Light of Awareness,** [b] **has the nature of the** continuously arising **Great Mantra** ['I'], [c] **consists of fully expanded 'I'-consciousness, and** [d] **is pregnant with the entire circle of fifty** [phonemic] **powers from *a* to *kṣa*.**

To explain how we are deluded by the powers of our own awareness, Kṣema first has to explain what those powers are.

First, he starts by invoking the Supreme Goddess (Parā Devī) as the Power of the Word (*vāk-śakti*; from the Greek *logos*), that is to say, *the power of consciousness to represent itself to itself*, especially in the form of thought and speech. This power, he tells us, naturally inheres within the Light of Awareness (*cit-prakāśa*), which is another way of saying that consciousness instinctively engages in self-representation—and another way of saying Śiva (the Light of Awareness) and Śakti (its Power of Reflection or Representation) are one.

Second, he tells us that the fundamental form of this Power of the Word is the 'continuously arising Great Mantra (*mahā-mantra*)', which, though he doesn't tell us so here, is AHAṂ, which means 'I' or 'I am' in Sanskrit. Here the term 'mantra' is being used in an esoteric way. We are not being advised to repeat the word AHAṂ; rather, Kṣema is saying that the deepest, most subtle, most fundamental form of the Divine Word is the *basic sense of one's own existence*, the wordless awareness that one has of one's own being, the innate subjectivity that is experienced by all sentient beings in every moment. We know he means this because he says that the Great Mantra is 'continuously arising' (*nityodita*)—and the sense of one's own being is the only constant in the ever-changing flux of human experience.[82] This teaching anticipates that of more recent masters like Ramana Maharṣi and Nisargadatta Mahārāj, who advises us to attend to the fundamental sense of 'I am' that underlies all experience.

Third, he tells us that the Supreme Word "consists of the fully expanded 'I'-consciousness" (*pūrṇāhaṃ-vimarśa*), a beautiful phrase subtly layered with meaning. It primarily refers to the *awareness of the all-inclusive 'I'*, a felt sense of oneself as including and encompassing all that one perceives. This, we are told, is the true 'I'—any sense of 'I' that is not all-inclusive is merely a mental construct. But the phrase *pūrṇāhaṃ-vimarśa* can also be translated as:

» the reflective awareness 'I am whole/complete/perfect', *or*
» the awareness of the perfectly full 'I', *or*
» the perfected 'I'-consciousness.

The last translation is seen in an extraordinary poem cited without attribution by Gurumayī Chidvilāsānandā in her book *Kindle My Heart*:

Where has my ecstasy brought me?
It has brought me to a place
Where nothing is left but the pure 'I',
*Pūrṇāham-vimarśa*, the perfect 'I'-consciousness.
Now I know what my existence is all about:
Nothing remains but the ecstasy of my true Self.

It is so astonishing and so unique!
I have not taken a drink, but I feel so intoxicated.
There is no one except *pūrṇāham-vimarśa*,
the perfect 'I'-consciousness.
My Guru's grace did a wondrous thing:
It ripped open the veil of duality.[83]

This phrase, then, refers to an experience of unity-consciousness, whereby the adept feels "There is nothing that is not my Self," where 'Self' refers not to the personal self but a pure sense of Being without limitations or labels, without all the mind-created divisions and boundaries.

Fourth, the Goddess that is the Supreme Word is described by Kṣemarāja as 'pregnant' with the 'circle' of all the powers (*śaktis*) from *a* to *kṣa*, which is to say the Sanskrit alphabet ('*a* to *kṣa*' is equivalent to an English speaker saying 'A to Z'). In the linguistic mysticism of the Trika, the fifty phonemes of the Sanskrit syllabary (≈ the sounds of the alphabet) are thought to express and embody the powers and principles that make up all of reality through their endless combinations (thirty-four *tattvas* + sixteen fundamental *śaktis* = fifty).[84] These fifty powers combine and recombine in 'interference patterns' that, when interpreted through the sensory apparatus of embodied conscious beings, give rise to the total range of phenomenal experience. The Goddess that is the Supreme Word is 'pregnant' with all these powers in the sense that She contains them all in embryonic form (as well as in full expression)—thus 'the Word' (*vāk*) really means the fundamental *pattern* of reality, the pattern that makes possible both language and the experiences of phenomena to which language refers.

Language, or rather discursive thought, is also fundamental in the formation of dualistic consciousness and the illusion of personal selfhood, Kṣema tells us:

**That same Power manifests the role** (or level) **of the limited perceiver** (*māyā-pramātā*) **through the Visionary, Intermediate, and Corporeal** [stages of the articulation of the Word]**.**

Since the Word is the fundamental pattern of reality, it also manifests as the mind, the limited perceiver, the personal self (these three terms being near-synonyms). As discussed in Chapter Six, the limited perceiver is one who takes duality and difference to be fundamentally real, seeing things in terms of me *versus* you, us *versus* them, good *versus* bad, and so on. Such a view of reality is constructed through language, so it is appropriate that Kṣema says that the limited perceiver is constructed *through* the stages of linguistic formation. These three non-ultimate levels of the Word are explained on pages 166–173 of *Tantra Illuminated*. Briefly, the Visionary, Intermediate, and Corporeal stages are the levels of subconscious conditioning (socially and culturally constructed belief patterns engraved at a deep level), of mentalese (the fragments of language and imagery with which the conscious mind thinks to itself), and of spoken (or written) language respectively. Conditioned discursive thought not only shapes how we experience reality, but even creates our sense of separate self. Your very sense of who you are is largely constructed out of everything anyone ever said to you about yourself, along with a flood of culturally constructed images of what a boy or girl or man or woman or white person or black person is *supposed* to be like in general. And, you might notice if you reflect on it now, when other people described you, they never actually told the truth. They didn't know how. For example, instead of saying "I don't feel pleasure when I look at your face, though that surely has more to do with me than with you," they say "You're ugly." Instead of saying "I feel pleased and appreciative when you help me solve my problem," they say "You're smart." And out of these very distorted expressions of the truth, we build a sense of self, an image of who we are, a mental world filled with shameful self-images we hope to live down and prideful self-images we have to live up to. We live in and from this world. Is it any wonder we suffer so much? This socially constructed self is a limited perceiver in the sense that she cannot see herself as she really is, nor can she see reality as it truly is.

**In that process, by not manifesting Herself in Her highest** (*parā*) **nature, She brings into play the differentiating cognitive activity** (*vikalpa-kriyā*) **of the limited perceiver. This activity changes moment-to-moment, and creates pictures of reality that are unclear and unshared.**[85]

'She' here is still the Supreme Word, the fundamental patterning of reality, appropriately personified as a Goddess because that pattern is not separate from universal Consciousness. In her contracted or non-ultimate form, she brings into play the cognitive activity that divides up the world into categories shaped by language. This dualistic cognitive activity or 'thought' represents the world of direct experience, but nowhere near as accurately as we like to think it does. This internal representation of reality is unstable, unclear, and unshared, but we tend to see it as much more stable, clear, and universally applicable than it really is.

To explain, the world of discursive thought (*vikalpa*) with which the mind represents reality is just like the world of dreams. Dreams are unstable and ever fluctuating, usually hazy and distorted, and usually the products of a single mind separated from other minds. Our mental world is just the same, with the key difference that we *know* dreams are distorted and unreliable pictures of reality, but we take our thoughts and opinions to be more or less accurate representations of reality. A little reflection shows us that our thoughts and opinions are (a) always changing, (b) usually not clearly reasoned-out and tested against reality, and (c) precisely what divide one from all other human beings, since no one else shares exactly the same set of opinions and views. Since our thoughts and opinions about things are unstable, not clearly defined, and idiosyncratic, why do we put so much stock in them? Why do you argue your point of view so vehemently, and believe others to be wrong about the objective reality that apparently you alone see accurately? Why, in relating to others, do we sacrifice human connection to the idol of being 'right' or 'justified' more often than not? Why do we define ourselves through the thoughts called 'self-images'? Why do we feel so frightened when we are shown, even briefly, that everything we think about reality and ourselves is a veil of illusion?

When dreams do convey truth, they do so via pointers, via metaphor rather than literalism. The mind-world is the same. It's not that there is no truth to be found there: it's that thoughts, when they are something more than white-noise, reveal truth in terms of their form rather than their content. That is, we can find truth by investigating 'where' the thought is arising from, 'where' it might be leading us, how it makes us feel, and the quality of 'vibration' it has (warm/cool, hard/soft, smooth/spiky, sweet/sour, etc.), not the literal words it has to say.

*Contemplation Exercise*

Investigate a thought or story that is troubling you or that you are attached to. If you consider the thought as a vibration of energy, what are its qualities? If it had a temperature... If it had a color... If it had a texture... If it had a smell...

If you believe this thought, what does reality feel like? How do things appear to you from within the thought? If you believe this thought, how are you likely to behave?

If this thought is really an expression of an unresolved experience from your past, and/or an unexamined self-image, which experience or self-image is it likely to be?

Now consider: what if the fact that a thought *feels* true doesn't mean that it is true? What if there is no truth to the thought *per se*, but it is true that it can lead you to more suffering or greater joy? Which thoughts do you want to hold close, and which do you want to lay aside?

Now Kṣemarāja reaches his key point in the section, that sums up the thesis he wishes us to consider:

**Moreover, this causes the prediscursive level** [of direct experience]—**though it is always pure** [undifferentiated awareness of reality]—**to appear concealed by that cognitive activity.**

Though we believe we directly contact the world-as-it-is through our senses, in fact that prediscursive, unconstructed (*avikalpa*) level of reality remains mostly inaccessible, concealed as it is by the countless ways we project our subconscious beliefs about reality onto reality. In considering this subtle teaching, we must understand that even general categories and labels like 'tree' and 'man' are beliefs. Living as we do from the mind-world, we are more likely to see a tree as just another instantiation of the category 'tree', dissimilar in only minor particulars to other trees we have seen, than as an irreducibly unique, miraculously complete, patterned manifestation of life energy in perfect harmony with its total environment. A botanist who loves trees sees them more clearly and fully (note the connection between love and increased awareness), but still tends to categorize them into classes like beech, oak, elm, pine, and sees them in terms of those categories. Our obsession with names, labels, and diagnoses shows the extent to which we strive to feel in control by reducing each irreducible experience to known and relatively safe categories.

In certain magical moments, however, we glimpse reality-as-it-is, and those are among the most precious of our lives. In those moments, we see that reality is immeasurably more vivid and immediate, more sharp and clear, more real and present, more undivided and intimate, than the world seen through the mind-filter. Sometimes those moments are forced upon us and we are broken open to the truth, as when we witness a birth or death, and other times they sneak up on us and feel like a gift of grace. Sometimes, people who have this experience of clear seeing in fullness say that everything is 'opened up' or 'laid bare' and they themselves feel naked, but unafraid because everything is 'naked'. In this clear seeing, then, reality-as-it-is stands unconcealed and unfiltered, exquisitely—for some unbearably—intimate.

In opposition to the common view in psychology today, this philosophy argues that a continuous or nearly continuous direct experience of reality, free from all mental filters, is possible. It is precisely this that we call awakeness or Awareness (*bodha*) in nondual Tantra.

*Awareness Cultivation Exercise: Easy Access to Nonduality*

Reality is simple. It's delusion that's complicated. Nondual perception is easy to access: just take a quick sidestep out of your habitual dualistic perception. Remember: reality is whatever's happening *before* you have a thought about it. So just ask yourself, with real curiosity:

*What's the quality of this moment before I have a thought about it?*

When the resulting experience is no longer fresh (which is always because labels have consciously or subconsciously crept in), then ask the question again. Every time you ask the question with honest intent, really curious to know the answer, you immediately experience nondual reality for at least a moment. It may also work to ask,

*Who am I, really? What is 'me'?*

If you're ready to ask that question, that is, if you really want to know the answer, there comes a moment of stillness or blankness or openness right after asking. In that moment lies the wordless answer. Keep visiting that moment. *Feel* it open up to you. Feel it connect to everything.

Kṣemarāja continues:

**And in this context, unaware people—who are deluded by the various powers of the** [eight] **classes of phonemes, which are animated by the** [eight] **Mother goddesses beginning with Brāhmī—identify themselves only with limited aspects of the Self** (the body, *prāṇa*, etc.)**, because they are powerless to do otherwise.***

In this sentence we find both theological and philosophical points. Here the Goddess of the Supreme Word subdivides into the ancient

* Or we could translate this as "**they think themselves limited and powerless, being only the body, breath, etc.**"

Eight Mother Goddesses, each one seen as presiding over and animating a subset of the Sanskrit alphabet, which here stands in for all language generally. What is the point to divinizing language in this way? Sometimes we feel helpless and at the mercy of our own negative thoughts or 'sticky' stories; in those moments, for some it can help to pray to the Mother Goddesses for the ability to see through the stories and recognize which emotional states are story-generated and which are spontaneously arising. Historically, Tantrik philosophy probably linked the phonemes of language to these preexisting Mother Goddesses partially because images of them were ubiquitous all over India at that time, and every time the initiate 'in the know' saw them, he or she would be reminded of this powerful teaching: that misidentification with one of the limited aspects of selfhood is a function of mental constructs based in language, and cannot persist once the latter are uprooted. We have already considered how this works: believing thoughts like "I'm fat" or "I'm skinny" reinforces identification with the body, believing thoughts like "I'm smart" or "I'm stupid" reinforces identification with the mind, and so on. What is extraordinary to contemplate is the teaching that, when these beliefs are seen through and thus dissolved, identification with a limited aspect of the self can no longer continue, and without such identification, one's true wholeness, one's radiant being, automatically stands revealed.

Finally, language is here divinized as the goddesses that reside within all of us because that serves to remind us of the basic teaching that delusion is a condition of being deluded by our own powers. We become deluded by our power of thinking when we believe the contents of our thoughts instead of encountering them as forms of energy (remember that *śakti* means both 'goddess' and 'energy'). To emancipate ourselves from this mental slavery, we take advantage of every avenue available: we contemplate and meditate and self-reflect, we identify the stories while allowing the release of the raw emotion, we digest the self-images and the *saṃskāra*s, and having done all this inner work, sometimes all that is left to us is to open to the power of grace, letting our longing be naked and raw, and coming to our knees, pray to the Mother Goddesses that we may finally be free of our self-delusion and confusion.

For those interested in all the geeky details, this is the schema that in all probability Kṣemarāja had in mind (though the order of the goddesses is uncertain):

| Mother Goddess | Phonemes |
|---|---|
| Brāhmī | the velar class (k, kh, g, gh, ṅ) |
| Māheśvarī | the palatal class (c, ch, j, jh, ñ) |
| Kaumārī | the retroflex class (ṭ, ṭh, ḍ, ḍh, ṇ) |
| Vaiṣṇavī | the dental class (t, th, d, dh, n) |
| Vārāhī | the labial class (p, ph, b, bh, m) |
| Indrāṇī | the semivowels (y, r, l, v) |
| Mahālakṣmī | the sibilants (ś, ṣ, s) |
| Cāmuṇḍā | kṣ |

In this schema, Śiva is the vowels (a, ā, i, ī, etc.) and the goddesses are the consonants, for only by joining a consonant and vowel does one have a pronounceable phoneme. So just as Śiva and Śakti, awareness and energy, come together to manifest the world of our experience, vowels and consonants joined together create the building blocks of language with which we represent that experience.

In summary, then:

**In the state of the bound soul, these goddesses** [of language and thought] **manifest emission and stasis of the sphere of duality and retraction of the sphere of nonduality, and thereby make a person into a vessel for limited dualistic cognitions** (*vikalpas*).

**However, in the state of the Lord, they manifest retraction of duality and the emission and stasis of nonduality. By the gradual diminishing of *vikalpas*, they cause the great unconstructed** (*avikalpa*) **domain to open up; which is synonymous with entry into the sacred *Bhairava-mudrā*.**

How do the very same powers that condition us to see in a limited, distorted, and dualistic mode also cause us to connect with reality-as-it-is, free of all cognitive distortion? In other words, how do the same powers that bind us also liberate us? Briefly, the same powers of awareness that allow us to construct mental models of reality also allow us to see that they *are* mental models, and not reality itself. When we see clearly that our stories are just stories, that is, conditioned frameworks of interpretation with no necessary relationship to reality itself, we begin to become free of them. When we stop looking for truth in our mental models and conditioned thoughts, their power begins to weaken and diminish. Then the 'great unconstructed domain', the *avikalpa-bhūmi*, begins to open up, which means that you increasingly access direct experience of reality prior to all interpretation. Here 'unconstructed' refers to *what is* before we construct any interpretation or narrative about it (we could also translate *avikalpa* as 'prediscursive').

Kṣemarāja tells us that this is the state which the tradition calls the *Bhairava-mudrā*, where *mudrā* refers not to a position of the hands but a disposition of one's whole being; an attitudinal posture, if you will. In traditional iconography, Bhairava is depicted with wide-open eyes, so in this mudrā that bears his name (also known as *śāmbhavī mudrā*), one sees the external world clearly while remaining grounded in the inner reality. Bhairava's wide-open eyes also suggest the sense of wonder or astonishment (*camatkāra*) which frequently accompanies direct perception of reality. As one goes deeper into direct perception, into the great unconstructed domain, it becomes undeniably apparent that the dichotomy of self versus not-self is actually a mental construct, and that in reality, everything is an expression of what you are, and what you truly are contains everything. In this state of *Bhairava-mudrā*, one of my teachers commented, "Consciousness perceives everything as the outflow of its own stainless internal identity." This is why Kṣemarāja next quotes this verse from his great-grand-teacher's masterpiece:

> **One whose self is the whole, knowing fully that 'All this is the expansion of what I am', experiences the divine state even in the flow of differential cognitions.** || [*Stanzas on the Recognition of the Divine* IV.12]

In pre-Tantrik yoga, such as the *Yoga-sūtra* of Patañjali, it was argued that the flow of cognitions needs to cease for the practitioner to see the Truth. In this nondual View, however, by recognizing your true nature as infinitely malleable autonomous Awareness itself, one comes to recognize all phenomena as an expression of that true nature. Therefore, differentiating cognitions (*vikalpas*) have no power to rob you of this true self-awareness: they are seen as nothing but another permutation of the One energy, the singular power of Awareness, no more and no less significant than a cloud or a blade of grass. Utpala Deva describes the felt-sense of this experience with the phrase *sarvo mamāyaṃ vibhava*,

'All this is the expansion of what I am', or 'This whole is [simply] the expansion of [the real] me'. In other words, there's nothing but what's looking out of your eyes: everything is a perfect expression of what you are. (This, then, is a first-person statement of *pūrṇāham-vimarśa*, 'the fully expanded "I"-consciousness', discussed above.)

You might have already thought of a significant objection to this teaching: if mistaking mental representations of reality for reality is such a key 'problem' in the spiritual life, then how can we understand the role of these spiritual teachings? However beautiful sounding, are not they, too, mental constructs, and therefore problematic? Is not this critique of *vikalpa*s itself a *vikalpa*? To address this implicit objection, Kṣemarāja now invokes the teaching of his guru, Abhinava Gupta: there is such a thing as a *śuddha-vikalpa*, a mental construct that accurately points toward reality. Though it is true that no *vikalpa* can capture or encompass the truth, some point us in the right direction and some don't. Just as a compass is different from the North Pole, yet unerringly enables us to find the North Pole, the spiritual teachings do not express or explain reality (which is inexpressible), yet they unerringly enable us to find our way to the direct experience of reality. Such carefully considered, fine-tuned, well-aligned articulations that point us toward truth are called *śuddha-vikalpa*s, 'pure' mental constructs.

**As taught in statements such as** [the above]**, the goddesses** [of one's own awareness] **bring into play the power of 'pure' mental constructs: a power that is utterly saturated with the Joy of Awareness (*cid-ānanda*).**

From the awakened perspective, the power that Awareness has to represent itself to itself is a form of creativity or art: it delights in crafting words (or other forms of representation) that, while failing to capture the truth, point in its direction. As Picasso said so well, "Art is a lie that makes us realize the truth." Though even the best words can only point in the right direction, there is something deeply satisfying in a pointer that 'clicks', that is aligned with the actual pattern of Reality. However, we should always remember that the pleasure we derive from well-articulated representations of the truth is but a pale shadow of the joy of direct experience. However fascinating and delightful a model train set is, you can't ride that train; however well drawn the blueprint of a house, you can't live in the blueprint. The spiritual teachings bear only as much relationship to Truth as the blueprint of a house does to an actual house.

Finally, remember that only direct experience can give rise to truly reliable pointers. The blueprint analogy breaks down on that point, because in this case, only one who has seen the 'territory' with his own eyes can draw a map to that territory.

**Therefore, by the principle taught** [here]**, the state of being a *saṃsārin* is nothing other than that of being deluded by one's own powers.**

The key teaching of the sūtra is fundamentally empowering: if you are deluded only by, and about, the powers of your own consciousness, then you can become truly and totally free of that delusion. We'll find out more about *how* you become free in Chapters Sixteen to Eighteen. Now we proceed to the second of Kṣemarāja's three interpretations of Sūtra Twelve.

The Krama Reading

**Moreover** [there is another way of interpreting the sūtra, in accordance with the Great Truth]**: the** [Supreme] **Goddess, who is simply the Power of Awareness, is called Vāmeśvarī because She pours forth** (*vam*) **the universe and because Her flow counters** (*vāma*) **the cycles of suffering** (*saṃsāra*).

This interpretation is grounded in the Kālīkula lineage of the Krama, also known as the Mahārtha or 'Great Truth' (see *Tantra Illuminated*, page 248*ff*). In this inflection, the Supreme Goddess who is universal Awareness is called by the name Vāmeśvarī, for the two reasons Kṣemarāja gives. (This is an example of a *nirukta*, an explanation of why the Sanskrit name for something is appropriate.) Note the symmetry of the teaching here: on the one hand, Goddess Awareness pours forth the whole world of experience, and on the other, She draws us inward to the core of being, in a flow that naturally counters the movement of the cycle of suffering. These two complementary flows define Her essential nature. Yet She also vibrates into being as all the aspects of embodied consciousness and the objects of its experience:

**She vibrates as the totality, in the form of the** [four other] **Flow Goddesses [2]Khecarī, [3]Gocarī, [4]Dikcarī, and [5]Bhūcarī,* who respectively are the inner nature of the [2]subjective knower, [3]the mental faculties, [4]the** [ten] **outer faculties, and the [5]objects of awareness.**

The singular Power of Awareness vibrates in ever-denser frequencies of manifestation as individual subjects like you and I, their faculties, and all the 'objects' of experience (including intangible objects like feelings) that their faculties contact. These are worshiped in this system as expressions of the Goddesses named above, who in ancient times were thought to rule over spirits of the sky, animals, and the earth, and who acquired a new identity and function in the sophisticated Krama school. I am using superscripted numbers to help you keep easy track of what corresponds with what; they start with #2 because #1 is always Vāmeśvarī, transpersonal Awareness, the ground of the whole process. Now Kṣemarāja explains how these four 'goddesses' express themselves in two modes: the mode of partial concealment, and the mode of the full revelation, respectively called the condition of the 'bound soul' (*paśu*) and the condition of 'the Lord' (*pati*), since these terms are inherited from the earlier tradition.[86]

**On the level of the bound soul,** [first] **reposing in the state of the Void** [then taking on successively greater degrees of contraction]**,**

2) **She shines forth as the Khecarī-circle, consisting of the powers of the five *kañcukas* (limited agency, etc.), thereby** [partially] **concealing Her ultimate nature, which is to move freely in the Sky of Awareness.**

Why is Awareness said to 'repose in the state of the Void' prior to manifesting itself as the levels of everyday embodied consciousness? In this system, the inner Void is the locus of the root of individuality, because individuality is not ultimately real. (It is this doctrine that makes nondual Śaiva Tantra stand a little closer to Buddhism than to Hinduism.) Having set the context, Kṣemarāja then maps the levels of increasing 'densification' of Awareness. The first circle of powers

* Literally, She who moves in the sky, She who moves over the range, She who moves in all directions, and She who moves on the earth.

(*śakti-cakra*) is that of Khecarī (pronounced KAY-char-ee), and these are none other than the five 'armors' or 'veils' (*kañcukas*) already discussed in Chapter Nine. These are limited powers, and therefore they partially conceal Khecarī's ultimate nature, which as her name implies is to roam unimpeded in the 'Sky of Awareness', the unlimited realm of infinite possibility in which Awareness fully knows itself. In terms of the five-layered self model, the Khecarī-circle is associated with *prāṇa* or life-force, because all embodied living things are limited by the five *kañcukas*. The next level corresponds to the mind and the subtle body:

> **3) She manifests as the Gocarī-circle, consisting of the goddesses of the three mental faculties, i.e., those predominantly concerned with dualistic judgment, egoic identification (*abhimāna*), and selective differentiating attention (*saṅkalpana*); thereby concealing her ultimate nature, which is to manifest a nondual mode of judgment, nondual sense of self, and undivided attentiveness to the whole field of perception.**

The three faculties mentioned are *buddhi*, *ahaṃkāra*, and *manas* under different names (see *Tantra Illuminated*, pages 129–133). Here Kṣema introduces an intriguing teaching: that liberation does not entail the annihilation of ego and judgment, but rather their reconfiguration in a nondual mode. Dualistic judgment, which causes suffering, appears in the nondual mode as skillful discernment; a kind of discernment based in utility, not discrimination. In other words, discerning that in a given context (such as the pursuit of a specific aim) some things are effective and others are not does not require one to label the former as 'good' and the latter as 'bad', nor does it require one to perceive one thing as less expressive of the Divine than another. Thus discernment can operate in a nondual mode. Similarly, though self-referencing and egoic identification causes suffering, it is possible to retain a sense of self in a nondual mode: the experience of the all-inclusive 'I' (*pūrṇāham-vimarśa*). Self-referencing ceases to cause pain only when *everything* is equally seen as a manifestation of the Self. Finally, the mind's attention is normally pulled this way and that, picking and choosing among the sense-field on the basis of its saṃskārically encoded attachments and aversions, fixating on some things (or people) and neglecting others;

whereas attention in the nondual mode gives itself to the whole sensory field, awake and alert to whatever calls for response without necessity for the belief that any one thing is intrinsically more important than any other.

> 4) **She vibrates as the Dikcarī-circle, consisting of the divinities of the** [ten] **external faculties, which predominantly see dualistically,** [hear dualistically,] **and so on; thereby concealing her ultimate nature, which is to manifest these sense-fields in a nondual mode.**

This, of course, is the level of the body. For the five sense-faculties and the five faculties of action, see *Tantra Illuminated*, page 128. What is it like to see or hear or taste nondualistically? Whatever you see, you see it as an expression of what you are; whatever you hear, you hear as a vibration of your own Self; whatever you taste, it tastes like another flavor of the one Consciousness; whatever you touch, it feels like God in another form. It is also possible to walk in a nondual mode, to speak, to make love, even to have a bowel movement in a nondual mode (for these are the *karmendriyas* or faculties of action), though Kṣema invites us to consider these possibilities without spelling them out.

> 5) **She shines as the Bhūcarī-circle, consisting of objects of awareness that appear thoroughly differentiated, thereby concealing** [the fact that] **Her/your true nature is one with everything; thus deluding the heart of the bound soul.**

This is the level of the actual 'stuff' that populates the field of awareness; the 'known' as opposed to the 'knower' (#2 above) or the faculties of knowing (#3 and #4 above). While the prior levels of manifestation had five, three, and ten components respectively, the Bhūcarī-circle is infinite, for it is comprised of all possible objects of awareness, whether tangible or intangible. In the mode of concealment, these objects appear to be thoroughly differentiated from each other and from the awareness that contacts them; it is not obvious to the individuated experiencer that everything she experiences is a vibration *within* awareness and a vibration *of* awareness. The appearance of a world external to awareness—something 'other' which forces itself upon awareness—is just that, an appearance. Belief that how things appear to the conditioned mind is how they actually *are* is the delusion that pains the heart of the bound soul; indeed, it is what defines a bound soul. However, the same powers of awareness that operate in the mode of concealment can also operate in the mode of revelation already alluded to at every step.

**But on the level of the Lord, She vibrates**

> **2) as Khecarī, moving freely in the Sky of Awareness, with her** [five] **powers of total agency and the rest;***
> **3) as Gocarī, whose nature is nondual judgment, nondual ego, and holistic attention;**
> **4) as Dikcarī, whose nature is nondualistic vision, hearing, and so on; and**
> **5) as Bhūcarī, whose nature is to manifest objects of awareness in their nondual essence, as if part of one's own body;**[87]

**thus revealing the Heart of the Lord.**

As already noted, 'the level of the Lord' is simply antiquated language for the mode of revelation or grace (*anugraha*). The very same Goddess Awareness Vāmeśvarī in Her full expansion expresses as the four other Flow Goddesses joyously articulating their innate potential to operate in a fully nondual mode. In actuality, the nondual mode is constantly being expressed, though initial encounters with it certainly feel like a revelation. The truth is always hidden in plain sight; the kingdom of heaven is spread out upon the earth, though people don't see it.[88] Indeed, once you experience for yourself that everything is internal to awareness and is a vibration of the same awareness that you fundamentally are, it is sometimes hard to understand why everyone doesn't see it. What else could any given object possibly *be* if not a vibration of awareness? The thought that anything could be 'other' is too bizarre for words. Someone once asked Jed McKenna, "So there isn't a universe external to consciousness?" and he replied, bemused, "Of course not! Where would they *put* it?" That quip always makes me smile.

---

* See Chapter Nine.

So the 'Heart of the Lord' being referred to here is simply Awareness in its natural state: clear and open, unsullied by any trace of superimposed conditioned beliefs, and delighting in its seamless unity with all things, all things being the direct expression of its stainless essence. From the perspective of that Heart, all objects of awareness are as if part of one's body. To put it another way, the whole world and everything in it is your body, insofar as you have a body. What you habitually call your body is simply the set of sensations that occur in the center of a vast field of harmonically vibrating energy, all internal to your awareness.

This is why Kṣemarāja juxtaposes 'the deluded heart of the bound soul' with 'the expanded Heart of the Lord' (note that the word translated as 'revealing' above can also be rendered 'expanding'): it is the same reality seen from the perspective of two very different paradigms. From the conditioned perspective, consciousness is in your brain and your brain is in your body and your body is in the world, which exists independently of you. From the awakened perspective, everything is within consciousness and is an expression of what you are, and that seems as clear and obvious as anything could be.

But since both paradigms seem obviously true when you are inhabiting them, how do you know that the second is actually true and the first is not? Well, no one I've met who has actually entered the second paradigm ever seriously asks that question, which in itself is telling, but there is also a logical answer. Abhinava Gupta argues that the first paradigm can successfully be subverted and eliminated through relentless empirical investigation wedded to awareness cultivation, but the second paradigm, once established, cannot be so subverted. Reality is what doesn't go away even if you stop believing in it, and as it turns out, if you stop believing in separation and otherness thoroughly enough, it goes away, but if you stop believing in unity, it doesn't go away.

Next Kṣemarāja cites a master who is otherwise unknown to us today, showing us that the central teaching of Chapter Twelve is attested by other realized beings as well.

**A similar idea is taught by Bhaṭṭa Dāmodara—who had a genuine enthusiastic devotion created by** [his experience of] **spontaneous wonder** (*sahaja-camatkāra*)**—in his** [verses called] ***Pearls*:**

**The five Goddesses, Vāmeśvarī and the rest—
manifesting as the [1]expanded and [2]limited knowers,
the [3]inner and [4]outer faculties, and [5]objects of
experience—bestow liberation or bondage, depending
on whether they are recognized or not. ||**

**In this way as well, the state of being a *saṃsārin* is nothing but that of being deluded by one's own powers.**

Next we have the third interpretation of the sūtra, based on the yogic teachings found in the latter part of the original *Recognition* text, the *Stanzas on the Recognition of [oneself as] the Divine* (the *Īśvara-pratyabhijñā-kārikā*s).

Pratyabhijñā Reading

**Moreover** [there is another way of interpreting the sūtra]**: the Highest Divinity, which is Awareness, has an innate, constant, unitary Power of Sovereignty** (*aiśvarya-śakti*)**, i.e., an agency whose essence is vibrant dynamism** (*sphurattā*)**.**

This doctrine is one of the key points of difference between Tantrik and Vedāntic nondualism. In the latter, Consciousness is said to be wholly inactive (*niṣprapañca*), possessing no agency, and so all activity is said to be illusory, unreal, like a magic trick or an optical illusion. In the Tantra, by contrast, Awareness is understood to be inherently dynamic and possessing agency. This means that activity is real, that Awareness is a pulsating, oscillating, vibrating, dynamic force (*spanda*) that accomplishes everything and transforms itself into all the objects of experience. Vedānta says, "There is no doer," because nothing ever actually happens; whereas Tantra says, "There is One actor, One source of all action, whom we call God, or the essence-nature of each and every being." This key difference explains why some Vedāntins proclaim, "There's nothing to do; we're all already enlightened," whereas in the Tantrik path it is understood that though each of us is already perfectly divine, *sādhanā* (spiritual practice) is necessary for those who wish to experientially realize and embody that truth. This is what Kṣemarāja will allude to next.

**When that Power, concealing Her true nature, functions delusively on the level of the bound soul, she does so through the states of the**

**energies of *prāṇa*, *apāna*, and *samāna*; through the levels of waking, dreaming, and deep sleep, and through the limited powers of the body, energy-body** (*puryaṣṭaka*)**, and Prāṇa. In that context, one exists in the state of a *saṃsārin*, i.e., that of being deluded by** [identification with] **those** [states, levels, and powers].

Here we are again taking a slightly different slice of the same pie. The Power of Sovereignty, i.e., Dynamic Agency (*aiśvarya-śakti*) also functions in modes of concealment and revelation (in the latter mode, She is called *kuṇḍalinī*). In the former mode, it's as if Awareness is so enamored of the miraculous phenomenon of embodiment, it falls into identification with the basic aspects of that phenomenon. Understanding it this way removes the unnecessary negative association. Identification with the body, thoughts and feelings, and life force is simply a natural phase in Awareness' relationship with embodiment. It's like when falling in love with someone leads to codependence and thus to suffering, at which point you're motivated to find your own center without rejecting the love. That's Tantrik *sādhanā* in a nutshell: having become all wrapped up in the embodiment-and-personality game, due to being understandably fascinated by it, we seek to stabilize in our deepest Center without relinquishing the body or running away from the conditions of embodiment.

What, then, are the aspects of embodiment with which we become identified and attached? The life force (*prāṇa*), the feeling of being alive in a body (attachment to which generates intense fear of death), the body itself (attachment to which generates anxiety concerning appearance, aging, etc.), and the energy-body, which here denotes the whole inner world of thoughts, feelings, memories, and fantasies (attachment to which generates many types of suffering).[89] Kṣema also mentions two other triads that we become identified with: the three primary phases of awareness (waking, dreaming, and deep sleep) and the three primary subdivisions of life-force energy (*prāṇa*, *apāna*, and *samāna*). The former are treated in *Tantra Illuminated* (page 176*ff*), and I invite you to contemplate for yourself what releasing overidentification with any of those three states might look like by asking the question, "What would my life-experience be like if I didn't believe that any of these three states (waking, dreaming, deep sleep) were more (or less) important than the others?" Or "What would my self-image be like if it was equally informed by all three states?" For this is a contemplation that the Tantrik View invites. Most of us are overidentified with the waking state, and see the earnest inquiry of philosophers like Zhuang-tzu* as an amusing trifle, but some of us are infatuated with the world of dreams, dreamlike imagery or dreamlike psychoactive substances, and a few seek escape from both waking and dream in the realm of deep sleep, sensationless *samādhi*, or other similar soporific states.

Finally, Kṣema talks about the states of the energies of *prāṇa*, *apāna*, and *samāna*. (Note that these are three out of five subdivisions of Prāṇa; confusingly, the same word is used for the whole class and the first member of the class.) The first of these corresponds to the exhale, to 'solar' or active outward-moving energy, and to *yang* in the *yin-yang* of Daoism. The second (i.e., *apāna*) corresponds to the inhale, to 'lunar' inward-turning contemplative energy, and to *yin* in the *yin-yang*.† Clearly many people are more identified with one of these than the other, but in this case the goal is not to equalize identification but to release identification with both entirely. That's where *samāna* comes in. In Āyurvedic medical theory, *samāna* is associated with equilibrioception (balance) and digestion. It is understood to function at the balance point between *prāṇa* and *apāna*, and in part depends on them having approximately equal flow.

In Tantrik Yoga, *samāna* serves another function: it actualizes the fusion of *prāṇa* and *apāna* that must occur prior to the rise of *udāna* (which will be explained shortly). To put it simply, in meditation the exhale and the inhale become balanced and equal in length and quality (either spontaneously or through gentle effort), then slowly become more and more subtle, until it feels like one is barely breathing at all (though without being consciously aware of it, usually). The breath and the mind are scarcely moving. Then the breath spontaneously pauses (this is called *kumbhaka*) in a timeless moment of stillness and centeredness. Then there may be a gentle or dramatic surge of energy up the

---

* To paraphrase: "I slept, and dreamt that I was a butterfly; or am I now a butterfly asleep, dreaming it is a man?" Zhuang-tzu (莊子) was a Daoist master, and Daoism and Tantra have some key parallels, as well as many differences.

† Please note that modern postural yoga has reversed *prāṇa* and *apāna*, taking them as inhale and exhale respectively, but all branches of Tantra and Āyurveda are unanimous in describing them as I have done here.

central channel. This is the topic to which we now turn, for this is the operation of the Power of Dynamic Agency in the mode of revelation.

**But when, due to the activation** [and/or expansion] **of the Radiant Domain of the Center** (*madhya-dhāman*)**, She unfolds the energy of *udāna*, and the energy of *vyāna*, whose essence is** [its capacity to] **pervade everything—corresponding to the State of the Transcendent Fourth** (*turya*) **and the State Beyond the Fourth** (*turyātīta*) **respectively,** [both] **replete with the Joy of Awareness—then arises liberation-while-living** (*jīvan-mukti*)**,** [also known as] **the state of the Lord, even under the conditions** [imposed by] **the body, mind, etc.** [and the states of waking, dreaming, etc.]**.**

There are five subdivisions of Prāṇa in total, often known as the five *prāṇa-vāyus*. The fourth and fifth are *udāna* and *vyāna*. In Āyurveda, *udāna* is responsible for the necessary functions of belching and coughing, the ability to exert energy, and speech & singing; while *vyāna* is responsible for circulation to the extremities and flexion of the limbs. In Tantrik Yoga, these two acquire a mystical function. *Udāna* is the upward-rising force of *kuṇḍalinī*, a fiery energy experienced in the central channel that rises toward liberation and dissolves into infinite transcendent Presence; while *vyāna* is the nectarean pervasion of that Presence into all the layers of embodiment. *Udāna* has a strong upward vector and is associated with fire, and *vyāna* has a downward, outward, and ultimately all-pervasive movement, described as a flood of nectar.

*Udāna* leads us to the experience of the Fourth State (beyond the three states of waking, dreaming, and deep sleep), and *vyāna* brings the Fourth into the other three. This pervasion of the Fourth, transcendent Presence, into the three ordinary states is called 'Beyond the Fourth' (*turyātīta*). While both the Fourth State and that Beyond the Fourth are 'replete with the Joy of Awareness (*cid-ānanda-ghana*),' it is *turyātīta* that makes this yoga uniquely Tantrik, for the ultimate goal is not to transcend everything, but to experience the transcendent in the apparently mundane conditions of embodiment. It is in touching the highest heavens, *then* coming all the way back down to Earth—and bringing one's realization fully into the everyday world—that one becomes a truly Tantrik yogī. Deep humility balanced with self-respect, softness balanced with steadiness, gentleness without passivity, loving intimacy with the 10,000 things of everyday life: these are the marks of a Tantrik yogī who has integrated her realization. This alone is *jīvan-mukti*, embodied liberation, according to Tantra. The 'highest' state is the realization of God in the thick of the conditions imposed by the body, the psyche, and so on.

**Thus, the state of delusion by one's own powers has been explained in three ways** [Kaula, Krama, and Pratyabhijñā]. **In the Ninth Sūtra, it was stated that the *saṃsārin* is none other than the Light of Awareness having taken on contraction; here, the same thing is said from another angle, i.e., that one enters the state of a *saṃsārin* by means of delusion by** [and about] **one's own powers.**

**Thus, I have taught indirectly that when one is not deluded by one's own powers, though they are contracted (**[because] **one possesses *Prāṇa*, etc.) then that person is Lord Śiva himself, as taught in** [our] **tradition, e.g.,**

**This person is the Highest Divinity in bodily form.**

**As** [said in another] **scripture:**

> **They are the Highest Divinity in disguise, having taken on human bodies.**[90]

**And, in** [my *parameṣṭhī guru* Utpala's] **commentary on his own *Stanzas on the Recognition of the Divine*:**

> **They too are perfected who see their very body,**
> **or even pots and other objects, as a form of God,**
> **composed of all thirty-six *tattvas*.**[91] ||

As we have seen before, Kṣemarāja wishes to corroborate his teachings with citations from scripture and from previous masters in his lineage. First Kṣema wishes us to understand that the powers of consciousness do not need to return to their fully expanded state (which requires shedding the body) for self-realization to be complete; the latter is possible even while possessing a body-mind. This state of 'living liberation' (*jīvan-mukti*) is a unique teaching of the nondual Tāntrikas that has become very popular in mainstream Indian religion.

The scriptural citations here given emphasize the doctrine that one who is fully self-realized is absolutely identical to God. However, in the more refined nondual teachings, it is acknowledged that *everyone* is absolutely identical to God, and that this scriptural teaching must be construed to mean that the self-realized being is to be venerated as divine, unlike unrealized persons. (This veneration is of course not for the saint's benefit, but for the disciple's, since such veneration opens a wider channel for transmission.) Note that the quote from Utpala Deva solves the issue by referring to people with nondual vision as 'perfected' or 'accomplished' (*siddha*) rather than as 'God' (*parameśvara*).

This concludes our study of Sūtra Twelve and its commentary.

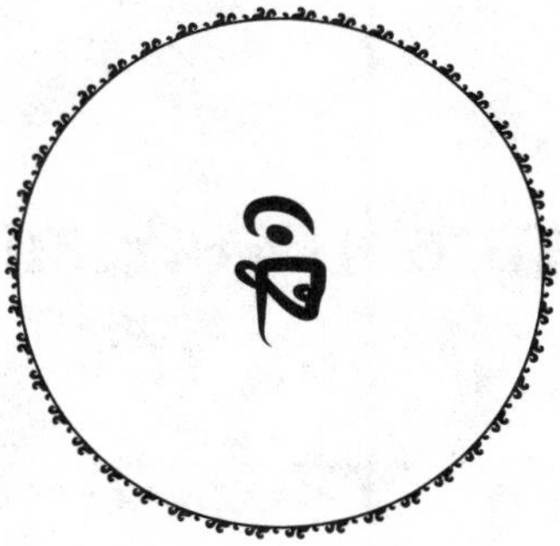

उक्तसूत्रार्थप्रातिपक्ष्येण तत्त्वदृष्टिं दर्शयि-
तुमाह

**तत्परिज्ञाने चित्तमेव अन्तर्मु-
खीभावेन चेतनपदाध्यारो-
हात् चितिः ॥१३॥**

पूर्वसूत्रव्याख्याप्रसङ्गेन प्रमेयदृष्ट्या वितत्य

व्याख्यातप्रायमेतत् सूत्रम्; शब्दसंगत्या तु अधुना व्याख्यायते। 'तस्य' आत्मीयस्य पञ्चकृत्यकारित्वस्य 'परिज्ञाने' सति अपरिज्ञानलक्षणकारणापगमात् स्वशक्तिव्यामोहिततानिवृत्तौ स्वातन्त्र्यलाभात् प्राक् व्याख्यातं यत् 'चित्तं' तदेव संकोचिनीं बहिर्मुखतां जहत्, 'अन्तर्मुखीभावेन चेतनपदाध्यारोहात्,—ग्राहकभूमिकाक्रमणक्रमेण संकोचकलाया अपि विगलनेन स्वरूपापत्त्या 'चितिर्' भवति; स्वां[14] चिन्मयीं परां भूमिमाविशति इत्यर्थः ॥ १३ ॥

# CHAPTER THIRTEEN

*Kṣemarāja's original text*

To explain the perspective on Reality that is the inverse of the meaning of the previous *sūtra*, it is taught:

**When there is full realization of that, the mind, by turning within, ascends to its expanded state and is revealed as nothing but Awareness.** || 13 ||

Reading this sūtra in light of the explanation of the previous sūtra almost fully explains it. So now I will expound it simply through its syntax.

**When there is full realization of that,** i.e., that you are the author of the Five Acts, the state of being deluded by your own powers ceases, because the cause—which is the absence of recognition—has disappeared. When that occurs, due to attaining one's autonomy the **mind** discussed above relinquishes its contracted state of outward focus and **by turning within, ascends to its expanded state.** Through this process of reaching the level of the expanded perceiver by dissolving even the last remaining trace of contraction, the mind becomes **Awareness**, attaining its true nature. This means that it becomes immersed in its own highest expression, which is Awareness. || 13 ||

# CHAPTER THIRTEEN

*with explanation*

In terms of the arc of the text, Chapters One through Twelve charted the 'movement' of divine Awareness from its unparticularized, fully expanded state of absolute potential to its condition of contraction and confusion. (Of course this loose narrative structure should not be taken to imply an actual linear progression: in truth, all aspects of the process are happening at every moment.) In dialectical terms, he has stated both *thesis* and apparent *antithesis*. With Chapter Thirteen, Kṣemarāja initiates a turn: the movement toward full awakeness and seamless unity with all things. This is the required *synthesis* of the dialectic.[92]

**To explain the perspective on Reality that is the inverse of the meaning of the previous *sūtra*, it is taught:**

**|| TAD-PARIJÑĀNE CITTAM EVĀNTARMUKHĪBHĀVENA CETANA-PADĀDHYĀROHĀC CITIḤ || 13 ||**

**When there is full realization of that, the mind, by turning within, ascends to its expanded state and is revealed as nothing but Awareness.**

**Reading this sūtra in light of the explanation of the previous sūtra almost fully explains it. So now I will expound it** [simply] **through its syntax.**

Here Kṣema does an interesting thing: he tells us that this sūtra is the inverse of the previous sūtra when in fact, apart from its first phrase, it's actually a precise inversion of Sūtra Five.* This tells us that he regards a contracted mind as the normal state of affairs when one is deluded by one's own powers, and that the disappearance of that de-

* "Awareness itself, descending from its [expanded] state of pure consciousness, becomes contracted by the object perceived: this is [called] the mind."

lusion is concomitant with the mind attaining its expanded, fully conscious state (*cetana-pada*). So in his commentary, he weaves together the inverse of both Sūtras Five and Twelve to describe the condition known as 'enlightenment' (*bodha*, literally awakeness or awareness), according to the Recognition school. Here he is simply giving us a brief outline of the nature of the awakened state *vis-à-vis* the mind; in later chapters we will receive a much more detailed account.

**When there is full realization of *that*, i.e., that you are the author of the Five Acts, the state of being deluded by your own powers ceases, because the cause** [of such delusion]—**which is the absence of recognition** [of your true nature]—**disappears. When that occurs, due to attaining one's** [innate] **autonomy the mind discussed above** [in Sūtras Five and Six] **relinquishes its contracted state of outward focus and by turning within, ascends to its expanded state. Through this process of reaching the level of the** [expanded] **perceiver by** [gradually] **dissolving even the last remaining trace of contraction,** [the mind] **becomes Awareness, attaining its true nature. This means that it becomes immersed in its own highest expression, which is Awareness.**

Here Kṣema argues that the key element of recognition of your true nature is realizing that you—the real you, not your mental construct of selfhood we call ego—is the performer of all five Divine Acts. You are creator, in that everything you experience emanates from your essence-nature, and sustainer, in that whatever you pay attention to in your field of experience is magnified by that attention (and tends to persist longer and recur more often), and dissolver, in that everything that dies or disappears dissolves back into the ground of being with which you are one, and concealer, in that you have veiled your own authorship of the previous three Acts, and revealer, in that, when you are ready, you reveal to yourself your authorship of all Five Acts. This is self-realization. We must note that *believing* the statements in the sentence before last is not realization; rather, we speak here of a direct nonverbal *seeing* of the truth of what you are, made possible (but not caused) by deep spiritual practice and contemplation.

In this state, delusion falls away, and when it does, your innate autonomy is revealed. In this awakened mode of being free of confusion and connected to freedom, the mind tends to behave differently. It no longer looks to external things, people, and situations for fulfillment, driven by contracted desire and fear; it begins to turn inward and repose in its deeper/wider self, Awareness. Another way to say the same thing is that contracted-mind is immersed in Awareness-self and eventually dissolves into Awareness-self (though beneficial forms of contraction, like the ability to focus, still remain). There is an indefinite (but finite) amount of time between the mind attaining its natural state of reposing in Awareness and the dissolution of all non-beneficial contraction. This is a gradual process, since for the 'last remaining trace of contraction' to dissolve, your deepest *saṃskāra*s need to be digested and resolved. But that's okay, because if your mind is truly settled in its natural state, then you will be content with however long it takes. As described in Chapter Eleven, this process, which many teachers today call *integrating* your awakening, is contingent on a willingness to see and feel whatever needs to be seen and felt, as well as an ability to rapidly digest/dissolve the stories and self-images that often form out of the *saṃskāra*s that surface in the process.

This concludes our study of Sūtra Thirteen and its commentary.

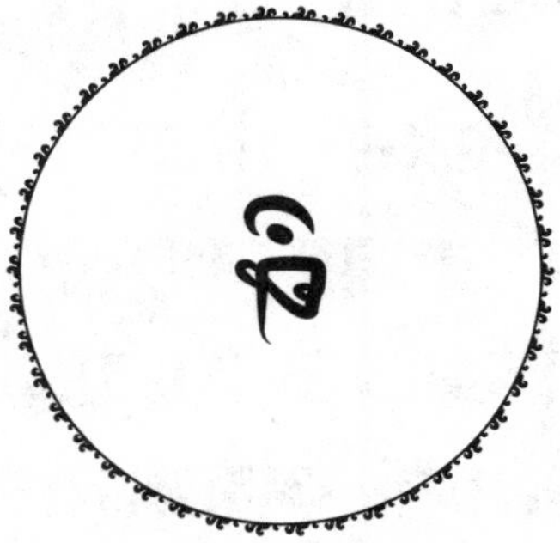

ननु यदि पारमार्थिकं चिच्छक्तिपदं सकलभेदकवलनस्वभावं, तत् अस्य मायापदेऽपि तथारूपेण भवितव्यं यथा जलदाच्छादितस्यापि भानोः भावावभासकत्वम् ।—इत्याशङ्क्य आह

चितिवह्निरवरोहपदे छन्नोऽपि
मात्रया मेयेन्धनं प्लु-
ष्यति ॥ १४ ॥

'चितिरेव' विश्वग्रसनशीलत्वात् 'वह्निः;' असौ एव 'अवरोहपदे'—मायाप्रमातृतायां 'छन्नोऽपि'—स्वातन्त्र्यात् आच्छादितस्वभावोऽपि, भूरिभूतिच्छन्नाग्निवत् 'मात्रया'—अंशेन, नीलपीतादिप्रमेयेन्धनं 'प्लुष्यति'—स्वात्मसात् करोति । मात्रापदस्य इदम् आकूतम्—यत् कवलयन् अपि सार्वात्म्येन न ग्रसते, अपि तु अंशेन संस्कारात्मना उत्थापयति । ग्रासकत्वं च सर्वप्रमातृणां स्वानुभवत एव सिद्धम् । यदुक्तं श्रीमदुत्पलदेवपादैः निजस्तोत्रेषु

'वर्तन्ते जन्तवोऽशेषा अपि ब्रह्मेन्द्रविष्णवः ।
ग्रसमानास्ततो वन्दे देव विश्वं भवन्मयम् ॥'

इति ॥ १४ ॥

# CHAPTER FOURTEEN

*Kṣemarāja's original text*

Objection: "Surely, if the essence of the ultimately significant and desirable state of the Power of Awareness is its capacity to devour all kinds of things, then it must do so even on the level of Māyā, just as the sun retains its capacity to illuminate things even when it is obscured by clouds."

To address this concern, it is taught:

> **The Fire of Awareness, though obscured in its descended state, still partially consumes the 'kindling' of knowable objects.** || 14 ||

**Awareness** itself is a '**fire**' in that its characteristic behavior is to devour all things. That same Awareness, **though obscured** (i.e., though its true nature is concealed out of its own freedom) **in its descended state** (i.e., on the level of one who perceives primarily in terms of duality), like glowing embers covered with ash **still consumes** (i.e., makes one with itself) **the 'kindling' of knowable objects** (like 'blue' or 'pleasure') **partially**. The point of the word 'partially' is this: though swallowing them, it does not devour them entirely. Rather, it deposits a portion as a subtle impression.

The fact that all knowers are *absorbers* can be demonstrated simply through one's own experience. As our revered master Utpala Deva sang in his hymns:

> All creatures, even Brahmā, Indra, and Viṣṇu, are continuously devouring; therefore, O Playful One, I worship the universe made of You.

|| 14 ||

# CHAPTER FOURTEEN

*with explanation*

Even though I revere this text as a divine transmission, and Kṣemarāja as a guru, I retain my capacity for critical thinking, as I think we all should. I say this because I am critical of Chapter Fourteen, for two reasons. First, I'm not sure what it really adds to the discussion, and second, its placement seems odd to me. It would better fit the arc of the text if it went between Chapters Eleven and Twelve, since it describes how the ordinary, unawakened condition still demonstrates the nature of the Power of Awareness, but as noted above, a turn is initiated by Chapter Thirteen and it continues in Fifteen. At any rate, let's see what we can tease out of the brief and perhaps unnecessary Chapter Fourteen. Kṣemarāja once again invokes his perennial objectioner:

**Surely, if the essence of the ultimately significant and desirable state of the Power of Awareness is its capacity to 'devour' all kinds** [of things], **then it must do so even on the level of Māyā, just as the sun retains its capacity to illuminate things even when it is obscured by clouds.**

Kṣema describes the state of full access to the Power of Awareness as *pāramārthika*, a difficult-to-translate word that simultaneously expresses three concepts in English: 'absolutely real', 'ultimately significant', and 'the highest goal'. The imagined objectioner correctly states that since this divine Awareness is the ever-present power by which any of us are aware of anything whatsoever, it should exhibit its capacity to devour and absorb all objects of awareness even when the contracted mind that perceives duality is dominant. Kṣema responds that indeed it does, to some extent.

**To address this concern, it is taught:**

## || CITI-VAHNIR AVAROHA-PADE CHANNO 'PI MĀTRAYĀ MEYENDHANAṂ PLUṢYATI || 14 ||

**The Fire of Awareness, though obscured in its descended state, still partially consumes the kindling of knowable objects.**

The 'descended state' is that described in Chapter Five, that is, the everyday contracted mind-state. The Power of Awareness, here usefully compared to fire, displays part of its character through 'consuming' the objects of consciousness. To explain: when one inquires, in contemplative meditation (*bhāvanā*), into the question of where thoughts, sensations, and other percepts *go* when they disappear or subside, one sees that they dissolve into the space of Awareness itself. Prior to actualizing spiritual liberation, however, this dissolution is not total, since, as already explained in Chapter Eleven, experiences tend to leave a subtle trace called a *saṃskāra* or *vāsanā* in Sanskrit.

**Awareness itself is a 'fire' in that its characteristic behavior is to devour all things. That same Awareness, though obscured (i.e., though its true nature is concealed out of its own freedom) in its descended state (i.e., on the level of one who perceives primarily in terms of duality), like glowing embers covered with ash it still consumes (i.e., makes one with itself) the 'kindling' of knowable objects (like 'blue' or 'pleasure') partially. The point of the word 'partially' is this: though swallowing** [them], **it does not devour them entirely. Rather, it deposits a portion as a subtle impression** (*saṃskāra*).

**The fact that all knowers are *absorbers* can be demonstrated simply through one's own experience.**

Again Kṣemarāja wishes to distinguish the Śaiva view of the self from that of the Vedāntins and Sāṅkhyas, who describe it as a passive witness, unaffected by what it witnesses. In the Śaiva view, the essential self is an experiencer and an absorber, sympathetically vibrating with the energy of whatever it experiences and digesting that energy, though often incompletely. This is a necessary corollary of a view in which the core self is not ultimately divisible from the mental-emotional body, though not everything that pertains to one pertains to the other. For example, the essential self is untainted by whatever one experiences, whereas the mental-emotional body (*puryaṣṭaka*) stores traces of those experiences in direct proportion to how incompletely they were digested at the time of occurrence. Due to identification with the mental–emotional body, it might seem as if severe trauma damages a person to the core, but if, through spiritual practice, that person is able to access the deepest place within, they experience for themselves that there is a part of them as unscarred and open, as loving and forgiving, as an innocent child.

Since Awareness is a 'devourer', meaning it is that space in which all things converge, in which all things are dissolved and ultimately resolved, and since all beings exhibit that capacity, we know that all beings are forms of that same divine Consciousness.

**As our revered master Utpala Deva sang in his hymns** (*Śiva-stotrāvalī* 20.17):

> **All creatures, even Brahmā, Indra, and Viṣṇu, are continuously devouring; therefore, O Playful One, I worship the universe made of you.** ||

The last phrase could also be translated as 'I venerate everything as You,' or 'I worship the universe [because it is] full of you.' Utpala's hymns beautifully express how a liberated being's experience can include devotion and reverence even though he is a radical nondualist. He loved to praise and honor the Divine, even though he didn't experience any separation or difference between himself and God. His hymns have been translated in a book published by Constantina Rhodes Bailly.

This concludes our study of Sūtra Fourteen and its commentary.

**यदा पुनः करणेश्वरीप्रसरसंकोचं संपाद्य सर्गसंहारक्रमपरिशीलनयुक्तिम् आविशति तदा**

**बललाभे विश्वमात्मसात्क-**

**रोति ॥ १५ ॥**

चितिरेव देहप्राणाद्याच्छादननिमज्जनेन स्वरूपम् उन्मग्नत्वेन स्फारयन्ती बलम्; यथोक्तं

'तदाक्रम्य बलं मन्त्राः............... ।

इति । एवं च 'बललाभे'–उन्मग्नस्वरूपाश्रयणे, क्षित्यादि-सदाशिवान्तं 'विश्वम् आत्मसात् करोति'–स्वस्वरूपाभेदेन निर्भासयति । तदुक्तं पूर्वगुरुभिः स्वभाषामयेषु क्रमसूत्रेषु

'यथा वह्निरुद्बोधितो दाह्यं दहति, तथा विषयपाशान् भक्षयेत्'

इति ।

'न चैवं वक्तव्यम्,–विश्वात्मसात्काररूपा समावेशभूः कादाचित्की, कथम् उपादेया इयं स्यात् इति; यतो देहाद्युन्मज्जननिमज्जनवशेन इदम् अस्याः कादाचित्कत्वम् इव आभाति । वस्तुतस्तु चितिस्वातन्त्र्यावभासितदेहाद्युन्मज्जनात् एव कादाचित्कत्वम् । एषा तु सदैव प्रकाशमाना; अन्यथा तत् देहादि अपि न प्रकाशेत । अत एव देहादिप्रमातृताभिमाननिमज्जनाय अभ्यासः, न तु सदा प्रथमानतासारप्रमातृताप्राप्त्यर्थम्'

इति श्रीप्रत्यभिज्ञाकाराः ॥ १५ ॥

# CHAPTER FIFTEEN

*Kṣemarāja's original text*

When one immerses oneself in the practice of mindfully attending to the process of emission and reabsorption while bringing about the expansive outflow and contraction of the goddesses of the senses, then:

**Attaining one's innate power,**
**one absorbs everything into oneself.** || 15 ||

Awareness is referred to as **innate power** when it submerges the veils of identification with the body, *prāṇa*, etc. and allows its true nature to expansively emerge. As it is taught:

> Mantras, attaining that innate power, become suffused with Divine force, enabling them to perform their respective functions, like the senses of embodied beings. ||

Thus, **upon attaining one's innate power**, i.e., upon taking refuge in one's emergent essence-nature, **one assimilates everything,** from Earth to Sadāśiva, **into oneself,** i.e., causes it to appear as it really is, non-different from one's own essence-nature.

As said by an earlier master in the *Krama-sūtra*, which uses its own special language,

> Just as a fire inflamed burns all its fuel, he will certainly devour the bonds of the sense-objects. |

Nor should one say "This state of Immersion—this making everything one with the self—is merely an occasional experience, so how can it be the Goal?" since it only *appears* to be occasional because of the arising and subsiding of identification with the body, etc., manifested through the innate autonomy of Awareness. Actually, this oneness with Awareness is ever present; otherwise, even the body, etc. could not appear. For this very reason, the author of the original *Recognition* text taught:

> Daily meditative practice has the purpose of submerging the egoic identification of subjectivity with the body and so on, not to attain subjectivity (the state of the Knower), since the very essence of the latter is its quality of being continually manifest. || 15 ||

# CHAPTER FIFTEEN

*with explanation*

From this point forward, Kṣemarāja's discourse is like a snowball rolling down a mountain, gaining speed and size until it finally reaches the limit of its journey and explodes in a dazzling climax. First, in Chapters Fifteen and Sixteen, he explains where we're headed (already hinted at in Chapter Thirteen); then in Chapters Seventeen, Eighteen, and Nineteen, he tells us how to get there; in Chapter Twenty, he gives a fascinating description of 'there': that is, fully awakened and liberated Awareness harmoniously integrated with the body-mind and the entire world.

First he gives us a sublime and subtle mindfulness practice, and describes its result. This is a key practice in Kṣema's system, and for reasons best known to him, he slips it in here without fanfare. Though it is esoteric and perhaps elusive, he will give us more concrete techniques in Chapter Eighteen that will help us connect more fully with what he says here.

**When one immerses oneself in the practice of mindfully attending to the process of emission and reabsorption while bringing about the** [normal] **expansive outflow** [toward 'objectivity'] **and contraction** [inward to subjectivity] **of the goddesses of the senses...**

The 'sense-goddesses' are the faculties of visual perception and so on, understood not as passive receptors of data, but as vital energies that flow in two directions. When they flow outward, they expand, and function as the means by which Awareness creates a world for itself to experience. When they flow inward, they contract—in the sense of pulling in toward the core—and if they are allowed to contract sufficiently through meditative practice, Awareness reposes in innate subjectivity, tasting the sweetness of pure Being. This is the *spanda*, or natural oscillation, of the sense-goddesses: outward toward Becoming, inward toward Being. This is happening all the time on different scales: such as in the cycles of waking and sleeping, and in the alternation of introversive contemplative moments (where the world, if still seen, is like background wallpaper) and extroversive active moments (which often include a kind of self-forgetfulness).

Here, though, Kṣemarāja invites a somewhat advanced nondual mindfulness practice: throughout any example of this *spanda*, pay devotional attention to it as a process of the emission and reabsorption of the Power of Awareness that you are. This is a kind of reconditioning or reconfiguring of your very sense of the nature of reality. Instead of your habitual mental image of a more-or-less static world 'out there' that you encounter with your senses, open to the possibility of experiencing that *what-you-are* blossoms forth into what you see (or hear, etc.) at the moment that you see it. When you open your eyes, *what-you-are* manifests as everything you see. When you close your eyes, those phenomena dissolve into *what-you-are.* As quantum physicists have now thoroughly demonstrated, it is meaningless to talk of the existence of even a particle of matter without an observer; before observation, there is only probability, potentiality.[93] *Observation is creation.* When we open the sense-gates, we emit phenomena, in the sense that nothing coalesces into being without an observer. Each embodied locus of Awareness (you and me) manifests a unique world of experience that overlaps with all the other 'worlds' to a greater or lesser extent, but always to some extent, because no form of Awareness is separable from any other.

When we close the doors of perception, phenomena relinquish their manifest form and dissolve into the field of absolute potential; the part that physics has not yet demonstrated is that in your deepest nature, you *are* that field of absolute potential. Therefore, whatever dissolves, dissolves into *what you are.* Now you might say, "When I close my eyes, things don't *really* dissolve into me, because someone else is observing them and thereby maintaining them." But this objection pivots on your conditioned belief in objective reality. Each of us constitutes a unique vantage point that the One has on itself, which means that no one else sees phenomena exactly the way you do—so when you close the sense-gates or go unconscious, phenomena as seen uniquely by you *do* in fact dissolve, reabsorbed into the field of absolute potential that you ultimately are.[94]

Test this out: wherever you are, close your eyes and put down the book, then orient yourself to the view that when you open your eyes, Awareness flashes forth and becomes everything you see. When you close your eyes again, don't you feel the impression of those visual phenomena inside you? If you hear a sound, just after it ceases, don't you feel its vibration within you? If you smell a redolent scent, doesn't it perfume your awareness for a few moments after it's gone? Taste, touch, words, all the same. Phenomena are dissolving into you. That's where they go. There's nowhere else for them to go.

Once you've got the feel of things dissolving into you, it's easier to start experiencing that things arise from you, as an expression of *what-you-are*. But that's the advanced practice, because it takes a strong energy body to digest the realization that everything—all the beauty and all the misery that you directly experience—is an ever-changing kaleidoscopic expression of what you are.[95]

The more basic practice, then, was already described in the first paragraph of this section: simply pay attention to the *spanda* by which the energy of your awareness moves outward, then inward. Outward toward 'objectivity'; inward toward subjectivity. It happens many times a day. When awareness pulls inward, whenever that happens in your day, let it pull further in than you usually do; if possible, all the way in to the core. Let it rest there for a timeless moment. A sacred still point. You may find that when it moves outward again, reality is a little clearer, a little fresher, a little more vivid. Contemplate the implications of that fact.

Kṣemarāja uses a when/then clause to set up the sūtra. *When* one immerses sufficiently in the sublime mindfulness practice here described,

**then:**

### || BALA-LĀBHE VIŚVAM ĀTMASĀTKAROTI || 15 ||

### Attaining one's innate power, one absorbs everything into oneself.

What is this innate power or force (*bala*) of which Kṣema speaks? As he will explain in a moment, it is Awareness in its awakened/inflamed/activated mode. Immersing in the practice described above causes Awareness to enter this mode of predominance. In this mode, Kṣema says, *viśvam ātmasātkaroti*—'one absorbs everything into oneself', or, we could translate, 'one makes the whole universe one's own'. This is the state of unity-consciousness, of the all-inclusive 'I'. Though you may have had a spiritual experience of unity-consciousness that came over in a moment, coming to abide in unity-awareness as your default state is a process that takes time, as we shall see.

**Awareness is** [referred to as] **'innate power'** (*bala*) **when it submerges the veils of** [identification with] **the body, *prāṇa*, etc. and allows its true nature to expansively emerge.**

Again we return to the theme of the predominance of Awareness versus the predominance of habitual identification with the body, mind, *prāṇa*, etc. Here we learn that when the former (i.e., *citi*) is predominant or 'emergent', it becomes activated and is then referred to as *bala*, innate power. Spacious Awareness and flowing Energy become the primary context for life-experience, as opposed to dense matter or thought-content being primary.

Kṣema then cites a parallel case: *mantra*s also become activated and potent when they access this same power of awakened Awareness.

**As it is taught** [in the *Spanda-kārikā*s, 2.1]:

> **Mantras, attaining that innate power, become suffused with Divine force,[96] enabling them to perform their respective functions, like the senses of embodied beings.** ||

In the mantra-theory of the nondual Tāntrikas, even divinely revealed mantras are said to be inert and ineffective (*jaḍa*) until and unless they are infused with *mantra-vīrya*. This generally happens when a being with awakened Awareness does *sādhanā* (spiritual practice) with a particular mantra, thereby potentizing it, after which she can pass it on to her students in this activated or alive (*caitanya*) state. A *caitanya* mantra is the 'sonic body' of the deity it names and thus can manifest the qualities of that particular deity or pattern of Awareness. For example, a Lakṣmī mantra infused with *mantra-vīrya* is said to be able to manifest material and/or spiritual abundance and prosperity. The verse cited above (note that Kṣema cites only its first phrase, expecting his audience to know it by heart) argues that just as well-functioning eyes only give rise to actual sight if consciousness is present, in the same way properly intoned mantras only effect their results when imbued with the innate power of awakened Awareness.

Next Kṣema glosses the sūtra, which means he provides a word-by-word explanation of each phrase. First he cites a phrase from the sūtra, then he gives alternate words that express the same idea, to make sure we're clear on the meaning. Note that in the sūtra and in the following paragraph, the actual subject-word is left unstated: I supply the abstract third person ('one'), referring to the hypothetical practitioner, but could just as easily have put 'it', referring of course to Awareness.

**Thus, upon attaining** [one's] **innate power, i.e., upon taking refuge in** [one's] **emergent essence-nature, one absorbs everything, from Earth to Sadāśiva, into oneself, i.e., causes it to appear as** [it really is,] **non-different from one's own essence-nature. As said by an earlier master in the *Krama-sūtra*, which uses its owns special language:**

> **Just as a fire inflamed** (*udbodhita*) **burns** [all] **its fuel,**
> **he will certainly devour the bonds of the sense-**
> **objects.** |

'Attaining one's innate power' is glossed with 'taking refuge in one's emergent essence-nature', where *emergent* (the opposite of *submerged*) refers to the mode in which Awareness is predominant and therefore potentiated. In other words, having awakened (to some degree) to the truth of Awareness as your essence-nature, you attain your innate power by focusing on, seeing the significance of, and centering in that Awareness. Increasingly accessing your innate power thereby, you become capable of digesting any experience and becoming one with anything. These two are intimately related, because when by virtue of your increased power and capacity, you can recognize that whatever you experience is an aspect of *what-you-are*, then you are able to 'digest' that experience fully, which means allow all its energy to pass through your system without resistance. Remember that resistance not only means the attitude 'I don't like this and don't want to feel it' but also can take the subtler form of making a story out of the experience, even a 'positive' story, if the latter helps you avoid feeling a painful experience fully. Now if you say that you can recognize that experience X is an aspect of what you are, but you still resist it, I would respond that you're only thinking or believing that it's an aspect of what you are; if you actually *recognize* that truth, resistance naturally falls away. If then you ask exactly *how* to recognize it, the only answer is to continue to marinate in the spiritual teachings and practices. Recognition comes when it comes. However, it helps to thoroughly divest yourself of the wrong view that there are certain kinds of energy that are somehow fundamentally *other* than your essence-nature. When you have that view, this recognition is not possible. Note that Kṣemarāja tells us that to 'absorb' anything into oneself is to see it (literally, cause it to appear) as non-different from one's essence-nature (*sva-svarūpa*). He tells us that this includes anything and everything from tattva #3 to tattva #36, in other words, the entirety of reality. In this way he teaches that *nothing* is other than *what-you-are*. Only when this is truly recognized can you absorb/digest/process anything.

Notice, by the way, that Kṣema indirectly tells us what our essence-nature is: by describing the 'absorption' of everything into oneself in terms of tattvas #3 to #36, he clearly yet indirectly states that our essence-nature is tattvas #1 and #2, that is, Śiva/Śakti, *cid-ānanda*, Awareness blissfully reposing in itself. Everything that appears is an appearance *within* Awareness and a vibration *of* Awareness, and therefore everything is an expression of your essence-nature. (The bliss element only becomes apparent through the direct recognition of that truth.)

A metaphor for this absorption process is given in a citation from the *Krama-sūtra* (a scripture now lost), in which awakened Awareness is compared to intensified fire that more effectively burns through its fuel (note that the word *udbodhita* can mean 'awakened' or 'intensified'). Here the 'fuel' is the 'bonds of the sense-objects'. The things our senses perceive become like bonds when we see them as other than self, for then we grasp after them in desire or push them away out of fear. To 'devour' the bonds of the sense-objects is to dissolve their binding properties by seeing those objects as an expression of what you are. If the whole universe is yours, what's the point of grasping after anything or pushing anything away?

If we wish to abide in this state of unity-consciousness as our default state, we must gain full access to our innate power, since it takes energy to absorb everything into oneself, or as Nisargadatta put it, "devour the world". (See his quote on page 250 above.) Why should it take energy when in actuality this seamless unity is already the way things are? Because to stabilize this as our default state, we have to overcome our ingrained tendency to identify with a tiny portion of the whole, a portion called 'me'—a tendency reinforced over countless lifetimes. Ultimately, as Kṣema describes in Chapters Sixteen and Nineteen, everything has to be re-seen and recalibrated in light of your essence-nature. Recalibration (also called integration) is a subtle process not adequately addressed in most nondualist literature that wrongly imagines the attainment of unity-consciousness as being like the flip of a perceptual switch. To put this teaching simply, once you have recognized what you are, then everything that was previously experienced in the dualistic mode of being must be re-seen as an expression of what you are, then it is recalibrated and integrated. And it doesn't work to just think of something and realize, "Ah, that too am I," because in that case you are recognizing only your mental image of the thing, not the thing-in-itself. Post-awakening, the *saṃskāra*s of duality are gradually effaced through the process of seeing everything, internal or external, with fresh eyes and recalibrating each perception and experience in the light of your true nature, until a tipping point is reached and the totality integrates in a flood.

**Nor should one say, "This state of Immersion—this making everything one with the self—is merely an occasional** [experience], **so how can it be the Goal?" since it only *appears* to be occasional because of the arising and subsiding of identification with the body, etc., manifested through the innate autonomy of Awareness. Actually, this oneness with Awareness is ever present; otherwise, even the body,** [mind,] **etc. could not manifest.**

Here Kṣema raises a very important objection. Most people who experience unity-consciousness experience it in the form of a rare, relatively brief mystical experience. So having defined unity-consciousness as a level of Immersion (*samāveśa*),* a term frequently used to denote powerful spiritual experience in the nondualist literature, he then addresses the question of how it can be a goal† of practice. After all, no experience is ever constant; everything that arises must subside sooner

* Specifically, it is *śākta-samāveśa*.

† The word *upādeya*, here translated as 'goal', literally means 'that which is worthy of being sought' or 'that which ought to be held close'.

or later. Therefore, an experience, however beautiful or amazing, cannot be the goal of spiritual practice. To this problem Kṣema replies that it is actually *body-identification* that arises and subsides. Like a veil being drawn back and then replaced, body-identification (here as usual standing in for identification with any nonultimate layer of selfhood) usually obscures all-inclusive Awareness, and by temporarily dissolving, that Awareness seems to manifest, though in reality it is ever present. Indeed, it is by virtue of the very same Awareness that the body manifests as an experiential phenomenon. Everything that manifests is a manifestation of Awareness; everything that vibrates is a vibration of Awareness; nothing can be experienced, seen, measured, or felt unless it appears within Awareness. And that Awareness is continuous, everything being equally a part of it; notice that awareness of the sound of a passing car and of a twinge in your knee is not different in kind once the mental labels *me* versus *not me* are removed. Whatever arises is just another vibration within Awareness, and clearly, the specific vantage point that each locus of Awareness has does not entail that things appearing as closer are qualitatively different from things appearing as farther.[97] Your body is always in the middle of your awareness-field from your vantage point, but that does not demonstrate that it is any more *you* than anything else in your awareness-field.

Having established that the all-inclusive nature of Awareness is ever present, Kṣemarāja lets his teacher's teacher's teacher make the point that the purpose of a daily practice in this context can only be to remove wrong view, e.g., body-identification, not to attain the essential self, since that by definition is ever present.

**For this very reason,** [Utpala Deva,] **the author of the original *Recognition* text taught** [in a section of his lost commentary]:

> **Daily meditative practice has the purpose of submerging the egoic identification of subjectivity with the body, etc., not to *attain* subjectivity** (the state of the Knower), [since] **the very essence of the latter is its quality of being continually manifest.** ||

The orientation one has to daily practice partially determines the effect of that practice. If one is seeking God, or seeking the innermost Self, one must presume that they are not already present for that seeking to have any sense. One must, in other words, begin by implicitly denying the presence of that which one seeks. This orientation to practice would clearly not be fruitful in the context of a nondual view. Therefore, it's important to get an effective orientation to practice: spiritual practice is that which wears away the ingrained identification with a small portion of the Whole called 'me', little by little every day. The falling away of that identification automatically reveals your oneness with the Whole, which has after all always been the case. True unity-consciousness does not need to be triggered or maintained by an affirmation or belief; it is simply total intimacy with reality.

Daily practice (the Sanskrit word for practice, *abhyāsa*, specifically implies that it is daily) functions like river water running over a piece of hardwood stuck between two rocks: though you can't see the wood disappearing, it is, gradually but inexorably. When the culturally conditioned story "This is what I am" (whatever 'this' is for you) is totally worn away, your ever-present seamless unity with the Whole is revealed. It's already there right now, staring you in the face, hidden in plain sight, waiting to be recognized.

This concludes our study of Sūtra Fifteen and its commentary.

एवं च

चिदानन्दलाभे देहादिषु चेत्यमाने-
ष्वपि चिदैकात्म्यप्रतिपत्तिदार्ढ्यं
जीवन्मुक्तिः ॥ १६ ॥

विश्वात्मसात्कारात्मनि समावेशरूपे 'चिदानन्दे लब्धे' व्युत्थानदशायां दलकल्पतया देहप्राणनीलसुखादिषु आभासमानेषु अपि, यत्समावेशसंस्कारबलात् प्रतिपादयिष्यमाणयुक्तिक्रमोपबृंहितात् 'चिदैकात्म्यप्रतिपत्तिदार्ढ्यम्'–अविचला चिदेकत्वप्रथा, सैव 'जीवन्मुक्तिः'–जीवतः प्राणान् अपि धारयतो मुक्तिः; प्रत्यभिज्ञातनिजस्वरूपविद्रावितारोषपाशराशित्वात् । यथोक्तं स्पन्दशास्त्रे

'इति वा यस्य संवित्तिः क्रीडात्वेनाखिलं जगत् ।
स पश्यन्सततं युक्तो जीवन्मुक्तो न संशयः ॥'

इति ॥ १६ ॥

# CHAPTER SIXTEEN

*Kṣemarāja's original text*

**When one discovers this Joy of Awareness, and stabilizes the realization that Awareness is one with body, etc.—even while they are perceivable—that is called 'embodied liberation'.**

|| 16 ||

**When one** has discovered **this Joy of Awareness**—i.e., the kind of Immersion in which one absorbs everything into oneself—*and* then, in the phase of emerging from it, one **stabilizes the realization that Awareness is one with body**, *prāṇa*, blue, pleasure, **etc.**, seeing them as extensions of that state **even while they are** still appearing, then **that** and that alone can be called '**embodied liberation**'.

One manifests this unity of Awareness in a consistent manner when the impression of Immersion is strengthened by the sequence of methods that will be taught below.

'Embodied liberation' is defined as the freedom that arises for one who has recognized her own essence-nature when the entire mass of bonds melts away yet she continues to maintain the *prāṇas* of the body. As it is said in the Spanda teachings:

> One who has this kind of realization, and thereby becomes permanently connected, seeing the whole world as a divine play, is liberated while embodied, without a doubt.

|| 16 ||

# CHAPTER SIXTEEN

*with explanation*

Having realized that your own essence-nature is the sole author of the Five Acts, and the mind as a result having come to rest in its natural state as Awareness (Chapter Thirteen), and having next accessed your innate power and seen (however briefly) that everything is an expression of what you are (Chapter Fifteen), the next step is to *stabilize* that realization so that it becomes your default state, not just an occasional experience. Here he introduces what at the time was a unique doctrine of nondual Tantra: the possibility of stabilized realization while still in the body, called the *jīvan-mukti* state.[98]

**|| CID-ĀNANDA-LĀBHE DEHĀDIṢU CETYAMĀNEṢV API CID AIKĀTMYA-PRATIPATTI-DĀRḌHYAṂ JĪVAN-MUKTIḤ || 16 ||**

**When one discovers this Joy of Awareness, and stabilizes the realization that Awareness is one with body, etc.—even while they are** [still] **perceivable—that is** [called] ***jīvan-mukti*: 'embodied liberation'.**

**When one has discovered this Joy of Awareness—i.e., the kind of Immersion** [described above] **in which one absorbs everything into oneself—and** [then,] **in the** [subsequent] **phase of emerging** [from it], one **stabilizes the realization that Awareness is one with** [the various phenomena that appear, such as] **body, *prāṇa*, blue, pleasure, etc., seeing them as extensions of that state even while they are still appearing, then that and that alone can be called 'embodied liberation'.**

Here the intensified, empowered, awakened Consciousness described in Chapter Fifteen is given the name *cid-ānanda*, the Joy of Awareness. To be crystal clear about the stages of this process, first you recognize that divine Awareness or Śiva-nature (the author of the Five Acts) is your own essence-nature, then you access your innate power (*bala*; = *śakti*) by centering yourself in that essence-nature, which makes possible the 'absorption' of all things into yourself. It is in this second phase that the Joy aspect of your inherent being becomes apparent. Kṣemarāja here clarifies that the blissful experience of the all-encompassing 'I', the Immersion (*samāveśa*) into the Whole, is also named the Joy of Awareness. This term is particularly resonant because it suggests both *prakāśa-vimarśa* (for which see *Tantra Illuminated*, pages 60–61) and unified Śiva-Śakti.

The experience of unity-consciousness is delightful, but it is in the *transition* back to supposedly normal consciousness that the opportunity lies and the work must be done. The Tantrik tradition is particularly concerned with transitional or liminal states as vital opportunities for furthering realization. In the *samāveśa* experience, unity reveals itself with no effort. Then, after a short or a long time, this mystical state gives way to a more habitual mode of perception. It is this transition, called *vyutthāna*, which is a golden opportunity for integrating and furthering the experience. In the transition, whatever one notices—the sensations of the body, an emotion arising (such as sadness at the experience ebbing away), a thought arising ("Have I lost it?") or an ordinary perception—should be seen as further expressions of that same unitary Awareness that a moment ago effortlessly pervaded. A gentle effort is necessary here, a firm intention to see whatever arises or whatever you notice as an expression of that same Awareness, a vibration of that same Energy, an extension of that same state. The word Kṣema uses for 'extension' literally means 'petal', so the image suggested is one in which unity-consciousness is the center of the flower, and whatever arises when effortless unity-consciousness subsides should be seen as 'petals' of that same flower. In this way, you start to erase the false boundaries between the peak experience and 'ordinary' experience.

Cultivating this understanding during all transitions out of spiritual experiences or spiritual practice periods allows one to increasingly carry the flavor of the unity-experience into everyday interactions. Little by little, everything tastes more and more like Awareness. Nothing stands outside it, nothing is excluded, nothing is divorced from divine Consciousness. When this experiential realization becomes stabilized, that is, when it becomes your default state, that is what we call *jīvan-mukti*, living liberation. 'Default state' means it is your baseline, your normal experience, the state you naturally come back to. It need not be constant, but it is not yet your default state when a stimulus—such as a spiritual teaching or practice—must be applied to activate it. For most people, some key *saṃskāra*s must be healed and digested for the unity of Awareness to become their default state.

Since no one can make Immersion into unity-consciousness happen on cue, what are we to do? How are we to cultivate it?

**One manifests this unity of Awareness in a consistent manner when the impression of the Immersion** [experience] **is strengthened by the sequence of methods that will be taught below.**

If you have experienced the all-encompassing 'I' even once, then you can move forward on this path.* If you want an unwavering manifestation of the unity of Awareness, says Kṣemarāja, then simply strengthen the impression (*saṃskāra*) of that experience through the methods (*yukti*s) he will teach in Chapter Eighteen, until that impression overwhelms the impressions of limited, dualistic, adversarial experience. (He will discuss this same process in terms of the 'expansion of the Center' in the next chapter.)

Finally, Kṣema wishes to define *jīvan-mukti* more specifically, seeing as how it was not yet a widespread doctrine in his time, though it later became one of the most salient contributions of Tantra to mainstream Hinduism.

**'Embodied liberation' is** [defined as] **the** [natural] **freedom that arises for one who has recognized her own essence-nature when the entire mass of bonds melts away yet she continues to maintain the *prāṇa*s of the body.**

Here we have an unusually clear statement that awakening—experiential recognition of your essence-nature—precedes liberation and does not necessarily entail it. For one to be liberated, the 'mass of bonds'

---

* But, I argue, the prerequisite to cultivating unity-consciousness (*śākta-samāveśa*) as your default state is cultivating centeredness in your core, your essence-nature (*āṇava-samāveśa*). Consistent access to *cit* precedes consistent access to *cid-ānanda*. However, as we will see, the practices of Chapter Eighteen are appropriate to both phases of the spiritual journey.

must melt away or be driven off (the Sanskrit word *vidrāvita* means both, and is sometimes used when an enemy army is put to flight). According to some yogic authorities, this would sever the link to the physical body, which is why Kṣema stresses that this state can coexist with full embodiment ("maintaining [all five primary and five secondary] *prāṇas*"). What does it mean for the mass of bonds to melt away? It means the dissolution of ignorance (skewed perspective), of attachment and aversion based in ignorance, and of compulsive self-referencing, but these dissolve (quickly or gradually) of their own accord when reality is seen, and met, as it is. It also means digestion of *saṃskāras*, and therefore anyone who desires embodied liberation must be willing to meet whatever is unmet in the depths of the body-mind.

**As it is said in the Spanda teachings (2.5),**

> **One who has this kind of realization, and thereby becomes permanently connected, seeing the whole world as a divine play, is liberated while embodied, without a doubt. ||**

You may recall that Kṣema cited the Spanda verses that occur right before this one back at the end of Chapter Four. The immediately preceding verse reads: "The state that is not Śiva does not exist in word, thing, or thought. Śiva is everywhere and at all times established as the experiencer in the form of the felt-sense of whatever is experienced" (2.4). So it is this kind of realization that the verse cited above is referring to. One who recognizes that God is all experiencers and all that is experienced sees the whole world as a divine play, and in time becomes permanently connected, constantly yoked, to that realization. Such a one is truly free, even while inhabiting the apparent cage of the body. For such a one, there are no cages, no bonds, and death holds no fear, for he sees that every ending is also a beginning. For such a one nothing needs to be done, yet everything is accomplished. He is at peace while moving and alive while still.

This concludes our study of Sūtra Sixteen and its commentary.

---

अथ कथं चिदानन्दलाभो भवति?—इत्याह

**मध्यविकासाच्चिदानन्द-
लाभः ॥ १७ ॥**

सर्वान्तरतमत्वेन वर्तमानत्वात् तद्भित्तिलग्नतां विना च कस्यचित् अपि स्वरूपानुपपत्तेः संविदेव भगवती 'मध्यम्'। सा तु मायादशायां तथाभूतापि स्वरूपं गूहयित्वा

'प्राक् संवित्प्राणे परिणता'

इति नीत्या प्राणशक्तिभूमिं[15] स्वीकृत्य, अवरोहक्रमेण बुद्धिदेहादिभुवम् अधिशयाना, नाडीसहस्रसरणिम् अनुसृता। तत्रापि च पलाशपर्णमध्यशाखान्यायेन आ ब्रह्मरन्ध्रात् अधोवक्त्रपर्यन्तं प्राणशक्तिब्रह्माश्रयमध्यमनाडीरूपतया प्राधान्येन स्थिता; तत एव सर्ववृत्तीनाम् उदयात्, तत्रैव च विश्रामात्। एवंभूतापि एषा पशूनां[16] निमीलितस्वरूपैव स्थिता।

यदा तु उक्तयुक्तिक्रमेण सर्वान्तरतमत्वे मध्यभूता संविद्भगवती विकसति, यदि वा वक्ष्यमाणक्रमेण मध्यभूता ब्रह्मनाडी विकसति, तदा 'तद्विकासात्' 'चिदानन्दस्य' उक्तरूपस्य 'लाभः'—प्राप्तिर्भवति। ततश्च प्रागुक्ता जीवन्मुक्तिः ॥ १७ ॥

# CHAPTER SEVENTEEN

*Kṣemarāja's original text*

Now, how is this Joy of Awareness discovered? It is taught:

**The Joy of Awareness is discovered through the expansion of the Center.** || 17 ||

The Blessed Goddess who is simply Awareness is called the 'Center' because she continuously exists as the most intimate core of all, and because it is impossible that anything could exist separately from that ground, or have an essential nature of an entirely different kind.

But in the state of differentiation (*māyā*), although she remains Herself, she conceals her real nature, making the realm of life-force energy (*prāṇa-śakti*) her own, as taught by Kallaṭa: "Consciousness is first transformed into Prāṇa." Through a process of further 'descent', she inhabits the levels of the intellect, the body, and so on, flowing into the paths of the thousands of channels (*nāḍīs*).

Though that is the case, as life-force energy she is primarily present in the form of the Central Channel, the Divine Abode extending from 'Brahma's opening' to the 'lower mouth'. This is because all processes arise from and subside into that Channel, like all the veins connect to the midrib of the flame tree leaf. Her precise nature remains concealed from bound souls, although she abides as the very core of their being.

But when the Goddess Awareness, who is the Center, that which is innermost in all, expands through the process of the methods already taught, or, alternately, when the divine Channel that is the Center expands through the methods that are yet to be explained, then, **because of the expansion of** that Center, **the Joy of Awareness** (whose nature has already been taught) **is discovered**, that is, attained. From that discovery arises the aforementioned embodied liberation. || 17 ||

# CHAPTER SEVENTEEN

*with explanation*

From the point of view of the spiritual journey, Kṣemarāja now backtracks. Having already introduced the all-inclusive unity-consciousness characterized as the Joy of Awareness (*cid-ānanda*), which when stabilized manifests as embodied liberation, he now raises the question of how one discovers *cid-ānanda* in the first place. This leads him to discuss the spiritual teaching of the Core or Center. Becoming centered in the core of your being (which is *cit*) is a prerequisite to expanding it, which gives rise to *cid-ānanda*,[99] which eventually becomes all-inclusive. Therefore, Chapter Seventeen introduces some yogic theory, teaching us about the Center, and thereby laying the groundwork for the eleven *yukti*s (practices) of Chapter Eighteen, several of which are yogic.

**Now, how is this Joy of Awareness discovered? It is taught:**

**|| MADHYA-VIKĀSĀC CID-ĀNANDA-LĀBHAḤ || 17 ||**

**The Joy of Awareness is discovered through the expansion of the Center.**

**The Blessed Goddess who is simply Awareness is** [called] **the 'Center' because** [a] **She continuously exists as the most intimate core of all and** [b] **it is impossible that anything could exist separately from that ground (*bhitti*), or have an essential nature of an entirely different kind.**[100]

First Kṣema presents the metaphorical sense of the term Center (*madhya*): Goddess Awareness is appropriately called the center of all living creatures because simple awareness of being is their most fundamental attribute. Even animals are aware of their existence (though they cannot reflect on that fact, lacking *vimarśa*). When you settle into the 'place' within yourself that has been there as long as you can remember, the place where you feel most *you*, free of judgments and stories and self-images, the place where you just let yourself *be* and enjoy being, that is the Center. (See also *Tantra Illuminated*, page 386.) That is why an indispensable element of any spiritual practice is cultivating one's ability to let go of all doing and simply be. To be able to sit and do nothing, truly nothing, is a remarkable spiritual attainment. When we relax into being, we may notice that awareness of being is the only constant in our ever-changing experience, another reason it is appropriately called the Center.

However, 'center' is an imperfect metaphor unless we understand that the center is everywhere: the nonlocalizable ground of being. For this reason, Kṣema identifies the Center with the ground of being metaphorically called 'canvas' (*bhitti*) in Sūtra Two. Nothing can exist separate from Awareness, which is why we call it the ground of being. Another way of saying the same thing is that nothing can have an essential nature (*svarūpa*) other than Awareness, or else it would not appear as an aspect of anyone's awareness and thus would form no part of anyone's experience. Here Kṣema is touching upon the more philosophical discussions of the first two chapters.

There is a less metaphorical sense of the term Center as well: the core of the subtle bodies of sentient beings, an energy column that is related to but not identical to the spinal column of the physical body. This column, called variously the *madhya-nāḍī* ('central channel'), the *suṣumnā-nāḍī* ('graceful channel'), and the *brahma-nāḍī* ('divine channel'), is explained next.

**But in the state of differentiation** (*māyā*)**, although she remains Herself, She** [partially] **conceals Her real nature, making the realm of life-force energy** (*prāṇa-śakti*) **her own, as taught** [in Bhaṭṭaśrī Kallaṭa's *Tattvārtha-cintāmaṇi*]**: "Consciousness is first transformed into Prāṇa." Through a process of further 'descent', she inhabits the levels of the intellect, the body, and so on, flowing into the paths of the thousands of channels** [that animate living organisms].

**Though that is the case, as life-force energy** [in human beings] **she is primarily present in the form of the Central Channel, the Divine Abode** [extending] **from 'Brahma's opening'** [at the crown] **to the 'lower mouth'** [at the pelvic floor]. **This is because all** [biological and cognitive] **processes arise from and subside into that** [Channel], **like** [all the veins connect to] **the midrib of the flame tree leaf.**[101] **Her**

**precise nature remains concealed from bound souls, although she abides as the very core of their being.**

When divine Awareness flows forth into manifestation, it first becomes *prāṇa-śakti* or life-force energy, present in (and making possible) all forms of life from bacteria to the blue whale.[102] (The word 'first' is not used chronologically here, but in the sense of 'most fundamental'.) In yogic theory, *prāṇa* is thought to animate living things, flowing in complex patterns of subtle energy that underlie and interconnect all ecosystems. All eukaryotic living things possess *nāḍī*s or subtle channels along which *prāṇa-śakti* flows, and some of these channels connect to the channels of other beings, forming a great web of life.

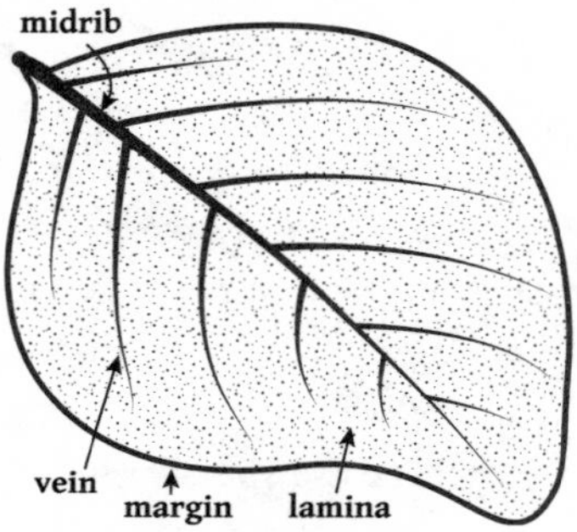


In human beings, the most important *nāḍī* is the central channel, for all other channels connect to it (usually at nexus points called *cakra*s) and it is the basis for all neurological activity. Though lacking the scientific terminology, Kṣemarāja's lineage intuited that the various cognitive processes (*vṛtti*s) arose from and converged at the central channel, which of course is the subtle version of the spinal column. Regardless of the accuracy of their quasi-scientific speculations (which were based exclusively on meditation, not dissection), it is this channel that is of the greatest concern to yogīs. Causing the *prāṇa* to flow freely in an expanded and activated central channel is the yogic equivalent of attaining 'enlightenment'. For this reason there are a variety of meditations and yogic techniques involving the central channel. In yogic theory, during ordinary habitual states of consciousness, *prāṇa* flows almost exclusively in the lateral channels called *iḍā* and *pingalā*, whereas if a person is abiding in Presence, *prāṇa* is flowing primarily in the central channel. Kṣemarāja endorses both the gnostic (insight-based) and yogic paths, and indeed encourages us to see them as aspects of one path, as the following comments demonstrate.

**But when Goddess Awareness, who is the Center, that which is innermost in all, expands through the process of the** [gnostic] **methods already taught, or, alternately, when the divine Channel that is the Center expands through the** [yogic] **methods that are yet to be explained, then, because of the expansion of that** [Center]**, the Joy of Awareness (whose nature has already been taught) is discovered, that is, attained. From that** [discovery arises] **the aforementioned embodied liberation. ||**

Whether the Center is conceived as fundamental Awareness or as the central channel or both doesn't much matter. What matters is that it must be expanded to access the Joy of Awareness. When you contemplate your essence-nature as author of the Five Acts, it expands your sense of what you are. Contemplating awareness as that which emits, sustains, and dissolves phenomena (instead of just passively registering them) expands your sense of what you are. This is the 'gnostic' method of expansion, as is the cultivation of any wisdom-teachings given in the text so far. Both gnostic and yogic methods for the expansion of the central channel will be given in Chapter Eighteen, the longest chapter in the text.

This concludes our study of Sūtra Seventeen and its commentary.

Let's see where we're at by looking at the structure of the last five chapters of the text. First I'll list them in the order Kṣemarāja gives, listing the main point of each sūtra rather than the exact translation.

| | |
|---|---|
| Fifteen: | Attaining innate power (= accessing awakened awareness/being centered in essence-nature) → unity-consciousness (= the Joy of Awareness), but not yet stabilized |
| Sixteen: | *Stabilized* realization of the oneness of Awareness with body, etc. = *jīvan-mukti* |
| Seventeen: | The Joy of Awareness is discovered through the expansion of the Center |
| Eighteen: | Ten ways to expand the Center |
| Nineteen: | Integrate everything with awakened Awareness (recalibration) → *nityodita samādhi* (= *samāveśa*; = continuously arising Joy of Awareness) |
| Twenty: | Fully integrated liberation |

Here we can clearly see what is synonymous with what, an important point in a tradition that frequently states the same thing in different words. For example, Sūtras Sixteen and Ninteen both address the same goal of the path but with different language. The main difference between Sūtras Sixteen and Nineteen is that in the former, the emphasis is on seeing the oneness of Awareness with the body, the mind, and the other layers of selfhood, whereas in Sūtra Nineteen, it is on the oneness of Awareness with all things whatsoever. Seeing the synonymity of Sūtras Sixteen and Nineteen enables us to see how Sūtras Seventeen and Eighteen are a pedagogically motivated backtrack (from the point of view of the individual's spiritual journey). So now let's look at the basic points of each sūtra in the order that the practitioner actually experiences them:

| | |
|---|---|
| Eighteen: | Practice ten ways to expand the Center (= attain innate power) |

| | |
|---|---|
| Seventeen: | Through expansion of the Center, Joy of Awareness is discovered |
| Fifteen: | Through attaining innate power comes unity-consciousness (not yet stabilized) |
| Sixteen: | *Stabilized* realization of the oneness of Awareness with body, etc. = *jīvan-mukti* |
| Nineteen: | Integrate everything within Awareness (re-calibration) → *nityodita samādhi* |
| Twenty: | Fully integrated liberation |

Now that we put things in this order, we can more clearly see that Sūtras Seventeen and Fifteen are stating essentially the same thing in different words, as are Sūtras Sixteen and Nineteen. Furthermore, this order better reflects the stages of the spiritual journey. So why didn't Kṣemarāja put them in this sequence? Because the sequence he uses reflects the common Indian pedagogical structure of question-and-answer. If you go back and look at Sūtras Fifteen to Eighteen again, along with the phrase that introduces each sūtra, you will easily see the logical question-and-answer structure. However, once someone has read this book and comprehended the theory, clearly the thing to do is to focus on the practices of Chapter Eighteen, since Kṣemarāja is very clearly teaching us that without practice, all of this will remain theoretical.

मध्यविकासे युक्तिमाह

विकल्पक्षय-शक्तिसंकोचविकास-
वाहच्छेदाद्यन्तकोटिनिभाल-
नादय इहोपायाः ॥ १८ ॥

'इह' मध्यशक्तिविकासे 'विकल्पक्षयादय उपायाः'। प्रागुपदिष्टपञ्चविधकृत्यकारित्वाद्यनुसरणेन सर्वमध्यभूतायाः संविदो विकासो जायते—इति अभिहितप्रायम् । उपायान्तरम् अपि तु उच्यते;—प्राणायाम-मुद्राबन्धादिसम-

## CHAPTER EIGHTEEN

*Kṣemarāja's original text*

The methods for the expansion of the Center are [now] taught:

**The skillful means here are: dissolving mental constructs, contraction and expansion of energy, pausing the flows, focusing on the beginning and ending point, and so on.**

**|| 18 ||**

**Here**, i.e., in the matter of the expansion of the Central Power, **the skillful means are the dissolution of mental constructs** and the rest. It has already been suggested that the expansion of Awareness—which is the Center of all [beings]—arises by paying attention to one's authorship of the Five Acts and other methods already taught. But here, another means is taught, a quite easeful set of methods that shatters the necessity for all the systems of control such as *prāṇāyāma*, *mudrā*, and *bandha*.

स्तथन्त्रणातन्त्रत्रोटनेन सुखोपायमेव, हृदये निहितचित्तः, उक्तयुक्त्या स्वस्थितिप्रतिबन्धकं विकल्पम् अकिंचिच्चिन्तकत्वेन प्रशमयन्, अविकल्पपरामर्शेन देहाद्यकलुषस्वचित्प्रमातृतानिभालनप्रवणः, अचिरादेव उन्मिषद्विकासां तुर्य-तुर्यातीतसमावेशदशाम् आसादयति। यथोक्तम्

'विकल्पहानेनैकाग्र्यात्क्रमेणेश्वरतापदम् ।'

इति श्रीप्रत्यभिज्ञायाम् । श्रीस्पन्देऽपि

'यदा क्षोभः प्रलीयेत तदा स्यात्परमं पदम् ॥'

इति । श्रीज्ञानगर्भेऽपि

'विहाय सकलाः क्रिया जननि मानसीः सर्वतो
विमुक्तकरणक्रियानुसृतिपारतन्त्र्योज्ज्वलम् ।
स्थितैस्त्वदनुभावतः सपदि वेद्यते सा परा
दशा नृभिरतन्द्रितासमसुखामृतस्यन्दिनी ॥'

इति। अयं च उपायो मूर्धन्यत्वात् प्रत्यभिज्ञायां

[1. *vikalpa-kṣaya*]

One whose mind is fixed on and entrusted to the Heart (through bringing attention to the fact of Awareness), by thinking of nothing in particular, stills the mind's storytelling (which hinders the ability to abide in oneself, as has been explained), and through cultivating conscious contact with prediscursive reality becomes intent on the perception that the one and only Knower is his own awareness, untainted by body-identification and so on.

Through this nonconceptual self-reflective awareness, in very little time one reaches Immersion into the Fourth State and the State Beyond the Fourth, the development of which continually opens up and gradually intensifies.

As it is said in the sacred *Recognition* text:

> Through letting go of mental constructs with one-pointedness, one gradually adopts the standpoint of Divinity. |

Also in the sacred *Spanda* scripture:

> When the agitation of *vikalpa* dissolves, there is the supreme state. |

And in the sacred *Hymn to the Womb of Wisdom*:

> O Mother, having completely relinquished attachment to all mental activities, radiant from releasing enslavement to the pursuit of sense-objects, the people who abide in that freedom rapidly realize, through experiencing Your grace, that supreme state that flows with the nectar of an unremitting, unequalled joy. ||

And this skillful means of *vikalpa-kṣaya* is taught first because it is the primary one, and because it was presented in the original *Recognition* text.

प्रतिपादितत्वात् आदौ उक्तः। शक्तिसंकोचाद-
यस्तु यद्यपि प्रत्यभिज्ञायां न प्रतिपादिताः,
तथापि आम्नायिकत्वात् अस्माभिः प्रसङ्गात्
प्रदर्श्यन्ते; बहुषु[१७] हि प्रदर्शितेषुँ कश्चित् केनचित्
प्रवेक्ष्यति इति।

'शक्तेः संकोच'—इन्द्रियद्वारेण प्रसरन्त्या एव आकुञ्चनक्रमेण उन्मुखीकरणम्। यथोक्तम् आथर्वणिकोपनिषत्सु कठवल्ल्यां चतुर्थवल्लीप्रथममन्त्रे

'पराञ्चि खानि व्यतृणत्स्वयंभू-
स्तस्मात्पराङ्पश्यति नान्तरात्मन्।
कश्चिद्धीरः प्रत्यगात्मानमैक्षद्
आवृत्तचक्षुरमृतत्वमश्नन्॥'

इति। प्रसृताया अपि वा कूर्माङ्गसंकोचवत् त्रासमये हृत्प्रवेशवच्च सर्वतो निवर्तनम्। यथोक्तम्

'तदपोद्धृते नित्योदितस्थितिः।'

इति।

As for the methods of contraction of energy, etc. which follow, they were not presented in the original *Recognition* text; nonetheless, because they are part of our scriptural tradition I will teach them as the occasion demands. For if many methods are taught, someone will enter into Immersion by at least one of them.

[2. *śakti-saṅkoca*]

[a.] 'Contraction of energy' means becoming more conscious of it through the process of bending it back toward the Center, even as it is flowing out through the doors of the senses.

In the first mantra of the fourth chapter of the Kaṭha division of the *Upaniṣads* of the *Ātharvaṇikas*, it is taught:

> The Creator pierced [us with] outward-facing apertures; therefore, one looks out, not to the inner self. A rare wise man, turning the gaze around, looked inward to the self, and tasted immortality. ||

[b.] Or rather, 'contraction of energy' is completely turning back and pulling in the energy that has flowed out, as a tortoise suddenly pulls in his limbs, or like the penetration of *prāṇa* into the core on an occasion of terror. As has been taught:

> When that has dispersed, one abides in the eternally arising. |

‘शक्तेर्विकासः’ अन्तर्निगूढाया अक्रममेव सकलकरणचक्रविस्फारणेन

‘अन्तर्लक्ष्यो बहिर्दृष्टिर्निमेषोन्मेषवर्जितः ।’

इति । भैरवीय[१८]मुद्रानुप्रवेशयुक्त्या बहिः प्रसरणम् । यथोक्तं कक्ष्यास्तोत्रे

‘सर्वाः शक्तीश्चेतसा दर्शनाद्याः
स्वे स्वे वेद्ये यौगपद्येन विष्वक् ।
क्षिप्त्वा मध्ये हाटकस्तम्भभूत-
स्तिष्ठन्विश्वाधार एकोऽवभासि ।।’

इति । श्रीभट्टकल्लटेनापि उक्तम्

‘रूपादिषु परिणामात् तत्सिद्धिः ।’

[3. *śakti-vikāsa*]

'Expansion of energy' means the flowing outward of the energy that has been hidden within through an instantaneous expansion of the entire circuit of the faculties without losing connection to the Center, in accordance with the method of entering into *Bhairava-mudrā*, as in the scriptural quote "Attention within while gazing outward, neither closing nor opening one's eyes."

This is also taught in the *Kakṣyā-stotra*:

> Simultaneously casting all the sense-powers, together with the heart-mind, in all directions, each to their respective sense-field, and standing in the center, as a golden pillar, you shine forth as the singular support of all things. ||

As Bhaṭṭaśrī Kallaṭa also taught:

> Through the transformation of Awareness into form, etc., each thing attains its nature.

इति । शक्तेश्च संकोचविकासौ, नासापुटस्प-न्दनक्रमोन्मिषत्सूक्ष्मप्राणशक्त्या भ्रूभेदनेन क्रमासादितोर्ध्वकुण्डलिनीपदे प्रसरविश्रान्ति-दशापरिशीलनम्; अधःकुण्डलिन्यां च षष्ठ-वक्त्ररूपायां प्रगुणीकृत्य शक्तिं, तन्मूल-तदग्र-त-न्मध्यभूमिस्पर्शावेशः । यथोक्तं विज्ञानभट्टारके

'वह्नेर्विषस्य मध्ये तु चित्तं सुखमयं क्षिपेत् ।
केवलं वायुपूर्णं वा स्मरानन्देन युज्यते ॥'

इति । अत्र वह्निः अनुप्रवेशक्रमेण संकोचभूः, विषस्थानम् प्रसरयुक्त्या विकासपदम्, 'विष्लृ व्याप्तौ' इति अर्थानुगमात् ।

[4. *śakti-saṅkoca-vikāsa*]

[a.] And the 'expansion and contraction of energy' means cultivating & attending to the modes of 'flowing out' and 'coming to rest' in the upper abode of the Kuṇḍalinī. This abode is gradually reached through the piercing of the center between the eyebrows by the subtle *prāṇa-śakti*, which intensifies gradually through the vibration of the mantra in the nasal cavity.

[b.] And, by nourishing the energy in the region of the lower Kuṇḍalinī—that is, the 'sixth face'—there occurs an immersion into sensation on the levels of its root, its tip, and its center.

As taught in the sacred *Vijñāna-Bhairava*,

> One should cast one's heart-mind, full of pleasure, into the center between the 'fire' and the 'poison', with either *kevala-kumbhaka* or *pūraka-kumbhaka*; thus one is connected to the bliss of passion. ||

Here 'fire' is the place of contraction through penetration; the 'site of poison' is the place that expands through outflow. Here the verb *viṣ* is used in the sense of 'pervasion'—this is necessary to understand the sense.

'वाहयोः'—वामदक्षिणगतयोः प्राणापानयोः 'छेदो'—हृदयविश्रान्तिपुरःसरम् अन्तः ककार-हकारादिप्रायानच्कवर्णोच्चारेण विच्छेदनम् । यथोक्तं ज्ञानगर्भे

'अनच्ककककृतायतिप्रसृतपार्श्वनाडीद्वय-
च्छिदो विधृतचेतसो हृदयपङ्कजस्योदरे ।
उदेति तव दारितान्धतमसः स विद्याङ्कुरो
य एष परमेशतां जनयितुं पशोरप्यलम् ॥'

इति ।

'आदिकोटिः' हृदयम्, 'अन्तकोटिः' द्वादशान्तः; तयोः प्राणोल्लासविश्रान्त्यवसरे 'निभालनं'—चित्तनिवेशनेन परिशीलनम् । यथोक्तं विज्ञानभैरवे

'हृद्याकाशे निलीनाक्षः पद्मसंपुटमध्यगः ।
अनन्यचेताः सुभगे परं सौभाग्यमाप्नुयात् ॥'

इति । तथा

'यथा तथा यत्र तत्र द्वादशान्ते मनः क्षिपेत् ।
प्रतिक्षणं क्षीणवृत्तेर्वैलक्षण्यं दिनैर्भवेत् ॥'

[5. *vāha-cheda*]

Pausing the 'flows', i.e., the *apāna* and *prāṇa* moving in the left and right channels, means interrupting them—after bringing them to rest in the heart—with the internal utterance of a vowelless phoneme, something close to k, h, etc. As taught in the *Hymn to the Womb of Wisdom*:

> When one's two lateral channels have flowed to their fullest extent, and one 'cuts' them by a vowelless 'k', keeping attention focused on the inner recess of the lotus of the heart, then the veil of blind darkness is torn, and there arises the sprout of Your wisdom that can produce the state of highest Divinity, even for the bound soul. ||

[6. *ādyanta-koṭi-nibhālana*]

The 'beginning point' is the heart; the 'ending point' is the *dvādaśānta*. Focusing on them at the moment of the emerging and coming to rest of the *prāṇa* is cultivating the practice of settling the mind.

As taught in the *Vijñāna-Bhairava*:

> With one's sense-faculties dissolved in the space of the Heart—in the innermost recess of the Lotus—with one's attention on nothing else: O blessed Lady, one will obtain blessedness. || 49

> Wherever you may be, whatever you may be doing, cast your attention into the *dvādaśānta*. As your mental agitation dissolves moment by moment, you will be transformed in a matter of days. || 51

इति । आदिपदात् उन्मेषदशानिषेवणम् । यथोक्तम्

'उन्मेषः स तु विज्ञेयः स्वयं तमुपलक्षयेत् ॥'

इति स्पन्दे । तथा रमणीयविषयचर्वणादयश्च संगृहीताः । यथोक्तं श्रीविज्ञानभैरवे एव

'जग्धिपानकृतोल्लासरसानन्दविजृम्भणात् ।
भावयेद्भरितावस्थां महानन्दमयो भवेत् ॥
गीतादिविषयास्वादासमसौख्यैकतात्मनः ।
योगिनस्तन्मयत्वेन मनोरूढेस्तदात्मता ॥
यत्र यत्र मनस्तुष्टिर्मनस्तत्रैव धारयेत् ।
तत्र तत्र परानन्दस्वरूपं संप्रकाशते ॥'

इति । एवमन्यदपि आनन्दपूर्णस्वात्मभावनादिकम् अनुमन्तव्यम् । इत्येवमादयः अत्र मध्यविकासे उपायाः ॥ १८ ॥

[7. *unmeṣa-daśā-niṣevaṇa*]

The phrase **'and so on'** [in the sūtra refers to] the practice of attending to the 'unfolding' phase [of each new energy state].

As it is said in the *Spanda-kārikā*:

> That should be known as the 'arising'; let him focus on that in himself.

[8. *ramaṇīya-viṣaya-carvaṇa*]

Likewise encompassed by the phrase 'and so on' are practices such as the relishing of a beautiful sense-object. As taught in the *Vijñāna-Bhairava* itself:

> One should meditate on the state of fullness that expands due to the delight of savoring good food and drink, and that joy will become sublime. ||
>
> The yogin who relishes music and song to the extent that he merges with it becomes filled with unparalleled happiness, attains heightened awareness, and thus experiences oneness with the Divine. ||
>
> Wherever the mind delights, let your attention linger there. In any such experience, the true nature of supreme bliss may shine forth. ||

Thus, one may infer other similar practices as well, such as meditation on oneself when full of joy. These and other ways not here taught are the means in our system for the expansion of the Center. || 18 ||

## CHAPTER EIGHTEEN

*with explanation*

**The methods for the expansion of the Center are** [now] **taught:**

|| VIKALPA-KṢAYA-ŚAKTI-SAṄKOCA-VIKĀSA-VĀHA-CCHEDĀDYANTA-KOṬI-NIBHĀLANĀDAYA IHOPĀYĀḤ || 18 ||

**The skillful means here are: dissolving mental constructs, contraction and expansion of energy, pausing the flows, focusing on the beginning and ending point, and so on.**

Along with Sūtra Seven, this sūtra proves that the Recognition Sūtras cannot be read without their commentary. Sūtra Eighteen gives five out of the eight main practices Kṣemarāja teaches here, and even those five cannot be understood without the commentary.

**Here, i.e., in the matter of the expansion of the Central Power** (*madhya-śakti*)**, the skillful means are the dissolution of mental constructs and the rest.**

**It has already been suggested that the expansion of Awareness—which is the Center of all** [beings]**—arises by paying attention to one's authorship of the Five Acts and other** [gnostic] **methods already taught. But here, another means is taught, a quite easeful** [set of] **method**[s] **that shatters** [the necessity for] **all the systems** (*tantra*) **of control such as *prāṇāyāma, mudrā,* and *bandha*.**

Here Kṣema introduces the Recognition teaching of the *sukhopāya* or 'easy method'—easy, that is, compared to mastering the difficult yogic techniques of *prāṇāyāma* (breath control), *mudrā* (posture), and *bandha* (internal muscular 'lock'), not to mention other 'systems of control' (where control, *yantraṇā*, refers mainly to controlling and channeling energy) such as the complex rituals Tantrik initiates were required to perform. The 'easy method', inspired by Krama teachings, was a significant innovation in nondual Tantra of the tenth century. It provided an alternative path to liberation, one that dramatically shattered the necessity for the more arduous and protracted methods. Yet the powerfully effective teachings of the 'easy method' were mostly forgotten, since they did not enter mainstream Hinduism. Though they continued to be taught through oral transmission in a handful of lineages throughout India, in the main what prevailed was exactly the kind of strenuous yoga and elaborate ritual that these Krama teachings sought to transcend. So it is probable that even with years of experience doing various kinds of yoga, you might not have been exposed to these practices, though if you are an intuitive type, you might have discovered one or two of them on your own. Kṣemarāja explains eight specific practices, mentions a ninth, and alludes to more. Let's encounter them, one by one. I hope you're interested and open, because these practices are truly life-transforming.

### 1. *vikalpa-kṣaya*: dissolving mental constructs

**One whose mind is fixed on and entrusted to the Heart** [through bringing attention to the fact of Awareness]**, by thinking of nothing in particular stills the mind's storytelling** (*vikalpa*) **which hinders the ability to abide in oneself (as has been explained), and through** [cultivating] **conscious contact with prediscursive reality** (*avikalpa-parāmarśena*) **becomes intent on the perception that the** [one and only] **Knower is his own awareness, untainted by body**[-identification] **and so on.**

The first, subtlest, and most important practice is that of dissolving mental constructs, or 'stories' (*vikalpa*), already briefly discussed in Chapters Six and Twelve. Though a little reflection shows you that all your thoughts and narratives about reality are at best imperfect representations of it, not windows onto it, you simply cannot see the extent to which they distort things until you are able to dissolve them and see without them. Since these stories operate even subconsciously, you see through their thick lenses most of your life, starting almost as soon as you can understand language. If as an adult you have had more than a moment of seeing without story, then you *know* you have, because the experience is positively revelatory. It's like a veil being stripped away, one that's been there as long as you can remember, and the world it reveals is bright, clear, vivid, startlingly real, delightfully meaningless, and almost unbearably beautiful.

It's not thoughts *per se* that we are concerned with here; only when a thought is *believed* does it have power to alter and distort your experience of reality. The most insidious kinds of *vikalpa*s are the believed thoughts that connect to all kinds of subconscious baggage. For example, if you believe the seemingly innocent thoughts "I'm a man," or "I'm a mother," or "I'm a spiritual person," they become a source of bondage because you have a huge amount of subconscious programming about what a 'man' or a 'mother' or a 'spiritual person' is supposed to be like.

But the "I am ____" beliefs are among the last vikalpas to fall away; more relevant for a daily practice are the stories arising currently in your daily life. Your unresolved *saṃskāra*s are revealed by the assumptions you make about what other people's words and actions mean. These assumptions are *vikalpas*. Especially in relation to friends, family, lovers, roommates, or partner(s), pay close attention to the difference between exactly what was said or done, and your assumption about what it meant or where it was coming from. Is your interpretation the only possible interpretation of those words? (If you answered yes, then put down the book and start praying for the *śaktipāta* that will awaken you to reality, because you are trapped in the mind-world.) If you pause and reflect for a moment, you admit that there are a range of possible interpretations. But notice the way you feel compelled to believe your interpretation, and regard others as distant possibilities: this is because of the power of your unresolved *saṃskāra*s. In truth, you simply don't know. If you subtract the influence of your *saṃskāra*s, you actually have *no idea* which interpretation, if any, aligns closest to truth. Only when you're not at all triggered do you have any ability to intuit which interpretation points toward truth (this is why you're so much better at coaching other people on their relationships than coping with your own). If you're soft and open, centered and relaxed, you might be able to access the inner intuitive wisdom (called *pratibhā* in this tradition) which regards all stories as communication tools at best and can see which tool is most beneficial in the present situation—benefit being measured in terms of loving and compassionate human connection.

It's when your *saṃskāras* are triggered that it's most crucial to remember, if you can, that the thought you are currently believing about the other person (or people), or about yourself, has no necessary connection to reality. It's kind of like realizing that you're on drugs, and compensating for that fact, though the latter is more obvious and therefore easier. With practice, you can feel the emotional charge of the triggered *saṃskāra*, see the associated thought or projection, and *at the same time* acknowledge to yourself that you don't know for sure where that other person is coming from, or what they think of you, or whether it matters. If you can really feel the truth of unknowing, you'll taste freedom and openness. A sense of freedom and openness is the evidence that you *know* that you don't know (as opposed to just thinking it).

Now, this radical skepticism about *vikalpa*s does not discount your direct experience. When people speak and act, they do so with a certain energy, a certain 'vibe'. You sense that vibe, and prior to having an interpretation of it, you might simply feel uncomfortable, or you might glow with warmth, you might snap to attention or relax into softness. Though it's always possible that those reactions might be connected to very deep-seated *saṃskāra*s, they might also be natural responses. Reactivity comes from *saṃskāra*s, but even if you become totally free of them, there's still natural response, and natural response is a part of your life even now. So you can be skeptical about your interpretations about what you feel, while still acknowledging and even honoring what you feel. If you're feeling fear, it's beneficial to acknowledge to yourself and others that you're afraid, even while you regard skeptically any stories that arise in your mind to explain or justify that fear. So becoming free of *vikalpa*s does *not* mean that you lose all basis for action. Quite the contrary—stories tend to paralyze us and mire us in self-doubt or endless speculation and analysis. (Not all of them, though: as discussed above on page 278, the spiritual teachings are themselves 'stories' that point you toward truth and freedom, for which reason they are called 'pure *vikalpa*s'.)

Furthermore, as Kṣema points out, believing your stories hinders and obstructs your ability to abide in yourself, in your center (*sva-sthiti-pratibandhaka*). Notice how believing a painful thought pulls you off-center; or how believing any compelling thought, even a pleasant one, easily pulls you into a mind-world that is abstracted from present-moment reality. Worry, fantasy, anxiety, or expectation: they all make you a stranger to yourself. Notice the difference in your whole energy-field between those states and that of being established in your center, seated in your core. Do you notice how in the latter condition you are more ready and able to meet reality, whatever it may be? Do you notice how much easier it is to be content and accepting, open and alive? What more evidence do you need that the path to freedom is not picking your way through your stories in search of truth, but rather raising your gaze to the shining horizon of simple being, simple story-free intimacy with reality?

You are not your story about yourself. He is not your story about him. They are not your story about them. Life is not your story about it. Reality is what's happening *before* you have a thought about it. If these statements don't yet seem joyously liberating, then dig deeper to uproot your too-well-cultivated stories. One powerful resource for this is Byron Katie's Work;* another is the spiritual teacher Ādyashānti. Both are expert in helping people become free of *vikalpa*s. With patience, with persistence, you really can be free.

The intention of the foregoing discussion is mainly to convince you of the value of "stilling the mind's storytelling" and "cultivating contact with prediscursive reality", in Kṣemarāja's words. Now we can explore the specific practice instructions that he gives us for *vikalpa* dissolution. First, he invites you to place your mind in the Heart. In the specific language of the nondual Śaiva Tāntrikas, the Heart is a synonym for *bodha*, awareness. So to place the mind in the Heart, or entrust the mind to the Heart, is simply to bring reverent attention to awareness itself—to focus on the fact of being aware. Habitually, we tend to focus on the objects of consciousness, so it takes some gentle effort to focus on the fact of awareness itself; or, we could say, focus on the fact of being itself. However, the term 'awareness' includes not only all that is, but all that could be, and so the field of awareness feels full of all the phenomena one perceives and yet has room for more. It includes all that is yet is somehow indefinably more than the sum of its parts.

---

* Everything you need to do The Work is available free on the website thework.com.

Having entrusted the mind to the Heart that is Consciousness by bringing attention to the essential fact of being-awareness, we are then instructed to "Think of nothing in particular." How is one to do this? The only way, in my experience, is by becoming disinterested in the contents of thought, and fascinated by the context in which thought occurs. If you find your thoughts clever or compelling or morbidly fascinating, it is very difficult to focus on the field of awareness in which they arise and subside. If, however, you realize that for the most part thoughts are tawdry and trivial regurgitations of conditioning, you might become interested in and drawn to what lies beyond. If you are not hypnotized by the content of thought, then you will think of "nothing in particular", content to watch the eddies and currents of thought, feeling, and sensation, while resting in the wider field in which they vibrate. In this way, the *vikalpa*s subside and come to rest.

Next Kṣema invites us to "cultivate conscious contact with prediscursive reality" and by doing so "become intent on the perception that the Knower is one's own awareness". Let's take these one at a time. If in the previous step the mind's storytelling subsided, then it is relatively easy to make conscious contact with prediscursive or unconstructed reality (*avikalpa-parāmarśa*), for this simply means allowing intimacy with *what is.* Prediscursive reality is whatever's happening before you have a thought about it, and if you are interested enough in touching it with your awareness, you can do so for at least a few moments many times a day. Just ask yourself, "What's the quality of the present moment *before* I have a thought about it?" In your daily meditation practice, this can take the form of noticing all present-moment phenomena without labeling them. Notice all the feelings, sensations, sounds, light, color, without labeling them or separating them from each other. To notice thoughts in this way without getting caught up in them, you must give your attention to the *form* of the thought rather than its content. That is, see the thought as a vibration of energy, and notice its qualities without labeling them, the way you would notice the texture of something you touch without having to categorize it. Or put it this way: if someone spoke to you in a language you didn't understand, you could be present with the 'vibe' of that person, perhaps even more easily than if you did understand; in the same way, you can (with practice) notice the vibrational quality of a thought without engaging its content. As soon as you give any attention to the content of the thought, you're in the *vikalpa* realm, and here we're cultivating the *avikalpa*. Of course, it takes practice to observe without labeling, analyzing, or commenting. But it doesn't take so very long if you become convinced that your 'inner commentator' is not as authoritative or valuable or correct as he is generally assumed to be. In fact, what he's doing most of the time is *confabulating*. That means making up plausible explanations for things, including one's own behavior, that actually have little to no basis in fact, *while concealing to oneself that the explanation is fabricated*.

To understand why Kṣemarāja's lineage was so correct and so prescient in advising us to be skeptical of our habitual thoughts and to focus on greater intimacy with the nonverbal aspect of reality, it helps to take a page or so to discuss confabulation, a breakthrough in cognitive science research of the last thirty years. This breakthrough was made possible by test subjects who had undergone a surgical procedure to cure severe epilepsy in which the two hemispheres of the brain are surgically separated. You need to know two simple facts to understand the experiment I'm about to describe: first, that all language-processing happens in the left hemisphere, and second, that the left hemisphere processes visual information only from the right half of the field of vision, and the right hemisphere processes visual information only from the left half. In the classic 1985 experiment by Michael Gazzaniga, he showed these 'split-brain' people different images on a screen to the left and to the right. When he showed them a chicken claw on the right screen (seen only by the left hemisphere) and a snowbank on the left screen (seen only by the right hemisphere) and asked them to then grab a plastic toy corresponding with what they had seen, they grabbed a chicken with their right hand (which is controlled by the left hemisphere) and a shovel with the left hand (which is controlled by the right hemisphere). So far so good (but if you need to, read the last sentence several times and visualize the scene in front of you to get it straight, because if you understand what I'm about to say, it will rock your world). Next Gazzaniga asked them (I say 'them' to indicate that the experiment was replicated, though it was done with one person at a time) why they picked up those two objects. The response was invariably something like, "Oh, that's easy. The chicken goes with the chicken claw, and you need a shovel to clean out the chicken shed."[103] Since only the left brain has access to language and did not see the snowbank, it spontaneously fabricated an explanation for why the left hand picked up the shovel, *without knowing it was a fabrication*. That's called confabulation. In another example, the right brain of a person was shown the instruction "Walk," and the person stood up and started walking; upon being asked "Why are you walking?" the response (from the left brain) was "Oh, I'm going to get a Coke." If you don't have chills yet, consider this: further experimentation has shown that this is not only a behavior seen in split-brain people: we're all confabulating, every day. We feel an impulse to do something, *then* make up a plausible reason why we're doing it. Gazzaniga argued, on the basis of his experiments, that there is an 'interpreter module' in the left hemisphere that gives a running commentary on whatever the self is doing, even though it has little to no access to the real causes or motives of the self's behavior.[104]

Are you getting the picture? It turns out that our fascination with our own randomly arising thoughts is misplaced, and we would be better served by becoming fascinated with other, nonverbal, features of our experience. Now, this is *not* to dismiss the value of careful, systematic reasoning, which is so highly valued in the Tantrik tradition that it is given as one of the 'limbs of yoga' (i.e., *tarka* is a *yogāṅga* in Tantra). But most of our thoughts are randomly arising expressions of our past conditioning. So if you are now thoroughly convinced in the value of the *vikalpa* dissolution practice, let's return to Kṣema's formal practice instructions.

To review, first, we 'place the mind in the Heart' by bringing more attention to the fact of awareness than what we are aware of.

Second, we view the thoughts arising within awareness as insignificant and meaningless, and thereby enter a state of 'thinking of nothing in particular' in which the mind's storytelling naturally subsides, and all kinds of thoughts fade into the background.

Third, we become engrossed with 'prediscursive reality'—whatever presents itself before we have a thought about it. We notice phenomena without labeling, and thus become intimate with raw experience, meeting it and touching it with our awareness (this is called *avikalpa-parāmarśa*).

Fourth, we are instructed to "become intent on the perception that the Knower is one's own awareness." This statement seems mysterious only because the phrase *sva-cit-pramātṛtā* is difficult to translate. It literally means 'the fact that one's awareness is the Knower' but the connotation in Kṣemarāja's usage is that 'awareness is the agent of all experience'. What this means is that everything you experience is arising spontaneously from the formless Awareness that you are in essence. This can most easily be recognized in meditation: if we slow way down, suspend storytelling and analysis, and observe phenomena arise and subside, they cannot be seen to arise from or subside into anything but Awareness.

Finally, Kṣema invites us to notice that this Awareness, in and of itself, is 'stainless': that is, untainted by body-identification, mind-identification, or any other kind of identification. This means that it is not limited to or contingent on any of those more peripheral layers of selfhood. If you look to your direct experience, it is obvious that body, mind, etc. are phenomena arising within awareness, not the other way around. And those phenomena, even when afflicted by pain, do not alter or corrupt the nature of Awareness itself. Check this against your own experience.

Kṣemarāja has given us subtle and powerful instructions. If you implement them with a sense of openness and curiosity, you *will* find your way to the state they point toward. What, then, is the result of this practice of *vikalpa-kṣaya*?

**Through this nonconceptual self-reflective awareness (*avikalpa-parāmarśa*), in very little time one reaches Immersion (*samāveśa*) into the Fourth State and the State Beyond the Fourth, the development of which continually opens up and gradually intensifies** [until it is complete].

I translate the phrase *avikalpa-parāmarśa* a second time because it is so rich: it equally means both 'conscious contact with prediscursive reality' and 'nonconceptual self-reflective awareness'. Both describe the opposite of living in a *vikalpa*-determined world. The second translation points to the nondual aspect of nonconceptual experience: when you suspend the analytical judgmental mind, you see that there is no actual boundary where 'self' ends and 'other' begins. Everything is a reflection of the self, and the self is a reflection of everything. To reflect on anything is to reflect on *what-you-are* in the form of that thing (or person).

Kṣemarāja makes us an extraordinary promise here: committing to the practice of *vikalpa-kṣaya*, we can "in very little time" enter into the state of Immersion, or oneness with reality as it is. There are two versions of this Immersion mentioned here. Briefly, 'the Fourth State' (*turya*) refers to the ability to abide in your core, your essence-nature; it is sometimes called *samādhi*. It is called the Fourth because it lies beyond the standard three states of waking, dreaming, and deep sleep. 'Beyond the Fourth' (*turyātīta*) refers to the experience of essence-nature pervading everything, in other words it is the unity-consciousness already discussed in Chapters Fifteen and Sixteen. When the Fourth State pervades the three normal states, it is called 'Beyond the Fourth' because it is not a fifth state, but just that pervasion of the three by the Fourth. (For more on this, see *Tantra Illuminated*, page 180.) Kṣemarāja is simply saying here that the practice of *vikalpa* dissolution can take you 'all the way', though it must become extremely subtle to do so. The process keeps opening up more and more (*unmiṣat-vikāsa*), until the process itself leads you onward, beyond anything that can be taught or explained.

Next Kṣema quotes scriptural support for his point, as is his wont.

**As it is said in the sacred *Recognition* text:**

> **Through letting go of mental constructs with one-pointedness, one gradually** [adopts] **the standpoint of Divinity.** [*Īśvara-pratyabhijñā-kārikā* IV.11]

Once upon a time, an old folktale goes, two mice in search of sustenance fell into a vat of milk. They swam about desperately, but could not get out, being unable to find any purchase for their little legs on the smooth sides of the vat. One mouse said to the other forlornly, "It's no use; can't you see? There is clearly no way out of this!" And he sank beneath the surface and drowned in the milk. The other mouse could not see any way out either, but he swam and swam, wondering if there was a way he could not see. Finally, as he was getting very tired, his swimming began churning the milk into butter, and he found purchase, and just managed to leap out before his last gasp.

In the American version of this folktale, the moral is "Never give up." But the yogic version is more concerned with why the first mouse died. The answer is clear: he died of a *vikalpa*. (And so, too, do many,

many humans. *Vikalpas* are the number one cause of violent death.) The second mouse remained in unknowing, and trusting the unknown was his salvation. When you know you don't know, you remain open. When you know you don't know, anything is possible. That is the yogic moral to the story.

As the quote above from the *Stanzas on the Recognition of the Divine* states, you need one-pointedness (*ekāgratā*) or dedicated focus, like the mouse who lived, to dissolve the power that mental constructs have over you. The fruit of that dedication is attaining the standpoint of Divinity, because being free of bondage to the mind's stories, you see with a divine eye. You experience things as they are, without conceptual overlay. You encounter reality as a raw revelation, as an inexplicable awesome mystery inseparable from the mystery of your own existence.

Specifically, 'the standpoint of Divinity' (*īśvaratā-pada*) refers to the nonconceptual experience 'I am this whole reality'; in other words, unity-consciousness.[105] This clarification is offered by the great master Utpala Deva in his explanation of the verse quoted above. (See also Chapter Twelve, page 277 above, where the verse that follows this one is quoted.) In that commentary, Utpala further explains the kind of one-pointedness needed to become free of *vikalpas*:

> By applying oneself and intensely cultivating those moments when one's mental construct(s) become attenuated, which occur sporadically in everyday life, conscious beings in the power of *saṃsāra* gradually attain—through the emergence of the divine power of dynamic agency (*aiśvarya*) in its purest distillation—the dissolution of the state of limited individuality.[106]

The practice Utpala describes here requires vigilance and presence of mind. We are to be on the lookout, in the course of everyday life, for moments when our *vikalpas* are weaker, and value those moments, cherish those moments, attribute significance to those moments. This is counter-intuitive in the sense that it goes totally against our conditioning, which would have us cling to our stories that make sense of the world (even though they generate and perpetuate suffering as well), because we feel safer when we believe we know 'what's going on', even if that narrative is confabulated, a mere regurgitation of cultural conditioning. Usually, when a fundamental narrative you hold is undermined in some way, you feel disoriented, destabilized, and perhaps fearful as you brush up against the Great Unknown. But after the awakening process begins, that fear (at least partially) translates into excitement and wonder. Utpala wants us to value the temporary disorientation that necessarily precedes full story-dissolution. ('Story-dissolution' is a convenient shorthand. In fact, what we seek to dissolve is *compulsive belief* in our stories. We do not seek to control our minds so tightly that stories have no room to arise.) A rapidly spinning top looks stable, and slowing down it becomes more chaotic before it comes to rest. In the same way, when you begin fully deconstructing your narratives, you might feel disoriented for awhile, a bit lost at sea, wondering what's real and what can be trusted. This is normal. (It can help in this phase to go for walks in nature, touching leaves and hearing birds and sitting on earth and otherwise having experiences of reality that are undeniable and do not compel interpretation.)

Utpala's phrasing suggests that we notice and cultivate *both* versions of *vikalpa*-weakening in everyday life. When a train of thought we've been riding peters out, giving rise to the possibility of a moment of just *being*, we are to seize those precious moments, instead of, say, immediately reviewing the thought-train to see how we got from point A to point Z. With practice, every time a train of thought loses steam, you will wake up to the glorious opportunity of just being present to your total environment (including, of course, your body and your energy-state). This entails becoming less and less enraptured by the free-association thought-stream of the conditioned mind. This is the simpler version of the practice. The second, subtler one, already alluded to in the previous paragraph, is being open to new information that disconfirms what you think you know, or being open to a different perspective that undermines your established narrative about something. (Incidentally, this is an attitude that's beneficial to all your relationships as well.) Not only being open to it, but inviting it in and letting it destabilize your established view on whatever the subject is, thereby opening you up to the wonder and aliveness of not knowing anything for sure, and to the greater flexibility that comes with that openness.

Instead of passing over these opportunities and retrenching in the apparent safety of your fixed opinions, realize that they are walls between you and others, and between you and the world as-it-is. Take delight in the many opportunities life offers you to see that your static mental pictures of things don't even begin to capture a fluid, complex reality that is continuously reconfiguring itself. Resolve to escape the musty museum rooms and concrete corridors of the mind-world, and taste the joy of being inconceivably *what-you-are*, in fluid patterns of intuitive relating with an ever-fresh universe of being.

**Also in the sacred *Spanda*** [scripture it is said]*:*

> **When the agitation** [of *vikalpa*] **dissolves, there is** [nothing but] **the supreme state.** | 1.9cd

The mind-world is one of anxiety and agitation. Anxiety due to a subconscious knowing that one's stories are inadequate, distorted, and self-serving, and agitation due to the pressing need to better 'figure things out' and thus be safer and more secure. Here Kṣema quotes a half-verse from the *Stanzas on Vibration*. The agitation mentioned in the quote is specifically that of a person preoccupied with stories of 'what should be done'. We know this from the first half of the verse, not quoted here, in which a person is said to be incapacitated by these 'should' stories: rendered powerless by the anxiety and agitation that accompanies the belief that one 'should' conform to extrinsically determined obligations or norms of behavior. But perhaps Kṣema quotes only half the verse because he wants to make a more general point: that when the confused mêlée of *vikalpas* subsides through these practices, it naturally reveals the still ocean of peaceful being here called 'the supreme state'. What a relief to be free of 'shoulds' and 'should nots', to be free to meet others' needs out of the joy of contributing to their well-being instead of out of the burden of guilt and obligation! It is not overpraising such a mode of being to call it the supreme state. And in this state, so much more energy and aliveness is available to you. It is probably not a coincidence that the verse of the *Spanda-kārikā* quoted here occurs immediately after a verse (1.8) that is parallel to our Sūtra Fifteen, extolling as it does the value of *ātma-bala-sparśa*, 'contacting the innate power of the [innermost] self'. Free of the belief in obligation, that you 'should' or 'have to' behave a certain way, you actually have much more ability to make life more wonderful for others as well as yourself.

Kṣemarāja climaxes this section by citing an exquisite verse from a lost text. It praises the Goddess as the 'womb of wisdom'; he will cite it again further on.

**And in the sacred *Hymn to the Womb of Wisdom*** (*Jñāna-garbha-stotra*):

> **O Mother, having completely relinquished attachment to all mental activities,** [and thereby] **radiant from releasing enslavement to the pursuit of sense-objects, the people who abide** [in that condition of freedom] **rapidly realize, through experiencing Your grace, that supreme state that flows with the nectar of an unremitting, unequalled joy.** ||

This verse describes *sādhaka*s who have seen the futility of attaching significance to the mind's regurgitations of its conditioning, and who have likewise seen that no interpretation or mental model of things could possibly capture more than a fleeting fragment of the supremely complex reality of this magnificently mysterious universe. These *sādhaka*s are further said to be radiant, positively glowing with the joy of finally throwing off their dependence on running around after pleasurable experiences. While clearly Tantra has nothing against sensual experience, here the key word is 'enslavement' to their pursuit, and that is what we are invited to free ourselves from. Indeed, the hunger for certain experiences (whether related to wealth, power, status, or sex) effectively pulls us out of our natural center. It may be the case that the author of this verse sees the second clause as dependent on the first; that is, throwing off enslavement to the pursuit of those experiences is much easier if one has deconstructed the social conditioning that makes us believe we need them to be happy. A raft of studies have now shown that because humans habituate so rapidly to new situations, no one is fulfilled by more money, power, status, or sex for very long.[107]

Those who abide in the condition of freedom just described 'rapidly realize the supreme state'. The words chosen for 'supreme state', *parā daśā*, suggest that the Goddess this hymn has in mind is Parā Devī, the Supreme Goddess of the Trika branch of Śaiva Tantra. People are said to actualize the supreme state, the condition of full awakeness, through experiencing her divine grace. What does this mean in a nondual context? Well, Parā Devī is said to be the personification of *pratibhā*, which simultaneously means intuitive insight, embodied instinct, and creative inspiration. So I propose that 'experiencing [Her] grace' means accessing that intuitive faculty. If *pratibhā* is indeed being subtly implied here, that is both significant and apropos—for it is this faculty that takes the place of *vikalpas* in guiding the actions of an awakened being. In other words, one who has broken free from social and cultural conditioning would be cast adrift with no sound basis for decision-making if not for the fact that such freedom gives greatly increased access to the deep, nonverbal intuitive faculty that all of us have but few of us get quiet enough to sense.* Since *pratibhā* is a kind of compass to sense the natural flow of the deeper Pattern, it provides a far sounder basis for action than our narrow, provincial, ephemeral, and idiosyncratic cultural conditioning. Since the Pattern always naturally moves toward harmony, following your deepest inner intuition is always the most beneficial course for all beings. The 'voice' of *pratibhā*, unlike that of the mind, doesn't speak loudly, doesn't defend or explain itself, but simply offers itself as a gift. It often feels like a deep current, a persistent quiet pull toward anything that aligns with your essence-nature, and thus is different from desires, whims, or fancies. Following that pull immediately yields a feeling of 'rightness', though not following it doesn't necessarily feel wrong, just less right. Following it consistently makes your whole life feel permeated by 'flow' (even though there may be challenges), because you are in harmony with the greater Pattern.

But is "experiencing Her grace" only a code for accessing your innate intuitive faculty? On the contrary, the phrase also conveys something closer to its literal meaning, because there is always acknowledgment in this tradition that we can and do have experiences of what feels like a higher power flowing through us. Even though all is one and nothing is other, we can feel profoundly blessed by a benevolent force that seems awesome in its scope and power. Though you are in your deepest nature non-different from that force, don't you savor and value that experience? In the nondual view, there is not a separate divine personality that you must abase yourself to, but that doesn't mean God/dess isn't real. From the perspective of the embodied individual,

---

* Those raised in the Judeo-Christian tradition might compare *pratibhā* to the "still small voice" with which God spoke to Elijah (1 Kings 19).

opening into one's deeper nature is like surrendering into an ocean of Presence, far vaster than you ever imagined yourself to be. The habitual 'small self' or constructed identity 'dies' into that Presence, and in that way is graced. Contrary to what you ever expected, the 'death' of the person you thought you were is joyous beyond compare. There may be a little nostalgic regret in letting it go, but if so, it is soon carried away on the current of flowing nectar—"the nectar of an unremitting, unequalled joy".

What price must we pay to abide in this Presence and access its concomitant joy? Here I must come clean with you: the price of Truth is everything. That is to say, to realize and *abide in* the supreme state, you must be willing to let go of anything, to sever any attachment, to digest all your self-images and see through all your stories, including the ones that give you comfort. You don't get to retain the self-images and stories that make you feel good and just relinquish the so-called 'negative' ones. They are inseparably part and parcel of the same mind-world, and you can't become free of it until and unless you burn the whole house of cards. To do that, you have to want Truth more than you want anything else.

Having said that, you can deconstruct, dissolve, and relinquish your obviously negative stories first, but eventually you must see how your 'positive' stories are always sown with the seeds of future suffering. (Take for example the stories "He makes me so happy!" or "I have a blessed life"—do you see the seeds of suffering in them? What happens when he moves on? When tragedy strikes? The enjoyment you derive from the 'positive' story is cancelled out by the suffering of the subsequent reversal. The degree to which you're attached to the 'positive' is proportional to the suffering you experience when it is undermined or disconfirmed in some way. Check this against other 'positive' stories you hold.) Even if you have only 'positive' self-images, you suffer when they are challenged (in a degree proportional to your attachment to them), because they are nothing but static representations of tiny aspects of your infinite being, and they stand between you and direct experience of your essence-nature just as much as 'negative' self-images. The only difference is they feel better, which makes them harder to let go of. But trust me—the unconditioned free-flowing joy of abiding in essence-nature makes attachment to the pleasure of positive self-images seem like the pathetic dependency of a drug addict. Being free of the need for self-images, self-referencing, and egoic narratives is a high with no comedown and no side-effects. It is indeed a state that flows with the nectar of an unremitting, unequalled joy.

**And this skillful means** [of *vikalpa-kṣaya*] **is taught first because it is the primary one, and because it was presented in the** [original] ***Recognition* text.**

**As for the** [methods of] **contraction of energy, etc.** [which follow], **although they were not presented in the** [original] ***Recognition* text, nonetheless, because they are part of our scriptural tradition I will teach them as the occasion demands. For if many** [methods] **are taught, someone will enter into** [Immersion] **by** [at least] **one** [of them].

These sentences are self-explanatory, but note the last sentence, which explains the Tantrik strategy of teaching many practices and techniques: though just a handful (or even one) of them—if cultivated deeply enough—could take you all the way, to do so they must really 'click' with you. Hence a wide enough range must be offered so that each student can experiment and play with the practices until one or several indicate that they will bear fruit. Let us then encounter the sampling of Tantrik practices that Kṣemarāja has chosen. They are a mix of standard and esoteric techniques, of the simple and the subtle, and of the formal and the informal. It is a selection unique to Kṣema's teaching.

### 2. *śakti-saṅkoca*

[a.] **'Contraction of energy' means becoming more conscious of it through the process of bending it back toward** [the Center]**, even as it is flowing out through the doors of the senses.**

This subtle practice is a kind of 'second attention': that is, a practice that can be cultivated while doing other things, while out and about in the world or at home. It's simple enough to learn: simply take a moment to slow down and feel the energy pouring out into the world from within you. Without judgment or evaluation, ask yourself, with what kind of energy are my senses meeting the world? Is it desirous? Is it anxious? Is it excited? Is it grasping? Is it grateful? Is it needy? Is it loving? Is it manipulative? Is it accepting? (With practice, you won't need to label it to feel its qualities.) Whatever the kind of energy flowing out, 'bend' some of it back inward to feel it more fully, kind of like how planet Earth's magnetic energy moves out then arcs back in: Do not attempt to transmute or change the energy—that impulse arises from judgment of it. Instead, just be with it for a couple of minutes, and if it spontaneously transmutes, fine. If not, equally fine.

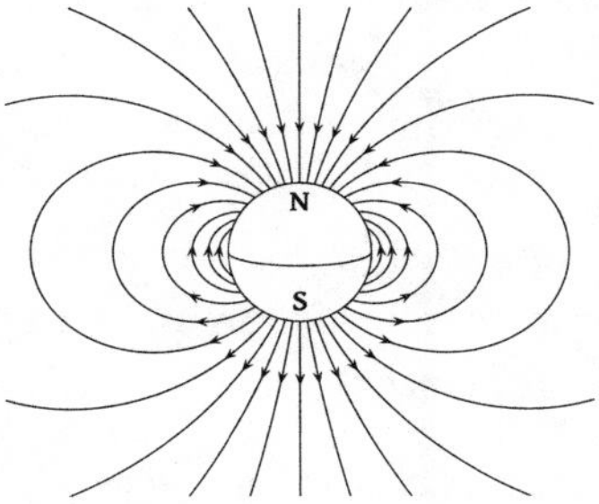


If you're not energy-sensitive and the instruction to bend some of the energy back toward the center doesn't make practical sense to you, then you can accomplish much the same effect by simply placing secondary attention in your heart center while you're doing whatever you're doing. While doing the dishes, or talking to someone, or preparing food, or surfing the Internet, keep your primary attention on what you're doing while simultaneously being aware of the feeling in the heart center. Then become aware of the connection (or lack thereof) between the heart center and what you're doing, without judgment. Are you feeling frustration and heartache? How is that manifesting in your actions and the way you see things? Are you feeling open and alive? How is that manifesting in your actions and the way you see things? Get curious. Here I'm using words, but let your awareness of your energy be as nonverbal as possible. If your attention shifts onto thoughts and stories about *why* you're feeling a certain way, you've lost the practice. Come back to the energy itself, and how it's affecting your relationship with your environment, without judgment. If noticing that spontaneously shifts the energy to a different frequency, fine. But it's crucial to practice *being with what is*, without trying to change *or* resisting change. Just see the thoughts and stories that arise, if any, as the epiphenomena resulting from your *saṃskāras* reacting to the energy moving through you, and remember that energy itself is neither bad nor good. (If you blame others for your energy state, your words and actions might become harmful, but that doesn't mean the energy itself is bad.) You don't need to engage the stories or decide if they're true or not; let them spin off like energy dust devils and just keep feeling the quality of the energy. Get intimate with your energy. As the practice progresses, let go of naming or labeling the energy and instead be aware of what it feels like: its 'temperature', 'texture', 'color', and 'frequency of vibration', as it were (these are metaphors).

There are many forms of second attention.[108] If you see the value in this practice, but can't remember to do it periodically throughout the day, then you might set an alarm to remind yourself. Ideally, you would do the practice for a few minutes every hour throughout the day. The increase of self-awareness, compassion for yourself, and sensitivity to your total environment repays the time invested ten times over.

As usual, Kṣema gives a proof-text for the practice, but unusually, he cites an ancient *Upaniṣad* (c. 300 BCE) instead of a Tantrik source.

**In the first mantra of the fourth chapter of the Kaṭha division of the *Upaniṣads* of the *Ātharvaṇikas*,[109] it is taught:**

> **The Creator pierced** [us with] **outward-facing apertures; therefore, one looks out, not to the inner self. A rare wise man, turning the gaze around, looked inward to the self, and tasted immortality.** ||
> [*Kaṭha Upaniṣad* 4.1]

Not only does our culture encourage us to look outside of ourselves for what we seek, but even most religions and spiritual paths encourage us to keep looking outward: to dogmatically rely on this or that text, to model ourselves after this or that teacher, to compare ourselves to other practitioners, to study our astrological chart, to receive this or that attunement, to ingest this or that psychotropic 'medicine', to acquire the right talismans or crystals or holy relics ... the list goes on. But the fundamental orientation of a seeker of the truth is *inward*, not *outward*. To see everything there is to see by looking within. To penetrate through layer after layer, until there's no further to go: and then, intimate with the whole of yourself, discerning the difference between core and periphery, between abiding essence-nature and its shifting clothing, you 'taste immortality', meaning you experience directly the part of yourself that is unborn and undying. The verse following the one above, *Kaṭha Upaniṣad* 4.2, states bluntly:

Childish people pursue outward desires,
and enter the noose of death spread wide.
But the wise know what constitutes the immortal,
and do not seek the stable in unstable things of this world. ||[110]

[b.] **Or rather,** [contraction of energy] **is completely turning back and pulling in the** [energy] **that has flowed out, as a tortoise** [suddenly] **pulls in his limbs, or like the** [instinctive] **penetration** [of *prāṇa*] **into the core on an occasion of terror.**

Now Kṣema gives another version of the *śakti-saṅkoca* practice. This is not a form of second attention, for here we are invited to pull *all* our energy strongly inward toward the core, the central channel. Try it this way: when you're feeling scattered, or ungrounded, or anxious, or confused, or destabilized, or enraged, or overjoyed, close the sense-gates (eyes, etc.) and pull all your energy in toward your center, toward the inner core of your being, and feel it fully while letting it stabilize. Even if you can't close your eyes in the situation you're in at that moment, it can still be beneficial to pull everything in toward the center. You may experience your central channel (which runs through your gut, heart, throat, and head) intensify with the vibration of the rage or confusion or joy or whatever you're feeling. After a moment of feeling it fully, cultivate the sense that there are openings at the pelvic floor and the crown of the head so that excess energy can discharge down or up if it's ready to (but don't try to *make* it discharge; it's important to let go of the need for control motivated by fear of your feelings).[111]

When feeling joy or excitement, it's a powerful practice to pull it all into the core for a few minutes and feel it totally, feel it as pure energy. That's one way to avoid laying down an attachment-saṃskāra. But to do this practice with so-called 'negative' emotions, you must relinquish the culturally conditioned idea that they are harmful or bad in some way. All emotions are just energy (*śakti*), and we only flow that energy into harmful actions when we *believe our story* about someone else being to blame for how we feel. It's vikalpas that can be harmful, not emotions. If you can experience a 'negative' (read: unpleasant or challenging) emotion nonjudgmentally as pure energy, it becomes 'food' for the energy-body. It is digested, and then one experiences the subtle vibration of pure being in the middle of everything. This is taught in the text Kṣema cites next.

**As has been taught:**

> **When that has dispersed, one abides in the eternally arising.** |

While the text cited here is lost, it is probably teaching something similar to the practice found in the *Stanzas on Vibration* at verse 1.22 (with commentary). Briefly, when one experiences the arising of rage, joy, confusion, or any other intense emotion, one is to dive into it immediately, before the mind starts confabulating stories about it, and feel it fully. If successful in letting the energy into your very center and feeling it fully, then it will soon settle and subside, revealing the very subtle yet very alive pulsation that is the pure awareness of being called *spanda.* (This is the very same thing as the subtle pulsation of the *mahā-mantra* 'I am' discussed in Chapter Twelve.) The text cited just above calls that pulsation, that basic awareness of being, the 'eternally arising' (*nityodita*), meaning that it is dynamically ever renewing itself even though it is eternal. In fact, the Sanskrit phrase used here, *nityodita-sthiti* (which could also be translated as 'stably situated within the eternally arising'), suggests that this *spanda* state is simultaneously still and pulsing, implying the perfect fusion of Śiva and Śakti. Though being very still and pulsing at the same time might seem like a paradox to the mind, it does describe a real experience. Try the practice and see for yourself (you might need several attempts to get the hang of it).

Let's review then. The *Spanda* verse I paraphrased above reads as follows:

> Enraged or overjoyed, panicked or confused, and wondering what to do: when one fully enters into states like these, the innate vibrancy of Awareness is demonstrated.* || 1.22

The key practice points found only in the Sanskrit commentary on this verse and in Kṣemarāja's teaching above involve: (1) diving into the feeling when it first arises, before the mind starts making stories about it; (2) pulling it all the way into the center to feel it more fully; and (3) the fact that the innate vibrancy of Awareness is experienced when the

* Or one could translate, "The innate vibrancy of awareness is situated within the states of rage, joy, panic, or confusion that one fully enters into."

emotional energy subsides.[112] So when it starts to pass, don't be so quick to turn your attention to the next thing, but rather let yourself abide in the gently pulsing stillness—that's the core of your being.[113]

This is not to say that you need to wait for an intense emotion to arise to do this second *śakti-saṅkoca* practice. Anywhere, anytime that you want to stabilize yourself in the Center, you can pull all your energy into your core and just be with whatever you feel. And if your circumstances are not conducive to that, you can always do the first *śakti-saṅkoca* practice described above (2.a.), where you bend part of your energy back inward while still being engaged in the world.

Before moving on, let us remember that *all* the practices in Chapter Eighteen are said to accomplish the 'expansion of the Center'. Since the Center can mean 'fundamental Awareness' it's clear enough how the story-dissolution practice accomplishes that, but what about *śakti-saṅkoca*, the contraction of energy practices? Recall that the Center also means the central channel, the energetic core of one's being. Becoming more aware of your energy, and pulling some or all of it into the Center is a way of expanding your access to that Center. Only when you've accessed it can you then expand outward in a stable and sustainable manner—and that's our next practice.

### 3. *śakti-vikāsa*

**'Expansion of energy' means the flowing outward of the** [energy] **which has been hidden within through an instantaneous expansion of the entire circuit of the faculties** [without losing connection to the Center], [in accordance] **with the method of entering into *Bhairava-mudrā*, as in** [the scriptural quote] "Attention within [while] gazing outward, neither closing nor opening one's eyes."

The wording here implies that this practice should be done subsequent to the second *śakti-saṅkoca* practice described just above, since the energy is said to be "hidden within". If these practices are done in succession, that constitutes a larger-scale *spanda*, an oscillation from inward contraction to outward expansion. It's important when expanding awareness that you expand out from the Center. Here we are invited to suddenly fling the net of awareness wide, meeting everything in the whole field of perception. The Sanskrit word used, *visphāra*, means not only 'expansion' and 'opening wide' but is also used to describe a bird spreading its wings and the sudden twanging of a bowstring. So it describes a sudden expansion of awareness from the center to its widest circumference. It is described above as "an expansion of the entire circuit of faculties" because all the sense-gates are open and all the senses are fully engaged. (This will be described more fully below.) While fully embracing the whole field of perception, you retain awareness of what is subtle and internal as well: your felt sense of the Center. Kṣema makes this explicit by telling us that this practice is identical to what is called *Bhairava-mudrā* or *śāmbhavī mudrā*, in which one has eyes wide open but retains attentiveness to the inner world. He gives a quote from a lost scripture about *Bhairava-mudrā* that specifies that one is to have "Gaze outward, [yet] attention within, without closing or opening the eyes". Doubtless, the last phrase is not an injunction to avoid blinking; rather, it suggests that one's attention should not turn so far inward that one loses touch with the 'external' world, nor should it turn outward to the extent that one loses awareness of the Center.

You might think this virtually identical to the 'second attention' practice described above (under 2.a.), but the difference is that here you cannot do the practice while engaged in a specific task since you are to be equally aware of the *whole* field of perception. Thus, this practice is in fact a more advanced version of the *tattva-bhāvanā* practice given in Chapter Eight. The differences are: (a) here you expand awareness to the whole field of perception suddenly (which is much easier if you've been cultivating the *tattva-bhāvanā* practice), and (b) you retain constant awareness of the Center. Fortunately, Kṣema gives us a bit more guidance about the practice by quoting a Vaiṣṇava *tāntrika* who lived perhaps a century earlier.[114]

**This is** [also] **taught in the *Kakṣyā-stotra*** [of Divākara Vatsa]:

> **Simultaneously casting all the sense-powers,**
> **together with the heart-mind, in all directions, each**
> **to their respective sense-field, and standing in the**
> **center, as a golden pillar, you shine forth as the**
> **singular support of all things.** ||

Though this verse's author was probably addressing the deity Viṣṇu, here Kṣema clearly understands the 'you' in the verse to refer to the practitioner, and reads it as prescription rather than description. One is to simultaneously 'cast' the power of sight to the whole visual field, the power of hearing to the whole auditory field, the power of touch to the whole tactile field, and so on. The heart-mind is also included, meaning that the vibrations of energy we call thoughts and emotions should be embraced to the same degree as the images, sensations, sounds, and smells. But precisely to the same degree, mind you: in this practice, you are not to see your thoughts and emotions as any more significant than whatever sounds you happen to hear, images you see, or sensations you feel. The goal is to embrace the whole field of perception equally, experiencing *everything* as a vibration of Awareness. Every vibration deserves the same amount of attention, but simultaneously, not individually and sequentially. For this you must be quite relaxed, or your attention cannot go into 'soft focus' and embrace everything together.

In the second half of the verse we are given a poetic instruction to retain awareness of the Center: we are given an evocative image of the central channel as a golden column of light. You do not need to try to visualize it as such; with practice, you can feel as if your central channel is glowing with golden light, and this helps you retain awareness of the Center while embracing the whole field of perception. Even more so if you can feel that the Center is the 'singular support of all things' (*viśvādhāra*). That is, as you do this practice, you can cultivate the sense that the core of awareness, the central channel, the golden column of light, is actually emanating and sustaining all the phenomena you perceive. All perceptible things are a form of energy, and all that energy is a radiant expression of the Center. This is exactly what is meant by the following quote.

**As Bhaṭṭaśrī Kallaṭa also taught:**

> **through the transformation** [of Awareness] **into form, etc.,** [each thing] **attains its** [nature].

Kallaṭa, you may recall, is the much-revered author of the *Stanzas on Vibration*. Though we are given only a fragment of a lost text by him here, it is clear from context that what is meant is that: (a) Awareness transforms itself into all the objects of its experience (visual, auditory, tactile, cognitive, etc.), and (b) through this transformation (really more of a permutation) of Awareness, each thing attains its nature, i.e., becomes what it is and performs its natural function. The word used here for attains/becomes/performs is *siddhi*, the same key word found in Sūtra One.

So this practice culminates in the direct realization that Awareness causes each and every thing to appear and express its nature *by becoming that thing.* Can you imagine any greater intimacy? Goddess Awareness, we might say, so loves all the potentialities inherent in her being that She becomes them all. For God so loved the world, She became it. And you are She.

4. *śakti-saṅkoca-vikāsa*

[a.] **And the 'expansion and contraction of energy'** [in the first instance] **means cultivating and attending to the** [two] **modes of 'flowing out' and 'coming to rest' in the upper abode of the Kuṇḍalinī. This abode is gradually reached through the piercing of the** [center] **between the eyebrows by the subtle *prāṇa-śakti*, which intensifies gradually through the vibration** [of the *anusvāra* of the mantra] **in the nasal cavity.**

Practices 4a and 4b activate the central channel fully through stimulating the upper and lower Kuṇḍalinī respectively. Since these teachings were closely guarded, Kṣemarāja uses allusive, elliptical, and cryptic language to describe them. I spent a couple of years researching Sanskrit passages that might explain these half-a-dozen lines of his text, and though I can't be sure of 100% accuracy, I think most of what I'm about to say is verifiably correct. At any rate, here these two practices are explained for the first time in print.

First off, we encounter in this passage the esoteric Kaula doctrine of not one but *two* Kuṇḍalinīs, an upper and a lower, each of which need to be activated so that, flowing freely in the central channel, they may merge. In this way, the sexual energy (≈ lower Kuṇḍalinī) is sublimated, and the urge to transcend to a higher plane (≈ upper Kuṇḍalinī) is grounded, and each balances the other in the state of embodied liberation.

In Kṣema's teaching, the upper Kuṇḍalinī is stimulated through the esoteric Tantrik technique called *uccāra*, in which a single-syllable mantra is raised up the central channel and then vibrated intensely in the nasal cavity (see *Tantra Illuminated*, pages 393). To unify the upper Kuṇḍalinī with the rest of the life-force energy (*prāṇa-śakti*), that energy must be focused through the *uccāra* practice to such an extent that it penetrates both the psychic knot in the center of the head, sometime called the *māyā-granthi*, and the *ājñā-cakra* (the 'center between the eyebrows') above it. The *prāṇa-śakti* yoked to the appropriate *bīja* mantra is said to form a 'sound-needle' (*nāda-sūcī*) that pierces the knot of duality, which is sometimes analogized to the dense part at the base of a flower. Once it is pierced, the *ājñā* center opens up like a flower blooming (this is sometimes called the 'opening of the third eye'), and there is a free flow of energy to the higher *cakras* at the crown and above. Even more important than the opening up of the third eye is the opening of the *brahma-randhra* (the 'gateway to God') at the crown, as a result of which energy can be drawn in and emitted through it easefully. Then one can practice 'attending to the modes of flowing out and coming to rest' that Kṣema speaks of, which probably refers to a *spanda* in which upper Kuṇḍalinī expands and fills the body with nectarean joy, then contracts and comes to a sweet place of repose, subtly pulsing at the crown.

Having said all that, you are still probably asking, "But what exactly am I supposed to *do*?" The practice of *uccāra* cannot be fully taught in a book. One selects the appropriate *bīja* mantra and utters it in a prolonged fashion, using an entire controlled exhale, while feeling its energy rise up the central channel from the lower abdomen to the nasal cavity.

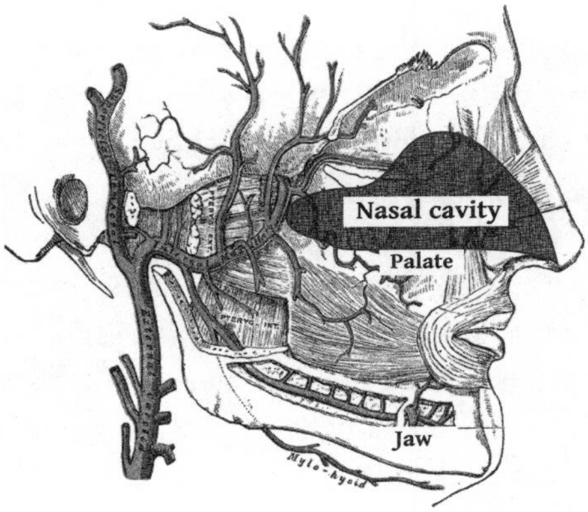


When it reaches that region, it vibrates there in the form of a pure nasal, similar to a hum. This sound is denoted in mantras transliterated into our alphabet with the character ṃ or ṁ, as in OṂ or HŪṀ. But what specific seed-mantra should you use for this practice? That question brings us to the origin of the word *kuṇḍalinī*, which is a feminine possessive word literally meaning 'having a ring' (a *kuṇḍala*), formed in the same way as *yoginī*, a feminine word meaning 'having yoga'. So what is the ring alluded to by the word's etymology? It was almost definitely a reference to an old way of writing the character ह्र *hr*, which as you can see has a ring formation. You see, in the oldest usage of the word *kuṇḍalinī* (c. eighth century), it refers to a mantric power, a secret seed syllable, probably HRĪṀ. Later, when this usage was forgotten, *kuṇḍalinī* came to be called 'the serpent power' only because a serpent sleeps in a coiled shape like a ring. It's possible, even likely, that Kṣemarāja has two seed-mantras in mind, one for the upper and one for the lower Kuṇḍalinī. If so, the most probable candidates are HRAUṀ and HRĪṀ respectively.

This is about all I can say about the practice here. Please do not attempt to undertake *uccāra* practice without guidance, because doing it incorrectly or overdoing it can have undesirable results, up to and including temporary psychosis. There are a number of important details to performing it correctly and beneficially.

[b.] **And, by nourishing and sublimating the energy in** [the region of] **the lower Kuṇḍalinī—that is, the 'sixth face'—there occurs an 'immersion into sensation' on the levels of its root, its tip, and its center.**

This practice is parallel to the previous one, in that it seeks to intensify the energy such that it may break open a subtle knot (the *brahma-granthi*) and thereby allow the Kuṇḍalinī to flow freely into the central channel. The details, though, are obscured by the vague and elliptical language, because this is a sexual practice and as such secret. In the interest of transparency, I will say that this is the only practice in Chapter Eighteen that I have not personally worked with in any depth. Hence my translation of the details of the practice is still provisional, though I have given it much thought, and I am reasonably confident of the interpretation I am about to give.

The first coded term that attracts our attention is the 'sixth face'. This alludes to the ancient teaching of the five faces of Śiva, one for each of the four cardinal directions and an upward face, that speak the various streams of Śaiva scripture. The radical, nondual, transgressive

Kaula branch of Tantra propounded a 'secret' teaching of a sixth, lower face that uttered the esoteric Kaula scriptures, an undercurrent of revelation considered both more powerful and potentially dangerous in the hands of those with immature understanding. The mouth of this 'face' metaphorically lies at the lower terminus of the central channel, and is also called the *yoginī-vaktra*, the 'mouth of the yoginī', where the latter term has a richer range of meanings than in mainstream discourse, since the Kaulas honored female practitioners and feminine spirits more than any other branch of Tantra.[115] In yogic practice, then, the 'sixth face' is the area of the body and subtle body from the *kanda* to the perineum.

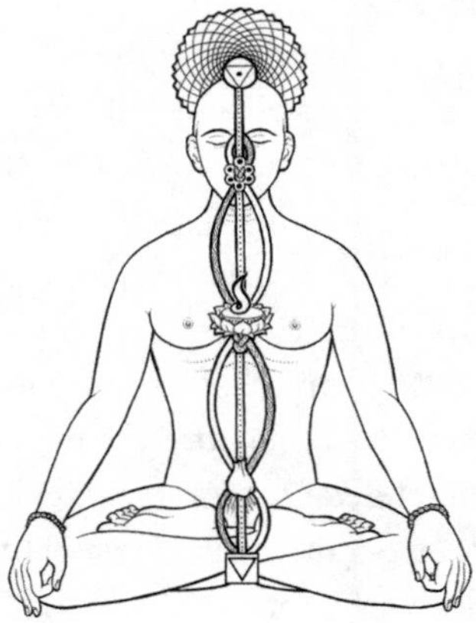

The *kanda* (literally, 'bulb', like a tulip bulb) is the second *cakra* in the Kaula Trika's five-cakra system, located in the lower abdomen midway between the genitals and the navel (three or four finger-widths below the navel and two or three finger-widths inward). It is one of the most important energy centers in the subtle body, though it is mostly forgotten today, since it is not included in the popular seven-cakra system currently being used worldwide. (Though some versions of that system place *svādhiṣṭhāna* in the location just described instead of at the genitals, in which case it is a synonym for the *kanda*.) It is identical to the so-called 'secret place' in Tantrik Buddhism, and corresponds exactly to the *dan tian* (Xià Dāntián) in Daoist practice. There are two reasons why the *kanda* is so important: more *nāḍīs* or subtle channels run through it than any other center, and it is considered the source of sexual energy.

So the 'sixth face' is the area from the *kanda* to the perineum (or perineal body,[116] to be more precise). In most people, especially the sexually repressed, sexual energy remains localized to this area. The practice here discussed allows the energy to flow upward (as well as radiate in all directions), which is important in Tantrik Yoga because: (a) sexual energy is a huge source of power that yogīs seek to incorporate into their spiritual practice, and (b) it must be fully integrated into the total energy system to become internally undivided and harmonious. So how does the practice effect the energy in this region to achieve these goals? Interestingly, Kṣema here uses the verb *praguṇīkṛ*, which means 'to nourish/develop', 'to intensify', 'to make smooth and even', 'to make virtuous', and 'to bring up', in the way one brings up children. He probably has most or all of these meanings in mind when he uses the verb with *śakti* as its object, and though the first meaning is primary, I work in the last two meanings with the word 'sublimate'.[117] So we are to "nourish and sublimate the energy in [the region of] the lower Kuṇḍalinī" which gives rise to "an immersion into sensation on the levels of its root, its tip, and its center". The sensation is, no doubt, an orgasmic one, but what are these three 'levels'? Examination of parallel passages reveals that they are the *kanda*, the penis, and the perineum in men, and the *kanda* (= the cervix), the clitoris, and the perineum for women. To obtain an 'immersion into sensation' in these three areas powerful enough for the energy to flow into the central channel, we are advised to use the yogic methods of breath-pause and mantra-awareness.

Though Kṣema doesn't mention mantra here, remember that in his time, the very use of the word Kuṇḍalinī implied a mantra. The mantra is probably HRĪṂ or ऐं AIṂ (note that the central element of the latter is a downward-pointing triangle, commonly used to symbolize the *yoni*). The second mantra derives from a parallel source, specifically a scripture of the Śrīvidyā sect (which once specialized in sexual energy cultivation) called the *Vāmakeśvarī-mata*, in which we find this verse:

> One should focus on the Goddess of the Word,* who is Parā, vibrating radiantly in the form of the *bīja*, awakening the joy of awareness, having shattered the *brahma-granthi*. ||
> [*Visuddhi-magga* 4.23d–24c]

The importance of the breath-pause in this practice is made explicit by Kṣemarāja's citation of a verse from the *Vijñāna-Bhairava*, the most esoteric scripture of the Trika.

**As taught in the sacred *Vijñāna-Bhairava*,**

> **One should cast one's heart-mind, full of pleasure, into the center** [point] **between the 'fire'** [at the root] **and the 'poison'** [at the tip] **with either *kevala-kumbhaka* or *pūraka-kumbhaka*; thus one is connected to the bliss of passion.**[118] || 68

It's possible that this verse in its original context is simply teaching one how to intensify orgasm as a means to intensify awareness, but by quoting it, Kṣema implies we should incorporate its instructions into the practice under consideration. This verse too uses code or so-called 'twilight language', and thus is impossible to translate correctly without researching parallel passages. One such passage is the commentary on the *Vāmakeśvarī-mata* verse I quoted above:

> The Goddess of the Word in the form of the *bīja* awakens the joy of awareness, that is, activates the resonance of consciousness, since she is in fact Parā, the power of the Center vibrating radiantly, having pierced the *brahma-granthi* totally ... [which is] situated [above] the base of the 'locus of generation/birth' (*janma-sthāna*), between the 'fire' and 'poison'. [119]

Through this and other sources we can discern that 'fire' is a code word for the *kanda*,[120] and 'poison' for the penis, and the center point between them is the perineum.[121] Thus the *Vijñāna-Bhairava* is telling us to focus our attention and enjoyment at the pelvic floor and perineal body,

* The Goddess of the Word is invoked because in this text, the sexual energy is sublimated into creative energy in the form of literary talent and eloquence.

away from the place of maximum sensation (the head of the penis for men, the clitoris and/or G-spot for women; note the *Vijñāna* verse is not gendered). It also tells us to pause the breath, either at the end of an inhale (*vāyu-pūrṇa* meaning *pūraka-kumbhaka*) or at any random moment (*kevala-kumbhaka*). Now in terms of the proper focal point, though the scripture clearly advises us to focus on the center, Kṣema mentions becoming absorbed in all three levels (root, tip, and center), so there is a lack of clarity here. However, since the *brahma-granthi* is definitely situated above the perineum, and the practice is implicitly supposed to pierce and open up that knot, we probably ought to focus on the center point primarily if not exclusively.

Kṣema's final words on the practice, supposedly explaining the *Vijñāna* verse above, if anything leave us a bit more mystified.

**Here 'fire' is the place of contraction through penetration; the 'site of poison' is the place that expands through outflow. Here the verb *viṣ* is used in the sense of 'pervasion'** (*vyāpti*)**—this** [fact] **is necessary to understand the sense.**

Though the English word 'penetration' is suggestive of intercourse, it translates as *anupraveśa*, which is ambiguous. The 'contraction' mentioned could be the spontaneous partial *uḍḍīyāna-bandha* that occurs during sex and/or the onset of orgasm (especially for women), or it could refer to a yogic practice of penetrating the *kanda* with extra *prāṇa* (by means of *kumbhaka* and focused attention) until it 'ignites' and reveals its full power.

In treating the problematic word 'poison' (*viṣa*) as code for the genital tip (which of course is inherited from a much older tradition), Kṣema wishes to remove any negative association by telling us that the verbal root must be taken in the sense of 'pervasion' or 'flow', suggesting again that *viṣa* denotes the head of the penis because it is the place that expands due to the outflow of sexual fluid. But it is also possible that here we have a subtle allusion to the experience of 'nectar-pervasion' (*amṛta-vyāpti*) in which blissful energy pervades the whole body due to the fire of Kuṇḍalinī reaching the crown and spontaneously transmuting to the nectarean bliss that transcends mortality (*amṛta*). One reason this is a possible allusion is that in the *Vāmakeśvarī-mata*, a text primarily about love and sex magic (which I quoted above), *viṣa* is a code-word for the first stage of the emanation of Kuṇḍalinī. Thus

Kṣema may be implying here that at the moment of orgasm, if the practice was done correctly, Kuṇḍalinī can enter the central channel and surge upward.

Thus, if Kuṇḍalinī does surge up the central channel, something remarkable happens: since the energy previously confined to the pelvis has entered the *suṣumnā*, now the root is the *kanda*, the center is the heart, and the 'tip' is the crown of the head. In this second phase of the experience, the "place that expands through outflow" is the crown, and the flow in question is the nectar-pervasion, as implied by Kṣema's gloss of *viṣa* as *vyāpti*.[122]

To understand all the elements of the practice, we have had to combine three sources: Kṣemarāja's words, the scripture he quotes, and another scripture he doesn't. Let us then state the practice in the simplest possible terms. When sexual energy is activated (i.e., during lovemaking or masturbation), focus your attention at the perineum (with a gentle *mūla-bandha*) while remaining secondarily aware of the whole region from the *kanda* downward. When you feel orgasm approaching, pause the breath and feel/visualize your seed-mantra vibrating just above the pelvic floor. If orgasm retreats again, repeat the process. If orgasm occurs,[123] continue to hold the breath and feel the mantra while consciously letting the blissful sensation permeate the *kanda* and the perineal area as well as the genitals. As soon as the orgasm starts to fade, let the energy rise up the central channel with an exhale.

The practice will be more successful if the *kanda* has already been 'warmed up' through repeated breath retention, focused attention, and visualization practice (e.g., seeing the *kanda* as a ball of red fire) before sexual activity.

Both these practices (4a and 4b) involve both expansion and contraction, but their overall effect is the expansion of the central channel and the unimpeded flow of energy within it.

### 5. *vāha-cheda*

**Pausing the 'flows', i.e., the *apāna* and *prāṇa* moving in the left and right** [channels], **means interrupting them—after bringing them to rest in the heart—with the internal utterance of a vowelless phoneme, something close to k, h, etc. As taught in the *Hymn to the Womb of Wisdom:***

> **When one's two lateral channels have flowed to their fullest extent, and** [one] **'cuts' them by a vowelless 'k', keeping the mind focused on the inner recess of the heart-lotus, then the** [veil of] **blind darkness is torn, and there arises the sprout of Your wisdom, which can produce the state of highest Divinity, even for the bound soul.** ||

This practice presumes a basic understanding of the three primary channels, discussed on pages 387–389 of *Tantra Illuminated.* It is a simple but esoteric practice that, like the previous one, is said to awaken Kuṇḍalinī. Note that while practice four focused on the energy centers in the lower belly and the head, this one focuses on the heart, and thus all three major centers along the central channel have a corresponding activation practice. For your awakening to be complete, you must awaken on the levels of head, heart, and gut (and then integrate the awakenings).

This practice is deceptively simple: assume a yogic posture and take a few long, deep breaths, then after the most complete exhale you can comfortably do, inhale into the heart region, focusing the *prāṇa-śakti* there, then when you feel full, pause the breath and still the *prāṇa* by hovering right on the edge of saying the letter 'k' (or a word beginning with k, such as Kālī) while staying acutely aware of the innermost point of the heart-center. (You don't have to worry about the anatomy; just focus on whatever *feels* like the innermost point.) You should experience a kind of 'pregnant pause' combined with profound stillness for at least a few seconds. When holding the breath becomes uncomfortable, exhale (without actually saying the k-word) and repeat.

The text Kṣema quotes, you may recall from an earlier citation (under practice one) is a hymn to the Goddess, so the 'sprout of Your wisdom' is meant to suggest Kuṇḍalinī. We more commonly encounter the expression 'sprout of flame', but the word used here for 'wisdom', *vidyā,* also means 'goddess mantra' in Tantrik terminology; therefore, I am confident that when Kṣema describes the practice as "the internal utterance of a vowelless phoneme, something close to k, h, etc." he is subtly implying that the practitioner should in fact hover on the edge of saying not a *letter*, but a mantra beginning with that letter. This can be a powerful way to access the energy of an esoteric goddess-mantra without uttering it. If you stay present with the experience of being *about* to say the mantra, while retaining the heart-center awareness, the practice can be powerful indeed.

### 6. *ādyanta-koṭi-nibhālana*

**The 'beginning point' is the heart; the 'ending point' is the *dvādaśānta*** [above the crown]**. Focusing on them at the moment of the emerging and coming to rest of the *prāṇa* is cultivating the practice of settling the mind.**

This is a beautiful, simple, powerful practice. As you may know, the flow of life-force energy (*prāṇa-śakti*) is strongly linked to but not identical to the flow of the breath. In this practice, you simply feel as if the exhale is beginning from the base of the heart and flowing vertically up the central channel, out the crown of the head, and 'coming to rest' at a point about eight inches above the head, the upper limit of the energy-body. Then imagine that the inhale is beginning from that same point, traveling down the central channel, and coming to rest in the base of the heart. Through focused attention, you can direct the subtle energy of the *prāṇa* in this way, even though the physical breath is moving out the nose or mouth. (With practice, you may even feel that the middle of the top of your head is slightly cooler on the inhale.) For some people, it helps them focus to imagine a tiny point of light (*bindu*) riding on the current of *prāṇa* and moving between the two points. Whether you use the *bindu* or not, if you can get absorbed in this practice, it does indeed settle the mind remarkably well.

Next Kṣema quotes that central practice text of the Trika, the *Vijñāna-Bhairava*. Curiously, he does not quote the famous verse with which that scripture begins its practice instructions though it would seem appropriate here, since it describes essentially the same practice. Perhaps this was because he assumed his audience knew it so well. Instead he quotes a couple of verses that describe the benefits of focusing attention on the two points of the practice, the heart and the *dvādaśānta*. Though he doesn't quote the verse in between these two, I include it here because it is relevant.

**As taught in the *Vijñāna-Bhairava*:**

> **With one's sense-faculties dissolved in the space of the Heart—in the innermost recess of the Lotus—with one's attention on nothing else: O blessed Lady, one will obtain blessedness (*saubhāgya*).** || 49

Though any of the *cakras* can be visualized as a lotus, the heart is described as such much more frequently than the others. This verse advises the *yogin* to focus awareness deep in the subtle center of the heart, like a bee nestled in the enfolding petals of a half-opened lotus, with such one-pointed attention that it is as if all the sense-faculties—vision, hearing, etc.—dissolve into that inner space. But the purpose of citing the verse here is just to establish the significance of the lower of the two breath-points: where the exhale emerges and the inhale comes to rest.

> By thoroughly dissolving the mind into the *dvādaśānta* of one's own body, the goal of Reality becomes certain for one of steady discernment. || 50

> **Wherever you may be, whatever you may be doing, cast your attention into the *dvādaśānta*. As your mental agitation dissolves moment by moment, you will be transformed in a matter of days.** || 51

As noted, the *dvādaśānta* (literally, 'end-of-twelve') is the uppermost limit of the energy-body, depicted in many religions as a halo. The literal meaning derives from using the width of a finger as a measurement; twelve finger-widths being about eight inches above the head. The exact measurement is not too important, however. As the verse suggests, you can simply practice casting your attention to the point that feels like that upper limit. To experience the transformation the verse promises, however, you must do the practice constantly: whenever you notice you're having a thought that you don't absolutely need to be having, you throw your attention up to the *dvādaśānta*. If you do this a hundred times a day or more, within a few days you can indeed experience an altered state, one that includes greater awareness of the energy-body. But the purpose of citing the verse here is again simply to establish the significance of the *dvādaśānta*. Kṣemarāja invites us to experience the *relationship* between these two subtle points, connected by the movement of *prāṇa*. The practice he gives is much more effective than either of the two *Vijñāna-Bhairava* verses he cites considered separately. However, as I mentioned, that scripture does have a well-known verse (or two) that gives almost exactly the same practice, curiously not cited by Kṣema:

> The Supreme Goddess [constantly] articulates herself
> as the life-giving flow of breath: the exhale rising up,
> and the inhale—the movement into embodiment—
> descending. By pausing at the two points of their arising,
> and filling them [with silent awareness], [one abides in]
> the still state of fullness. || 24
>
> By not turning back the inner and outer breaths too
> soon from the pair of spaces [where the breath pauses],
> the still space of awareness underlying the movement of
> *prāṇa* is revealed. || 25

The only nuance Kṣema has added to the practice as given in these two verses is that we are invited to pay attention not only to the pause between the breaths, but also to the *emerging* of the breath-energy after each pause, and the *coming to rest* of the breath-energy just before each pause. Thus the spatial elements of the heart and the *dvādaśānta* are more significant than in the verses just above, for it is at those points that the breath-energy emerges and comes to rest. For this reason Kṣema calls the practice *ādyanta-koṭi-nibhālana*, 'focusing on the beginning and ending points'.

### 7. *unmeṣa-daśā-niṣevaṇa*

**The phrase 'and so on'** [in the sūtra] **is** [referring to] **the practice of attending to the 'unfolding' phase** [of each new cognition or energy-state]. **As it is said in the *Stanzas on Vibration*:**

> [When one is occupied with one cognition, and another (unrelated) cognition arises (spontaneously)], **that should be known as the 'unfolding'** (*unmeṣa*)**; one should focus on that in oneself.** || 3.9

Considering the very few words Kṣemarāja uses to describe this practice, one might think it must be very simple. But in fact it is so subtle and so nonconceptual that Kṣema no doubt thinks it pointless to try to explain it in words. In terms of his teacher's schema of the three *upāyas* (covered in detail in *Tantra Illuminated*), this practice belongs to the nonconceptual *śāmbhava-upāya*, about which little can be said. However, I did my best to explain it on pages 349–355 of *Tantra Illuminated*. Here we can investigate it more precisely.

Kṣema again quotes a verse from the *Stanzas on Vibration* (*Spanda-kārikā*), one that defines the technical term *unmeṣa*. The verse has an implicit argument that our fundamental awareness is not static, actionless, and unchanging as some nondualists argue, but rather is the source of the various shifts in energy state, mood, thought, or focus that occur throughout the day in everyday life. If the cause of a new cognition were simply the previous cognition (as some Buddhists argue), how—while one is occupied with a particular train of thought—could a novel, unrelated, or unexpected thought or impulse arise? The cause of each new thought, impulse, or shift in energy state is simply your essence-nature (*svabhāva*), which expresses itself through this innate vibrancy, this creative upsurge called *unmeṣa*. This is how it is explained in the commentaries.[124] But here's where it gets subtle: it's not that essence-nature is responsible for the *content* of the thought that arises, which, after all, is inevitably expressive of one's conditioning—rather, it is the source of the urge to shift one's attention in a different direction, whether that manifests as a different line of thought, a desire to eat or to stretch, a pull to reach out to another person, or whatever. In other words, it is the source of the impulse to shift in some general direction (such as toward outward activity, inward contemplation, or connection) which is then immediately interpreted by the conditioned body-mind in some specific way. Thus *unmeṣa* is variously translated as 'creative upsurge' or 'emerging expansion' (Sanderson), 'burgeoning of consciousness' (Paul Muller-Ortega), and 'initial unfolding' (Mark Dyczkowski).

But what is the actual practice? It is very subtle, because we are invited to be so self-aware that we can sense the feeling of our deeper consciousness *being about to produce* a new thought or energy-state or shift of some kind, like a bubble rising through the water just before it reaches the surface, or like a belch a few seconds before it happens, only more subtle. Now, for most people this practice requires slowing down so much, and cultivating such continuous self-awareness, that it can only be done on retreat rather than in day-to-day life. However, the practice should not require removing oneself from society nor should it involve obsessive self-monitoring. Rather, it invites a spirit of real curiosity and fascination with the shifting currents of consciousness in everyday life. To make it a part of your daily practice, you can approach it through an easier version. If you can't or don't notice the feeling of your deeper self being about to give rise to a shift, you can at least catch hold of the first moment of perception of that shift when it arises. In this somewhat easier version of the practice, you simply notice when a different mood or energy-state starts to steal over you, and try to feel what it feels like *without labeling or analyzing it* for as long as possible (even if that's just a few seconds). If you're not clear what I'm talking about, examples might be: a shift from energized to tired, or *vice versa*; from not-hungry to hungry, or *vice versa*; from feeling discouraged to feeling determined, or *vice versa*; or countless other possibilities—but try to feel the shift without labeling it. Try to be with the 'vibe' of the new state or mood without labeling or interpreting it for a few seconds or a few minutes. Also, when you suddenly have a great idea or realization, notice that it spontaneously arose out of nowhere—that 'nowhere' is your essence-nature! In fact, haven't all the best ideas you've had arisen in such a way, rather than through worrying over a problem?

Technically, it's the pure energy of inspiration that arises from essence-nature, not the verbal content of the idea. If the wave of energy is strong enough, it 'attracts' to itself cognitive structure as it rises through the subconscious and then the conscious mind, like a magnet attracts iron filings as it slides across a table. To increase the frequency of such inspiration, meditate more—because it is when you give everything more space, and let your system settle into stillness and openness, that essence-nature has 'room' to produce more waves of inspiration. In Abhinava Gupta's formulation, the creative upsurge (*unmeṣa*), when unimpeded, gives rise to the wave of inspiration (*ūrmi*) that culminates in action (*kriyā-śakti*) that expresses your essence-nature.

What is the benefit to this practice of "attending to the unfolding of each new cognition or energy-state"? Perhaps surprisingly, the *Stanzas on Vibration* (3.8) claim that it destroys *glāni*: depression, lethargy, inertia, torpor, apathy, and/or cynical pessimism. This is because in the Tantrik view, these states are the result of ignorance of your real nature. Feeling disempowered, with an attitude of "What's the point?" can only occur when you don't have full access to the innate power of your deeper self. *Glāni*, then, is the opposite of the *bala* discussed in Chapter Fifteen. If you do the practice here discussed assiduously, you start to experience for yourself that *you* (what you really are), not your circumstances or life-situation, are the source of all spontaneous inspirations and all possible shifts in energy. This realization is empowering, and it sweeps away the various depressive states of *glāni*. If the realization goes deep enough, then *glāni* can no longer gain a foothold.

But, you might say, if essence-nature, the fundamental vibration of my awareness, is the cause of all the various shifts in energy, doesn't that mean it also triggers the shift from enthusiasm to tiredness, from confidence to doubt, not just the another way around? Yes and no. In the mode of concealment (lack of self-awareness), any 'downshifting' initiated by deeper awareness can be interpreted by the conditioned mind negatively. However, once you start accessing your innate power, though of course you still experience downshifting, it is now seen for what it is: an invitation to rest, or to inward contemplation, or to softening and listening, or to caring for the body, all of which are so necessary to a life lived as an empowered and effective expression of your essence-nature. In other words, if you can respect the *spanda* or natural oscillation between energized and tired, between full and empty, then over the long term you will have more total energy, and more enjoyment of life as well.

Though of course I can't be sure of a cause-and-effect relationship, I certainly experience much less *glāni* and more confidence, self-acceptance, and enthusiasm since I began these practices. The *Spanda-kārikā* verse Kṣema quotes above says, speaking of *unmeṣa* (the initial arising of each new state), *svayaṃ tam upalakṣayet*, which means both 'one should focus on that in oneself' and 'one should experience it for oneself'. And so you should, if you want to access your innate power and joy more fully. A Krama text, describing the fruit of this practice, speaks of "the immersion into the feeling of wonder at each new form of awareness".[125] In attending to the unfolding of each new cognition or energy-state, a sense of wonder does begin to arise as you start to realize that every state you experience is irreducibly unique, and only the reductive mental filter made it seem otherwise.

It takes patience, of course, and real curiosity. If the variations on the practice discussed above seem too subtle or difficult, you can prepare for the full practice by just checking in with yourself a dozen or more times a day (set an alarm if you have to): slow down, take a breath, look inward, and ask, "What does it feel like to be me right now?" When you ask this, try to just *feel* the answer instead of responding to yourself in words. Do this for a few weeks, and you may find that everything written above makes more sense, and you can begin experimenting with it.

### 8. *ramaṇīya-viṣaya-carvaṇa*

**Likewise encompassed** [by the phrase 'and so on'] **are** [practices] **such as the relishing of a beautiful sense-object.**

This kind of micro-meditation is straightforward and easy to do, so it is rather surprising that few yogīs do it every day. You simply take a few minutes to go fully into the experience of tasting good food or drink, or listening to beautiful music, or smelling a flower, or feeling a caress. We all enjoy these things, but how often do we give them one-pointed attention for at least a few minutes at a stretch? Despite the fact that such presence increases the pleasure of the experience, we feel so much scarcity around time that we compulsively multitask, whether reading our newsfeed while eating, or listening to music only while doing other work. It nourishes the soul to become completely absorbed in good food or drink or music for even just three or five or nine minutes.

Tantrik Śaivas regarded *ramaṇīya-viṣaya-carvaṇa*, relishing a beautiful sense-object, as an important spiritual practice, sometimes referred to as 'feeding the goddesses of the senses'. All the 'sense-goddesses' should be regularly nourished with beauty, such that they bestow their 'blessing', which is an increased capacity to see the whole world as beautiful.

Rather than explain the practice himself, Kṣema lets scripture speak, citing again one of his favorite practice texts.

**As taught in the *Vijñāna-Bhairava* itself:**

> **One should meditate on the state of fullness that expands due to the delight of savoring good food and drink, and that joy will become sublime.** || 72
>
> **The yogin who relishes music and song to the extent that he merges with it becomes filled with unparalleled happiness, attains heightened awareness, and experiences oneness with the Divine.** || 73
>
> **Wherever the mind delights, let your attention linger there. In any such experience, the true nature of supreme bliss may shine forth.** || 74

These verses are self-explanatory, though a word about the context of the last of them may be helpful. This summary verse (74) gives the basic principle of the practice, which involves a shift from *appetitive consumption* to *aesthetic awareness*. To explain, when your attitude is one of 'consuming' experiences, you look to the next one as soon as the peak of intensity of the previous one has passed but before it is complete. By contrast, the Tantrik yogī cultivates aesthetic awareness, a different mode of experience in which one savors not only the peak of the experience, but the sublime way in which as it slowly fades, it merges into one's very being. For example, when enjoying a single piece of fine chocolate, if you stay with the experience for as long as possible, you will notice that even when the actual taste has dissolved, there remains, for several moments or a minute, an impression of the delicious taste within awareness—'chocolate-flavored consciousness', if you will. Absorbing and digesting *that*, as well as the food-stuff itself, means not only enjoying the experience to the full, but also that it will not leave the residue of an attachment-saṃskāra. (Just as, if you digest a painful experience, it will not leave an aversion-saṃskāra; review Chapter Eleven if this is not crystal clear to you.) Thus the verse says, "Wherever the mind delights, *let your attention linger there.*" This is cultivating aesthetic awareness—slowing down, going deeper into the experience, and being intimate with each phase of it. It only takes a few extra minutes, but it orients you to all of life differently. You notice and savor beauty more fully. You begin to see with the eye of the great poets and artists (anyone can, as it turns out). You feel more deeply fulfilled by less. You realize that in the appetitive mode you chased after more and 'better' experiences only because you didn't let the ones you already had *all the way in*. You felt half-empty much of the time only because you didn't let the beauty around you fill you completely. Cultivating this practice, you come to know that there is so much beauty all around, more than enough to satiate you on any given day, if you just know how to look, and "let your attention linger." In any such experience, anywhere, anytime, the true nature of supreme bliss may shine forth.

**Thus, one may infer other** [similar practices] **as well, such as meditation on oneself when full of joy.**

Since Kṣema tells us that we may "infer" other practices, and gives the example of "meditating on oneself when full of joy" (*ānanda-pūrṇa-svātma-bhāvanā*, where *bhāvanā* can mean 'fully experiencing' as well as 'meditating' or 'contemplating'), he is indirectly suggesting that we look to the *Vijñāna-Bhairava* for yet more practices that are effective for the expansion of the Center. For in that text, the first to teach micro-meditations, we find two verses on meditating on oneself when full of joy:

> Meditate on your own body, or the whole world, as full of your innate joy. Through that inner 'nectar', you will suddenly experience sublime bliss. || 65
>
> When you feel great joy, as when seeing a [beloved] relative after a long time, meditate on it. Let the mind dissolve into it; become one with it. || 71

Because Kṣemarāja points us toward this text for further practices, I am planning the publication of a full translation of the *Vijñāna-Bhairava* as a sequel to this book, to be released at the end of 2018. That book will also include *The Flowering of One's Innate Awareness* (*Svabodha-mañjarī*), which is itself a short sequel to the *Vijñāna-Bhairava*, and like it is full of micro-meditations.[126]

**These** [nine practices] **and other** [ways not here taught] **are the means in our system for the expansion of the Center.** || 18 ||

We have seen that the nine practices (actually eleven, because #2 and #4 include two distinct practices each) of Chapter Eighteen constitute a variety of ways to increase one's access to the Center—the metaphorical and literal core of one's being—*and* to the Central Power of the *kuṇḍalinī-śakti*. Not only do they increase access to that inner reality, they also nourish and expand its energy. Practices #4a, #4b, and #5 activate the three primary centers along the central channel and all three of those practices are said to stimulate or nourish the Kuṇḍalinī. Practice #6 moves *prāṇa* up and down the central channel, touching its uppermost limit. Practice #7 greatly increases self-awareness (*vimarśa*) and thus 'expands the Center' metaphorically, as did Practice #1. Practice #8 literally expands that central domain, by feeding the goddesses of the senses, whose energies converge and merge into the central channel, the abode of Awareness. You can review the practices through the summary below.

This concludes our study of Sūtra Eighteen and its commentary.

*Summary of the practices given in Chapter Eighteen:*

1) Dissolution of mental constructs: *vikalpa-kṣaya*
2) Contracting energy: *śakti-saṅkoca* (two varieties)
    a) turning awareness within even as sense-energy is flowing out (= second attention)
    b) completely turning back the energy; pulling all the way into core
3) Expanding energy: *śakti-vikāsa* (contacting the entire sense-field while connected to center; = *tattva-bhāvanā*)
4) Expanding and contracting energy: *śakti-saṅkoca-vikāsa*
    a) *uccāra*: stimulate the upper *kuṇḍalinī* through mantric vibration in the nasal cavity, thus piercing the *māyā-granthi*, allowing for energy flow out from and back to *dvādaśānta*
    b) stimulate lower *kuṇḍalinī* (sexual energy), to give rise to an immersion into 'inner sensation' in root, center, and tip, especially center
5) Pausing the flows: *vāha-cheda* (bringing *prāṇa-apāna* to stillness thru accessing *icchā* in the heart-center by means of the 'vowel-less k')
6) Settling the mind by paying attention to the breath's point of emergence and its point of coming to rest (in heart and *dvādaśānta*): *ādyanta-koṭi-nibhālana*
7) Bringing attention to the moment of unfolding, the initial arising of any energy state: *unmeṣa-daśā-niṣevaṇa*
8) Relishing a beautiful experience (food, drink, music, etc.): *ramaṇīya-viṣaya-carvaṇa*
9) Meditating on oneself when full of bliss: *ānanda-pūrṇa-svātma-bhāvanā*

मध्यविकासाच्चिदानन्दलाभः, स एव च परमयोगिनः समावेशसमापत्त्यादिपर्यायः समाधिः, तस्य नित्योदितत्वे युक्तिमाह

समाधिसंस्कारवति व्युत्थाने भूयो भूयश्चिदैक्यामर्शान्नित्योदित-समाधिलाभः ॥ १९ ॥

आसादितसमावेशो योगिवरो व्युत्थाने अपि समाधिरससंस्कारेण क्षीव इव सानन्दं घूर्णमानो, भावराशिं शरदभ्रलवम् इव चिद्गगन एव लीयमानं पश्यन्, भूयो भूयः अन्तर्मुखताम् एव समवलम्बमानो, निमीलनसमाधिक्रमेण चिदैक्यमेव विमृशन्, व्युत्थानाभिमतावसरे अपि समाध्येकरस एव भवति। यथोक्तं क्रमसूत्रेषु

'क्रममुद्रया अन्तःस्वरूपया बहिर्मुखः समाविष्टो भवति साधकः। तत्रादौ बाह्यात् अन्तः प्रवेशः, आभ्यन्तरात् बाह्यस्वरूपे प्रवेशः आवेशवशात् जायते;—इति सबाह्याभ्यन्तरोऽयं मुद्राक्रमः'

इति। अत्रायमर्थः सृष्टि-स्थिति-संहृतिसंविच्च-

# CHAPTER NINETEEN

*Kṣemarāja's original text*

The Joy of Awareness discovered through the expansion of the Center is the *samādhi* of the Tantrik yogī, also known as *samāveśa* and *samāpatti.* Now the method to make it continuous (*nityodita*) is taught:

**When emerging slowly from deep meditation, while still feeling its effect, contemplate the oneness with Awareness: practicing this again and again, one will attain a *samādhi* that continuously arises.** || 19 ||

The Tantrik yogī,

who has attained Immersion into the Center,

in the post-meditative state as well,

swaying blissfully—as if drunk—with the afterglow of the sweet taste of *samādhi*,

sees the mass of existent things dissolving into the Sky of Awareness like wisps of autumn cloud.

Again and again taking the support of the turn within,

touching pure oneness with Awareness through the method of inward-turning *samādhi*,

eventually there is no longer a 'post'-meditative state:

he has become one for whom *samādhi* is the One Taste.

As it is taught in the *Krama-sūtra*,

> By means of the *krama-mudrā*, whose nature is internal, the practitioner becomes immersed even while focused outward. [How?] In this process, first one enters within from the external; then, because of that Immersion, from the interiorized state an 'entry' into external forms comes about. Thus the 'seal-sequence' has both internal and external aspects.

क्रात्मकं क्रमं मुद्रयति, स्वाधिष्ठितम् आत्मसात् करोति येयं तुरीया चितिशक्तिः, तया 'क्रममुद्रया'; 'अन्तरिति'—पूर्णाहन्तास्वरूपया; 'बहिर्मुख'—इति, विषयेषु व्यापृतः अपि; 'समाविष्टः'—साक्षात्कृतपरशक्तिस्फारः 'साधकः'—परमयोगी भवति। तत्र च 'बाह्याद्' ग्रस्यमानात् विषयग्रामात् 'अन्तः'—परस्यां चिति भूमौ, ग्रसनक्रमेणैव 'प्रवेशः'—समावेशो भवति। 'आभ्यन्तरात्' चितिशक्तिस्वरूपात् च साक्षात्कृतात् 'आवेशवशात्'—समावेशसामर्थ्यात् एव 'बाह्यस्वरूपे'—इदन्तानिर्भासे विषयग्रामे, वमनयुक्त्या 'प्रवेशः'—चिद्रसाश्यानताप्रथनात्मा समावेशो जायते;—इति। 'सबाह्याभ्यन्तरः अयं' नित्योदितसमावेशात्मा, 'मुदो'—हर्षस्य वितरणात् परमानन्दस्वरूपत्वात्, पाशद्रावणात्, विश्वस्य अन्तः

तुरीयसत्तायां मुद्रणात् च मुद्रात्मा, क्रमः अपि सृष्ट्यादिक्रमाभासकत्वात् तत्क्रमाभासरूपत्वात् च 'क्रम' इति अभिधीयते इति ॥ १९ ॥

This is the meaning of this passage: It is called *krama-mudrā*, the 'seal of the sequence', because the Fourth, the Power of Awareness 'seals the sequence' consisting of the emission, stasis, and retraction cycles of cognition: that is to say, it makes one with itself the sequence that it governs. By means of this *krama-mudrā*, whose nature is 'internal' in the sense that it is perfect 'I'-awareness, the 'practitioner' (i.e., the Tantrik yogī) is 'immersed', meaning he directly experiences the expansion of the Supreme Power of the Center, even while 'focused outward', i.e., engaged with sense-objects.

In that process, 'one enters within from the external', meaning that from the normal state of devouring the mass of sense-objects one enters into the most fundamental plane of Awareness, an Immersion that takes place simply through that 'devouring'. By the power of that inward Immersion alone, meaning from direct experience of the essential nature of the Power of Awareness, "an 'entry' into external forms comes about", meaning an Immersion into the mass of sense-objects appearing as objectivity is produced through the act of 'flowing forth'. This extroversive Immersion has as its essence the revelation that everything is the 'crystallized' form of the dynamic flowing essence of Awareness (*cid-rasa*).

Thus, this continuously arising, ever-fresh Immersion has both internal and external forms. It is called a *mudrā* because it bestows joy (*mud*)—given that its very nature is the highest bliss—and because it dispels (*drā*) bonds. And it is called *mudrā* because it 'seals' everything within the Fourth State. This *mudrā* is furthermore called a *krama* (sequence), because it manifests of the sequences of emission, stasis, reabsorption, and because its nature is to appear *as* those sequences. || 19 ||

## CHAPTER NINETEEN

*with explanation*

**The Joy of Awareness discovered through the expansion of the Center is the *samādhi* of the Tantrik yogī, also known as *samāveśa* and *samāpatti*. Now the method to make it continuous (*nityodita*) is taught.**

Here Kṣemarāja uses three key terms for spiritual experience, specifically the kind of spiritual experience that results from awareness cultivation and meditative practice. He tells us that he regards the three terms as synonyms, which is ecumenical of him, since each term belongs to a different branch of the Yoga tradition: *samāveśa* is unique to Tantrik Yoga, while *samādhi* is the term of choice in Classical Yoga (i.e., that of Patañjali and similar teachers), and *samāpatti* the preferred term in Buddhist yogic discourse.[127] Here Kṣema also reveals his particular bias, because he says that these terms are also synonymous with *cid-ānanda*, the Joy of Awareness, which as we have already seen refers in his teaching to the experience of unity-consciousness, of the all-inclusive 'I'-sense. But in fact, while *samāveśa* is often used in other sources in this very sense, *samādhi* and *samāpatti* more usually refer to deeply interiorized states, sometimes so interiorized that one loses awareness of the external world. As we will see, Kṣema does address this apparent discrepancy, since his main point in Chapter Nineteen is to present the Tantrik teaching of two primary types of *samādhi*, an introversive one and an extroversive one, and to explain the relation between the two. While his lineage acknowledges as many as 150 subtypes of spiritual experience, he wants to emphasize the primacy of these two. In describing their relation, he gives us an incredibly powerful tool for integrating whatever degree of self-realization one has into the fabric of one's daily life.

Now, recall that he already addressed the importance of integration in Chapter Sixteen, where we learned about the significance of experiencing all the layers of apparent selfhood—the body, heart-mind, *prāṇa*, and the Void—as expressions of the unborn undying clear light of Awareness that you fundamentally are. Here in Chapter Nineteen, the emphasis is on seeing everything whatsoever as expressions of that same essence-nature. This shift in perception is accomplished by a daily practice of turning deep within and touching the core of your being, and then turning outward into the world, bringing the nectar of that Presence with you and infusing it into all that you perceive and experience. Note that the key practice of Chapter Nineteen presumes success with the techniques of Eighteen, because to infuse the energy of the Center—the Core of being—into every cognition, perception, and action, you must be actually touching into that Core. By contrast, if you are accessing only a mental construct of your essence-nature, and attempting to integrate all your perceptions and actions with that mental construct, you are heading down the road of building yourself a spiritual ego—a dangerous path indeed.

How do you know that you are authentically touching into the Core, and not just a subtle and refined mental construct thereof? Well, this is the hardest thing to point to in words, but here are some clues. First of all, the effect of accessing the Core is more humbling than exalting; it softens you, makes you more open, more receptive, more willing to be with what is. There is unwavering strength in the Core, but it never needs to make a show of force or bravado. There is a kind of inner knowing that doesn't speak in words, that doesn't argue or justify or explain itself. The dominant experience of the Core, however, is stillness and silence—a deep, nourishing, silent stillness pervaded by the wordless awareness of *being*. It is an *alive* silence. A stillness quietly full with presence. A spacious openness quietly full of infinite possibility. Being 'there' can feel like gently balancing on the leading edge of the present moment, in sweet anticipation—of nothing in particular. Or it can feel like reposing in the place of absolute groundedness: the ocean floor under all the currents, or the still point at the center of the turning world.

This tradition is also careful to distinguish the Awareness of the Center from that of the Void, though the difference is very subtle. The inner Void, which many people experience at some point in their meditation practice, is also completely still and silent, but compared to the stillness of Core, it has an empty feeling, like interstellar space, whereas Core is permeated with aliveness. The Void *per se* has no energy, whereas Core very gently pulsates with the wordless 'I am'. And lastly, the Void is empty of any desire or will, whereas, as Kṣemarāja will suggest, reposing in our true Center gives rise to an impulse to engage with the world from that place of centeredness. Remember though, you can be in the Center/Core at the same time as experiencing anything else, and when you experience the Void from the perspective of the Center, it reveals itself as *shining* emptiness, *radiant* nothingness, and/or *alive* stillness, as described above. But how do we learn to experience any layer of being—from the Void to external objects—from the perspective of the Center? Sūtra Nineteen (and its commentary) has the answer.

This sūtra presents us with a crucial and powerful practice almost unrecognized today. It addresses the unique moment known as *vyutthāna*—the several-minutes-long process of coming out of deep meditation, of moving from fully introversive awareness to the extroversive state. It is in this *vyutthāna* phase that we have a golden opportunity to integrate the former with the latter. Kṣema teaches us that the way we transition out of deep meditation (*samādhi*) is just as important as the meditation itself.

### || SAMĀDHI-SAṂSKĀRAVATI VYUTTHĀNE BHŪYO BHŪYAŚ CID-AIKYĀMARŚĀN NITYODITA-SAMĀDHI-LĀBHAḤ || 19 ||

**When emerging slowly from deep meditation, while still feeling its effect, contemplate the oneness** [of whatever is perceived] **with Awareness: practicing this again and again, one will attain a *samādhi* that continuously arises.**

And here is the sūtra again with word-by-word breakdown:

**When emerging slowly** (*vyutthāne*) **from deep meditation** (*samādhi*)**, while still feeling its effect** (*saṃskāra*)**, contemplate** (*āmarśa*; = *vimarśa*) **the oneness** (*aikya*) [of whatever is perceived] **with Awareness** (*cit*)**: practicing this again and again** (*bhūyo bhūyas*)**, one will attain** (*lābhaḥ*) **a *samādhi* that continuously arises** (*nityodita-samādhi*)**.**

The practice described here is simple: if in meditation you abide in your true Center (as described above), even only for a few moments, then, when coming out of meditation and opening the senses to the 'external' world, let yourself perceive whatever you perceive as a direct expression of the fundamental Awareness of the Center. In other words, let yourself perceive whatever you perceive as a direct expression of what you are at Core. Everything you experience, without exception, is a direct expression of the simple, sweet, quietly alive sense of *being* at the Center. But you don't necessarily realize this automatically, hence the practice given here. The moments of *vyutthāna*—the liminal space between *samādhi* and the state of being actively engaged with the world—are the golden opportunity to integrate whatever arises in the sphere of perception into the ever-expanding sense of 'I'-ness until it becomes totally all-inclusive. Then your *samādhi* becomes continuous, for the word *samādhi* really means 'intimate union with'; in the first instance, intimate union with the Center, and in the second, through the practice given here, intimate union with the totality of reality.

Kṣema then restates his sūtra in very poetic terms, while adding more information. Notice that, on page 389, I have arranged his words as poetry to bring out their full *rasa* (poetic flavor).[128] Here are those same words presented as prose, in two sections.

**The Tantrik yogī, who has attained Immersion** (*samāveśa*) [into the Center]**, in the post-meditative** (*vyutthāna*) **state as well, swaying blissfully—as if drunk—with the afterglow** (*saṃskāra*; literally, impression) **of the sweet taste of *samādhi*, sees the mass of existent things, beings, feelings, and mental states dissolving into the Sky of Awareness like wisps of autumn cloud.**

The passage is beautiful and evocative, as befits the state it describes. But Kṣema is also using some technical terms: for example, 'swaying' translates as *ghūrṇi*, which usually refers to a mystical experience that is considered a sign of very high attainment, one in which the adept feels a kind of divine intoxication, combined with pleasant sensations of floating, whirling, swaying, or spinning (which are sometimes thought to indicate that the subtle body is moving quasi-independently of the physical body).[129] Note also that here Kṣema replaces the word *samādhi* with *samāveśa*, because, as noted above, he regards them as synonyms.[130] Finally, note that the word *saṃskāra* (impression, imprint, after-effect, afterglow), commonly assumed in modern yoga to have only negative connotations, can actually denote something highly beneficial. In this case, the *saṃskāra* of the *samādhi* state is what allows for the practice of integrating all that is perceived with the fundamental Awareness of that state. It is precisely when you are bathing in "the afterglow of the sweet taste of deep meditation" (the *saṃskāra* of the *rasa* of *samādhi*) that you have the natural ability to "see the mass of existent things, beings, feelings, and mental states (*bhāvas*) dissolving into the Sky of Awareness (*cid-ākāśa*) like wisps of autumn cloud". The description is not literal, because what dissolves is actually one's *perception* that any particular thing is different from or other than Awareness. That is, both one's belief and one's felt-sense that any thing or being or feeling or mental state (the Sanskrit word *bhāva* conveniently denoting all four) is other than Awareness dissolves. It is separation itself that dissolves. Otherness dissolves. They dissolve 'like wisps of autumn cloud', because in India, unlike in Europe or America, autumn is the relatively hot post-monsoon season in which clouds can't hold together easily, and dissolve again almost as soon as they are formed. In the same way, for one who experiences intimate union with the Center, the illusion of otherness can't hold together easily, and the experience of any given object or being as 'other' dissolves into Oneness.

Lastly, we should note that Kṣema's explanation of his sūtra teaches us that when emerging from meditation, we should regard 'external' objects and people (*bhāvas*) *and* our own 'internal' thoughts and feelings (*bhāvas*) as manifestations of Awareness to precisely the same degree. The whole mass of *bhāva*s dissolve into the Sky of Awareness like wisps of autumn cloud.

Many meditation teachers today use the analogy of sky and clouds for awareness and mental-emotional phenomena respectively. They invite us to release our obsession with the 'weather' (thoughts and feelings) and bring attention to the stainless 'sky' of consciousness, which holds unconditional space for any and all weather, or none. While the phrase 'the Sky of Awareness' or 'the Space of Consciousness' (*cid-ākāśa, cid-gagana*) was already old by Kṣemarāja's time, the metaphor of sky versus clouds might have begun with him.[131]

**Again and again taking the support of the turn within, contemplating the oneness** [of everything] **with Awareness itself through the method of inward-turning *samādhi*, eventually there is no longer a 'post'-meditative state: he has become one for whom *samādhi* is the One Taste (*eka-rasa*).**

Kṣema specifies that we must take the support of "the turn within", i.e., meditation, "again and again". This is something that must be cultivated. Only in the context of this repeated introversion can we effectively contemplate the oneness of *everything* with the Awareness experienced at the Core. Kṣema makes this explicit when he says that it is "through the method of inward-turning *samādhi*" that we become able to contemplate this oneness.[132] We must meditate daily *not* because meditation is the only way to contact the Center (which, being the core of what you are, is contactable anywhere and anytime, once you've got the feel of it), but because it gives us the repeated opportunity for the *vyutthāna* practice that we need to realize Oneness: the practice of opening our eyes and ears to see and hear everything as the spontaneous outflow of our own pure innermost identity.

How does Kṣema expect us to attain this introversive *samādhi*, this experience of abiding in the Center? Any of the practices given in Chapter Eighteen are a doorway. They are 'skillful means', or *upāyas*, to expand our access to the Core. Once 'there', however, the practice is simply to abide in *being*. The practices are all subtle forms of *doing* that must give way to pure *being*. Though most of us can simply *be* for a few seconds, to stay in *being* (as opposed to doing)—sometimes known as 'nonconceptual meditation'—is harder than it sounds. Since most of us need some coaching to be able to abide in *being*, I recommend the book *True Meditation* by Ādyashānti. I know of no simpler or better guide to nonconceptual meditation.

As we cultivate our ability to abide in the Center, and subsequently experience all that we perceive as one with that Center, "eventually there is no longer a 'post'-meditative state,"[133] meaning that the *vyutthāna* state, in which experience is flavored by nondual awareness, becomes continuous. At that tipping point, the practitioner has "become one for whom *samādhi* is the One Taste (*eka-rasa*)." One Taste is a technical term in the literature, referring to the state of unity-consciousness in which every thing and every experience 'tastes' like a different flavor of the One. In other words, it refers to 'extroversive' *samādhi*, also known in this text as the Joy of Awareness. As already mentioned, this category of open-eyed, engaged and active *samādhi* was originally a unique teaching of nondual Tantra.

Once established in this state, one continually experiences the joy of being aware, and of each new form of awareness. It is a *samādhi* that is *nityodita*, continuously arising and ever refreshing itself, because at last reality is seen as it truly is: each moment (and everything 'in' it) spontaneously arising as a direct expression of the Absolute, complete and whole in itself and irreducibly unique.

The twentieth-century master Bhagavān Nityānanda was established in *nityodita-samādhi*. He once ecstatically exclaimed while walking with someone, "Look! Look at the miracle of Consciousness! Here, it has become a rock! Here, a tree! And here (pointing to his companion) a human being."

The rest of Chapter Nineteen consists of a close analysis of a quote from the *Krama-sūtra* or *Aphorisms on the Phases of Consciousness*. Sadly, this scripture is now lost to us, and only this quotation survives. Clearly, Kṣema holds it in high esteem, since he analyzes its teaching in minute detail. In keeping with the style of most *sūtra*-type texts, the quotation is compressed and elliptical, requiring analysis.

Bhagavān Nityānanda holding a miracle of consciousness

**As it is said in the *Krama-sūtra*,**

> **By means of the *krama-mudrā*, whose nature is internal, the practitioner becomes immersed even while focused outward.** [How does this happen?] **In this process, first one enters within from the external;** [then,] **because of that Immersion, from**

**the interiorized** [state] **an 'entry' into external forms comes about. Thus the 'seal-sequence'** (*mudrā-krama*) **has both internal and external** [aspects].

Simply put, this passage is about just what we've been discussing: introversive and extroversive forms of Immersion (*samāveśa*) or *samādhi.* Kṣemarāja will explain it for us, though his explanation may need some explaining. Here he performs a gloss, meaning that he explains the meaning of each and every word in the original quote.

**This is the meaning of this** [passage]: [It is called *krama-mudrā*, the 'seal of the sequence', because] **the Fourth, the Power of Awareness 'seals' the sequence consisting of the emission, stasis, and retraction cycles of cognition: that is to say, it makes one with itself the sequence that it governs.**

This sentence explains the meaning of the term *krama-mudrā.* I'll briefly explain the key terms used here. A *mudrā* is literally a seal, sign, or imprint, like the red wax seals you've seen used on important letters in historical dramas. Here, the word *mudrā* is used in a special esoteric sense to refer to an internal state (a state that is a sign of self-realization), though Kṣema—who, like his guru, loves wordplay—explains that state with reference to the original meaning of the word. More confused? I'll take you through it.

The 'Fourth' (a term first introduced near the end of Chapter Eight) refers to the fundamental Power of Awareness we've been discussing all along. It is usually called the Fourth with reference to the three states of waking, dreaming, and deep sleep, since it is their source and ground. Here, though, it is the Fourth with reference to the three phases (*krama*) of cognition: emission, stasis, and retraction (which in other contexts are known as the first three of the Five Acts). Kṣema tells us that the Fourth 'seals' the three in the sense that it imprints them with its nature, or rather makes them one with itself, for each of the three are actually expressions of the underlying Fourth. In other words, Awareness spontaneously emits any given cognition (concept or percept), maintains it through its power of attention, and dissolves it into itself once again.

Thus, Awareness "makes one with itself the sequence that it governs", meaning it is both the author of the threefold act and its ground.

The metaphorical term 'ground' refers to the teaching that Awareness is that from which cognition arises, that which maintains it, and that into which it dissolves once again. (And here 'cognition' means the experience of anything whatsoever.)

**By means of this *krama-mudrā*, whose nature is 'internal' in the sense that it is perfect 'I'-consciousness** (*pūrṇāhaṃtā*)**, the 'practitioner' (i.e., the Tantrik yogī) is 'immersed', meaning he directly experiences the expansion of the Supreme Power** (*parā śakti*) [of the Center]**, even while 'focused outward', i.e., engaged with sense-objects.**

I'll give you the essence of this sentence, shorn of its parenthetical information: "By means of his innermost Awareness, the practitioner can experience the activation of his innermost Power even while engaged in the 'external' world." That's all it's saying. It seems confusing only because in the twenty-first century, we're no longer familiar with the science of textual exegesis, or its primary tools such as glossing. At any rate, here Kṣema is saying that the *Krama-sūtra* is telling us that when we contact our fundamental Awareness of being—the non-separate and non-exclusive 'I'-sense—and cultivate it in the ways already taught, we can experience the expansion of the Power of the Center even while moving about the everyday world. This was already discussed in Chapter Eighteen, practice three (it is *Bhairava-mudrā* under another name). So there's not any new teaching here; he's just providing scriptural support for what he's already taught.

But so far he has just explained the first sentence of the scriptural quote. In expounding on the rest of the quote—which explains exactly *how* one can experience everything as a form of one's own divine Awareness—he will summarize some key teachings of the Krama.

**In that** [process]**, 'one enters within from the external', meaning that from** [the normal state of] **devouring the mass of sense-objects one enters into the most fundamental plane of Awareness, an Immersion** (*samāveśa*) **that takes place simply through that very 'devouring'.**

This is simply a description of the introversive *samādhi* already discussed above, with a brief instruction on how to achieve it. That instruction is the Krama teaching already hinted at in various places throughout Kṣema's text: that by staying fully present with the experience of any given sense-object, one can trace its inward trajectory to where its energy-pattern dissolves into core Awareness. In other words, one simply rides the flow of absorption of the sense-object inward to the core of subjectivity. Whether it be music, poetry, chocolate, a sharp pain, or a foul stench, the process is the same: as the sense-experience starts to fade, if you gently stay with it, it dissolves into the fundamental inner Awareness that was its true source in the first place. For more on this key teaching, see Kṣema's fifth interpretation of Sūtra One (page 39), and his second interpretation of Sūtra Eight (page 189–192).

This is what Kṣema means when he says that Immersion into the 'most fundamental plane of Awareness' occurs through the everyday process by which consciousness 'devours' its content. (You may recall that the Krama teachings use devouring and digesting as metaphors for the way awareness absorbs and assimilates whatever it is aware of.) This teaching is the great leveler: no one needs any privilege, advantage, or specialized knowledge to investigate the relationship between sensory experience and fundamental Awareness. Any experience, when fully (and non-discursively) investigated, can lead you toward realization of your fundamental nature.

**By the power of that** [inward] **Immersion alone, meaning from direct experience of the essential nature of the Power of Awareness, "an 'entry' into external forms comes about", meaning an Immersion into the mass of sense-objects appearing as objectivity is produced through the act of flowing forth. This** [extroversive] **Immersion has as its essence the revelation that everything is the 'crystallized' form of the dynamic flowing essence of Awareness** (*cid-rasa*).

Kṣema is saying three important things in his analysis of the second sentence of the scriptural quotation. First, that realization of the true nature of the 'external' world is only possible by *first* touching the real core of being within. This is because the entire perceptible world is in truth nothing but an expansion of that which lies at the core of awareness. Second, that reposing in the still point of the innermost center of being eventually generates a spontaneous 'wave' of expansion that propels one outward into engagement with the world again. This 'wave' carries with it the energy-signature of that innermost state, and as a result one's experience of the external world is radically transformed. (This transformation is usually gradual, requiring repetition as Sūtra Nineteen suggests, but can for some be rapid and dramatic. The latter often gives rise to premature claims of 'enlightenment' when in fact it requires more integration work than the gradual version of the process.) Kṣemarāja here implies that if one does not experience this 'wave', this undeniable impetus to reenter the manifest world but with a new understanding, then that is evidence that one has not in fact reached the real core of being but has instead only penetrated to the level of the Void. To put it in traditional terms, only the experience of *pūrṇāhaṃtā*, not *śūnyāhaṃtā*,* inevitably leads to this extroversive *samāveśa/samādhi*. This is a key feature that distinguishes the teaching of Tantrik Shaivism from that of Tantrik Buddhism.

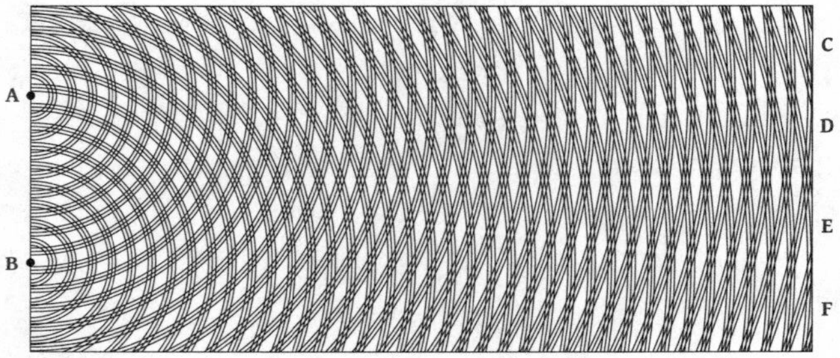


This image depicts the simplest kind of wave interference pattern: one with only two energy sources, depicted in two dimensions. Now imagine the complexity of the 'interference pattern' created by uncountable trillions of energy sources in four dimensions. Wait: you don't have to imagine it. Just look around. ~ But when you do so, you still aren't seeing the full picture, unless you can sense that you yourself are one of the point-sources that generate the Pattern. All sentient beings are point-sources for the pattern, because they constitute the nodes where Awareness intersects itself, thereby initiating the waves that combine to make the Pattern.

Kṣema's third key point in this paragraph is a definition of the nature of this extroversive Immersion. He says that in this way of ex-

---

* Where the first term denotes the full, complete and whole 'I'-sense, that is, the non-separate and non-exclusive 'I', and the second term denotes the realization that the 'I'-concept is completely empty and void (*śūnya*) of any meaning or referent. These are not necessarily contradictory; one can first realize that the 'I'-concept one had is empty of reality (*śūnyāhaṃtā*) and subsequently experience the true 'I', the pure sense of being that is non-separate from everything else (*pūrṇāhaṃtā*). This distinction is at the heart of Shaivism's debate with Buddhism.

periencing reality, everything is seen to be the 'crystallization' of the 'dynamic flowing essence' of Awareness. This is a metaphor he first introduced in Chapter Four. Here he makes clear that it is another way of understanding the experience of unity-consciousness discussed in Chapters Fifteen and Sixteen. To put it simply, the idea here is that the total field of Awareness is permeated by flowing patterns of energy (much like complex wave interference patterns) which constitute all that is perceptible, and that all apparently static forms are in fact temporary condensations or crystallizations of the ever-dynamic flowing energy field.

Therefore the yogī who accesses direct perception of reality sees/feels/senses it as an ocean of patterned energy permeated by flowing currents, all of which express his innate being, without any separation whatsoever. His 'self' is completely immersed in that ocean.

In this perception of reality, everything is vibrating, pulsating, and positively oozing with sublimely sweet nectar (this is another meaning of *rasa*). The nectar of Awareness inundates everything; indeed, the manifestation of form (*all* form) is nothing but the brimming over of this nectar with which Awareness is replete.

Kṣema's final paragraph sums up what we've learned and provides a further explanation of what a *mudrā* is, and why the word *mudrā* is appropriate for the state(s) of Immersion. I'll break down the paragraph into three parts.

**Thus, this continuously arising, ever-fresh Immersion has** [both] **internal and external** [forms].

Again, the internal Immersion is simply reposing in essence-nature, in the still point at the center of your being. When stabilized, it is called *āṇava-samāveśa*, Immersion into the soul or innermost point (the word *āṇava* refers to both). The next step is to experience all the layers of your being from the perspective of that Center, and align them with it (Sūtra Sixteen); this process generates a momentum that eventually causes *everything* to be absorbed into the Self (Sūtra Fifteen), or rather, realized as an aspect of the Self (Sūtra Nineteen). The 'external' Immersion is this very unity-consciousness, which grants the ever-fresh Joy of

Awareness. It is sometimes called *śākta-samāveśa*, immersion into the total energy-field.

Kṣema's great-grand-guru, Utpala, wrote poetry about the state of Immersion (*samāveśa*). A radical nondualist, he held that 'Śiva' or 'God' means nothing but innate autonomous Awareness, yet he used the dualistic language of devotional poetry to express the intensity of his feelings:

> Due to immersion in You, may I be free of desires for anything but what is; may I be utterly filled with delight, considering every thing and being I see as consisting only of You.
>
> [Truly, O blessed Lord, there is no other prayer that arises within me but this: may the extraordinary state of immersion into devotion be ever mine. Intoxicated with devotion, let me be enraged by the cycle of suffering yet also intimate with it. May I laugh, and sing, and cry "O Śiva!" and fall silent.]
>
> ~ Utpala Deva's *Garland of Hymns to Śiva*

Now, the *Krama-sūtra* called this state of Immersion the *krama-mudrā*. Why is the word *mudrā*, which usually refers to sacred hand gestures and bodily postures, appropriate for the mystical mode of awareness more usually denoted by the words *samāveśa* or *samādhi*?

**It is called a *mudrā* because it bestows joy (*mud*)—given that its very nature is the highest bliss—and because it dispels (*drā*) bonds. And** [it is called a *mudrā*] **because it 'seals' everything within the Fourth State.**

First Kṣema explains that the word *mudrā* is appropriate to what it designates because of the roots that make it up. Since the state of Immersion bestows joy (√*mud*), and, when stabilized, dissolves (√*drā*) the dreamstate of bondage, it can be called a *mudrā*. Furthermore, even the original literal meaning of the word (i.e., 'seal') is applicable, because the experience of the twofold Immersion reveals that everything is 'sealed' within the Fourth State (the fundamental Power of Awareness), or, we could say, 'imprinted' with that State.

He concludes with:

**This *mudrā* is furthermore called a *krama* (sequence), because it manifests of the sequences of emission, stasis, reabsorption, and because its nature is to appear *as* those sequences.** || 19 ||

In this final sentence, Kṣema is explaining the term *mudrā-krama*. This mysterious phrase from the *Krama-sūtra* passage he cites conceals a secret teaching that Kṣema only hints at here (but that we have already discussed in this book): that Immersion into one's essence-nature reveals that it actually manifests the cycles of creation, stasis, and dissolution that constitute one's entire experience of reality. In other words, what-you-really-are is the 'Nameless Fourth' that is the source and ground of all these cycles of the phenomena of being—cycles that the Krama tradition worships as aspects of the infinite Goddess, Kālī. What-you-are not only manifests these cycles, it expresses itself *as* these cycles. You are the infinite interlocking pattern, in which every creation necessitates a dissolution, and every dissolution a creation, with a perfect pause of seeming stasis as the balance point between the two. The perfection of the Pattern can only be seen from the perspective of the ground, the Nameless Fourth.

This concludes our study of Sūtra Nineteen and its commentary.

इदानीम् अस्य समाधिलाभस्य फलमाह

तदा प्रकाशानन्दसारमहामन्त्रवीर्या-
त्मकपूर्णाहन्तावेशात्सदा सर्वसर्ग-
संहारकारिनिजसंविद्देवताच-
क्रेश्वरताप्राप्तिर्भवतीति
शिवम् ॥ २० ॥

नित्योदिते समाधौ लब्धे सति, 'प्रकाशा-नन्दसारा'–चिदाह्लादैकघना 'महती मन्त्रवीर्यात्मिका'–सर्वमन्त्रजीवितभूता 'पूर्णा' पराभट्टारिकारूपा या इयम् 'अहन्ता'–अकृत्रिमः स्वात्मचमत्कारः, तत्र 'आवेशात्' 'सदा' कालाग्न्यादेः चरमकलापर्यन्तस्य विश्वस्य यौ 'सर्गसंहारौ'–विचित्रौ सृष्टिप्रलयौ 'तत्कारि' यत् 'निजं संवि-

# CHAPTER TWENTY

*Kṣemarāja's original text*

Now is described the fruit of the attainment of this type of *samādhi*:

**Then, due to continuous Immersion into the fully expanded 'I'—which is in essence the fusion of Illumination and Joy, and is the great potency of mantras—one attains the state of being the Lord of the innate circle of the goddesses of awareness, who are constantly engaged in the emanation and reabsorption of all things.**
**~ All this is Śiva. May it be a blessing.**

|| 20 ||

This is the brief gloss of the sūtra:

When one attains this continuously arising *samādhi*, it manifests as **Immersion into the fully expanded 'I'**—'fully expanded' because it is one with the Lady Parā, and 'I' in the sense that it is the natural state of wonder at one's essence-nature. It is '**in essence the fusion of Illumination and Joy**', i.e., overflowing with Awareness and innate Delight, and it is '**the great potency of mantra**', i.e., it animates all living mantras.

By immersing in That, the Tantrik yogī (the implicit subject of the sentence) attains sovereignty over the **innate circle of the goddesses of awareness**, who are **eternally engaged** in the manifold **emissions and reabsorptions of all things**, from the Fire of Time to the final Power. Thus, this whole reality is nothing but God—that is the summary and the conclusion.

देवताचक्रं' 'तदैश्वर्यस्य' 'प्राप्तिः'—आसादनं 'भवति,' प्राकरणिकस्य परमयोगिन इत्यर्थः; 'इति' एतत् सर्वं शिवस्वरूपमेव इति उपसंहारः—इति संगतिः। तत्र यावत् इदं किंचित् संवेद्यते, तस्य संवेदनमेव स्वरूपं; तस्यापि अन्तर्मुखविमर्शमयाः प्रमातारः तत्त्वम्; तेषामपि विगलितदेहाद्युपाधिसंकोचाभिमाना अशेषशरीरा सदाशिवेश्वरतैव सारम्; अस्या अपि प्रकाशैकसद्भावापादिताशेषविश्वचमत्कारमयः श्रीमान् महेश्वर एव परमार्थः;—नहि पारमार्थिकप्रकाशावेशं विना कस्यापि प्रकाशमानता घटते—स च परमेश्वरः स्वातन्त्र्यसारत्वात् आदि-क्षान्तामायीयशब्दराशिपरामर्शमयत्वेनैव एतत्स्वीकृतसमस्तवाच्य-वाचकमयाशेषजगदानन्दस-

To explain in more detail: whatever one is aware of in this world, its nature is nothing but that awareness. The underlying reality of these acts of awareness are the various conscious perceivers, whose distinguishing feature is their capacity for internally directed awareness. Their essence, in turn, is the supreme Perceiver who embodies all, whether in Sadāśiva or Īśvara aspect, in whom egoic identification with the contraction caused by apparently limiting factors such as the body is totally dissolved. The ultimate reality of those aspects, in turn, is simply Śrīmān Maheśvara, who consists of the state of joyful wonder toward the entire universe, which is simply the Light of Awareness.

And that Highest Divinity, by virtue of the fact that it consists of the forms of reflective awareness known as the 'transcendent mass of sounds' underlying the letters from *a* to *kṣa*—because it has Autonomy as its essence—brings about oneness with the bliss of the whole world made up of all the names and objects to which names refer (both of which are included within the scope of that transcendent alphabet), because of which it is supreme, that is, replete with floods of joy, by virtue of the fact that it is empty of all need or desire due to being completely full.

न्द्रावापादनात् परं परिपूर्णत्वात् सर्वाकाङ्क्षा-शून्यतया आनन्दप्रसरनिर्भरः; अत एव अनु-त्तराकुलस्वरूपात् अकारात् आरभ्य शक्तिस्फा-ररूपह[२०]कलापर्यन्तं यत् विश्वं प्रसृतं, क्षकारस्य प्रसरशमनरूपत्वात्; तत् अकार-हकाराभ्यामेव संपुटीकारयुक्त्या प्रत्याहारन्यायेन अन्तः स्वी-कृतं सत् अविभागवेदनात्मकबिन्दुरूपतया स्फुरितम् अनुत्तर एव विश्राम्यति;—इति शब्द-राशिस्वरूप एव अयम् अकृतको विमर्शः। यथोक्तं

'प्रकाशस्यात्मविश्रान्तिरहं-भावो हि कीर्तितः।
उक्ता च सैव विश्रान्तिः सर्वापेक्षानिरोधतः॥
स्वातन्त्र्यमथ कर्तृत्वं मुख्यमीश्वरतापि च।'

इति। एषैव च अहन्ता सर्वमन्त्राणाम् उदयवि-

For this very reason, the universe that has flowed forth from the transcendent alphabet—beginning with A, the own-form of the Absolute (*anuttara*) and Transcendent (*akula*), and ending with *HA*, the fullest expansion of Power (since *kṣa* is merely the dying out of that outward flow)—is internalized by bringing together A and *HA*, manifested with the Point (for it signifies undivided awareness) and coming to rest in the silence of the Absolute itself. This natural self-awareness—AHAṂ—thus is the very nature of the complete mass of phonemes.

As it is said in *Proof of the Conscious Knower*:

> It is taught that the 'I'-sense is where the Light of Awareness comes to rest in itself. That state is called 'repose in groundedness', for in it all sense of need or want vanishes. It is *this* that is Freedom, this is the fundamental Agency, and this too is the state of Sovereignty.

And this same fundamental 'I'-ness is the great Domain of Potency, because it is the place from which all effective mantras arise and in which they come to rest, and because it is only by Its power that they can perform their various functions.

श्रान्तिस्थानत्वात् एतद्बलेनैव च तत्तदर्थक्रियाकारित्वात् महती वीर्यभूमिः । तदुक्तम्

'तदाक्रम्य बलं मन्त्रा ........................।'

इत्यादि

........................त एते शिवधर्मिणः ॥'

इत्यन्तम् श्रीस्पन्दे । शिवसूत्रेषु अपि

'महाह्रदानुसंधानान्मन्त्रवीर्यानुभवः, (१उ०२२सू०)

इति। तदत्र महामन्त्रवीर्यात्मिकायां पूर्णाहन्तायाम् 'आवेशो'—देहप्राणादिनिमज्जनात् तत्पदावास्यवष्टम्भेन देहादीनां नीलादीनामपि तद्रसाप्लावनेन तन्मयीकरणम्। तथा हि—देहसुखनीलादि यत् किंचित् प्रथते, अध्यवसीयते, स्मर्यते संकल्प्यते वा, तत्र सर्वत्रैव भगवती चितिशक्तिमयी प्रथा भित्तिभूतैव स्फुरति;—तदस्फुरणे कस्यापि अस्फुरणात् इति उक्तत्वात्। केवलं तथा स्फुरन्त्यपि सा, तन्मायाशक्त्या

This is taught in the sacred *Stanzas on Vibration*:

> Mantras, attaining that power ... having performed their functions, completely dissolve into that same power, becoming quiescent and stainless, along with the mind of the one who worships (them). Therefore, these mantras have the nature of Śiva himself.

And, in the *Śiva-sūtra* as well, we find:

> The experience of the potency of mantras arises from investigating and uniting with the Great Lake of Awareness. (1.22)

So here in our system, it is Immersion into fully expanded 'I'-ness that constitutes the great potency of all mantras. This Immersion results from subordinating false identification with body, *prāṇa*, etc. Through stabilizing the attainment of that state, everything one experiences—not only the layers of apparent selfhood such as body, but even 'external' phenomena—becomes merged with it by being flooded with the nectar of its bliss.

To explain: whatever is manifest—such as the body, inner experiences, or outer perceptions; whatever is ascertained; whatever is remembered; whatever is imagined & desired: in every case without exception, the Goddess who is the Power of Awareness is manifest as the 'ground' upon which it vibrates. As has been taught, "If She were not manifest, nothing could manifest."

अवभासितदेहनीलाद्युपरागदत्ताभिमानवशात् भिन्नभिन्नस्वभावा इव भान्ती ज्ञानसंकल्पाध्यवसायादिरूपतया मायाप्रमातृभिः अभिमन्यते; वस्तुतस्तु एकैव असौ चितिशक्तिः । यथोक्तम्

'या चैषा प्रतिभा तत्तत्पदार्थक्रमरूषिता ।
अक्रमानन्तचिद्रूपः प्रमाता स महेश्वरः ॥'

इति । तथा

'मायाशक्त्या विभोः सैव भिन्नसंवेद्यगोचरा ।
कथिता ज्ञानसंकल्पाध्यवसायादिनामभिः ॥'

इति। एवम् एषा सर्वदशासु एकैव चितिशक्तिः विजृम्भमाणा यदि तदनुप्रवेश-तदवष्टम्भयुक्त्या समासाद्यते, तत् तदावेशात् पूर्वोक्तयुक्त्या करणोन्मीलननिमीलनक्रमेण सर्वस्य सर्वमयत्वात् तत्तत्संहारादौ अपि 'सदा सर्वसर्गसंहारकारि' यत् 'सहजसंवित्तिदेवताचक्रम्'—अमायीयान्तर्बहिष्करणमरीचिपुञ्जः, तत्र 'ईश्वरता'—

Though She is always manifesting solely in this way, because of the egoic perception conferred by the influence of body, etc.—manifested by Her power of self-concealment-in-plurality—She appears to have various different natures. Those who perceive through the lens of subject–object differentiation wrongly perceive Her in terms of discrete cognitions, imaginations, judgments, etc., when in fact there is but One, this Power of Awareness.

As it is taught:

> And this creative power, this intuitive light, colored though it may be by the phases of the cognitions of the various objects that words denote, is in fact both the Knower, whose nature is nonsequential undying Awareness, and the universal Actor (Maheśvara), the creator of the world of experience that is its 'body'. ||

Likewise:

> That Divine Power of Awareness, through its capacity for Self-concealment-in-plurality, becomes a field of differentiated perceptibles, and thus is called by names such as 'cognition', 'imagination', 'judgment', and so on. ||

Thus, if this singular Power of Awareness—which is constantly revealing itself in every state of consciousness—is attained by entering into it and becoming established in it, then, due to that Immersion, the Tantrik yogin need only practice the method previously taught of turning the sense-faculties inward and outward to attain sovereignty over the natural and innate circle of the goddesses of his own consciousness—that is, the mass of rays of inner and outer faculties in their unlimited aspect—which is constantly bringing about the emissions and reabsorptions of phenomena in each and every experience, because the pattern of the whole is contained in every part.

साम्राज्यं परभैरवात्मता, तत्प्राप्तिः भवति परमयोगिनः । यथोक्तम्

'यदा त्वेकत्र संरूढस्तदा तस्य लयोद्भवौ ।
नियच्छन्भोक्तृतामेति ततश्चक्रेश्वरो भवेत् ॥'

इति । अत्र एकत्र इति

'एकत्रारोपयेत्सर्वम्……………………………।'

इति । चित्सामान्यस्पन्दभूः उन्मेषात्मा व्याख्यातव्या । तस्य इति अनेन

'पुर्यष्टकेन संरुद्ध……………………………।'

इति । उपक्रान्तं पुर्यष्टकम् एव परामष्टव्यम्; न तु यथा विवरणकृतः 'एकत्र सूक्ष्मे स्थूले शरीरे वा' इति व्याकृतवन्तः । स्तुतं च मया

'स्वतन्त्रश्चितिचक्राणां चक्रवर्ती महेश्वरः ।
संवित्तिदेवताचक्रजुष्टः कोऽपि जयत्यसौ ॥'

इति । इतिशब्द उपसंहारे, यत् एतावत् उक्तप्रकरणशरीरं तत् सर्वं 'शिवम्'—शिवप्राप्तिहेतुत्वात्, शिवात् प्रसृतत्वात् शिवस्वरूपाभिन्नत्वात् च, शिवमयमेव इति शिवम् ॥

Experiencing such sovereignty, one becomes identical to the awe-inspiring supreme Divinity.

It is taught [in the final verse of the *Stanzas on Vibration*]:

> But when he is firmly rooted in the One, then, being capable of bringing about the arising and dissolving of his mind and sense faculties, he attains the state of the Experiencer, and as a result becomes Lord of the Circle. ||

Here, "in the One" refers us back to "he should attribute everything to the One," which should be interpreted as referring to the level of the universal pulsation (*spanda*) of Awareness, also known as the Unfolding.

As I have hymned:

> The extraordinary Maheśvara, the autonomous emperor of the territories of Awareness, served and adored by the circle of the goddesses of cognition, is triumphant! ||

The word *iti* indicates we have arrived at the summation and conclusion of the entire text. The whole body of the treatise here taught is Śiva—because it is a means of obtaining Śiva,

because it has flowed forth from Śiva, and because it is not different from Śiva's nature, it is an embodiment of Śiva. Hence,

*iti śivam*! ~ **'All this is Śiva.'/'May it be a blessing.'** || 20 ||

# CHAPTER TWENTY

*with explanation*

At last we come to the final chapter. It is longest chapter of the work, in many ways the most subtle, and perhaps, if one can fully grasp it, the most sublime. For this chapter describes the final fruit of the Tantrik path: the mode of being toward which all the teachings point and all the practices aim.

**Now is described the fruit of the attainment of this** [type of] ***samādhi*:**

|| TADĀ PRAKĀŚĀNANDA-SĀRA-MAHĀ-MANTRA-VĪRYĀTMAKA-PŪRṆĀHAṂTĀVEŚĀT SADĀ-SARVA-SARGA-SAṂHĀRA-KĀRI-NIJA-SAṂVID-DEVATĀ-CAKREŚVARATĀ-PRĀPTIR BHAVATĪTI ŚIVAM || **20** ||

**Then, due to** [continuous] **Immersion into the fully expanded 'I'—which is in essence** [the fusion of] **Illumination and Joy, and is the great potency of** [all] **mantras—one attains the state of being the Lord of the innate circle of the goddesses of awareness, who are constantly engaged in the emanation and reabsorption of all things. All this is Śiva. May it be a blessing.**

Whatever doesn't yet make sense in this sūtra will be explained thoroughly as we proceed through the commentary. First Kṣema gives a brief explanation of the sūtra, then a much more thorough and detailed one.[134]

**This is the brief gloss of the sūtra:**

**When one attains this continuously arising *samādhi*, it manifests as Immersion into the fully expanded 'I'** (*pūrṇāhaṃtā*)—**'fully expanded' because it is one with the Lady Parā, and 'I' in the sense that it is the natural state of wonder at one's essence-nature. It is 'in essence** [the fusion of] **Illumination and Joy', i.e., overflowing with Awareness**

**and** [innate] **Delight, and it is 'the great potency of mantra', i.e., it animates all** [living] **mantras.**

The gloss divides the sūtra into two sections. In the first, the Immersion into the fully expanded 'I' is explained again with some new information, and in the second (below), the full fruition of that Immersion is described.

Here are the points of interest in the first section of the gloss. It is affirmed that the *nityodita-samādhi* of Chapter Nineteen is another name for 'Immersion into the fully expanded 'I'' (*pūrṇāhaṃtā-samāveśa*). We already know that the fully expanded 'I' is the 'I'-sense that includes everything whatsoever. Here Kṣema analyzes the first part of the compound, *pūrṇa*, as being suggestive of the full-bodied Goddess Parā, who contains all things because she is the personification of Awareness itself. The second part of the compound, *ahaṃtā* or 'I'-ness, is explained in terms of its most essential characteristic: wonder. Specifically, we learn that inherent in our essential being is the capacity for *camatkāra*, wonder or aesthetic rapture. This wonder activates in response to the miracle of our existence itself, first and foremost, and secondarily in response to the countless forms that Awareness takes on in the world of our experience.

Saying that the fully expanded 'I' is in essence the fusion of Illumination and Joy is really just saying the same thing (as in the previous paragraph) in different words (because Illumination refers to the manifesting power of Awareness, and Joy = *camatkāra*), except that it adds the nuance that our essence-nature can be understood as the fusion of Śiva and Śakti, for Illumination and Joy are also abstractions of the divine masculine and feminine.

Finally, we are told that this fully expanded self-awareness is the power that animates mantras. This means it is that which makes mantras effective. This will be discussed in more detail below.

Next we learn that the *nityodita-samādhi* described in Chapter Nineteen is not a static state (as the word *nityodita* implies: 'ever fresh', 'continually arising anew'), but continues developing until it culminates in the state of being described in the next section:

**By immersing in That, the Tantrik yogī (the implicit subject of the sentence) attains sovereignty (*aiśvarya*) over the innate circle of the goddesses of awareness,**[135] **who are eternally engaged in the manifold**

**emanations and reabsorptions of all things, from the Fire of Time to the final Power.**[136] **Thus, this whole reality is nothing but God—that is the summary and the conclusion.**

This section will be explained in much greater depth further on. Suffice to say here that the imagery used here depends on the long-established central image of Tantrik spirituality: that of the *maṇḍala* or wheel of sacred power, in which the main deity (or deity pair) is in the center at the hub of the wheel, and rays of energy (*śakti*) radiate out, forming the spokes, with an array of subsidiary deities (or deity pairs) on the rim of the wheel, each of them nuanced expressions of the central deity. Here, in Kṣemarāja's evocation of final realization, *you* are the central deity, and the goddesses emanating from that center are the various faculties of cognition and action. But now you realize that to cognize something is also to manifest it, since Awareness manifests as everything that is experienced. Thus there is no difference at all between *to be aware of* and *to manifest*, just as there is no difference at all between *to be unaware of* and *to dissolve*. Creation is nothing but emanation from the timeless ground of Awareness within you, and dissolution is reabsorption into that same formless Awareness.

However, it is important to realize that this is a necessarily clumsy attempt to describe the subtle realization that is the fruit of the path; it is *not* describing an attitude that one should cultivate along the way, since that would likely result in spiritual bypassing. If having read this, you decided "Okay, so whatever I'm not aware of doesn't exist, so I don't need to worry about it," it could be problematic to say the least. After all, something residing in the subconscious is still part of consciousness—just on the 'sub' level of it. And to be in denial about something is to be, on some level, aware of it, without wanting to be. And furthermore, if someone tells you, "I think you're in denial about X," then according to this view of reality, *what-you-are* is manifesting that experience—in other words, you're trying to tell yourself something. I say these things only to point toward the danger of interpreting these teachings simplistically, and the danger of taking a description of the *result* of practice as a description of something one should practice.

It's safe to say that in much of Chapter Twenty, the reality being pointed to is so subtle and indescribable that Kṣema can use only metaphorical images, and therefore the mental construct you form by reading the words of the chapter probably bears virtually no relation to what you will actually experience, should you arrive at the state of being 'the lord (or lady) of the innate circle of Awareness'.

Now we will move on to Kṣemarāja's in-depth explanation of all that is hinted at in the sūtra. His primary project here is to recap and review nearly all of the key concepts he has introduced throughout the work—in a style that makes them feel fresh—while weaving his prose together with citations from his most important primary sources. In this way Chapter Twenty forms a kind of sustained crescendo to the whole work. However, Kṣema writes even more elliptically than usual (omitting all the words he thinks the intelligent and intuitive reader ought to be able to fill in), possibly to make the chapter difficult to comprehend for anyone not ready to access its teachings.

The first compound of the sūtra is *prakāśānanda-sāra*, 'the essence of Illumination and Joy'. He now proceeds to explain both those key terms in detail.

Topic 1. The Innate Hierarchy of Awareness.

**To explain** [in more detail]**: whatever one is aware of in this world, its nature is nothing but that awareness. The** [underlying] **reality** [of these acts of awareness] **are the** [various] **conscious perceivers, whose distinguishing feature is** [their capacity for] **internally directed awareness. Their essence, in turn, is** [the supreme Perceiver] **who embodies all,** [whether in] **Sadāśiva or Īśvara aspect, in whom egoic identification with the contraction caused by apparently limiting factors such as the body is totally dissolved. The ultimate reality of those aspects, in turn, is simply Śrīmān Maheśvara, who consists of** [the state of] **joyful wonder (*camatkāra*) toward the entire universe, which is simply the Light of Awareness.**[137]

This fascinating paragraph echoes the spirit of the doctrine of the Seven Perceivers presented back in Chapter Three. My speculation is that if Kṣemarāja could have jettisoned that ancient and traditional doctrine, he would have, and would have replaced it with this more lucid account of the innate hierarchy of Awareness.

The first thing we have to note is that this is not a hierarchy in the usual sense. It proceeds not higher and higher, but deeper and deeper, explicating what is dependent on what. It presents five layers in total:

$^{5}$knowables → $^{4}$acts of awareness → $^{3}$perceivers → $^{2}$Supreme Perceiver → $^{1}$Divine Ground with its Śrī

Each of the first four aspects of awareness named here is grounded in, and derives its reality from, the following aspect. So as we proceed, there is a kind of collapsing of layers happening, until we arrive at the ultimate ground. (This is an epistemological parallel of the *Mālinī-vijayottara-tantra*'s 'yoga of apperception' that utilizes the Seven Perceivers. See endnote 37.)

First we learn that there are no knowables apart from knowing. Check this against your own experience, since it's easily verified. Have you ever been able to prove to yourself that things exist independently of your awareness of them? Have you ever tried? If you can look at the situation clearly, you'll soon realize that you've simply been conditioned to assume that things exist independently of your awareness of them, but there has never been any proof whatsoever that they do. And there never could be. Like most people, you take observer-independent reality on *faith*. But the apparent common sense of that assumption has now been deconstructed by the most advanced branch of science we have, that of quantum physics. It has demonstrated that the belief in observer-independent reality is nothing other than that: a belief. And one without any evidence whatsoever to support it. Kṣemarāja reveals this truth in these words: "Whatever one is aware of in this world, its nature is nothing but that awareness." Another way of saying the same thing is: there is no reality to whatever you are aware of *apart from your awareness of it.*

"But wait a second," you say. "If I experience a specific thing, let's say a tree, and then when I'm not there my friend experiences the same thing and reports it to me, surely that proves its existence is independent of my awareness?" No—it only demonstrates that perceivers are coordinated, which we discussed back in Chapter Three. They agree on the tangible aspects of reality because their awarenesses co-create that reality, giving rise to the illusion of objectivity. But perceivers are and must be coordinated simply because they are all instantiations of a single underlying Perceiver. They are all facets in a single jewel, as it were; all rays of the one light. This is what Kṣema is trying to show in this paragraph. The reality underlying acts of perception is simply their perceivers, he tells us, who have the power to look within and discover this fact for themselves. And the essence of all these perceivers is the One Perceiver who embodies all. The only way you can experience the 'level' of the One Perceiver, Kṣema implies, is by completely dissolving egoic identification with the apparent loci of contraction: the body, mind, etc.

The One Perceiver can manifest in either of two aspects (but not at the same time: thus it is still One). These two aspects are called Sadāśiva and Īśvara (tattvas #3 and #4, for those who know the *tattva* map).[138] The difference between them is subtle: both exist in a relationship of identity with all that they perceive, experiencing *I am all this*, but with Sadāśiva, the emphasis is on the *I*, and with Īśvara, the emphasis is on *this*. (Review Chapter Three, pages 94–95, if this doesn't make sense to you.) Now, if you abide in the state of the One Perceiver, and directly experience that the multiplicity of perceivers is not ultimately real—since in truth there is only one consciousness looking out through every pair of eyes—then you have attained awakeness (*bodha*) and liberation (*mokṣa*), according to the Tantrik View. And yet there is 'further' you can go, because the One Perceiver is itself grounded in an even deeper reality.

How can this be? What could be more fundamental than One Consciousness? Recall that the One Perceiver described above is in relationship with the whole, all that is or can be perceived. The even more fundamental ground is the Awareness that is absolute potential, unnameable in truth but here called Śrīmān Maheśvara, a phrase I'll explain presently. (In *tattva* terms, it's the perfect fusion and balance of tattvas #1 and #2, also known as tattva #0.) The main point is, at this 'level' (that is not in any way a level), there is no relationship of identity (*I am this*), since there is **only** the 'I', no 'this' whatsoever. In other words, from the perspective of Śrīmān Maheśvara, nothing has ever manifested. There is only the singular Light of Awareness pervaded by unconditional rejoicing in its own being.[139] This pure Light-of-being does nothing, because suffused with wonder (*camatkāra*) in relation to being itself, no becoming is necessary—so it never becomes anything. From this 'level' of perception, no separation ever occurred and no forgetting ever occurred. The Light of Awareness never departed from itself in the smallest degree, and this is seen with utmost clarity. The real 'game' is not one of forgetting and remembering, concealing and revealing, but rather the game of make-believing that there is a game at all, when in truth the One can never cease to be itself or to be aware of itself.

But why does Kṣema use the phrase Śrīmān Maheśvara (literally, 'the Great Lord possessing radiant power') to denote this ultimate ground? Why such a pedestrian theistic phrase, utilized by the devoted god-fearing masses? For three reasons, I think. First, that Maheśvara is the preferred term for the Divine in his source text (Utpala's *Stanzas on the Recognition of the Divine*, which though rigorously philosophical, has a devotional background). Second, to subvert our expectations by avoiding an abstract term and thereby remind us that the real nature of the Divinity we refer to in everyday language is none other than this very Light of Awareness. Third, by saying *Śrīmān* Maheśvara, he can imply the union of Śiva and Śakti: 'the Great Lord with his Śrī'. The implication of this is significant: that the ground of being, the timeless Light of Awareness, is inseparably joined with its innate power. It is by virtue of this that we can accurately call it 'absolute potential', whether we experience it as manifest or unmanifest.

Topic 2. The Mystic Alphabet and Its Essence.

**And that Highest Divinity, by virtue of the fact that it consists of** [the forms of] **reflective awareness known as the 'transcendent mass of sounds'** [underlying the letters] **from *a* to *kṣa*—because it has Autonomy as its essence—, brings about oneness with the bliss of the whole world made up of all the names and objects** [to which names refer, both of which are] **included within** [the scope of] **that** [transcendent alphabet]—**because of which it is supreme (*para*), that is, replete with floods of joy, by virtue of the fact that it is empty of all need or desire due to being completely full.**

This paragraph seems complex because it exhibits classic Sanskritic precision and concision. The grammar of the language is such that one can tie together any number of clauses in a precise way, which flows nicely in Sanskrit but when rendered into English gives the impression of being needlessly dense. First I'll state the gist of this paragraph in simple language, then unpack it.

The Light of Awareness, in its freedom, takes the form of the fundamental constituents of language, which are really nothing but products of our capacity for self-reflection. These fundamental constituents (which linguists today call *phonemes*) manifest as the alphabets of the various languages, especially Sanskrit, here seen as the paradigmatic language. Understanding that the same capacity for self-reflection underlies both our ability to formulate language and our ability to identify the things to which language refers gives rise to a unique joy, a joy that encompasses and pervades the whole world of one's experience. Fully accessing this self-reflective capacity reveals that it is both innately joyful and self-sufficient.

Let's unpack that a little more. Since the previous topic was mainly about the Light of Awareness (*prakāśa*), Kṣema nows turns to its counterpart, the power of self-reflection and representation (*vimarśa*), represented in the sūtra itself by the word Joy (*ānanda*), for reasons that will become clear. One way that *vimarśa* expresses is as the discrete yet interdependent pulsations of reflective awareness (*parāmarśa*) that take concrete form as the fundamental constituents of language, the phonemes.[140] Now, the phonemes of Sanskrit are thought, in Tantrik linguistic mysticism, to have a 'transcendent' aspect that is free from the 'taint' of dualistic cognition. This 'transcendent alphabet' (*amāyīya-śabda-rāśi*) cannot be spoken, but underlies the letters that can be spoken, just as the true vibration of *Oṃ* cannot be captured by a person enunciating the word 'Oṃ', however accurately. Realization of the nature of this transcendent alphabet gives rise to an all-encompassing joy (*jagad-ānanda*), because one realizes it as the source not only of the words that denote things but also of the cognitive acts by which discrete moments of experience are comprehended. To put it another way, it is our fundamental capacity to reflect on our experience that gives rise both to the *category of experience* represented by the word 'tree' and the word itself. So the 'transcendent alphabet' consists precisely of those forms of reflective (and reflexive) awareness that make possible words *and* the categories of experience to which the words refer. To put it yet another way, it would be impossible for us to experience a tree as a specific phenomenon if we were unable to formulate the word-concept 'tree', regardless of whether the word occurs during the experience or not. So this self-reflective capacity, which only humans display on this planet,[141] is the source of *all* forms of representation—art and imagination as well as language. One and the same capacity, *vimarśa*, underlies all these: the simple act by which awareness becomes aware of *itself* and reflects on its experience. Realizing this truth, one can experience a bliss that encompasses the whole world, because that world is made up entirely of word-concepts and the categories of direct experience to which they refer.

In the final clause of Kṣema's paragraph, he argues that it is because of the potential of *vimarśa* to connect us to this all-pervasive joy that it can be called 'supreme'. And here Kṣema is playing his own subtle language game, since the Sanskrit words he chooses are calculated to suggest the divine identity of this aspect of Awareness: that is, Parā Devī, the supreme (*para*) Goddess of the Trika, who is also known as Vāgīśvarī, the Goddess of Speech. For he describes the aspect of divine Awareness under consideration as *paripūrṇa*, 'completely full', implicitly taking Parā and *pūrṇa* as deriving from the same root (√*pṝ*). Thus we are meant to understand that if we realize our capacity for *vimarśa* in full measure, we realize the nature of the Goddess: full beyond measure, free of all need and desire by virtue of her fullness, and replete with floods of joy. Full realization of your capacity for *vimarśa* and intimate union with this Goddess are one and the same thing.[142]

Thus, Topic 1 explored *prakāśa*, associated in this lineage with Śiva, and Topic 2 explored *vimarśa*, associated with *ānanda* and with the Goddess. (If you don't thoroughly understand these two basic categories by now, please review pages 60–62 in *Tantra Illuminated*.) But we are not yet done with Topic 2! The next paragraph (which also foreshadows Topic 3) explains how the Sanskrit alphabet encodes the most fundamental form of self-awareness, the sense of 'I am' which is the basis for all other forms of *vimarśa*.

**Therefore, the universe that has flowed forth** [from the divine Awareness in the form of the transcendent alphabet]**—beginning with *a*, the own-form of the Absolute** (*anuttara*) **and Transcendent** (*akula*),[143] **and ending with *ha*, the** [fullest] **expansion of Power (since *kṣa* is merely the dying out of that outward flow)—is internalized by bringing together A and HA, manifested with the Point (for it signifies undivided awareness) and coming to rest in** [the silence of] **the Absolute itself. This natural self-awareness** [AHAṂ] **is thus the very nature of the** [complete] **mass of phonemes.**

Kṣema's guru, Abhinava Gupta, argues that the structure of the Sanskrit language is in certain ways parallel to the structure of reality itself. Here we see evidence for that assertion. Even though Sanskrit evolved organically, it so happens that the first and last letters of its alphabet—its alpha and omega—form the word 'I' when brought together with a *bindu* or dot, like so: अहं (*ahaṃ*). Furthermore, since Sanskrit has a grammatical rule that the verb 'be' is assumed if no verb is stated, *ahaṃ* also means 'I am'. In Abhinava Gupta's linguistic mysticism, the first letter of the alphabet, अ *a*, signifies the Absolute, and the last letter, ह *ha*, signifies tangible concrete physical reality (the Earth element), which as Kṣema says is "the fullest expansion of *śakti*".[144] Thus the word *ahaṃ* encompasses everything, from the most subtle and transcendent to the most obvious and palpable. This teaching points to the fact that when the true 'I' is experienced, it is seen (and felt) to encompass everything, and to the fact that this is only possible through the attainment of undivided awareness, here appropriately designated by the dot called *bindu*—for what could be more indivisible than a single point? It is only with this dot, this nondual awareness, that अह *aha* ('certainly' or 'it is true') becomes अहं *ahaṃ* ('I' or 'I am').

If you remember that this philosophy denies (or is agnostic about) the existence of any 'objective' reality separate from awareness, then the assertion made here, that the whole universe exists within the 'I', seems less fantastic—because the only reality about which we can meaningfully speak is the universe experienced by specific consciousnesses, and it is undeniably true that the whole universe of your experience is unified by one and only one feature—it is all internal to, and pervaded by, your awareness, which is the only consistent referent of the word 'I'. To put it another way, since there is no observer-independent reality, all phenomena arise and subside within awareness, within the 'I', and this 'I', unlike one's conditioned self-image, is naturally all-encompassing. Thus this 'natural self-awareness' encompasses 'the complete mass of phonemes' and the principles of reality they represent and express.

When reciting *bīja-mantras* (such as OṂ or HRĪṂ) in the *uccāra* style* one always pauses and rests in the stillness after each enunciation. Here AHAṂ is being treated like a *bīja-mantra* (otherwise, M not Ṃ would

* See *Tantra Illuminated*, page 393.

terminate the word), and thus Kṣema mentions "coming to rest in the Absolute itself", for in the silence following each bīja enunciation there is precisely that opportunity. But of course that is not the only meaning intended here, for Kṣema speaks of AHAṂ as "natural self-awareness", and thus AHAṂ as mantra is really just symbolic for AHAṂ as wordless self-reflection, and there too we have the opportunity to come to rest in the Absolute. The poet Alfred Lord Tennyson discovered this independently, as attested by this quotation:

> I have never had any revelations through [drugs], but a kind of waking trance—this for lack of a better word—I have frequently had, quite up from boyhood, when I have been all alone. This has come upon me through repeating my own name to myself silently, till all at once, as it were out of the intensity of the consciousness of individuality, individuality itself seemed to dissolve and fade away into boundless being, and this not a confused state but the clearest, the surest of the surest, utterly beyond words—where death was an almost laughable impossibility—the loss of personality (if so it were) seeming no extinction, but the only true life. I am ashamed of my feeble description. Have I not said the state is utterly beyond words?[145]

Clearly, the magic was not in the word 'Alfred' but in the deep self-reflection underlying it, a sense of fascinated wonder at the mystery of his own existence. Incidentally, this quote is one of many that provide important evidence that some (rare) individuals can discover independently some of what is taught in texts like the one we are studying here.

The reader who wishes to fully understand the linguistic mysticism unique to Abhinava Gupta and Kṣemarāja's teaching will need to consult Chapter Three of the *Tantrāloka*.[146] However, here Kṣema suggests that if we practice and cultivate the most fundamental form of self-reflection, we will eventually access all the insights that lie hidden within the 'transcendent alphabet'. The most fundamental form of self-reflection, taught in the twentieth century by Ramana Maharṣi and Nisargadatta Mahārāj, is to access and abide in 'I am'-consciousness. As above, this doesn't mean repeating the words 'I am' (though for some, that can function as an effective mantra), but rather becoming absorbed in awareness of your own being, your own presence. As in Lord Tennyson's example, this kind of meditation tends to be more effective when you realize that you don't actually understand what you are (I mean, come on, you don't even understand how your body works, and that's the *least* subtle layer of your being) and thus you become curious and fascinated with investigating the nature of awareness itself (the only common element in all your experiences, and thus the best contender for your true nature). For more on this, please read Nisargadatta's amazing book *I Am That.*

Next Kṣema cites a text by his grand-guru that both finishes this topic and foreshadows the next one.

**As it is said** [in the *Proof of the Conscious Knower* by Utpala Deva]:

> **For it is taught that the 'I'-sense** (*ahaṃbhāva*) **is where the Light of Awareness comes to rest in itself. That state is called 'repose in groundedness'** (*viśrānti*)**, for in it all sense of need or want vanishes. Now it is this** [state] **that is** [rightly called] **Freedom, this is the fundamental Agency, and this too is the state of Sovereignty.**

The Light of Awareness manifests all things, but it only comes to rest in itself through the act of *vimarśa*, self-awareness or self-reflection. Not the cogitative kind of self-reflection, but rather the wordless reflection on one's own fundamental being. The word *ahaṃbhāva* means not only ''I'-sense', but also 'the feeling of *I*' and 'the existence of *I*'. To become absorbed in this wordless self-reflection (said to be possible only after *śaktipāta*)* is to repose in the ground of one's being, where it is easy to sense the sheer miracle of existence and to feel contented and grateful. Kṣema talks about the "cessation of all *apekṣā*", where the latter word, translated here as 'need or want' implies a sense of lack, for it literally connotes the act of looking to something (not already present) for fulfillment. The only true repose in human life is when all one's needs are met and/or one is confident they will be met. But essence-nature has no needs *per se*; or perhaps it is more accurate to say that its needs

* See *Tantra Illuminated*, page 321ff.

are fulfilled simply by existing. As astonishing as it may sound if you haven't experienced it, when you repose in being itself, there is a kind of fulfillment that could never be bought or attained, and a kind of peace that passeth all understanding. (And if you haven't experienced it, the first step is to learn to relax, truly relax, in both mind and body.) Kṣema follows his guru in using the word *viśrānti* to refer to reposing in the center of one's being, which is also the ground.

When abiding in the Center becomes your default state, you experience your innate Freedom, Agency, and Sovereignty (the last of these three words, *īśvaratā*, also translates as Divinity). This comes as a revelation, for, as neuroscience is now showing, none of these are a feature of the body-mind complex. That is, individual agency is actually an illusion.[147] The Śaiva Tantrik tradition, unique among Indian philosophies, taught exactly that; more specifically, it taught that Agency (the power to act freely) belongs only to Awareness, not to the body-mind. To put it another way, there is only one Actor behind all actions, and that is God. (Note that these are, in this system, two ways of describing the exact same thing.) To put it a third way, the you that you think you are has no free will, but the You you really are is nothing *but* free will. Now, the mind, as if jealous, generates an artificial correlate of the freedom that Awareness has: the felt-sense 'I chose A, but I *could have* chosen B.' Both neuroscience and quantum physics have shown this to be a mind-created illusion.[148] The mind will always choose what seems to be the best option available to it, given all the information that it has. (And if, at your next apparent choice-point, you choose what is clearly not the best option in order to prove this theory wrong, *that* is simply the mind trying to preserve the sense of free will, because having such a sense is adaptive and empowering even if false, and thus the mind is still choosing the 'best option'.) But if our sense of being able to choose freely between A and B is false, where is action arising from? Biologists will say the body. Cognitive scientists will say the subconscious mind, or more precisely the adaptive unconscious.[149] In this tradition, both body and mind are seen as expressions of a deeper underlying power, *cit-śakti*, which we imperfectly translate as Awareness.

This might be the simplest way to explain this: Freedom and Agency are real, but they are features of the *transindividual* aspect of your being. Since they are not features of the individual aspect of your being, the sense of free will that your mind and body have is illusory.

(You can verify this for yourself: just track how often you do something you plan to do, big or small, and if you do it over enough time, you'll see that which plans are executed and which aren't is so unpredictable as to be almost random. Oh and it doesn't count if you *do* do something you planned to do, but in a very different manner from how you planned to do it. Because the point is that your imagination, which is linked to your personal will and illusion of separate individuality, predicts the future no better than random chance,[150] even though you *plan* to act on each imagined scheme that seems like a good idea at the time. The verifiable fact is that imagination is only right about the future by chance, or when it (occasionally) expresses an *intuition* about the trajectory your life is taking.) But that illusion is itself a simulacrum of the true Freedom and Agency that exist on the transindividual level. You can approximately measure the degree to which you're identified with body-mind versus Awareness by the degree to which you can feel deep acceptance and gratitude for your whole life situation in any given moment. (I'm not talking about acceptance of a static snapshot of your life at any given moment, because in truth every given moment is a part of a larger *flow*, a flow that is sensed by Awareness at every moment, but cannot be understood by the mind. The 'static snapshot' is just a mental image, not a felt-sense of your existence.)

That is to say, Awareness freely chooses *what is* in any given moment; if it didn't, what is would be what isn't. The power of Awareness to manifest all the objects of its experience is here called Freedom. But what about action? For some people, action is what feels the most individual. In truth, however, all your actions express either your mental and psychological conditioning, or arise as spontaneous expressions of Awareness. Either way, they're not 'yours' in any meaningful sense. And since conditioned action (what the tradition calls 'bondage') is also freely chosen by Awareness, we can accurately say that all actions arise solely from the power of Awareness called Agency.[151] In other words, in truth all actions arise as a spontaneous expression of the power of the One to act. (And of course, the moment when Awareness chooses to begin unravelling its state of bondage also happens spontaneously: it's called *śaktipāta* by this tradition.)

So we can speak of the agency of individual actors only in a figurative sense, as a verbal convenience. There is only one agent of all action and activity, and that is Awareness. This is why the world's spiritual paths encourage us to surrender the personal will by merging it with Divine Will; not only because that will make us happier and more content, but because personal will is itself an illusion, a mistaken belief that generates struggle, striving, and resistance. The feeling of merging the personal will with the Divine Will is such a blessed relief because it is simply surrendering to the fact of how this reality is constituted. Instead of asking "What do I want to do with my life?" we ask the saner question "What does Life want to do with me?"

And that's what prevents the state of surrender from being a passive one. Nearly everyone who honestly asks the question "What does Life want to do through me?" discovers that Life *does* want to do something specific through them, nearly every day. Exactly what it wants to do might be surprising, or even disappointing to one's ego. But there can be such sweet joy in doing it—whatever it is.

The final of the three terms with which the primary source passage presents us is Sovereignty (though *īśvaratā* might also be intended in the sense of 'Divinity'). We will discuss this further, but briefly: though it's true that the you you think you are (named so-and-so) is not in control of anything, at least not anything of the slightest significance, the deeper underlying transindividual You is 'sovereign', is Lord of all it surveys, as it were. This statement simply points to the fact that one who abides in essence-nature does not feel in the least disempowered or helpless; on the contrary, despite the body-mind-personality's inability to control anything, s/he feels totally empowered in the true sense: totally connected to all the powers of Awareness. Such a one freely chooses, moment to moment, intimate engagement with this world, in which one of the conditions of embodiment is the inability of any individual body-mind to determine any specific outcome. It is in this sense that one experiences 'sovereignty'.

But if Utpala Deva means the word *īśvaratā* in the sense of 'Divinity', then he is simply saying, in effect, "Possessing this innate Freedom and Agency is what it means to be God in our tradition."

Topic 3. The Potency of Mantra.

**And this same** [fundamental] **'I'-ness is the great domain of potency** (*vīrya-bhūmi*)**, because it is the place from which all** [effective] **mantras arise and in which they come to rest, and because it is only by Its power that they can perform their various functions.**

Adherents of the nondual Tantrik tradition noticed that some who attempt to use mantras find them ineffective and others find them effective, not only for internal practice but also to accomplish tangible goals in the world. The explanation given for this is that some masters possess *mantra-vīrya*, the power that potentizes mantras, as a result of their awakened awareness and spiritual attainment generally. So here Kṣema explains that it is specifically self-awareness that is the true potentizer. One who has spiritual realization knows that the power of mantras, if they have any, arises from one's awakened self-awareness, through which s/he is in touch with the true potencies of consciousness. It is only through the power of self-realization that the full power of mantras is actualized, and any degree of self-realization (even a glimmer) potentizes mantras to that degree. This, of course, creates a positive feedback loop when the power of the mantras is directed toward further and deeper self-realization.

This teaching explains why, whenever possible, one should receive a mantra from a self-realized being, and the more self-realized the better. In that way, the mantra comes to you already potentized, already pulsing with the energy of Awareness. This is sometimes called a *caitanya* mantra. Such a mantra can hasten the aspirant's process of awakening to his essence-nature (but it cannot accomplish that process in and of itself).

**This is taught in the sacred *Stanzas on Vibration*** (2.1–2)**:**

> **"Mantras, attaining that power ... [having performed their functions, completely dissolve into that same** [power]**, becoming quiescent and stainless, along with the mind of the one who worships** (them)**.] Therefore, these mantras have the nature of Śiva** [himself]**."**

As is his wont, here Kṣema gives only the very beginning and end of a quotation that he expects his audience to have memorized. Therefore I have filled in the relevant portions of this two-verse quotation from the *Spanda-kārikā*. Note that the first verse of this quote was already cited back in Chapter Fifteen. By citing this passage here, Kṣema is teaching that the 'power' the verse alludes to is precisely this awakened self-awareness we have been discussing.[152] What is interesting about this passage is that it implies that the main reason for utilizing a mantra (assuming an enlivened mantra here) is precisely that it dissolves into Awareness when its task (here, worship) is complete, and thus the mind of the worshiper that is firmly joined to the mantra will likewise dissolve, becoming as quiescent and peaceful as the mantra does when it is no longer functioning. This is even more effective in the case of the person who is worshiping the mantras themselves by repeating them (rather than using them as instruments): for s/he attains the state from which they arose and into which they dissolve. But even in the case of someone using a mantra for a prosaic end, such as neutralizing the poison from a snakebite,[153] the same opportunity exists, for if the mantra is effective it must have arisen from and will dissolve into the power of awake awareness. For these reasons, mantras ought to be regarded as non-different from Śiva—or God—himself. In this context I recall the twentieth-century yoga master Swāmī Muktānanda's assertion that a mantra will only be fully effective if the practitioner regards the mantra, the deity to which it refers, *and* his own true nature as one and the same.

**And, in the *Śiva-sūtra* as well,** [we find:]

> **The experience of the potency of mantras** [arises]
> **from investigating and uniting with the Great Lake**
> [of Awareness]**.** (1.22)

Here Kṣema is simply reinforcing his point by citing another prooftext. In his commentary on this sūtra found in his *Śiva-sūtra-vimarśinī*, he clarifies that the metaphor of a great mountain lake is appropriate for Awareness because both are pure, clear, and deep, and both contain subtle currents. (In the case of Awareness, these are the flows called Khecarī and so on, covered back in Chapter Twelve.) He also clarifies that 'uniting' is figurative here; in reality, one realizes one's already-existent unity with That. Finally, he explains that the "potency of mantras" (*mantra-vīrya*) refers to the awareness of the perfect (and all-inclusive) 'I', which expands into the mass of phonemic sounds (*śabda-rāśi*) known as the 'transcendent alphabet'. So his commentary there almost duplicates his comments here.

Now Kṣema sums up the topic and foreshadows the next one:

**So here** [in our system]**, it is Immersion into fully expanded 'I'-ness that constitutes the great potency of all mantras. This Immersion**

**results from subordinating** [false identification with] **body, *prāṇa*, etc. Through stabilizing the attainment of that state, everything one experiences**—[not only the layers of apparent selfhood] **such as body, etc. but even 'external' phenomena—becomes merged with it by being flooded with the nectar** [of its bliss].

Mantras become fully effective only when one becomes fully immersed in the true 'I'. And that immersion, he reiterates, can only occur through a systematic, sustained, thorough process of releasing identification with the impermanent aspects of one's being, which means releasing all self-images associated with the body, mind, etc. This process is both necessary and sufficient to attain immersion into one's true nature. Then that state must be stabilized, as discussed in Chapter Sixteen. When it is, *everything* is experienced as an expression of the one universal Awareness that you yourself are, as discussed in Chapter Nineteen. As Kṣema poetically says here, it is as if everything becomes flooded, inundated, saturated with the *rasa* or sweet juiciness of that state; in other words, everything tastes like God.

Next Kṣema explains why this experience is not a pleasant daydream, but conforms to the nature of reality itself. Through both logical reasoning and the authority of the scriptures, we can verify that this experience of the total unity of oneself, the universe, and God is indeed a veridical one.

Topic 4. The Nature of Reality.

**To explain: whatever is manifest—such as the body, inner experiences, or outer perceptions; whatever is ascertained; whatever is remembered; whatever is imagined or desired: in every case without exception, the Goddess who is the Power of Awareness is manifest as the 'ground' upon which it vibrates. As has been taught, "If She were not manifest, nothing could manifest."***

Of the six topics in Chapter Twenty, only Topic 4 is not an explanation of some portion of Sūtra Twenty (unless it be an explication of

* We could also translate, "If She did not vibrate, nothing else could vibrate" or "If She did not shine, nothing could shine", for *sphuraṇa* means vibrate, shine, and manifest more or less equally.

the word *bhavati*, 'there is'). I think Kṣema included this topic to bring his concluding chapter back to the putative source of his whole text, the *Stanzas on the Recognition of the Divine*. In the paragraph above, he reminds us that Awareness is the ground of being, the context for all experience, and that within which whatever is manifest manifests. The word he uses for 'ground' is precisely that which was translated as 'canvas' back in Sūtra Two.

**Though She is always manifesting solely in this way, because of the egoic perception conferred by the influence of body, pleasure, blue, etc.—manifested by Her power of self-concealment-in-plurality** (*māyā-śakti*)**—She appears to have various different natures. Those who perceive through the lens of subject–object differentiation wrongly perceive Her in terms of** [discrete] **cognitions, imaginations, judgments, etc., when in fact there is but One, this Power of Awareness** (*citi-śakti*)**.**

A few points of explanation here, in order of their appearance in the above paragraph. 'In this way'—that is, as the ground for all forms of manifestation. 'Egoic perception' (*abhimāna*) develops on the basis of three types of manifestation (which were also mentioned in the preceding paragraph): 'body' stands for all the layers of everyday personhood (body, heart-mind, *prāṇa*, and Void), 'pleasure' stands for the whole range of mental-emotional states, and 'blue' stands for all forms of sense perception, that is, all apparently external phenomena perceived by the senses. There's a nice ambiguity to the referent of the word 'manifested': body, pleasure, and blue are manifested as apparently separate objects through Awareness's power of *māyā* (which in this system means 'self-concealment-in-plurality'), but that power also manifests the egoic perception that appropriates the first two categories to itself but denies the third. In other words, the self-image-manufacturer we call 'ego' claims body, heart-mind, *prāṇa*, pleasure, pain, etc. as part of itself, but denies that status to other aspects of its experience (aspects labeled as 'external'). Because of this egoic mode of perception, Awareness appears to have 'various different natures': my awareness versus your awareness. A person afflicted with *māyīya-mala* (see Chapter Nine) perceives habitually and exclusively through the lens of this subject–object differentiation—'me' versus 'not me'—and thus cannot see all forms of conscious experience as aspects and expressions of the singular Power of Awareness. Since it is the mind that is conditioned to see in terms of subject–object duality, when we see from the perspective of core Awareness, we see without boundaries and the seamless unity of all is obvious.

**As it is taught:**

> **And this creative power, this intuitive light** (*pratibhā*)**, colored** [though it may be] **by the phases** [of cognition] **of the various objects that words denote, is** [in fact both] **the Knower, whose nature is nonsequential undying Awareness, and the universal Actor** (*Maheśvara*)**, the creator of the world of experience that is its 'body'.**[154] || [*Stanzas on the Recognition of the Divine* I.7.1]

The singular Power of Awareness is identified in this system as *pratibhā*, the capacity for supramental intuitive insight described in Chapter Eighteen, and as the innermost Knower, that self that pervades and connects the various thoughts and feelings that arise and subside. That same Knower is not defined or limited by the sequentiality of time, but exists atemporally, as can be directly experienced. The mind is exclusively temporal: that is, it experiences things within linear time and in terms of sequentiality, and it constructs time-bound narratives about reality, like cause and effect. The Knower is atemporal, since its perception is not time-bound. When perceiving as the Knower, everything exists in an eternal Now, and 'then' is merely a mental construct also existing within the Now. (This key distinction between temporal and atemporal perception is one way to distinguish the mind and the Knower, and to check whether you've actually experienced the latter.) Furthermore, the Knower is unborn and undying. It never came into being and can never cease to be.

This 'intuitive light' of Awareness is furthermore identical to God, the singular Actor behind all actions, the fundamental action being of course the creation of the world of experience that constitutes the 'body' in relation to the 'soul' that is Awareness.

All this is stated or implied in Utpala's verse quoted above.

**Likewise:**

> **That Divine** [Power of Awareness]**, through its power of Self-concealment-in-plurality,** [becomes] **a field of differentiated perceptibles, and thus is called by names such as 'cognition', 'imagination', 'judgement', and so on.** || [*Stanzas on the Recognition of the Divine* I.5.18]

This verse adds no new information; Kṣema is citing it as a proof-text for what he has already said.

Topic 5. The Experience of Complete Liberation.

**Thus, if this singular Power of Awareness—which is** [constantly] **revealing itself in every state** [of consciousness]—**is attained by entering into it and becoming established in it, then, due to that Immersion, the Tantrik yogin** [need only] **practice the method previously taught of turning the sense-faculties inward and outward to attain sovereignty over the natural and innate circle of the goddesses of his own consciousness—that is, the mass of rays of inner and outer faculties in their unlimited aspect—**[which is] **constantly bringing about the emissions and reabsorptions** [of phenomena] **in each and every experience, because the pattern of the whole is contained in every part.** [Experiencing such sovereignty]**, one becomes identical to the awe-inspiring supreme Divinity (*para-bhairava*).**

This paragraph translates one long and complex sentence in the Sanskrit, which is glossing and expounding the second half of Sūtra Twenty. The grammar is difficult, and it's almost as if Kṣema did not want it to be easily understood. If so, that would be because this is the paragraph in which he attempts to describe the experience of complete liberation, and he doesn't want the reader to think he can grasp that state with the mind. That he might be using such a strategy is not much of a speculative stretch, since his guru, Abhinava Gupta, often would employ more difficult Sanskrit grammar in passages that he wanted the reader to have to work to understand. So here we must carefully contemplate what is being said.

Let's organize the key points of the paragraph. First Kṣema reminds us that we need not await any special circumstances to awaken to our true nature and become liberated beings—for by definition, the Power of Awareness is constantly revealing itself in every cognition and perception. Second, we are invited to enter into that Power and stabilize ourselves there. This seems paradoxical, for that Power is what we are and always have been. Yet it makes sense, because what is shifting is our locus of identification, our sense of what we fundamentally are. As long as you assume, even subconsciously, that your identity centers on your thoughts, memories, emotions, etc., a kind of existential angst pervades your life, whether obviously or subtly. Something's always somehow a bit off—"There must be more to life than *this*"—even if all your needs are met. By contrast, when we identify with what we really are and always have been, when we take up residence at the true center of our being, everything somehow feels *right*, even if our needs are not always met.

Entering into your true nature is not difficult. You can do it many times a day through any centering practice that works for you, such as those in Chapter Eighteen.[155] Stabilizing there ("becoming established in it", as Kṣema says) is harder, for that refers to the process though which abiding in your Center becomes your default state. This process can take some time, but if it is your top priority, it doesn't take more than a few years.[156]

The third key point in the paragraph is that whenever we are in our Center, we can practice the method of "turning the sense-faculties inward and outward". Here he uses an ambiguous phrase, since it could be referring to the practice given at the beginning of Chapter Fifteen, or the twofold *samādhi* of Chapter Nineteen, or even practices two and three of Chapter Eighteen in immediate succession. Perhaps he is purposefully ambiguous because he wants us to see these different passages as variations on a single theme. (If so, the underlying theme would be *spanda*.) At any rate, if this method or methods are practiced by someone who already has access to the Center, s/he will attain through them complete empowerment and liberation. I will discuss the metaphor he uses to describe this state below, but first we should note his fourth key point: that this method works "because the pattern of the whole is contained in every part". This teaching was first propounded by the originator of the Pratyabhijñā lineage, Utpala's guru

Somānanda, who taught that "everything is in everything"—that the nature of reality is *holographic* in the sense that each part contains the pattern of the whole, and *nonseparable* in the sense that each thing is entangled, or inseparably connected, with all things.[157] (This is, in part, a Śaiva version of the Buddhist teaching of interdependent origination (*pratītya-samutpāda*), which says that everything arises and subsides in interdependence on everything else.) Since everything is in everything, in the apparently simple practice of "turning the sense-faculties inward and outward" you are expressing and recapitulating the fundamental pulsation of reality, which creates and dissolves every thought and experience, and every world and universe, and everything in between.

To put it another way: because everything has the nature of all things, to attain sovereignty over one's world of experience, one does not have to learn the individual nature of each and every item in existence; one merely has to become intimate with one's own nature. To put it another way still, to experience unity with the whole of reality you do not have to individually learn the specific patterns of how clouds move, trees grow, birds migrate, ants build, etc. If you become fully one with your*self*, you become one with everything, because the pattern of the whole is contained within you. You instinctively and intuitively feel connected to and consonant with the rhythms of clouds, trees, birds, ants, and everything else, because you are connected to the underlying Pattern from which all those patterns—and the pattern of your life—arise. But what does it mean to become one with yourself? It means to be: (a) fully intimate with the whole of yourself and (b) internally undivided, that is, integrated as opposed to fragmented, and thus internally harmonious and at peace with yourself. A person who is truly and completely at peace with themselves automatically experiences that same harmony with the whole world. Such a person is also free of the curse of compulsive self-referencing (the nearly constant conscious or subconscious thoughts: "How does this relate to *me*?"—"What about *me*?"—or even just "*I* am the one who's experiencing this"). A person who is integrated (*samāhita*) has by definition digested their self-images, and without self-image, self-referencing cannot continue. Without the veils of self-image and self-referencing fogging up everything you see, you finally perceive with crystal clarity. You see that nothing happening *now* has any noteworthy connection to the you

you thought you were, and yet everything in the *now* is an expression of the One you actually are. With this clarity of view (which of course the last sentence almost completely failed to describe) comes a deep and wondrous willingness to be with things *as they are*, and to be with people as they are, instead of as they relate to the fictitious 'I' which has now ebbed away on the inexorable tide of realization. And here is a seeming paradox: every thing (and person) presents with a unique nature that cannot be named, defined, or described, and yet absolutely everything is nothing but a different form of what *you* are. Each thing being perfectly unique, it is different from everything else—and yet, inexplicably, it's exactly the same as everything else, because it is God, and so is everything else. And nothing is more God than anything else, nothing is more worthy of reverence, nothing shines with divine light more than anything else. And everything shines. Everything exquisitely whispers God's name just by being what it is. Everyone radiates God's light just by being what they are. (Yes, everyone. It's inexplicable, yet it's true, and you can directly see this truth for yourself if you wish.) So being with things and people *as they are* somehow means being with them in their uniqueness, in the particularity they express in any given moment, *and* in their oneness, in the way they are nothing but a mirror of you, of what you are, in every moment. And their Divinity is expressed in both their uniqueness *and* their universality, not just the latter.

As one of the greatest of American spiritual poets, Walt Whitman, wrote:

> What do you suppose Creation is? What do you suppose will satisfy the Soul, except to walk free, and own no superior? What do you suppose I would intimate to you in a hundred ways, but that there is no God any more divine than Yourself? And that that is what the oldest and newest myths finally mean?
>
> I am he who places over you no master, owner, better, God, beyond what waits intrinsically in yourself. There is no endowment in man or woman that is not tallied in you; there is no virtue, no beauty, in man or woman, but as good is in you; no pluck, no endurance in others, but as good is in you; no pleasure waiting for others, but an equal pleasure waits for you.

As for me, I give nothing to any one, except I give the like carefully to you; I sing the songs of the glory of none, not God, sooner than I sing the songs of the glory of you.

Whoever you are! claim your own at any hazard![158]

Kṣemarāja speaks of spiritual liberation as 'sovereignty' because it was the best metaphor he knew for the experience of the opposite of victimhood, where the word 'victimhood' stands not only for the sense that life's not fair, that one is at the mercy of forces and fates far beyond one's control, but also for the feeling that the universe is indifferent to your existence, that you are merely a bit of flotsam floating on the waves of a world you never made and that will wipe you away at some point without a second thought. The term sovereignty (*īśvaratā* or *sāmrājya*) refers to the opposite of this experience: that the world does not exist independently of you, but rather as an expression of your innate joy. From the clear seeing of the liberated perspective, it is *just as true* to say that the world exists because of you as to say that you exist because of the world. And everything is as it is because you—the real You—wants it that way. (Remember that 'what is' does not refer to how things are in a static snapshot or sliver of time, since change is the most salient and obvious feature of what is. Consciousness-as-world is constantly reinventing itself within a field of infinite possibility, and that's just how You want it.) The real You is already in perfect harmony with reality. The real You is the contented Lord of all s/he surveys, as it were. You know everything you need to know, and you have control over all that needs controlling (which isn't much, as it turns out). *This* is the sovereignty to which Kṣemarāja refers.

This sovereignty in relation to your world arises as a direct result of inner sovereignty, "sovereignty over the natural and innate circuit of the goddesses of your own awareness", as Kṣema eloquently puts it. Part of what you realize at this stage is that the inner world *is* the outer world. There isn't really the slightest difference. So let's look at the nature of this inner world. In Kṣema's metaphor, it consists of a 'circuit' (*cakra*; he could have said *maṇḍala* as well) of powers personified as goddesses. These goddesses constitute the various potencies and capacities of consciousness. Note that he clarifies his meaning by defining this circle of goddesses as "the mass of rays of inner and outer faculties in their unlimited (literally, non-māyic) aspect". So they are the powers that underlie the five faculties of action, the five faculties of perception, the five subtle elements in the energy-body,[159] the tripartite mind or psychic instrument, the five primary *śakti*s of awareness, and the overarching meta-power of Autonomy, giving us the image of a twenty-three-spoked wheel of energy (with Autonomy as the outer rim, connecting the various powers), at the hub of which is core Awareness, your essence-nature, the Lord of the unbroken Wheel of Consciousness.[160] For the circle is eternally unbroken (*akhaṇḍa-maṇḍala*), and it only seems otherwise when you are not aware of one or more of your innate powers. Thoughts and emotions vibrate along just three of these twenty-three spokes, and when we are overly caught up in them, we easily lose sight of our other powers, potencies, and capacities. In such a condition, we cannot experience ourselves as Lord of the Circle (*cakreśvara*). That Lordship—your real nature—can only be accessed at the hub of the Circle. Only from the perspective of the hub can all the powers be seen and accessed equally. If you are situated in your true home at the hub of the Circle, you realize that only a gentle effort is needed to keep the Wheel turning, to keep everything in beautiful flow. By contrast, if you are identified with the elements of your being that occupy the spokes, you feel as if you can't keep up with life and are at constant risk of being tangled in the spokes and crushed under the turning Wheel of what is, ironically, your very own being in its true form.

Readers of *Tantra Illuminated* may recall that the Wheel of Energies is an important image for Kṣema's teacher Abhinava Gupta as well; he gives us a specific meditation exercise utilizing a Fire-Wheel visualization, which I discussed in some detail on pages 385–387 of *Tantra Illuminated*.

There is another metaphor at play in Kṣema's paragraph: a feudal one. Since the temple worship rites for deities in India are modelled closely on how medieval Indian kings were treated, it is not surprising that in a spiritual system in which one attains identity with the Deity, the metaphor of kingship is sometimes used. I have already alluded to it above in discussing the word sovereignty, but to spell it out, *cakra* means 'territory' as well as 'circle' and *īśvara* means 'Lord' in both a spiritual and worldly sense. I need not dwell on this feudal metaphor, since its importance in Tantrik discourse has been documented in detail by scholar Ron Davidson in his book *Indian Esoteric Buddhism*.

So let us come to the last key point of Kṣema's paragraph. The innate Circle of Powers, he tells us, is "constantly bringing about the emissions and reabsorptions [of phenomena] in each and every experience". This is why, if you attain Lordship over the innate circle of the powers of awareness, you attain Lordship over your whole life. The Circle of Powers creates, sustains, and dissolves not only internal experience but all that you regard as external as well. This makes sense in light of the fact that in reality, there is no dividing line between internal and external except the line you draw in your imagination. Erase that line, and if you have successfully situated yourself at the 'hub' of the 'wheel' of Awareness, you see that your 'sovereignty' extends to the entire world of your experience. Kṣema says, "Experiencing such sovereignty, one becomes identical to the awe-inspiring supreme Divinity (*para-bhairava*)." Let us here remember the crucial fact that the concept of divinity in play here bears no resemblance to the god of the Old Testament, who blesses, curses, and wreaks terrible vengeance on wrongdoers. When Kṣemarāja says that the culmination of this process is becoming God, he is speaking of the result of *recognizing* your true nature and integrating that recognition, not of becoming some elevated kind of being who can control the fates of others. Indeed, in the Six Realms teaching of Tantrik psychology, there is a name for the delusion of believing that spiritual attainment sets you above others or in some way makes you special: it's called 'god delusion'. According to this view, you can become supreme Bhairava—nothing but God—without necessarily producing any change that others would notice.[161] As mentioned above, in this liberated state you are 'omniscient' only in the sense that you know whatever you need to know, you are 'omnipotent' only in the sense that you can do whatever needs to be done by you, and your 'sovereignty' extends only to having control over everything you actually need to control. In that sense, you are unlimited and you correctly feel that all your powers are unimpeded. You can't accomplish something that Life is not calling for from you, but in the liberated state it would never even *occur* to you to try to accomplish something Life isn't calling for. So your feeling of being everywhere unimpeded and free continues constantly. In the liberated state, you are the contented Lord of all you survey, if we understand the term Lord (*īśvara*) as 'steward' rather than 'dictator'. Even the feudal metaphor remains intact in this interpretation, because of course a good ruler is one who is a servant of all the people in his territory/circle (*cakra*).

Next Kṣema cites his main proof-text for this Topic, together with some brief explanatory comments of the verse he cites.

**It is taught** [in the final verse of the *Stanzas on Vibration*]:

> **But when he is firmly rooted in the One, then,** [being capable of] **bringing about** (*niyam*) **the arising and dissolving of his** [mind and sense faculties (*puryaṣṭaka*)], **he attains the state of the Experiencer, and as a result becomes Lord of the Circle.** || 3.19

**Here, "in the One" refers us back to** [a line in verse 3.12,] **"he should attribute everything to the One," which should be interpreted as referring to the level of the universal pulsation of Awareness** (*cit-sāmānya-spanda*)**,** [also known in the *Stanzas*] **as *unmeṣa*.**[162]

To clarify: "the One" in the verse refers to the *spanda* principle. Since *spanda* (literally, pulsation, oscillation) can refer to a range of phenomena, Kṣema here specifies that we are speaking of the "universal pulsation of Awareness" common to all sentient beings. This is the same as the fundamental 'I'-sense (*purṇāhaṃtā*) that we have already discussed. But Kṣema also adds—and we have not yet seen this equivalence—that another synonym for this universal pulsation is *unmeṣa*, a term we encountered back in practice seven of Chapter Eighteen. *Unmeṣa* (literally, opening, expanding, blossoming) is a technical term that refers to the initial upsurge of consciousness, the prediscursive burgeoning of awareness being *about to* present content. It is, in brief, the creative potential that inheres within the fundamental 'I'-sense, the universal pulsation of Awareness.

The line Kṣema cites from an earlier verse in the *Stanzas on Vibration* gives us a specific practice: we are to "attribute everything to the One." Kṣema explains this in his *nirṇaya* commentary as follows:

> One should realize that [whatever one experiences,] it is not other than the vibration of awareness (*spanda*), in either its contracted or expanded state. If one can firmly stabilize the realization that [the given cognition arises from Awareness and dissolves into the same Awareness

> through paying close attention to] the beginning and ending points [of each cognition or perception], then one can come to see that the fully concrete manifestation [of any given phenomenon] is nothing but the crystallization into form of the dynamic flowing essence of Awareness.[163]

This is very similar to practice seven of Chapter Eighteen, except that there we were invited to pay attention to the arising of each new cognition, and here we are invited to pay attention to the subsiding as well. Doing so will cause us to realize that everything we experience is nothing but one form or another of Awareness itself. This is the practice of correctly "attributing everything to the One". Repetition of the practice will lead us to attain the state of being "firmly rooted in the One" mentioned in the verse cited above.

Since Kṣema doesn't give us a commentary on that verse (*Stanzas on Vibration* 3.19), we must turn to another work of his, the *Spanda-nirṇaya*, in which he does. The information in the following paragraph comes from that source. I draw on it because the *Vibration* stanza he cites demands interpretation, and because it is the final substantive teaching of Chapter Twenty.

Being firmly rooted in the One (the fundamental pulsation of Awareness), one becomes capable of bringing about the dissolving and arising of the mind and sense faculties through the introversive and extroversive *samāveśa*s described in Chapter Nineteen. Achieving facility with this (Kṣema says in his *Spanda-nirṇaya* on this verse), makes one capable of bringing about the manifestation and dissolution of everything (which perhaps means the realization that one is already doing so), since the microcosm of the energy body is the portal to everything: what you can do with your energy-body (which consists primarily of the tripartite mind and fivefold sense-powers) you can do with the universe. The creation (or emission) and dissolution (or retraction) of the universe arises from the singular divine essence-nature that you are. Realization of this is here called 'attaining the state of the Experiencer' (where the word translated as Experiencer also means Enjoyer). Kṣema adds in his *nirṇaya* that one becomes the Experiencer by 'devouring' or assimilating to oneself all experiencable things (which we discussed in Chapter Fifteen). In other words, Kṣema tells us, "One attains (*avalam-*

*bate*) the state of the Supreme Perceiver—which in truth one already is—through the process of Recognizing [oneself in and as all things]. Then one becomes the great Lord of the *śakti-cakra*, i.e., of the mass of one's own powers, and attains divinity (*maheśvaratva*) in this very body." As you can see, his commentary on this verse closely parallels his language here in Chapter Twenty.

Let's sum up (which in this case necessitates oversimplifying). Through the practice of seeing everything as a form of the pulsation of Awareness, you become firmly rooted in the One (that same Awareness manifest in the Center as the perfect or non-egoic 'I'-sense), subsequent to which you can master the introversive and extroversive *samādhis* of Chapter Nineteen, as a result of which you see the truth that everything arises from and dissolves into what you are. As a result of that seeing, you 'devour' all things or recognize them as an expression of your true nature. This is the state of completion, in which you abide as Lord of Wheel of Powers, with not even a shred of apparent difference between you and the Divine.

Remember that feudal metaphor I mentioned a few pages back? It returns in a stronger form in Kṣema's final citation, this time from a hymn he himself wrote but that is now lost. His wordplay in this verse is evident.

**As I have hymned:**

> **The extraordinary Maheśvara, the autonomous emperor (*cakravartin*) of the territories (*cakra*) of Awareness, served and adored by the circle (*cakra*) of the goddesses of consciousness, is triumphant!**

The verse adds no new information, apart from the idea that the sense-faculties and other powers of consciousness "serve and adore" the fundamental awareness (*pūrṇāhaṃtā*) at the Center. This is perhaps a Śaiva version of the Sāṅkhya idea that the mind's job is to present the objects of consciousness to the inner witness, but here, of course, the image is more sensual and emotive: the word *juṣṭa* means 'embrace' as well as 'serve' and 'adore'.

Topic 6. Conclusion: the Nature of this Work.

**The word *iti*** [in the sūtra] **indicates** [we have arrived] **at the summation and conclusion** [of the entire text]**. The whole body of the treatise here taught is Śiva.** [How so?] **Because it is a means of obtaining Śiva, because it has flowed forth from Śiva, and because it is not different from Śiva's nature, it is an embodiment of Śiva.**

This final paragraph explains the last two words of Sūtra Twenty, *iti śivam*, a proverbial expression into which Kṣemarāja wants to read multiple meanings. He says that this whole work is an embodiment of Śiva (God) in three senses. First, through studying and practicing its techniques, we attain *śiva*, where that word has a double meaning: both 'God' and 'blessings' (note that Sanskrit has no capital letters). Second, the text we have read is faithfully based on the scriptures and treatises that Śiva has revealed and inspired, and in that sense the present work has flowed forth from Him. Third, like everything else it is one with the Divine. So for these three reasons, it is appropriate to call this *Pratyabhijñā-hṛdaya* an 'embodiment of Śiva'. And thus we can use the proverbial Sanskrit expression *iti śivam*, which usually just means 'may it be auspicious' or 'may it be a blessing', with a double meaning:

**All this is Śiva. / May it be a blessing.**

This concludes our study of Sūtra Twenty and its commentary.

देहप्राणसुखादिभिः प्रतिकलं संरुध्यमानो जनः
पूर्णानन्दघनामिमां न चिनुते माहेश्वरीं स्वां चितिम् ।
मध्येबोधसुधाब्धि विश्वमभितस्तत्फेनपिण्डोपमं
यः पश्येदुपदेशतस्तु कथितः साक्षात्स एकः शिवः ॥

समाप्तमिदं प्रत्यभिज्ञाहृदयम् ॥

कृतिस्तत्रभवन्महामाहेश्वराचार्यवर्यश्रीमदभिनवगुप्तपादपद्मोपजीविनः श्रीमतो राजानकक्षेमराजाचार्यस्य ॥

शुभमस्तु ॥

# EPILOGUE

*Kṣemarāja's original text*

*deha-prāṇa-sukhādibhiḥ pratikalaṃ saṃrudhyamāno janaḥ*
*pūrṇānanda-ghanām imāṃ na cinute māheśvarīṃ svāṃ citim* |

People who are constrained every moment by the bonds of identification with body, *prāṇa*, pleasure, pain, and so on, do not recognize what is right here—their own Divine Awareness, thick with the joy of perfect wholeness.

*madhye-bodha-sudhābdhi viśvam abhitas tat-phena-piṇḍopamaṃ*
*yaḥ paśyed upadeśatas tu kathitaḥ sākṣāt sa ekaḥ śivaḥ* ||

But one who, through this teaching, sees the universe all around him as nothing more than a mass of foam on the surface of the nectarean ocean of Awareness—he alone is said to be Śiva made fully manifest. ||

This 'Heart of the [Teachings on] Recognition' is concluded.

It was written by the Reverend Teacher Rājānaka Kṣemarāja in dependence on the lotus feet of His Honor the Reverend Abhinava Gupta, the best of Śaiva gurus.

May it be for a blessing.

# EPILOGUE

*with explanation*

Kṣemarāja's epilogue is a single, beautifully constructed, complex verse.

> **People who are constrained every moment by** [the bonds of identification with] **body, *prāṇa*, pleasure, pain, and so on, do not recognize what is right here—their own Divine Awareness, thick with the joy of perfect wholeness** (*pūrṇānanda*). |
>
> **But one who, through this teaching, sees the universe all around him as** [nothing more than] **a mass of foam on** [the surface of] **the nectarean ocean of Awareness—he alone is said to be Śiva made** [fully] **manifest.** ||

This is the perfect verse to end on, because it hints at a further spiritual attainment beyond that described in Chapter Twenty. I'll explain. In the *Mālinī-vijayottara-tantra*, the root text of the Trika lineage of which Kṣema was an initiate, we learn of three phases or stages in the awakening process: *āṇava-samāveśa* (literally, immersion into one's soul), *śākta-samāveśa* (literally, immersion into *śakti*, the total energy-field), and *śāmbhava-samāveśa* (literally, immersion into [Supreme] Śiva). I'll briefly summarize these as I understand them.[164] The first refers to the condition of being centered in your essence-nature; it is stabilized when abiding the Center is your default state. (This is the state of final liberation in some systems, such as that of Patañjali.) The second refers to the condition of unity-consciousness, in which reality is perceived as nothing but patterns of flowing energy from which the perceiver is never even slightly separate. We have discussed this attainment of unity-consciousness at some length in Chapter Fifteen, Chapter Sixteen, and elsewhere, since for Kṣema it is the primary goal of the practice of Tantrik Yoga (though, as he implies, it presupposes the attainment of *āṇava-samāveśa*, the ability to abide in one's Center). Chapter Twenty, it seems to be, describes the fullest expression of that same state. Kṣema has not alluded to the third phase of *śāmbhava-samāveśa* until now, probably because the *Mālinī-vijayottara-tantra* says that it is completely indescribable.

Though indescribable, we can point toward it simply in the following manner. If *śākta-samāveśa* constitutes unity with all that is, *śāmbhava-samāveśa* constitutes unity with all that is *and* all that isn't. That is to say, it constitutes unity with Śiva as the field of absolute potential. It is the state 'beyond existence and nonexistence'. A glimpse of this state before one is ready can be terrifying, but abiding in it is ultimate liberation. From the perspective of this state, the entire manifest universe is like a tiny ripple on the surface of an infinitely vast ocean of pure potentiality. That is to say, what exists, all the trillions of galaxies and everything they contain, expresses only the tiniest fraction of the field of potential energy. (This assertion agrees with modern physics as well.) Kṣemarāja poetically describes exactly this perspective in the verse above. I'll tease out some of the subtler elements in the verse.

Most importantly, the structure of the Sanskrit suggests that this attainment can only be considered real from within the midst (*madhye*) of the world. It's easy enough to dwell in a mental construct of this attainment while removed from society. Seated on a silent mountaintop, one can easily say to oneself, "Ah yes, this whole universe is like a tiny ripple or a bit of foam on the ocean of Consciousness"—but experiencing the truth of that in the midst of society is much more difficult. One who is stabilized in that experience exhibits what meditation master Ādyashānti calls 'divine indifference', which is the nonconceptual awareness that *everything is infinitely precious* and yet *nothing really matters*. Experiencing these modes of perception sequentially is not uncommon, but it is not divine indifference unless one experiences them simultaneously and in balance. If either has the upper hand, as it were, it is not yet divine indifference.

One who is united with the field of absolute potential has travelled the spiritual path as far as it goes. S/he is united with what Meister Eckhart called "the simple ground [of being], the desert of stillness, where distinction never gazed".[165] S/he alone is said to be Śiva made [fully] manifest, Kṣema tells us. That last phrase (*kathitaḥ sākṣāt sa ekaḥ śivaḥ*) could also be translated as 'he is said to be the One Śiva before your very eyes' or 'he alone can [rightly] be called Śiva in bodily form'.

Kṣemarāja's teacher, Abhinava Gupta, summarizes all three *samāveśas* as a single process in this exquisitely beautiful verse from his *Light on the Tantras*:

> The Truth, unfolding spontaneously without intellection, suddenly subordinates the 'subject', [the illusory self,] which is [merely] reflected in the mirror of the [real] Subject, and remains continuously revealing ever-greater degrees of its innate glory within the abundant purity of the Heart.[166]

May you, gentle reader, experience that for yourself in its fullness.

**This *Pratyabhijñā-hṛdaya*,**
**'The Heart of** [the Teachings on] **Recognition',**
**is concluded.**[167]

**It was written by the Reverend Teacher Rājānaka Kṣemarāja in dependence on the lotus feet of His Honor the Reverend Abhinava Gupta, the best of Śaiva gurus.**

**May it be for a blessing.**

Completed at Esalen Institute, Big Sur, CA, North America,
on the second night of Navarātra (Chandra Darshan),
Dvitīya-tithi of Śukla Pakṣa, month of Aśvin,
in the year 2073 (Vikram Saṃvat)
(October 2, 2016, of the Common Era)

# THE TWENTY SŪTRAS

*We present the sūtras here separately, because it's a powerful experience to read them and let them take you into a deep state of awareness and presence.*

चितिः स्वतन्त्रा विश्वसिद्धिहेतुः ॥१॥

**|| CITIḤ SVATANTRĀ VIŚVA-SIDDHI-HETUḤ || 1 ||**

Awareness, free and independent, is the cause
of the performance of everything.

स्वेच्छया स्वभित्तौ विश्वमुन्मीलयति ॥२॥

**|| SVECCHAYĀ SVABHITTAU VIŚVAM UNMĪLAYATI || 2 ||**

Through Her own Will, Awareness unfolds the
universe on the 'canvas' that is Herself.

तन्नानानुरूपग्राह्यग्राहकभेदात् ॥३॥

**|| TAN NĀNĀNURŪPA-GRĀHYA-GRĀHAKA-BHEDĀT || 3 ||**

It is diverse because it is divided into mutually adapted subjects and objects.

चितिसंकोचात्मा चेतनोऽपि संकुचितविश्वमयः ॥४॥

**|| CITI-SAṄKOCĀTMĀ CETANO 'PI SAṄKUCITA-VIŚVA-MAYAḤ || 4 ||**

The individual conscious being, as a contraction of universal
Awareness, consists of the entire universe in a microcosmic form.

चितिरेव चेतनपदादवरूढा चेत्यसंकोचिनी चित्तम् ॥५॥

**|| CITIR EVA CETANA-PADĀD AVARŪḌHĀ
CETYA-SAṄKOCINĪ CITTAM || 5 ||**

Awareness itself, descending from its state of pure consciousness,
becomes contracted by the object perceived: this is [called] the mind.

तन्मयो मायाप्रमाता ॥६॥

**|| TAN-MAYO MĀYĀ-PRAMĀTĀ || 6 ||**

One who consists of the mind perceives duality.

स चैको द्विरूपस्त्रिमयश्चतुरात्मा सप्तपञ्चकस्वभावः ॥७॥

**|| SA CAIKO DVI-RŪPAS TRI-MAYAŚ CATUR-ĀTMĀ SAPTA-PAÑCAKA-SVABHĀVAḤ || 7 ||**

It is one, and yet it is two; it consists of three, has a quadruple being, and is seven, five, and seven times five in its nature.

तद्भूमिकाः सर्वदर्शनस्थितयः ॥८॥

**|| TAD-BHŪMIKĀḤ SARVA-DARŚANA-STHITAYAḤ || 8 ||**

The positions held by all the philosophical Views are Its various roles, the levels of Its self-expression.

चिद्वत्तच्छक्तिसंकोचान्मलावृतः संसारी ॥९॥

**|| CIDVAT-TACCHAKTI-SAṄKOCĀN MALĀVṚTAḤ SAṂSĀRĪ || 9 ||**

Due to the contraction of those Powers belonging to Awareness, It becomes a *saṃsārin*, veiled by Impurity.

तथापि तद्वत्पञ्चकृत्यानि करोति ॥१०॥

**|| TATHĀPI TADVAT PAÑCA-KṚTYĀNI KAROTI || 10 ||**

Even then s/he performs the Five Acts in the same way.

आभासनरक्तिविमर्शनबीजावस्थापनविलापनतस्तानि ॥११॥

**|| ĀBHĀSANA-RAKTI-VIMARŚANA-BĪJĀVASTHĀPANA-VILĀPANATAS TĀNI || 11 ||**

S/he performs those Five Acts through manifestation, attachment, subjective awareness, laying down the 'seed', and dissolving it.

तदपरिज्ञाने स्वशक्तिव्यामोहितता संसारित्वम् ॥१२॥

**|| TAD-APARIJÑĀNE SVA-ŚAKTI-VYĀMOHITATĀ SAṂSĀRITVAM || 12 ||**

When one lacks realization of this, one exists in the state of a *saṃsārin*: that of being deluded by one's own powers.

तद्परिज्ञाने चित्तमेवान्तर्मुखीभावेन चेतनपदाध्यारोहाच्चितिः ॥१३॥

**|| TAD-PARIJÑĀNE CITTAM EVĀNTARMUKHĪBHĀVENA CETANA-PADĀDHYĀROHĀC CITIḤ || 13 ||**

When there is full realization of that, the mind, by turning within, ascends to its expanded state, and is revealed as nothing but Awareness.

चितिवह्निरवरोहपदे छन्नो ऽपि मात्रया मेयेन्धनं प्लुष्यति ॥१४॥

**|| CITI-VAHNIR AVAROHA-PADE CHANNO 'PI MĀTRAYĀ MEYENDHANAṂ PLUṢYATI || 14 ||**

The Fire of Awareness, though obscured in its descended state, still partially consumes the 'kindling' of knowable objects.

बललाभे विश्वमात्मसात्करोति ॥१५॥

**|| BALA-LĀBHE VIŚVAM ĀTMASĀTKAROTI || 15 ||**

Attaining one's innate power, one absorbs everything into oneself.

चिदानन्दलाभे देहादिषु चेत्यमानेष्वपि चिदैकात्म्यप्रतिपत्तिदार्ढ्यं जीवन्मुक्तिः ॥१६॥

**|| CID-ĀNANDA-LĀBHE DEHĀDIṢU CETYAMĀNEṢV API CID AIKĀTMYA-PRATIPATTI-DĀRḌHYAṂ JĪVAN-MUKTIḤ || 16 ||**

When one discovers this Joy of Awareness, and stabilizes the realization that Awareness is one with body, etc.—even while they are perceivable—that is called 'embodied liberation'.

मध्यविकासाच्चिदानन्दलाभः ॥१७॥

**|| MADHYA-VIKĀSĀC CID-ĀNANDA-LĀBHAḤ || 17 ||**

The Joy of Awareness is discovered through the expansion of the Center.

विकल्पक्षयशक्तिसंकोचविकासवाहच्छेदाद्यन्तकोटिनिभालनादय इहोपायाः ॥१८॥

**|| VIKALPA-KṢAYA-ŚAKTI-SAṄKOCA-VIKĀSA-VĀHA-CCHEDĀDYANTA-KOṬI-NIBHĀLANĀDAYA IHOPĀYĀḤ || 18 ||**

The skillful means here are: dissolving mental constructs, contraction and expansion of energy, pausing the flows, focusing on the beginning and ending point, and so on.

समाधिसंस्कारवति व्युत्थाने भूयो भूयश्चिदैक्यामर्शान्नित्योदितसमाधिलाभः ॥१९॥

**|| SAMĀDHI-SAṂSKĀRAVATI VYUTTHĀNE BHŪYO BHŪYAŚ CID-AIKYĀMARŚĀN NITYODITA-SAMĀDHI-LĀBHAḤ || 19 ||**

When emerging slowly from deep meditation, while still feeling its effect, contemplate the oneness with Awareness: practicing this again and again, one will attain a *samādhi* that continuously arises.

तदा प्रकाशानन्दसारमहामन्त्रवीर्यात्मकपूर्णाहंतावेशात्सदासर्वसर्गसंहारकारिनिजसंविद्देवताचक्रेश्वरताप्राप्तिर्भवतीति शिवम् ॥२०॥

**|| TADĀ PRAKĀŚĀNANDA-SĀRA-MAHĀ-MANTRA-VĪRYĀTMAKA-PŪRṆĀHAṂTĀVEŚĀT SADĀ-SARVA-SARGA-SAṂHĀRA-KĀRI-NIJA-SAṂVID-DEVATĀ-CAKREŚVARATĀ-PRĀPTIR BHAVATĪTI ŚIVAM || 20 ||**

Then, due to continuous Immersion into the fully expanded 'I'—which is in essence the fusion of Illumination and Joy, and is the great potency of all mantras—one attains the state of being the Lord of the innate circle of the goddesses of awareness, who are constantly engaged in the emanation and reabsorption of all things. All this is Śiva. May it be a blessing.

*"There are no subjects, it's only Consciousness. Consciousness arranges it like this, exactly as you experience it; with intersubjectivity, external reality—all that is presented by Consciousness to Consciousness, including the plurality of individual agents."*

*With eternal gratitude to the greatest Indologist of our time,*
Alexis Sanderson

## To You

by Walt Whitman

Whoever you are, I fear you are walking the walks of
dreams,
I fear these supposed realities are to melt from under your
feet and hands,
Even now your features, joys, speech, house, trade, manners,
troubles, follies, costume, crimes, dissipate away from you,
Your true soul and body appear before me,
They stand forth out of affairs, out of commerce, shops,
work, farms, clothes, the house, buying, selling, eating,
drinking, suffering, dying.

Whoever you are, now I place my hand upon you, that you
be my poem,
I whisper with my lips close to your ear,
I have loved many women and men, but I love none better
than you.

O I have been dilatory and dumb,
I should have made my way straight to you long ago,
I should have blabb'd nothing but you, I should have chanted
nothing but you.

I will leave all and come and make the hymns of you,
None has understood you, but I understand you,
None has done justice to you, you have not done justice to
yourself,
None but has found you imperfect, I only find no
imperfection in you,
None but would subordinate you, I only am he who will
never consent to subordinate you,
I only am he who places over you no master, owner, better,
God, beyond what waits intrinsically in yourself.

Painters have painted their swarming groups and the centre-figure of all,
From the head of the centre-figure spreading a nimbus of gold-color'd light,
But I paint myriads of heads, but paint no head without its nimbus of gold-color'd light,
From my hand from the brain of every man and woman it streams, effulgently flowing forever.

O I could sing such grandeurs and glories about you!
You have not known what you are, you have slumber'd upon yourself all your life,
Your eyelids have been the same as closed most of the time,
What you have done returns already in mockeries,
(Your thrift, knowledge, prayers, if they do not return in mockeries, what is their return?)

The mockeries are not you,
Underneath them and within them I see you lurk,
I pursue you where none else has pursued you,
Silence, the desk, the flippant expression, the night, the accustom'd routine, if these conceal you from others or from yourself, they do not conceal you from me,
The shaved face, the unsteady eye, the impure complexion, if these balk others they do not balk me,
The pert apparel, the deform'd attitude, drunkenness, greed, premature death, all these I part aside.

There is no endowment in man or woman that is not tallied in you,
There is no virtue, no beauty in man or woman, but as good is in you,
No pluck, no endurance in others, but as good is in you,

No pleasure waiting for others, but an equal pleasure waits
for you.

As for me, I give nothing to any one except I give the like
carefully to you,
I sing the songs of the glory of none, not God, sooner than
I sing the songs of the glory of you.

Whoever you are! claim your own at an hazard!
These shows of the East and West are tame compared to you,
These immense meadows, these interminable rivers, you are
immense and interminable as they,
These furies, elements, storms, motions of Nature, throes of
apparent dissolution, you are he or she who is master or
mistress over them,
Master or mistress in your own right over Nature, elements,
pain, passion, dissolution.

The hopples fall from your ankles, you find an unfailing
sufficiency,
Old or young, male or female, rude, low, rejected by the rest,
whatever you are promulges itself,
Through birth, life, death, burial, the means are provided,
nothing is scanted,
Through angers, losses, ambition, ignorance, ennui—what
you are picks its way.

## CRITICAL EDITION OF THE SANSKRIT TEXT

*Based on the unpublished edition of Jürgen Hanneder, with additional emendations by Alexis Sanderson. See the last page for conventions.*

oṃ namo maṅgala-mūrtaye |
atha
pratyabhijñā-hṛdayam ||
namaḥ śivāya satataṃ pañca-kṛtya-vidhāyine |
cid-ānanda-ghana-svātma-paramārthāvabhāsine ||
śāṅkaropaniṣat-sāra-pratyabhijñā-mahodadheḥ |
uddharāmi paraṃ sāraṃ saṃsāra-viṣa-śāntidam* ||
iha, ye sukumāra-matayo,
'kṛta-tīkṣṇa-tarka-śāstra-pariśramāḥ,
śaktipāta-vaśonmiṣat†-pārameśvara-samāveśābhilāṣāḥ,‡
katicid bhakti-bhājas teṣām īśvara-pratyabhijñopadeśa-tattvaṃ manāg unmīlyate |
tatra svātma-devatāyā eva sarvatra kāraṇatvaṃ, sukhopāya-
prāpyatvaṃ, mahā-phalatvaṃ, cābhivyaṅktum āha:
**citiḥ svatantrā viśva-siddhi-hetuḥ || 1 ||**
viśvasya → sadāśivāder bhūmyantasya, « siddhau [sṛṣṭau§] → niṣpattau,
prakāśane → sthityātmani, para-pramātṛ-viśrāntyātmani ca ← saṃhāre, »
parā-śakti-rūpā ← citir eva bhagavatī
svatantrā → anuttara-vimarśa-mayī śiva-bhaṭṭārakābhinnā
hetuḥ → kāraṇam |
asyāṃ hi prasarantyāṃ jagad unmiṣati vyavatiṣṭhate ca
nivṛtta-prasarāyāṃ ca nimiṣatīti svānubhavaivātra sākṣī |

---

* For this line, the KSTS Edition (hereafter Ed.) prints *kṣemeṇoddhriyate sāraḥ saṃsāra-viṣa-śāntaye*, though it is the inferior reading, and only one MS has it. This would translate: "Kṣema has extracted the essence ... in order to neutralize the poison of the cycle of suffering." Or (assuming *śleṣa*): "The essence ... is extracted by contentment (*kṣema*)."

† Reading *śaktipāta-vaśonmiṣat* with MS $K_4$ : *śaktipātonmiṣita* Ed.

‡ *-abhilāṣāḥ* MS $K_3$, $A_{1,2}$ : *abhilāṣiṇaḥ* Ed. This reading is to be construed as a *bahuvrīhi*. If we retained the KSTS reading here and in the previous instance, we would translate "[those devotees] who desire an immersion into the Highest Divinity, [of the sort] revealed through a Descent of Power." This would imply that they had not yet experienced a *śaktipāta*, which seems hardly likely for Kṣemarāja (hereafter K)'s intended audience.

§ It seems to me that the section from *siddhau* to *saṃhāre* is corrupt; the insertion of the needed word *sṛṣṭau* is a conjectural emendation that does not solve all the problems of the sentence.

anyasya tu māyā-prakṛtyādeś cit-prakāśa-bhinnasyāprakāśamānatvenāsattvān na
kvacid api hetutvaṃ prakāśamānatve tu,
prakāśaikātmyāt prakāśa-rūpā citir eva hetur, na tv asau kaścit |
ata eva deśa-kālākārā etat-sṛṣṭā etad-anuprāṇitāś ca naitat-svarūpaṃ bhettum alam
iti vyāpaka-nityodita-paripūrṇa-rūpeyam |
ity artha-labhyam evaitat |
nanu—jagad api cito bhinnaṃ naiva kiñcid, abhede ca, kathaṃ hetu-hetumad-bhāva?
ucyate—cid eva bhagavatī, svaccha-svatantra-rūpā,
tat-tad-ananta-jagad-ātmanā sphurati
ity etāvat paramārtho 'yaṃ kārya-kāraṇa-bhāvaḥ |
[2] yataś ceyam eva pramātṛ-pramāṇa-prameya-mayasya ← viśvasya
siddhau → prakāśane hetus,
tato 'syāḥ svatantrāparicchinna-svaprakāśa-rūpāyāḥ siddhāv abhinavārtha-
prakāśana-rūpaṃ na pramāṇa-varākam upayuktam upapannaṃ vā |
tad uktam *Trika-sāre*:
svapadā svaśiraś chāyāṃ yadval laṅghitum īhate |
pādoddeśe śiro na syāt tatheyaṃ baindavī kalā || iti |
[3] yataś ceyaṃ viśvasya siddhau parādvaya-sāmarasyāpādanātmani
ca saṃhāre hetus tata eva svatantrā |
[4] pratyabhijñāta-svātantryā satī* bhoga-mokṣa-svarūpāṇāṃ ←
viśva-siddhīnāṃ hetuḥ | ity āvṛttyā vyākhyeyam |
[5] api ca viśvaṃ → nīla-sukha-deha-prāṇādi,
tasya yā siddhiḥ → pramānopāroha†-krameṇa vimarśamaya-pramātrāveśaḥ
saiva hetuḥ → parijñāne upāyo yasyāḥ |
anena ca sukhopāyatvam uktam |
yad uktaṃ Śrī-*Vijñāna*-bhaṭṭārake:
grāhya-grāhaka-saṃvittiḥ sāmānyā sarva-dehinām |
yogināṃ tu viśeṣo 'yaṃ saṃbandhe sāvadhānatā || iti [v. 106] |
citir ity eka-vacanaṃ deśa-kālādyanavacchinnatām abhidadhat
samasta-bheda-vādānām avāstavatāṃ vyanakti |
svatantra-śabdo brahma-vāda-vailakṣaṇyam ācakṣāṇaś
cito māheśvarya-sāratāṃ brūte |

---

* I retain *satī* from the Ed., supported by five MSS, though Hanneder drops it.
† Some MSS read 'offering' (*upahāra*), e.g. $K_1$, $K_3$, IOL San Ms 2528, BORI No. 467.

viśvetyādi-padam
aśeṣa-śaktitvaṃ, sarva-kāraṇatvaṃ, sukhopāyatvaṃ, mahā-phalatvaṃ*
cāha || 1 ||
nanu—viśvasya yadi citir hetus tad asyā upādānādyapekṣāyāṃ,
bheda-vādā-parityāgaḥ syāt
ity āśaṅkyāha:

**svecchayā sva-bhittau viśvam unmīlayati || 2 ||**

svecchayā → na tu brahmādivad anyecchayā,
tayaiva ca na tūpādānādyapekṣayā,
evaṃ hi prāg-ukta-svātantrya-hānyā cittvam eva na ghaṭeta |
svabhittau na tu anyatra kvāpi, prāk nirṇītaṃ viśvaṃ darpaṇe nagaravad abhinnam
api bhinnam iva unmīlayati |
unmīlanaṃ ca avasthitasyaiva prakaṭīkaraṇaṃ |
ity anena jagataḥ prakaśaikātmyenāvasthānam uktam || 2 ||
atha viśvasya svarūpaṃ vibhāgena pratipādayitum, āha:

**tan nānānurūpa-grāhya-grāhaka-bhedāt || 3 ||**

tad → viśvaṃ nānā → aneka-prakāram |
katham? anurūpāṇāṃ → parasparaucityāvasthīnāṃ grāhyāṇāṃ grāhakāṇāṃ ca
bhedād → vaicitryāt |
tathā ca sadāśiva-tattve 'hantācchāditā-sphuṭedantā-mayaṃ yādṛśaṃ parāpara-
rūpaṃ viśvaṃ grāhyaṃ tādṛg eva śrī-sadāśiva-bhaṭṭārakādhiṣṭhito mantra-
maheśvarākhyaḥ pramātṛ-vargaḥ
parameśvarecchāvakalpita-tathāvasthānaḥ |
īśvara-tattve sphuṭedantāhantā-sāmānādhikaraṇyātma yādṛg viśvaṃ grāhyaṃ
tathā-vidha eva īśvara-bhaṭṭārakādhiṣṭhito mantreśvara-vargaḥ |
vidyā-pade śrīmad-ananta-bhaṭṭārakādhiṣṭhitā bahu-śākhāvāntara-
bheda-bhinnā yathā-bhūtā mantrāḥ pramātāraḥ
tathā-bhūtam eva bhedaika-sāraṃ viśvam api prameyam |
māyordhve yādṛśā vijñānākalāḥ kartṛtā-śūnya-śuddha-bodhātmānaḥ
tādṛg eva tad-abheda-sāraṃ sakala-pralayākalātmaka-
pūrvāvasthā-paricitam eṣāṃ prameyam |
māyāyāṃ śūnya-pramātṝṇāṃ pralaya-kevalināṃ svocitaṃ pralīna-kalpaṃ prameyam
|
kṣiti-paryantāvasthitānāṃ tu sakalānāṃ sarvato bhinnānāṃ parimitānāṃ
tathā-bhūtam eva prameyam |
tad-uttīrṇa-śiva-bhaṭṭārakasya prakāśaika-vapuṣaḥ prakāśaika-rūpā eva bhāvāḥ |
śrīmat-paramaśivasya punar viśvottīrṇa-viśvātmaka-paramānanda-maya-prakāśaika-

* *-phalatvam* conj. em. : *-phalam* Ed. ~ Note: K must intend the *svātma-devatāyāḥ* in his introduction to Sūtra One to construe with the abstract nouns here as well.

ghanasya, evaṃ-vidham eva śivādi-dharaṇyantam akhilaṃ abhedenaiva sphurati |
na tu vastutaḥ anyat kiṃcid grāhyaṃ grāhakaṃ vā,
api tu śrī-paramaśiva-bhaṭṭāraka evetthaṃ nānā-vaicitrya-sahasraiḥ sphurati
ity abhihita-prāyam || 3 ||
yathā ca bhagavān viśva-śarīras tathā
**citi-saṃkocātmā cetano 'pi saṃkucita-viśva-mayaḥ || 4 ||**
śrī-paramaśivaḥ svātmaikyena sthitaṃ viśvaṃ sadāśivādyucitena rūpena
avabibhāsayiṣuḥ pūrvaṃ cid-aikyākhyāti-mayānāśrita-śiva-paryāya-
śūnyātiśūnyātmatayā prakāśābhedena prakāśamānatayā sphurati |
tataś cid-rasāśyānatā-rūpāśeṣa-tattva-bhuvana-bhāva-tat-tat-pramātrādyātmatayāpi
prathate |
yathā caivaṃ bhagavān viśva-śarīras
tathā citi-saṃkocātmā saṃkucita-cid-rūpaḥ cetano grāhako 'pi vaṭa-dhānikāvat
saṃkucitāśeṣa-viśva-rūpaḥ |
tathā ca siddhānta-vacanam
vigraho vigrahī caiva sarva-vigraha-vigrahī | iti |
*Triśiro-mate* 'pi
sarva-deva-mayaḥ kāyas taṃ cedānīṃ śṛṇu priye |
pṛthivī kaṭhinatvena dravatve 'mbhaḥ prakīrtitam ||
ity upakramya
triśiro-bhairavaḥ sākṣād vyāpya viśvaṃ vyavasthitaḥ |
ity antena granthena grāhakasya saṃkucita-viśvamayatvam eva vyāharati |
ayaṃ cātrāśayo—grāhako 'pi ayaṃ prakāśaikātmyena uktāgama-yuktyā ca
viśva-śarīra-śivaika-rūpa eva kevalaṃ tan-māyā-śaktyā
anabhivyakta-svarūpatvāt saṃkucita ivābhāti,
saṃkoco 'pi vicāryamāṇaś cid-aikātmyena prathamānatvāt cinmaya eva,
anyathā tu na kiṃcit
iti sarvo grāhako viśva-śarīraḥ śiva-bhaṭṭāraka eva |
tad uktaṃ mayaiva
akhyātir yadi na khyāti khyātir evāvaśiṣyate |
khyāti cet khyāti-rūpatvāt khyātir evāvaśiṣyate || iti |
anenaivāśayena śrī-*Spanda*-śāstreṣu
yasmāt sarva-mayo jīvaḥ .......................... |
ity upakramya
tena śabdārtha-cintāsu na sāvasthā na yaḥ śivaḥ |
ityādinā śiva-jīvayor abheda evoktaḥ |
etat-tattvaparijñānam eva muktiḥ,
etat-tattvāparijñānam eva ca bandha iti bhaviṣyati eva etat || 4 ||
nanu grāhako 'yaṃ vikalpa-mayo vikalpanaṃ ca citta-hetukaṃ sati ca citte
katham asya śivātmakatvaṃ iti śaṅktvā cittam eva nirṇetum āha:

**citir eva cetana-padād avarūḍhā cetya-saṃkocinī cittam || 5 ||**

na cittaṃ nāma anyat kiṃcid api tu saiva bhagavatī tat |
tathā hi sā svaṃ svarūpaṃ gopayitvā yadā saṃkocaṃ gṛhṇāti tadā dvayī gatiḥ |
kadācid ullasitam api saṃkocaṃ guṇīkṛtya cit-prādhānyena sphurati |
kadācit saṃkoca-pradhānatayā |
cit-prādhānya-pakṣe sahaje prakāśa-mātra-pradhānatve vijñānākalatā |
prakāśa-parāmarśa-pradhānatve tu vidyā-pramātṛtā |
tatrāpi krameṇa saṃkocasya tanutāyāṃ īśa-sadāśivānāśrita-rūpatā |
samādhi-prayatnopārjite tu cit-pradhānatve śuddhādhva-pramātṛtā kramāt-kramaṃ prakarṣavatī |
saṃkoca-prādhānye tu śūnyādi-pramātṛtā |
evam avasthite sati citir eva saṃkucita-grāhaka-rūpā cetana-padād avarūḍhā artha-grahaṇonmukhī satī cetyena nīla-sukhādinā saṃkocinī ubhaya-saṃkoca-saṃkucitaiva cittam |
tathā ca
svāṅga-rūpeṣu bhāveṣu patyur jñānaṃ kriyā ca yā |
māyā-tṛtīye te eva paśoḥ sattvaṃ rajas tamaḥ ||
ityādinā svātantryātmā citi-śaktir eva jñāna-kriyā-māyā-śakti-rūpā paśu-daśāyāṃ saṃkoca-prakarṣāt sattva-rajas-tamaḥ-svabhāva-cittātmatayā sphurati iti śrī-*Pratyabhijñā*yām uktam |
ata eva śrī-*Tattva-garbha-stotre* vikalpa-daśāyām api tāttvika-svarūpa-sadbhāvāt tad-anusaraṇābhiprāyeṇoktam
ata eva tu ye kecit paramārthānusāriṇaḥ |
teṣāṃ tatra svarūpasya svajyotiṣṭvaṃ na lupyate || iti
|| 5 ||
cittam eva tu māyā-pramātuḥ svarūpam ity āha:

**tan-mayo māyā-pramātā || 6 ||**

deha-prāṇa-padaṃ tāvat citta-pradhānam eva |
śūnya-bhūmir api citta-saṃskāravaty eva |
anyathā tato vyutthitasya svakartavyānudhāvanābhāvaḥ syād iti citta-maya eva māyīyaḥ pramātā |
amunaivāśayena *Śiva*-sūtreṣu vastu-vṛttānusāreṇa 'caitanyam ātmā' ity abhidhāya māyā-pramātṛ-lakṣaṇāvasare punaḥ 'cittam ātmā' ity uktam || 6 ||
asyaiva samyak svarūpa-jñānād yato muktiḥ asamyak tu saṃsāras tataḥ tilaśa etat-svarūpaṃ nirbhaṅktum āha:

**sa caiko dvi-rūpas tri-mayaś catur-ātmā sapta-pañcaka-svabhāvaḥ || 7 ||**

nirṇīta-dṛśā cid-ātmā śiva-bhaṭṭāraka eva ekātmā na tv anyaḥ kaścit prakāśasya deśa-kālādibhir bhedāyogāt,
jaḍasya tu grāhakatvānupapatteḥ |
prakāśa eva yataḥ svātantryād gṛhīta-prāṇādi-saṃkocaḥ

saṃkucitārtha-grāhakatām aśnute tato 'sau
prakāśarūpatva-saṃkocāvabhāsavattvābhyāṃ dvi-rūpaḥ |
āṇava-māyīya-kārma-malāvṛtatvāt tri-mayaḥ |
śūnya-prāṇa-puryaṣṭaka-śarīra-svabhāvatvāt catur-ātmā |
sapta-pañcakāni śivādi-pṛthivyantāni pañca-triṃśat-tattvāni tat-svabhāvaḥ |
tathā śivādi-sakalānta-pramātṛ-saptaka-svarūpaḥ |
cid-ānandecchā-jñāna-kriyā-śakti-rūpatve 'pi akhyāti-vaśāt
kalā-vidyā-rāga-kāla-niyati-kañcuka-valitatvāt pañcaka-svarūpaḥ |
evaṃ ca śivaikatvena pañca-triṃśat-tattva-mayatvena pramātṛ-saptaka-
svabhāvatvena cid-ādi-śakti-pañcakātmakatvena ca
ayaṃ pratyabhijñāyamāno mukti-daḥ |
anyathā tu saṃsāra-hetuḥ ||
evaṃ ca

**tad-bhūmikāḥ sarva-darśana-sthitayaḥ || 8 ||**

sarveṣāṃ Cārvākādi-darśanānāṃ sthitayaḥ → siddhāntāḥ, tasya → etasya ātmano
naṭasyeva svecchāvagṛhītāḥ kṛtrimā bhūmikāḥ |
tathā ca 'caitanya-viśiṣṭaṃ śarīram ātmā' iti Cārvākāḥ |
Naiyāyikādayo jñānādi-guṇa-gaṇāśrayaṃ buddhi-tattva-prāyam eva ātmānaṃ
saṃsṛtau manyante, apavarge tu tad ucchede śūnya-prāyam |
ahaṃ-pratīti-pratyeyaḥ sukha-duḥkhādyupādhibhis tiraskṛtātmā iti manvānā
Mīmāṃsakā 'pi buddhāv eva niviṣṭāḥ |
jñāna-santāna eva tattvaṃ iti Saugatā buddhi-vṛttiṣv eva paryavasitāḥ |
prāṇa evātmeti kecit Śrutyanta-vidaḥ |
asad eva idam āsīd ity abhāva-brahma-vādinaḥ śūnya-bhuvam avagāhya sthitāḥ |
mādhyamikā apy evam eva |
parā prakṛtir bhagavān vāsudevas tad-visphuliṅga-prāyā eva jīvā iti
Pāñcarātrāḥ parasyāḥ prakṛteḥ pariṇāmābhyupagamād avyakta evābhiniviṣṭāḥ |
Sāṃkhyādayas tu vijñānakala-prāyāṃ bhūmiṃ avalambante |
sad eva idam agra āsīd iti īśvara-tattva-padam āśritā apare Śrutyanta-vidaḥ |
śabda-brahma-mayaṃ paśyantī-rūpaṃ ātma-tattvam
iti vaiyākaraṇāḥ śrī-sadāśiva-padam adhyāsitāḥ |
evam anyad api anumantavyam* |
etac ca āgameṣu
buddhi-tattve sthitā Bauddhā guṇeṣv evĀrhatāḥ sthitāḥ |
sthitā Veda-vidaḥ puṃsi avyakte Pāñcarātrikāḥ ||
ity ādinā nirūpitam |
viśvottīrṇam ātma-tattvam iti tāntrikāḥ |
viśva-mayam iti kulādyāmnāya-niviṣṭāḥ |
viśvottīrṇaṃ viśva-mayaṃ ca iti trikādi-darśana-vidaḥ |

* MSS A1,2 read *anusartavyam.*

evaṃ ekasyaiva cid-ātmano bhagavataḥ svātantryāvabhāsitāḥ sarvā imā bhūmikāḥ svātantrya-pracchādanonmīlana-tāratamya-bheditāḥ |
ata ekaiva etāvad-vyāptikātmā |
mita-dṛṣṭayas tv aṃśāṃśikāsu tad-icchayaivābhimānaṃ grāhitāḥ yena dehādiṣu bhūmiṣu pūrva-pūrva-pramātṛ-vyāpti-sāratā-prathāyām apy ukta-rūpāṃ mahā-vyaptiṃ para-śaktipātaṃ vinā na labhante |
yathoktaṃ
Vaiṣṇavādyās tu ye kecit vidyā-rāgeṇa rañjitāḥ |
na vidanti paraṃ devaṃ sarvajñaṃ jñāna-śālinam || iti |
tathā
bhramayaty eva tān māyā hy amokṣe mokṣa-lipsavaḥ* | iti |
ta ātmopāsakāḥ śaivaṃ na gacchanti paraṃ padam | iti ca |
[2] api ca sarveṣāṃ darśanānāṃ samastānāṃ nīla-sukhādi-jñānānāṃ yāḥ sthitayo 'ntar-mukha-rūpā viśrāntayas tās tad-bhūmikāḥ cid-ānanda-ghana-svātma-svarūpābhivyakty-upāyāḥ |
tathā hi yadā yadā bahir-mukhaṃ rūpaṃ svarūpe viśrāmyati tadā tadā bāhya-vastūpasaṃhāro 'ntaḥ-praśānta-padāvasthitiḥ tat-tad-udeṣyat-saṃvit-santaty-āsūtraṇaṃ iti sṛṣṭi-sthiti-saṃhāra-melana-rūpā iyaṃ turīyā saṃvid-bhaṭṭārikā tat-tat-sṛṣṭyādi-bhedān udvamantī saṃharantī ca sadā pūrṇā ca kṛśā ca ubhaya-rūpā ca anubhayātmā ca akramam eva sphurantī sthitā |
uktaṃ ca śrī-*Pratyabhijñā-ṭīkā*yāṃ
tāvad arthāvalehena uttiṣṭhati pūrṇā ca bhavati | iti |
eṣā ca bhaṭṭārikā kramāt-kramaṃ adhikam anuśīlyamānā svātmasātkaroty eva bhakta-janam || 8 ||
yadi evaṃbhūtāsyātmano† vibhūtis tat kathaṃ ayaṃ malāvṛto 'ṇuḥ kalādi-valitaḥ saṃsārī abhidhīyate? ity āha:

**cidvat-tac-chakti-saṃkocāt malāvṛtaḥ saṃsārī || 9 ||**

yadā cid-ātmā parameśvaraḥ sva-svātantryād abheda-vyāptiṃ nimajjya bheda-vyāptim avalambate
tadā tadīyā icchādi-śaktayaḥ asaṃkucitā api saṃkocavatyo bhānti |
tadānīm eva ayaṃ malāvṛtaḥ saṃsārī bhavati |
tathā ca apratihata-svātantrya-rūpā icchā-śaktiḥ saṃkucitā satī apūrṇaṃ-manyatā-rūpam āṇavaṃ malam |
jñāna-śaktiḥ krameṇa saṃkocād bhede sarvajñatvasya kiṃcijjñatvāpteḥ

* *mokṣa-lipsavaḥ* em. Sanderson (following the Nepalese MSS) : *mokṣa-lipsayā* Ed. The translation takes the liberty of using both readings.

† *evaṃbhūtāsyātmano* em. Sanderson : *evaṃbhūtasyātmano* Ed.

antaḥkaraṇa-buddhīndriyatāpatti-pūrvaṃ atyanta*-saṃkoca-grahaṇena
bhinna-vedya-prathā-rūpaṃ māyīyaṃ malam |
kriyā-śaktiḥ krameṇa bhede sarva-kartṛtvasya kiṃcit-kartṛtvāpteḥ
karmendriya-rūpa-saṃkoca-grahaṇa-pūrvaṃ atyanta-parimitatāṃ prāptā
śubhāśubhānuṣṭhāna-mayaṃ kārmaṃ malam |
tathā sarvakartṛtva-sarvajñatva-pūrṇatva-nityatva-vyāpakatva-śaktayaḥ
saṃkocaṃ gṛhṇānā yathā-kramaṃ kalā-vidyā-rāga-kāla-niyati-rūpatayā bhānti |
tathā-vidhaś cāyaṃ śakti-daridraḥ saṃsārī ucyate |
sva-śakti-vikāse tu śiva eva || 9 ||
nanu: saṃsāryavasthāyām asya kiṃcit śivatocitaṃ abhijñānam asti yena
śiva eva tathāvasthita ity udghoṣyate? asti. ity āha:

**tathāpi tadvat pañcakṛtyāni karoti || 10 ||**

iha īśvarādvaya-darśanasya brahma-vādibhyo 'yam eva viśeṣaḥ, yat
sṛṣṭi-saṃhāra-kartāraṃ vilaya-sthiti-kārakam |
anugraha-kāraṃ devaṃ praṇatārti-vināśanam || iti
śrimat-*Svacchand*ādi-śāsanokta-nītyā sadā pañca-vidha-kṛtya-kāritvaṃ
cid-ātmano bhagavataḥ |
yathā ca bhagavān śuddhetarādhva-sphāraṇa-krameṇa
svarūpa-vikāsa-rūpāṇi sṛṣṭy-ādīni karoti
tathā saṃkucita-cic-chaktitayā saṃsāra-bhūmikāyām api pañca-kṛtyāni vidhatte |
tathā hi
tad evaṃ vyavahāre 'pi prabhur dehādim āviśan |
bhāntam evāntararthaugham icchayā bhāsayed bahiḥ ||
iti *Pratyabhijñā-kārik*oktārtha-dṛṣṭyā, deha-prāṇādi-padam āviśan cid-rūpo
maheśvaro bahir-mukhī-bhāvāvasare nīlādikam arthaṃ niyata-deśa-kālāditayā
yadā ābhāsayati tadā niyata-deśakālādyābhāsāṃśe 'sya sraṣṭṛtā,
anya-deśa-kālādyābhāsāṃśe 'sya saṃhartṛtā,
nīlādyābhāsāṃśe sthāpakatā,
bhedena ābhāsāṃśe vilaya-kāritā,
prakāśaikyena prakāśane 'nugrahītṛtā |
yathā ca sadā pañca-vidha-kṛtya-kāritvaṃ bhagavataḥ
tathā mayā vitatya *Spanda-sandohe* nirnītam |
evam idaṃ pañca-kṛtya-kāritvaṃ ātmīyaṃ sadā dṛḍha-pratipattyā pariśīlyamānaṃ
māheśvaryaṃ unmīlayaty eva bhakti-bhājām |
ata eva ye sadā etat pariśīlayanti te svarūpa-vikāsa-mayaṃ
viśvaṃ jānānā jīvanmuktā ity āmnātāḥ |
ye tu na tathā te sarvato vibhinnaṃ meya-jātaṃ paśyanto baddhātmanaḥ ||

---

* The edition has *atyantaṃ saṃkoca-grahaṇena*, which I now think is a better reading, but I translated the reading printed here.

na cāyam eva prakāraḥ pañca-vidha-kṛtya-kāritve
yāvad anyo 'pi kaścid rahasya-rūpo 'sti, ity āha:

**ābhāsana-rakti-vimarśana-bījāvasthāpana-vilāpanatas tāni || 11 ||**

pañca-kṛtyāni karotīti pūrvataḥ saṃbadhyate |
śrīman-mahārtha-dṛṣṭyā dṛg-ādi-devī-prasaraṇa-krameṇa
yad yad ābhāti tat tat sṛjyate |
tathā sṛṣṭi-pade* tatra yadā praśānta-nimeṣaṃ kaṃcit kālaṃ rajyati
tadā « sthiti-devyā » tat sthapyate |
camatkārāpara-paryāya-vimarśana-samaye tu saṃhriyate |
yathoktaṃ śrī-rāmena
samādhi-vajreṇāpy anyair abhedyo bheda-bhūdharaḥ |
parāmṛṣṭaś ca naṣṭaś ca tvad-bhakti-bala-śālibhiḥ || iti |
yadā tu saṃhriyamāṇam api etad antar vicitrāśaṅkādi-saṃskāraṃ ādhatte
tadā tat punar-udbhaviṣyat-saṃsāra-bīja-bhāvam āpannaṃ vilaya-padam adhyāropitam |
yadā punas tat tathāntaḥ sthāpitaṃ anyad vānubhūyamānam eva haṭha-pāka-krameṇālaṃgrāsa-yuktyā cid-agni-sādbhāvam āpadyate
tadā pūrṇatāpādanena anugṛhyata eva |
īdṛśaṃ ca pañca-vidha-kṛtya-kāritvaṃ sarvasya sadā
saṃnihitam api sadgurūpadeśaṃ vinā na prakāśata iti sadguru-saparyaiva etat-prathārtham anusartavyā || 11 ||
yasya punaḥ sadgurūpadeśaṃ vinā etat-parijñānaṃ nāsti
tasyāvacchādita-sva-svarūpābhir nijābhiḥ śaktibhir vyāmohitatvaṃ bhavati, ity āha:

**tad-aparijñāne sva-śaktibhir vyāmohitatā saṃsāritvam || 12 ||**

tasya → etasya sadā saṃbhavataḥ pañca-vidha-kṛtya-kāritvasya
aparijñāne śaktipāta-hetuka-sva-balonmīlanābhāvāt aprakāśane svabhiḥ śaktibhir
vyāmohitatvaṃ vividha-laukika-śāstrīya-śaṅkā-śaṅku-kīlitatvaṃ
yat idam eva saṃsāritvam |
tad uktaṃ śrī-*Sarva-vīra*-bhaṭṭārake
ajñānāc chaṅkate lokas tataḥ sṛṣṭiś ca saṃhṛtiḥ | iti |
mantrā varṇātmakāḥ sarve sarve varṇāḥ śivātmakāḥ | iti ca |
[1] tathā hi cit-prakāśād avyatiriktā nityodita-mahā-mantra-rūpā
pūrṇāhaṃ-vimarśa-mayī yā iyaṃ parā-vāk-śaktiḥ
ādikṣānta-rūpāśeṣa-śakti-cakra-garbhiṇī
sā tāvat paśyantī-madhyamādi-krameṇa grāhaka-bhūmikāṃ bhāsayati |
tatra ca parā-rūpatvena svarūpam aprathayantī māyā-pramātuḥ

* *sṛṣti-pade* conj. em. Sanderson : *sṛṣṭe pade* Ed. See *Spanda-nirṇaya* KSTS p. 12.

asphuṭāsādhāraṇārthāvabhāsa-rūpāṃ pratikṣaṇaṃ nava-navāṃ vikalpa-kriyāṃ ullāsayati
śuddhām api ca avikalpa-bhūmiṃ tad-ācchāditām eva darśayati |
tatra ca brāhmy-ādi-devatādhiṣṭhita-kakārādi-vicitra-śaktibhir vyāmohito
deha-prāṇādim eva parimitam avaśyam* ātmānaṃ manyate mūḍha-janaḥ |
brāhmy-ādi-devyaḥ paśu-daśāyāṃ bheda-viṣaye sṛṣṭi-sthity abheda-viṣaye ca
saṃhāraṃ prathayantyaḥ parimita-vikalpa-pātratām eva saṃpādayanti |
pati-daśāyāṃ tu bhede saṃhāraṃ abhede ca sarga-sthitī prakaṭayantyaḥ
kramāt-kramaṃ vikalpa-nirhrāsanena śrīmad-bhairava-mudrānupraveśa-mayīṃ
mahatīm avikalpa-bhūmim eva unmīlayanti |
sarvo mamāyaṃ vibhava ity evaṃ parijānataḥ |
viśvātmano vikalpānāṃ prasare 'pi maheśatā ||
ity ādi-rūpāṃ cid-ānandāveśa-magnāṃ śuddha-vikalpa-śaktim ullāsayanti |
tataḥ ukta-nītyā sva-śakti-vyāmohitataiva saṃsāritvam |
[2] kiṃca citi-śaktir eva bhagavatī viśva-vamanāt saṃsāra-vāmācāratvāc ca
Vāmeśvary-ākhyā sati Khecarī-Gocarī-Dikcarī-Bhūcarī-rūpaiḥ aśeṣaiḥ
pramātṛ-antaḥkaraṇa-bahiṣkaraṇa-bhāva-svabhāvaiḥ parisphurantī |
paśu-bhūmikāyāṃ śūnya-pada-viśrāntā
kiṃcit-kartṛtvādy-ātmaka-kalādi-śakty-ātmanā Khecarī-cakreṇa
gopita-pāramārthika-cid-gagana-carītva-svarūpeṇa cakāsti |
bheda-niścayābhimāna-kalpana†-pradhānāntaḥkaraṇa-devī-rūpeṇa Gocarī-cakrena
gopitābheda-niścayādy-ātmaka-pāramārthika-svarūpeṇa prakāśate |
bhedālocanādi-pradhāna-bahiṣkaraṇa-devatātmanā ca Dikcarī-cakreṇa
gopitābheda-prathātmaka-pāramārthika-svarūpeṇa sphurati |
sarvato-vyavacchinnābhāsa-svabhāva-prameyātmanā ca Bhūcarī-cakreṇa
gopita-sārvātmya-svarūpeṇa paśu-hṛdaya-vyāmohinā bhāti |
pati-bhūmikāyāṃ tu
sarva-kartṛtvādi-śakty-ātmaka-cid-gagana-carītvena
abheda-niścayādy-ātmanā Gocarītvena abhedālocanādy-ātmanā Dikcarītvena
svāṅga-kalpādvaya-prathā-sāra-prameyātmanā ca Bhūcarītvena
pati-hṛdaya-vikāsinā sphurati |
tathā coktaṃ sahaja-camatkāra-parijanitākṛtakādareṇa
bhaṭṭa-Dāmodareṇa vimuktakeṣu
pūrṇāvacchinna-mātrāntar-bahiṣ-karaṇa-bhāva-gāḥ |
Vāmeśyādyāḥ parijñānājñānāt syur mukti-bandha-dāḥ || iti |
evaṃ ca nija-śakti-vyāmohitataiva saṃsaritvam |
[3] api ca cidātmanaḥ parameśvarasya svānapāyinī ekaiva
sphurattā-sāra-kartṛtātmā aiśvarya-śaktiḥ |

---

* *avaśyam* em. Sanderson : *avaśam* Ed.

† *(saṃ)kalpana* conj. Sanderson : *vikalpana* Ed.

sā yadā svarūpaṃ gopayitvā pāśave pade
prāṇāpāna-samāna-śakti-daśābhiḥ jāgrat-svapna-suṣupta-bhūmibhir deha-prāṇa-puryaṣṭaka-kalābhiś ca vyāmohayati
tadā tad-vyāmohitatā saṃsāritvam |
yadā tu madhya-dhāmollāsād* udāna-śaktiṃ viśva-vyāpti-sārāṃ ca vyāna-śaktiṃ turya-daśā-rūpāṃ turyātīta-daśā-rūpāṃ ca cidānanda-ghanāṃ unmīlayati,
tadā dehādy-avasthāyām api pati-daśātmā jīvan-muktir bhavati |
evaṃ tridhā sva-śakti-vyāmohitatā vyākhyātā |
cidvad iti sūtre cit-prakāśo gṛhīta-saṃkocaḥ saṃsārī ity uktam |
iha tu sva-śakti-vyāmohitatvenāsya saṃsāritvaṃ bhavati
iti bhaṅgyantareṇa uktam |
evaṃ saṃkucita-śaktiḥ, prāṇādimān api,
yadā sva-śakti-vyāmohito na bhavati,
tadā ayaṃ, 'śarīrī parameśvaraḥ' ity āmnāya-sthityā, śiva-bhaṭṭāraka eva
iti bhaṅgyā nirūpitaṃ bhavati |
yadāgamaḥ
manuṣya-deham āsthāya channās te parameśvarāḥ
[nirvīryam api ye hārdaṃ trikārthaṃ samupāsate] | iti |
uktam ca *Pratyabhijñā-ṭīkā*yāṃ
śarīram eva {ghaṭādy api vā} ye ṣaṭ-triṃśat-tattva-mayaṃ
śiva-rūpatayā paśyanti [arcayanti ca] te 'pi sidhyanti
[ghaṭādikam api tathābhiniviśanti te 'pīti nasty atra vivāda]†
iti || 12 ||
ukta-sūtrārtha-prātipakṣyeṇa tattva-dṛṣṭiṃ darśayitum āha:

**tat-parijñāne cittam evāntar-mukhī-bhāvena cetana-padādhyārohāc citiḥ || 13 ||**

pūrva-sūtra-vyākhyā-prasaṅgena prameya-dṛṣṭyā vitatya vyākhyāta-prāyam etat sūtram, śabda-saṃgatyā tv adhunā vyākhyāyate |
tasya → ātmīyasya pañca-kṛtya-kāritvasya parijñāne sati aparijñāna-lakṣaṇa-kāraṇāpagamāt sva-śakti-vyāmohitatā-nivṛttau
svātantrya-labhāt prāg vyākhyātaṃ yat cittaṃ

---

* *-ullāsād* em. Sanderson (following MSS $K_1$ and $P_2$) : *-ullāsām* Ed. If we retained the Ked's reading, it would be a *bahuvrīhi* translated as "in which there is the expansion/flaring up/activation of the central Radiant Abode (*dhāmā*)."

† The Telegu and Kashmiri MSS give very different versions of this citation. I have translated the version in the KSTS edition, while Hanneder has preferred the Telegu version in his edition, which I have translated in Endnote 91. The {curly brackets} enclose material not in the Telegu version, while the [square brackets] enclose material not in the Kashmiri version. Of course it is impossible to know which is correct, because Utpala's *ṭīkā* commentary (aka *vivṛti*) on his ĪPK is now lost.

tad eva saṃkocinīṃ bahir-mukhatāṃ jahat
antarmukhībhāvena cetana-padādhyārohāt
grāhaka-bhūmikākramaṇa-krameṇa saṃkoca-kalāyā api vigalanena
svarūpāpattyā citir bhavati |
svāṃ cin-mayīṃ parāṃ bhūmim āviśatīty arthaḥ || 13 ||
nanu: yadi pāramārthikaṃ cic-chakti-padaṃ sakala-bheda*-kavalana-svabhāvaṃ
tad asya māyā-pade 'pi tathā-rūpeṇa bhavitavyaṃ
yathā jaladācchāditasyāpi bhānor bhāvāvabhāsakatvaṃ |
ity āśaṅkyāha:
**citi-vahnir avaroha-pade channo 'pi mātrayā**
**meyendhanaṃ pluṣyati || 14 ||**
citir eva viśva-grasana-śīlatvāt vahniḥ,
asau eva avaroha-pade māyā-pramātṛtāyāṃ
channo 'pi svātantryāt ācchādita-svabhāvo 'pi bhūri-bhūti-channāgnivat
mātrayā aṃśena nīla-sukhādi†-prameyendhanaṃ pluṣyati svātmasātkaroti |
mātrā-padasyedam ākūtaṃ yat kavalayann api sārvātmyena na grasate,
api tv aṃśena saṃskārātmanā tat-sthāpayati‡ |
grāsakatvaṃ ca sarva-pramātṝṇāṃ svānubhavata eva siddham |
yad uktaṃ śrīmad-Utpaladeva-pādaiḥ nija-stotreṣu:
vartante jantavo 'śeṣā api brahmendra-viṣṇavaḥ |
grasamānās tato vande deva viśvaṃ bhavan-mayam || iti
|| 14 ||
yadā punaḥ karaṇeśvarī-prasara-saṃkocaṃ saṃpādya
sarga-saṃhāra-krama-pariśīlana-yuktiṃ āviśati, tadā
**bala-lābhe viśvam ātmasātkaroti || 15 ||**
citir eva deha-prāṇādy-ācchādana-nimajjanena
svarūpaṃ unmagnatvena sphārayantī balam |
yathoktam
tadākramya balaṃ mantrāḥ ... | iti |
evaṃ ca bala-lābhe → unmagna-svarūpāśrayaṇe kṣityādi-sadāśivāntaṃ ← viśvaṃ
ātmasātkaroti → svasvarūpābhedena nirbhāsayati |
tad uktaṃ pūrva-gurubhiḥ svabhāṣā-mayeṣu krama-sūtreṣu
yathā vahnir udbodhito dāhyaṃ dahati tathā viṣaya-pāśān bhakṣayet | iti |
na caivaṃ vaktavyam—viśvātmasātkāra-rūpā samāveśa-bhūḥ kādācitkī,
kathaṃ upādeyā iyaṃ syād? iti, yato dehādy-unmajjana-nimajjana-vaśena
idam asyāḥ kādācitkatvam ivābhāti |

---

* Perhaps *bheda* should be emended to *bhāva*?

† *sukhādi* conj. : *pītādi* Ed.

‡ *tat-sthāpayati* em. Sanderson (following MSS $K_{1,3}$, $P_2$, and $A_{1-4}$) : *utthāpayati* Ed.

vastutas tu « citi-svātantryāvabhāsita-dehādy-unmajjanād eva kādācitkatvam »,*
eṣā tu sadaiva prakāśamānā, anyathā tad dehādy api na prakāśeta |
ata eva
dehādi-pramātṛtābhimāna-nimajjanāyābhyāsaḥ,
na tu sadā-prathamānatā-sāra-pramātṛtā-prāptyartham |
iti śrī-*Pratyabhijñā*-kārāḥ || 15 ||
evaṃ ca

**cid-ānanda-lābhe dehādiṣu cetyamāneṣv api**
**cid-aikātmya-pratipatti-dārḍhyaṃ jīvan-muktiḥ || 16 ||**

viśvātmasātkārātmani samāveśa-rūpe cid-ānande labdhe
vyutthāna-daśāyāṃ dala-kalpatayā deha-prāṇa-nīla-sukhādiṣv ābhāsamāneṣv api
yat samāveśa-saṃskāra-balāt pratipādayiṣyamāṇa-yukti-kramopabṛṃhitāt
cid-aikātmya-pratipatti-dārḍhyam avicalā cid-ekatva-prathā
saiva jīvan-muktiḥ « jīvataḥ prāṇān api dhārayato » muktiḥ
pratyabhijñāta-nija-svarūpe† vidrāvitāśeṣa-pāśa-rāśitvāt |
yathoktaṃ *Spanda*-śāstre
iti vā yasya saṃvittiḥ krīḍātvenākhilaṃ jagat |
sa paśyan satataṃ yukto jīvan-mukto na saṃśayaḥ || iti
|| 16 ||
atha, kathaṃ cid-ānanda-lābho bhavati? ity āha:

**madhya-vikāsāc cid-ānanda-lābhaḥ || 17 ||**

sarvāntaratamatvena vartamānatvāt tad-bhitti-lagnatāṃ vinā ca kasyacid api
svarūpānupapatteḥ saṃvid eva bhagavatī madhyam |
sā tu māyā-daśāyāṃ tathābhūtāpi svarūpaṃ gūhayitvā,
'prāk saṃvit prāṇe pariṇatā' iti nītyā, prāṇa-śakti-bhūmiṃ svīkṛtya,
avaroha-krameṇa buddhi-dehādi-bhuvaṃ adhiśayānā,
nāḍī-sahasra-saraṇim anusṛtā |
tatrāpi ca palāśa-parṇa-madhya-śākhā-nyāyena
ābrahmarandhrād adho-vaktra-paryantaṃ
prāṇa-śaktir‡ brahmāśraya-madhyama-nāḍī-rūpatayā prādhānyena sthitā
tata eva sarva-vṛttīnām udayāt tatraiva ca viśrāmāt |
evaṃbhūtāpy eṣā paśūnāṃ nimīlita-svarūpaiva sthitā |
yadā tūkta-yukti-krameṇa sarvāntaratamatvena
madhya-bhūtā saṃvid bhagavatī vikasati,

---

* I suspect that *citi... kādācitkatvam* is a scribe's marginal gloss that got incorporated into the text, since it is largely redundant; but I have incorporated the non-redundant portion, *citi-svātantryāvabhāsita,* into my translation.

† *-svarūpe* em. Sanderson (following the reading of MSS $K_1$ and $P_2$) : *-svarūpa-* Ed.

‡ *prāṇa-śaktir* conj. em. Sanderson (supported by MS $K_1$) : *prāṇaśakti-* Ed.

yadi vā vakṣyamāṇa-[yukti]-krameṇa madhya-bhūtā brahma-nāḍī vikasati,
tadā tad-vikāsāc cid-ānandasya ukta-rūpasya lābhaḥ prāptir bhavati |
tataś ca prāg uktā jīvan-muktiḥ || 17 ||

madhya-vikāse yuktim āha:

**vikalpa-kṣaya-śakti-saṃkoca-vikāsa-vāha-cchedādyanta-koṭi-nibhālanādaya ihopāyāḥ || 18 ||**

iha madhya-śakti-vikāse vikalpa-kṣayādaya upāyāḥ |
prāg-upadiṣṭa-pañca-vidha-kṛtya-kāritvādy-anusaraṇena sarva-madhya-bhūtāyāḥ saṃvido vikāso jāyata ity abhihita-prāyam |
upāyāntaram api tūcyate
prāṇāyāma-mudrā-bandhādi-samasta-yantraṇā-tantra-troṭanena sukhopāyam eva

[1. *vikalpa-kṣaya*]

hṛdaye nihita-cittaḥ
ukta-yuktyā sva-sthiti-pratibandhakaṃ vikalpam akiṃcic-cintakatvena praśamayan
avikalpa-parāmarśena dehādy-akaluṣa-sva-cit-pramātṛtā-nibhālana-pravaṇaḥ
acirād eva unmiṣad-vikāsāṃ turya-turyātīta-samāveśa-daśāṃ āsādayati |
yathoktam

vikalpa-hānenaikāgryāt krameṇeśvaratā-padam |
iti śrī-*Pratyabhijñā*yām [IV.11]

śrī-*Spande* 'pi

yadā kṣobhaḥ pralīyeta tadā syāt paramaṃ padam | iti [1.9]

*śrī-Jñāna-garbhe* 'pi

vihāya sakalāḥ kriyā janani mānasīḥ sarvato
vimukta-karaṇa-kriyānusṛti-pāratantryojjvalam |
sthitais tvad-anubhāvataḥ sapadi vedyate sā parā
daśā nṛbhir atandritāsama-sukhāmṛta-syandinī || iti |

ayaṃ ca upāyo mūrdhanyatvāt *Pratyabhijñā*yāṃ ca pratipāditatvād ādāv uktaḥ |
śakti-saṃkocādayas tu yady api *Pratyabhijñā*yāṃ na pratipāditāḥ
tathāpy āmnāyikatvād asmābhiḥ prasaṅgāt pradarśyante,
bahuṣu hi pradarśiteṣu kaścit kenacit pravekṣyatīti |

[2.] śakteḥ saṃkoca

[a.] indriya-dvāreṇa prasarantyā evākuñcana-krameṇa unmukhīkaraṇam |
yathoktam Ātharvaṇikopaniṣatsu Kaṭha-vallyāṃ caturtha-vallī-prathama-mantre

parāñci khāni vyatṛṇat svayaṃbhūḥ
tasmāt parāṅ paśyati nāntarātman |
kaścid dhīraḥ pratyag ātmānam aikṣad
āvṛtta-cakṣur amṛtatvam aśnan* || iti [Kaṭha Up. IV.1] |

* The standard reading has *icchan* instead of *aśnan*, but the Kaśmīrī recension may preserve an older reading, and *aśnan* is certainly not an inferior one.

[b.] prasṛtāyā api vā kūrmāṅga-saṃkocavat trāsa-samaye hṛt-praveśavac ca
sarvato nivartanam |
yathoktaṃ 'tad-apoddhṛte nityodita-sthitiḥ' iti |
[3.] śakter vikāsaḥ
antar-nigūḍhāyā akramam eva sakala-karaṇa-cakra-visphāraṇena
'antar-lakṣyo bahir-dṛṣṭiḥ nimeṣonmeṣa-varjitaḥ' iti
bhairavīya-mudrānupraveśa-yuktyā bahiḥ prasaraṇam |
yathoktaṃ *Kakṣya-stotre*
sarvāḥ śaktīḥ cetasā darśanādyāḥ
sve sve vedye yaugapadyena viṣvak |
kṣiptvā madhye hāṭaka-stambha-bhūtas
tiṣṭhan viśvādhāra eko 'vabhāsi || iti |
śrībhaṭṭa-Kallaṭenāpi uktam 'rūpādiṣu pariṇāmāt tat-siddhiḥ' iti |
[4.] śakteś ca saṃkoca-vikāsau
[a.] nāsāpuṭa-spandana-kramonmiṣat-sūkṣma-prāṇa-śaktyā bhrū-bhedanena
kramāsāditordhva-kuṇḍalinī-pade prasara-viśrānti-daśā-pariśīlanam |
[b.] adhaḥ-kuṇḍalinyāṃ ca ṣaṣṭa-vaktra-rūpāyāṃ praguṇīkṛtya śaktiṃ
tan-mūla-tad-agra-tan-madhya-bhūmi-sparśāveśaḥ |
yathoktaṃ *Vijñāna*-bhaṭṭārake:
vahner viṣasya madhye tu cittaṃ sukha-mayaṃ kṣipet |
kevalaṃ vāyu-pūrṇaṃ vā smarānandena yujyate || iti | [68]
atra vahniḥ anupraveśa-krameṇa saṃkoca-bhūḥ |
viṣa-sthānaṃ prasara-yuktyā vikāsa-padaṃ
'viṣḷ vyāptau' ity arthānugamāt |
[5. vāha-ccheda]
vāhayoḥ vāma-dakṣiṇa-gatayoḥ prāṇāpānayoś chedo
hṛdaya-viśrānti-puraḥsaraṃ
antaḥ-kakāra-hakārādi-prāyānacka-varṇoccāreṇa vicchedanam |
yathoktaṃ *Jñāna-garbhe*
anacka-kakṛtāyati-prasṛta-pārśva-nāḍī-dvaya-
cchido vidhṛta-cetaso hṛdaya-paṅkajasyodare |
udeti tava dāritāndha-tamasaḥ sa vidyāṅkuro
ya eṣa parameśatāṃ janayituṃ paśor api alam || iti |
[6. *ādyanta-koṭi-nibhālana*]
ādi-koṭiḥ hṛdayam, anta-koṭiḥ dvādaśāntaḥ |
tayoḥ prāṇollāsa-viśrānty-avasare nibhālanaṃ citta-niveśanena pariśīlanam |
yathoktaṃ *Vijñāna-bhairave*
hṛdy-ākāśe nilīnākṣaḥ padma-saṃpuṭa-madhya-gaḥ |
ananya-cetāḥ subhage paraṃ saubhāgyam āpnuyāt || iti [49]

tathā

yathā tathā yatra tatra dvādaśānte manaḥ kṣipet |
pratikṣaṇaṃ kṣīṇa-vṛtter vailakṣaṇyaṃ dinair bhavet || iti [51]

ādi-padād

[7.] unmeṣa-daśā-niṣevaṇam

yathoktaṃ

unmeṣaḥ sa tu vijñeyaḥ svayaṃ tam upalakṣayet |

iti *Spande* |

tathā [8.] ramaṇīya-viṣaya-carvaṇādayaś ca saṃgṛhītāḥ |

yathoktaṃ śrī-*Vijñāna-bhairava* eva

jagdhi-pāna-kṛtollāsa-rasānanda-vijṛmbhaṇāt |
bhāvayed bharitāvasthāṃ mahānanda-mayo bhavet || 72
gītādi-viṣayāsvādāsama-saukhyaikatātmanaḥ |
yoginas tanmayatvena mano-rūḍhes tad-ātmatā || 73
yatra yatra manas tuṣṭir manas tatraiva dhārayet |
tatra tatra parānanda-svarūpaṃ saṃprakāśate || 74 | iti |

evam anyad api [9.] ānanda-pūrṇa-svātma-bhāvanādikaṃ anumantavyam* |

ity evam ādayaḥ atra madhya-vikāse upāyāḥ || 18 ||

madhya-vikāsāc cidānanda-lābhaḥ, sa eva ca parama-yoginaḥ samāveśa-samapattyādi-paryāyaḥ samādhiḥ, tasya nityoditatve yuktim āha:

**samādhi-saṃskāravati vyutthāne bhūyo bhūyaḥ cid-aikyāmarśān nityodita-samādhi-lābhaḥ || 19 ||**

āsādita-samāveśo yogi-varo vyutthāne 'pi samādhi-rasa-saṃskāreṇa kṣīva iva sānandaṃ ghūrṇamāno bhāva-rāśiṃ śarad-abhra-lavam iva cid-gagana eva līyamānaṃ paśyan bhūyo bhūyaḥ antarmukhatāṃ eva samavalambamāno nimīlana-samādhi-krameṇa cid-aikyam eva vimṛśan vyutthānābhimatāvasare 'pi samādhy-eka-rasa eva bhavati |

yathoktaṃ *Krama-sūtreṣu*

krama-mudrayā antaḥ-svarūpayā bahir-mukhaḥ samāviṣṭo bhavati sādhakaḥ |
tatrādau bāhyād antaḥ praveśaḥ
ābhyantarād bāhya-svarūpe praveśaḥ āveśa-vaśāt jāyate
iti sabāhyābhyantaro 'yaṃ mudrā-kramaḥ | iti |

atrāyam arthaḥ

sṛṣṭi-sthiti-saṃhṛti-saṃvic-cakrātmakaṃ kramaṃ mudrayati svādhiṣṭhitaṃ ātmasātkaroti yeyaṃ turīyā citi-śaktiḥ |

tayā krama-mudrayā, antar iti pūrṇāhaṃtā-svarūpayā bahir-mukha iti viṣayeṣu vyāpṛto 'pi samāviṣṭaḥ → sākṣāt-kṛta-para-śakti-sphāraḥ sādhakaḥ → parama-yogī bhavati |

tatra ca bāhyād → grasyamānāt viṣaya-grāmāt

---

* Sanderson reads *anusartavyam.*

antaḥ → parasyāṃ citi-bhūmau, grasana-krameṇaiva, praveśaḥ → samāveśo bhavati |
ābhyantarāt → citi-śakti-svarūpāt ca
sākṣāt-kṛtāt āveśa-vaśāt → samāveśa-sāmarthyād eva
bāhya-svarūpe → idaṃtā-nirbhāse viṣaya-grāme
vamana-yuktyā praveśaś cid-rasāśyānatā-prathanātmā samāveśo jāyate |
iti sabāhyābhyantaro 'yaṃ → nityodita-samāveśātmā |
mudo harṣasya vitaraṇāt paramānanda-svarūpatvāt pāśa-drāvaṇāt [ca]
viśvasya antaḥ-turīya-sattāyāṃ mudraṇāt ca
mudrātmāpi* sṛṣṭyādi-kramābhāsakatvāt tat-kramābhāsa-rūpatvāt ca
krama iti abhidhīyata iti || 19 ||
idānīm asya samādhi-lābhasya phalam āha

**tadā prakāśānanda-sāra-mahā-mantra-vīryātmaka-pūrṇāhaṃtāveśāt sadā sarva-sarga-saṃhāra-kāri-nija-saṃvid-devatā-cakreśvaratā-prāptir bhavatīti śivam || 20 ||**

nityodite samādhau labdhe sati
prakāśānanda-sārā → cid-āhlādaika-ghanā
mahatī† mantra-vīryātmakā → sarva-mantra-jīvita-bhūtā
pūrṇā → parā-bhaṭṭārikā-rūpā
yeyaṃ ahaṃtā → akṛtrimaḥ svātma-camatkāraḥ;
tatrāveśāt sadā kālāgnyādeḥ carama-kalā-paryantasya viśvasya
yau sarga-saṃhārau → vicitrau sṛṣṭi-pralayau tat-kāri
yat nijaṃ‡ saṃvid-devatā-cakraṃ
tad-aiśvaryasya prāptiḥ → āsādanaṃ bhavati |
prākaraṇikasya [parama]-yogina ity arthaḥ |
iti etat sarvaṃ śiva-svarūpam eva ity upasaṃhāra iti saṃgatiḥ |
tatra yāvad§ idaṃ kiṃcit saṃvedyate tasya saṃvedanam eva svarūpam |
tasyāpi antar-mukha-vimarśa-mayāḥ pramātāraḥ tattvam |
teṣām api vigalita-dehādy-upādhi-saṃkocābhimānā aśeṣa-śarīrā
sadāśiveśvarataiva sāram |
asyā api prakāśaika-« sadbhāvāpādita »¶-aśeṣa-viśva-camatkāra-mayaḥ
śrīmān maheśvara eva paramārthaḥ |
« na hi pāramārthika-prakāśāveśaṃ vinā kasyāpi prakāśamānatā ghaṭate » |

---

* *mudrātmāpi* diag. conj. Sanderson : *mudrātmā kramo 'pi* Ed.

† *mahatī* is probably a scribal corruption for *mahā-*, in order to clarify that the latter modifies *vīryātmakā* not *mantra*.

‡ *nijaṃ* is likely a corruption for *nija-*.

§ Many MSS read *yad* for *yāvad*.

¶ Sanderson sees a textual problem due to awkward phrasing.

sa ca parameśvaraḥ svātantrya-sāratvāt
ādi-kṣāntāmāyīya-śabda-rāśi-parāmarśa-mayatvenaiva
etat-svīkṛta-samasta-vācya-vācaka-mayāśeṣa-jagad-ānanda-sadbhāvāpādanāt
paraḥ paripūrṇatvāt sarvākāṅkṣāśūnyatayā ānanda-prasara-nirbharaḥ |
ata eva anuttarākula-svarūpāt akārāt ārabhya śakti-sphāra-rūpa-hakāra*-paryantaṃ
yat viśvaṃ prasṛtaṃ « kṣakārasya prasara-śamana-rūpatvāt »
tat akāra-hakārābhyām eva saṃpuṭīkāra-yuktyā « pratyāhāra-nyāyena »†
antaḥ-svīkṛtaṃ sat,
avibhāga-vedanātmaka-bindu-rūpatayā sphuritam anuttara eva viśrāmyati |
iti śabda-rāśi-svarūpa eva ayaṃ akṛtako vimarśaḥ |
yathoktam [*Ajaḍa-pramātṛ-siddhyām*]
prakāśasyātma-viśrāntir ahaṃ-bhāvo hi kīrtitaḥ |
uktā ca saiva viśrāntiḥ sarvāpekṣā-nirodhataḥ || 22
svātantryam atha kartṛtvaṃ mukhyam īśvaratāpi ca | 23ab |
eṣaiva ca ahantā sarva-mantrāṇāṃ udaya-viśrānti-sthānatvāt etad-balenaiva ca
tat-tad-arthakriyā-kāritvāt mahatī vīrya-bhūmiḥ |
tad uktam
tad-ākramya balaṃ mantrā... | ityādi
...tenaite śiva-dharmiṇaḥ | ityantaṃ śrī-*Spande* [II. 1-2]
*Śiva-sūtreṣu* api
mahā-hrādānusaṃdhānān mantra-vīryānubhavaḥ | 1.22
tad atra mahā-mantra-vīryātmakāyāṃ
pūrṇāhantāyāṃ āveśo deha-prāṇādi-nimajjanāt
tat-padāvāptyavaṣṭambhena dehādīnāṃ nīlādīnām api
tad-rasāplāvanena tanmayīkaraṇam |
tathā hi
deha-sukha-nīlādi yat kiṃcit prathate, adhyavasīyate, smaryate, saṃkalpyate vā
tatra sarvatraiva bhagavatī citi-śakti-mayī prathā bhitti-bhūtaiva sphurati |
'tad-asphuraṇe kasyāpi asphuraṇāt' iti uktatvāt
kevalaṃ tathā sphuranty api sā,
tan-māyā-śaktyāvabhāsita-deha-nīlādy-uparāga-dattābhimāna-vaśāt
bhinna-bhinna-svabhāvā iva bhāntī
jñāna-saṃkalpādhyavasāyādi-rūpatayā māyā-pramātṛbhiḥ abhimanyate |
vastutas tu ekaiva asau citi-śaktiḥ |

---

* *hakāra* em. (supported by MSS $K_{2,4}$ and $A_{1,2,4}$) : *hakalā* Ed.

† The two cruxes in this paragraph mark probable marginal glosses that were incorporated into the main text. The first appears in my translation, albeit parenthetically, and the second does not. The latter refers to the Pāninean convention that all the letters between the two that are mentioned are to be included.

yathoktam
yā caiṣā pratibhā tat-tat-padārtha-krama-rūṣitā |
akramānanta-cid-rūpaḥ pramātā sa maheśvaraḥ || I.7.1
tathā
māyā-śaktyā vibhoḥ saiva bhinna-saṃvedya-gocarā |
kathitā jñāna-saṃkalpādhyavasāyādi-nāmabhiḥ || I.5.18
evam eṣā sarva-daśāsu ekaiva citi-śaktiḥ vijṛmbhamāṇā
yadi tad-anupraveśa-tad-avaṣṭambha-yuktyā samāsādyate
tat tad-āveśāt pūrvokta-yuktyā karaṇonmīlana-nimīlana-krameṇa
sarvasya sarvamayatvāt tat-tat-saṃhārādau api sadā sarva-sarga-saṃhāra-kāri
yat sahaja*-saṃvitti-devatā-cakraṃ → amāyīyāntar-bahiṣ-karaṇa-marīci-puñjaḥ
tatra īśvaratā → sāmrājyaṃ para-bhairavātmatā tat-prāptir bhavati parama-yoginaḥ |
yathoktam
yadā tv ekatra saṃrūḍhas tadā tasya layodbhavau |
niyacchan bhoktṛtām eti tataś cakreśvaro bhavet || 3.19
atra ekatra iti 'ekatrāropayet sarvam' iti
cit-sāmānya-spanda-bhūḥ unmeṣātmā vyākhyātavyā |
« tasya iti anena 'puryaṣṭakena saṃruddha' iti
upakrāntaṃ puryaṣṭakam eva parāmraṣṭavyam » |
« na tu yathā vivaraṇa-kṛtaḥ ekatra sūkṣme sthūle śarīre vā iti vyākṛtavantaḥ »† |
stutaṃ ca mayā
svatantraś citi-cakrāṇāṃ cakravartī maheśvaraḥ |
saṃvitti-devatā-cakra-juṣṭaḥ ko 'pi jayaty asau ||
iti-śabda upasaṃhāre |
yat etāvat ukta-prakaraṇa-śarīraṃ tat sarvaṃ śivaṃ
śiva-prāpti-hetutvāt, śivāt prasṛtatvāt, śiva-svarūpābhinnatvāc ca śiva-mayam eva
iti śivam |
[Epilogue:]
deha-prāṇa-sukhādibhiḥ pratikalaṃ saṃrudhyamāno janaḥ
pūrṇānanda-ghanām imāṃ na cinute māheśvarīṃ svāṃ citim |
madhye-bodha-sudhābdhi viśvam abhitas tat-phena-piṇḍopamaṃ
yaḥ paśyed upadeśatas tu kathitaḥ sākṣāt sa ekaḥ śivaḥ ||

---

* Perhaps we should read *sahajaṃ* here.

† These lines (*tasya...vyākṛtavantaḥ*), which may be interpolations, are translated in Endnote 162, not in the main body of the text. The case for being a marginal annotation that was later incorporated into the main text is stronger for the first sentence (*tasya...parāṃraṣṭavyam*) than for the second (*na tu yathā...vyākṛtavantaḥ*), for which cf. Rāma's *Spandakārikā-vivṛti*, page 134 of the Dyczkowski translation.

yeṣāṃ vṛttaḥ śāṅkaraḥ śaktipāto
ye 'nabhyāsāt tīkṣṇa-yuktiṣv ayogyāḥ |
śaktā jñātuṃ neśvara-pratyabhijñām
uktas teṣām eṣa tattvopadeśaḥ ||

————————

samāptam idaṃ pratyabhijñā-hṛdayam |
kṛtis tatrabhavan-mahā-māheśvarācārya-varya-śrīmad-abhinavagupta-pāda-padmopajīvinaḥ śrīmato rājānaka-kṣemarājācaryasya ||

————————

śubham astu ||

## *Conventions and Abbreviations*

| | |
|---|---|
| - | Compounds are hyphenated where *sandhi* permits |
| « ... » | Encloses a doubtful passage or marks possible corruption |
| → | Marks a gloss (points from the word glossed to the gloss) |
| *italics* | Title of a text |
| Ed. | Kashmīr Series of Texts and Studies edition, 1911 |
| em. | emendation |
| conj. em. | conjectural emendation |
| diag. conj. | diagnostic conjecture |
| MS | manuscript |
| MSS | manuscripts |

Following the convention of the KSTS, *sandhi* has not been applied in every possible instance, in order to help the beginning Sanskritist read the text. It has, however, been applied much more frequently than in the KSTS Ed.

# List of Primary Sources Cited

*Ajaḍapramātṛsiddhi (Proof of the Conscious Knower)* by Utpaladeva (translation: Lawrence 2009).

*Īśvarapratyabhijñākārikā (Stanzas on the Recognition of the Divine)* by Utpaladeva (recommended translation: Torella 1994).

*Ūrmikaulārṇava (The Kaula Ocean of Waves)*, circa 9th century, exists only in manuscript (National Archives Kathmandu 5-5207).

*Kakṣyā-stotra* by Divākara Vatsa, lost Vaiṣṇava text surviving only in citations.

*Kaṭha Upaniṣad*, 2nd century BCE (recommended translation: Olivelle 1998).

*Kramasūtra*, a lost Krama text surviving only in citations.

*Jñānagarbhastotra (Hymn to the Womb of Wisdom)*, lost Kaula text surviving only in citations.

*Tattvagarbhastotra (Hymn on the Core of Reality)*, lost Kaula text surviving only in citations.

*Tantrasāra (The Essence of the Tantras)* by Abhinavagupta (recommended translations: Chakravarty 2012 and Wallis *forthcoming*).

*Tantrāloka (Light on the Tantras)* by Abhinavagupta, with the commentary (*viveka*) of Jayaratha (recommended translation: none, but several forthcoming; partial translations by Sanderson, Dyczkowski, and Wallis).

*Trikasāra (The Essence of the Trinity)*, lost Trika scripture.

*Triśiromata (The Doctrine of the Three-Headed Bhairava)*, lost Trika scripture.

*Mālinīvijayottaratantra (The Latter Triumph of the Garlanded Goddess)*, 8th century Trika text published only in Sanskrit (partial translation in Vāsudeva 2004).

*Yoga-sūtra (Aphorisms on Yoga)* by Patañjali (recommended translations: Bryant 2009, Stoler Miller 1998, Hartranft 2003, and Wallis *forthcoming*).

*Vākyapadīya* by Bhartṛhari, 5th century (translation: Pillai 1971).

*Vijñānabhairavatantra*, c. 9th century Trika scripture (recommended translations: Semenov 2010, Singh 2002 [1979], and Wallis *forthcoming*).

*Vimuktakāḥ (Pearls of Liberation)*, a lost Krama text by Bhaṭṭa Dāmodara.

*Śiva-sūtra (Aphorisms of Śiva)*, 9th century (recommended translations: Dyczkowski 1998, Singh 2012, and Lakshmanjoo 2007).

*Sarvavīrasamāyoga (Union of All Heroes)*, a lost Krama text surviving only in citations.

*Spandakārikā (Stanzas on Vibration)* by Kallaṭa (recommended translations: Dyczkowski 1992 and Wallis *forthcoming*).

*Spandanirṇaya (An Investigation into the Doctrine of Vibration)* by Kṣemarāja (recommended translation: Singh, 1991).

*Spandasandoha* (*The Essence of Spanda*) by Kṣemarāja (recommended translations: Dyczkowski 1992 and Wallis *forthcoming*).

*Svabodhodayamañjarī (The Flowering of One's Innate Awareness)* by Vīranātha (recommended translations: Torella 2001 and Wallis *forthcoming*).

# Endnotes

1 Jeffrey J. Kripal, 2007, *Esalen: America and the Religion of No Religion*, Chicago: University of Chicago Press, p. 61.

2 The equivalence between *namas* and *samāveśa* is established in Kṣemarāja's commentaries on the *Śiva-stotrāvalī* and other hymns; see the doctoral dissertation on the subject by Hamsa Stainton (Columbia University).

3 As we will see, the Krama is this author's favorite Tantrik lineage, and so he positions its teachings as the esoteric center of the present work—esoteric in the sense that because they were closely guarded, he does not expound them fully here.

4 We might consider a topographic analogy here: that of a Klein bottle, on the continuous surface of which one can travel indefinitely, experiencing both 'inside' and 'outside' without ever coming up against a boundary.

5 If this paragraph seems confusing, I don't blame you for being confused. I'm convinced that the passage *siddhau .... saṃhāre* is corrupt, meaning that scribal errors have probably distorted whatever Kṣemarāja originally wrote.

6 See Chapter One of the *Tantrāloka* and the *Tantrasāra*, both soon to be released in my own translation. The *Tantrasāra* is also available in a translation by Hemendra Nath Chakravarty and Boris Marjanovic.

7 Sanderson's spontaneous paraphrase of Kṣemarāja given during a lecture on the present text, delivered at the University of Leipzig, 2008.

8 I use the two English words interchangeably, but prefer 'awareness' because it comes from the Old English *gewær* (which itself comes from Proto-Germanic **ga-waraz*, 'to be very careful or attentive', itself deriving from the 4,000-year-old Proto-Indo-European root **wer-* ('to perceive, watch out for'), whereas 'consciousness' is a relatively recent import from Old French *conscience*, and originally was not differentiated in meaning from conscience, i.e., 'moral sense' or 'awareness of wrongdoing', which is not a connotation of Sanskrit *cit* or *saṃvit*.

9 I translate *parādvaya-sāmarasya-āpādana* twice to more fully bring out the meaning of this difficult-to-translate expression: first as '[she] brings about the fusion of everything in complete nonduality', and then as 'causing [one] to relish all things as a seamless unity'. The latter translation derives from Sanderson.

10 The speed of light in a vacuum, 299,792,458 meters per second, is absolute, which means that even if you are traveling 200,000,000 meters per second in the same direction as the light, if you measure its speed, it will still be 299,792,458 meters per second—not 99,792,458. Light thus has an absolute value. The widespread misinterpretation of Einstein that states "everything is relative" is meaningless. Everything is relative *in relation to a constant*, an absolute value, which makes order possible in an otherwise fluxing, relativistic universe. The speed of light is not the only constant; it seems there is at least one mathematical constant in any given frame of reference—a truth that would not have surprised the Tantrik masters.

11 To clarify (because many today would dispute this point), there have certainly been Vedāntic thinkers since Kṣemarāja's time that endow *brahman* with action capacity, i.e., with some version of *kriyā-śakti*. This development within Vedānta was almost certainly due to Tantrik influence. In classical Vedānta, however, all action and activity is illusory: nothing has ever happened and nothing ever could, since divine consciousness, which is all that exists, is completely static and quiescent (*niṣprapañca* and *śānta*).

12 This is the standard paradigm in the Krama school, which Kṣemarāja seems to regard as holding the ultimate (i.e., truest) teachings. See *Tantra Illuminated,* pages 248–269.

13 *Tantrāloka* 3.100

14 On this basis, one could construct an argument for analyzing the degree of self-reflective awareness a life-form possesses through its creativity and unpredictability. For example, elephants surprised us when we discovered they could paint (see www.elephantartgallery.com), but the range of expression in their abstract paintings is extremely narrow compared to that of humans.

15 Kṣemarāja's teacher, Abhinava Gupta, gives precisely this teaching in Chapter Three of his *Tantrasāra*, soon to be published in my translation.

16 The original source for the doctrine of the Seven Perceivers is the Trika scripture called *The Latter Triumph of the Garlanded Alphabet Goddess* (*Mālinī-vijayottara-tantra*), Chapter One, verses 14–17. My teacher Somadeva Vāsudeva has written a whole book on the Seven Perceivers as taught in this scripture (see the bibliography).

17 In the tradition Kṣemarāja inherits, there are eight Great Lords of Mantra (traditionally named as Ananta, Sūkṣma, Śivottama, Ekanetra, Ekarudra, Trinetra, Śrīkaṇṭha, and Śikhaṇḍin). We can compare this to other traditions: for Roman Catholics, there are three archangels; for Muslims, four; and for some branches of the Eastern Orthodox Church, seven. In Zoroastrianism, which has common roots with the Indian tradition, there are six 'divine sparks' of the Supreme Being. In all of these religions, the 'archangels' are emanations of God, not really separate beings.

18 If we were to take *mantra* very literally as 'an instrument for the mind', we could perhaps translate *Mantreśvara* literally as '[a] lord of the instrumentality of cognition', which in fact is just the kind of exegetical strategy that Kṣemarāja employs.

19 It is important to note that Kṣemarāja has changed his view from his earlier writings, in which he has the following sequence (from *Sadāśiva* to *Īśvara* to *śuddhavidyā-tattva*): first 'This am I', then 'I am this', then 'I am this; this am I'.

20 Where *maya* is translated as 'consists of' but could even be rendered 'is'. *Maya*, that is, not *māyā*: in Sanskrit, a change in vowel length makes a different word, which is why the diacritic markings (those horizontal lines) are necessary to spell a Sanskrit word correctly with the Roman alphabet.

21 Due to a *sandhi* ambiguity, we can read either *ākhyāti* or *akhyāti*. Grammatically speaking, it has to be one or the other; however, it seems to me too perfect of a construction for the ambiguity to be unintentional on Kṣemarāja's part.

22 See, e.g., the Buddhist *Guhyasamāja-tantra* for parallel expressions.

23 The text has *deva* where we might expect *tattva*, since it is a list of the tattvas that follows, but I have not seen a manuscript with *tattva* yet.

24 See *Tantrāloka-viveka* after verse 1.5: "'Individuality' has difference as a primary [characteristic], is interpenetrated [or fractured] with infinite various images, and is [fundamentally] a contracted form of the [infinite] Self." (*bheda-pradhānaṃ tattad-anantābhāsa-saṃbhinnaṃ saṅkucitātma-rūpaṃ naratvam*)

25 *Spanda-kārikā* 28–29b/2.3–4b.

26 Actually, he just cites the beginning and end of the quote, assuming his audience knows the verse in question. I have filled in the missing part from Kṣema's *Spanda-nirṇaya.*

27 In another work (his commentary on the *Svacchanda-tantra*), Kṣemarāja humorously mocks the Sāṅkhya/Yoga view of the self as witness, saying "In a self which is not an active experient there is no possibility at all for any [real] experience, [whether] mediated by the intellect or [other faculties]. For an [actual] experience of 'cold' is not possible, even by some secondary operation, simply because [the cognition of] snow is internally 'reflected' in somebody." The translation follows that of my teacher Somadeva Vāsudeva, to whom I am indebted for reading the *Spanda-nirṇaya* passage with me, and illuminating me on the subject of *bhoktṛ* versus *sākṣin*. He has now published an article on this topic, "The Unconscious Experiencer: Bhoktṛtva in the Pramātṛbheda of the Trika," in the *Journal of Indological Studies*, No. 24 (2012–2014), pp. 203–230.

28 Note, however, that *cit* and *citi* are used interchangeably in this philosophy, perhaps because *citi* cannot be fully grasped through the $H_2O$ metaphor.

29 However, the Sanskrit is ambiguous at this point (perhaps due to scribal error), so it could be that Kṣema is actually saying "if there is a predominance of the *innate* Light of Awareness alone..." *Sahaja* can mean either 'spontaneous' or 'innate', and if it was in fact meant to be compounded (as *sahaja-prakāśa-mātra-pradhānatve*), then 'innate' would be the correct translation, and the subtle critique I mentioned would not be present.

30 Kṣemarāja's term (for he seems to have coined *vidyā-pramātā* or 'Wisdom-perceiver') is probably derived from the fact that the first level of the Pure Realm is called *[śuddha-]vidyā tattva.*

31 Presumably, this process of gradual awakening cannot go beyond tattva #1 (or, more accurately, tattva #0), but Kṣema does not mention that here, instead emphasizing an ongoing process with no static goal.

32 This verse parallels *Īśvara-pratyabhijñā-kārikā* IV.12, which is cited in Chapter Twelve.

33 If the reader has an emotional attachment to any of the *vikalpa*s mentioned in this list, or indeed to the glucose-heavy diet that helps fuel them, his own reactivity might be evidence in favor of the hypothesis briefly advanced here. I for one have never seen such foaming-at-the-mouth emotional reactivity than

when one of these *vikalpa*-structures is challenged in someone for whom it is a central part of his or her identity. And no challenge is more fundamental than one that strikes at the very root of the *vikalpa*-structure: the fact that it is all made up. Finally, another feature of the mind-world is right versus wrong, a black-and-white mentality, which if operative may incline the reader to think that I am condemning out of hand all the *vikalpa*-structures mentioned, as if they were intrinsically bad or wrong. If you think that is what is being said here, you have missed the point entirely.

34 There is a precisely parallel theory among the Buddhists. The Yogācāra school proposed the *ālaya-vijñāna* or 'substratum consciousness' as a repository for the subtle impressions of past experience that survive the meditational state of complete dissolution of the mind (*nirodha-samāpatti*).

35 Alan Watts, solely on the basis of his enlightened insight, argued that this is because both past and future flow forth from the present, and are both created by the present.

36 See the work of Sean Carroll, who argues that time only appears to flow in a single direction because of entropy, which creates 'the arrow of time'. (You'll find some fascinating video lectures of his online.) Another way of stating the argument is that time only exists as a form of perception had by beings like us; we perceive in terms of linear consecutive time, which does not suggest it actually exists that way. Yet another way of stating the argument is that we move through an already existent unified spacetime, and perceive time 'passing' due to our spacetime trajectory. See also www.exactlywhatistime.com/physics-of-time/the-arrow-of-time.

37 Note that in the original scriptural source for the doctrine of the Seven Perceivers (the *Mālinī-vijayottara-tantra*), *śakti* is present at each level as the power by which each of the Perceivers perceive. Here are the details of the practice described in that text:

One traverses the seven layers of Consciousness in two stages each (since each Perceiver has its *śakti*) plus an initial starting point, which is the contemplation of any one of the five primary elements (so fifteen stages total). This is done through the traditional yogic method of one-pointed attention on an interiorized visualization. Each stage is to be practiced until it is mastered (which usually takes one to twelve months):

i. Visualize the *maṇḍala* or symbolic diagram of the element (for example, if one is starting from the Earth element, one visualizes a yellow square with double *vajra*s on all four sides). Here one is the ordinary Sakala-self knowing an object.

ii. Visualize your body floating above the *maṇḍala* of the element (all the following stages subdivide into two phases; in the first phase the visualization is unclear and/or unsteady, in the second clear and steady). Here one is accessing the Pralayākala level, observing one's ordinary level of consciousness and the object fused together.

iii. Visualize yourself in a smaller version seated in the relevant *cakra* (heart for Earth, throat for Water, palate for Fire, third eye for Wind, crown for Space). Here one is accessing the Vijñānākala level, viewing one's lower two layers collapsed into unity.

iv. Visualize yourself as an orb of the relevant color (yellow-gold for Earth, etc.), partially shrouded in dark clouds. Here one is accessing the Mantra layer, viewing one's Vijñānākala-self, fused with the other layers.

v. Visualize yourself as the icon of Lord Śiva seated in the relevant center. Here one is accessing the Mantreśvara layer (a.k.a. Īśvara-tattva).

vi. Visualize an orb of the relevant color, now unshrouded. Here one is accessing the Mantra-maheśvara layer.

vii. Visualize pure light of the color of the original element, pervading oneself completely. Here one is accessing the Śiva layer, the root Perceiver.

viii. Visualize all-pervasive pure light, filling the entire universe. Here one is accessing the Śrī-Paramaśiva, the transcendent-yet-immanent meta-perceiver.

38 See, for example, *Tantrāloka* 9.8: "In reality, supreme Śiva is the agent of all phenomena, for agency is completely impossible for one who is not autonomous" (translation by Vasudeva). Remember that it is only Awareness that is completely autonomous (free and independent); indeed, it *is* autonomy. See also *Tantrāloka* 9.38cd–39ab: "Therefore in the creation of each and every thing, Śiva—who singly embodies the universe—is the agent, and the soul's make-believe (*abhimāna*) at agency is also the Lord's doing" (translation by Vasudeva). We could also translate *abhimāna* as 'egoic identification with'.

39 But we must distinguish here between holding an opinion and following a gut instinct. You cannot explain the reasons for your gut instinct (which is why we call it that), but it may still be trustworthy. You don't need to be able to explain it for it to be valid. However, gut instincts are situationally specific and situationally sensitive, unlike opinions. The latter are thought-structures we develop over time, concerning the general patterns of human life. They must be defendable in order to have some validity.

40 Though being atheistic, they didn't think the Veda was revealed by God or by the gods; rather, they held that it was *self-revealed*. The Exegetes (*Mīmāṃsakas*) and other Vedicists (*Vaidikas*) believed in a kind of 'apotheosis of scripture'—the Veda itself is functionally equivalent to Deity, and owes its existence to no other being.

41 Thanks to Professor Alexis Sanderson for this explanation, and for teaching me about Kumārila and his significance generally.

42 For an examination of these arguments see Alex Watson's book *The Self's Awareness of Itself* and Rafaelle Torella's *Īśvara-pratyabhijñā-kārikā*.

43 The traditional Buddhist example is that of a chariot (we would use a car). Are the wheels the car? No. Is the frame without the engine the car? No. Is the engine the car? No. Are all these things together the car? Yes, you might say, but by that definition, any time a part is missing, you can't call it a car, and you do, which proves that 'car' is nothing more than a convenient verbal designation. The same goes for 'self'. Furthermore, you keep replacing many different parts over time, but you still consider it the same car, because you are relating to it more in terms of a mental construct ('my car') than the thing as it is. Same goes for yourself, nearly all the 'parts' of which have been replaced many times.

44 He adds that this is true as long as they do not deny that the Void—their description of the ultimate principle—is permeated with Awareness. The Yogācārins who do deny it do not attain final liberation because their false view impedes it. This information comes from a lecture by Alexis Sanderson, and so far I have not been able to trace the textual passage(s) to which he refers.

45 Translation by Patrick Olivelle, whose work on the Upaniṣads is definitive as of this writing. The doctrine that *prāṇa* is the *brahman* is presented in the fourth book of the *Bṛhad-āraṇyaka Upaniṣad* as originating with Udaṅka Śaulbāyana, about whom we know nothing else. We also see *prāṇa* described as "immortal" at *Bṛhad-āraṇyaka Upaniṣad* 1.6.3.

46 Specifically *Chāndogya Upaniṣad* 3.19.1 and *Taittirīya Upaniṣad* 2.7.1.

47 We don't know for sure whether Kṣema is characterizing this early form of the Pañcarātra accurately, since its literature has not survived.

48 Note that in some sources, the Yogins are placed slightly above the Sāṅkhyas, because of their emphasis on practice over theory, but this is an academic point, since they still do not attain liberation.

49 Called *sat*, 'the Existent', in Sanskrit; pronounce it as to rhyme with 'cut'.

50 See Johannes Bronkhorst, 2001, "The Peacock's Egg: Bhartṛhari on Language and Reality," *Philosophy East and West*, 51(4), pp. 474–491.

51 See, e.g., Steven Pinker's *The Language Instinct*.

52 *Vākyapadīya* 1.167: *avibhāgā tu paśyantī sarvataḥ saṃhṛtakramā / svarūpajyotir evāntaḥ sūkṣmā vāg anapāyinī*. Utpala Deva comments on the first half of this verse at *Śiva-dṛṣṭi -vṛtti* 2.11ab; see also Harivṛṣabha's commentary on this verse.

53 The Kulamārga (historically derived from the Kāpālika or Soma Siddhānta tradition) emphasizes the following: initiation through *āveśa* (direct experience of the śakti), *ādya-yāga* ('consort practice'), sacrifice, the *vīra-melāpa*, prohibition of external signs of the *kapāla-vrata* ('skull-vow') except in the Kālīkula, and worship of Bhairava and the Goddess as Kuleśvara and Kuleśvarī (either together or separate), surrounded by eight Mothers, attended by Gaṇeśa and Vaṭuka, with ancillary worship of the Siddhas and Mahāsiddhas (*siddha-santāna*) and their consorts. It is divided into four Āmnāyas or Anvayas ('transmissions') or Gharāmnāyas ('lodge teachings'):

- E. Kuleśvarī (see *Tantrāloka* 29.1–55): first of the four
- W. Kubjikā: influenced by Trika; successful for several centuries; influenced early *haṭha-yoga*
- S. Kāmeśvarī/Tripurā: early tradition of erotic magic; includes worship of consort Kāmadeva and 11 Nityās; now extinct but gave rise to Śrīvidyā, worship of Tripurasundarī
- N. Kālīkula: flourished for several centuries in north and south; maintained the *kapāla-vrata*

This Kula or Kaula tradition, founded by Macchanda Nātha and Koṅkanāmbā, along with their six lineage-holding sons, comes to 'colonize' many of the Mantramārga traditions, which then display both Kaula and non-Kaula forms (the Trika is one example); thus one can be initiated via the *tantra-prakriyā* or the *kula-prakriyā*. Note that 'Tantrik' was originally an antonym to 'Kaula'. The elements that most people think of as Tantrik today are in fact Kaula.

54 *mukhyatvaṃ kartṛtāyās tu bodhasya ca cid-ātmanaḥ* | *śūnyādau tad-guṇe jñānaṃ tat-samāveśa-lakṣaṇam* || [Īśvara-pratyabhijñā-kārikā III.23]

55 Here we have a textual problem. Kṣema cites a half-verse, but without the other half, the citation doesn't make much sense. Therefore, I have supplied the missing half (the part that is unbolded). This translation follows the reading of the Nepali manuscript (*mokṣa-lipsavaḥ*) because it makes more sense, but if we retain the KSTS reading (*mokṣa-lipsayā*), then we would translate "Māyā causes them to wander in non-liberation by means of their desire for liberation." Less likely, but an intriguing possibility: that in those addicted to dry, fruitless argumentation, their desire for liberation actually works against them.

56 The importance of this quote is suggested by the fact that it is found in both the *Netra-tantra* and the *Svacchanda-tantra*.

57 But note that in some interpretations of Trika philosophy, there are three stages of awakening/realization/liberation, corresponding to the soul, Śakti, and Śiva respectively, and it is only in the third stage that the 'I' disappears. The second stage is the one in which one says "I am one with the universe," and the first stage, the realization of the divinity of the soul, is the one reached by 'worshipers of the self', who are not fully liberated if they do not proceed to the other stages.

58 You might argue otherwise, saying, "I can validly make the statement 'That leaf is green,' a statement characterizing objective reality, not my inner state." But a little reflection reveals this is not in fact true. You are characterizing an inner state when you say "That leaf is green," because you really mean "I am having the visual experience that I characterize as green," and you cannot know for sure that what you see as green is experienced in the same way by someone else (such as a colorblind person to whom your statement is purely abstract). Nor does 'green' exist objectively: the word represents the uniquely human experiential quale resulting from the way our visual cortex processes light vibrating at wavelengths between 495 nanometers and 570 nanometers. But more to the point, everything that we can say in normal words represents an aspect of someone's conscious experience. Science strives to extrapolate objective (i.e., universally applicable) reality from individual conscious expe-

riences and only really succeeds in doing so when it resorts to purely formal language such as that of mathematics.

59 *tāvad arthāvalehena uttiṣṭhati pūrṇā ca bhavati.* Note that *avaleha* is cognate with *lelihāna*, which when denoting a *yogini mudrā* means "to melt the senses" (see Serbaeva 2009), and is also a name for Kālī in the *Ūrmikaulārṇava* (see the next note).

60 *lelihānā sadā devī sadā pūrṇā ca bhāsate | ūrmir eṣā vibodhābdheḥ śaktir icchātmikā prabhoḥ* ||, a verse anonymously cited in the *Spanda-sandoha*, but which Jayaratha tells us (in his commentary on Chapter Four of the *Tantrāloka*) comes from the *Ūrmikaulārṇava*, a Kaula scripture allegedly revealed by Macchanda Nātha himself.

61 Cf. *Tantrāloka* 9.62b, 65a, and *Īśvara-pratyabhijñā-kārikā* 3.15 (where *āṇava-mala* = *svātantryasya abodhaḥ*).

62 This also means that the uncontracted Will is 'pre-cognitive', here meaning not directed toward a mental image of what is desirable, and the contracted will is the opposite ('post-cognitive', perhaps).

63 Kṣemarāja is here implicitly responding to a philosophical problem in his system, namely the fact that the *tattva* map, which was supposedly comprehensive, does not include the three Impurities. The presentation here is clearly meant to suggest that the Impurities of Action, Differentiation, and Individuality are implicit in the *kañcukas* of *kalā* (limited agency), *vidyā* (limited power of knowledge), and *rāga* (craving, or appetitive desire for worldly experience).

64 Cf. the anonymous *Mahānaya-prakāśa*: "On the basis of the principle expressed in the oral tradition of the Siddhas in the words: 'Since things do not have a nature of their own—as may be seen from a correct analysis of reality—I render homage to the self's mode of being that is full of the bliss deriving from the rising of consciousness', there is no real nature in which time exists and acts as impeller and measurer. The whole universe is merely the self's mode of being, whose essence is its own expansion" (9.52c–54, translation by Rafaelle Torella, "On Vāmanadatta", page 494). The verse quoted by the *Mahānaya-prakāśa* here is the opening verse of the *Svabodhodaya-mañjari*, which I have translated and will soon publish.

65 From www.edge.org/responses/what-do-you-believe-is-true-even-though-you-cannot-prove-it; see also www.edge.org/memberbio/donald_d_hoffman.

66 Rather than referring to his own tradition as the Trika or the Śaiva-śāsana, Kṣemarāja follows his teacher in calling it the *īśvarādvaita-darśana*, the View of the Nonduality of the Divine, or the Way based on the teaching that nothing is separate from Divine Consciousness. In this way he can present teachings of the Trika, Krama, and Kaula traditions under a single rubric.

67 An example of how this plays out in 'real life': modern Advaita Vedāntins and yogīs influenced by Vedānta, when confronted by racial difference, are more likely to declare themselves 'colorblind' (e.g., "I don't see you as black; I just see you as a person"), thinking that *overlooking* difference is socially and spiritually beneficial, whereas Tāntrikas are more likely to realize that seeing and honoring difference *while* maintaining an egalitarian stance is most socially and spiritually beneficial. For more on this, please see my blog post "Yoga Philosophy, Race, and 'Colorblindness'" at tantrikstudies.org/blog/2016/7/14/yoga-philosophy-race-and-colorblindness.

68 Sanskrit scholars will recognize here a possible debt to the linguistic/epistemological theory of *apoha* proposed by Dignāga and elaborated by others such as Ratnakīrti. See the relevant journal articles by Chien-Hsing Ho, Mark Siderits, and Parimal Patil.

69 This way of languaging the results of these experiments comes from the impressive *Quantum Enigma: Physics Encounters Consciousness* by Rosenblum and Kuttner; see also Brian Greene's *The Fabric of the Cosmos.*

70 The principle that makes this all much more complicated is that of *entanglement.* For example, we don't claim that the moon disappears when not visually being observed because it is constantly being observed in other ways, for example through its effect on the ocean tides. The atoms of the moon, though 225,000 miles away, are *entangled* with those of the Earth, and the two bodies constantly affect each other. We can easily understand this as long as the moon remains in orbit around the Earth, but when it escapes the Earth's gravitational pull and flies off into deep space (as it one day will), quantum physics tells us that it will *still* be entangled with Earth, affecting it in unknown ways forever. Once entangled, there is no disentangling! And some physicists argue that everything in the universe is entangled with everything else, because in

the early minutes of the universe, everything was in contact with everything else. If this is true (and Tantrik philosophy asserts that it is), then *nothing* is separable from anything else; that is, acting on any part of the whole somehow effects the whole.

71 And this does not invalidate the science relating to the subconscious or unconscious mind. From a strict idealist perspective, we would say that reality consistently appears in such a way as to suggest the existence of an unconscious mind, and the models we form of that unconscious mind can be effective and instructive without actually having to posit that anything exists outside of consciousness in a literal sense.

72 Though usually each cognitive experience includes four out of the Five Acts, it could express all five if one was aware that the object of perception was nothing but Consciousness while simultaneously being aware of one's capacity to see it as separate.

73 See *Quantum Enigma: Physics Encounters Consciousness* by Rosenblum and Kuttner.

74 A mental version of the cycle usually goes something like this: you say, "These guys are really good" (manifestation of a thought-form), become invested in your opinion (attachment phase), attribute it to yourself (subjective awareness), and feel disappointed if your friend doesn't agree with you, which closes your heart slightly (concealment phase, which we haven't come to in the main text yet). But it can also go like this: manifestation of the thought is followed by a moment of fascination with the power of consciousness to represent its experience in words, however paltry, then you look to the space of inward presence from which the thought arose, which causes the thought itself to dissolve, then you have a *camatkāra* moment, and the heart opens slightly (grace or revelation phase). These two examples of a mental cycle both go through manifestation → attachment →subjective awareness, but respectively end with concealment or revelation (a.k.a. 'laying down the seed' or dissolving it), which we are about to discuss in more detail. As your awakening process continues, you experience more of the second example.

75 Curiously, the very history of the English word 'aesthetic' is illustrative of a parallel line of thinking: it originally meant 'relating to perception by the senses' (from the Greek *aisthētikos*, 'perceptible things') and only later came to mean 'concerned with beauty'.

76 For a clear nontechnical account of *saṃskāras* from a modern spiritual teacher, see Chapter Six of Michael Singer's *The Untethered Soul*. See also my blog post "The Power of Subtle Impressions" (http://tantrikstudies.squarespace.com/blog/2015/9/21/impressions-of-past-lives).

77 See Chapter Seven of the anonymous *Mahānaya-prakāśa* (not yet available in English).

78 You might think that depression and related states of consciousness are different, that since there is no discernible energy surging inside, the practice described here would be ineffectual. This is not true. You can become fascinated with the qualities of the depressive state: how dense and thick and immobile it is, for example. And you can let yourself be amazed, wondering at what subconscious story could possibly produce such a petrification of consciousness. If you can find a shred of curiosity about it, nurture that until it becomes a powerful desire to know how you become depressed; while noticing and tracking the very subtle changes in the depressive state. Then these changes will start to accelerate, and you will experience the dissolution of that state.

79 *tanmukhenaiva tat tasya haṭhapākena līyate | viśvaṃ prakāśādhīnatvāt tanmayatvāc ca vastutaḥ* || 7.36

80 See Endnote 69 in Sanderson's "Purity and Power."

81 The fuller version of the quote is found in Jayaratha's *viveka* commentary on the *Tantrāloka*, specifically after verse 12.24. Jayaratha adds a parallel from the *Niśācara*: "Due to mental constructs, there is anxious inhibition, which becomes bondage. Further bondage will not occur without anxious inhibition born of mental constructs."

82 Not only for that reason; the teaching on AHAM is important for Kṣemarāja's teacher Abhinava Gupta, who discusses it in Chapter Three of the *Tantrāloka* and his commentary on the *Thirty Verses of Parā* (*Parātriṃśikā-vivaraṇa*). In the latter, he calls the Great Mantra AHAM the 'roar' (*rava*) of self-awareness which gives Bhairava (the Tantrik name for Śiva, i.e., God) his name. Scholar Eivind Kahrs comments: "Bhairava is aware of himself in this inner language which is the instinct of consciousness, the instinct of the light of reality. So his nature is a constant roaring of the Great Mantra of 'I', AHAM. Thus the term 'Bhairava' refers to unconditioned subjectivity as the essence of all phenomena."

83 Swāmi[nī] Chidvilāsānandā, *Kindle My Heart*, page 291. My suspicion is that the poem is Chidvilāsānandā's own but she was too humble to say so at that time.

84 In this particular schema, elaborated in Chapter Three of the *Tantrāloka* and *Tantrasāra*, there are thirty-four tattvas because *kāla* and *niyati* are not included as *tattvas*, being emergent properties of *māyā* and the three primary *kañcukas*.

85 This paragraph specifically alludes to verses IV.9–10 of the original *Recognition* text (the *Īśvara-pratyabhijñā-kārikā*).

86 Cf. the reinterpretation of the two terms at *Īśvara-pratyabhijñā-kārikā* III.2.3: "The perceiver is called 'Lord' when things appear to him as constituting his own body. When they appear to him differentiated due to *māyā*, the subject ... is called 'bound soul'" (translation by Rafaelle Torella, 1994).

87 Cf. *Śiva-sūtra* 1.14: *dṛśyaṃ sarīram*, "All that is perceptible is (one's own) body," and *Īśvara-pratyabhijñā-kārikā* III.2.3: "The perceiver is called 'Lord' when things appear to him as constituting his own body."

88 Saying 113 of the secret teachings of Jesus written down by Judas Didymus Thomas (known as the *Gospel of Thomas* in the Nag Hammadi Library).

89 Note that here Kṣemarāja uses the term *puryaṣṭaka* for the energy-body, which emphasizes its role as a locus of thoughts and feelings (the eight elements of the *puryaṣṭaka* being the three aspects of the heart-mind already discussed above in the Krama section, and the five *tanmātras* or subtle senses of the inner world).

90 First half of the verse: "They who venerate (*samupāsate*) the teaching of the Trika in the Heart, even though they are bereft of *mantra-vīrya*..."

91 The Telegu manuscripts read instead: "Seeing and venerating their very body as Śiva in the form of all thirty-six *tattvas*, [such] extraordinary people are perfected. In this way, some people penetrate (*abhiniviś*) even pots and so on. There is no argument on this point."

92 The dialectical formulation of thesis-antithesis-synthesis commonly ascribed to Hegel actually derives from Kant and Fichte. Hegel preferred the less obvious terminology of abstract-negative-concrete because, as a Wikipedia author puts it, "The formula, thesis-antithesis-synthesis, does not explain why

the thesis requires an antithesis. However, the formula, abstract-negative-concrete, suggests a flaw, or perhaps an incompleteness, in any initial thesis—it is too abstract and lacks the 'negative' of trial, error, and experience. For Hegel, the concrete, the synthesis, must always pass through the phase of the negative, in the journey to completion, that is, mediation. This is the essence of what is popularly called Hegelian Dialectics" (https://en.wikipedia.org/wiki/Dialectic#Hegelian_dialectic). I feel no compunction whatsoever to assimilate Indian philosophical discourse to European, but in case of the present work, it fits the dialectical structure well, and the structure seems a helpful pedagogical tool.

93 For a proper scientific treatment of these issues (as opposed to the goofy New Age treatment), see *Quantum Enigma*, which as noted above, argues that quantum physics has now experimentally proven that reality cannot be both objective (observer-independent) and separable (a non-unified state of affairs whereby something can happen in one part of the universe and not affect all the other parts) and is very probably neither.

94 Those familiar with the three Phases of Awakening taught in the Trika should note that immersion into the field of absolute potential constitutes the third phase (*śāmbhava-samāveśa*), which should not be sought before phases one and two are stabilized.

95 Notice I said "that you directly experience". If you read about horrors in a country far away, it would be wrong to say that those horrors are an expression of what you are, because they are not arising in your field of experience; only a *vikalpa* (mental construct) about them is arising in your field. So only the *vikalpa* is an expression of what you are. But, you might say, "Those things are really happening!" Perhaps so, but not in your field of experience, and more importantly, not the way you're imagining them. A *vikalpa* sometimes *represents* reality, but it never *presents* reality. More on this in Chapter Eighteen.

96 This phrase could also be translated as "become endowed with the power of the Omniscient One".

97 To explore these issues as they have appeared in Western philosophy, compare Kant's discussion of the transcendental unity of apperception with Berkeley's subjective idealism.

98 Note that the correct spelling is *jīvan-mukti*, not jivamukti. A popular New York yoga studio, by using the latter misspelling, has inadvertently been named 'letting go of life' or 'releasing the soul', a euphemism for death.

99 Note that by the rules of Sanskrit euphony, 't' becomes 'd' before a vowel.

100 I have translated the Sanskrit phrase *tad-bhitti-lagnatāṃ vinā ca kasyacid api svarūpānupapatteḥ* twice to capture fully what Kṣemarāja means by it.

101 The *palāśa* tree (*Butea monosperma*) is called 'flame of the forest' after its brilliant red flowers, though its leaves are the point of comparison here.

102 Though the blue whale is the largest animal, the largest living thing on Earth is either the self-cloning aspen tree colony called Pando in south-central Utah (also the oldest living thing at 80,000 years) or the honey fungus colony in eastern Oregon, depending on whether you are considering mass or area.

103 From the account of the experiment in Jonathan Haidt's *The Happiness Hypothesis*, Chapter One, "The Divided Self", but I've also benefitted from the discussion of this research in the work of Antonio Damasio and others.

104 Paraphrased from Haidt, *loc. cit.*; these findings are confirmed by Jill Bolte Taylor's astonishing *My Stroke of Insight* (both a book and a TED talk).

105 Since *aham idam* ('I am [all] this') is the experience that characterizes awakening/liberation at the level of Īśvara.

106 Translation by Torella, 1994: 216, with minor modifications.

107 The only exception to this rule concerns those in poverty, whose happiness is measurably increased by a modicum of financial security. However, once basic needs are consistently met, more money has rapidly diminishing returns, correlating to happiness less and less. This may be common folk wisdom, but now it's been proven: see Jonathan Haidt, *The Happiness Hypothesis*.

108 "You may use an awareness anchor from one of these categories: awareness of a body part or location in the body, awareness of a sensation in the body, awareness of embodying a virtue, awareness of the actions of the body, awareness of breathing, awareness of the texture of the breath, awareness of *cakra*, *nāḍī*, *bindu* or entire body as translucent light, awareness of a mantra, awareness of the visual of your chosen deity or *mahāsiddha* in your heart, awareness of the presence of the deity, *mahāsiddha* or guru in your heart

without the visual image, etc." From www.dharmainc.org/teachings/practice/form-and-energy-meditation/second-attention, retrieved April 2, 2015.

109 Note that in Kṣemarāja's time and region, the *Kaṭha Upaniṣad* was associated with the Atharva Veda rather than the Yajur Veda.

110 Translation by Patrick Olivelle (1998), with minor emendations.

111 Though of course Tantra teaches techniques for control and channeling of energy, these can only be mastered when the immature fear-based impulse to exert control and thereby avoid certain aspects of reality has been transcended.

112 The verb translated here as "subsides" (*pratyastamaya-*, from Kallaṭa's auto-commentary) is that usually used to describe the setting of the sun.

113 In citing *Spanda-kārikā* 1.22 (and *vṛtti* commentary) as a parallel here, I follow Professor Sanderson's suggestion. If he is correct, then Kṣemarāja here provides a crucial piece of the puzzle of how to do the practice alluded to in that famous verse.

114 That he quotes a Vaiṣṇava is noteworthy because back then, the standard Śaiva doctrine was that true liberation was not accessible to the members of other faiths. But Abhinava Gupta and Kṣemarāja exhibit the rather enlightened attitude that anyone who manages, by whatever means, to attain true insight into the nature of reality is liberated as far as their insight extends, because Consciousness is not and cannot be bound by rules formed from *vikalpas*.

115 The primary classical sects of Kaulism, a.k.a. the Kulamārga, are the Krama, the Kaubjikā, the Śrīvidyā, and a Kaula-influenced version of the Trika, the first and last of these being central to Abhinava Gupta and Kṣemarāja's thought and practice. They are discussed in *Tantra Illuminated.* See also n. liii.

116 The perineal body is a pyramidal fibromuscular mass in the middle line of the perineum.

117 'Sublimate' literally means 'to raise to a higher status' and in psychoanalytic theory refers to transmuting problematic or immature impulses (especially sexual) into creative energy; here I use it in a more general sense, free of the Freudian implication that sexual energy is problematic in and of itself, and more aligned with Jung's reinterpretation (as seen in his letters) where it is seen as an "alchemical transformation" that does not necessitate or benefit

from demonizing sexual energy in any way. The literal/etymological meaning of 'sublimate' is very close to *praguṇīkṛ*.

118 Contemporary Tantrik yogī Dharmabodhi (Kolbjorn Martens) comments: "The bliss experience had when the energy is brought down volitionally to the root, then center, then tip, is crucial to the experience being authentic. It is *not* sexual arousal desiring object (which is the often warned of 'demonic' flow or downward direction of improper *kuṇḍalinī* descent). The bliss means full integration. Stabilizing and enhancing the experience of bliss in all the centers comes next" (personal communication, 2011).

119 This is from Jayaratha's thirteenth-century commentary; I owe the discovery of this passage to the Oxford Master of Studies thesis of Anna Golovkova (pages 60–61).

120 In an interesting synchronicity, Jung wrote in private correspondence that sublimation was not as Freud described, but rather "an alchemical transformation for which *fire* and *prima materia* are needed".

121 Though Dharmabodhi argues, on the basis of oral transmission, that the 'center' (for men) is the point in the pubic symphysis where the penile ligament connects to the pelvis, which in subtle body physiology is the point where the *vajra-nāḍī* exits to traverse the length of the penis. He adds, "Control of this marma point is important in authentic sexualized *sādhanā*. ... Success equals complete transition and transference of the limited desire of [the] individual to the unbroken experience of pure Śakti-desire at [its] root without [the] need for object satiation" (personal communication, 2011). While it may be true that the marma point he references is also important, I still maintain that the 'center' most probably refers to the pelvic floor here.

122 Tantrik yogī Dharmabodhi argues: "Now, the key here is that unless one has had the actual experience of *amṛta* flowing from the crown into the whole body, literally *irreversibly* transforming the tissues and energies (and there are demonstrative signs to prove this) and therefore the 'mind', the whole process of the [cultivation of] *sva-kuṇḍalinī* becomes sorcery [i.e., sidetracked by fascination with *siddhis*]" (personal communication, 2011).

123 Men should have no concern about trying to withhold ejaculation; doing so is not, contrary to popular belief, a Tantrik practice (except when pursuing certain magical powers).

124 Rājānaka Rāma glosses *unmeṣa* as *sva-svabhāvābhāsa-vikāsa*—"the unfolding of a [new] expression of one's own essence-nature".

125 *navīna-cic-camatkāra-sparśāveśa*, in verse 77 of *A Hundred Verses on the Unity of Wisdom and Practice*.

126 It was written by Kṣemarāja's guru's guru's guru's guru in the Krama lineage, and is about fifty verses in length. I will be publishing it in my own translation in the near future.

127 This is necessarily a simplification, since *samādhi* and *samāpatti* are used in all three traditions, and *samāveśa* appears in Buddhist Tantra as well (often as *vajrāveśa*), but the assertion that each tradition has its preferred term is in general true.

128 Marshall McLuhan taught us that "the medium is the message", and this is a simple but effective example of how we can experience the same words differently when presented in a different visual layout. Compare page 389 with pages 395–396.

129 *Ghūrṇi* is the fifth and highest of the five mystic states of Kaula teaching, for which see Chapter Five of my forthcoming translation of *The Essence of Tantra* (*Tantrasāra*).

130 But the latter term has a double meaning that the former does not. It can be read not only as immersion *into* the Center, but also as 'possession' *by* one's essence-nature; in other words, Self-possession. The term *samāveśa* has as its ancient background the quasi-shamanic rites in which a deity was invited to beneficially possess the practitioner. Here, in so-called 'high' or 'classical' Tantra, the term is repurposed to imply that the most beneficial form of possession is Self-possession.

131 And note that in Tantra, one term for a liberated being is 'Sky-walker' (*khecara*), meaning one who roams freely in the Sky of Awareness. See also Peter Kingsley's book *A Story Waiting to Pierce You* for an explanation of why the term Skywalker might have come originally from Mongolian shamanism.

132 You might notice that in the poetic presentation on page 389, we have 'touching', whereas in the bolded passage above we have 'contemplating'; this is because both correctly translate the word *vimṛśan*.

133 This is a free translation of *vyutthānābhimatāvasare 'pi*, literally "even in the state previously considered to be *vyutthāna*".

134 Though it may be the case that the brief explanation is not Kṣemarāja's. When I read this chapter with Professor Alexis Sanderson at the University of Leipzig, he raised some doubts about the authorship of this short *saṅgati* section, which is rather pedantic and could have been a marginal annotation by a scribe or *paṇḍit* that was later incorporated into the main text by a subsequent scribe, as often happens.

135 Here (and in the sūtra itself) we have a textual problem: is it "innate circle of the goddesses..." or "circle of the innate goddesses..."? The former is what we have in the commentary, if it is not a corruption; if the latter is correct, it implies that these are not the gross faculties (seeing, hearing, etc.), but the *śakti*s underlying them.

136 The 'Fire of Time' (*kālāgni*) and the 'final Power' (*samanā*) refer respectively to the bottom and top of the ontological hierarchy of Shaivism. The Fire of Time simmers away until it flares up at the end of a cosmic aeon to consume all things (before the universe is re-created anew, in an endless cycle). The final Power is the *śakti* of equalization (entropy, we might say) that constitutes the highest and most subtle power within the universe of emanation and resorption. 'Beyond' that is only *unmanā*, the transmental power outside spacetime.

137 Here we have a problem in the text, best solved by assuming interpolation. Most likely a later scribe has added the phrase *sadbhāvāpādita* found in the Kashmir Series of Texts and Studies edition), which would mean "**transformed into its real nature as** nothing but the Light of Awareness". (The Sanskrit is marked with cruxes in the appendix.) If, however, we presume that Kṣema did write this awkward phrase, we could just about make it work by explaining that, for one attaining liberation at the level of Śrīmān Maheśvara (tattvas #1 and #2), it is *as if* the whole universe is 'transformed' into the pure Light of Awareness, even though in actuality no transformation occurs; one realizes that it has never been anything other than that Light. Against this argument one might simply point to the lack of an *iva*, a common Sanskrit particle meaning 'as if'. But note that I have retained the words *prakāśa-eka* before the crux, since this is the only mention of the word that the whole paragraph serves to explain.

Additionally, subsequent to the phrase just discussed is found in the text another sentence that I regard as a later interpolation: "**For nothing can come into being that is not immersed in the ultimately real Light of Awareness.**"

In defense of my cruxing of this sentence I can only say that it certainly doesn't add anything to the argument, and more importantly, to me it doesn't *feel* like Kṣema's words, and it does feel like a marginal annotation by a scribe that got incorporated into the main text.

138 From the perspective of the process of creation–emanation (*sṛṣṭi-krama*), "the first stirring of Consciousness in its dynamic self-projection is to produce this oscillation between Sadāśiva and Īśvara" (transcribed from Sanderson's lectures at the University of Leipzig, 2008).

139 You might think that it would be impossible to experience this reality while in the body and still be functional, but it's not so. I'm aware of two people who perceive from this perspective, and they both are not only functional in the world, but are the most natural, easeful, down-to-earth people I've ever known. If you're surprised by that statement, I invite you to question your assumption that full realization of ultimate reality would somehow distance one from the rhythms and patterns of everyday life. Why should that be so? Ultimate reality, by definition, must be fully present in every aspect of the everyday, or else it wouldn't be ultimately real.

140 Note that in this lineage (and only in this lineage), *parāmarśa* is a technical term that means both 'form of reflective awareness' (or 'self-reflective cognition') *and* 'phoneme'. We see this usage in Abhinava Gupta's extensive treatment of linguistic mysticism in Chapter Three of the *Tantrāloka* (summarized in Chapter Three of the *Tantrasāra*, which I plan to publish soon as *The Essence of Tantra*).

141 Though some readers may resist this point, arguing that (say) dolphins have language, only humans display **all** the various major manifestations of *vimarśa*: questioning, representational and abstract art, unimpeded imagination, and widely diverse forms of language. *Vimarśa*, remember, is the self-reflective aspect of awareness, so if we say that other animals don't possess it, that is not to say that they aren't *aware*. Clearly, all other animals display the signs of *prakāśa* to some degree, just not *vimarśa*. For example, gorillas can develop a sign-language vocabulary of hundreds of words, but they never use their linguistic facility to ask a question of another gorilla or a human.

142 Parā Devī is more specifically associated with *pratibhā*, the intuitive faculty, which of course is only available to a person in direct proportion to their cultivation of self-awareness or *vimarśa*.

143 Cf. *Tantrāloka* 3.67: *akulasyāsya devasya kula-prathana-śālinī kaulikī sā parā śaktir aviyukto yayā prabhuḥ* →"The Supreme Power of this Transcendent Deity (*akula deva*) is the *kaulikī-śakti*, from which the Lord is never separate, and which manifests the *kula*, the universe." Note that this *kaulikī-śakti* is another name for *parā pratibhā*, 'supreme intuition'/'creative upsurge', that is, the 'unsurpassed Goddess' (*anuttarā devī*) from the previous verse, 3.66. *Pratibhā* also means creative genius, embodied instinct, and intuitive insight: that which has the capacity to constantly reveal something new.

144 In this homology of the tattvas with the syllables of the alphabet, all the vowels together constitute Śiva (for each vowel is a specific *śakti* and Śiva is nothing but the coherence of the *śakti*s), Mahāmāyā is not counted as a *tattva*, and only the three *kañcuka*s common to all the tantras (*kalā, vidyā,* and *rāga*) are counted, and therefore *ha* aligns with the Earth element. But even if this is regarded as an artificial schema, the fact remains that the Sanskrit alphabet actually ends with *ha*, for *kṣa* is a conjunct consonant whose elements are already accounted for elsewhere in the alphabet, and it is only used when fifty letters are needed for numerological reasons.

145 Quoted in William James, *The Varieties of Religious Experience*.

146 Since that is not yet available in English, please refer to its summary in Chapter Three of the *Tantrasāra*, forthcoming in my own translation (*The Essence of Tantra*).

147 For an introduction to the subject, see Sam Harris's *Free Will*, 2012.

148 For the former, see *Free Will*, and for the latter, see *Quantum Enigma*.

149 See Timothy Wilson's *Strangers to Ourselves: Discovering the Adaptive Unconscious*, 2002.

150 See Daniel Gilbert's *Stumbling on Happiness*, 2005.

151 The Pratyabhijñā lineage calls *kriyā-śakti* 'Agency' (*kartṛtva*) when discussing it as a fundamental principle, rather than as one of a triad of powers.

152 Kallaṭa, the author of the verse, has the same view, for he explains the word 'power' as 'unveiled and unimpeded Awareness' in his auto-commentary.

153 In the original tradition, mantras were frequently used for worldly ends, and no one doubted they were effective for those ends. In fact, we frequently find the argument that since mantras are seen to bring about visible and

verifiable effects in worldly life, one should not doubt that they can also bring about the invisible effect of spiritual liberation! The ubiquity of this claim and the fact that no arguments against it are discussed (in a tradition rich with debate) can only mean, to my mind, that most people of that time *had* seen mantras accomplish what must be termed magical effects. The fact that they could commonly do so then, and not so commonly (or at all) now, leads me to formulate the hypothesis that a very large percentage of the population of a given culture must believe in magic for it to work (which, if true, would be a specific instantiation of the general theory that Awareness creates reality and individuals are thus co-creators).

154 Incorporating the explanation of *maheśvara* from the author's *vṛtti: svāṅga-bhūte prameye nirmātṛtayā*. Note also that *pramātṛ* is glossed as *sarva-saṃvit-kāla-vyāpī...ātma-saṃjñaḥ*, "known as the Self, it is that which pervades the [various] moments of all the cognitive acts".

155 This is assuming that *śaktipāta*, the initial awakening that commences the spiritual path as such, has already occurred.

156 My Soul Immersion program is aimed at this goal. For more information, see hareesh.org and livetru.org.

157 According to this view of *sarva-sarvātma-vāda*, "All things have the essence of all others, because every thing has the nature of all things" (paraphrased by Torella [1994: xvi] from Somānanda's *Śiva-dṛṣṭi* 5.107–108). As Torella comments, "Here [this view] acquires very special importance and implications because it serves as the theoretical context for the experience of the Tantric adept who has set out on the path of the expansion of consciousness and energy" (1994: xv).

158 The first paragraph comes from "Song of Myself", the rest from "To You", the whole of which is found at the end of this book.

159 These five are the element underlying sound (*śabda*), the element underlying touch (*sparśa*), the element underlying appearance (*rūpa*), the element underlying taste (*rasa*), and the element underlying scent (*gandha*).

160 If the Five Acts are meant to be construed as Powers here, then the Wheel would have 28 spokes.

161 To be more precisely accurate, some who complete their *sādhanā* and attain the Bhairava-state undergo changes that are obvious to others, and

others do not exhibit such changes. I propose that the reason for the difference lies in the degree to which the person's life and conduct already reflected her or his essence-nature prior to completing her or his *sādhanā*.

162 An aside, like a footnote, occurs at this point in the text, which is probably just a scribe's marginal note from a previous stage in the manuscript transmission that got incorporated into the main text at a subsequent stage, but in case it is actually Kṣemarāja's words, I translate it here: "**'His' in the present verse refers** [back] **to** [*Spanda-kārikā* 3.17c]**, 'constrained by his *puryaṣṭaka*'** (subtle body)**, i.e., the *puryaṣṭaka* should be understood as the antecedent here.**" This is followed by another parenthetical aside of dubious authenticity: "**Nor should *ekatra* be interpreted as the author of the *vivaraṇa* commentary** [Rājānaka Rāma] **has done, saying that 'to that one' means to the subtle body or the physical body.**"

163 This is an explanatory translation of Kṣemarāja's very elliptical Sanskrit: *nimīlanonmīlana-daśayoḥ tad-abhedena jānīyāt, pūrvāpara-koṭy-avaṣṭambha-dārḍhyān madhya-bhūmim api cid-rasāśyānatā-rūpatayaiva paśyed iti arthaḥ*. One must know his work well to translate such a passage with any accuracy.

164 Since the *Mālinī-vijayottara-tantra* does not describe these *samāveśa*s, but only hints at how to attain them, my understanding of them was developed through discussions, transmissions, and practice with two master practice teachers.

165 Alternate translation, with context: "The light [of the soul] is not content with the simple divine essence in its repose, as that neither gives nor receives; it wants to know the source of this essence. It wants to go into the simple ground [of being], into the quiet desert, into which distinction never gazed" (Meister Eckhart, Sermon 48).

166 *Tantrāloka* 1.174c–6b.

167 At this point we have a verse I regard as a later interpolation, because it does nothing but repeat what Kṣema said in the introduction, which is not his style. It reads: "**This teaching on Reality was composed for those who have experienced Śiva's Descent of Grace, but, through lack of training, are not adept in rigorous** [philosophical] **reasoning and are thus unable to understand the *Recognition of the Lord* texts.**"

## Glossary of Key Sanskrit Terms

*abhimāna*: egoic identification, egoic perception
*aiśvarya*: agency, sovereignty
*amṛta*: Nectar of Immortality
*ānanda*: joy
*āṇava-mala*: the Impurity of Individuality
*anugraha*: grace, revelation, remembering (one of the Five Acts)
*apāna*: inhale, inward-turning contemplative energy
*avikalpa*: prediscursive, unconstructed
*avikalpa-parāmarśa*: prediscursive reality, nonconceptual self-reflective awareness
*bhāva*: thing, being, feeling, mental state
*bhāvanā*: contemplative meditation
*bhoga*: happiness
*bodha*: awakeness or awareness
*brahma-granthi*: subtle knot located above the perineum
*brahman*: divine consciousness
*caitanya*: activated, alive
*cakra*: circle, territory
*camatkāra*: expansive, awestruck wonder
*cetana*: pure consciousness
*citi*: Awareness, Consciousness
*cit-śakti*: the Power of Awareness
*citta*: the mind
*dvādaśānta*: "end-of-twelve", uppermost limit of the energy body
*glāni*: depression, lethargy, inertia, torpor, apathy, cynical pessimism
*guṇa*: quality, constituent
*icchā*: will, desire, urge
*icchā-śakti*: God's Will, the Power of Will
*īśvara*: Lord, God
*īśvaratā*: divinity, sovereignty
*jīva*: the embodied soul
*jīvan-mukti*: embodied liberation, living liberation
*jñāna-śakti*: the Power of Knowing
*kalā*: limited power, limited agency
*kāla*: limited time
*kañcuka*: armors, veils
*kanda*: bulb, the second cakra in the Kaula Trika's five-cakra system, located in the lower abdomen midway between the genitals and the navel
*kārma-mala*: the Impurity of Action
*krama-mudrā*: the seal of the sequence
*kriyā-śakti*: the Power of Action
*kuṇḍalinī*: inner intuitive power, innate intelligence
*madhya*: central, Center
*mahā-mantra*: the Great Mantra
*mahā-vyāpti*: the Great Pervasion
*mala*: impurity
*maṇḍala*: wheel, circle
*Mantra*: the liberated perceiver of diversified (and dominant) objectivity as an expression of underlying subjectivity (one of the Seven Perceivers)

*Mantra-maheśvara*: the liberated perceiver of objectivity enveloped by a greater subjectivity (one of the Seven Perceivers)
*Mantreśvara*: the liberated perceiver of subjectivity and objectivity as mirrors of each other, in appositional balance (one of the Seven Perceivers)
*mantra-vīrya*: the potency of mantras
*māyā*: illusion, the state of differentiation
*māyā-pramātā*: limited perceiver
*māyā-śakti*: self-concealment-in-plurality
*māyīya-mala*: the Impurity of Differentiation
*mokṣa*: liberation
*mudrā*: posture
*mukti*: liberation
*nāḍī*: channel
*nigraha*: concealment, occlusion, forgetting (one of the Five Acts)
*nimeṣa*: concealing, infolding
*nityodita*: continuous, continuously arising
*niyati*: causality, localization
*parā*: supreme
*parāmarśa*: reflective awareness
*paramārtha*: ultimate reality
*parameśvara*: the Highest Divinity
*paśu*: unliberated being, bound soul
*prakāśa*: the Light of Awareness, the Light of Creation
*prakāśana*: manifestation
*Pralayākala*: the unliberated perceiver who is temporarily partially free by virtue of existing in the Void
*prāṇa*: life force (one of the Seven Perceivers)
*prāṇa-śakti*: life-force energy
*prāṇāyāma*: breath control
*pratibhā*: intuition, intuitive light
*pūrṇa*: fullness, completeness, wholeness
*pūrṇāhaṃtā*: fully expanded 'I', 'I'-consciousness
*pūrṇatā*: complete fullness
*pūrṇatva*: fullness of being
*puruṣa*: pure consciousness, perceiving witness
*puryaṣṭaka*: energy-body, subtle body
*rāga*: desire, craving
*rajas*: passion, energy
*rasa*: taste, poetic flavor
*sādhanā*: gradual awakening through spiritual practice
*Sakala*: the unliberated perceiver who sees duality as the basic reality, perceiving himself as separate from the whole (one of the Seven Perceivers)
*śākta-samāveśa*: immersion into the total energy-field
*śakti*: energy field
*śaktipāta*: initial awakening experience
*samādhi*: deep meditation
*samāveśa*: immersion into reality
*śāmbhava-samāveśa*: immersion into [Supreme] Śiva

*saṃhāra*: dissolution, retraction, reabsorption (one of the Five Acts)
*saṃsāra*: the cycle of suffering
*saṃsārin*: one who wanders aimlessly, one who is bound up in suffering
*saṃskāra*: subtle trace, subliminal impression
*śaṅkā*: anxiety, doubt, inhibition
*sattva*: lightness, purity, clarity
*siddhi*: performance, completion, fulfillment
*Śiva*: absolute nondual Awareness (one of the Seven Perceivers)
*sṛṣṭi*: creation, emission, manifestation, flowing forth (one of the Five Acts)
*sthiti*: stasis, maintenance, preservation (one of the Five Acts)
*śūnya*: the Void
*svabhāva*: essence-nature
*svarūpa*: one's essential nature
*svātantrya*: autonomy, freedom
*svātma*: one's own self
*tamas*: heaviness, darkness, inertia
*tattva*: principle, level, reality
*uccāra*: esoteric Tantrik technique in which a single-syllable mantra is raised up the central channel and then vibrated intensely in the nasal cavity
*udāna*: upward rising force of kuṇḍalinī
*unmeṣa*: unfolding
*upaniṣads*: esoteric teachings, hidden connections
*vāk*: the Word
*Vijñānākala*: the unliberated perceiver who is almost free by virtue of his insight, but unwilling to surrender his separate identity (one of the Seven Perceivers)
*vikalpa*: conditioned interpretive thought-matrix, differential thought-construct
*vikāsa*: expansion, blossoming, unfolding
*vimarśa*: self-reflection
*vimarśana*: subjective awareness
*vimarśa-śakti*: the Power of Self-reflection
*viśrānti*: repose in the center of one's being
*viśva*: everything, the Everything
*vyāna*: a downward, outward, and ultimately all-pervasive movement, described as a flood of nectar
*vyāpti*: pervasion
*vyutthāna*: post-meditative state

# Bibliography


Allione, Tsultrim. *Feeding Your Demons: Ancient Wisdom for Resolving Inner Conflict.* Little, Brown and Company, 2008.

Bronkhorst, Johannes. 2001. "The Peacock's Egg: Bhartṛhari on Language and Reality," Philosophy East and West, 51(4), pp. 474–491.

Carroll, Sean. "The Arrow of Time" [Blog post], 2004. http://www.preposterousuniverse.com/blog/2004/10/27/the-arrow-of-time/

Chidvilasananda, Swami. *Kindle My Heart*. Prentice Hall Press, 1989.

Colledge, Edmund and McGinn, Bernard (Trans.). *Meister Eckhart: The Essential Sermons, Commentaries, Treatises, and Defense.* Paulist Press, 1981.

Davidson, Ron. *Indian Esoteric Buddhism: A Social History of the Tantric Movement*. Columbia University Press, 2002.

Dharma Inc. "Second Attention" www.dharmainc.org/teachings/practice/form-and-energy-meditation/second-attention

Edge.org. "2005: What Do You Believe Is True Even Though You Cannot Prove It?" [Blog post], 2005. https://www.edge.org/responses/what-do-you-believe-is-true-even-though-you-cannot-prove-it

Exactly What Is...Time? "The Arrow of Time" [Blog post], n.d. http://www.exactlywhatistime.com/physics-of-time/the-arrow-of-time

Gilbert, Daniel. *Stumbling on Happiness*. Knopf, 2006.

Golovkova, Anna. *The Cult of the Goddess Tripurasundarī Vāmakeśvarīmata*. Unpublished thesis submitted for the degree of Masters of Studies at Oxford University, 2010.

Greene, Brian. *The Fabric of the Cosmos: Space, Time, and the Texture of Reality*. Vintage, 2004.

Haidt, Jonathan. *The Happiness Hypothesis: Finding Modern Truth in Ancient Wisdom*. Basic Books, 2006.

Harris, Sam. *Free Will.* Free Press, 2012.

James, William. *The Varieties Of Religious Experience: A Study In Human Nature.* Longmans, Green, and Co, 1917.

Kingsley, Peter. *A Story Waiting to Pierce You: Mongolia, Tibet and the Destiny of the Western World.* The Golden Sufi Center, 2010.

Kripal, Jeffrey J. *Esalen: America and the Religion of No Religion.* University of Chicago Press, 2007.

Marjanovic, Boris and Chakravarty, Hemendra Nath. *Tantrasāra of Abhinavagupta.* Rudra Press, 2012.

McKenna, Jed. *Jed McKenna's Theory of Everything: The Enlightened Perspective.* Wisefool Press, 2013.

Olivelle, Patrick. *Upaniṣads.* Oxford University Press, 1998.

Pinker, Steven. *The Language Instinct: How the Mind Creates Language.* William Morrow and Company, 1994.

Rhodes Bailly, Constantina. *Shaiva Devotional Songs of Kashmir.* State University of New York Press, 1987.

Rosenblum, Bruce and Kutter, Fred. *Quantum Enigma: Physics Encounters Consciousness.* Oxford University Press, 2011.

Sanderson, Alexis. "Purity and Power among the Brahmans of Kashmir," in *The Category of the Person: Anthropology, Philosophy, History*, M. Carrithers, S. Collins and S. Lukes, eds. Cambridge University Press, 1985.

Schrödinger, Erwin. *My View of the World.* Cambridge University Press, 1951.

Singer, Michael A. *The Untethered Soul.* New Harbinger Publications, 2007.

Stainton, Hamsa. *Poetry and Prayer: Stotras in the Religious and Literary History of Kashmir* [Doctoral dissertation]. Columbia University, 2013.

Taylor, Jill Bolte. *My Stroke of Insight.* Penguin Books, 2009.

Torella, Raffaele. *The Īśvarapratyabhijñākārikā of Utpaladeva with the Author's Vṛtti.* Motilal Banarsidass, 2002.

Torella, Raffaele. "On Vāmanadatta," in *Pandit N.R. Bhatt, Felicitation Volume*, P-S. Filliozat, C.P. Bhatta and S.P. Narang, eds. Motilal Banarsidass, 1994, pp. 481–498.

Vāsudeva, Somadeva. *The Yoga of the Mālinīvijayottaratantra.* IFP/EFEO, 2004.

Wallis, Christopher. "The Power of Subtle Impressions" [Blog post], 2015. http://tantrikstudies.squarespace.com/blog/2015/9/21/impressions-of-past-lives

Wallis, Christopher. "Yoga Philosophy, Race, and 'Colorblindness'" [Blog post], 2016. tantrikstudies.org/blog/2016/7/14/yoga-philosophy-race-and-colorblindness

Watson, Alex. *The Self's Awareness of Itself: Bhatta Ramakantha's Arguments Against the Buddhist Doctrine of No-Self.* Wien, 2006.

Watts, Alan. *The Book: On the Taboo Against Knowing Who You Are.* Random House, 1966.

Whitman, Walt. *Leaves of Grass.* David McKay, c1900.

Wikipedia. "Dialectic: Hegelian Dialectic," n.d. https://en.wikipedia.org/wiki/Dialectic#Hegelian_dialectic

Wilson, Timothy D. *Strangers to Ourselves: Discovering the Adaptive Unconscious.* Harvard University Press, 2004.

# Index

Note: *Italics* indicate footnotes; **bold** indicates illustrations.

creation *(unmeṣa)*, 228, 343, 380–83, 420
"Critical Edition of the Sanskrit Text," 463–83

Dāmodara, Bhaṭṭa, 259, 284–85
delusion
  cessation of, 293
  and contraction, 294–95
  god, 444
  and Mother Goddesses, 275
  and *saṃsārin*, 255–61, 264–67, 279, 285–90
depression, 497N78
Descent of Grace/Power, 31, 161, 186, 207, 225, 262, 508N167. *See also śaktipāta* (awakening)
'detached witness' teaching, 119
detachment, 119
Divine, the, 113–14
DNA, 111
*Doctrine of the Three-Headed Bhairava, The (Triśiro-mata)*, 105–7, 113–14
dreams, 49, 271–72, 286–87
dualism
  consequences of, 208
  as illusion, 68–69, 75
  perceived as real, 131
  and recalibration, 312
  and Spirit and Matter, 87–88
  and thought constructs, 257, 276–77

Eckhart, Meister, 453, 508N165
Einstein, 62
embodied liberation *(jīvan-mukti)*
  defined, 317, 320–21
  and Joy of Awareness, 327
  and realization, 289, 323
  and *saṃskāras*, 321
  spelling, 500N98
  and stability, 318–20, 324
emotions, demonization of, 116
energy, contraction and expansion of *(śakti-saṅkoca-vikāsa)*, 339, 368–75
energy, contraction of *(śakti-saṅkoca)*, 335, 360–65, **361**
energy, expansion of *(śakti-vikāsa)*, 337, 365–68
energy-body, 286, 379, 443, 498N89, 507N159
entanglement, principle of, 495N70
*Essence of Spanda, The*, 197, 219, 228
*Essence of the Tantras, The*, *148*, 150–51
*Essence of the Trinity, The*, 39, 59
essence-nature
  and awareness, 310–12
  cultivation of centeredness, *320*
  and downshifting, 382
  and embodied liberation, 317, 320–21
  and Five Acts, 327
  and immersion, 405
  and mantras, 433
  and perception, 393
  stabilized, 403
  and thoughts, 380
Exegetes, 157, 170–71, 172, 491N40
exercises
  on *ānanda*, 102, 192–93
  on Awareness, 135, 198
  on the Divine seeking to know itself, 120
  on freedom to choose, 65
  on fulfillment, 78
  merging awareness and divine nature, 23
  on nonduality, 274
  on opposing Views, 185
  on *saṃskāras*, 253
  self-awareness and freedom, 46
  on self-image, 110
  on Śiva and Śakti, 181
  on thoughts and truth, 272
experience, spiritual, 118, 154, 186, 197, 312, 392

*Feeding Your Demons*, *116*
Fire of Awareness, 299, 301
Fire of Consciousness, 237, 246–51, 263
Fire of Time, 407, 420, 504N136
Five Acts
  and cognition, 25–29, 225–28, 496N72

Five Acts (*continued*)
and Consciousness, 11
and contemplative practice, 229–31
defined, 21, 22, 24
and essence-nature, 327
and mental constructs, 24
performance of, 23–24, 228–29
performance of (esoteric), 235–37, 251
and *saṃsārin* (sufferer), 217–19, 220, 223–24
and self-realization, 26–29, 295–96
five 'armors' *(kañcukas)*, 147, 155, 175, 203, 204, 212–13, 214, 281
flame tree leaf, 325, **326**, 500N101
*Flowering of One's Innate Awareness, The*, 385, 503N126
'flows,' pausing, practice of *(vāha-cheda)*, 341, 375–77
freedom
and Agency, 430–32
as autonomy of Awareness, 161, 166, 172
and Awareness, 42–43, 45–46, 62, 76–77
and choice, 64–65
and sleep, 99
and suffering, 148
and supreme state, 357–60
*See also* autonomy of Awareness
fulfillment, 61–70, 77–78, 207, 429–30

Gazzaniga, Michael, 350–51
God
and individual, 117–19
as the only thing that exists, 149–51
and self-expression, 110
and self-realization, 289–90
and universe, 111
Goddess
as awareness, 44–45
as Awareness, 163, 197–99, 323, 324–27, 368, 413–17
and contraction, 123–25, 128–29
different forms of, 196
and 'I am,' 195–96
as Kālī, 238, 405
and perceiver and perceived, 88
and pronouns, 47
and self-expression, 74
and Śiva, 46–47
as Supreme, 379
and supreme state, 357–59
as Supreme Word, 268–71, 274–75
Vāmeśvarī, 257, 259, 279–80, 283, 285
Goddesses, Flow, 257–59, 280–83, 285
Goddesses, Mother, 274–76
goddesses, of the senses, 305, 306–7, 383
Grammarians, 159, 176–78
Great Lords of Mantra, 83, 93, 487N17
Great Mantra, 268, 497N82
Great Pervasion, 161, 186–88
Gurumayī Chidvilāsānandā, 269, 498N83

Harris, Sam, *192*
Heart of the Lord, 259, 283–84
*Heart of the Teachings on Recognition*, 1, 7, 21, 26
Heart Sūtra, 176
Hegel, 294, 498N92
Heisenberg, 89
*Hymn on the Core of Reality*, 125, 134
*Hymn to the Womb of Wisdom*, 333, 341, 357, 375–76

'I,' expanded, 407, 411–13, 418–21, 429–32, 434–35
'I am,' 195–96, 268, 393, 426, 427, 428–29, 497N82
*I Am That*, 429
*icchā*, as the urge to express, 45, 75–76
'I'-concept, *402*
'I'-consciousness, 255, 268, 269, 309, 400, 445, 447
*idam aham* ('I am this'), 94, 96
ignorance, as knowing, 115
Immersion
and Awareness, 317, 318–20, 438–39
into essence-nature, 405
into expanded 'I,' 407–17, 418–21, 434–35
and Fourth State, 333–35, 352–53

fruition of, 419–21
internal and external, 389–91, 395–404
as occasional, 306, 312–13
phases of, 452–54, 508n164
as spiritual experience, 154
and stability, 317
*See also samādhi* (contentless meditation); *samāpatti; samāveśa* (immersion)
Impure Realm, 175, 217, 223–24
Impurities, 97, 203, 204–5, 205–6, 206–7, 207–9
independence, 42–43, 45–46, 62, 76–77
intention, and practice, 64

Jains, 178
Jayaratha, *98*
Jesus, secret teachings of, 498n88
Joy of Awareness
accessing, 163, 190, 193, 288
discovery of, 323, 324–25, 327, 389
and embodied liberation, 317, 327, 392
and 'pure' mental constructs, 278–79
and transitional states, 318–20
*See also* Consciousness

*Kakṣyā-stotra,* 337, 366
Kallaṭa, Bhaṭṭaśrī, 506n152
Kashmīr, history of, 2–7
*Kaṭha Upaniṣad,* 362–63, 501n109
Katie, Byron, 248, 348
Kaula
and anxiety, 266–67
and female practitioners, 371
initiation, 492n53
and Kuṇḍalinī, 368–72
reading of Sūtra Twelve, 268–79
sects of, 501n115
on Self, 159, 178–79
*Kaula Ocean of Waves, The,* 197
*Kindle My Heart,* 269, 498n83
knowing, and awakening, 208–9
Krama tradition
and cognition, 25, 26, 190–96
and interpretation of Sūtra Eight, 189
on liberation, 251
and Mahārtha ('Great Truth'), 65, 190, 238, 239
and means to realization, 66–67
and reading of Sūtra Twelve, 279–85
secret teachings of, 65, 238, 405, 485n3
and Vedānta, 69
*krama-mudrā,* 391, 398, 399–400, 404–5
*Krama-sūtra,* 305, 310, 311, 389–91, 398–405
Kṣemarāja (Kṣema), writings of, 1, 31–32. *See also* Sūtras, Prologue; Sūtra One, Sūtra Two, etc.; Sūtras, Epilogue
Kula. *See* Kaula
Kulamārga. *See* Kaula
Kumārila, 171
Kuṇḍalinī, 14, 286, 288, 339, 368–72, 374–75, 376

Lakṣman-jū, Swāmī, 6, 99
language, 176–77, 232, 270, 275–76, 350–51, 424–26
Larson, Gerry, 5–6
light, speed of, 62, 486n10
Light of Awareness *(prakāśa)*
and consciousness, 268
and contraction, 114–15, 151
and dualism, 68–69
expression of, 51–54, 55
and language, 424–26
and nonduality, 92–93
and object, 227
and oneness, 73, 80, 149–51
as perceiver, 145–47, 151
separation from, 57, 115
and Śiva, 85, 100–102, 105–7
as universe, 409
and *vimarśa,* 28, 129–31
Logicians and Atomists, 157, 169–70
*Lord Vijñāna-Bhairava,* 41, 67
"Lord's Club, The," 165

Mādhyamika, 173–74
Mahārtha ('Great Truth'), 65, 190, 238, 239

on mind as self, 143
Sūtra Seven
on aspects of selfhood, 151–54
on God as the only thing that exists, 149–51
Kṣemarāja's original text, 145–47
on liberation, 155
Sūtra Eight
on autonomy of Awareness, 181–82
on Buddhists, 171–72
on cognition, 190–96
and Exegetes, 170–71
on the Goddess, 196–99
on Grammarians, 176–78
on the Great Pervasion, 186–88
and hierarchy of philosophies, 164–68, 178
Kṣemarāja's original text, 157–63
on Logicians and Atomists, 169–70
on Mādhyamika, 173–74
on Materialists, 168–69
on Sāṅkhyas and Pātañjala Yogins, 174–75
on self as contraction of universal Principle, 188–89
on those of limited views, 182–85
on transcendence and immanence, 178–80
on Vaiṣṇava Pāñcarātrikas, 174
on Vedāntins, 172–73, 175–76
Sūtra Nine
on expansion of Powers of Awareness, 214
on five 'armors,' 212–13
Kṣemarāja's original text, 201–3
on Power of Action, 209–12
on Power of Knowing, 207–9
on Power of Will, 206–7
and *saṃsārin*, 204–6
Sūtra Ten
on bondage, 232–33
on contemplative practice, 229–31
on creation and dissolution, 228–29
on Five Acts and cognition, 225–28
on Five Acts as *saṃsārin*, 223–24
Kṣemarāja's original text, 217–19
on Śaiva Tantra/Vedānta, 220–23
on *saṃsārin*, 220
on *vikāsa*, 231–32
Sūtra Eleven
on *camatkāra*, 240–43
on consciousness, 239–40
on Fire of Consciousness, 246–51
Kṣemarāja's original text, 235–37
on *saṃskāra*, 244–46
on teachers, 251–52
Sūtra Twelve
on anxiety and inhibition, 264–67
on delusion, 285–90
on Flow Goddesses, 280–83, 285
on Heart of the Lord, 283–84
Kaula Trika reading, 268–79
Krama reading, 279–85
Kṣemarāja's original text, 255–61
on limited perceiver, 270–72
on Mother Goddesses, 274–76
Pratyabhijñā reading, 285–90
on 'pure' mental constructs, 278–79
on reality-as-it-is, 273–74
on *śaktipāta*, 262–64
on Supreme Goddess, 279–80
on Supreme Word, 268–70
on *vikalpas*, 276–78
Sūtra Thirteen
on disappearance of delusion, 294–95
Kṣemarāja's original text, 293
on self-realization, 295–96
Sūtra Fourteen
critique of, 300
Kṣemarāja's original text, 299
on Power of Awareness, 300–302
Sūtra Fifteen
on Awareness activated, 308–9
on Immersion *(samāveśa)*, 312–13
Kṣemarāja's original text, 305
on mantras, 309–10
on mindfulness practice, 306–8, 313–14
on one's essence-nature, 310–12

Void (*śūnya*)
and Awareness, 186–87
distinct from Core, 393–94, 402
and individuality, 280
and mind, 137
passing through, 99
and *saṃskāras*, 142–43, 489N34
and selfhood, 151, 152, 173
supreme, 109
and transcendentalists, 98
*vyutthāna* (transitional state), 319, 394, 395, 397
Watts, Alan, 209, 489N35
wave, 401–3, **402**
*what-you-are*, 307–8, 310–11, 352, 356, 405, 420
Whitman, Walt, 441, 460
will, free, 430
Wisdom-perceiver, 123, 130, 131, 138, 488N30
'witness-consciousness,' *222*
Word-absolute, 176–78
Work, The, 248, 348

Yoga, Classical, 134, 175, 392
Yoga, Tantrik, 247, 287–88, 392, 452
Yogācārins, 172, 491N44
*Yoga-sūtra*, 134, 175, 277

Zhuang-tzu, 287, *287*